COLLECTED
POEMS
1947-1997

ALSO BY ALLEN GINSBERG

POETRY

Howl and Other Poems, 1956
Kaddish and Other Poems, 1961
Empty Mirror, Early Poems, 1961
Reality Sandwiches, 1963
Planet News, 1968
The Fall of America, Poems of These States, 1972
The Gates of Wrath: Rhymed Poems 1948–52, 1973
Iron Horse, 1973
First Blues, 1975
Mind Breaths, Poems 1971–76, 1978
Plutonian Ode, Poems 1977–1980, 1982
Collected Poems 1947–1980, 1984
White Shroud, Poems 1980–1985, 1986
Cosmopolitan Greetings, Poems 1986–1992, 1994
Selected Poems 1947–1995, 1996
Death & Fame: Poems 1993–1997, 1999

PROSE

The Yage Letters (with William Burroughs), 1963
Indian Journals, 1970, 1996
Gay Sunshine Interview (with Allen Young), 1974
Allen Verbatim: Lectures on Poetry, Politics, Consciousness, 1974
Chicago Trial Testimony, 1975
To Eberhart from Ginsberg, 1976
As Ever: Collected Correspondence Allen Ginsberg & Neal Cassady, 1977
Neal Cassady, 1977
Journals Early Fifties Early Sixties 1977, 1993

Composed on the Tongue: Literary Conversations 1967–1977, 1980
Straight Hearts Delight, Love Poems and Selected Letters 1947–1980 (with Peter Orlovsky), 1980
Howl, Original Draft Facsimile, Fully Annotated, 1986, 1995
The Visions of the Great Rememberer (with Visions of Cody, Jack Kerouac), 1993
Journals Mid-Fifties: 1954–1958, 1994
Luminous Dreams, 1997
Deliberate Prose: Selected Essays 1952–1995, 2000
Spontaneous Mind: Selected Interviews, 1958–1996, 2001

PHOTOGRAPHY

Photographs, 1991
Snapshot Poetics, 1993

VOCAL WORDS & MUSIC

First Blues, 1981, 2006
The Lion For Real, 1989, 1996
Howls, Raps & Roars, 1993
Hydrogen Jukebox (opera with Philip Glass), 1993
Holy Soul Jelly Roll: Poems & Songs 1949–1993, 1994
The Ballad of the Skeletons, with Paul McCartney, Philip Glass, 1996
Howl, U.S.A., Kronos Quartet, Lee Hyla score, 1996
Howl & Other Poems, 1998
Wichita Vortex Sutra, 2004
The Allen Ginsberg Poetry Collection, 2004
Allen Ginsberg Reads Kaddish, 2006

ALLEN GINSBERG

COLLECTED POEMS

1947–1997

HARPER**PERENNIAL** MODERN**CLASSICS**

NEW YORK • LONDON • TORONTO • SYDNEY

HARPER**PERENNIAL** ◐ MODERN**CLASSICS**

A hardcover edition of this book was published in 2006 by HarperCollins Publishers.

FIRST HARPER PERENIAL MODERN CLASSICS EDITION PUBLISHED 2007.

The Library of Congress has catalogued the hardcover edition as follows:

Ginsberg, Allen, 1926–1997.
  [Poems]
  Collected poems, 1947–1997 / Allen Ginsberg.— 1st ed.
    p. cm.
  Includes indexes.
  ISBN-13: 978-0-06-113974-1
  ISBN-10: 0-06-113974-2
    I. Title.

PS3513.I74 2006
811'.54—dc22
                                           2006041191

ISBN: 978-0-06-113975-8 (pbk.)
ISBN-10: 0-06-113975-0 (pbk.)

11 NMSG/RRD 10 9 8 7 6

Collected Poems 1947–1997 is a compilation of the texts of
Collected Poems 1947–1980, White Shroud: Poems 1980–1985,
Cosmopolitan Greetings: Poems 1986–1992, and
Death & Fame: Poems 1993–1997.

The Estate would like to express gratitude to Eliot Katz for his dedication
and assistance in preparation of this manuscript, Danny Mulligan at
HarperCollins for attentive coordinating, and Jeffrey Posternak at the
Wylie Agency for his tireless intermediation.

Contents

COLLECTED POEMS 1947–1980

Author's Preface, Reader's Manual   5

I. EMPTY MIRROR : GATES OF WRATH *(1947–1952)*

In Society   11
The Bricklayer's Lunch Hour   12
Two Sonnets   13
On Reading William Blake's "The Sick Rose"   14
The Eye Altering Alters All   15
A Very Dove   15
Vision 1948   16
Do We Understand Each Other?   17
The Voice of Rock   18
Refrain   19
A Western Ballad   21
The Trembling of the Veil   22
A Meaningless Institution   23
A Mad Gleam   24
Complaint of the Skeleton to Time   25
Psalm I   26
An Eastern Ballad   26
Sweet Levinsky   27
Psalm II   28
Fie My Fum   31
Pull My Daisy   32
The Shrouded Stranger   34
Stanzas: Written at Night in Radio City   35
After All, What Else Is There to Say?   37
Sometime Jailhouse Blues   38
Please Open the Window and Let Me In   39
"Tonite all is well"   40
Fyodor   40
Epigram on a Painting of Golgotha   41
"I attempted to concentrate"   41
Metaphysics   41

In Death, Cannot Reach What Is Most Near   42
This Is About Death   43
Hymn   44
Sunset   45
Ode to the Setting Sun   46
Paterson   48
Bop Lyrics   50
A Dream   52
Long Live the Spiderweb   54
The Shrouded Stranger   55
An Imaginary Rose in a Book   57
Crash   57
The Terms in Which I Think of Reality   58
The Night-Apple   60
Cézanne's Ports   61
The Blue Angel   62
Two Boys Went Into a Dream Diner   63
A Desolation   64
In Memoriam: William Cannastra, 1922–1950   65
Ode: My 24th Year   67
How Come He Got Canned at the Ribbon Factory   68
The Archetype Poem   69
A Typical Affair   71
A Poem on America   72
After Dead Souls   73
Marijuana Notation   74
Gregory Corso's Story   75
I Have Increased Power   76
Walking home at night   78
"I learned a world from each"   78
"I made love to myself"   78
A Ghost May Come   79
"I feel as if I am at a dead end"   79
An Atypical Affair   80
345 W. 15th St.   81
A Crazy Spiritual   83
Wild Orphan   86

II. THE GREEN AUTOMOBILE (1953–1954)

The Green Automobile   91
An Asphodel   96
My Alba   97
Sakyamuni Coming Out from the Mountain   98

Havana 1953   100
Green Valentine Blues   103
Siesta in Xbalba   105
Song ("The weight of the world")   119
In back of the real   121
On Burroughs' Work   122
Love Poem on Theme by Whitman   123
Over Kansas   124

III. HOWL, BEFORE & AFTER: SAN FRANCISCO BAY AREA *(1955–1956)*

Malest Cornifici Tuo Catullo   131
Dream Record: June 8, 1955   132
"Blessed be the Muses"   133
Howl   134
Footnote to Howl   142
A Strange New Cottage in Berkeley   143
A Supermarket in California   144
Four Haiku   145
Sunflower Sutra   146
Transcription of Organ Music   148
Sather Gate Illumination   150
America   154
Fragment 1956   157
Afternoon Seattle   158
Tears   159
Scribble   160
In the Baggage Room at Greyhound   161
Psalm III   163
Many Loves   164
Ready to Roll   167

IV. REALITY SANDWICHES: EUROPE! EUROPE! *(1957–1959)*

POEM Rocket   171
Squeal   173
Wrote This Last Night   174
Death to Van Gogh's Ear!   175
Europe! Europe!   179
The Lion for Real   182
The Names   184
At Apollinaire's Grave   188
Message   191
To Lindsay   191
To Aunt Rose   192

American Change   194
'Back on Times Square, Dreaming of Times Square'   196
Laughing Gas   197
Funny Death   208
My Sad Self   209
Ignu   211
Battleship Newsreel   214

V. KADDISH AND RELATED POEMS *(1959–1960)*

Kaddish: Proem, Narrative, Hymmnn, Lament, Litany
    and Fugue   217
Mescaline   236
Lysergic Acid   239
I Beg You Come Back & Be Cheerful   243
Psalm IV   246
To an Old Poet in Peru   247
Aether   250
Magic Psalm   263
The Reply   265
The End   267
Man's glory   268
Fragment: The Names II   269

VI. PLANET NEWS: TO EUROPE AND ASIA *(1961–1963)*

Who Will Take Over the Universe   273
Journal Night Thoughts   275
Television Was a Baby Crawling Toward That Deathchamber   280
This Form of Life Needs Sex   292
Sunset S.S. Azemour   295
Seabattle of Salamis Took Place off Perama   296
Galilee Shore   297
Stotras to Kali Destroyer of Illusions   298
To P. O.   301
Heat   302
Describe: The Rain on Dasaswamedh Ghat   303
Death News   305
Vulture Peak: Gridhakuta Hill   306
Patna–Benares Express   308
Last Night in Calcutta   309
Understand That This Is a Dream   311
Angkor Wat   314
The Change: *Kyoto–Tokyo Express*   332

VII. KING OF MAY: AMERICA TO EUROPE *(1963–1965)*

    Nov. 23, 1963: Alone   341
    Why Is God Love, Jack?   343
    Morning   345
    Waking in New York   347
    After Yeats   351
    I Am a Victim of Telephone   352
    Today   353
    Message II   356
    Big Beat   357
    Café in Warsaw   358
    The Moments Return   360
    Kral Majales   361
    Guru   364
    Drowse Murmurs   365
    Who Be Kind To   367
    Studying the Signs   371
    Portland Coliseum   373

VIII. THE FALL OF AMERICA *(1965–1971)*

  Thru the Vortex West Coast to East (1965–1966)
    Beginning of a Poem of These States   377
    Carmel Valley   381
    First Party at Ken Kesey's with Hell's Angels   382
    Continuation of a Long Poem of These States   383
    These States: into L.A.   384
    A Methedrine Vision in Hollywood   388
    Hiway Poesy: L.A.–Albuquerque–Texas–Wichita   390
    Chances "R"   401
    Wichita Vortex Sutra   402
    Auto Poesy: On the Lam from Bloomington   420
    Kansas City to Saint Louis   421
    Bayonne Entering NYC   427
    Growing Old Again   431
    Uptown   432
    The Old Village Before I Die   433
    Consulting I Ching Smoking Pot Listening to the Fugs
      Sing Blake   434
  Zigzag Back Thru These States (1966–1967)
    Wings Lifted over the Black Pit   435
    Cleveland, the Flats   437
    To the Body   439

Iron Horse   440
City Midnight Junk Strains   465
A Vow   468
Autumn Gold: New England Fall   469
Done, Finished with the Biggest Cock   474
Holy Ghost on the Nod over the Body of Bliss   475
Bayonne Turnpike to Tuscarora   476
An Open Window on Chicago   481
Returning North of Vortex   484
Wales Visitation   488
Pentagon Exorcism   491
Elegy Che Guevara   492
War Profit Litany   494

Elegies for Neal Cassady (1968)
Elegy for Neal Cassady   495
Chicago to Salt Lake by Air   498
Kiss Ass   501
Manhattan Thirties Flash   501
Please Master   502
A Prophecy   504
Bixby Canyon   505
Crossing Nation   507
Smoke Rolling Down Street   509
Pertussin   509
Swirls of black dust on Avenue D   510
Violence   511
Past Silver Durango Over Mexic Sierra-Wrinkles   512
On Neal's Ashes   513
Going to Chicago   514
Grant Park: August 28, 1968   515
Car Crash   516

Ecologues of These States (1969–1971)
Over Denver Again   519
Imaginary Universes   520
Rising over night-blackened Detroit Streets   521
To Poe: Over the Planet, Air Albany–Baltimore   522
Easter Sunday   524
Falling Asleep in America   525
Northwest Passage   526
Sonora Desert-Edge   530
Reflections in Sleepy Eye   532
Independence Day   534
In a Moonlit Hermit's Cabin   535

Rain-wet asphalt heat, garbage curbed cans overflowing   537
Death on All Fronts   538
Memory Gardens   539
Flash Back   542
Graffiti 12th Cubicle Men's Room Syracuse Airport   543
After Thoughts   544
G. S. Reading Poesy at Princeton   545
Friday the Thirteenth   546
Anti–Vietnam War Peace Mobilization   549
Ecologue   550
Guru Om   561
"Have You Seen This Movie?"   563
Milarepa Taste   565
Over Laramie   566
Bixby Canyon to Jessore Road (1971)
Bixby Canyon Ocean Path Word Breeze   567
Hūm Bom!   576
September on Jessore Road   579

IX. MIND BREATHS ALL OVER THE PLACE *(1972–1977)*
Sad Dust Glories (1972–1974)
Ayers Rock / Uluru Song   587
Voznesensky's "Silent Tingling"   588
These States: to Miami Presidential Convention   590
Xmas Gift   595
Thoughts Sitting Breathing   597
"What would you do if you lost it?"   600
Who   603
Yes and It's Hopeless   604
Under the world there's a lot of ass, a lot of cunt   606
Returning to the Country for a Brief Visit   607
Night Gleam   609
What I'd Like to Do   610
On Illness   611
News Bulletin   613
On Neruda's Death   615
Mind Breaths   617
Flying Elegy   620
Teton Village   620
Sweet Boy, Gimme Yr Ass   621
Jaweh and Allah Battle   622
Manifesto   625
Sad Dust Glories   626

Ego Confessions (1974–1977)

    Ego Confession   631
    Mugging   633
    Who Runs America?   636
    Thoughts on a Breath   637
    We Rise on Sun Beams and Fall in the Night   640
    Written on Hotel Napkin: Chicago Futures   641
    Hospital Window   642
    Hadda Be Playing on the Jukebox   643
    Come All Ye Brave Boys   645
    Sickness Blues   647
    Gospel Noble Truths   649
    Rolling Thunder Stones   651
    Cabin in the Rockies   653
    Reading French Poetry   654
    Two Dreams   655
    C'mon Jack   657
    Pussy Blues   658
    Don't Grow Old   659
    "Junk Mail"   665
    "You Might Get in Trouble"   668
    Land O'Lakes, Wisc.   669
    "Drive All Blames into One"   669
    Land O'Lakes, Wisconsin: Vajrayana Seminary   670
    For Creeley's Ear   671
    Haunting Poe's Baltimore   672
    Contest of Bards   673
    I Lay Love on My Knee   688
    Stool Pigeon Blues   690
    Punk Rock Your My Big Crybaby   691
    Love Replied   692

X. PLUTONIAN ODE *(1977–1980)*

What's Dead   697
Grim Skeleton   698
Ballade of Poisons   700
Lack Love   701
Father Guru   702
Manhattan May Day Midnight   703
Adapted from Neruda's "Que dispierte el leñador"   704
Nagasaki Days   707
Plutonian Ode   710
Old Pond   715

Blame the Thought, Cling to the Bummer   717
"Don't Grow Old"   718
Love Returned   720
December 31, 1978   722
Brooklyn College Brain   725
Garden State   726
Spring Fashions   727
Las Vegas: Verses Improvised for El Dorado H.S. Newspaper   728
To the Punks of Dawlish   729
Some Love   730
Maybe Love   731
Ruhr-Gebiet   734
Tübingen–Hamburg Schlafwagen   736
Love Forgiven   737
Verses Written for Student Antidraft Registration Rally 1980   738
Homework   739
After Whitman & Reznikoff   740
Reflections at Lake Louise   741
τεθνάκην δ' ὀλίγω 'πιδενής φαίνομ' ἀλαία   743
Fourth Floor, Dawn, Up All Night Writing Letters   744
Ode to Failure   745
Birdbrain!   746
Eroica   748
"Defending the Faith"   750
Capitol Air   751

Appendix for *Collected Poems 1947–1980*
    Notes   757
    Epigraphs from Original Editions   809
    Dedications   810
    Acknowledgments   813
    Introduction by William Carlos Williams to Empty Mirror   817
    Introduction by William Carlos Williams to Howl   819
    Author's Cover Writ   821
    Index of Proper Names   827

WHITE SHROUD: POEMS 1980–1985

    Acknowledgments   841

Porch Scribbles   843
Industrial Waves   845
Those Two   849

Homage Vajracarya   850
Why I Meditate   851
Love Comes   852
Old Love Story   856
Airplane Blues   859
Do the Meditation Rock   863
The Little Fish Devours the Big Fish   865
Happening Now?   868
A Public Poetry   869
"What You Up To?"   870
Maturity   872
"Throw Out the Yellow Journalists of Bad Grammar & Terrible
    Manner"   873
Going to the World of the Dead   875
Irritable Vegetable   877
Thoughts Sitting Breathing II   878
What the Sea Throws Up at Vlissingen   880
I Am Not   881
I'm a Prisoner of Allen Ginsberg   882
221 Syllables at Rocky Mountain Dharma Center   883
Fighting Phantoms Fighting Phantoms   884
Arguments   885
Sunday Prayer   886
Brown Rice Quatrains   887
They're All Phantoms of My Imagining   888
White Shroud   889
Empire Air   893
Surprise Mind   895
Student Love   896
The Question   897
In My Kitchen in New York   898
It's All So Brief   899
I Love Old Whitman So   900
Written in My Dream by W. C. Williams   901
One Morning I Took a Walk in China   903
Reading Bai Juyi—I. II. III. IV. V. *China Bronchitis* VI. VII.
    Transformation of Bai's "A Night in Xingyang"   905
Black Shroud   911
World Karma   913
Prophecy   915
Memory Cousins   916
Moral Majority   917
The Guest   918

After Antipater   921
Jumping the Gun on the Sun   922
Cadillac Squawk   925
Things I Don't Know   926

Notes   *929*

COSMOPOLITAN GREETINGS: POEMS 1986–1992

Acknowledgments   935
Preface: Improvisation in Beijing   937
Prologue: Visiting Father & Friends   941

You Don't Know It   943
On the Conduct of the World Seeking Beauty Against Government
    947
Hard Labor   948
Velocity of Money   949
Sphincter   950
Spot Anger   951
London Dream Doors   952
Cosmopolitan Greetings   954
Fifth Internationale   957
Europe, Who Knows?   959
Graphic Winces   960
Imitation of K.S.   961
I Went to the Movie of Life   962
When the Light Appears   966
On Cremation of Chögyam Trungpa, Vidyadhara   967
Nanao   969
Personals Ad   970
Proclamation   971
To Jacob Rabinowitz   972
Grandma Earth's Song   973
Salutations to Fernando Pessoa   976
May Days 1988   979
Numbers in U.S. File Cabinet   982
Return of Kral Majales   984
Elephant in the Meditation Hall   985
Poem in the Form of a Snake That Bites Its Tail   987
Mistaken Introductions   995

CIA Dope Calypso   997
  N.S.A. Dope Calypso   1000
  Just Say Yes Calypso   1002
Hum Bom!   1004
Supplication for the Rebirth of the Vidyadhara   1009
After the Big Parade   1010
Big Eats   1011
Not Dead Yet   1012
Yiddishe Kopf   1013
John   1014
A Thief Stole This Poem   1016
Lunchtime   1017
Deadline Dragon Comix   1018
After Lalon   1019
Get It?   1024
Angelic Black Holes   1025
Research   1026
Put Down Your Cigarette Rag   1029
Violent Collaborations   1033
Calm Panic Campaign Promise   1035
Now and Forever   1036
Who Eats Who?   1037
The Charnel Ground   1038
Everyday   1042
Fun House Antique Store   1043
News Stays News   1045
Autumn Leaves   1046
In the Benjo   1047
American Sentences   1048

Notes   1051

DEATH & FAME: POEMS 1993–1997

Acknowledgments   1059
Foreword   1061

New Democracy Wish List   1063
Peace in Bosnia-Herzegovina   1066
After the Party   1068
After Olav H. Hauge   1069
These knowing age   1070

C'mon Pigs of Western Civilization Eat More Grease   1071
Here We Go 'Round the Mulberry Bush   1073
Tuesday Morn   1074
God   1076
Ah War   1077
Excrement   1078
New Stanzas for *Amazing Grace*   1080
City Lights City   1081
Newt Gingrich Declares War on "McGovernik Counterculture"   1082
Pastel Sentences (Selections)   1083
Nazi Capish   1087
Is About   1089
The Ballad of the Skeletons   1091
"You know what I'm saying?"   1096
Bowel Song   1097
Popular Tunes   1098
Five A.M.   1100
Power   1101
Anger   1102
Multiple Identity Questionnaire   1103
Don't Get Angry with Me   1104
Swan Songs in the Present   1105
Gone Gone Gone   1106
Reverse the rain of Terror   1108
Sending Message   1110
No! No! It's Not the End   1112
Bad Poem   1115
Homeless Compleynt   1116
Happy New Year Robert & June   1117
Diamond Bells   1118
Virtual Impunity Blues   1119
Waribashi   1120
Good Luck   1121
Some Little Boys Dont   1122
Jacking Off   1123
Think Tank Rhymes   1124
Song of the Washing Machine   1125
World Bank Blues   1126
Richard III   1129
Death & Fame   1130
Sexual Abuse   1133
Butterfly Mind   1134
A fellow named Steven   1135

Half Asleep   1136
Objective Subject   1137
Kerouac   1138
Hepatitis Body Itch . . .   1139
Whitmanic Poem   1140
American Sentences 1995–1997   1141
Variations on Ma Rainey's See See Rider   1144
Sky Words   1145
Scatalogical Observations   1147
My Team Is Red Hot   1149
Starry Rhymes   1150
Thirty State Bummers   1151
"I have a nosebleed . . ."   1156
"Timmy made a hot milk"   1156
"This kind of Hepatitis can cause ya"   1156
"Giddy-yup giddy-yup giddy-yap"   1156
"Turn on the heat & take a seat"   1157
Bop Sh'bam   1158
Dream   1159
Things I'll Not Do (Nostalgias)   1160

Afterword   *1163*
Notes   *1167*

Index of Titles, First Lines, and Original Book Sources   *1175*

COLLECTED
POEMS
1947–1980

"Things are symbols of themselves."

Portions of this work have appeared in the following Allen Ginsberg books:

Airplane Dreams. House of Anasi, Toronto/City Lights Books, San Francisco, 1968.
Angkor Wat. Fulcrum Press, London, 1968.
As Ever: Collected Correspondence Allen Ginsberg & Neal Cassady. Creative Arts Book Company, Berkeley, 1977.
Empty Mirror, Early Poems. Totem/Corinth, New York, 1961.
The Fall of America, Poems of These States 1965–1971. City Lights Books, San Francisco, 1973.
The Gates of Wrath: Rhymed Poems, 1948–1951. Grey Fox Press, 1972.
Howl & Other Poems. City Lights Books, San Francisco, 1956.
Indian Journals. City Lights Books, San Francisco, 1970.
Iron Horse. City Lights Books, San Francisco, 1974.
Journals: Early Fifties Early Sixties. Grove Press, New York, 1977.
Kaddish and Other Poems, 1958–1960. City Lights Books, San Francisco, 1978.
Mind Breaths: Poems 1972–1977. City Lights Books, San Francisco, 1978.
Planet News. City Lights Books, San Francisco, 1968.
Plutonian Ode: Poems 1977–1980. City Lights Books, San Francisco, 1982.
Poems All Over the Place: Mostly Seventies. Cherry Valley Editions, Cherry Valley, NY, 1978.
Reality Sandwiches: 1953–1960. City Lights Books, San Francisco, 1963.
Sad Dust Glories: Poems Work Summer in Woods 1974. Workingmans Press, 1975.
Straight Hearts' Delight: Love Poems & Selected Letters, by Allen Ginsberg and Peter Orlovsky. Edited by Winston Leyland. Gay Sunshine Press, 1980.

To
Naomi Ginsberg
1894–1956

———

Louis Ginsberg
1896–1976

Author's Preface, Reader's Manual

Arrangement of Text

Herein author has assembled all his poetry books published to date rearranged in straight chronological order to compose an autobiography. *Collected Poems* includes seven volumes published in City Lights Pocket Poets series: *Howl, Kaddish, Reality Sandwiches, Planet News, The Fall of America, Mind Breaths,* and *Plutonian Ode,* backbone of three decades' writing.

Books circulated less widely by delicate small presses (excepting song experiments in *First Blues*) fill gaps in the sequence. Youthful poetries were printed in *Empty Mirror* and *The Gates of Wrath.* Three odd books, *Angkor Wat, Iron Horse* and *Airplane Dreams,* interleaf poems of the 1960s. *Poems All Over the Place* flash on spots of time from President Kennedy's assassination day, through 1972 Presidentiad, to author's meditation practice in his fiftieth year.

Among half-dozen poems taken from prose journal and letter books, one singular rhapsody, "The Names," falls into place, with motifs from "Howl" particularized in 1958.

"Many Loves" manuscript, detailing first erotic encounter with a lifelong friend, not printed till now for reasons of prudence and modesty, completes a sequence of writing that included "Sunflower Sutra" and "America," Berkeley 1956.

Advantages of Chronological Order

The Gates of Wrath's imperfect literary rhymes are interspersed with *Empty Mirror*'s raw-sketch practice poems. Disparate simultaneous early styles juxtaposed aid recognition of a grounded mode of writing encouraged by Dr. Williams, "No ideas but in things."

"A Strange New Cottage in Berkeley" precedes "A Supermarket in California" because it was composed on top of the same page, originally one poem in two parts, here rejoined.

Travel poems Calcutta-Saigon-Angkor Wat-Japan, 1963, mixed through three separate books, now cohere in sequence.

Cross-country Auto Poesy chronicle starts 1965 at Northwest border *(The Fall of America),* continues through Wichita vortex East *(Planet News),* recrosses U.S.A. Oakland to New York *(Iron Horse)* and tarries 1966 East, returns via Chicago North of vortex 1967, and comes back through Northwest passage 1969 *(The Fall of America).*

* * *

Reader exploring *Collected Poems'* mass of writing will find Contents divided into ten sections, roughly indicating time, geography, and motif or "season" of experience.

Reader may further observe poetic energy as cyclic, the continuum a panorama of valleys and plateaus with peaks of inspiration every few years. This chain of strong-breath'd poems links "The Song of the Shrouded Stranger of the Night," 1949, with "The Green Automobile," 1953, "Siesta in Xbalba," 1954, "Howl," "Sunflower Sutra" and "Many Loves," 1955–1956, "The Names," 1958, "Kaddish," 1959, "TV Baby," 1960, "The Change," 1963, "Kral Majales," 1965, "Wichita Vortex Sutra," 1966, "Wales Visitation," 1967, "On Neal's Ashes," 1968, "September on Jessore Road," 1971, "Mind Breaths," 1973, "Father Death Blues," 1976, "Contest of Bards," 1977, "Plutonian Ode," 1978, "Birdbrain!" and "Capitol Air," 1980.*

Texture of Texts

"First thought, best thought." Spontaneous insight—the sequence of thought-forms passing naturally through ordinary mind—was always motif and method of these compositions.

Syntax punctuation Capitalization remain idiosyncratic, retaining the variable measure of nervous systematics. In many poems, semi-irregular indentation of verse conforms to divisions of original notation or spacings of first thought-speech mindfully recollected. "Mind is shapely, Art is shapely."

Nevertheless some touches are added here and there, adjustments made after years of reading works aloud, changes few and far between. Defective passages or words are excised from several poems, including "Sunflower Sutra" and "Wales Visitation." Author has altered a dozen or more phrases that consistently annoyed him over years, eliminated half-dozen foggy adjectives or added a half-dozen factual epithets to clear up the sense of dated verses, notably in "America."

Typographical errors, misalignment of verse on pages of previous printings, and unintended grammatic quirks are corrected. Apparent solecisms were judged, approved or cast out.

Assembled Appendixes

"Notes" transmit cultural archetypes to electronic laser TV generations that don't read Dostoyevsky Buddha bibles. Karma wants understanding, Moloch needs noting. Mini-essays hint further reading for innocent-eyed

---

*"White Shroud," 1983, dream epilogue to "Kaddish" and title poem of book subsequent to *Collected Poems,* is late work of true inspiration in this sequence.

youths. Author took opportunity to verify ephemera in his poetry, interpret recurrent reference images for peers and elders.

Dante, Milton, Blake and Smart footnotes were made by scholars. Mary Wollstonecraft Shelley wrote extensive commentaries for Percy Shelley's posthumous collections. Wordsworth and Eliot favored readers by composing their own notes; their practice had precedents.

The back of this book preserves old title-page "Epigraphs" and "Dedications," artifacts of original pamphlets which played their part in the drama of breakthrough from closed form to open form in American poetry. A small-press culture revolution helped change hyper-industrialized public consciousness from provincial wartime nationalist-history-bound egoic myopia to panoramic awareness of planet news, eternal view of both formal charm and empty nature of local identity. "Acknowledgments" alphabetize an extravagant list of publications that first printed these poems throughout three decades of explosive humor during which legal censorship broke down. Present gratitudes find place here. Artisans who collaborated on this volume are specified. William Carlos Williams's "Introductions" to two early books are retained, as well as "Author's Writ," jacket-blurb prose-poetries once composed as précis for each book.

"Index of Proper Names" is designed to make this large volume "user friendly." *Collected Poems* may be read as a lifelong poem including history, wherein things are symbols of themselves. Cross-reference between texts and notes can serve as rough concordance to the book's mythic actualities, from Cassady to CIA to Sakyamuni. "Index of Proper Names" and "Index of Titles, First Lines, and Original Book Sources" complete the work.

ALLEN GINSBERG

New York City
June 26, 1984

I
EMPTY MIRROR: GATES OF WRATH
(1947–1952)

In Society

I walked into the cocktail party
room and found three or four queers
talking together in queertalk.
I tried to be friendly but heard
myself talking to one in hiptalk.
"I'm glad to see you," he said, and
looked away. "Hmn," I mused. The room
was small and had a double-decker
bed in it, and cooking apparatus:
icebox, cabinet, toasters, stove;
the hosts seemed to live with room
enough only for cooking and sleeping.
My remark on this score was under-
stood but not appreciated. I was
offered refreshments, which I accepted.
I ate a sandwich of pure meat; an
enormous sandwich of human flesh,
I noticed, while I was chewing on it,
it also included a dirty asshole.

More company came, including a
fluffy female who looked like
a princess. She glared at me and
said immediately: "I don't like you,"
turned her head away, and refused
to be introduced. I said, "What!"
in outrage. "Why you shit-faced fool!"
This got everybody's attention.
"Why you narcissistic bitch! How
can you decide when you don't even
know me," I continued in a violent
and messianic voice, inspired at
last, dominating the whole room

Dream New York–Denver, Spring 1947

The Bricklayer's Lunch Hour

Two bricklayers are setting the walls
of a cellar in a new dug out patch
of dirt behind an old house of wood
with brown gables grown over with ivy
on a shady street in Denver. It is noon
and one of them wanders off. The young
subordinate bricklayer sits idly for
a few minutes after eating a sandwich
and throwing away the paper bag. He
has on dungarees and is bare above
the waist; he has yellow hair and wears
a smudged but still bright red cap
on his head. He sits idly on top
of the wall on a ladder that is leaned
up between his spread thighs, his head
bent down, gazing uninterestedly at
the paper bag on the grass. He draws
his hand across his breast, and then
slowly rubs his knuckles across the
side of his chin, and rocks to and fro
on the wall. A small cat walks to him
along the top of the wall. He picks
it up, takes off his cap, and puts it
over the kitten's body for a moment.
Meanwhile it is darkening as if to rain
and the wind on top of the trees in the
street comes through almost harshly.

Denver, Summer 1947

Two Sonnets

After Reading Kerouac's Manuscript
The Town and the City

I

I dwelled in Hell on earth to write this rhyme,
I live in stillness now, in living flame;
I witness Heaven in unholy time,
I room in the renownèd city, am
Unknown. The fame I dwell in is not mine,
I would not have it. Angels in the air
Serenade my senses in delight.
Intelligence of poets, saints and fair
Characters converse with me all night.
But all the streets are burning everywhere.
The city is burning these multitudes that climb
Her buildings. Their inferno is the same
I scaled as a stupendous blazing stair.
They vanish as I look into the light.

II

Woe unto thee, Manhattan, woe to thee,
Woe unto all the cities of the world.
Repent, Chicagos, O repent; ah, me!
Los Angeles, now thou art gone so wild,
I think thou art still mighty, yet shall be,
As the earth shook, and San Francisco fell,
An angel in an agony of flame.
City of horrors, New York so much like Hell,
How soon thou shalt be city-without-name,
A tomb of souls, and a poor broken knell.
Fire and fire on London, Moscow shall die,
And Paris her livid atomies be rolled
Together into the Woe of the blazing bell—
All cities then shall toll for their great fame.

New York, Spring 1948

On Reading William Blake's "The Sick Rose"

Rose of spirit, rose of light,
Flower whereof all will tell,
Is this black vision of my sight
The fashion of a prideful spell,
Mystic charm or magic bright,
O Judgement of fire and of fright?

What everlasting force confounded
In its being, like some human
Spirit shrunken in a bounded
Immortality, what Blossom
Gathers us inward, astounded?
Is this the sickness that is Doom?

East Harlem, June–July 1948

The Eye Altering Alters All

Many seek and never see,
anyone can tell them why.
O they weep and O they cry
and never take until they try
unless they try it in their sleep
and never some until they die.
I ask many, they ask me.
This is a great mystery.

East Harlem, June–July 1948

A Very Dove

A very Dove will have her love
    ere the Dove has died;
the spirit, vanity approve,
    will even love in pride;

and cannot love, and yet can hate,
    spirit to fulfill;
the spirit cannot watch and wait,
    the Hawk must have his kill.

There is a Gull that rolls alone
    over billows loud;
the Nightingale at night will moan
    under her soft shroud.

East Harlem, July 1948

Vision 1948

Dread spirit in me that I ever try
        With written words to move,
    Hear thou my plea, at last reply
        To my impotent pen:
    Should I endure, and never prove
        Yourself and me in love,
Tell me, spirit, tell me, O what then?

And if not love, why, then, another passion
        For me to pass in image:
    Shadow, shadow, and blind vision.
        Dumb roar of the white trance,
    Ecstatic shadow out of rage,
        Power out of passage.
Dance, dance, spirit, spirit, dance!

Is it my fancy that the world is still,
        So gentle in her dream?
    Outside, great Harlems of the will
        Move under black sleep:
    Yet in spiritual scream,
        The saxophones the same
As me in madness call thee from the deep.

I shudder with intelligence and I
        Wake in the deep light
    And hear a vast machinery
        Descending without sound,
    Intolerable to me, too bright,
        And shaken in the sight
The eye goes blind before the world goes round.

                        East Harlem, July 1948

Do We Understand Each Other?

My love has come to ride me home
To our room and bed.
I had walked the wide sea path,
For my love would roam
In absence long and glad
All through our land of wrath.
We wandered wondrously,
I, still mild, true and sad,
But merry, mad and free
My love was. Look! yet come love hath.
Is this not great gentility?

I only remembered the ocean's roll,
And islands that I passed,
And, in a vision of death and dread,
A city where my soul
Visited its vast
Passage of the dead.
My love's eternity
I never entered, when, at last
"I blush with love for thee,"
My love, renewed in anger, said.
Is this not great gentility?

Over the road in an automobile
Rode I and my gentle love.
The traffic on our way was wild;
My love was at the wheel,
And in and out we drove.
My own eyes were mild.
How my love merrily
Dared the other cars to rove:
"But if they stop for me,
Why, then, I stop for them, my child."
Is this not great gentility?

East Harlem, July 1948

The Voice of Rock

I cannot sleep, I cannot sleep
until a victim is resigned;
a shadow holds me in his keep
and seeks the bones that he must find;
and hoveled in a shroudy heap
dead eyes see, and dead eyes weep,
dead men from the coffin creep,
nightmare of murder in the mind.

Murder has the ghost of shame
that lies abed with me in dirt
and mouths the matter of my fame.
With voice of rock, and rock engirt,
a shadow cries out in my name;
he struggles for my writhing frame;
my death and his were not the same,
what wounds have I that he is hurt?

This is such murder that my own
incorporeal blood is shed,
but shadow changes into bone,
and thoughts are doubled in my head;
for what he knows and I have known
is, like a crystal lost in stone,
hidden in skin and buried down,
blind as the vision of the dead.

Paterson, August 1948

Refrain

The air is dark, the night is sad,
I lie sleepless and I groan.
Nobody cares when a man goes mad:
He is sorry, God is glad.
Shadow changes into bone.

Every shadow has a name;
When I think of mine I moan,
I hear rumors of such fame.
Not for pride, but only shame,
Shadow changes into bone.

When I blush I weep for joy,
And laughter drops from me like stone:
The aging laughter of the boy
To see the ageless dead so coy.
Shadow changes into bone.

Paterson, August 1948

A Western Ballad

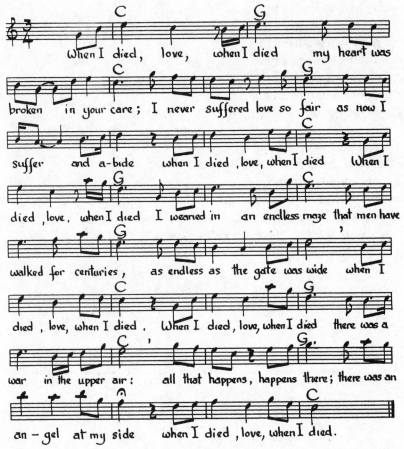

When I died, love, when I died my heart was
broken in your care; I never suffered love so fair as now I
suffer and a-bide when I died, love, when I died When I
died, love, when I died I wearied in an endless maze that men have
walked for centuries, as endless as the gate was wide when I
died, love, when I died. When I died, love, when I died there was a
war in the upper air: all that happens, happens there; there was an
an-gel at my side when I died, love, when I died.

A Western Ballad

When I died, love, when I died
my heart was broken in your care;
I never suffered love so fair
as now I suffer and abide
when I died, love, when I died.

When I died, love, when I died
I wearied in an endless maze
that men have walked for centuries,
as endless as the gate was wide
when I died, love, when I died.

When I died, love, when I died
there was a war in the upper air:
all that happens, happens there;
there was an angel at my side
when I died, love, when I died.

Paterson, August 1948

The Trembling of the Veil

Today out of the window
the trees seemed like live
organisms on the moon.

Each bough extended upward
covered at the north end
with leaves, like a green

hairy protuberance. I saw
the scarlet-and-pink shoot-tips
of budding leaves wave

delicately in the sunlight,
blown by the breeze,
all the arms of the trees
bending and straining downward

at once when the wind
pushed them.

Paterson, August 1948

A Meaningless Institution

I was given my bedding, and a bunk
in an enormous ward,
surrounded by hundreds of weeping,
decaying men and women.

I sat on my bunk, three tiers up
next to the ceiling,
looking down the gray aisles.
Old, crippled, dumb people were

bent over sewing. A heavy girl
in a dirty dress
stared at me. I waited
for an official guide to come

and give me instructions.
After awhile, I wandered
off down empty corridors
in search of a toilet.

Dream, Paterson, Fall 1948

A Mad Gleam

Go back to Egypt and the Greeks,
Where the Wizard understood
The spectre haunted where man seeks
And spoke to ghosts that stood in blood.

Go back, go back to the old legend;
The soul remembers, and is true:
What has been most and least imagined,
No other, there is nothing new.

The giant Phantom is ascending
Toward its coronation, gowned
With music unheard, but unending:
Follow the flower to the ground.

New York, January 1949

Complaint of the Skeleton to Time

Take my love, it is not true,
So let it tempt no body new;
Take my lady, she will sigh
For my bed where'er I lie;
Take them, said the skeleton,
  But leave my bones alone.

Take my raiment, now grown cold,
To give to some poor poet old;
Take the skin that hoods this truth
If his age would wear my youth;
Take them, said the skeleton,
  But leave my bones alone.

Take the thoughts that like the wind
Blow my body out of mind;
Take this heart to go with that
And pass it on from rat to rat;
Take them, said the skeleton,
  But leave my bones alone.

Take the art which I bemoan
In a poem's crazy tone;
Grind me down, though I may groan,
To the starkest stick and stone;
Take them, said the skeleton,
  But leave my bones alone.

Early 1949

Psalm I

These psalms are the workings of the vision haunted mind and not that reason which never changes.

I am flesh and blood, but my mind is the focus of much lightning.

I change with the weather, with the state of my finances, with the work I do, with my company.

But truly none of these is accountable for the majestic flaws of mind which have left my brain open to hallucination.

All work has been an imitation of the literary cackle in my head.

This gossip is an eccentric document to be lost in a library and rediscovered when the Dove descends.

New York, February 1949

An Eastern Ballad

I speak of love that comes to mind:
The moon is faithful, although blind;
She moves in thought she cannot speak.
Perfect care has made her bleak.

I never dreamed the sea so deep,
The earth so dark; so long my sleep,
I have become another child.
I wake to see the world go wild.

1945–1949

Sweet Levinsky

Sweet Levinsky in the night
Sweet Levinsky in the light
do you giggle out of spite,
or are you laughing in delight
sweet Levinsky, sweet Levinsky?

Sweet Levinsky, do you tremble
when the cock crows, and dissemble
as you amble to the gambol?
Why so humble when you stumble
sweet Levinsky, sweet Levinsky?

Sweet Levinsky, why so tearful,
sweet Levinsky don't be fearful,
sweet Levinsky here's your earful
of the angels chirping cheerful-
ly Levinsky, sweet Levinsky,
sweet Levinsky, sweet Levinsky.

New York, Spring 1949

Psalm II

Ah, still Lord, ah, sweet Divinity
Incarnate in our grave and holy substance,
Circumscribed in this hexed endless world
Of Time, that turns a triple face, from Hell,
Imprisoned joy's incognizable thought,
To mounted earth, that shudders to conceive,
Toward angels, borne unseen out of this world,
Translate the speechless stanzas of the rose
Into my poem, and I vow to copy
Every petal on a page; perfume
My mind, ungardened, and in weedy earth;
Let these dark leaves be lit with images
That strike like lightning from eternal mind,
Truths that are not visible in any light
That changes and is Time, like flesh or theory,
Corruptible like any clock of meat
That sickens and runs down to die
With all those structures and machinery
Whose bones and bridges break and wash to sea
And are dissolved into green salt and coral.

A Bird of Paradise, the Nightingale
I cried for not so long ago, the poet's
Phoenix, and the erotic Swan
Which descended and transfigured Time,
And all but destroyed it, in the Dove
I speak of now are here, I saw it here,
The Miracle, which no man knows entire,
Nor I myself. But shadow is my prophet,
I cast a shadow that surpasses me,
And I write, shadow changes into bone,
To say that still Word, the prophetic image
Beyond our present strength of flesh to bear,
Incarnate in the rain as in the sea,
Watches after us out of our eyes.
What a sweet dream! to be some incorruptible
Divinity, corporeal without a name,
Suffering metamorphosis of flesh.

Holy are the Visions of the soul
The visible mind seeks out for marriage,
As if the sleeping heart, agaze, in darkness,
Would dream her passions out as in the Heavens.
In flesh and flesh, imperfect spirits join
Vision upon vision, image upon image,
All physical and perishing, till spirit
Driven mad by Time, a ghost still haunted
By his mortal house, goes from the tomb
And drops his body back into the dirt.
I fear it till my soul remembers Heaven.
My name is Angel and my eyes are Fire!
O wonder, and more than wonder, in the world!
Now I have built my Love a sepulchre
Of whitened thoughts, and sat a year in ash,
Grieving for the lost entempled dead,
And Him who appeared to these dead eyes,
And Him my wakened beating mind remembered,
And Love that moved in substance clear as bone,
With beautiful music, at the fatal moment,
And clock stopped by its own, or hidden, hand.
These are the hollow echoes of His word.

Ah, but to have seen the Dove of still
Divinity come down in silken light of summer sun
In ignorance of the body and bone's madness.
Light falls and I fail! My youth is ending,
All my youth, and Death and Beauty cry
Like horns and motors from a ship afar,
Half heard, an echo in the sea beneath,
And Death and Beauty beckon in the dawn,
A presage of the world of whitening shadows
As another pale memorial.
Ah! but to have seen the Dove, and then go blind.

I will grow old a grey and groaning man,
Hour after hour, with each hour a thought,
And with each thought the same denial. Am I to spend
My life in praise of the idea of God?
Time leaves no hope, and leaves us none of love;
We creep and wait, we wait and go alone.
When will the heart be weary of its own

Indignity? Or Time endured destroy
The last such thoughts as these, the thoughts of Dove?
Must ravenous reason not be self-consumed?
Our souls are purified of Time by Time,
And ignorance consumes itself like flesh.

Bigger and bigger gates, Thou givest, Lord,
And vaster deaths, and deaths not by my hand,
Till, in each season, as the garden dies,
I die with each, until I die no more
Time's many deaths, and pass toward the last gates,
Till come, pure light, at last to pass through pearl.
Take me to thy mansion, for I house
In clay, in a sad dolor out of joy.

Behold thy myth incarnate in my flesh
Now made incarnate in Thy Psalm, O Lord.

New York, March 1949

Fie My Fum

Pull my daisy,
Tip my cup,
Cut my thoughts
For coconuts,

Bone my shadow,
Dove my soul,
Set a halo
On my skull,

Ark my darkness,
Rack my lacks,
Bleak my lurking,
Lark my looks,

Start my Arden,
Gate my shades,
Silk my garden,
Rose my days,

Whore my door,
Stone my dream,
Milk my mind
And make me cream,

Say my oops,
Ope my shell,
Roll my bones,
Ring my bell,

Pope my parts,
Pop my pot,
Poke my pap,
Pit my plum.

New York, Spring 1949

Pull My Daisy

Pull my daisy
tip my cup
all my doors are open
Cut my thoughts
for coconuts
all my eggs are broken
Jack my Arden
gate my shades
woe my road is spoken
Silk my garden
rose my days
now my prayers awaken

Bone my shadow
dove my dream
start my halo bleeding
Milk my mind &
make me cream
drink me when you're ready
Hop my heart on
harp my height
seraphs hold me steady
Hip my angel
hype my light
lay it on the needy

Heal the raindrop
sow the eye
bust my dust again
Woe the worm
work the wise
dig my spade the same
Stop the hoax
what's the hex
where's the wake
how's the hicks
take my golden beam

Rob my locker
lick my rocks
leap my cock in school
Rack my lacks
lark my looks
jump right up my hole
Whore my door
beat my boor
eat my snake of fool
Craze my hair
bare my poor
asshole shorn of wool

Say my oops
ope my shell
bite my naked nut
Roll my bones
ring my bell
call my worm to sup
Pope my parts
pop my pot
raise my daisy up
Poke my pap
pit my plum
let my gap be shut

Allen Ginsberg, Jack Kerouac & Neal Cassady
New York, Spring–Fall 1949

The Shrouded Stranger

Bare skin is my wrinkled sack
When hot Apollo humps my back
When Jack Frost grabs me in these rags
I wrap my legs with burlap bags

My flesh is cinder my face is snow
I walk the railroad to and fro
When city streets are black and dead
The railroad embankment is my bed

I sup my soup from old tin cans
And take my sweets from little hands
In Tiger Alley near the jail
I steal away from the garbage pail

In darkest night where none can see
Down in the bowels of the factory
I sneak barefoot upon stone
Come and hear the old man groan

I hide and wait like a naked child
Under the bridge my heart goes wild
I scream at a fire on the river bank
I give my body to an old gas tank

I dream that I have burning hair
Boiled arms that claw the air
The torso of an iron king
And on my back a broken wing

Who'll go out whoring into the night
On the eyeless road in the skinny moonlight
Maid or dowd or athlete proud
May wanton with me in the shroud

Who'll come lie down in the dark with me
Belly to belly and knee to knee
Who'll look into my hooded eye
Who'll lie down under my darkened thigh?

New York, 1949–1951

Stanzas: Written at Night
in Radio City

If money made the mind more sane,
Or money mellowed in the bowel
The hunger beyond hunger's pain,
Or money choked the mortal growl
And made the groaner grin again,
Or did the laughing lamb embolden
To loll where has the lion lain,
I'd go make money and be golden.

Nor sex will salve the sickened soul,
Which has its holy goal an hour,
Holds to heart the golden pole,
But cannot save the silver shower,
Nor heal the sorry parts to whole.
Love is creeping under cover,
Where it hides its sleepy dole,
Else I were like any lover.

Many souls get lost at sea,
Others slave upon a stone:
Engines are not eyes to me,
Inside buildings I see bone.
Some from city to city flee,
Famous labors make them lie;
I cheat on that machinery,
Down in Arden I will die.

Art is short, nor style is sure:
Though words our virgin thoughts betray,
Time ravishes that thought most pure,
Which those who know, know anyway;
For if our daughter should endure,
When once we can no more complain,
Men take our beauty for a whore,
And like a whore, to entertain.

The city's hipper slickers shine,
Up in the attic with the bats;

The higher Chinamen, supine,
Wear a dragon in their hats:
He who seeks a secret sign
In a daze or sicker doze
Blows the flower superfine;
Not a poppy is a rose.

If fame were not a fickle charm,
There were far more famous men:
May boys amaze the world to arm,
Yet their charms are changed again,
And fearful heroes turn to harm;
But the shambles is a sham.
A few angels on a farm
Fare more fancy with their lamb.

No more of this too pretty talk,
Dead glimpses of apocalypse:
The child pissing off the rock,
Or woman withered in the lips,
Contemplate the unseen Cock
That crows all beasts to ecstasy;
And so the Saints beyond the clock
Cry to men their dead eyes see.

Come, incomparable crown,
Love my love is lost to claim,
O hollow fame that makes me groan;
We are a king without a name:
Regain thine angel's lost renown,
As, in the mind's forgotten meadow,
Where brightest shades sleep under stone,
Man runs after his own shadow.

New York, March 1949

After All, What Else
Is There to Say?

When I sit before a paper
    writing my mind turns
in a kind of feminine
    madness of chatter;
but to think to see, outside,
in a tenement the walls
    of the universe itself
I wait: wait till the sky
    appears as it is,
wait for a moment when
    the poem itself
is my way of speaking out, not
declaiming of celebrating, yet,
    but telling the truth.

New York, Early 1949

Sometime Jailhouse Blues

Sometime I'll lay down my wrath,
As I lay my body down
Between the ache of breath and breath,
Golden slumber in the bone.

Thought's a stone, though sweet or sorry,
Run-down from an uphill climb:
Money, money, work and worry,
And all the aimless toil of Time.

Sometime I look up in light
And see the weary sun go West;
Sometime I see the moon at night
Go hidden in her cloudy rest.

Sometime tears of death will blind
All that was worldly, wise or fair,
And visioned by the death of mind
My ghost will wander in the air,

And gaze upon a ghostly face,
Not knowing what was fair or lost,
Remembering not what flesh lay waste,
Or made him kind as ghost to ghost.

Brooklyn, April 24, 1949

Please Open the Window and Let Me In

Who is the shroudy stranger of the night,
Whose brow is mouldering green, whose reddened eye
Hides near the window trellis in dim light,
And gapes at old men, and makes children cry?

Who is the laughing walker of the street,
The alley mummy, stinking of the bone,
To dance unfixed, though bound in shadow feet,
Behind the child that creeps on legs of stone?

Who is the hungry mocker of the maze,
And haggard gate-ghost, hanging by the door,
The double mummer in whose hooded gaze
World has beckoned unto world once more?

Paterson, May 1949

Tonite all is well . . . What a
terrible future. I am twenty-three,
year of the iron birthday,
gate of darkness. I am ill,
I have become physically and
spiritually impotent in my madness this month.
I suddenly realized that my head
is severed from my body;
I realized it a few nights ago
by myself,
lying sleepless on the couch.

Paterson, Summer 1949

Fyodor

The death's head of realism
and superhuman iron mask
that gapes out of *The Possessed*,
sometimes: Dostoievski.
My original version of D.
before I read him, as the dark
haunted-house man, wild, agèd,
spectral Russian. I call him
Dusty now but he is
Dostoyevsky. What premonitions
I had as a child.

Paterson, June 1949

Epigram on a Painting of Golgotha

On a bare tree in a hollow place,
A blinded form's unhaloed face;
Sight, where Heaven is destroyed,
The hanging visage of the void.

New York, Summer 1949

"The road to a true philosophy of life seems to lie in humbly recording diverse readings of its phenomena."
—*Thos. Hardy*

I attempted to concentrate
the total sun's rays in
each poem as through a glass,
but such magnification
did not set the page afire.

New York, Summer 1949

Metaphysics

This is the one and only
firmament; therefore
it is the absolute world.
There is no other world.
The circle is complete.
I am living in Eternity.
The ways of this world
are the ways of Heaven.

New York, Mid-1949

In Death, Cannot Reach
What Is Most Near

We know all about death that
we will ever know because
we have all experienced
the state before birth.
Life seems a passage between
two doors to the darkness.
Both are the same and truly
eternal, and perhaps it may
be said that we meet in
darkness. The nature of time
is illuminated by this
meeting of eternal ends.

It is amazing to think that
thought and personality
of man is perpetuated in
time after his passage
to eternity. And one time
is all Time if you look
at it out of the grave.

New York, Mid-1949

This Is About Death

Art recalls the memory
of his true existence
to whoever has forgotten
that Being is the one thing
all the universe shouts.

Only return of thought to
its source will complete thought.
Only return of activity
to its source will complete
activity. Listen to that.

Mid-1949

Hymn

No hyacinthine imagination can express this clock of meat bleakly pining for
      its sweet immaterial paradise which I have celebrated in one gone
      dithyramb after another and have elevated to that highest place in the
      mind's angelical empyrean which shall in the course of hot centuries
      to come come to be known as the clock of light:
the very summa and dove of the unshrouding of finality's joy whence cometh
      purely pearly streams of reves and honey-thoughts and all like
      dreamy essences our hearts therefrom so filled with such incompara-
      ble and crownly creaminess one never knew whence it came,
whether from those foul regions of the soul the ancients named Malebolge
      or the Dank or the icicle-like crystal roads of cloudless sky called
      Icecube or Avenue where the angels late fourteen there convened
      hang on and raptly gaze on us singing down
in mewing voices liturgies of milk and sweet cream sighing no longer for
      the strawberries of the world whence in pain and wit's despair they
      had ascended stoops of light up the celestial fire escape no more to
      sit suffering as we do one and all on the thorn
nor more we shall when the final gate is opened and the Diamond Seraph
      armed with 3 forks of lightning 7 claps of thunder 11 bursts of
      laughter and a thousand tears rolling down his silken cheeks bares his
      radiant breast and asks us in the Name of the Lord to share that Love
      in Heaven which on Earth was so disinherited.

September 1949

Sunset

The whole blear world
of smoke and twisted steel
around my head in a railroad
car, and my mind wandering
past the rust into futurity:
I saw the sun go down
in a carnal and primeval
world, leaving darkness
to cover my railroad train
because the other side of the
world was waiting for dawn.

New York–Paterson, November 1949

Ode to the Setting Sun

*The Jersey Marshes in rain, November evening,
seen from Susquehanna Railroad*

The wrathful East of smoke and iron
Crowded in a broken crown;
The Archer of the Jersey mire
Naked in a rusty gown;
Railroad creeping toward the fire
Where the carnal sun goes down.

Apollo's shining chariot's shadow
Shudders in the mortal bourn;
Amber shores upon the meadow
Where Phaëthon falls forlorn
Fade in somber chiaroscuro,
Phantoms of the burning morn.

Westward to the world's blind gaze,
In funeral of raining cloud,
The motionless cold Heavens blaze,
Born out of a dying crowd;
Daybreak in the end of days,
Bloody light beneath the shroud.

In vault dominion of the night
The hosts of prophecy convene,
Till, empire of the lark alight,
Their bodies waken as we dream,
And put our raiment on, and bright
Crown, still haloed though unseen.

Under the earth there is an eye
Open in a sightless cave,
And the skull in Eternity
Bares indifference to the grave:
Earth turns, and the day must die,
And the sea accepts the wave.

My bones are carried on the train
Westward where the sun has gone;

Night has darkened in the rain,
And the rainbow day is done;
Cities age upon the plain
And smoke rolls upward out of stone.

New York–Paterson, November 1949–1950

Paterson

What do I want in these rooms papered with visions of money?
How much can I make by cutting my hair? If I put new heels on my shoes,
bathe my body reeking of masturbation and sweat, layer upon layer of
    excrement
dried in employment bureaus, magazine hallways, statistical cubicles, factory
    stairways,
cloakrooms of the smiling gods of psychiatry;
if in antechambers I face the presumption of department store supervisory
    employees,
old clerks in their asylums of fat, the slobs and dumbbells of the ego with
    money and power
to hire and fire and make and break and fart and justify their reality of wrath
and rumor of wrath to wrath-weary man,
what war I enter and for what a prize! the dead prick of commonplace
    obsession,
harridan vision of electricity at night and daylight misery of thumb-sucking
    rage.

I would rather go mad, gone down the dark road to Mexico, heroin dripping
    in my veins,
eyes and ears full of marijuana,
eating the god Peyote on the floor of a mudhut on the border
or laying in a hotel room over the body of some suffering man or woman;
rather jar my body down the road, crying by a diner in the Western sun;
rather crawl on my naked belly over the tincans of Cincinnati;
rather drag a rotten railroad tie to a Golgotha in the Rockies;
rather, crowned with thorns in Galveston, nailed hand and foot in Los
    Angeles, raised up to die in Denver,
pierced in the side in Chicago, perished and tombed in New Orleans and
    resurrected in 1958 somewhere on Garret Mountain,
come down roaring in a blaze of hot cars and garbage,
streetcorner Evangel in front of City Hall, surrounded by statues of agonized
    lions,
with a mouthful of shit, and the hair rising on my scalp,
screaming and dancing in praise of Eternity annihilating the sidewalk, an-
    nihilating reality,
screaming and dancing against the orchestra in the destructible ballroom of
    the world,
blood streaming from my belly and shoulders

flooding the city with its hideous ecstasy, rolling over the pavements and
    highways
by the bayoux and forests and derricks leaving my flesh and my bones
    hanging on the trees.

New York, November 1949

Bop Lyrics

When I think of death
  I get a goofy feeling;
Then I catch my breath:
  Zero is appealing,
    Appearances are hazy.
    Smart went crazy,
    Smart went crazy.

      *

A flower in my head
  Has fallen through my eye;
Someday I'll be dead:
  I love the Lord on high,
    I wish He'd pull my daisy.
    Smart went crazy,
    Smart went crazy.

      *

I asked the lady what's a rose,
  She kicked me out of bed.
I asked the man, and so it goes,
  He hit me on the head.
    Nobody knows,
    Nobody knows,
  At least nobody's said.

      *

The time I went to China
To lead the boy scout troops,
They sank my ocean liner,
And all I said was "Oops!"

      *

All the doctors think I'm crazy;
The truth is really that I'm lazy:
I made visions to beguile 'em
Till they put me in th'asylum

      *

I'm a pot and God's a potter,
And my head's a piece of putty.
    Ark my darkness,
    Lark my looks,
I'm so lucky to be nutty.

New York, March–December 1949

A Dream

I waked at midmost in the night,
Dim lamp shuddering in the bell,
House enwracked with natal light
That glowed as in a ghostly shell.

I rose and darked the hornlike flare,
And watched the shadows in the room
Crawl on walls and empty air
Through the window from the moon.

I stared in phantom-attic dark
At such radiant shapes of gloom,
I thought my fancy and mind's lark
So cried for Death that He had come.

As sleepy-faced night walkers go,
Room to room, and down the stair,
Through the labyrinth to and fro,
So I paced sleepless in nightmare.

I walked out to the city tower,
Where, as in a stony cell,
Time lay prisoned, and twelfth hour
Complained upon the midnight bell.

I met a boy on the city street,
Fair was his hair, and fair his eyes,
Walking in his winding sheet,
As fair as was my own disguise.

He walked his way in a white shroud,
His cheek was whiter than his gown.
He looked at me, and spoke aloud,
And all his voice was but a groan:

"My love is dreaming of me now,
For I have dreamed him oft so well
That in my ghostly sleep I go
To find him by the midnight bell.

And so I walk and speak these lines
Which he will hear and understand.
If some poor wandering child of time
Finds me, let him take my hand,

And I will lead him to the stone,
And I will lead him through the grave,
But let him fear no light of bone,
And let him fear no dark of wave,

And we will walk the double door
That breaks upon the ageless night,
Where I have come, and must once more
Return, and so forsake the light."

The darkness that is half disguised
In the Zodiac of my dream
Gazed on me in his bleak eyes,
And I became what now I seem.

Once my crown was silk and black;
I have dreamed, and I awake.
Now that time has wormed my cheek,
Horns and willows me bespeak.

Paterson, December 1949

Long Live the Spiderweb

Seven years' words wasted
waiting on the spiderweb:
        seven years' thoughts
harkening the host,
        seven years' lost
sentience naming images,
narrowing down the name
to nothing,
        seven years':
fears
in a web of ancient measure;
the words dead
flies, a crop
of ghosts,
        seven years':
the spider is dead.

Paterson, Spring 1950

The Shrouded Stranger

1
The Shroudy Stranger's reft of realms.
Abhorred he sits upon the city dump.
His broken heart's a bag of shit.
The vast rainfall, an empty mirror.

2
A Dream

He climbed over the rim
of the huge tower
looking down afraid,
descended the escarpment

over sheaves of rock,
crossed railyard gullies
and vast river-bridges
on the groundward slope

under an iron viaduct,
coming to rivulet
in a still meadow
by a small wood

where he stood trembling
in the naked flowers,
and walked under oak
to the house of folk.

3
I dreamed I was dreaming again
and decided to go down the years
looking for the Shrouded Stranger.
I knew the old bastard
was hanging around somewhere.
I couldn't find him for a while;
went looking under beds,
pulling mattresses off,
and finally discovered him

hiding under the springs
crouched in the corner:

met him face to face at last.
I didn't even recognize him.

"I'll bet you didn't think
it was me after all," he said.

4
Fragmenta Monumenti

It was to have a structure, it
was going to tell a story;
it was to be a mass of images
moving on a page, with
a hollow voice at the center;
it was to have told of Time
and Eternity; to have begun
in the rainfall's hood and moon,
and ended under the street light
of the world's bare physical
appearance; begun among vultures
in the mountains of Mexico,
traveled through all America
and ended in garbage on River Street;
its first line was to be
"Be with me Shroud, now—"
and the last "—naked
on broken bottles
between the brick walls,"
being THE VISION OF
THE SHROUDED STRANGER OF THE NIGHT.

Paterson–New York, 1949–September 1950

An Imaginary Rose in a Book

Oh dry old rose of God,
that with such bleak perfume
changed images to blood
and body to a tomb,

what fragrance you have lost,
and are now withered mere
crimson myth of dust
and recollection sere

of an unfading garden
whereof the myriad life
and all that flock in blossom,
none other met the knife.

Paterson, Early 1950

Crash

There is more to Fury
Than men imagine
Who drive a pallid jury
On a pale engine.

In a spinning plane,
A false machine,
The pilot drops in flame
From the unseen.

Paterson, Early 1950

The Terms in Which
I Think of Reality

a.
Reality is a question
of realizing how real
the world is already.

Time is Eternity,
ultimate and immovable;
everyone's an angel.

It's Heaven's mystery
of changing perfection:
absolutely Eternity

changes! Cars are always
going down the street,
lamps go off and on.

It's a great flat plain;
we can see everything
on top of the table.

Clams open on the table,
lambs are eaten by worms
on the plain. The motion

of change is beautiful,
as well as form called
in and out of being.

b.
Next: to distinguish process
in its particularity with
an eye to the initiation

of gratifying new changes
desired in the real world.
Here we're overwhelmed

with such unpleasant detail
we dream again of Heaven.
For the world is a mountain

of shit: if it's going to
be moved at all, it's got
to be taken by handfuls.

c.
Man lives like the unhappy
whore on River Street who
in her Eternity gets only

a couple of bucks and a lot
of snide remarks in return
for seeking physical love

the best way she knows how,
never really heard of a glad
job or joyous marriage or

a difference in the heart:
or thinks it isn't for her,
which is her worst misery.

Paterson, Spring 1950

The Night-Apple

Last night I dreamed
of one I loved
for seven long years,
but I saw no face,
only the familiar
presence of the body:
sweat skin eyes
feces urine sperm
saliva all one
odor and mortal taste.

Paterson, Spring 1950

Cézanne's Ports

In the foreground we see time and life
swept in a race
toward the left hand side of the picture
where shore meets shore.

But that meeting place
isn't represented;
it doesn't occur on the canvas.

For the other side of the bay
is Heaven and Eternity,
with a bleak white haze over its mountains.

And the immense water of L'Estaque is a go-between
for minute rowboats.

Paterson, Summer 1950

The Blue Angel

Marlene Dietrich is singing a lament
for mechanical love.
She leans against a mortarboard tree
on a plateau by the seashore.

She's a life-sized toy,
the doll of eternity;
her hair is shaped like an abstract hat
made out of white steel.

Her face is powdered, whitewashed and
immobile like a robot.
Jutting out of her temple, by an eye,
is a little white key.

She gazes through dull blue pupils
set in the whites of her eyes.
She closes them, and the key
turns by itself.

She opens her eyes, and they're blank
like a statue's in a museum.
Her machine begins to move, the key turns
again, her eyes change, she sings

—you'd think I would have thought a plan
to end the inner grind,
but not till I have found a man
to occupy my mind.

Dream, Paterson, Mid-1950

Two Boys Went Into a Dream Diner

and ate so much the bill was five dollars,
but they had no idea
what they were getting themselves into,
so they shoveled

garbage into a truck in the alley
to make up for the food.
After about five minutes, wondering
how long they would have

to work off what it cost, they asked
the diner owner when
their penance or pay would be over.
He laughed.

Little did they realize—they were
so virginal—
that a grown worker works half a day
for money like that.

Paterson, Mid-1950

A Desolation

Now mind is clear
as a cloudless sky.
Time then to make a
home in wilderness.

What have I done but
wander with my eyes
in the trees? So I
will build: wife,
family, and seek
for neighbors.

          Or I
perish of lonesomeness
or want of food or
lightning or the bear
(must tame the hart
and wear the bear).

And maybe make an image
of my wandering, a little
image—shrine by the
roadside to signify
to traveler that I live
here in the wilderness
awake and at home.

Paterson, Mid-1950

In Memoriam:
William Cannastra, 1922–1950

He cast off all his golden robes
and lay down sleeping in the night,
and in a dream he saw three fates
at a machine in a shroud of light.

He yelled "I wait the end of Time;
be with me, shroud, now, in my wrath!
There is a lantern in my grave,
who hath that lantern all light hath."

Alas! The prophet of this dream
is sunken in the dumbing clime:
much is finished, much forgotten
in the wrack and wild love of time.

It's death that makes man's life a dream
and heaven's splendor but a wave;
light that falls into the sea
is swallowed in a starving cave.

Skin may be visionary till the crystal
skull is coaled in aged shade,
but underground the lantern dies,
shroud must rot, and memory fade.

Who talks of Death and Angel now,
great angel darkened out of grace?
The shroud enfolds your radiant doom,
the silent Parcae change the race,

while the man of the apocalypse
shall with his wrath lie ever wed
until the sexless womb bear love,
and the grave be weary of the dead,

tragical master broken down
into a self-embodied tomb,
blinded by the sight of death,
and woven in the darkened loom.

Paterson, September 1950

Ode: My 24th Year

Now I have become a man
and know no more than mankind can
and groan with nature's every groan,
transcending child's blind skeleton
and all childish divinity,
while loomed in consanguinity
the weaving of the shroud goes on.

No two things alike; and yet
first memory dies, then I forget
one carnal thought that made thought grim:
but that has sunk below time's rim
and wonder ageing into woe
later dayes more fatal show:
Time gets thicker, light gets dim.

And I a second Time am blind,
all starlight dimmed out of the mind
that was first candle to the morn,
and candelabra turned to thorn.
All is dream till morn has rayed
the Rose of night back into shade,
Messiah firmament reborn.

Now I cannot go be wild
or harken back to shape of child
chrystal born into the aire
circled by the harte and bear
and agelesse in a greene arcade,
for he is down in Granite laid,
or standing on a Granite stair.

No return, where thought's completed;
let that ghost's last gaze go cheated:
I may waste my days no more
pining in spirituall warre.
Where am I in wilderness?
What creature bore my bones to this?
Here is no Eden: this is my store.

September 1950–1951

How Come He Got Canned at the Ribbon Factory

Chorus of Working Girls

There was this character come in
to pick up all the broken threads
and tie them back into the loom.

He thought that what he didn't know
would do as well as well did, tying
threads together with real small knots.

So there he was shivering in his shoes,
showing his wish to be a god of all the knots
we tended after suffering to learn them up.

But years ago we were employed by Mr. Smith
to tie these knots which it took us all
of six months to perfect. However he showed

no sign of progress learning how after five
weeks of frigid circumstances of his own
making which we made sure he didn't break

out of by freezing up on him. Obviously
he wasn't a real man anyway but a goop.

New York, Late 1950

The Archetype Poem

Joe Blow has decided
he will no longer
        be a fairy.
He involves himself
in various snatches
        and then hits
a nut named Mary.

He gets in bed with her
        and performs
as what in his mind
would be his usual
        okay job,
which should be solid
        as a rock
        but isn't.

What goes wrong here?
        he says
to himself. I want
        to take her
but she doesn't want
        to take me.

I thought I was
        giving her * * *
and she was giving
        me a man's
position in the world.

Now suddenly she lays
        down the law.
I'm very tired, she says,
        please go.

Is this it? he thinks.
        I didn't want it
to come to that but
I've got to get out
        of this situation.

So the question
resolves itself: do
          you settle for her
or go? I wouldn't
          give you a nickel,
you aren't much of a doll
          anyway. And he

picks up his pride
and puts on his pants
          —glad enough
to have pants to wear—
          and goes.

Why is it that versions
          of this lack
of communication are
          universal?

New York, Late 1950

A Typical Affair

Living in an apartment with a gelded cat
I found a maiden—and left her there.
I seek a better bargain; and that aunt,
that aunt of hers was an awful nuisance.

Seriously, between us, I think I did right
in all things by her. And I'll see her again,
and we'll become friendly (not lovers) because
I have to work with her in the shoestore.

She knows, too. And it will be interesting
tomorrow to see how she acts. If she's
friendly (or even loving) I will resist:
albeit so politely she'll think she has

been complimented. And one night
drunk maybe we'll have a ball.

Paterson, December 1950

A Poem on America

America is like Russia.
Acis and Galatea sit by the lake.
We have the proletariat too.

Acis and Galatea sit by the lake.
Versilov wore a hair shirt
and dreamed of classical pictures.

The alleys, the dye works,
Mill Street in the smoke,
melancholy of the bars,
the sadness of long highways,
negroes climbing around
the rusted iron by the river,
the bathing pool hidden
behind the silk factory
fed by its drainage pipes;
all the pictures we carry in our mind

images of the thirties,
depression and class consciousness
transfigured above politics
filled with fire
with the appearance of God.

Early 1951

After Dead Souls

Where O America are you
going in your glorious
automobile, careening
down the highway
toward what crash
in the deep canyon
of the Western Rockies,
or racing the sunset
over Golden Gate
toward what wild city
jumping with jazz
on the Pacific Ocean!

Spring 1951

Marijuana Notation

How sick I am!
          that thought
always comes to me
          with horror.
Is it this strange
          for everybody?
But such fugitive feelings
have always been
          my métier.

Baudelaire—yet he had
great joyful moments
          staring into space,
looking into the
          middle distance,
contemplating his image
          in Eternity.
They were his moments
          of identity.
It is solitude that
produces these thoughts.

          It is December
almost, they are singing
          Christmas carols
in front of the department
stores down the block on
          Fourteenth Street.

New York, November 1951

Gregory Corso's Story

The first time I went
     to the country to New Hampshire
when I was about eight
     there was a girl
I always used to paddle with a plywood stick.

We were in love,
     so the last night there
we undressed in the moonlight
     and showed each other our bodies,
then we ran singing back to the house.

December 10, 1951

I Have Increased Power

over knowledge of death.
(See also Hemingway's
preoccupation.) My
dreamworld and realworld
become more and more
distinct and apart.
I see now that what
I sought in X seven years
ago was mastery or
victimage played out
naked in the bed.

Renewal of nostalgia
for lost flair of those days,
lost passions . . .
                    Trouble with
me now, no active life
in realworld. And Time,
as realworld, appearing vile,
as Shakespeare says:
ruinous, vile, dirty Time.

As to knowledge of death:
and life itself as without
consummation foreseeable
in ideal joy or passion
(have I exaggerated the
terror of catastrophe?
reality can be joy or terror—
and have I exaggerated the joy?):
life as vile, as painful,
as wretched (this pessimism
which was X's jewel),
as grim, not merely bleak:
the grimness of chance. Or as
Carl wrote, after bughouse,
    "How often have I
    had occasion to see
    existence display

A Ghost May Come

Elements on my table—
    the clock.
All life reduced to this—
    its tick.
Dusty's modern lamp,
all shape, space and curve.
Last attempts at speech.
    And the carved
serpentine knife of Mexico,
    with the childish
eagle head on the handle.

New York, December 30, 1951

I feel as if I am at a dead
end and so I am finished.
All spiritual facts I realize
are true but I never escape
the feeling of being closed in
and the sordidness of self,
the futility of all that I
have seen and done and said.
Maybe if I continued things
would please me more but now
I have no hope and I am tired.

New York, Early 1952

An Atypical Affair

—Long enough to remember the girl
who proposed love to me in the neon
light of the Park Avenue Drugstore
(while her girl friends walked
giggling in the night) who had
such eerie mental insight into my
coldness, coupled with what seemed
to me an untrustworthy character,

and who died a few months later,
perhaps a month after I ceased
thinking of her, of an unforeseen
brain malignancy. By hindsight,
I should have known that only such
a state of deathliness could bare
in a local girl such a luminous
candor. I wish I had been kinder.
This hindsight is the opposite,
after all, of believing that even
in the face of death man can be
no more than ordinary man.

New York, January 1952

345 W. 15th St.

I came home from the movies with nothing on my mind,
Trudging up 8th Avenue to 15th almost blind,
Waiting for a passenger   ship to go to sea.
I live in a roominghouse attic near the Port Authority,

An enormous City warehouse   slowly turning brown
Across from which old brownstones'   fire escapes hang down
On a street which should be Russia   outside the Golden gates
Or back in the middle ages   not in United States.

I thought of my home in the suburbs, my father who wanted me home,
My aunts in the asylum   myself in Nome or Rome.
I opened the door downstairs & Creaked up the first flight.
A Puerto Rican in the front room   was laughing in the night.

I saw from the second stairway the homosexual pair
That lived in different cubicles   playing solitaire,
And I stopped on the third landing and said hello to Ned,
A crooked old man like Father Time   who drank all night in bed.

I made it up to the attic room   I paid $4.50 for.
There was a solitary   cockroach on my door.
It passed me by. I entered.   Nothing of much worth
Was hung up under the skylight.   I saw what I had on earth.

Bare elements of Solitude: table, chair & clock;
Two books on top of the bedspread,   Jack Woodford and Paul de Kock.
I sat down at the table   & read a holy book
About a super City   whereon I cannot look.

What misery to be guided   to an eternal clime
When I yearn for sixty   minutes of actual time.
I turned on the Radio   voices strong and clear
described the high fidelity   of a set without a peer.

Then I heard great musicians   playing the Mahogany Hall
Up to the last high chorus. My neighbor beat on the wall.
I looked up at the Calendar   it had a picture there
Showing two pairs of lovers   and all had golden hair.

I looked into the mirror   to check my worst fears.
My face is dark but handsome   It has not loved for years.
I lay down with the paper   to see what Time had wrought:
Peace was beyond vision,   war too much for thought.

Only the suffering shadow   of DREAM DRIVEN BOY, 16
Looked in my eyes from the Centerfold   after murdering High School
                                                            Queen.
I stripped, my head on the pillow   eyes on the cracked blue wall.
The same cockroach or another   continued its upward crawl.

From what faint words, what whispers   did I lie alone apart?
What wanted consummation?   What sweetening of the heart?
I wished that I were married   to a sensual thoughtful girl.
I would have made a wedded   workmanlike tender churl.

I wished that I were working   for $10,000 a year.
I looked all right in business suits   but my heart was weak with fear.
I wished I owned an apartment   uptown on the East Side,
So that my gentle breeding   nurtured, had not died.

I wished I had an Aesthetic   worth its weight in gold.
The myth is still unwritten.   I am getting old.
I closed my eyes and drifted   back in helpless shame
To jobs & loves wasted   Disillusion itself was lame.

I closed my eyes and drifted   the shortening years ahead,
Walk home from the movies   lone long nights in bed,
Books, plays, music,   spring afternoons in bars,
The smell of old Countries,   the smoke of dark cigars.

February 1952

[According to biographer Bill Morgan, the actual address where this poem was written
was 346 West 15th Street.—The Allen Ginsberg Trust, May 2006]

A Crazy Spiritual

A faithful youth
with artificial legs
drove his jalopy
through the towns of Texas.

He got sent out
of the Free Hospital
of Galveston, madtown
on the Gulf of Mexico

after he recovered.
They gave him a car
and a black mongrel;
name was Weakness.

He was a thin kid
with golden hair
and a frail body
on wire thighs,

who never traveled
and drove northward
timid on the highway
going about twenty.

I hitched a hike
and showed him the road.
I got off at Small Town
and stole his dog.

He tried to drive away,
but lost control,
rode on the pavement
near a garage,

and smashed his doors
and fenders on trees
and parked cars,
and came to a halt.

The Marshal came,
stopping everything
pulled him out
of the wreck cursing.

I watched it all
from the lunch cart,
holding the dog
with a frayed rope.

"I'm on my own
from the crazyhouse.
Has anybody
seen my Weakness?"

What are they saying?
"Call up the FBI.
Crazy, ha? What
is he a fairy?

He must do funny
things with women,
we bet he * * *
them in the * * *."

Poor child meanwhile
collapsed on the ground
with innocent expression
is trying to get up.

Along came a Justice
of the Supreme Court,
barreling through town
in a blue limousine.

He stopped by the crowd
to find out the story,
got out on his pegleg
with an angry smile.

"Don't you see
he has no legs?

That's you fools
what crazy means."

He picked the boy
up off the ground.
The dog ran to them
from the lunch cart.

He put them both in
the back seat of his car
and stood in the square
hymning at the crowd:

"Rock rock rock
for the tension
of the people
of this country

rock rock rock
for the craziness
of the people
of America

tension is a rock
and god will
rock our rock

craziness is a rock
and god will
rock our rock

Lord we shall all
be sweet again."

He showed his wooden leg
to the boy, saying:
"I promise to drive you
home through America."

Paterson, April 1952

Wild Orphan

Blandly mother
takes him strolling
    by railroad and by river
—he's the son of the absconded
    hot rod angel—
and he imagines cars
    and rides them in his dreams,

so lonely growing up among
    the imaginary automobiles
and dead souls of Tarrytown

    to create
out of his own imagination
    the beauty of his wild
forebears—a mythology
    he cannot inherit.

Will he later hallucinate
    his gods? Waking
among mysteries with
    an insane gleam
of recollection?

    The recognition—
something so rare
    in his soul,
met only in dreams
    —nostalgias
of another life.

A question of the soul.
    And the injured
losing their injury
    in their innocence
—a cock, a cross,
    an excellence of love.

And the father grieves
    in flophouse
complexities of memory
    a thousand miles
away, unknowing
    of the unexpected
youthful stranger
    bumming toward his door.

New York, April 13, 1952

II
THE GREEN
AUTOMOBILE
(1953–1954)

The Green Automobile

If I had a Green Automobile
      I'd go find my old companion
      in his house on the Western ocean.
            Ha! Ha! Ha! Ha! Ha!

I'd honk my horn at his manly gate,
      inside his wife and three
      children sprawl naked
            on the living room floor.

He'd come running out
      to my car full of heroic beer
      and jump screaming at the wheel
            for he is the greater driver.

We'd pilgrimage to the highest mount
      of our earlier Rocky Mountain visions
      laughing in each other's arms,
            delight surpassing the highest Rockies,

and after old agony, drunk with new years,
      bounding toward the snowy horizon
      blasting the dashboard with original bop
            hot rod on the mountain

we'd batter up the cloudy highway
      where angels of anxiety
      careen through the trees
            and scream out of the engine.

We'd burn all night on the jackpine peak
      seen from Denver in the summer dark,
      forestlike unnatural radiance
            illuminating the mountaintop:

childhood youthtime age & eternity
      would open like sweet trees
      in the nights of another spring
            and dumbfound us with love,

for we can see together
        the beauty of souls
        hidden like diamonds
                in the clock of the world,

like Chinese magicians can
        confound the immortals
        with our intellectuality
                hidden in the mist,

in the Green Automobile
        which I have invented
        imagined and visioned
                on the roads of the world

more real than the engine
        on a track in the desert
        purer than Greyhound and
                swifter than physical jetplane.

Denver! Denver! we'll return
        roaring across the City & County Building lawn
        which catches the pure emerald flame
                streaming in the wake of our auto.

This time we'll buy up the city!
        I cashed a great check in my skull bank
        to found a miraculous college of the body
                up on the bus terminal roof.

But first we'll drive the stations of downtown,
        poolhall flophouse jazzjoint jail
        whorehouse down Folsom
                to the darkest alleys of Larimer

paying respects to Denver's father
        lost on the railroad tracks,
        stupor of wine and silence
                hallowing the slum of his decades,

salute him and his saintly suitcase
        of dark muscatel, drink

and smash the sweet bottles
        on Diesels in allegiance.

Then we go driving drunk on boulevards
        where armies march and still parade
        staggering under the invisible
            banner of Reality—

hurtling through the street
        in the auto of our fate
        we share an archangelic cigarette
            and tell each other's fortunes:

fames of supernatural illumination,
        bleak rainy gaps of time,
        great art learned in desolation
            and we beat apart after six decades . . .

and on an asphalt crossroad,
        deal with each other in princely
        gentleness once more, recalling
            famous dead talks of other cities.

The windshield's full of tears,
        rain wets our naked breasts,
        we kneel together in the shade
            amid the traffic of night in paradise

and now renew the solitary vow
        we made each other take
        in Texas, once:
            I can't inscribe here. . . .

        •   •   •   •   •
        •   •   •   •   •

How many Saturday nights will be
        made drunken by this legend?
        How will young Denver come to mourn
            her forgotten sexual angel?

How many boys will strike the black piano
            in imitation of the excess of a native saint?
            Or girls fall wanton under his spectre in the high
                        schools of melancholy night?

While all the time in Eternity
            in the wan light of this poem's radio
            we'll sit behind forgotten shades
                        hearkening the lost jazz of all Saturdays.

Neal, we'll be real heroes now
            in a war between our cocks and time:
            let's be the angels of the world's desire
                        and take the world to bed with us before we die.

Sleeping alone, or with companion,
            girl or fairy sheep or dream,
            I'll fail of lacklove, you, satiety:
                        all men fall, our fathers fell before,

but resurrecting that lost flesh
            is but a moment's work of mind:
            an ageless monument to love
                        in the imagination:

memorial built out of our own bodies
            consumed by the invisible poem—
            We'll shudder in Denver and endure
                        though blood and wrinkles blind our eyes.

So this Green Automobile:
            I give you in flight
            a present, a present
                        from my imagination.

We will go riding
            over the Rockies,
            we'll go on riding
                        all night long until dawn,

then back to your railroad, the SP
            your house and your children

and broken leg destiny
you'll ride down the plains

in the morning: and back
to my visions, my office
and eastern apartment
I'll return to New York.

New York, May 22–25, 1953

An Asphodel

O dear sweet rosy
        unattainable desire
. . . how sad, no way
        to change the mad
cultivated asphodel, the
        visible reality . . .

and skin's appalling
        petals—how inspired
to be so lying in the living
        room drunk naked
and dreaming, in the absence
        of electricity . . .
over and over eating the low root
        of the asphodel,
gray fate . . .

        rolling in generation
on the flowery couch
        as on a bank in Arden—
my only rose tonite's the treat
        of my own nudity.
                                    Fall 1953

My Alba

Now that I've wasted
five years in Manhattan
life decaying
talent a blank

talking disconnected
patient and mental
sliderule and number
machine on a desk

autographed triplicate
synopsis and taxes
obedient prompt
poorly paid

stayed on the market
youth of my twenties
fainted in offices
wept on typewriters

deceived multitudes
in vast conspiracies
deodorant battleships
serious business industry

every six weeks whoever
drank my blood bank
innocent evil now
part of my system

five years unhappy labor
22 to 27 working
not a dime in the bank
to show for it anyway

dawn breaks it's only the sun
the East smokes O my bedroom
I am damned to Hell what
alarmclock is ringing

New York, 1953

Sakyamuni Coming Out
from the Mountain

Liang Kai, Southern Sung

He drags his bare feet
        out of a cave
             under a tree,
eyebrows
        grown long with weeping
            and hooknosed woe,
in ragged soft robes
        wearing a fine beard,
            unhappy hands
clasped to his naked breast—
        humility is beatness
            humility is beatness—
faltering
        into the bushes by a stream,
            all things inanimate
but his intelligence—
        stands upright there
            tho trembling:
Arhat
        who sought Heaven
            under a mountain of stone,
sat thinking
        till he realized
            the land of blessedness exists
in the imagination—
        the flash come:
            empty mirror—
how painful to be born again
        wearing a fine beard,
            reentering the world
a bitter wreck of a sage:
        earth before him his only path.
            We can see his soul,
he knows nothing
        like a god:
            shaken

meek wretch—
      humility is beatness
            before the absolute World.

                   New York Public Library, 1953

Havana 1953

I
The night café—4 A.M.
     Cuba Libre 20c:
          white tiled squares,
triangular neon lights,
     long wooden bar on one side,
          a great delicatessen booth
on the other facing the street.
     In the center
          among the great city midnight drinkers,
by Aldama Palace
     on Gómez corner,
          white men and women
with standing drums,
     mariachis, voices, guitars—
          drumming on tables,
knives on bottles,
     banging on the floor
          and on each other,
with wooden clacks,
     whistling, howling,
          fat women in strapless silk.

Cop talking to the fat-nosed girl
     in a flashy black dress.
          In walks a weird Cézanne
vision of the nowhere hip Cuban:
     tall, thin, check gray suit,
          gray felt shoes,
blaring gambler's hat,
     Cab Calloway pimp's mustachio
          —it comes down to a point in the center—
rushing up generations late talking Cuban,
     pointing a gold-ringed finger
          up toward the yellowed ceiling,
other cigarette hand pointing
     stiff-armed down at his side,
          effeminate:—he sees the cop—

they rush together—they're embracing
　　　like long lost brothers—
　　　　　　fatnose forgotten.

Delicate chords
　　　from the negro guitarino
　　　　　　—singers at El Rancho Grande,
drunken burlesque
　　　screams of agony,
　　　　　VIVA JALISCO!
I eat a catfish sandwich
　　　with onions and red sauce
　　　　　20¢.

II
A truly romantic spot,
　　　more guitars, Columbus Square
　　　　　　across from Columbus Cathedral
—I'm in the Paris Restaurant
　　　adjacent, best in town,
　　　　　Cuba Libres 30¢—
weatherbeaten tropical antiquity,
　　　as if rock decayed,
　　　　　unlike the pure
Chinese drummers of black stone
　　　whose polished harmony can still be heard
　　　　　　(Procession of Musicians) at the Freer,
this with its blunt cornucopias and horns
　　　of conquest made of stone—
　　　　　a great dumb rotting church.

Night, lights from windows,
　　　high stone balconies
　　　　　on the antique square,
green rooms
　　　paled by fluorescent houselighting,
　　　　　a modern convenience.

I feel rotten.
　　　I would sit down with my servants and be dumb.
　　　　　I spent too much money.

White electricity
      in the gaslamp fixtures of the alley.
            Bullet holes and nails in the stone wall.
The worried headwaiter
      standing amid the potted palms in cans
            in the fifteen-foot wooden door looking at me.
Mariachi harmonica artists inside
      getting around to Banjo on My Knee yet.
            They dress in wornout sharpie clothes.

Ancient streetlights down the narrow Calle I face,
      the arch, the square,
            palms, drunkenness, solitude;
voices across the street,
      baby wail, girl's squeak,
            waiters nudging each other,
grumble and cackle of young boys' laughter
      in streetcorner waits,
            perro barking off-stage,
baby strangling again,
      banjo and harmonica,
            auto rattle and a cool breeze—

Sudden paranoid notion the waiters are watching me:
      Well they might,
            four gathered in the doorway
and I alone at a table
      on the patio in the dark
            observing the square, drunk.
25¢ for them
      and I asked for "Jalisco"—
            at the end of the song
oxcart rolls by
      obtruding its wheels
            o'er the music o' the night.

                              Christmas 1953

Green Valentine Blues

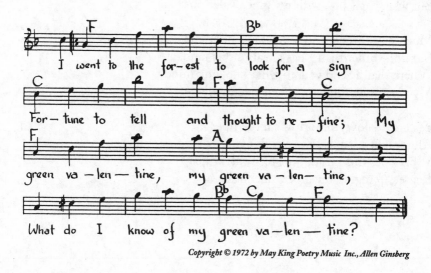

Green Valentine Blues

I went in the forest to look for a sign
Fortune to tell and thought to refine;
My green valentine, my green valentine,
What do I know of my green valentine?

I found a strange wild leaf on a vine
Shaped like a heart and as green as was mine,
My green valentine, my green valentine,
How did I use my green valentine?

Bodies I've known and visions I've seen,
Leaves that I gathered as I gather this green
Valentine, valentine, valentine, valentine;
Thus did I use my green valentine.

Madhouse and jailhouses where I shined
Empty apartment beds where I pined,
O desolate rooms! My green valentine,
Where is the heart in which you were outlined?

Souls and nights and dollars and wine,
Old love and remembrance—I resign
All cities, all jazz, all echoes of Time,
But what shall I do with my green valentine?

Much have I seen, and much am I blind,
But none other than I has a leaf of this kind.
Where shall I send you, to what knowing mind,
My green valentine, my green valentine?

Yesterday's love, tomorrow's more fine?
All tonight's sadness in your design.
What does this mean, my green valentine?
Regret, O regret, my green valentine.

Chiapas, 1954

Siesta in Xbalba

AND

Return to the States

For Karena Shields

I

Late sun opening the book,
        blank page like light,
invisible words unscrawled,
        impossible syntax
of apocalypse—
        Uxmal: Noble Ruins
No construction—

        let the mind fall down.

—One could pass valuable months
and years perhaps a lifetime
doing nothing but lying in a hammock
reading prose with the white doves
        copulating underneath
and monkeys barking in the interior
        of the mountain
and I have succumbed to this
        temptation—

'They go mad in the Selva—'
        the madman read
and laughed in his hammock

        eyes watching me:
unease not of the jungle
        the poor dear,
can tire one—
        all that mud
and all those bugs . . .
        ugh. . . .

Dreaming back I saw
an eternal kodachrome
souvenir of a gathering

of souls at a party,
crowded in an oval flash:
cigarettes, suggestions,
laughter in drunkenness,
broken sweet conversation,
acquaintance in the halls,
faces posed together,
stylized gestures,
odd familiar visages
and singular recognitions
that registered indifferent
greeting across time:
Anson reading Horace
with a rolling head,
white-handed Hohnsbean
camping gravely
with an absent glance,
bald Kingsland drinking
out of a huge glass,
Dusty in a party dress,
Durgin in white shoes
gesturing from a chair,
Keck in a corner waiting
for subterranean music,
Helen Parker lifting
her hands in surprise:
all posturing in one frame,
superficially gay
or tragic as may be,
illumined with the fatal
character and intelligent
actions of their lives.

And I in a concrete room
              above the abandoned
labyrinth of Palenque
              measuring my fate,
wandering solitary in the wild
              —blinking singleminded
at a bleak idea—
              until exhausted with
its action and contemplation
              my soul might shatter

at one primal moment's
            sensation of the vast
movement of divinity.

As I leaned against a tree
            inside the forest
expiring of self-begotten love,
I looked up at the stars absently,
            as if looking for
something else in the blue night
            through the boughs,
and for a moment saw myself
            leaning against a tree . . .

. . : back there the noise of a great party
            in the apartments of New York,
half-created paintings on the walls, fame,
            cocksucking and tears,
money and arguments of great affairs,
            the culture of my generation . . .

            my own crude night imaginings,
my own crude soul notes taken down
            in moments of isolation, dreams,
piercings, sequences of nocturnal thought
            and primitive illuminations

—uncanny feeling the white cat
            sleeping on the table
will open its eyes in a moment
            and be looking at me—

One might sit in this Chiapas
recording the apparitions in the field
            visible from a hammock
looking out across the shadow of the pasture
in all the semblance of Eternity

            . . . a dwarfed thatch roof
down in the grass in a hollow slope
under the tall crowd of vegetation
            waiting at the wild edge:

the long shade of the mountain beyond
            in the near distance,
its individual hairline of trees
traced fine and dark along the ridge
            against the transparent sky light,
rifts and holes in the blue air
            and amber brightenings of clouds
disappearing down the other side
            into the South . . .

            palms with lethargic feelers
rattling in presage of rain,
            shifting their fronds
in the direction of the balmy wind,
            monstrous animals
sprayed up out of the ground
            settling and unsettling
as in water . . .
            and later in the night
a moment of premonition
when the plenilunar cloudfilled sky
            is still and small.

So spent a night
            with drug and hammock
at Chichén Itzá on the Castle:—

            I can see the moon
moving over the edge of the night forest
            and follow its destination
through the clear dimensions of the sky
            from end to end of the dark
circular horizon.

            High dim stone portals,
entablatures of illegible scripture,
bas-reliefs of unknown perceptions:
            and now the flicker of my lamp
and smell of kerosene on dust-
            strewn floor where ant wends
its nightly ritual way toward great faces
            worn down by rain.

In front of me a deathshead
          half a thousand years old
—and have seen cocks a thousand
old grown over with moss and batshit
          stuck out of the wall
in a dripping vaulted house of rock—
          but deathshead's here
on portal still and thinks its way
          through centuries the thought
of the same night in which I sit
          in skully meditation
—sat in many times before by
          artisan other than me
until his image of ghostly change
          appeared unalterable—
but now his fine thought's vaguer
          than my dream of him:
and only the crude skull figurement's
          gaunt insensible glare is left
with broken plumes of sensation,
headdresses of indecipherable intellect
          scattered in the madness of oblivion
to holes and notes of elemental stone,
blind face of animal transcendency
          over the sacred ruin of the world
dissolving into the sunless wall of a blackened room
          on a time-rude pyramid rebuilt
          in the bleak flat night of Yucatán
where I come with my own mad mind to study
          alien hieroglyphs of Eternity.

A creak in the rooms scared me.

Some sort of bird, vampire or swallow,
          flees with little paper wingflap
around the summit in its own air unconcerned
          with the great stone tree I perch on.

          Continual metallic
whirr of chicharras,
          then lesser chirps

of cricket: 5 blasts
                of the leg whistle.
The creak of an opening
                door in the forest,
some sort of weird birdsong
                or reptile croak.

My hat woven of henequen
                on the stone floor
as a leaf on the waters,
                as perishable;
my candle wavers continuously
                and will go out.

Pale Uxmal,
                unhistoric, like a dream,
Tulum shimmering on the coast in ruins;
Chichén Itzá naked
                constructed on a plain;
Palenque, broken chapels in the green
                basement of a mount;
lone Kabah by the highway;
                Piedras Negras buried again
by dark archaeologists;
                Yaxchilan
resurrected in the wild,
and all the limbo of Xbalba still unknown—

                floors under roofcomb of branch,
foundation to ornament
                tumbled to the flowers,
pyramids and stairways
                raced with vine,
limestone corbels
                down in the river of trees,
pillars and corridors
                sunken under the flood of years:

Time's slow wall overtopping
                all that firmament of mind,
as if a shining waterfall of leaves and rain
were built down solid from the endless sky
                through which no thought can pass.

A great red fat rooster
mounted on a tree stump
in the green afternoon,
the ego of the very fields,
screams in the holy sunlight!

        —was looking back
with eyes shut to
        where they crawled
like ants on brown old temples
        building their minute ruins
and disappearing into the wild
        leaving many mysteries
of deathly volition
        to be divined.

I alone know the great crystal door
        to the House of Night,
a legend of centuries
        —I and a few Indians.

And had I mules and money I could find
        the Cave of Amber
and the Cave of Gold
        rumored of the cliffs of Tumbala.

I found the face of one
        of the Nine Guardians of the Night
hidden in a mahogany hut
        in the Area of Lost Souls
—first relic of kind for that place.
And I found as well a green leaf
        shaped like a human heart;
but to whom shall I send this
        anachronistic valentine?

Yet these ruins so much
        woke me to nostalgia
for the classic stations
        of the earth,
the ancient continent
        I have not seen

and the few years
       of memory left
before the ultimate night
       of war—

As if these ruins were not enough,
       as if man could go
no further before heaven
       till he exhausted
the physical round
       of his own mortality
in the obscure cities
       hidden in the aging world

. . . the few actual
       ecstatic conscious souls
certain to be found,
       familiars . . .
returning after years
       to my own scene
transfigured:
       to hurry change
to hurry the years
       bring me to my fate.

So I dream nightly of an embarkation,
       captains, captains,
iron passageways, cabin lights,
       Brooklyn across the waters,
the great dull boat, visitors, farewells,
       the blurred vast sea—
one trip a lifetime's loss or gain:

as Europe is my own imagination
       —many shall see her,
       many shall not—
though it's only the old familiar world
and not some abstract mystical dream.

And in a moment of previsioning sleep
       I see that continent in rain,
black streets, old night, a
       fading monument . . .

And a long journey unaccomplished
                    yet, on antique seas
rolling in gray barren dunes under
                    the world's waste of light
toward ports of childish geography
                    the rusty ship will
harbor in . . .

What nights might I not see
                    penniless among the Arab
mysteries of dirty towns around
                    the casbahs of the docks?
Clay paths, mud walls,
                    the smell of green cigarettes,
creosote and rank salt water—
                    dark structures overhead,
shapes of machinery and facade
                    of hull: and a bar lamp
burning in the wooden shack
                    across from the dim
mountain of sulphur on the pier.

                    Toward what city
will I travel? What wild houses
                    do I go to occupy?
What vagrant rooms and streets
                    and lights in the long night
urge my expectation? What genius
                    of sensation in ancient
halls? what jazz beyond jazz
                    in future blue saloons?
what love in the cafés of God?

I thought, five years ago
                    sitting in my apartment,
my eyes were opened for an hour
                    seeing in dreadful ecstasy
the motionless buildings
                    of New York rotting
under the tides of Heaven.

There is a god
dying in America

already created
in the imagination of men
made palpable
for adoration:
there is an inner
anterior image
of divinity
beckoning me out
to pilgrimage.

O future, unimaginable God.

                              *Finca Tacalapan de San
                                   Leandro, Palenque,
                               Chiapas, Mexico 1954–
                                 San Francisco 1955*

II

Jump in time
            to the immediate future,
another poem:

            return to the old land
penniless and with
            a disconnected manuscript,
the recollection of a few
            sensations, beginning:

logboat down Río Michol
            under plantain
and drifting trees
            to the railroad,

            darkness on the sea
looking toward the stations
            of the classic world—

another image descending
            in white mist
down the lunar highway
            at dawn, above

Lake Catemaco on the bus
            —it woke me up—
the far away likeness
            of a heavenly file
of female saints
            stepping upward
on miniature arches
            of a gold stairway
into the starry sky,
            the thousands of little
saintesses in blue hoods
            looking out at me
and beckoning:
            SALVATION!
            It's true,
simple as in the image.

            Then the mummies
in their Pantheon
            at Guanajuato—
a city of Cortesian
            mines in the first
crevasse of the Sierras,
            where I rested—

for I longed to see their
            faces before I left:
these weren't mythical rock
            images, tho stone
—limestone effigies out
            of the grave, remains
of the fatal character—

newly resurrected,
            grasping their bodies
with stiff arms, in soiled
            funeral clothes;
twisted, knock-kneed,
            like burning
screaming lawyers—
what hallucinations
            of the nerves?—

indecipherable-sexed;
        one death-man had
raised up his arms
        to cover his eyes,
significant timeless
        reflex in sepulchre:

apparitions of immortality
        consumed inward,
waiting openmouthed
        in the fireless darkness.
Nearby, stacked symmetrically,
        a skullbone wall ending
the whitewashed corridor
        under the graveyard
—foetid smell reminiscent
        of sperm and drunkenness—
the skulls empty and fragile,
        numerous as shells,
—so much life passed through
        this town . . .

The problem is isolation
        —there in the grave
or here in oblivion of light.

        Of eternity we have
a numbered score of years
        and fewer tender moments
—one moment of tenderness
        and a year of intelligence
and nerves: one moment of pure
        bodily tenderness—
I could dismiss Allen with grim
        pleasure.

Reminder: I knelt in my room
        on the patio at San Miguel
at the keyhole: 2 A.M.
        The old woman lit a candle.
Two young men and their girls
        waited before the portal,

news from the street. She
          changed the linen, smiling.

What joy! The nakedness!
          They dance! They talk
and simper before the door,
          they lean on a leg,
hand on a hip, and posture,
          nudity in their hearts,
they clap a hand to head
          and whirl and enter,
pushing each other,
          happily, happily,
to a moment of love. . . .

What solitude I've
          finally inherited.

          Afterward fifteen hours
on rubbled single lane,
          broken bus rocking along
the maws and continental crags
          of mountain afternoon,
the distant valleys fading,
          regnant peaks beyond
to days on the Pacific
          where I bathed—

then riding, fitful,
          gazing, sleeping
through the desert
          beside a wetback
sad-faced old-man-
          youth, exhausted
to Mexicali

          to stand
near one night's dark shack
          on the garbage cliffs
of bordertown overhanging
          the tin house poor

man's village below,
           a last night's
timewracked brooding
           and farewell,
the end of a trip.

—Returning
           armed with New Testament,
critic of horse and mule,
           tanned and bearded
satisfying Whitman, concerned
           with a few Traditions,
metrical, mystical, manly
. . . and certain characteristic flaws

           —enough!

The nation over the border
grinds its arms and dreams
           of war: I see
the fiery blue clash
           of metal wheels
clanking in the industries
           of night, and
detonation of infernal bombs

           . . . and the silent downtown
of the States
           in watery dusk submersion.

                         Guanajuato–Los Angeles, 1954

Song

The weight of the world
        is love.
Under the burden
        of solitude,
under the burden
        of dissatisfaction

        the weight,
the weight we carry
        is love.

Who can deny?
        In dreams
it touches
        the body,
in thought
        constructs
a miracle,
        in imagination
anguishes
        till born
in human—

looks out of the heart
        burning with purity—
for the burden of life
        is love,

but we carry the weight
        wearily,
and so must rest
in the arms of love
        at last,
must rest in the arms
        of love.

No rest
        without love,
no sleep
        without dreams

of love—
         be mad or chill
obsessed with angels
         or machines,
the final wish
         is love
—cannot be bitter,
         cannot deny,
cannot withhold
         if denied:

the weight is too heavy

         —must give
for no return
         as thought
is given
         in solitude
in all the excellence
         of its excess.

The warm bodies
         shine together
in the darkness,
         the hand moves
to the center
         of the flesh,
the skin trembles
         in happiness
and the soul comes
         joyful to the eye—

yes, yes,
         that's what
I wanted,
         I always wanted,
I always wanted,
         to return
to the body
         where I was born.

San Jose, 1954

In back of the real

railroad yard in San Jose
    I wandered desolate
in front of a tank factory
    and sat on a bench
near the switchman's shack.

A flower lay on the hay on
    the asphalt highway
—the dread hay flower
    I thought—It had a
brittle black stem and
    corolla of yellowish dirty
spikes like Jesus' inchlong
    crown, and a soiled
dry center cotton tuft
    like a used shaving brush
that's been lying under
    the garage for a year.

Yellow, yellow flower, and
    flower of industry,
tough spiky ugly flower,
    flower nonetheless,
with the form of the great yellow
    Rose in your brain!
This is the flower of the World

San Jose, 1954

On Burroughs' Work

The method must be purest meat
    and no symbolic dressing,
actual visions & actual prisons
    as seen then and now.

Prisons and visions presented
    with rare descriptions
corresponding exactly to those
    of Alcatraz and Rose.

A naked lunch is natural to us,
    we eat reality sandwiches.
But allegories are so much lettuce.
    Don't hide the madness.

San Jose, 1954

Love Poem on Theme by Whitman

I'll go into the bedroom silently and lie down between the bridegroom and
      the bride,
those bodies fallen from heaven stretched out waiting naked and restless,
arms resting over their eyes in the darkness,
bury my face in their shoulders and breasts, breathing their skin,
and stroke and kiss neck and mouth and make back be open and known,
legs raised up crook'd to receive, cock in the darkness driven tormented and
      attacking
roused up from hole to itching head,
bodies locked shuddering naked, hot hips and buttocks screwed into each
      other
and eyes, eyes glinting and charming, widening into looks and abandon,
and moans of movement, voices, hands in air, hands between thighs,
hands in moisture on softened hips, throbbing contraction of bellies
till the white come flow in the swirling sheets,
and the bride cry for forgiveness, and the groom be covered with tears of
      passion and compassion,
and I rise up from the bed replenished with last intimate gestures and kisses
      of farewell—
all before the mind wakes, behind shades and closed doors in a darkened
      house
where the inhabitants roam unsatisfied in the night,
nude ghosts seeking each other out in the silence.

San Jose, 1954

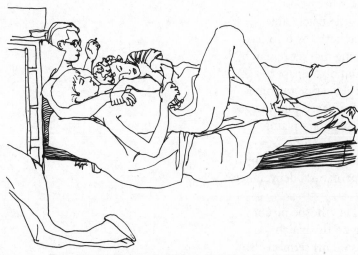

Drawing by Robert LaVigne, San Francisco, 1954

Over Kansas

Starting with eyeball kicks
on storefronts from bus window
on way to Oakland airport:
I am no ego
        these are themselves
stained gray wood and gilded
nigger glass and barberpole
          thass all.
But then, Kiss Me Again
in the dim brick lounge,
muted modern music.
Where shall I fly
not to be sad, my dear?
The other businessmen
bend heavily over armchairs
introducing women to cocktails
in fluorescent shadow—
gaiety of tables,
            gaiety of fat necks,
gaiety of departures,
gaiety of national business,
hands waving away jokes.
        I'm getting maudlin
on the soft rug watching,
mixed rye before me
on the little black table
whereon lieth my briefcase
containing market research
notes and blank paper—
that airplane ride to come
—or a barefaced pilgrimage
acrost imaginary plains
I never made afoot
into Kansas hallucination
and supernatural deliverance.

Later: Hawthorne mystic
waiting on the bench
composing his sermon also

with white bony fingers
bitten, with hometown gold
ring, in a blue serge suit
and barely visible blond
mustache on mental face,
blank-eyed: pitiful thin body
—what body may he love?—
My god! the soft beauty in
comparison—that football boy
in sunny yellow lovesuit
puzzling out his Xmas trip
death insurance by machine.
A virginal feeling again,
I'd be willing to die aloft now.

Can't see outside in the dark,
real dreary strangers about,
and I'm unhappy flying away.
All this facility of travel
too superficial for the heart
I have for solitude.
                          Nakedness
must come again—not sex,
but some naked isolation.

And down there's Hollywood,
the starry world below
—expressing nakedness—
that craving, that glory
that applause—leisure, mind,
appetite for dreams, bodies,
travels: appetite for the real,
created by the mind
and kissed in coitus—
that craving, that melting!
Not even the human
imagination satisfies
the endless emptiness of the soul.

The West Coast behind me
for five days while I return
to ancient New York—

ah drunkenness!
I'll see your eyes again.
Hopeless comedown!
Traveling thru the dark void
over Kansas yet moving nowhere
in the dark void of the soul.

Angel woke me to see
—past my own reflection,
bald businessman with hornrims
sleepy in round window view—
spectral skeleton of electricity
illuminated nervous system
floating on the void out
of central brainplant powerhouse
running into heaven's starlight
overhead. 'Twas over Hutchinson.
Engine passed over lights,
                              view gone.

Gorgeous George on my plane.

And Chicago, the first time,
smoking winter city
—shivering in my tweed jacket
walking by the airport
around the block on Cicero
under the fogged flat
supersky of heaven—
another project for the heart,
six months for here someday
to make Chicago natural,
pick up a few strange images.

Far-off red signs
on the orphan highway
glimmer at the trucks of home.
Who rides that lone road now?
What heart? Who smokes and loves
in Kansas auto now?
Who's talking magic
under the night? Who walks

downtown and drinks black beer
in his eternity? Whose eyes
collect the streets and mountain tops
for storage in his memory?
What sage in the darkness?

Someone who should collect
my insurance!
                    Better I make
a thornful pilgrimage on theory
feet to suffer the total
isolation of the bum,
than this hipster
business family journey
—crossing U.S. at night—
in a sudden glimpse
me being no one in the air
nothing but clouds in the moonlight
with humans fucking
underneath. . . .

San Francisco–New York, December 1954

III

HOWL, BEFORE & AFTER: SAN FRANCISCO BAY AREA

(1955–1956)

Malest Cornifici Tuo Catullo

I'm happy, Kerouac, your madman Allen's
finally made it: discovered a new young cat,
and my imagination of an eternal boy
walks on the streets of San Francisco,
handsome, and meets me in cafeterias
and loves me. Ah don't think I'm sickening.
You're angry at me. For all of my lovers?
It's hard to eat shit, without having visions;
when they have eyes for me it's like Heaven.

San Francisco, 1955

Dream Record: June 8, 1955

A drunken night in my house with a
boy, San Francisco: I lay asleep:
darkness:
        I went back to Mexico City
and saw Joan Burroughs leaning
forward in a garden chair, arms
on her knees. She studied me with
clear eyes and downcast smile, her
face restored to a fine beauty
tequila and salt had made strange
before the bullet in her brow.

We talked of the life since then.
Well, what's Burroughs doing now?
Bill on earth, he's in North Africa.
Oh, and Kerouac? Jack still jumps
with the same beat genius as before,
notebooks filled with Buddha.
I hope he makes it, she laughed.
Is Huncke still in the can? No,
last time I saw him on Times Square.
And how is Kenney? Married, drunk
and golden in the East. You? New
loves in the West—
        Then I knew
she was a dream: and questioned her
—Joan, what kind of knowledge have
the dead? can you still love
your mortal acquaintances?
What do you remember of us?
        She
faded in front of me— The next instant
I saw her rain-stained tombstone
rear an illegible epitaph
under the gnarled branch of a small
tree in the wild grass
of an unvisited garden in Mexico.

Blessed be the Muses

for their descent,
dancing round my desk,
crowning my balding head
  with Laurel.

1955

Howl

For Carl Solomon

I

I saw the best minds of my generation destroyed by madness, starving
    hysterical naked,

dragging themselves through the negro streets at dawn looking for an angry
    fix,

angelheaded hipsters burning for the ancient heavenly connection to the
    starry dynamo in the machinery of night,

who poverty and tatters and hollow-eyed and high sat up smoking in the
    supernatural darkness of cold-water flats floating across the tops of
    cities contemplating jazz,

who bared their brains to Heaven under the El and saw Mohammedan angels
    staggering on tenement roofs illuminated,

who passed through universities with radiant cool eyes hallucinating Arkan-
    sas and Blake-light tragedy among the scholars of war,

who were expelled from the academies for crazy & publishing obscene odes
    on the windows of the skull,

who cowered in unshaven rooms in underwear, burning their money in
    wastebaskets and listening to the Terror through the wall,

who got busted in their pubic beards returning through Laredo with a belt
    of marijuana for New York,

who ate fire in paint hotels or drank turpentine in Paradise Alley, death, or
    purgatoried their torsos night after night

with dreams, with drugs, with waking nightmares, alcohol and cock and
    endless balls,

incomparable blind streets of shuddering cloud and lightning in the mind
    leaping toward poles of Canada & Paterson, illuminating all the mo-
    tionless world of Time between,

Peyote solidities of halls, backyard green tree cemetery dawns, wine drunk-
    enness over the rooftops, storefront boroughs of teahead joyride neon
    blinking traffic light, sun and moon and tree vibrations in the roaring
    winter dusks of Brooklyn, ashcan rantings and kind king light of
    mind,

who chained themselves to subways for the endless ride from Battery to holy
    Bronx on benzedrine until the noise of wheels and children brought
    them down shuddering mouth-wracked and battered bleak of brain
    all drained of brilliance in the drear light of Zoo,

who sank all night in submarine light of Bickford's floated out and sat
    through the stale beer afternoon in desolate Fugazzi's, listening to the
    crack of doom on the hydrogen jukebox,

who talked continuously seventy hours from park to pad to bar to Bellevue to museum to the Brooklyn Bridge,

a lost battalion of platonic conversationalists jumping down the stoops off fire escapes off windowsills off Empire State out of the moon,

yacketayakking screaming vomiting whispering facts and memories and anecdotes and eyeball kicks and shocks of hospitals and jails and wars,

whole intellects disgorged in total recall for seven days and nights with brilliant eyes, meat for the Synagogue cast on the pavement,

who vanished into nowhere Zen New Jersey leaving a trail of ambiguous picture postcards of Atlantic City Hall,

suffering Eastern sweats and Tangerian bone-grindings and migraines of China under junk-withdrawal in Newark's bleak furnished room,

who wandered around and around at midnight in the railroad yard wondering where to go, and went, leaving no broken hearts,

who lit cigarettes in boxcars boxcars boxcars racketing through snow toward lonesome farms in grandfather night,

who studied Plotinus Poe St. John of the Cross telepathy and bop kabbalah because the cosmos instinctively vibrated at their feet in Kansas,

who loned it through the streets of Idaho seeking visionary indian angels who were visionary indian angels,

who thought they were only mad when Baltimore gleamed in supernatural ecstasy,

who jumped in limousines with the Chinaman of Oklahoma on the impulse of winter midnight streetlight smalltown rain,

who lounged hungry and lonesome through Houston seeking jazz or sex or soup, and followed the brilliant Spaniard to converse about America and Eternity, a hopeless task, and so took ship to Africa,

who disappeared into the volcanoes of Mexico leaving behind nothing but the shadow of dungarees and the lava and ash of poetry scattered in fireplace Chicago,

who reappeared on the West Coast investigating the FBI in beards and shorts with big pacifist eyes sexy in their dark skin passing out incomprehensible leaflets,

who burned cigarette holes in their arms protesting the narcotic tobacco haze of Capitalism,

who distributed Supercommunist pamphlets in Union Square weeping and undressing while the sirens of Los Alamos wailed them down, and wailed down Wall, and the Staten Island ferry also wailed,

who broke down crying in white gymnasiums naked and trembling before the machinery of other skeletons,

who bit detectives in the neck and shrieked with delight in policecars for committing no crime but their own wild cooking pederasty and intoxication, who howled on their knees in the subway and were dragged off the roof waving genitals and manuscripts,

who let themselves be fucked in the ass by saintly motorcyclists, and screamed with joy,

who blew and were blown by those human seraphim, the sailors, caresses of Atlantic and Caribbean love,

who balled in the morning in the evenings in rosegardens and the grass of public parks and cemeteries scattering their semen freely to whomever come who may,

who hiccuped endlessly trying to giggle but wound up with a sob behind a partition in a Turkish Bath when the blond & naked angel came to pierce them with a sword,

who lost their loveboys to the three old shrews of fate the one eyed shrew of the heterosexual dollar the one eyed shrew that winks out of the womb and the one eyed shrew that does nothing but sit on her ass and snip the intellectual golden threads of the craftsman's loom,

who copulated ecstatic and insatiate with a bottle of beer a sweetheart a package of cigarettes a candle and fell off the bed, and continued along the floor and down the hall and ended fainting on the wall with a vision of ultimate cunt and come eluding the last gyzym of consciousness,

who sweetened the snatches of a million girls trembling in the sunset, and were red eyed in the morning but prepared to sweeten the snatch of the sunrise, flashing buttocks under barns and naked in the lake,

who went out whoring through Colorado in myriad stolen night-cars, N.C., secret hero of these poems, cocksman and Adonis of Denver—joy to the memory of his innumerable lays of girls in empty lots & diner backyards, moviehouses' rickety rows, on mountaintops in caves or with gaunt waitresses in familiar roadside lonely petticoat upliftings & especially secret gas-station solipsisms of johns, & hometown alleys too,

who faded out in vast sordid movies, were shifted in dreams, woke on a sudden Manhattan, and picked themselves up out of basements hungover with heartless Tokay and horrors of Third Avenue iron dreams & stumbled to unemployment offices,

who walked all night with their shoes full of blood on the snowbank docks waiting for a door in the East River to open to a room full of steamheat and opium,

who created great suicidal dramas on the apartment cliff-banks of the Hudson under the wartime blue floodlight of the moon & their heads shall be crowned with laurel in oblivion,

who ate the lamb stew of the imagination or digested the crab at the muddy bottom of the rivers of Bowery, who wept at the romance of the streets with their pushcarts full of onions and bad music,

who sat in boxes breathing in the darkness under the bridge, and rose up to build harpsichords in their lofts,

who coughed on the sixth floor of Harlem crowned with flame under the tubercular sky surrounded by orange crates of theology,

who scribbled all night rocking and rolling over lofty incantations which in the yellow morning were stanzas of gibberish,

who cooked rotten animals lung heart feet tail borsht & tortillas dreaming of the pure vegetable kingdom,

who plunged themselves under meat trucks looking for an egg,

who threw their watches off the roof to cast their ballot for Eternity outside of Time, & alarm clocks fell on their heads every day for the next decade,

who cut their wrists three times successively unsuccessfully, gave up and were forced to open antique stores where they thought they were growing old and cried,

who were burned alive in their innocent flannel suits on Madison Avenue amid blasts of leaden verse & the tanked-up clatter of the iron regiments of fashion & the nitroglycerine shrieks of the fairies of advertising & the mustard gas of sinister intelligent editors, or were run down by the drunken taxicabs of Absolute Reality,

who jumped off the Brooklyn Bridge this actually happened and walked away unknown and forgotten into the ghostly daze of Chinatown soup alleyways & firetrucks, not even one free beer,

who sang out of their windows in despair, fell out of the subway window, jumped in the filthy Passaic, leaped on negroes, cried all over the street, danced on broken wineglasses barefoot smashed phonograph records of nostalgic European 1930s German jazz finished the whiskey and threw up groaning into the bloody toilet, moans in their ears and the blast of colossal steamwhistles,

who barreled down the highways of the past journeying to each other's hotrod-Golgotha jail-solitude watch or Birmingham jazz incarnation,

who drove crosscountry seventytwo hours to find out if I had a vision or you had a vision or he had a vision to find out Eternity,

who journeyed to Denver, who died in Denver, who came back to Denver & waited in vain, who watched over Denver & brooded & loned in Denver and finally went away to find out the Time, & now Denver is lonesome for her heroes,

who fell on their knees in hopeless cathedrals praying for each other's salvation and light and breasts, until the soul illuminated its hair for a second, who crashed through their minds in jail waiting for impossible criminals with golden heads and the charm of reality in their hearts who sang sweet blues to Alcatraz,

who retired to Mexico to cultivate a habit, or Rocky Mount to tender Buddha or Tangiers to boys or Southern Pacific to the black locomotive or Harvard to Narcissus to Woodlawn to the daisychain or grave,

who demanded sanity trials accusing the radio of hypnotism & were left with their insanity & their hands & a hung jury,

who threw potato salad at CCNY lecturers on Dadaism and subsequently presented themselves on the granite steps of the madhouse with shaven heads and harlequin speech of suicide, demanding instantaneous lobotomy,

and who were given instead the concrete void of insulin Metrazol electricity hydrotherapy psychotherapy occupational therapy pingpong & amnesia,

who in humorless protest overturned only one symbolic pingpong table, resting briefly in catatonia,

returning years later truly bald except for a wig of blood, and tears and fingers, to the visible madman doom of the wards of the madtowns of the East,

Pilgrim State's Rockland's and Greystone's foetid halls, bickering with the echoes of the soul, rocking and rolling in the midnight solitude-bench dolmen-realms of love, dream of life a nightmare, bodies turned to stone as heavy as the moon,

with mother finally ******, and the last fantastic book flung out of the tenement window, and the last door closed at 4 A.M. and the last telephone slammed at the wall in reply and the last furnished room emptied down to the last piece of mental furniture, a yellow paper rose twisted on a wire hanger in the closet, and even that imaginary, nothing but a hopeful little bit of hallucination—

ah, Carl, while you are not safe I am not safe, and now you're really in the total animal soup of time—

and who therefore ran through the icy streets obsessed with a sudden flash of the alchemy of the use of the ellipse the catalog the meter & the vibrating plane,

who dreamt and made incarnate gaps in Time & Space through images juxtaposed, and trapped the archangel of the soul between 2 visual images and joined the elemental verbs and set the noun and dash of consciousness together jumping with sensation of Pater Omnipotens Aeterna Deus

to recreate the syntax and measure of poor human prose and stand before you speechless and intelligent and shaking with shame, rejected yet

confessing out the soul to conform to the rhythm of thought in his
    naked and endless head,

the madman bum and angel beat in Time, unknown, yet putting down here
    what might be left to say in time come after death,

and rose reincarnate in the ghostly clothes of jazz in the goldhorn shadow
    of the band and blew the suffering of America's naked mind for love
    into an eli eli lamma lamma sabacthani saxophone cry that shivered
    the cities down to the last radio

with the absolute heart of the poem of life butchered out of their own bodies
    good to eat a thousand years.

II

What sphinx of cement and aluminum bashed open their skulls and ate up
    their brains and imagination?

Moloch! Solitude! Filth! Ugliness! Ashcans and unobtainable dollars! Chil-
    dren screaming under the stairways! Boys sobbing in armies! Old
    men weeping in the parks!

Moloch! Moloch! Nightmare of Moloch! Moloch the loveless! Mental Mo-
    loch! Moloch the heavy judger of men!

Moloch the incomprehensible prison! Moloch the crossbone soulless jail-
    house and Congress of sorrows! Moloch whose buildings are judg-
    ment! Moloch the vast stone of war! Moloch the stunned govern-
    ments!

Moloch whose mind is pure machinery! Moloch whose blood is running
    money! Moloch whose fingers are ten armies! Moloch whose breast
    is a cannibal dynamo! Moloch whose ear is a smoking tomb!

Moloch whose eyes are a thousand blind windows! Moloch whose skyscrap-
    ers stand in the long streets like endless Jehovahs! Moloch whose
    factories dream and croak in the fog! Moloch whose smokestacks and
    antennae crown the cities!

Moloch whose love is endless oil and stone! Moloch whose soul is electricity
    and banks! Moloch whose poverty is the specter of genius! Moloch
    whose fate is a cloud of sexless hydrogen! Moloch whose name is the
    Mind!

Moloch in whom I sit lonely! Moloch in whom I dream Angels! Crazy in
    Moloch! Cocksucker in Moloch! Lacklove and manless in Moloch!

Moloch who entered my soul early! Moloch in whom I am a consciousness
    without a body! Moloch who frightened me out of my natural ec-
    stasy! Moloch whom I abandon! Wake up in Moloch! Light stream-
    ing out of the sky!

Moloch! Moloch! Robot apartments! invisible suburbs! skeleton treasuries!

blind capitals! demonic industries! spectral nations! invincible mad-
houses! granite cocks! monstrous bombs!

They broke their backs lifting Moloch to Heaven! Pavements, trees, radios,
tons! lifting the city to Heaven which exists and is everywhere about
us!

Visions! omens! hallucinations! miracles! ecstasies! gone down the American
river!

Dreams! adorations! illuminations! religions! the whole boatload of sensitive
bullshit!

Breakthroughs! over the river! flips and crucifixions! gone down the flood!
Highs! Epiphanies! Despairs! Ten years' animal screams and sui-
cides! Minds! New loves! Mad generation! down on the rocks of
Time!

Real holy laughter in the river! They saw it all! the wild eyes! the holy yells!
They bade farewell! They jumped off the roof! to solitude! waving!
carrying flowers! Down to the river! into the street!

III
Carl Solomon! I'm with you in Rockland
    where you're madder than I am
I'm with you in Rockland
    where you must feel very strange
I'm with you in Rockland
    where you imitate the shade of my mother
I'm with you in Rockland
    where you've murdered your twelve secretaries
I'm with you in Rockland
    where you laugh at this invisible humor
I'm with you in Rockland
    where we are great writers on the same dreadful typewriter
I'm with you in Rockland
    where your condition has become serious and is reported on the radio
I'm with you in Rockland
    where the faculties of the skull no longer admit the worms of the
    senses
I'm with you in Rockland
    where you drink the tea of the breasts of the spinsters of Utica
I'm with you in Rockland
    where you pun on the bodies of your nurses the harpies of the Bronx
I'm with you in Rockland
    where you scream in a straightjacket that you're losing the game of
    the actual pingpong of the abyss

I'm with you in Rockland
> where you bang on the catatonic piano the soul is innocent and
> immortal it should never die ungodly in an armed madhouse

I'm with you in Rockland
> where fifty more shocks will never return your soul to its body again
> from its pilgrimage to a cross in the void

I'm with you in Rockland
> where you accuse your doctors of insanity and plot the Hebrew
> socialist revolution against the fascist national Golgotha

I'm with you in Rockland
> where you will split the heavens of Long Island and resurrect your
> living human Jesus from the superhuman tomb

I'm with you in Rockland
> where there are twentyfive thousand mad comrades all together sing-
> ing the final stanzas of the Internationale

I'm with you in Rockland
> where we hug and kiss the United States under our bedsheets the
> United States that coughs all night and won't let us sleep

I'm with you in Rockland
> where we wake up electrified out of the coma by our own souls'
> airplanes roaring over the roof they've come to drop angelic bombs
> the hospital illuminates itself   imaginary walls collapse   O skinny
> legions run outside   O starry-spangled shock of mercy the eternal
> war is here   O victory forget your underwear we're free

I'm with you in Rockland
> in my dreams you walk dripping from a sea-journey on the highway
> across America in tears to the door of my cottage in the Western
> night

San Francisco, 1955–1956

Footnote to Howl

Holy! Holy! Holy! Holy! Holy! Holy! Holy! Holy! Holy! Holy! Holy!
    Holy! Holy! Holy! Holy!
The world is holy! The soul is holy! The skin is holy! The nose is holy! The
    tongue and cock and hand and asshole holy!
Everything is holy! everybody's holy! everywhere is holy! everyday is in
    eternity! Everyman's an angel!
The bum's as holy as the seraphim! the madman is holy as you my soul are
    holy!
The typewriter is holy the poem is holy the voice is holy the hearers are
    holy the ecstasy is holy!
Holy Peter holy Allen holy Solomon holy Lucien holy Kerouac holy
    Huncke holy Burroughs holy Cassady holy the unknown buggered
    and suffering beggars holy the hideous human angels!
Holy my mother in the insane asylum! Holy the cocks of the grandfathers
    of Kansas!
Holy the groaning saxophone! Holy the bop apocalypse! Holy the jazzbands
    marijuana hipsters peace peyote pipes & drums!
Holy the solitudes of skyscrapers and pavements! Holy the cafeterias filled
    with the millions! Holy the mysterious rivers of tears under the
    streets!
Holy the lone juggernaut! Holy the vast lamb of the middleclass! Holy the
    crazy shepherds of rebellion! Who digs Los Angeles IS Los Angeles!
Holy New York Holy San Francisco Holy Peoria & Seattle Holy Paris Holy
    Tangiers Holy Moscow Holy Istanbul!
Holy time in eternity holy eternity in time holy the clocks in space holy the
    fourth dimension holy the fifth International holy the Angel in Mo-
    loch!
Holy the sea holy the desert holy the railroad holy the locomotive holy the
    visions holy the hallucinations holy the miracles holy the eyeball holy
    the abyss!
Holy forgiveness! mercy! charity! faith! Holy! Ours! bodies! suffering! mag-
    nanimity!
Holy the supernatural extra brilliant intelligent kindness of the soul!

Berkeley, 1955

A Strange New Cottage in Berkeley

All afternoon cutting bramble blackberries off a tottering brown
fence
    under a low branch with its rotten old apricots miscellaneous under
the leaves,
    fixing the drip in the intricate gut machinery of a new toilet;
    found a good coffeepot in the vines by the porch, rolled a big tire out
of the scarlet bushes, hid my marijuana;
    wet the flowers, playing the sunlit water each to each, returning for
godly extra drops for the stringbeans and daisies;
    three times walked round the grass and sighed absently:
    my reward, when the garden fed me its plums from the form of a
small tree in the corner,
    an angel thoughtful of my stomach, and my dry and lovelorn tongue.

1955

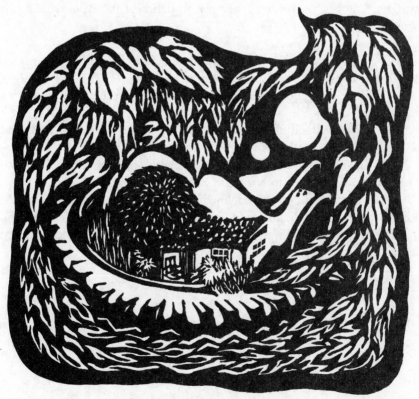

Block print by Robert LaVigne

A Supermarket in California

What thoughts I have of you tonight, Walt Whitman, for I walked down the sidestreets under the trees with a headache self-conscious looking at the full moon.

In my hungry fatigue, and shopping for images, I went into the neon fruit supermarket, dreaming of your enumerations!

What peaches and what penumbras! Whole families shopping at night! Aisles full of husbands! Wives in the avocados, babies in the tomatoes! —and you, García Lorca, what were you doing down by the watermelons?

I saw you, Walt Whitman, childless, lonely old grubber, poking among the meats in the refrigerator and eyeing the grocery boys.

I heard you asking questions of each: Who killed the pork chops? What price bananas? Are you my Angel?

I wandered in and out of the brilliant stacks of cans following you, and followed in my imagination by the store detective.

We strode down the open corridors together in our solitary fancy tasting artichokes, possessing every frozen delicacy, and never passing the cashier.

Where are we going, Walt Whitman? The doors close in an hour. Which way does your beard point tonight?

(I touch your book and dream of our odyssey in the supermarket and feel absurd.)

Will we walk all night through solitary streets? The trees add shade to shade, lights out in the houses, we'll both be lonely.

Will we stroll dreaming of the lost America of love past blue automobiles in driveways, home to our silent cottage?

Ah, dear father, graybeard, lonely old courage-teacher, what America did you have when Charon quit poling his ferry and you got out on a smoking bank and stood watching the boat disappear on the black waters of Lethe?

Berkeley, 1955

Four Haiku

Looking over my shoulder
my behind was covered
with cherry blossoms.

Lying on my side
in the void:
the breath in my nose.

I didn't know the names
of the flowers—now
my garden is gone.

On the porch
in my shorts—
auto lights in the rain.

Berkeley, Fall 1955

Sunflower Sutra

I walked on the banks of the tincan banana dock and sat down under the huge shade of a Southern Pacific locomotive to look at the sunset over the box house hills and cry.

Jack Kerouac sat beside me on a busted rusty iron pole, companion, we thought the same thoughts of the soul, bleak and blue and sad-eyed, surrounded by the gnarled steel roots of trees of machinery.

The oily water on the river mirrored the red sky, sun sank on top of final Frisco peaks, no fish in that stream, no hermit in those mounts, just ourselves rheumy-eyed and hung-over like old bums on the riverbank, tired and wily.

Look at the Sunflower, he said, there was a dead gray shadow against the sky, big as a man, sitting dry on top of a pile of ancient sawdust—

—I rushed up enchanted—it was my first sunflower, memories of Blake— my visions—Harlem

and Hells of the Eastern rivers, bridges clanking Joes Greasy Sandwiches, dead baby carriages, black treadless tires forgotten and unretreaded, the poem of the riverbank, condoms & pots, steel knives, nothing stainless, only the dank muck and the razor-sharp artifacts passing into the past—

and the gray Sunflower poised against the sunset, crackly bleak and dusty with the smut and smog and smoke of olden locomotives in its eye—

corolla of bleary spikes pushed down and broken like a battered crown, seeds fallen out of its face, soon-to-be-toothless mouth of sunny air, sunrays obliterated on its hairy head like a dried wire spiderweb,

leaves stuck out like arms out of the stem, gestures from the sawdust root, broke pieces of plaster fallen out of the black twigs, a dead fly in its ear,

Unholy battered old thing you were, my sunflower O my soul, I loved you then!

The grime was no man's grime but death and human locomotives,

all that dress of dust, that veil of darkened railroad skin, that smog of cheek, that eyelid of black mis'ry, that sooty hand or phallus or protuberance of artificial worse-than-dirt—industrial—modern—all that civilization spotting your crazy golden crown—

and those blear thoughts of death and dusty loveless eyes and ends and withered roots below, in the home-pile of sand and sawdust, rubber dollar bills, skin of machinery, the guts and innards of the weeping coughing car, the empty lonely tincans with their rusty tongues alack, what more could I name, the smoked ashes of some cock cigar, the cunts of wheelbarrows and the milky breasts of cars, wornout asses out of chairs & sphincters of dynamos—all these

entangled in your mummied roots—and you there standing before me in the sunset, all your glory in your form!

A perfect beauty of a sunflower! a perfect excellent lovely sunflower existence! a sweet natural eye to the new hip moon, woke up alive and excited grasping in the sunset shadow sunrise golden monthly breeze!

How many flies buzzed round you innocent of your grime, while you cursed the heavens of the railroad and your flower soul?

Poor dead flower? when did you forget you were a flower? when did you look at your skin and decide you were an impotent dirty old locomotive? the ghost of a locomotive? the specter and shade of a once powerful mad American locomotive?

You were never no locomotive, Sunflower, you were a sunflower!

And you Locomotive, you are a locomotive, forget me not!

So I grabbed up the skeleton thick sunflower and stuck it at my side like a scepter,

and deliver my sermon to my soul, and Jack's soul too, and anyone who'll listen,

—We're not our skin of grime, we're not our dread bleak dusty imageless locomotive, we're all golden sunflowers inside, blessed by our own seed & hairy naked accomplishment-bodies growing into mad black formal sunflowers in the sunset, spied on by our eyes under the shadow of the mad locomotive riverbank sunset Frisco hilly tincan evening sitdown vision.

Berkeley, 1955

Transcription of Organ Music

The flower in the glass peanut bottle formerly in the kitchen crooked to take
    a place in the light,
the closet door opened, because I used it before, it kindly stayed open waiting
    for me, its owner.

I began to feel my misery in pallet on floor, listening to music, my misery,
    that's why I want to sing.
The room closed down on me, I expected the presence of the Creator, I saw
    my gray painted walls and ceiling, they contained my room, they
    contained me
as the sky contained my garden,
I opened my door

    The rambler vine climbed up the cottage post, the leaves in the night
still where the day had placed them, the animal heads of the flowers where
they had arisen
    to think at the sun

    Can I bring back the words? Will thought of transcription haze my
mental open eye?

    The kindly search for growth, the gracious desire to exist of the
flowers, my near ecstasy at existing among them
    The privilege to witness my existence—you too must seek the
sun . . .

    My books piled up before me for my use
    waiting in space where I placed them, they haven't disappeared,
time's left its remnants and qualities for me to use—my words piled up, my
texts, my manuscripts, my loves.
    I had a moment of clarity, saw the feeling in the heart of things,
walked out to the garden crying.
    Saw the red blossoms in the night light, sun's gone, they had all
grown, in a moment, and were waiting stopped in time for the day sun to
come and give them . . .
    Flowers which as in a dream at sunset I watered faithfully not know-
ing how much I loved them.
    I am so lonely in my glory—except they too out there—I looked up
—those red bush blossoms beckoning and peering in the window waiting in

blind love, their leaves too have hope and are upturned top flat to the sky to receive—all creation open to receive—the flat earth itself.

The music descends, as does the tall bending stalk of the heavy blossom, because it has to, to stay alive, to continue to the last drop of joy.

The world knows the love that's in its breast as in the flower, the suffering lonely world.

The Father is merciful.

The light socket is crudely attached to the ceiling, after the house was built, to receive a plug which sticks in it allright, and serves my phonograph now . . .

The closet door is open for me, where I left it, since I left it open, it has graciously stayed open.

The kitchen has no door, the hole there will admit me should I wish to enter the kitchen.

I remember when I first got laid, H.P. graciously took my cherry, I sat on the docks of Provincetown, age 23, joyful, elevated in hope with the Father, the door to the womb was open to admit me if I wished to enter.

There are unused electricity plugs all over my house if I ever need them.

The kitchen window is open, to admit air . . .

The telephone—sad to relate—sits on the floor—I haven't the money to get it connected—

I want people to bow as they see me and say he is gifted with poetry, he has seen the presence of the Creator.

And the Creator gave me a shot of his presence to gratify my wish, so as not to cheat me of my yearning for him.

Berkeley, September 8, 1955

Sather Gate Illumination

Why do I deny manna to another?
Because I deny it to myself.
Why have I denied myself?
What other has rejected me?
Now I believe you are lovely, my soul, soul of Allen, Allen—
and you so beloved, so sweetened, so recalled to your true loveliness,
your original nude breathing Allen
will you ever deny another again?

Dear Walter, thanks for the message
I forbid you not to touch me, man to man, True American.

The bombers jet through the sky in unison of twelve,
the pilots are sweating and nervous at the controls in the hot cabins.
Over what souls will they loose their loveless bombs?

The Campanile pokes its white granite (?) innocent head into the clouds for
      me to look at.

A cripple lady explains French grammar with a loud sweet voice: Regarder
      is to look—
the whole French language looks on the trees on the campus.

      The girls' haunted voices make quiet dates for 2 o'clock—yet one of
them waves farewell and smiles at last—her red skirt swinging shows how
she loves herself.

      Another encased in flashy Scotch clothes clomps up the concrete in
a hurry—into the door—poor dear!—who will receive you in love's offices?

How many beautiful boys have I seen on this spot?
The trees seem on the verge of moving—ah! they do move in the breeze.
Roar again of airplanes in the sky—everyone looks up.

And do you know that all these rubbings of the eyes & painful gestures to
      the brow
of suited scholars entering Dwinelle (Hall) are Holy Signs?—anxiety and
      fear?

How many years have I got to float on this sweetened scene of trees &
     humans clomping above ground—
O I must be mad to sit here lonely in the void & glee & build up thoughts
     of love!
But what do I have to doubt but my own shiny eyes, what to lose but life
     which is a vision today this afternoon.

My stomach is light, I relax, new sentences spring forth out of the
scene to describe spontaneous forms of Time—trees, sleeping dogs, airplanes
wandering thru the air, negroes with their lunch books of anxiety, apples and
sandwiches, lunchtime, icecream, Timeless—

And even the ugliest will seek beauty—'What are you doing Friday night?'
asks the sailor in white school training cap & gilt buttons & blue coat,
and the little ape in a green jacket and baggy pants and overloaded school-
     book satchel says 'Quartets.'
Every Friday nite, beautiful quartets to celebrate and please my soul with all
     its hair—Music!
and then strides off, snapping pieces chocolate off a bar wrapped in Hershey
     brown paper and tinfoil,
eating chocolate rose.

& how can those other boys be them happy selves in their brown army study
     uniforms?

Now cripple girl swings down walk with loping fuck gestures of her hips
     askew—
let her roll her eyes in abandon & camp angelic through the campus bounc-
     ing her body about in joy—
someone will dig that pelvic energy for sure.

Those white stripes down your chocolate cupcake, Lady (held in front of
     your nose finishing sentence preparatory to chomp),
they were painted there to delight you by some spanish industrial artistic
     hand in bakery factory faraway,
expert hand in simple-minded messages of white stripes on millions of mes-
     sage cupcakes.
I have a message for you all—I will denote one particularity of each!

And there goes Professor Hart striding enlightened by the years
through the doorway and arcade he built (in his mind) and knows—he too
saw the ruins of Yucatán once—

followed by a lonely janitor in dovegray italian fruitpeddler Chico Marx hat
    pushing his rolypoly belly thru the trees.

N sees all girls
as visions of
their inner cunts,
yes, it's true!
and all men walking
along thinking
of their spirit cocks.

So look at that poor dread boy
with two-day black hair
all over his dirty face,
how he must hate his cock
        —Chinamen stop shuddering

and now to bring this to an end with a rise and an ellipse—

    The boys are now all talking to the girls 'If I was a girl I'd love all
boys' & girls giggling the opposite, all pretty everywhichway
and even I have my secret beds and lovers under another moonlight, be you
    sure

& any minute I expect to see a baby carriage pushed on to the scene
and everyone turn in attention like the airplanes and laughter, like a Greek
    Campus
and the big brown shaggy silent dog lazing openeyed in the shade
lift up his head & sniff & lower his head on his golden paws & let his belly
    rumble away unconcerned.

        . . . the lion's ruddy eyes
Shall flow with tears of gold.

Now the silence is broken, students pour onto the square, the doors are
    crowded, the dog gets up and walks away,
the cripple swings out of Dwinelle, a nun even, I wonder about her, an old
    lady distinguished by a cane,
we all look up, silence moves, huge changes upon the ground, and in the air
    thoughts fly all over, filling space.

My grief at Peter's not loving me was grief at not loving myself.
Huge Karmas of broken minds in beautiful bodies unable to receive love
    because not knowing the self as lovely—
Fathers and Teachers!

    Seeing in people the visible evidence of inner self thought by their
treatment of me: who loves himself loves me who love myself.

Berkeley, September 1955

America

America I've given you all and now I'm nothing.
America two dollars and twentyseven cents January 17, 1956.
I can't stand my own mind.
America when will we end the human war?
Go fuck yourself with your atom bomb.
I don't feel good don't bother me.
I won't write my poem till I'm in my right mind.
America when will you be angelic?
When will you take off your clothes?
When will you look at yourself through the grave?
When will you be worthy of your million Trotskyites?
America why are your libraries full of tears?
America when will you send your eggs to India?
I'm sick of your insane demands.
When can I go into the supermarket and buy what I need with my good
        looks?
America after all it is you and I who are perfect not the next world.
Your machinery is too much for me.
You made me want to be a saint.
There must be some other way to settle this argument.
Burroughs is in Tangiers I don't think he'll come back it's sinister.
Are you being sinister or is this some form of practical joke?
I'm trying to come to the point.
I refuse to give up my obsession.
America stop pushing I know what I'm doing.
America the plum blossoms are falling.
I haven't read the newspapers for months, everyday somebody goes on trial
        for murder.
America I feel sentimental about the Wobblies.
America I used to be a communist when I was a kid I'm not sorry.
I smoke marijuana every chance I get.
I sit in my house for days on end and stare at the roses in the closet.
When I go to Chinatown I get drunk and never get laid.
My mind is made up there's going to be trouble.
You should have seen me reading Marx.
My psychoanalyst thinks I'm perfectly right.
I won't say the Lord's Prayer.
I have mystical visions and cosmic vibrations.
America I still haven't told you what you did to Uncle Max after he came
        over from Russia.

I'm addressing you.
Are you going to let your emotional life be run by Time Magazine?
I'm obsessed by Time Magazine.
I read it every week.
Its cover stares at me every time I slink past the corner candystore.
I read it in the basement of the Berkeley Public Library.
It's always telling me about responsibility. Businessmen are serious.
      Movie producers are serious. Everybody's serious but me.
It occurs to me that I am America.
I am talking to myself again.

Asia is rising against me.
I haven't got a chinaman's chance.
I'd better consider my national resources.
My national resources consist of two joints of marijuana millions of genitals
      an unpublishable private literature that jetplanes 1400 miles an hour
      and twentyfive-thousand mental institutions.
I say nothing about my prisons nor the millions of underprivileged who live
      in my flowerpots under the light of five hundred suns.
I have abolished the whorehouses of France, Tangiers is the next to go.
My ambition is to be President despite the fact that I'm a Catholic.

America how can I write a holy litany in your silly mood?
I will continue like Henry Ford my strophes are as individual as his automo-
      biles more so they're all different sexes.
America I will sell you strophes $2500 apiece $500 down on your old strophe
America free Tom Mooney
America save the Spanish Loyalists
America Sacco & Vanzetti must not die
America I am the Scottsboro boys.
America when I was seven momma took me to Communist Cell meetings
      they sold us garbanzos a handful per ticket a ticket costs a nickel and
      the speeches were free everybody was angelic and sentimental about
      the workers it was all so sincere you have no idea what a good thing
      the party was in 1835 Scott Nearing was a grand old man a real
      mensch Mother Bloor the Silk-strikers' Ewig-Weibliche made me cry
      I once saw the Yiddish orator Israel Amter plain. Everybody must
      have been a spy.
America you don't really want to go to war.
America it's them bad Russians.
Them Russians them Russians and them Chinamen. And them Russians.
The Russia wants to eat us alive. The Russia's power mad. She wants to take
      our cars from out our garages.

Her wants to grab Chicago. Her needs a Red *Reader's Digest*. Her wants our
　　auto plants in Siberia. Him big bureaucracy running our fillingsta-
　　tions.
That no good. Ugh. Him make Indians learn read. Him need big black
　　niggers. Hah. Her make us all work sixteen hours a day. Help.
America this is quite serious.
America this is the impression I get from looking in the television set.
America is this correct?
I'd better get right down to the job.
It's true I don't want to join the Army or turn lathes in precision parts
　　factories, I'm nearsighted and psychopathic anyway.
America I'm putting my queer shoulder to the wheel.

Berkeley, January 17, 1956

Fragment 1956

Now to the come of the poem, let me be worthy
& sing holily the natural pathos of the human soul,
naked original skin beneath our dreams
& robes of thought, the perfect self identity
radiant with lusts and intellectual faces
Who carries the lines, the painful browed
contortions of the upper eyes, the whole body
breathing and sentient among flowers and buildings
open-eyed, self knowing, trembling with love—
Soul that I have, that Jack has, Huncke has
Bill has, Joan had, and has in me memory yet,
bum has in rags, madman underneath black clothes.
Soul identical each to each, as standing on
the streetcorner ten years ago I looked at Jack
and told him we were the same person—look
in my eyes and speak to yourself, that makes me
everybody's lover, Hal mine against his will,
I had his soul in my own body already, while
he frowned—by the streetlamp 8th Avenue & 27th
Street 1947—I had just come back from Africa
with a gleam of the illumination actually
to come to me in time as come to all—Jack
the worst murderer, Allen the most cowardly
with a streak of yellow love running through
my poems, a fag in the city, Joe Army screaming
in anguish in Dannemora 1945 jailhouse,
breaking his own white knuckle against the bars
his dumb sad cellmate beaten by the guards
an iron floor below, Gregory weeping in Tombs,
Joan eyes narrow-lidded under benzedrine
harkening to the paranoia in the wall,
Huncke from Chicago dreaming in Arcades
of hellish Pokerino blue skinned Times Square light,
Bill King yelling pale faced in the subway window
final minute gape-death struggling to return,
Morphy himself, archsuicide, expiring in blood
on the Passaic, tragic & bewildered in
last tears, attaining death that moment
human, intellectual, bearded, who else
was he then but himself?

Berkeley, 1956

Afternoon Seattle

Busride along waterfront down Yessler under street bridge to the old red Wobbly Hall—

One Big Union, posters of the Great Mandala of Labor, bleareyed dusty cardplayers dreaming behind the counter . . . 'but these young fellers can't see ahead and we nothing to offer'—

After Snyder his little red beard and bristling Buddha mind I weeping crossed Skid Road to 10¢ beer.

Labyrinth wood stairways and Greek movies under Farmers Market secondhand city, Indian smoked salmon old overcoats and dry red shoes,

Green Parrot Theater, *Maytime,* and down to the harborside the ships, walked on Alaska silent together—ferryboat coming faraway in mist from Bremerton Island dreamlike small on the waters of Holland to me

—and entered my head the seagull, a shriek, sentinels standing over rusty harbor iron dockwork, rocks dripping under rotten wharves slime on the walls—

the seagull's small cry—inhuman not of the city, lone sentinels of God, animal birds among us indifferent, their bleak lone cries representing our souls.

A rowboat docked and chained floating in the tide by a wharf. Basho's frog. Someone left it there, it drifts.

Sailor's curio shop hung with shells and skulls a whalebone mask, Indian seas. The cities rot from oldest parts. Little red mummy from Idaho Frank H. Little your big hat high cheekbones crosseyes and song.

The cities rot from the center, the suburbs fall apart a slow apocalypse of rot the spectral trolleys fade

the cities rot the fire escapes hang and rust the brick turns black dust falls uncollected garbage heaps the wall

the birds invade with their cries the skid row alley creeps downtown the ancient jailhouse groans bums snore under the pavement a dark Turkish bath the cornice gapes at midnight

Seattle!—department stores full of fur coats and camping equipment, mad noontime businessmen in gabardine coats talking on streetcorners to keep up the structure, I float past, birds cry,

Salvation Army offers soup on rotting block, six thousand beggars groan at a meal of hopeful beans.

February 2, 1956

Tears

I'm crying all the time now.
I cried all over the street when I left the Seattle Wobbly Hall.
I cried listening to Bach.
I cried looking at the happy flowers in my backyard, I cried at the sadness
      of the middle-aged trees.

Happiness exists I feel it.
I cried for my soul, I cried for the world's soul.
The world has a beautiful soul.
God appearing to be seen and cried over. Overflowing heart of Paterson.

Seattle, February 2, 1956

Scribble

Rexroth's face reflecting human
      tired bliss
White haired, wing browed
      gas mustache,
         flowers jet out of
           his sad head,
listening to Edith Piaf street song
      as she walks the universe
         with all life gone
         and cities disappeared
           only the God of Love
             left smiling.

Berkeley, March 1956

In the Baggage Room at Greyhound

I

In the depths of the Greyhound Terminal
sitting dumbly on a baggage truck looking at the sky waiting for the Los
     Angeles Express to depart
worrying about eternity over the Post Office roof in the night-time red
     downtown heaven,
staring through my eyeglasses I realized shuddering these thoughts were not
     eternity, nor the poverty of our lives, irritable baggage clerks,
nor the millions of weeping relatives surrounding the buses waving goodbye,
nor other millions of the poor rushing around from city to city to see their
     loved ones,
nor an indian dead with fright talking to a huge cop by the Coke machine,
nor this trembling old lady with a cane taking the last trip of her life,
nor the red-capped cynical porter collecting his quarters and smiling over the
     smashed baggage,
nor me looking around at the horrible dream,
nor mustached negro Operating Clerk named Spade, dealing out with his
     marvelous long hand the fate of thousands of express packages,
nor fairy Sam in the basement limping from leaden trunk to trunk,
nor Joe at the counter with his nervous breakdown smiling cowardly at the
     customers,
nor the grayish-green whale's stomach interior loft where we keep the bag-
     gage in hideous racks,
hundreds of suitcases full of tragedy rocking back and forth waiting to be
     opened,
nor the baggage that's lost, nor damaged handles, nameplates vanished,
     busted wires & broken ropes, whole trunks exploding on the concrete
     floor,
nor seabags emptied into the night in the final warehouse.

II

Yet Spade reminded me of Angel, unloading a bus,
dressed in blue overalls black face official Angel's workman cap,
pushing with his belly a huge tin horse piled high with black baggage,
looking up as he passed the yellow light bulb of the loft
and holding high on his arm an iron shepherd's crook.

III

It was the racks, I realized, sitting myself on top of them now as is my wont
      at lunchtime to rest my tired foot,
it was the racks, great wooden shelves and stanchions posts and beams
      assembled floor to roof jumbled with baggage,
—the Japanese white metal postwar trunk gaudily flowered & headed for
      Fort Bragg,
one Mexican green paper package in purple rope adorned with names for
      Nogales,
hundreds of radiators all at once for Eureka,
crates of Hawaiian underwear,
rolls of posters scattered over the Peninsula, nuts to Sacramento,
one human eye for Napa,
an aluminum box of human blood for Stockton
and a little red package of teeth for Calistoga—
it was the racks and these on the racks I saw naked in electric light the night
      before I quit,
the racks were created to hang our possessions, to keep us together, a tempo-
      rary shift in space,
God's only way of building the rickety structure of Time,
to hold the bags to send on the roads, to carry our luggage from place to place
looking for a bus to ride us back home to Eternity where the heart was left
      and farewell tears began.

IV

A swarm of baggage sitting by the counter as the transcontinental bus pulls
      in.
The clock registering 12:15 A.M., May 9, 1956, the second hand moving
      forward, red.
Getting ready to load my last bus.—Farewell, Walnut Creek Richmond
      Vallejo Portland Pacific Highway
Fleet-footed Quicksilver, god of transience.
One last package sits lone at midnight sticking up out of the Coast rack high
      as the dusty fluorescent light.

The wage they pay us is too low to live on. Tragedy reduced to numbers.
This for the poor shepherds. I am a communist.

Farewell ye Greyhound where I suffered so much,
hurt my knee and scraped my hand and built my pectoral muscles big as
      vagina.

May 9, 1956

Psalm III

To God: to illuminate all men. Beginning with Skid Road.

Let Occidental and Washington be transformed into a higher place, the plaza of eternity.

Illuminate the welders in shipyards with the brilliance of their torches.

Let the crane operator lift up his arm for joy.

Let elevators creak and speak, ascending and descending in awe.

Let the mercy of the flower's direction beckon in the eye.

Let the straight flower bespeak its purpose in straightness—to seek the light.

Let the crooked flower bespeak its purpose in crookedness—to seek the light.

Let the crookedness and straightness bespeak the light.

Let Puget Sound be a blast of light.

I feed on your Name like a cockroach on a crumb—this cockroach is holy.

Seattle, June, 1956

Many Loves

"Resolved to sing no songs henceforth but those of manly attachment"
—Walt Whitman

Neal Cassady was my animal: he brought me to my knees
and taught me the love of his cock and the secrets of his mind
And we met and conversed, went walking in the evening by the park
Up to Harlem, recollecting Denver, and Dan Budd, a hero
And we made shift to sack out in Harlem, after a long evening,
Jack and host in a large double bed, I volunteered for the cot, and Neal
Volunteered for the cot with me, we stripped and lay down.
I wore my underwear, my shorts, and he his briefs—
lights out on the narrow bed I turned to my side, with my back to his Irish
        boy's torso,
and huddled and balanced on the edge, and kept distance—
and hung my head over and kept my arm over the side, withdrawn
And he seeing my fear stretched out his arm, and put it around my breast
Saying "Draw near me" and gathered me in upon him:
I lay there trembling, and felt his great arm like a king's
And his breasts, his heart slow thudding against my back,
and his middle torso, narrow and made of iron, soft at my back,
his fiery firm belly warming me while I trembled—
His belly of fists and starvation, his belly a thousand girls kissed in Colorado
his belly of rocks thrown over Denver roofs, prowess of jumping and fists,
        his stomach of solitudes,
His belly of burning iron and jails affectionate to my side:
I began to tremble, he pulled me in closer with his arm, and hugged me long
        and close
my soul melted, secrecy departed, I became
Thenceforth open to his nature as a flower in the shining sun.
And below his belly, in white underwear, tight between my buttocks,
His own loins against me soft, nestling in comradeship, put forth & pressed
        into me, open to my awareness,
slowly began to grow, signal me further and deeper affection, sexual tender-
        ness.
So gentle the man, so sweet the moment, so kind the thighs that nuzzled
        against me smooth-skinned powerful, warm by my legs
That my body shudders and trembles with happiness, remembering—
His hand opened up on my belly, his palms and fingers flat against my skin
I fell to him, and turned, shifting, put my face on his arm resting,

my chest against his, he helped me to turn, and held me closer

his arm at my back beneath my head, and arm at my buttocks tender holding
me in,

our bellies together nestling, loins touched together, pressing and know-
ledgeable each other's hardness, and mine stuck out of my underwear.

Then I pressed in closer and drew my leg up between his, and he lay half
on me with his thighs and bedded me down close, caressing

and moved together pressing his cock to my thigh and mine to his

slowly, and slowly began a love match that continues in my imagination to
this day a full decade.

Thus I met Neal & thus we felt each other's flesh and owned each other
bodies and souls.

So then as I lay on his breast with my arms clasped around his neck and his
cheek against mine,

I put my hand down to feel his great back for the first time, jaws and pectorals
of steel at my fingers,

closer and stiller, down the silken iron back to his waist, the whole of his
torso now open

my hand at his waist trembling, waited delaying and under the elastic of his
briefs,

I first touched the smooth mount of his rock buttocks, silken in power,
rounded in animal fucking and bodily nights over nurses and school-
girls,

O ass of long solitudes in stolen cars, and solitudes on curbs, musing fist in
cheek,

Ass of a thousand farewells, ass of youth, youth's lovers,

Ass of a thousand lonely craps in gas stations ass of great painful secrecies
of the years

O ass of mystery and night! ass of gymnasiums and muscular pants

ass of high schools and masturbation ass of lone delight, ass of mankind, so
beautiful and hollow, dowry of Mind and Angels,

Ass of hero, Neal Cassady, I had at my hand: my fingers traced the curve
to the bottom of his thighs.

I raised my thighs and stripped down my shorts to my knees, and bent to
push them off

and he raised me up from his chest, and pulled down his pants the same,

humble and meek and obedient to his mood our silence,

and naked at long last with angel & greek & athlete & hero and brother and
boy of my dreams

I lay with my hair intermixed with his, he asking me "What shall we do
now?"

—And confessed, years later, he thinking I was not a queer at first to please
    me & serve me, to blow me and make me come, maybe or if I were
    queer, that's what I'd likely want of a dumb bastard like him.
But I made my first mistake, and made him then and there my master, and
    bowed my head, and holding his buttock
Took up his hard-on and held it, feeling it throb and pressing my own at
    his knee & breathing showed him I needed him, cock, for my dreams
    of insatiety & lone love.

—And I lie here naked in the dark, dreaming

Arctic, August 10, 1956

Ready to Roll

To Mexico! To Mexico! Down the dovegray highway, past Atomic City
    police, past the fiery border to dream cantinas!
Standing on the sunny metropolitan plateau, stranger prince on the street,
    dollars in my pocket, alone, free—genitals and thighs and buttocks
    under skin and leather.
Music! Taxis! Marijuana in the slums! Ancient sexy parks! Continental
    boulevards in America! Modern downtown for a dollar! Dungarees
    in Les Ambassadeurs! And here's a hard brown cock for a quarter!
Drunkenness! and the long night walks down brown streets, eyes, windows,
    buses, interior charnels behind the Cathedral, lost squares and hungry
    tacos, a calf's head cooked and picked apart for meat,
and the blackened inner roofs and tents of the Thieves' Market, street criss-
    crossed on street, a naked hipster labyrinth, stealing, pausing, loiter-
    ing, noticing drums, purchasing nothing
but a broken aluminum coffeepot with a doll's arm sticking up out of the
    mouth.
Haha! what do I want? Change of solitude, spectre of drunkenness in para-
    noiac taxicabs, fear and gaiety of unknown lovers
coming around the empty streetcorner dark-eyed and watching me make it
    there alone under the new hip moon.

San Francisco, October 1956

IV
REALITY
SANDWICHES:
EUROPE! EUROPE!
(1957–1959)

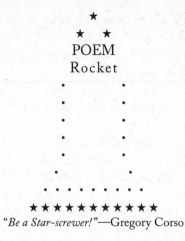

POEM
Rocket

"Be a Star-screwer!"—Gregory Corso

Old moon my eyes are new moon with human footprint
no longer Romeo Sadface in drunken river Loony Pierre eyebrow, goof
      moon
O possible moon in Heaven we get to first of ageless constellations of names
as God is possible as All is possible so we'll reach another life.

Moon politicians earth weeping and warring in eternity
tho not one star disturbed by screaming madmen from Hollywood
oil tycoons from Romania making secret deals with flabby green Plu-
      tonians—
slave camps on Saturn Cuban revolutions on Mars?
Old life and new side by side, will Catholic Church find Christ on Jupiter
Mohammed rave in Uranus will Buddha be acceptable on the stolid planets
or will we find Zoroastrian temples flowering on Neptune?
What monstrous new ecclesiastical design on the entire universe unfolds in
      the dying Pope's brain?
Scientist alone is true poet he gives us the moon
he promises the stars he'll make us a new universe if it comes to that
O Einstein I should have sent you my flaming mss.
O Einstein I should have pilgrimaged to your white hair!

O fellow travelers I write you a poem in Amsterdam in the Cosmos
where Spinoza ground his magic lenses long ago
I write you a poem long ago
already my feet are washed in death
Here I am naked without identity
with no more body than the fine black tracery of pen mark on soft paper

as star talks to star multiple beams of sunlight all the same myriad thought
in one fold of the universe where Whitman was
and Blake and Shelley saw Milton dwelling as in a starry temple
brooding in his blindness seeing all—
Now at last I can speak to you beloved brothers of an unknown moon
real Yous squatting in whatever form amidst Platonic Vapors of Eternity
I am another Star.
Will you eat my poems or read them
or gaze with aluminum blind plates on sunless pages?
do you dream or translate & accept data with indifferent droopings of anten-
     nae?
do I make sense to your flowery green receptor eyesockets? do you have
     visions of God?
Which way will the sunflower turn surrounded by millions of suns?

This is my rocket my personal rocket I send up my message Beyond
Someone to hear me there
My immortality
without steel or cobalt basalt or diamond gold or mercurial fire
without passports filing cabinets bits of paper warheads
without myself finally
pure thought
message all and everywhere the same
I send up my rocket to land on whatever planet awaits it
preferably religious sweet planets no money
fourth dimensional planets where Death shows movies
plants speak (courteously) of ancient physics and poetry itself is manufac-
     tured by the trees
the final Planet where the Great Brain of the Universe sits waiting for a poem
     to land in His golden pocket
joining the other notes mash-notes love-sighs complaints-musical shrieks of
     despair and the million unutterable thoughts of frogs
I send you my rocket of amazing chemical
more than my hair my sperm or the cells of my body
the speeding thought that flies upward with my desire as instantaneous as
     the universe and faster than light
and leave all other questions unfinished for the moment to turn back to sleep
     in my dark bed on earth.

Amsterdam, October 4, 1957

Squeal

He rises he stretches he liquefies he is hammered again
He's divided in shares he litters the floor of the Bourse
He's cut by adamantine snips and sent by railway car
Accumulated on the margin by bony Goldfinger has various
Visions of being an automobile consolidates
The fortune of spectral lawyers heirs weep over him
He melts he undergoes remarkable metamorphoses peculiar
Hallucinations he coughs up debentures beaten
By immense hammers in a vast loft pours in fire spurts
Upward in molten forges he levels he dreams and he cools
And the present adjusted steel squints.

A hunchback tuberculosis salesman drives him cackling to St. Louis
In the rain Hack no will of his own Creep next resale Crank
San Pedro tomorrow St. Joe Squeak will it never end Hohokus—

Crashes into a dirty locomotive the bastard never
Mind stock averages decline slightly here's the mechanic
Blam the junkyard Help the smelter later a merger pressure accumulates
He's had it now Eek he's an airplane Whine he wants to go home
Suddenly he dives on the market like a bomb.

Paris, December 1957

Wrote This Last Night

Listen to the tale of the sensitive car
who was coughed up out of earth in Pittsburgh.

She screamed like a Swedish Prime Minister
on her first flight down the red neon highway,

she couldn't stand the sirens and blind lights
of the male cars Fords Oldsmobiles Studebakers

—her assembly line foreman had prophesied wild wreck
on Sunset Boulevard headlights & eyeballs broken fenders & bones.

She rode all over Mexico avoiding Los Angeles
praying to be an old junkie in a bordertown graveyard

with rattly doors and yellow broken windowpanes
bent license plate weak brakes & unsalable motor

worn out by the slow buttocks of teen-age nightmare
panting under the impoverished jissum of the August moon,

Anything but that final joyride with the mad producer
and his bombshell intellectual star on the last night up from Mexicali.

Paris, December 1957

Death to Van Gogh's Ear!

POET is Priest
Money has reckoned the soul of America
Congress broken thru to the precipice of Eternity
the President built a War machine which will vomit and rear up Russia out
of Kansas
The American Century betrayed by a mad Senate which no longer sleeps
with its wife
Franco has murdered Lorca the fairy son of Whitman
just as Mayakovsky committed suicide to avoid Russia
Hart Crane distinguished Platonist committed suicide to cave in the wrong
America
just as millions of tons of human wheat were burned in secret caverns under
the White House
while India starved and screamed and ate mad dogs full of rain
and mountains of eggs were reduced to white powder in the halls of Con-
gress
no godfearing man will walk there again because of the stink of the rotten
eggs of America
and the Indians of Chiapas continue to gnaw their vitaminless tortillas
aborigines of Australia perhaps gibber in the eggless wilderness
and I rarely have an egg for breakfast tho my work requires infinite eggs to
come to birth in Eternity
eggs should be eaten or given to their mothers
and the grief of the countless chickens of America is expressed in the scream-
ing of her comedians over the radio
Detroit has built a million automobiles of rubber trees and phantoms
but I walk, I walk, and the Orient walks with me, and all Africa walks
and sooner or later North America will walk
for as we have driven the Chinese Angel from our door he will drive us from
the Golden Door of the future
we have not cherished pity on Tanganyika
Einstein alive was mocked for his heavenly politics
Bertrand Russell driven from New York for getting laid
immortal Chaplin driven from our shores with the rose in his teeth
a secret conspiracy by Catholic Church in the lavatories of Congress has
denied contraceptives to the unceasing masses of India.
Nobody publishes a word that is not the cowardly robot ravings of a de-
praved mentality
The day of the publication of the true literature of the American body will
be day of Revolution

the revolution of the sexy lamb

the only bloodless revolution that gives away corn

poor Genet will illuminate the harvesters of Ohio

Marijuana is a benevolent narcotic but J. Edgar Hoover prefers his deathly
 scotch

And the heroin of Lao-Tze & the Sixth Patriarch is punished by the electric
 chair

but the poor sick junkies have nowhere to lay their heads

fiends in our government have invented a cold-turkey cure for addiction as
 obsolete as the Defense Early Warning Radar System.

I am the defense early warning radar system

I see nothing but bombs

I am not interested in preventing Asia from being Asia

and the governments of Russia and Asia will rise and fall but Asia and Russia
 will not fall

the government of America also will fall but how can America fall

I doubt if anyone will ever fall anymore except governments

fortunately all the governments will fall

the only ones which won't fall are the good ones

and the good ones don't yet exist

But they have to begin existing they exist in my poems

they exist in the death of the Russian and American governments

they exist in the death of Hart Crane & Mayakovsky

Now is the time for prophecy without death as a consequence

the universe will ultimately disappear

Hollywood will rot on the windmills of Eternity

Hollywood whose movies stick in the throat of God

Yes Hollywood will get what it deserves

Time

Seepage of nerve-gas over the radio

History will make this poem prophetic and its awful silliness a hideous
 spiritual music

I have the moan of doves and the feather of ecstasy

Man cannot long endure the hunger of the cannibal abstract

War is abstract

the world will be destroyed

but I will die only for poetry, that will save the world

Monument to Sacco & Vanzetti not yet financed to ennoble Boston

natives of Kenya tormented by idiot con-men from England

South Africa in the grip of the white fool

Vachel Lindsay Secretary of the Interior

Poe Secretary of Imagination

Pound Secty. Economics
and Kra belongs to Kra, and Pukti to Pukti
crossfertilization of Blok and Artaud
Van Gogh's Ear on the currency
no more propaganda for monsters
and poets should stay out of politics or become monsters
I have become monsterous with politics
the Russian poet undoubtedly monsterous in his secret notebook
Tibet should be left alone
These are obvious prophecies
America will be destroyed
Russian poets will struggle with Russia
Whitman warned against this "fabled Damned of nations"
Where was Theodore Roosevelt when he sent out ultimatums from his castle
    in Camden
Where was the House of Representatives when Crane read aloud from his
    prophetic books
What was Wall Street scheming when Lindsay announced the doom of
    Money
Were they listening to my ravings in the locker rooms of Bickfords Employ-
    ment Offices?
Did they bend their ears to the moans of my soul when I struggled with
    market research statistics in the Forum at Rome?
No they were fighting in fiery offices, on carpets of heartfailure, screaming
    and bargaining with Destiny
fighting the Skeleton with sabers, muskets, buck teeth, indigestion, bombs
    of larceny, whoredom, rockets, pederasty,
back to the wall to build up their wives and apartments, lawns, suburbs,
    fairydoms,
Puerto Ricans crowded for massacre on 114th St. for the sake of an imitation
    Chinese-Moderne refrigerator
Elephants of mercy murdered for the sake of an Elizabethan birdcage
millions of agitated fanatics in the bughouse for the sake of the screaming
    soprano of industry
Money-chant of soapers—toothpaste apes in television sets—deodorizers on
    hypnotic chairs—
petroleum mongers in Texas—jet plane streaks among the clouds—
sky writers liars in the face of Divinity—fanged butchers of hats and shoes,
    all Owners! Owners! Owners! with obsession on property and van-
    ishing Selfhood!
and their long editorials on the fence of the screaming negro attacked by ants
    crawled out of the front page!

Machinery of a mass electrical dream! A war-creating Whore of Babylon
    bellowing over Capitols and Academies!
Money! Money! Money! shrieking mad celestial money of illusion! Money
    made of nothing, starvation, suicide! Money of failure! Money of
    death!
Money against Eternity! and eternity's strong mills grind out vast paper of
    Illusion!

Paris, December 1957

Europe! Europe!

World world world
I sit in my room
imagine the future
sunlight falls on Paris
I am alone there is no
one whose love is perfect
man has been mad man's
love is not perfect I
have not wept enough
my breast will be heavy
till death the cities
are specters of cranks
of war the cities are
work & brick & iron &
smoke of the furnace of
selfhood makes tearless
eyes red in London but
no eye meets the sun

Flashed out of sky it
hits Lord Beaverbrook's
white modern solid
paper building leaned
in London's street to
bear last yellow beams
old ladies absently gaze
thru fog toward heaven
poor pots on windowsills
snake flowers to street
Trafalgar's fountains splash
on noon-warmed pigeons
Myself beaming in ecstatic
wilderness on St. Paul's dome
seeing the light on London
or here on a bed in Paris
sunglow through the high
window on plaster walls

Meek crowd underground
saints perish creeps
streetwomen meet lacklove
under gaslamp and neon
no woman in house loves
husband in flower unity
nor boy loves boy soft
fire in breast politics
electricity scares downtown
radio screams for money
police light on TV screens
laughs at dim lamps in
empty rooms tanks crash
thru bombshell no dream
of man's joy is made movie
think factory pushes junk
autos tin dreams of Eros
mind eats its flesh in
geekish starvation and no
man's fuck is holy for
man's work is most war

Bony China hungers brain
wash over power dam and
America hides mad meat
in refrigerator Britain
cooks Jerusalem too long
France eats oil and dead
salad arms & legs in Africa
loudmouth devours Arabia
negro and white warring
against the golden nuptial
Russia manufacture feeds
millions but no drunk can
dream Mayakovsky's suicide
rainbow over machinery
and backtalk to the sun

I lie in bed in Europe
alone in old red under
wear symbolic of desire
for union with immortality

but man's love's not perfect
in February it rains
as once for Baudelaire
one hundred years ago
planes roar in the air
cars race thru streets
I know where they go
to death but that is OK
it is that death comes
before life that no man
has loved perfectly no one
gets bliss in time new
mankind is not born that
I weep for this antiquity
and herald the Millennium
for I saw the Atlantic sun
rayed down from a vast cloud
at Dover on the sea cliffs
tanker size of ant heaved
up on ocean under shining
cloud and seagull flying
thru sun light's endless
ladders streaming in Eternity
to ants in the myriad fields
of England to sun flowers
bent up to eat infinity's
minute gold dolphins leaping
thru Mediterranean rainbow
White smoke and steam in Andes
Asia's rivers glittering
blind poets deep in lone
Apollonic radiance on hillsides
littered with empty tombs

Paris, February 29, 1958

The Lion for Real

"Soyez muette pour moi, Idole contemplative . . ."

I came home and found a lion in my living room
Rushed out on the fire escape screaming Lion! Lion!
Two stenographers pulled their brunette hair and banged the window shut
I hurried home to Paterson and stayed two days.

Called up my old Reichian analyst
who'd kicked me out of therapy for smoking marijuana
'It's happened' I panted 'There's a Lion in my room'
'I'm afraid any discussion would have no value' he hung up.

I went to my old boyfriend we got drunk with his girlfriend
I kissed him and announced I had a lion with a mad gleam in my eye
We wound up fighting on the floor I bit his eyebrow & he kicked me out
I ended masturbating in his jeep parked in the street moaning 'Lion.'

Found Joey my novelist friend and roared at him 'Lion!'
He looked at me interested and read me his spontaneous ignu high poetries
I listened for lions all I heard was Elephant Tiglon Hippogriff Unicorn Ants
But figured he really understood me when we made it in Ignaz Wisdom's
     bathroom.

But next day he sent me a leaf from his Smoky Mountain retreat
'I love you little Bo-Bo with your delicate golden lions
But there being no Self and No Bars therefore the Zoo of your dear Father
     hath no Lion
You said your mother was mad don't expect me to produce the Monster for
     your Bridegroom.'

Confused dazed and exalted bethought me of real lion starved in his stink in
     Harlem
Opened the door the room was filled with the bomb blast of his anger
He roaring hungrily at the plaster walls but nobody could hear him outside
     thru the window
My eye caught the edge of the red neighbor apartment building standing in
     deafening stillness

We gazed at each other his implacable yellow eye in the red halo of fur
Waxed rheumy on my own but he stopped roaring and bared a fang greet-
    ing.
I turned my back and cooked broccoli for supper on an iron gas stove
boilt water and took a hot bath in the old tub under the sink board.

He didn't eat me, tho I regretted him starving in my presence.
Next week he wasted away a sick rug full of bones wheaten hair falling out
enraged and reddening eye as he lay aching huge hairy head on his paws
by the egg-crate bookcase filled up with thin volumes of Plato, & Buddha.

Sat by his side every night averting my eyes from his hungry motheaten face
stopped eating myself he got weaker and roared at night while I had night-
    mares
Eaten by lion in bookstore on Cosmic Campus, a lion myself starved by
    Professor Kandisky, dying in a lion's flophouse circus,
I woke up mornings the lion still added dying on the floor—'Terrible Pres-
    ence!' I cried 'Eat me or die!'

It got up that afternoon—walked to the door with its paw on the wall to
    steady its trembling body
Let out a soul-rending creak from the bottomless roof of his mouth
thundering from my floor to heaven heavier than a volcano at night in
    Mexico
Pushed the door open and said in a gravelly voice "Not this time Baby—but
    I will be back again."

Lion that eats my mind now for a decade knowing only your hunger
Not the bliss of your satisfaction O roar of the Universe how am I chosen
In this life I have heard your promise I am ready to die I have served
Your starved and ancient Presence O Lord I wait in my room at your Mercy.
                                                                    Paris, March 1958

The Names

Time comes spirit weakens and goes blank apartments shuffled through and
    forgotten
The dead in their cenotaphs locomotive high schools & African cities small
    town motorcycle graves
O America what saints given vision are shrouded in junk their elegy a
    nameless hoodlum elegance leaning against death's military garage
Huncke who first saw the sun revolve in Chicago survived into middle-age
    Times Square
Thief stole hearts of wildcat tractor boys arrived to morphine brilliance
    Bickford table midnight neon to take a fall
arrested 41 times late 40s his acned skin & black Spanish hair grown coy and
    old and lip bitten in Rikers Island Jail
as bestial newsprint photograph we shared once busted, me scared of black
    eye cops Manhattan
you blissful nothing to lose digging the live detectives perhaps even offering
    God a cigarette
I'll answer for you Huncke I never could before—admiring your natural tact
    and charm and irony—now sad Sing Sing
whatever inept Queens burglary you goofed again let God judge his sacred
    case
rather than mustached Time Judge steal a dirty photograph of your soul—
    I knew you when—
& you loved me better than my lawyer who wanted a frightened rat for
    official thousand buck mousetrap, no doubt, no doubt—
Shine in Cell free behind bars Immortal soul why not
Hell the machine can't sentence anyone except itself, have I to do that?
It gives jail I give you poem, bars last twenty years rust in a hundred
my handwork remains when prisons fall because the hand is compassion

Brilliant bitter Morphy stalking Los Angeles after his ghost boy
haunting basements in Denver with his Montmartre black beard
Charming ladies' man for gigolo purpose I heard, great cat for Shakespearean
    sex
first poet suicide I knew we sat on park benches I watched him despair his
    forehead star
my elder asked serious advice, gentle man! international queer pride hum-
    bled to pre-death cigarette gun fright
His love a young blond demon of broken army, his nemesis his own mad
    cock for the kids sardonic ass

his dream mouthful of white prick trembling in his head—woke a bullet in
      his side days later in Passaic
last moments gasping stricken blood under stars coughing intestines &
      lighted highway cars flowing past his eyes into the dark.

Joe Army's beauty forgotten that night, pain cops nightmare, drunken
      AWOL through Detroit
phonecalls angels backrooms & courtsmartial lawyers trains a kaleidoscope
      of instant change,
shrinkage of soul, bearded dead dreams, all Balzac read in jail,
late disappearance from the city hides metamorphosis to humancy loathing
      that deathscene.

Phil Black hung in Tombs, horsefaced junky, dreamy strange murderer,
      forgotten pistol three buck holdup, stoolpigeon suicide I save him
      from the grave

Iroquois his indian head red cock intelligence buried in miserous solitaire
      politics
his narcissistic blond haired hooknosed pride, I made him once he groaned
      and came
Later stranger chill made me tremble, I loved him hopeless years,
he's hid in Seattle consumed by lesbian hypochondrias' stealthy communion,
      green bullfighters envy age,
unless I save him from the grave, but he won't talk no more
much less fall in my arms or any mental bed forgiveness before we climb
      Olympics death

Leroi returning to bughouse monkishness & drear stinky soupdish his fatness
      fright & suffering mind insult a repetitious void
"I have done my best to make saintliness as uninteresting as possible"
and has succeeded, when did I last write or receive ambiguous message joky
      hangdog prophetic spade

Joan in dreams bent forward smiling asks news of the living
as in life the same sad tolerance, no skullbone judge of drunks
asking whereabouts sending regards from Mexican paradise garden where
      life & death are one
as if a postcard from eternity sent with human hand, wish I could see you
      now, it's happening as should
whatever we really need, we ought get, don't blame yourself—a photograph
      on reverse

the rare tomb smile where trees grow crooked energy above grass—

yet died early-old teeth gone, tequila bottle in hand, an infantile paralysis
        limp, lacklove, the worst—

I dreamed such vision of her secret in my frisco bed, heart can live the rest
        by my, or her, best desire—love

Bill King black haired sorry drunken wop lawyer, woke up trembling in
        Connecticut DT's among cows

Him there to recover I guess, but made his way back to New York shudder-
        ing to fuck stiff *Time* girls,

Death charm in person, sexual childlike radiant pain

See his face in old photographs & bandaged naked wrist leaning melancholy
        contemplating the camera

awkward face now calm, kind to me in cafeteria one sober morn looking for
        jobs at breakfast,

but mostly smiled at roof edge midnight, all 1920s elegance reincarnate in
        black vomit bestriven suit

& screechy records *Mahagonny* airplane crash, lushed young man of 1940s
        hated his fairy woe, came on Lizzie's belly or Ansen's sock in desper-
        ate orgies of music canopener

God but I loved his murdered face when he talked with a mouthful of rain
        in 14th St subway—

where he fell skull broken underground last, head crushed by the radiant
        wheel on iron track at Astor Place

Farewell dear Bill that's done, you're gone, we all go into the ancient void
        drunkard mouth

you made it too soon, here was more to say, & more to drink, but now too
        late to sit and talk

all night toward the eternity you sought so well so fearlessly in so much
        alcoholic pain with so much fire behind eyes with such

sweet manner in your heart that never won a happy fate thru what bleak
        years you saw your red skull burning deathshead in the U.S. sun

Mix living dead, Neal Cassady, old hero of travel love alyosha idiot seek-train
        poems, what crown you wear at last

what fameless reward for patience & pain, what golden whore come secret
        from the clouds, what has god bidden for your coffin and heart
        someday,

what will give back your famous arm, your happy catholic boy eye, orphan
        torso shining in poolhall & library, intimate spermworks with old
        girls downtown rockabelly energy,

what Paradise built high enough to hold your desire, deep enough to encompass your cock kindnesses, soft for your children to pray, 10 foot iron wheels you fell under?

what American heaven receive you? Christ allow sufferings then will he allow you His opening tinbarrel Iowa light as Jerusalem?

O Neal that life end we together on knees know harvest of prayers together,

Paradise autos ascend to the moon no illusion, short time earth life Bibles bear our eyes, make it dear baby

Stay with me Angel now in Shroud of railroad lost bet racetrack broke leg oblivion

till I get the shining Word or you the cockless cock to lay in my ass hope mental radiance—

It's all lost we fall without glory to empty tomb comedown to nothing but evil thinkless worm, but we know better

merely by old heart hope, or merely Desire, or merely the love whisper breathed in your ear on lawns of long gone by Denver,

merely by the night you leaned on my body & held me for All & called me to Adore what I wondered at as child age ten I

wandered by hopeless green hedges, when you sat under alley balcony garbagestair, ache in our breasts Futurity

meeting Love for Love, so wept as child now man I weep for true end,

Save from the grave! O Neal I love you I bring this Lamb into the middle of the world happily—O tenderness—to see you again—O tenderness—to recognize you in the middle of Time.

                                        Paris, Spring 1958

At Apollinaire's Grave

" . . . voici le temps
Où l'on connaîtra l'avenir
Sans mourir de connaissance"

I

I visited Père Lachaise to look for the remains of Apollinaire
the day the U.S. President appeared in France for the grand conference of
      heads of state
so let it be the airport at blue Orly a springtime clarity in the air over Paris
Eisenhower winging in from his American graveyard
and over the froggy graves at Père Lachaise an illusory mist as thick as
      marijuana smoke
Peter Orlovsky and I walked softly thru Père Lachaise we both knew we
      would die
and so held temporary hands tenderly in a citylike miniature eternity
roads and streetsigns rocks and hills and names on everybody's house
looking for the lost address of a notable Frenchman of the Void
to pay our tender crime of homage to his helpless menhir
and lay my temporary American Howl on top of his silent Calligramme
for him to read between the lines with Xray eyes of Poet
as he by miracle had read his own death lyric in the Seine
I hope some wild kidmonk lays his pamphlet on my grave for God to read
      me on cold winter nights in heaven
already our hands have vanished from that place my hand writes now in a
      room in Paris Git-le-Coeur
Ah William what grit in the brain you had what's death
I walked all over the cemetery and still couldn't find your grave
what did you mean by that fantastic cranial bandage in your poems
O solemn stinking deathshead what've you got to say nothing and that's
      barely an answer

You can't drive autos into a sixfoot grave tho the universe is mausoleum big
      enough for anything
the universe is a graveyard and I walk around alone in here
knowing that Apollinaire was on the same street 50 years ago
his madness is only around the corner and Genet is with us stealing books
the West is at war again and whose lucid suicide will set it all right
Guillaume Guillaume how I envy your fame your accomplishment for
      American letters
your Zone with its long crazy line of bullshit about death

come out of the grave and talk thru the door of my mind
issue new series of images oceanic haikus blue taxicabs in Moscow negro
    statues of Buddha
pray for me on the phonograph record of your former existence
with a long sad voice and strophes of deep sweet music sad and scratchy as
    World War I
I've eaten the blue carrots you sent out of the grave and Van Gogh's ear and
    maniac peyote of Artaud
and will walk down the streets of New York in the black cloak of French
    poetry
improvising our conversation in Paris at Père Lachaise
and the future poem that takes its inspiration from the light bleeding into
    your grave

II
Here in Paris I am your guest O friendly shade
the absent hand of Max Jacob
Picasso in youth bearing me a tube of Mediterranean
myself attending Rousseau's old red banquet I ate his violin
great party at the Bateau Lavoir not mentioned in the textbooks of Algeria
Tzara in the Bois de Boulogne explaining the alchemy of the machineguns
    of the cuckoos
he weeps translating me into Swedish
well dressed in a violet tie and black pants
a sweet purple beard which emerged from his face like the moss hanging
    from the walls of Anarchism
he spoke endlessly of his quarrels with André Breton
whom he had helped one day trim his golden mustache
old Blaise Cendrars received me into his study and spoke wearily of the
    enormous length of Siberia
Jacques Vaché invited me to inspect his terrible collection of pistols
poor Cocteau saddened by the once marvelous Radiguet at his last thought
    I fainted
Rigaut with a letter of introduction to Death
and Gide praised the telephone and other remarkable inventions
we agreed in principle though he gossiped of lavender underwear
but for all that he drank deeply of the grass of Whitman and was intrigued
    by all lovers named Colorado
princes of America arriving with their armfuls of shrapnel and baseball
Oh Guillaume the world so easy to fight seemed so easy
did you know the great political classicists would invade Montparnasse
with not one sprig of prophetic laurel to green their foreheads

not one pulse of green in their pillows no leaf left from their wars—Maya-
     kovsky arrived and revolted

III
Came back sat on a tomb and stared at your rough menhir
a piece of thin granite like an unfinished phallus
a cross fading into the rock 2 poems on the stone one Coeur Renversée
other Habituez-vous comme moi A ces prodiges que j'annonce Guillaume
     Apollinaire de Kostrowitsky
someone placed a jam bottle filled with daisies and a 5&10¢ surrealist typist
     ceramic rose
happy little tomb with flowers and overturned heart
under a fine mossy tree beneath which I sat snaky trunk
summer boughs and leaves umbrella over the menhir and nobody there
Et quelle voix sinistre ulule Guillaume qu'es-tu devenu
his nextdoor neighbor is a tree
there underneath the crossed bones heaped and yellow cranium perhaps
and the printed poems Alcools in my pocket his voice in the museum
Now middleage footsteps walk the gravel
a man stares at the name and moves toward the crematory building
same sky rolls over thru clouds as Mediterranean days on the Riviera during
     war
drinking Apollo in love eating occasional opium he'd taken the light
One must have felt the shock in St. Germain when he went out Jacob &
     Picasso coughing in the dark
a bandage unrolled and the skull left still on a bed outstretched pudgy fingers
     the mystery and ego gone
a bell tolls in the steeple down the street birds warble in the chestnut trees
Famille Bremont sleeps nearby Christ hangs big chested and sexy in their
     tomb
my cigarette smokes in my lap and fills the page with smoke and flames
an ant runs over my corduroy sleeve the tree I lean on grows slowly
bushes and branches upstarting through the tombs one silky spiderweb
     gleaming on granite
I am buried here and sit by my grave beneath a tree

Paris, Winter–Spring 1958

Message

Since we had changed
rogered spun worked
wept and pissed together
I wake up in the morning
with a dream in my eyes
but you are gone in NY
remembering me Good
I love you I love you
& your brothers are crazy
I accept their drunk cases
It's too long that I have been alone
it's too long that I've sat up in bed
without anyone to touch on the knee, man
or woman I don't care what anymore, I
want love I was born for I want you with me now
Ocean liners boiling over the Atlantic
Delicate steelwork of unfinished skyscrapers
Back end of the dirigible roaring over Lakehurst
Six women dancing together on a red stage naked
The leaves are green on all the trees in Paris now
I will be home in two months and look you in the eyes

Paris, May 1958

To Lindsay

Vachel, the stars are out
dusk has fallen on the Colorado road
a car crawls slowly across the plain
in the dim light the radio blares its jazz
the heartbroken salesman lights another cigarette
In another city 27 years ago
I see your shadow on the wall
you're sitting in your suspenders on the bed
the shadow hand lifts up a Lysol bottle to your head
your shade falls over on the floor

Paris, May 1958

To Aunt Rose

Aunt Rose—now—might I see you
with your thin face and buck tooth smile and pain
         of rheumatism—and a long black heavy shoe
                  for your bony left leg
limping down the long hall in Newark on the running carpet
         past the black grand piano
                  in the day room
                           where the parties were
         and I sang Spanish loyalist songs
         in a high squeaky voice
                  (hysterical) the committee listening
         while you limped around the room
                  collected the money—
Aunt Honey, Uncle Sam, a stranger with a cloth arm
         in his pocket
                  and huge young bald head
                           of Abraham Lincoln Brigade

—your long sad face
         your tears of sexual frustration
                  (what smothered sobs and bony hips
                           under the pillows of Osborne Terrace)
—the time I stood on the toilet seat naked
         and you powdered my thighs with calamine
                  against the poison ivy—my tender
                           and shamed first black curled hairs
what were you thinking in secret heart then
         knowing me a man already—
and I an ignorant girl of family silence on the thin pedestal
         of my legs in the bathroom—Museum of Newark.

         Aunt Rose
Hitler is dead, Hitler is in Eternity; Hitler is with
         Tamburlane and Emily Brontë

Though I see you walking still, a ghost on Osborne Terrace
         down the long dark hall to the front door
                  limping a little with a pinched smile
                  in what must have been a silken
                           flower dress

welcoming my father, the Poet, on his visit to Newark
　　　　—see you arriving in the living room
　　　　　　dancing on your crippled leg
　　　　and clapping hands his book
　　　　　　had been accepted by Liveright

Hitler is dead and Liveright's gone out of business
The Attic of the Past and *Everlasting Minute* are out of print
　　　　　　Uncle Harry sold his last silk stocking
　　　　Claire quit interpretive dancing school
　　　　　　Buba sits a wrinkled monument in Old
　　　　　　Ladies Home blinking at new babies

last time I saw you was the hospital
　　　　pale skull protruding under ashen skin
　　　　　　blue veined unconscious girl
　　　　　　　　in an oxygen tent
　　　　the war in Spain has ended long ago
　　　　　　Aunt Rose
　　　　　　　　　Paris, June 1958

American Change

 The first I looked on, after a long time far from home in mid Atlantic
on a summer day
 Dolphins breaking the glassy water under the blue sky,
 a gleam of silver in my cabin, fished up out of my jangling new pocket
of coins and green dollars
 —held in my palm, the head of the feathered indian, old Buck-Rogers
eagle eyed face, a gash of hunger in the cheek
 gritted jaw of the vanished man begone like a Hebrew with hairlock
combed down the side—O Rabbi Indian
 what visionary gleam 100 years ago on Buffalo prairie under the
molten cloud-shot sky, 'the same clear light 10000 miles in all directions'
 but now with all the violin music of Vienna, gone into the great slot
machine of Kansas City, Reno—
 The coin seemed so small after vast European coppers thick francs
leaden pesetas, lire endless and heavy,
 a miniature primeval memorialized in 5¢ nickel candy-store nostalgia
of the redskin, dead on silver coin,
 with shaggy buffalo on reverse, hump-backed little tail incurved, head
butting against the rondure of Eternity,
 cock forelock below, bearded shoulder muscle folded below muscle,
head of prophet, bowed,
 vanishing beast of Time, hoar body rubbed clean of wrinkles and
shining like polished stone, bright metal in my forefinger, ridiculous buffalo
—Go to New York.

 Dime next I found, Minerva, sexless cold & chill, ascending goddess
of money—and was it the wife of Wallace Stevens, truly?
 and now from the locks flowing the miniature wings of speedy
thought,
 executive dyke, Minerva, goddess of Madison Avenue, forgotten use-
less dime that can't buy hot dog, dead dime—

 Then we've George Washington, less primitive, the snub-nosed quar-
ter, smug eyes and mouth, some idiot's design of the sexless Father,
 naked down to his neck, a ribbon in his wig, high forehead, Roman
line down the nose, fat cheeked, still showing his falsetooth ideas—O Eisen-
hower & Washington—O Fathers—No movie star dark beauty—O thou
Bignoses—
 Quarter, remembered quarter, 40¢ in all—What'll you buy me when
I land—one icecream soda?—

poor pile of coins, original reminders of the sadness, forgotten money
of America—

nostalgia of the first touch of those coins, American change,

the memory in my aging hand, the same old silver reflective there,
the thin dime hidden between my thumb and forefinger

All the struggles for those coins, the sadness of their reappearance
my reappearance on those fabled shores

and the failure of that Dream, that Vision of Money reduced to this
haunting recollection

of the gas lot in Paterson where I found half a dollar gleaming in the
grass—

I have a $5 bill in my pocket—it's Lincoln's sour black head moled
wrinkled, forelocked too, big eared, flags of announcement flying over the
bill, stamps in green and spiderweb black,

long numbers in racetrack green, immense promise, a girl, a hotel, a
busride to Albany, a night of brilliant drunk in some faraway corner of
Manhattan

a stick of several teas, or paper or cap of Heroin, or a $5 strange
present to the blind.

Money money, reminder, I might as well write poems to you—dear
American money—O statue of Liberty I ride enfolded in money in my mind
to you—and last

Ahhh! Washington again, on the Dollar, same poetic black print, dark
words, The United States of America, innumerable numbers

R956422481 One Dollar This Certificate is Legal Tender (tender!)
for all debts public and private

My God My God why have you forsaken me

Ivy Baker Priest Series 1953 F

and over, the Eagle, wild wings outspread, halo of the Stars encircled
by puffs of smoke & flame—

a circle the Masonic Pyramid, the sacred Swedenborgian Dollar
America, bricked up to the top, & floating surreal above

the triangle of holy outstaring Eye sectioned out of the aire, shining

light emitted from the eyebrowless triangle—and a desert of cactus,
scattered all around, clouds afar,

this being the Great Seal of our Passion, Annuit Coeptis, Novus Ordo
Seclorum,

the whole surrounded by green spiderwebs designed by T-Men to
prevent foul counterfeit—

ONE

S.S. United States, July 1958

'Back on Times Square,
Dreaming of Times Square'

Let some sad trumpeter stand
         on the empty streets at dawn
and blow a silver chorus to the
         buildings of Times Square,
memorial of ten years, at 5 A.M., with
         the thin white moon just
           visible
     above the green & grooking McGraw
     Hill offices
a cop walks by, but he's invisible
     with his music

The Globe Hotel, Garver lay in
    gray beds there and hunched his
    back and cleaned his needles—
where I lay many nights on the nod
    from his leftover bloody cottons
    and dreamed of Blake's voice talking—
        I was lonely,
        Garver's dead in Mexico two years,
     hotel's vanished into a parking lot
And I'm back here—sitting on the streets
again—
    The movies took our language, the
        great red signs
    A DOUBLE BILL OF GASSERS
        Teen Age Nightmare
    Hooligans of the Moon

But we were never nightmare
    hooligans but seekers of
        the blond nose for Truth

Some old men are still alive, but
        the old Junkies are gone—

We are a legend, invisible but
        legendary, as prophesied
              New York, July 1958

Laughing Gas

To Gary Snyder
The red tin begging cup you gave me,
I lost it but its contents are undisturbed.

I
High on Laughing Gas
I've been here before
the odd vibration of
the same old universe

the nasal whine of the dentist's drill
      singing against the nostalgic
            piano Muzak in the wall
insistent, familiar, penetrating
      the teeth, where've I heard that
          asshole jazz before?

The universe is a void
   in which there is a dreamhole
   The dream disappears
         the hole closes

   It's the instant of going
   into or coming out of
   existence that is
   important—to catch on
   to the secret of the magic
       box

Stepping outside the universe
      by means of Nitrous Oxide
anesthetizing mind-consciousness

      the chiliasm was an impersonal dream—
one of many, being mere dreams.

      the sadness of birth
      and death, the sadness of
changing from dream to dream,
   the constant farewell

of forms . . .
            saying ungoodbye to what
didn't exist

The many worlds that don't exist
all which seem real
all joke
all lost cartoon

At that moment the whole goofy-spooky of the Universe WHAT?! Joke
Being slips into Nothing like the tail of a lizard disappearing into a crack in
the Wall with the final receding eyehole ending Loony Tunes accompanied
by Woody Woodpecker's hindoo maniac laughter in the skull. Nobody gets
hurt. They all disappear. They were never there. Beginningless perfection.

That's why Satori's accompanied by laughter
and the Zenmaster rips up the Sutras in fury.

And the pain of this contrariety
The cycles of scream and laughter
faces and asses Christs and Buddhas
each with his own universe dragged
over the snowy mental poles
like a sack mad Santa Clauses
Worst pain in the dentist's chair comes true
novocaine also arrives in the cycle
every hap will have its chance
even God will come Once or Twice
Satan will be my personal enemy

Relax and die—
The process will repeat itself
Be Born! Be Born!
Back to the same old smiling
            dentist—

The Bloomfield police car
        with its idiot red light
        revolving on its head
        balefully at Eternity
            gone in an instant
            —simultaneous

         appearance of Bankrobbers
     at the Twentieth Century Bank
The fire engines screaming
     toward an old lady's
     burned-in-her-bedroom
    today apocalypse
       tomorrow
    Mickey Mouse cartoons—

I'm disgusted! it's Unbelievable!
    What a funny horrible
      dirty joke!
    The whole universe a shaggy dog story!
      with a weird ending that begins again
        till you get the point
'It was a dark and gloomy night . . .'
    'in every direction in and
      out'
     'You take the high road
  and I'll take the low'
             —everybody lost
in Scotlands of mind-consciousness—

    Adonoi Echad!
It is not One, but Two,
    not two but Infinite—
the universe be born and die
    in endless series in the mind!

Gary Snyder, Jack, Zen thinkers,
    split open existence
    and laugh & Cry—
what's shock? what's measure?
    when the Mind's an irrational
     traffic light in
      Gobi—
follow the blinking lights of contrariety!

What's the use avoiding rats
and horror, hiding from Cops
    and dentists' drills?

Somebody will invent
        a Buchenwald next door
—an ant's dream's
        funnier than
                ours
—he has more of them
        faster and seems
        to give less of
                a shit—

O waves of probable
        and improbable
Universes—
        Everybody's right

I'll finish this poem
        in my next life.

II
. . . . . . .with eye opening
slowly to perceive
that I be coming out
        of a trance—
one look at the lipstick
        it's a nurse
in a dentist's office

        that first frog
thought leaping out of
        the void

                . . . a glimpse
out of which the whole
process unfolds this
universe & logically
and symmetrically next
unbuilds it in exact
reverse till you arrive
back at the Nothing
in which one chance
note was originally
struck . . .

, the Czardas
of Creation, the first banal chord
establishing Music forever in
    its mechanical jukebox
        . . . and the whole
    structure unfolds
itself inevitably and
    folds back into
Nothing again . . .

    —the same man
crossing the street looking
both ways watch out for
the cars—

and each time, returning
with a jerk of the face
(p'raps a dental touch)
dictated by the sinking
sensation, Oof! I've
been hoodwinked—

        again like
    someone in the Circus
defying death, got thrown
        into the orchestra—
            Note the music blaring
with an indifferent flourish of Triumph
        a nightmare Razz
        —as the acrobat leaps
out into the void—

Me! I made that Last Chance
    jump off the wire
way high up in the Big Top
        long ago . . .
            it's happening again!

    I wake up dazed . . .

    it being the dream
of someone in a dentist's

chair in a Universe he
imagines—coming out
of gas—
  it's only happening
in the closed universe of
  illusion

III

  A nice day in the Universe on Broad Street—sun shines today as it
never shone before and never will again—stillness in the blue sky—the
church's gold dome across the park sending and receiving flashes of light—
I feel heartsick to destroy this all—
  What hope have the children in their prams passing the white silent
doors of the houses—only the Public Library knows.

  Premonition in the dentist's chair—mechanical voices over the radio
singing Destination Moon—mysterious sorrow for the moon of this forgot-
ten universe—humans, singing, singing—of the moon—for money?—except
it's the imbecilic canned voice of eternity rocking & rolling in Space making
invisible announcements—
  The Doc's agreed to the experiment—novocaine, my mouth's begun
to disappear first—like the Cheshire Cat.

BACK: Endless cycles of conflict happening in nothingness
make it impossible to grasp for the perfection
which does not exist
but is not necessary
so everything is final and occurs over & over again
till we will finally blank out as expected.

  The First Note of Creation:
the only one there could be if there
weren't nothing but
an idea that there might
not be nothing—

Sherman Adams will resign
I'm holding my breath
the shiver run thru my belly
the nurse will be singing I love you
between breaths the Buddhists are right
a tear
siffle in the cheek

the possibility escape
the eye glare thru glasses
Nothing grasped at & ungrasped as its trance thought passes

I take my pen in hand
The same old way sings Sinatra
I'm writing to You give me understanding
I pray sings Sinatra
Can I never glimpse the round we have made?
Write me as soon as able sings Sinatra
O Lord burn me out of existence.

You've got a long body sings Sinatra
I refuse to breathe and return to form
I've seen every moment in advance before
I've turned my neck a million times
       & written this note
     & been greeted with fire and cheers
I refuse to stop
       —thinking—
    What Perfection has escaped me?

An endless cycle of possibilities clashing in Nothing
with each mistake in the writing inevitable from the beginning of time
The doctor's phone number is Pilgrim 1-0000
Are you calling me, Nothing?

The universe be smashed
to smithereens by the oncoming
atomic explosions with
Eisenhower as once President
of a place called U.S.
Gregory wrote the Bomb!
Russians dream of Mars &
when the cosmos goes and
all consciousness after the
final explosion of imagination
in the void it won't have
made any difference that it
all both did and did not
happen, whatever it was once
thought to be so real—
it will be—gone.

O that I might die on the spot
I'll have to go back
any prophecy might have been right
it's all a great Exception

My bus will arrive as foretold
it's the end of another September
war is on the radio ahead
we are all going to the inevitable beauty of doom
a firebox stands sentient before the library
it's hot sun now I'm crazy scribbling
—It began abstract and mindless nowhere
planets of thought have passed
it'll end where it began

I want to return to normal
—but there is no changelessness
but in Nirvana
                    Or is there
Ever Rest, Lord?—and what sages
know and sit.
                    I'm a spy
in Bloomfield on a park bench
    —frightened by buses—

What's that bee doing hanging round my shoe? my borrowed and inevitable
        shoe?
A vast red truck moving with boxes of dead television sets in the back

American flag waving over the library

On the bus I sit by a negress

This is an explosion

IV
Back in the same old black hole
        where Possibility closes the
            last door
        and the Great Void remains
            . . . a glass

in the dust reflecting the sun,
        fragment of a bottle
    that never knew it existed

        . . . under a tree
that sleeps all winter
        till it grows its eyes
            in May heat
and flowers upward with a thousand
            green sensations
dies, and forgets itself in Snow

    . . . Phantom in Phantom

If we didn't exist, God
would have to create this
        to leave no room for complaint
            by any of the birds & bees
who might have missed their
            chance (to be)

    Fate tells big lies.

        . . . And the big kind Dreamer
is on the nod again
            God sleeps!
He's in for a big surprise
one of his dreams is going to come true
        He'll get the answer too
        He'll get the answer too

Just a flash in the cosmic pan
—just an instant when there
            might have been a light
        had there been any pan
                to reflect it—

—we can lie on the bed and imagine
        ourselves away—

I'm afraid to stop breathing—
        first the pain in the

                body
        suffocation, then
                the Death.

V
The pain of gas flowing into the eye
the crooked tooth-drills hanging like gallows
                on a miniature Jupiter
Thru the open window, spring frozen
                in the young tree
the repeated bong of the doorbell
                opening elsewhere
I've come back to the same medicine
        cabinet in the universe—Bong,
I know I'm more real than the dentist!
a serious embarrassment, having grasped to one Self
though admittedly I'd seen it disappear
                over and over

TRACKLESS TRANSIT CORPORATION

runs a bus thru Bloomfield
        . . . blossoming
in the bottom of an unborn daisy
it will vanish into the Whist-not

History will keep repeating
itself forever like the woman
in the image on the Dutch Cleanser box

A way out of the mirror
        was found by the image
that realized its existence
        was only . . .
a stranger completely like myself

A way out for ever! has not been found
to enter the ground whence the images
        rise, and repeat themselves

        —————

The sadness is, that every leaf
        has fallen before—

At my feet an ant crawling
        in the broken asphalt—
and this exact white lollipop stick
        & twig of branch
lain next to that soggy match
        near those few grassblades . . .
and I've sat here and took this note
        before and tried to remember—
and now I do—remember what
I'm writing as I write it down
I know when I'm going to stop
I know when I'm forgetting and
know when I
        take a jump and change—
          Impossible
to do anything but right now in all
        the universe at once—
        which Art does, and
the Insight of Laughing Gas?

Ha Ha Ha Ha Ha
and the monk laughs
at the moon—
and everybody 10 miles round
in all directions wonders
why—he's just reminding
them—of what—of
the moon, the old dumb moon
of a million lives.

          New York, Fall 1958

```
FFFFF U      U NN    N
F     U      U N N   N
FFFFF U      U N  N  N
F        U  U  N   N N NY DEATH
F         U U   N    NN
F         UU    N     N
```

The music of the spheres—that ends in Silence
The Void is a grand piano
                          a million melodies
                one after another
          silence in between
                     rather an interruption
                   of the silence

                    Tho the music's beautiful
Bong Bong Bon————
                   gnob
                              gnob
                                  gno————

Bong Bong Bong
o   n
n   o
g   b
b   g
o   n
n   o
obgnobgnobgnob

                    THE circle of forms
                    Shrinks
                         and disappears
                    back into the piano.
                         New York, September 25, 1958

```
```

My Sad Self

To Frank O'Hara

Sometimes when my eyes are red
I go up on top of the RCA Building
    and gaze at my world, Manhattan—
        my buildings, streets I've done feats in,
        lofts, beds, coldwater flats
—on Fifth Ave below which I also bear in mind,
    its ant cars, little yellow taxis, men
    walking the size of specks of wool—
Panorama of the bridges, sunrise over Brooklyn machine,
    sun go down over New Jersey where I was born
    & Paterson where I played with ants—
my later loves on 15th Street,
    my greater loves of Lower East Side,
    my once fabulous amours in the Bronx
        faraway—
paths crossing in these hidden streets,
    my history summed up, my absences
    and ecstasies in Harlem—
—sun shining down on all I own
    in one eyeblink to the horizon
    in my last eternity—
        matter is water.

Sad,
    I take the elevator and go
    down, pondering,
and walk on the pavements staring into all man's
        plateglass, faces,
    questioning after who loves,
and stop, bemused
    in front of an automobile shopwindow
standing lost in calm thought,
    traffic moving up & down 5th Avenue blocks behind me
    waiting for a moment when . . .

Time to go home & cook supper & listen to
    the romantic war news on the radio

                    . . . all movement stops
& I walk in the timeless sadness of existence,
      tenderness flowing thru the buildings,
          my fingertips touching reality's face,
my own face streaked with tears in the mirror
      of some window—at dusk—
                    where I have no desire—
for bonbons—or to own the dresses or Japanese
          lampshades of intellection—

Confused by the spectacle around me,
      Man struggling up the street
          with packages, newspapers,
                    ties, beautiful suits
          toward his desire
      Man, woman, streaming over the pavements
          red lights clocking hurried watches &
              movements at the curb—

And all these streets leading
      so crosswise, honking, lengthily,
              by avenues
      stalked by high buildings or crusted into slums
          thru such halting traffic
                    screaming cars and engines
so painfully to this
      countryside, this graveyard
              this stillness
                    on deathbed or mountain
      once seen
              never regained or desired
                    in the mind to come
where all Manhattan that I've seen must disappear.

                              New York, October 1958

Ignu

On top of that if you know me I pronounce you an ignu
Ignu knows nothing of the world
a great ignoramus in factories though he may own or inspire them or even
    be production manager
Ignu has knowledge of the angel indeed ignu is angel in comical form
W. C. Fields Harpo Marx ignus Whitman an ignu
Rimbaud a natural ignu in his boy pants
The ignu may be queer though like not kind ignu blows archangels for the
    strange thrill
a gnostic women love him Christ overflowed with trembling semen for
    many a dead aunt
He's a great cocksman most beautiful girls are worshipped by ignu
Hollywood dolls or lone Marys of Idaho long-legged publicity women and
    secret housewives
have known ignu in another lifetime and remember their lover
Husbands also are secretly tender to ignu their buddy
oldtime friendship can do anything cuckold bugger drunk trembling and
    happy
Ignu lives only once and eternally and knows it
he sleeps in everybody's bed everyone's lonesome for ignu ignu knew soli-
    tude early
So ignu's a primitive of cock and mind
equally the ignu has written liverish tomes personal metaphysics abstract
images that scratch the moon 'lightningflash-flintspark' naked lunch fried
    shoes adios king
The shadow of the angel is waving in the opposite direction
dawn of intelligence turns the telephones into strange animals
he attacks the rose garden with his mystical shears snip snip snip
Ignu has painted Park Avenue with his own long melancholy
and ignu giggles in a hard chair over tea in Paris bald in his decaying room
    a black hotel
Ignu with his wild mop walks by Colosseum weeping
he plucks a clover from Keats' grave & Shelley's a blade of grass
knew Coleridge they had slow hung-up talks at midnight over mahogany
    tables in London
sidestreet rooms in wintertime rain outside fog the cabman blows his hand
Charles Dickens is born ignu hears the wail of the babe
Ignu goofs nights under bridges and laughs at battleships
ignu is a battleship without guns in the North Sea lost O the flowerness of
    the moment

he knows geography he was there before he'll get out and die already
reborn a bearded humming Jew of Arabian mournful jokes
man with a star on his forehead and halo over his cranium
listening to music musing happy at the fall of a leaf the moonlight of immor-
    tality in his hair
table-hopping most elegant comrade of all most delicate mannered in the Sufi
    court
he wasn't even there at all
wearing zodiacal blue sleeves and the long peaked conehat of a magician
harkening to the silence of a well at midnight under a red star
in the lobby of Rockefeller Center attentive courteous bare-eyed enthusiastic
    with or without pants
he listens to jazz as if he were a negro afflicted with jewish melancholy and
    white divinity
Ignu's a natural you can see it when he pays the cabfare abstracted
pulling off the money from an impossible saintly roll
or counting his disappearing pennies to give to the strange busdriver whom
    he admires
Ignu has sought you out he's the seeker of God
and God breaks down the world for him every ten years
he sees lightning flash in empty daylight when the sky is blue
he hears Blake's disembodied Voice recite the Sunflower in a room in Har-
    lem
No woe on him surrounded by 700 thousand mad scholars moths fly out of
    his sleeve
He wants to die give up go mad break through into Eternity
live on and teach an aged saint or break down to an eyebrow clown
All ignus know each other in a moment's talk and measure each other up at
    once
as lifetime friends romantic winks and giggles across continents
sad moment paying the cab goodbye and speeding away uptown
One or two grim ignus in the pack
one laughing monk in dungarees
one delighted by cracking his eggs in an egg cup
one chews gum to music all night long rock and roll
one anthropologist cuckoo in the Petén rainforest
one sits in jail all year and bets karmaic racetrack
one chases girls down East Broadway into the horror movie
one pulls out withered grapes and rotten onions from his pants
one has a nannygoat under his bed to amuse visitors plasters the wall with
    his crap

collects scorpions whiskies skies etc. would steal the moon if he could find
     it
That would set fire to America but none of these make ignu
it's the soul that makes the style the tender firecracker of his thought
the amity of letters from strange cities to old friends
and the new radiance of morning on a foreign bed
A comedy of personal being his grubby divinity
Eliot probably an ignu one of the few who's funny when he eats
Williams of Paterson a dying American ignu
Burroughs a purest ignu his haircut is a cream his left finger
pinkie chopped off for early ignu reasons metaphysical spells love spells with
     psychoanalysts
his very junkhood an accomplishment beyond a million dollars
Céline himself an old ignu over prose
I saw him in Paris dirty old gentleman of ratty talk
with longhaired cough three wormy sweaters round his neck
brown mould under historic fingernails
pure genius his giving morphine all night to 1400 passengers on a sinking
     ship
'because they were all getting emotional'
Who's amazing you is ignu communicate with me
by mail post telegraph phone street accusation or scratching at my window
and send me a true sign I'll reply special delivery
DEATH IS A LETTER THAT WAS NEVER SENT
Knowledge born of stamps words coins pricks jails seasons sweet ambition
     laughing gas
history with a gold halo photographs of the sea painting a celestial din in the
     bright window
one eye in a black cloud
and the lone vulture on a sand plain seen from the window of a Turkish bus
It must be a trick.   Two diamonds in the hand one Poetry one Charity
proves we have dreamed   and the long sword of intelligence
over which I constantly stumble like my pants at the age six—embarrassed.

New York, November 1958

Battleship Newsreel

I was high on tea in my fo'c'sle near the forepeak hatch listening to the stars
envisioning the kamikazes flapping and turning in the soiled clouds
ackack burst into fire a vast hole ripped out of the bow like a burning lily
we dumped our oilcans of nitroglycerine among the waving octopi
dull thud and boom of thunder undersea the cough of the tubercular ma-
        chinegunner
flames in the hold among the cans of ether the roar of battleships far away
rolling in the sea like whales surrounded by dying ants the screams the
        captain mad
Suddenly a golden light came over the ocean and grew large the radiance
        entered the sky
a deathly chill and heaviness entered my body I could scarce lift my eye
and the ship grew sheathed in light like an overexposed photograph fading
        in the brain.

New York, 1959

V
KADDISH
AND
RELATED POEMS
(1959–1960)

Kaddish

For Naomi Ginsberg, 1894–1956

I

Strange now to think of you, gone without corsets & eyes, while I walk on
the sunny pavement of Greenwich Village.
downtown Manhattan, clear winter noon, and I've been up all night, talking,
talking, reading the Kaddish aloud, listening to Ray Charles blues
shout blind on the phonograph
the rhythm the rhythm—and your memory in my head three years after—
And read Adonais' last triumphant stanzas aloud—wept, realizing
how we suffer—
And how Death is that remedy all singers dream of, sing, remember,
prophesy as in the Hebrew Anthem, or the Buddhist Book of An-
swers—and my own imagination of a withered leaf—at dawn—
Dreaming back thru life, Your time—and mine accelerating toward Apoca-
lypse,
the final moment—the flower burning in the Day—and what comes after,
looking back on the mind itself that saw an American city
a flash away, and the great dream of Me or China, or you and a phantom
Russia, or a crumpled bed that never existed—
like a poem in the dark—escaped back to Oblivion—
No more to say, and nothing to weep for but the Beings in the Dream,
trapped in its disappearance,
sighing, screaming with it, buying and selling pieces of phantom, worship-
ping each other,
worshipping the God included in it all—longing or inevitability?—while it
lasts, a Vision—anything more?
It leaps about me, as I go out and walk the street, look back over my shoulder,
Seventh Avenue, the battlements of window office buildings shoul-
dering each other high, under a cloud, tall as the sky an instant—and
the sky above—an old blue place.
or down the Avenue to the south, to—as I walk toward the Lower East Side
—where you walked 50 years ago, little girl—from Russia, eating the
first poisonous tomatoes of America—frightened on the dock—
then struggling in the crowds of Orchard Street toward what?—toward
Newark—
toward candy store, first home-made sodas of the century, hand-churned ice
cream in backroom on musty brownfloor boards—
Toward education marriage nervous breakdown, operation, teaching school,
and learning to be mad, in a dream—what is this life?

Toward the Key in the window—and the great Key lays its head of light
on top of Manhattan, and over the floor, and lays down on the
sidewalk—in a single vast beam, moving, as I walk down First toward
the Yiddish Theater—and the place of poverty
you knew, and I know, but without caring now—Strange to have moved
thru Paterson, and the West, and Europe and here again,
with the cries of Spaniards now in the doorstoops doors and dark boys on
the street, fire escapes old as you
—Tho you're not old now, that's left here with me—
Myself, anyhow, maybe as old as the universe—and I guess that dies with
us—enough to cancel all that comes—What came is gone forever
every time—
That's good! That leaves it open for no regret—no fear radiators, lacklove,
torture even toothache in the end—
Though while it comes it is a lion that eats the soul—and the lamb, the soul,
in us, alas, offering itself in sacrifice to change's fierce hunger—hair
and teeth—and the roar of bonepain, skull bare, break rib, rot-skin,
braintricked Implacability.
Ai! ai! we do worse! We are in a fix! And you're out, Death let you out,
Death had the Mercy, you're done with your century, done with
God, done with the path thru it—Done with yourself at last—Pure
—Back to the Babe dark before your Father, before us all—before the
world—
There, rest. No more suffering for you. I know where you've gone, it's good.
No more flowers in the summer fields of New York, no joy now, no more
fear of Louis,
and no more of his sweetness and glasses, his high school decades, debts,
loves, frightened telephone calls, conception beds, relatives, hands—
No more of sister Elanor,—she gone before you—we kept it secret—you
killed her—or she killed herself to bear with you—an arthritic heart
—But Death's killed you both—No matter—
Nor your memory of your mother, 1915 tears in silent movies weeks and
weeks—forgetting, agrieve watching Marie Dressler address human-
ity, Chaplin dance in youth,
or Boris Godunov, Chaliapin's at the Met, halling his voice of a weeping Czar
—by standing room with Elanor & Max—watching also the Capital-
ists take seats in Orchestra, white furs, diamonds,
with the YPSL's hitch-hiking thru Pennsylvania, in black baggy gym skirts
pants, photograph of 4 girls holding each other round the waste, and
laughing eye, too coy, virginal solitude of 1920
all girls grown old, or dead, now, and that long hair in the grave—lucky to
have husbands later—

You made it—I came too—Eugene my brother before (still grieving now and
    will gream on to his last stiff hand, as he goes thru his cancer—or kill
    —later perhaps—soon he will think—)
And it's the last moment I remember, which I see them all, thru myself, now
    —tho not you
I didn't foresee what you felt—what more hideous gape of bad mouth came
    first—to you—and were you prepared?
To go where? In that Dark—that—in that God? a radiance? A Lord in the
    Void? Like an eye in the black cloud in a dream? Adonoi at last, with
    you?
Beyond my remembrance! Incapable to guess! Not merely the yellow skull
    in the grave, or a box of worm dust, and a stained ribbon—Deaths-
    head with Halo? can you believe it?
Is it only the sun that shines once for the mind, only the flash of existence,
    than none ever was?
Nothing beyond what we have—what you had—that so pitiful—yet Tri-
    umph,
to have been here, and changed, like a tree, broken, or flower—fed to the
    ground—but mad, with its petals, colored, thinking Great Universe,
    shaken, cut in the head, leaf stript, hid in an egg crate hospital, cloth
    wrapped, sore—freaked in the moon brain, Naughtless.
No flower like that flower, which knew itself in the garden, and fought the
    knife—lost
Cut down by an idiot Snowman's icy—even in the Spring—strange ghost
    thought—some Death—Sharp icicle in his hand—crowned with old
    roses—a dog for his eyes—cock of a sweatshop—heart of electric
    irons.
All the accumulations of life, that wear us out—clocks, bodies, consciousness,
    shoes, breasts—begotten sons—your Communism—'Paranoia' into
    hospitals.
You once kicked Elanor in the leg, she died of heart failure later. You of
    stroke. Asleep? within a year, the two of you, sisters in death. Is
    Elanor happy?
Max grieves alive in an office on Lower Broadway, lone large mustache over
    midnight Accountings, not sure. His life passes—as he sees—and
    what does he doubt now? Still dream of making money, or that might
    have made money, hired nurse, had children, found even your Im-
    mortality, Naomi?
I'll see him soon. Now I've got to cut through—to talk to you—as I didn't
    when you had a mouth.
Forever. And we're bound for that, Forever—like Emily Dickinson's horses
    —headed to the End.

They know the way—These Steeds—run faster than we think—it's our own
life they cross—and take with them.

Magnificent, mourned no more, marred of heart, mind behind, mar-
ried dreamed, mortal changed—Ass and face done with murder.

In the world, given, flower maddened, made no Utopia, shut under
pine, almed in Earth, balmed in Lone, Jehovah, accept.

Nameless, One Faced, Forever beyond me, beginningless, endless,
Father in death. Tho I am not there for this Prophecy, I am unmarried, I'm
hymnless, I'm Heavenless, headless in blisshood I would still adore

Thee, Heaven, after Death, only One blessed in Nothingness, not
light or darkness, Dayless Eternity—

Take this, this Psalm, from me, burst from my hand in a day, some
of my Time, now given to Nothing—to praise Thee—But Death

This is the end, the redemption from Wilderness, way for the Won-
derer, House sought for All, black handkerchief washed clean by weeping
—page beyond Psalm—Last change of mine and Naomi—to God's perfect
Darkness—Death, stay thy phantoms!

II

Over and over—refrain—of the Hospitals—still haven't written your
history—leave it abstract—a few images

run thru the mind—like the saxophone chorus of houses and years—
remembrance of electrical shocks.

By long nites as a child in Paterson apartment, watching over your
nervousness—you were fat—your next move—

By that afternoon I stayed home from school to take care of you—
once and for all—when I vowed forever that once man disagreed with my
opinion of the cosmos, I was lost—

By my later burden—vow to illuminate mankind—this is release of
particulars—(mad as you)—(sanity a trick of agreement)—

But you stared out the window on the Broadway Church corner, and
spied a mystical assassin from Newark,

So phoned the Doctor—'OK go way for a rest'—so I put on my coat
and walked you downstreet—On the way a grammarschool boy screamed,
unaccountably—'Where you goin Lady to Death'? I shuddered—

and you covered your nose with motheaten fur collar, gas mask
against poison sneaked into downtown atmosphere, sprayed by Grandma—

And was the driver of the cheesebox Public Service bus a member of
the gang? You shuddered at his face, I could hardly get you on—to New
York, very Times Square, to grab another Greyhound—

where we hung around 2 hours fighting invisible bugs and jewish sickness—breeze poisoned by Roosevelt—

out to get you—and me tagging along, hoping it would end in a quiet room in a Victorian house by a lake.

Ride 3 hours thru tunnels past all American industry, Bayonne preparing for World War II, tanks, gas fields, soda factories, diners, locomotive roundhouse fortress—into piney woods New Jersey Indians—calm towns—long roads thru sandy tree fields—

Bridges by deerless creeks, old wampum loading the streambed—down there a tomahawk or Pocahontas bone—and a million old ladies voting for Roosevelt in brown small houses, roads off the Madness highway—

perhaps a hawk in a tree, or a hermit looking for an owl-filled branch—

All the time arguing—afraid of strangers in the forward double seat, snoring regardless—what busride they snore on now?

'Allen, you don't understand—it's—ever since those 3 big sticks up my back—they did something to me in Hospital, they poisoned me, they want to see me dead—3 big sticks, 3 big sticks—

'The Bitch! Old Grandma! Last week I saw her, dressed in pants like an old man, with a sack on her back, climbing up the brick side of the apartment

'On the fire escape, with poison germs, to throw on me—at night—maybe Louis is helping her—he's under her power—

'I'm your mother, take me to Lakewood' (near where Graf Zeppelin had crashed before, all Hitler in Explosion) 'where I can hide.'

We got there—Dr. Whatzis rest home—she hid behind a closet—demanded a blood transfusion.

We were kicked out—tramping with Valise to unknown shady lawn houses—dusk, pine trees after dark—long dead street filled with crickets and poison ivy—

I shut her up by now—big house REST HOME ROOMS—gave the landlady her money for the week—carried up the iron valise—sat on bed waiting to escape—

Neat room in attic with friendly bedcover—lace curtains—spinning wheel rug—Stained wallpaper old as Naomi. We were home.

I left on the next bus to New York—laid my head back in the last seat, depressed—the worst yet to come?—abandoning her, rode in torpor—I was only 12.

Would she hide in her room and come out cheerful for breakfast? Or lock her door and stare thru the window for sidestreet spies? Listen at keyholes for Hitlerian invisible gas? Dream in a chair—or mock me, by—in front of a mirror, alone?

12 riding the bus at nite thru New Jersey, have left Naomi to Parcae in Lakewood's haunted house—left to my own fate bus—sunk in a seat—all violins broken—my heart sore in my ribs—mind was empty—Would she were safe in her coffin—

Or back at Normal School in Newark, studying up on America in a black skirt—winter on the street without lunch—a penny a pickle—home at night to take care of Elanor in the bedroom—

First nervous breakdown was 1919—she stayed home from school and lay in a dark room for three weeks—something bad—never said what —every noise hurt—dreams of the creaks of Wall Street—

Before the gray Depression—went upstate New York—recovered—Lou took photo of her sitting crossleg on the grass—her long hair wound with flowers—smiling—playing lullabies on mandolin—poison ivy smoke in left-wing summer camps and me in infancy saw trees—

or back teaching school, laughing with idiots, the backward classes—her Russian specialty—morons with dreamy lips, great eyes, thin feet & sicky fingers, swaybacked, rachitic—

great heads pendulous over Alice in Wonderland, a blackboard full of C A T.

Naomi reading patiently, story out of a Communist fairy book—Tale of the Sudden Sweetness of the Dictator—Forgiveness of Warlocks—Armies Kissing—

Deathsheads Around the Green Table—The King & the Workers—Paterson Press printed them up in the '30s till she went mad, or they folded, both.

O Paterson! I got home late that nite. Louis was worried. How could I be so—didn't I think? I shouldn't have left her. Mad in Lakewood. Call the Doctor. Phone the home in the pines. Too late.

Went to bed exhausted, wanting to leave the world (probably that year newly in love with R——my high school mind hero, jewish boy who came a doctor later—then silent neat kid—

I later laying down life for him, moved to Manhattan—followed him to college—Prayed on ferry to help mankind if admitted—vowed, the day I journeyed to Entrance Exam—

by being honest revolutionary labor lawyer—would train for that—inspired by Sacco Vanzetti, Norman Thomas, Debs, Altgeld, Sandburg, Poe —Little Blue Books. I wanted to be President, or Senator.

ignorant woe—later dreams of kneeling by R's shocked knees declaring my love of 1941—What sweetness he'd have shown me, tho, that I'd wished him & despaired—first love—a crush—

Later a mortal avalanche, whole mountains of homosexuality, Matterhorns of cock, Grand Canyons of asshole—weight on my melancholy head—

meanwhile I walked on Broadway imagining Infinity like a rubber ball without space beyond—what's outside?—coming home to Graham Avenue still melancholy passing the lone green hedges across the street, dreaming after the movies—)

The telephone rang at 2 A.M.—Emergency—she'd gone mad—Naomi hiding under the bed screaming bugs of Mussolini—Help! Louis! Buba! Fascists! Death!—the landlady frightened—old fag attendant screaming back at her—

Terror, that woke the neighbors—old ladies on the second floor recovering from menopause—all those rags between thighs, clean sheets, sorry over lost babies—husbands ashen—children sneering at Yale, or putting oil in hair at CCNY—or trembling in Montclair State Teachers College like Eugene—

Her big leg crouched to her breast, hand outstretched Keep Away, wool dress on her thighs, fur coat dragged under the bed—she barricaded herself under bedspring with suitcases.

Louis in pajamas listening to phone, frightened—do now?—Who could know?—my fault, delivering her to solitude?—sitting in the dark room on the sofa, trembling, to figure out—

He took the morning train to Lakewood, Naomi still under bed—thought he brought poison Cops—Naomi screaming—Louis what happened to your heart then? Have you been killed by Naomi's ecstasy?

Dragged her out, around the corner, a cab, forced her in with valise, but the driver left them off at drugstore. Bus stop, two hours' wait.

I lay in bed nervous in the 4-room apartment, the big bed in living room, next to Louis' desk—shaking—he came home that nite, late, told me what happened.

Naomi at the prescription counter defending herself from the enemy —racks of children's books, douche bags, aspirins, pots, blood—'Don't come near me—murderers! Keep away! Promise not to kill me!'

Louis in horror at the soda fountain—with Lakewood girlscouts—Coke addicts—nurses—busmen hung on schedule—Police from country precinct, dumbed—and a priest dreaming of pigs on an ancient cliff?

Smelling the air—Louis pointing to emptiness?—Customers vomiting their Cokes—or staring—Louis humiliated—Naomi triumphant—The Announcement of the Plot. Bus arrives, the drivers won't have them on trip to New York.

Phonecalls to Dr. Whatzis, 'She needs a rest,' The mental hospital—State Greystone Doctors—'Bring her here, Mr. Ginsberg.'

Naomi, Naomi—sweating, bulge-eyed, fat, the dress unbuttoned at one side—hair over brow, her stocking hanging evilly on her legs—screaming for a blood transfusion—one righteous hand upraised—a shoe in it—barefoot in the Pharmacy—

The enemies approach—what poisons? Tape recorders? FBI? Zhda-nov hiding behind the counter? Trotsky mixing rat bacteria in the back of the store? Uncle Sam in Newark, plotting deathly perfumes in the Negro district? Uncle Ephraim, drunk with murder in the politician's bar, scheming of Hague? Aunt Rose passing water thru the needles of the Spanish Civil War?

till the hired $35 ambulance came from Red Bank——Grabbed her arms—strapped her on the stretcher—moaning, poisoned by imaginaries, vomiting chemicals thru Jersey, begging mercy from Essex County to Mor-ristown—

And back to Greystone where she lay three years—that was the last breakthrough, delivered her to Madhouse again—

On what wards—I walked there later, oft—old catatonic ladies, gray as cloud or ash or walls—sit crooning over floorspace—Chairs—and the wrinkled hags acreep, accusing—begging my 13-year-old mercy—

'Take me home'—I went alone sometimes looking for the lost Naomi, taking Shock—and I'd say, 'No, you're crazy Mama,—Trust the Drs.'—

And Eugene, my brother, her elder son, away studying Law in a furnished room in Newark—

came Paterson-ward next day—and he sat on the broken-down couch in the living room—'We had to send her back to Greystone'—

—his face perplexed, so young, then eyes with tears—then crept weeping all over his face—'What for?' wail vibrating in his cheekbones, eyes closed up, high voice—Eugene's face of pain.

Him faraway, escaped to an Elevator in the Newark Library, his bottle daily milk on windowsill of $5 week furn room downtown at trolley tracks—

He worked 8 hrs. a day for $20/wk—thru Law School years—stayed by himself innocent near negro whorehouses.

Unlaid, poor virgin—writing poems about Ideals and politics letters to the editor Pat Eve News—(we both wrote, denouncing Senator Borah and Isolationists—and felt mysterious toward Paterson City Hall—

I sneaked inside it once—local Moloch tower with phallus spire & cap o' ornament, strange gothic Poetry that stood on Market Street—replica Lyons' Hotel de Ville—

wings, balcony & scrollwork portals, gateway to the giant city clock, secret map room full of Hawthorne—dark Debs in the Board of Tax—Rembrandt smoking in the gloom—

Silent polished desks in the great committee room—Aldermen? Bd of Finance? Mosca the hairdresser aplot—Crapp the gangster issuing orders from the john—The madmen struggling over Zone, Fire, Cops & Backroom

Metaphysics—we're all dead—outside by the bus stop Eugene stared thru childhood—

where the Evangelist preached madly for 3 decades, hard-haired, cracked & true to his mean Bible—chalked Prepare to Meet Thy God on civic pave—

or God is Love on the railroad overpass concrete—he raved like I would rave, the lone Evangelist—Death on City Hall—)

But Gene, young,—been Montclair Teachers College 4 years—taught half year & quit to go ahead in life—afraid of Discipline Problems—dark sex Italian students, raw girls getting laid, no English, sonnets disregarded—and he did not know much—just that he lost—

so broke his life in two and paid for Law—read huge blue books and rode the ancient elevator 13 miles away in Newark & studied up hard for the future

just found the Scream of Naomi on his failure doorstep, for the final time, Naomi gone, us lonely—home—him sitting there—

Then have some chicken soup, Eugene. The Man of Evangel wails in front of City Hall. And this year Lou has poetic loves of suburb middle age—in secret—music from his 1937 book—Sincere—he longs for beauty—

No love since Naomi screamed—since 1923?—now lost in Greystone ward—new shock for her—Electricity, following the 40 Insulin.

And Metrazol had made her fat.

So that a few years later she came home again—we'd much advanced and planned—I waited for that day—my Mother again to cook &—play the piano—sing at mandolin—Lung Stew, & Stenka Razin, & the communist line on the war with Finland—and Louis in debt—suspected to be poisoned money—mysterious capitalisms

—& walked down the long front hall & looked at the furniture. She never remembered it all. Some amnesia. Examined the doilies—and the dining room set was sold—

the Mahogany table—20 years love—gone to the junk man—we still had the piano—and the book of Poe—and the Mandolin, tho needed some string, dusty—

She went to the backroom to lie down in bed and ruminate, or nap, hide—I went in with her, not leave her by herself—lay in bed next to her —shades pulled, dusky, late afternoon—Louis in front room at desk, waiting —perhaps boiling chicken for supper—

'Don't be afraid of me because I'm just coming back home from the mental hospital—I'm your mother—'

Poor love, lost—a fear—I lay there—Said, 'I love you Naomi,'—stiff, next to her arm. I would have cried, was this the comfortless lone union?—Nervous, and she got up soon.

Was she ever satisfied? And—by herself sat on the new couch by the front windows, uneasy—cheek leaning on her hand—narrowing eye—at what fate that day—

Picking her tooth with her nail, lips formed an O, suspicion—thought's old worn vagina—absent sideglance of eye—some evil debt written in the wall, unpaid—& the aged breasts of Newark come near—

May have heard radio gossip thru the wires in her head, controlled by 3 big sticks left in her back by gangsters in amnesia, thru the hospital—caused pain between her shoulders—

Into her head—Roosevelt should know her case, she told me—Afraid to kill her, now, that the government knew their names—traced back to Hitler—wanted to leave Louis' house forever.

One night, sudden attack—her noise in the bathroom—like croaking up her soul—convulsions and red vomit coming out of her mouth—diarrhea water exploding from her behind—on all fours in front of the toilet—urine running between her legs—left retching on the tile floor smeared with her black feces—unfainted—

At forty, varicosed, nude, fat, doomed, hiding outside the apartment door near the elevator calling Police, yelling for her girlfriend Rose to help—

Once locked herself in with razor or iodine—could hear her cough in tears at sink—Lou broke through glass green-painted door, we pulled her out to the bedroom.

Then quiet for months that winter—walks, alone, nearby on Broadway, read Daily Worker—Broke her arm, fell on icy street—

Began to scheme escape from cosmic financial murder plots—later she ran away to the Bronx to her sister Elanor. And there's another saga of late Naomi in New York.

Or thru Elanor or the Workmen's Circle, where she worked, addressing envelopes, she made out—went shopping for Campbell's tomato soup—saved money Louis mailed her—

Later she found a boyfriend, and he was a doctor—Dr. Isaac worked for National Maritime Union—now Italian bald and pudgy old doll—who was himself an orphan—but they kicked him out—Old cruelties—

Sloppier, sat around on bed or chair, in corset dreaming to herself—'I'm hot—I'm getting fat—I used to have such a beautiful figure before I went to the hospital—You should have seen me in Woodbine—' This in a furnished room around the NMU hall, 1943.

Looking at naked baby pictures in the magazine—baby powder advertisements, strained lamb carrots—'I will think nothing but beautiful thoughts.'

Revolving her head round and round on her neck at window light in summertime, in hypnotize, in doven-dream recall—

'I touch his cheek, I touch his cheek, he touches my lips with his hand, I think beautiful thoughts, the baby has a beautiful hand.'—

Or a No-shake of her body, disgust—some thought of Buchenwald —some insulin passes thru her head—a grimace nerve shudder at Involuntary (as shudder when I piss)—bad chemical in her cortex—'No don't think of that. He's a rat.'

Naomi: 'And when we die we become an onion, a cabbage, a carrot, or a squash, a vegetable.' I come downtown from Columbia and agree. She reads the Bible, thinks beautiful thoughts all day.

'Yesterday I saw God. What did he look like? Well, in the afternoon I climbed up a ladder—he has a cheap cabin in the country, like Monroe, N.Y. the chicken farms in the wood. He was a lonely old man with a white beard.

'I cooked supper for him. I made him a nice supper—lentil soup, vegetables, bread & butter—miltz—he sat down at the table and ate, he was sad.

'I told him, Look at all those fightings and killings down there, What's the matter? Why don't you put a stop to it?

'I try, he said—That's all he could do, he looked tired. He's a bachelor so long, and he likes lentil soup.'

Serving me meanwhile, a plate of cold fish—chopped raw cabbage dript with tapwater—smelly tomatoes—week-old health food—grated beets & carrots with leaky juice, warm—more and more disconsolate food—I can't eat it for nausea sometimes—the Charity of her hands stinking with Manhattan, madness, desire to please me, cold undercooked fish—pale red near the bones. Her smells—and oft naked in the room, so that I stare ahead, or turn a book ignoring her.

One time I thought she was trying to make me come lay her—flirting to herself at sink—lay back on huge bed that filled most of the room, dress up round her hips, big slash of hair, scars of operations, pancreas, belly wounds, abortions, appendix, stitching of incisions pulling down in the fat like hideous thick zippers—ragged long lips between her legs—What, even, smell of asshole? I was cold—later revolted a little, not much—seemed perhaps a good idea to try—know the Monster of the Beginning Womb— Perhaps—that way. Would she care? She needs a lover.

Yisborach, v'yistabach, v'yispoar, v'yisroman, v'yisnaseh, v'yishador, v'yishalleh, v'yishallol, sh'meh d'kudsho, b'rich hu.

And Louis reestablishing himself in Paterson grimy apartment in negro district—living in dark rooms—but found himself a girl he later married, falling in love again—tho sere & shy—hurt with 20 years Naomi's mad idealism.

Once I came home, after longtime in N.Y., he's lonely—sitting in the bedroom, he at desk chair turned round to face me—weeps, tears in red eyes under his glasses—

That we'd left him—Gene gone strangely into army—she out on her own in N.Y., almost childish in her furnished room. So Louis walked downtown to postoffice to get mail, taught in highschool—stayed at poetry desk, forlorn—ate grief at Bickford's all these years—are gone.

Eugene got out of the Army, came home changed and lone—cut off his nose in jewish operation—for years stopped girls on Broadway for cups of coffee to get laid—Went to NYU, serious there, to finish Law.—

And Gene lived with her, ate naked fishcakes, cheap, while she got crazier—He got thin, or felt helpless, Naomi striking 1920 poses at the moon, half-naked in the next bed.

bit his nails and studied—was the weird nurse-son—Next year he moved to a room near Columbia—though she wanted to live with her children—

'Listen to your mother's plea, I beg you'—Louis still sending her checks—I was in bughouse that year 8 months—my own visions unmentioned in this here Lament—

But then went half mad—Hitler in her room, she saw his mustache in the sink—afraid of Dr. Isaac now, suspecting that he was in on the Newark plot—went up to Bronx to live near Elanor's Rheumatic Heart—

And Uncle Max never got up before noon, tho Naomi at 6 A.M. was listening to the radio for spies—or searching the windowsill,

for in the empty lot downstairs, an old man creeps with his bag stuffing packages of garbage in his hanging black overcoat.

Max's sister Edie works—17 years bookkeeper at Gimbels—lived downstairs in apartment house, divorced—so Edie took in Naomi on Rochambeau Ave—

Woodlawn Cemetery across the street, vast dale of graves where Poe once—Last stop on Bronx subway—lots of communists in that area.

Who enrolled for painting classes at night in Bronx Adult High School—walked alone under Van Cortlandt Elevated line to class—paints Naomiisms—

Humans sitting on the grass in some Camp No-Worry summers yore —saints with droopy faces and long-ill-fitting pants, from hospital—

Brides in front of Lower East Side with short grooms—lost El trains running over the Babylonian apartment rooftops in the Bronx—

Sad paintings—but she expressed herself. Her mandolin gone, all strings broke in her head, she tried. Toward Beauty? or some old life Message?

But started kicking Elanor, and Elanor had heart trouble—came upstairs and asked her about Spydom for hours,—Elanor frazzled. Max away at office, accounting for cigar stores till at night.

'I am a great woman—am truly a beautiful soul—and because of that they (Hitler, Grandma, Hearst, the Capitalists, Franco, Daily News, the '20s, Mussolini, the living dead) want to shut me up—Buba's the head of a spider network—'

Kicking the girls, Edie & Elanor—Woke Edie at midnite to tell her she was a spy and Elanor a rat. Edie worked all day and couldn't take it— She was organizing the union.—And Elanor began dying, upstairs in bed.

The relatives call me up, she's getting worse—I was the only one left —Went on the subway with Eugene to see her, ate stale fish—

'My sister whispers in the radio—Louis must be in the apartment— his mother tells him what to say—LIARS!—I cooked for my two children —I played the mandolin—'

Last night the nightingale woke me / Last night when all was still / it sang in the golden moonlight / from on the wintry hill. She did.

I pushed her against the door and shouted 'DON'T KICK ELANOR!'—she stared at me—Contempt—die—disbelief her sons are so naive, so dumb—'Elanor is the worst spy! She's taking orders!'

'—No wires in the room!'—I'm yelling at her—last ditch, Eugene listening on the bed—what can he do to escape that fatal Mama—'You've been away from Louis years already—Grandma's too old to walk—'

We're all alive at once then—even me & Gene & Naomi in one mythological Cousinesque room—screaming at each other in the Forever— I in Columbia jacket, she half undressed.

I banging against her head which saw Radios, Sticks, Hitlers—the gamut of Hallucinations—for real—her own universe—no road that goes elsewhere—to my own—No America, not even a world—

That you go as all men, as Van Gogh, as mad Hannah, all the same —to the last doom—Thunder, Spirits, Lightning!

I've seen your grave! O strange Naomi! My own—cracked grave! Shema Y'Israel—I am Svul Avrum—you—in death?

Your last night in the darkness of the Bronx—I phonecalled—thru hospital to secret police

that came, when you and I were alone, shrieking at Elanor in my ear —who breathed hard in her own bed, got thin—

Nor will forget, the doorknock, at your fright of spies,—Law advancing, on my honor—Eternity entering the room—you running to the bathroom undressed, hiding in protest from the last heroic fate—

staring at my eyes, betrayed—the final cops of madness rescuing me
—from your foot against the broken heart of Elanor,

your voice at Edie weary of Gimbels coming home to broken radio
—and Louis needing a poor divorce, he wants to get married soon—Eugene
dreaming, hiding at 125 St., suing negroes for money on crud furniture,
defending black girls—

Protests from the bathroom—Said you were sane—dressing in a cot-
ton robe, your shoes, then new, your purse and newspaper clippings—no—
your honesty—

as you vainly made your lips more real with lipstick, looking in the
mirror to see if the Insanity was Me or a carful of police.

or Grandma spying at 78—Your vision—Her climbing over the walls
of the cemetery with political kidnapper's bag—or what you saw on the walls
of the Bronx, in pink nightgown at midnight, staring out the window on the
empty lot—

Ah Rochambeau Ave.—Playground of Phantoms—last apartment in
the Bronx for spies—last home for Elanor or Naomi, here these communist
sisters lost their revolution—

'All right—put on your coat Mrs.—let's go—We have the wagon
downstairs—you want to come with her to the station?'

The ride then—held Naomi's hand, and held her head to my breast,
I'm taller—kissed her and said I did it for the best—Elanor sick—and Max
with heart condition—Needs—

To me—'Why did you do this?'—'Yes Mrs., your son will have to
leave you in an hour'—The Ambulance

came in a few hours—drove off at 4 A.M. to some Bellevue in the night
downtown—gone to the hospital forever. I saw her led away—she waved,
tears in her eyes.

Two years, after a trip to Mexico—bleak in the flat plain near Brent-
wood, scrub brush and grass around the unused RR train track to the
crazyhouse—

new brick 20 story central building—lost on the vast lawns of mad-
town on Long Island—huge cities of the moon.

Asylum spreads out giant wings above the path to a minute black hole
—the door—entrance thru crotch—

I went in—smelt funny—the halls again—up elevator—to a glass
door on a Women's Ward—to Naomi—Two nurses buxom white—They
led her out, Naomi stared—and I gaspt—She'd had a stroke—

Too thin, shrunk on her bones—age come to Naomi—now broken
into white hair—loose dress on her skeleton—face sunk, old! withered—
cheek of crone—

One hand stiff—heaviness of forties & menopause reduced by one heart stroke, lame now—wrinkles—a scar on her head, the lobotomy—ruin, the hand dipping downwards to death—

O Russian faced, woman on the grass, your long black hair is crowned with flowers, the mandolin is on your knees—
Communist beauty, sit here married in the summer among daisies, promised happiness at hand—
holy mother, now you smile on your love, your world is born anew, children run naked in the field spotted with dandelions,
they eat in the plum tree grove at the end of the meadow and find a cabin where a white-haired negro teaches the mystery of his rainbarrel—
blessed daughter come to America, I long to hear your voice again, remembering your mother's music, in the Song of the Natural Front—
O glorious muse that bore me from the womb, gave suck first mystic life & taught me talk and music, from whose pained head I first took Vision—
Tortured and beaten in the skull—What mad hallucinations of the damned that drive me out of my own skull to seek Eternity till I find Peace for Thee, O Poetry—and for all humankind call on the Origin
Death which is the mother of the universe!—Now wear your naked-ness forever, white flowers in your hair, your marriage sealed behind the sky—no revolution might destroy that maidenhood—
O beautiful Garbo of my Karma—all photographs from 1920 in Camp Nicht-Gedeiget here unchanged—with all the teachers from Newark—Nor Elanor be gone, nor Max await his specter—nor Louis retire from this High School—

Back! You! Naomi! Skull on you! Gaunt immortality and revolution come—small broken woman—the ashen indoor eyes of hospitals, ward gray-ness on skin—
'Are you a spy?' I sat at the sour table, eyes filling with tears—'Who are you? Did Louis send you?—The wires—'
in her hair, as she beat on her head—'I'm not a bad girl—don't murder me!—I hear the ceiling—I raised two children—'
Two years since I'd been there—I started to cry—She stared—nurse broke up the meeting a moment—I went into the bathroom to hide, against the toilet white walls
'The Horror' I weeping—to see her again—'The Horror'—as if she were dead thru funeral rot in—'The Horror!'

I came back she yelled more—they led her away—'You're not Al-
len—' I watched her face—but she passed by me, not looking—

Opened the door to the ward,—she went thru without a glance back,
quiet suddenly—I stared out—she looked old—the verge of the grave—'All
the Horror!'

Another year, I left N.Y.—on West Coast in Berkeley cottage
dreamed of her soul—that, thru life, in what form it stood in that body, ashen
or manic, gone beyond joy—

near its death—with eyes—was my own love in its form, the Naomi,
my mother on earth still—sent her long letter—& wrote hymns to the mad
—Work of the merciful Lord of Poetry.

that causes the broken grass to be green, or the rock to break in grass
—or the Sun to be constant to earth—Sun of all sunflowers and days on
bright iron bridges—what shines on old hospitals—as on my yard—

Returning from San Francisco one night, Orlovsky in my room—
Whalen in his peaceful chair—a telegram from Gene, Naomi dead—

Outside I bent my head to the ground under the bushes near the
garage—knew she was better—

at last—not left to look on Earth alone—2 years of solitude—no one,
at age nearing 60—old woman of skulls—once long-tressed Naomi of
Bible—

or Ruth who wept in America—Rebecca aged in Newark—David
remembering his Harp, now lawyer at Yale—

or Svul Avrum—Israel Abraham—myself—to sing in the wilderness
toward God—O Elohim!—so to the end—2 days after her death I got her
letter—

Strange Prophecies anew! She wrote—'The key is in the window, the
key is in the sunlight at the window—I have the key—Get married Allen
don't take drugs—the key is in the bars, in the sunlight in the window.

                                        Love,
                                                your mother'

which is Naomi—

Hymmnn

In the world which He has created according to his will Blessed Praised
Magnified Lauded Exalted the Name of the Holy One Blessed is He!
In the house in Newark Blessed is He! In the madhouse Blessed is He! In
    the house of Death Blessed is He!
Blessed be He in homosexuality! Blessed be He in Paranoia! Blessed be He
    in the city! Blessed be He in the Book!
Blessed be He who dwells in the shadow! Blessed be He! Blessed be He!
Blessed be you Naomi in tears! Blessed be you Naomi in fears! Blessed
    Blessed Blessed in sickness!
Blessed be you Naomi in Hospitals! Blessed be you Naomi in solitude! Blest
    be your triumph! Blest be your bars! Blest be your last years' loneli-
    ness!
Blest be your failure! Blest be your stroke! Blest be the close of your eye!
    Blest be the gaunt of your cheek! Blest be your withered thighs!
Blessed be Thee Naomi in Death! Blessed be Death! Blessed be Death!
Blessed be He Who leads all sorrow to Heaven! Blessed be He in the end!
Blessed be He who builds Heaven in Darkness! Blessed Blessed Blessed be
    He! Blessed be He! Blessed be Death on us All!

III
Only to have not forgotten the beginning in which she drank cheap sodas
    in the morgues of Newark,
only to have seen her weeping on gray tables in long wards of her universe
only to have known the weird ideas of Hitler at the door, the wires in her
    head, the three big sticks
rammed down her back, the voices in the ceiling shrieking out her ugly early
    lays for 30 years,
only to have seen the time-jumps, memory lapse, the crash of wars, the roar
    and silence of a vast electric shock,
only to have seen her painting crude pictures of Elevateds running over the
    rooftops of the Bronx
her brothers dead in Riverside or Russia, her lone in Long Island writing a
    last letter—and her image in the sunlight at the window
'The key is in the sunlight at the window in the bars the key is in the
    sunlight,'
only to have come to that dark night on iron bed by stroke when the sun
    gone down on Long Island
and the vast Atlantic roars outside the great call of Being to its own

to come back out of the Nightmare—divided creation—with her head lain
    on a pillow of the hospital to die
—in one last glimpse—all Earth one everlasting Light in the familiar black-
    out—no tears for this vision—
But that the key should be left behind—at the window—the key in the
    sunlight—to the living—that can take
that slice of light in hand—and turn the door—and look back see
Creation glistening backwards to the same grave, size of universe,
size of the tick of the hospital's clock on the archway over the white
    door—

IV
O mother
what have I left out
O mother
what have I forgotten
O mother
farewell
with a long black shoe
farewell
with Communist Party and a broken stocking
farewell
with six dark hairs on the wen of your breast
farewell
with your old dress and a long black beard around the vagina
farewell
with your sagging belly
with your fear of Hitler
with your mouth of bad short stories
with your fingers of rotten mandolins
with your arms of fat Paterson porches
with your belly of strikes and smokestacks
with your chin of Trotsky and the Spanish War
with your voice singing for the decaying overbroken workers
with your nose of bad lay with your nose of the smell of the pickles of
    Newark
with your eyes
with your eyes of Russia
with your eyes of no money
with your eyes of false China
with your eyes of Aunt Elanor
with your eyes of starving India

with your eyes pissing in the park
with your eyes of America taking a fall
with your eyes of your failure at the piano
with your eyes of your relatives in California
with your eyes of Ma Rainey dying in an aumbulance
with your eyes of Czechoslovakia attacked by robots
with your eyes going to painting class at night in the Bronx
with your eyes of the killer Grandma you see on the horizon from the
        Fire-Escape
with your eyes running naked out of the apartment screaming into the hall
with your eyes being led away by policemen to an ambulance
with your eyes strapped down on the operating table
with your eyes with the pancreas removed
with your eyes of appendix operation
with your eyes of abortion
with your eyes of ovaries removed
with your eyes of shock
with your eyes of lobotomy
with your eyes of divorce
with your eyes of stroke
with your eyes alone
with your eyes
with your eyes
with your Death full of Flowers

V
Caw caw caw crows shriek in the white sun over grave stones in Long Island
Lord Lord Lord Naomi underneath this grass my halflife and my own as hers
caw caw my eye be buried in the same Ground where I stand in Angel
Lord Lord great Eye that stares on All and moves in a black cloud
caw caw strange cry of Beings flung up into sky over the waving trees
Lord Lord O Grinder of giant Beyonds my voice in a boundless field in
        Sheol
Caw caw the call of Time rent out of foot and wing an instant in the universe
Lord Lord an echo in the sky the wind through ragged leaves the roar of
        memory
caw caw all years my birth a dream caw caw New York the bus the broken
        shoe the vast highschool caw caw all Visions of the Lord
Lord Lord Lord caw caw caw Lord Lord Lord caw caw caw Lord

Paris, December 1957–New York, 1959

Mescaline

Rotting Ginsberg, I stared in the mirror naked today
I noticed the old skull, I'm getting balder
my pate gleams in the kitchen light under thin hair
like the skull of some monk in old catacombs lighted by
a guard with flashlight
followed by a mob of tourists
so there is death
my kitten mews, and looks into the closet
Boito sings on the phonograph tonight his ancient song of angels
Antinoüs bust in brown photograph still gazing down from my wall
a light burst from God's delicate hand sends down a wooden dove to the calm
        virgin
Beato Angelico's universe
the cat's gone mad and scraowls around the floor

What happens when the death gong hits rotting ginsberg on the head
what universe do I enter
death death death death death the cat's at rest
are we ever free of—rotting ginsberg
Then let it decay, thank God I know
thank who
thank who
Thank you, O lord, beyond my eye
the path must lead somewhere
the path
the path
thru the rotting shit dump, thru the Angelico orgies
Beep, emit a burst of babe and begone
perhaps that's the answer, wouldn't know till you had a kid
I dunno, never had a kid never will at the rate I'm going

Yes, I should be good, I should get married
find out what it's all about
but I can't stand these women all over me
smell of Naomi
erk, I'm stuck with this familiar rotting ginsberg
can't stand boys even anymore
can't stand
can't stand

and who wants to get fucked up the ass, really?
Immense seas passing over
the flow of time
and who wants to be famous and sign autographs like a movie star

I want to know
I *want I want* ridiculous *to know to know* WHAT rotting ginsberg
I want to know what happens after I rot
because I'm already rotting
my hair's falling out I've got a belly I'm sick of sex
my ass drags in the universe I know too much
and not enough
I want to know what happens after I die
well I'll find out soon enough
do I really need to know now?
is that any use at all use use use
death death death death death
god god god god god god god the Lone Ranger
the rhythm of the typewriter

What can I do to Heaven by pounding on Typewriter
I'm stuck change the record Gregory ah excellent he's doing just that
and I am too conscious of a million ears
at present creepy ears, making commerce
too many pictures in the newspapers
faded yellowed press clippings
I'm going away from the poem to be a drak contemplative

trash of the mind
trash of the world
man is half trash
all trash in the grave

What can Williams be thinking in Paterson, death so much on him
so soon so soon
Williams, what is death?
Do you face the great question now each moment
or do you forget at breakfast looking at your old ugly love in the face
are you prepared to be reborn
to give release to this world to enter a heaven
or give release, give release
and all be done—and see a lifetime—all eternity—gone over

into naught, a trick question proposed by the moon to the answerless earth
No Glory for man! No Glory for man! No glory for me! No me!

No point writing when the spirit doth not lead
New York, 1959

Lysergic Acid

It is a multiple million eyed monster
it is hidden in all its elephants and selves
it hummeth in the electric typewriter
it is electricity connected to itself, if it hath wires
it is a vast Spiderweb
and I am on the last millionth infinite tentacle of the spiderweb, a worrier
lost, separated, a worm, a thought, a self
one of the millions of skeletons of China
one of the particular mistakes
I allen Ginsberg a separate consciousness
I who want to be God
I who want to hear the infinite minutest vibration of eternal harmony
I who wait trembling my destruction by that aethereal music in the fire
I who hate God and give him a name
I who make mistakes on the eternal typewriter
I who am Doomed

But at the far end of the universe the million eyed Spyder that hath no name
spinneth of itself endlessly
the monster that is no monster approaches with apples, perfume, railroads,
        television, skulls
a universe that eats and drinks itself
blood from my skull
Tibetan creature with hairy breast and Zodiac on my stomach
this sacrificial victim unable to have a good time

My face in the mirror, thin hair, blood congested in streaks down beneath
        my eyes, cocksucker, a decay, a talking lust
a snaeap, a snarl, a tic of consciousness in infinity
a creep in the eyes of all Universes
trying to escape my Being, unable to pass on to the Eye
I vomit, I am in a trance, my body is seized in convulsion, my stomach
        crawls, water from my mouth, I am here in Inferno
dry bones of myriad lifeless mummies naked on the web, the Ghosts, I am
        a Ghost
I cry out where I am in the music, to the room, to whomever near, you, Are
        you God?
No, do you want me to be God?
Is there no Answer?

Must there always be an Answer? you reply,
and were it up to me to say Yes or No—
Thank God I am not God! Thank God I am not God!
But that I long for a Yes of Harmony to penetrate
to every corner of the universe, under every condition whatsoever
a Yes there Is . . . a Yes I Am . . . a Yes You Are . . . a We

A We
and that must be an It, and a They, and a Thing with No Answer
It creepeth, it waiteth, it is still, it is begun, it is the Horns of Battle it is
        Multiple Sclerosis
it is not my hope
it is not my death at Eternity
it is not my word, not poetry
beware my Word

It is a Ghost Trap, woven by priest in Sikkim or Tibet
a crossframe on which a thousand threads of differing color
are strung, a spiritual tennis racket
in which when I look I see aethereal lightwaves radiate
bright energy passing round on the threads as for billions of years
the thread-bands magically changing hues one transformed to another as if
        the
Ghost Trap
were an image of the Universe in miniature
conscious sentient part of the interrelated machine
making waves outward in Time to the Beholder
displaying its own image in miniature once for all
repeated minutely downward with endless variations throughout all of itself
it being all the same in every part

This image or energy which reproduces itself at the depths of space from the
        very Beginning
in what might be an O or an Aum
and trailing variations made of the same Word circles round itself in the same
        pattern as its original Appearance
creating a larger Image of itself throughout depths of Time
outward circling thru bands of faroff Nebulae & vast Astrologies
contained, to be true to itself, in a Mandala painted on an Elephant's hide,
or in a photograph of a painting on the side of an imaginary Elephant which
        smiles, tho how the Elephant looks is an irrelevant joke—
it might be a Sign held by a Flaming Demon, or Ogre of Transience,

or in a photograph of my own belly in the void
or in my eye
or in the eye of the monk who made the Sign
or in its own Eye that stares on Itself at last and dies

and tho an eye can die
and tho my eye can die
the billion-eyed monster, the Nameless, the Answerless, the Hidden-from-
     me, the endless Being
one creature that gives birth to itself
thrills in its minutest particular, sees out of all eyes differently at once
One and not One moves on its own ways
I cannot follow

And I have made an image of the monster here
and I will make another
it feels like Cryptozoids
it creeps and undulates beneath the sea
it is coming to take over the city
it invades beneath every Consciousness
it is delicate as the Universe
it makes me vomit
because I am afraid I will miss its appearance
it appears anyway
it appears anyway in the mirror
it washes out of the mirror like the sea
it is myriad undulations
it washes out of the mirror and drowns the beholder
it drowns the world when it drowns the world
it drowns in itself
it floats outward like a corpse filled with music
the noise of war in its head
a babe laugh in its belly
a scream of agony in the dark sea
a smile on the lips of a blind statue
it was there
it was not mine
I wanted to use it for myself
to be heroic
but it is not for sale to this consciousness
it goes its own way forever
it will complete all creatures

it will be the radio of the future
it will hear itself in time
it wants a rest
it is tired of hearing and seeing itself
it wants another form another victim
it wants me
it gives me good reason
it gives me reason to exist
it gives me endless answers
a consciousness to be separate and a consciousness to see
I am beckoned to be One or the other, to say I am both and be neither
it can take care of itself without me
it is Both Answerless (it answers not to that name)
it hummeth on the electric typewriter
it types a fragmentary word which is
a fragmentary word,

MANDALA

Gods dance on their own bodies
New flowers open forgetting Death
Celestial eyes beyond the heartbreak of illusion
I see the gay Creator
Bands rise up in anthem to the worlds
Flags and banners waving in transcendence
One image in the end remains myriad-eyed in Eternity
This is the Work! This is the Knowledge! This is the End of man!

Palo Alto, June 2, 1959

I Beg You Come Back & Be Cheerful

Tonite I got hi in the window of my apartment
        chair at 3 A.M.
gazing at Blue incandescent torches
        bright-lit street below
clotted shadows looming on a new laid pave
—as last week Medieval rabbiz
        plodded thru the brown raw
        dirt turned over—sticks
             & cans
  and tired ladies sitting on spanish
        garbage pails—in the deadly heat
           —one month ago
      the fire hydrants were awash—
the sun at 3 P.M. today in a haze—
now all dark outside, a cat crosses
        the street silently—I meow
and she looks up, and passes a
        pile of rubble on the way
to a golden shining garbage pail
        (phosphor in the night
           & alley stink)
      (or door-can mash)
—Thinking America is a chaos
Police clog the streets with their anxiety,
  Prowl cars creak & halt:

Today a woman, 20, slapped her brother
        playing with his infant bricks—
toying with a huge rock—
        'Don't do that now! the cops! the cops!'
And there was no cop there—
      I looked around shoulder—
a pile of crap in the opposite direction.

      Tear gas! Dynamite! Mustaches!

I'll grow a beard and carry lovely
    bombs,
I will destroy the world, slip in between
        the cracks of death
    And change the Universe—Ha!
I have the secret, I carry
      Subversive salami in
          my ragged briefcase
"Garlic, Poverty, a will to Heaven,"
    a strange dream in my meat:

Radiant clouds, I have heard God's voice in
      my sleep, or Blake's awake, or my own or
the dream of a delicatessen of snorting cows
    and bellowing pigs—
      The chop of a knife
      a finger severed in my brain—
        a few deaths I know—

      O brothers of the Laurel
Is the world real?
      Is the Laurel
a joke or a crown of thorns?—

      Fast, pass
      up the ass
      Down I go
      Cometh Woe

—the street outside,
    me spying on New York.
The dark truck passes snarling &
    vibrating deep—

What
    if
        the
            worlds
            were
            a
                series
                    of steps

                        What
                        if
                        the
                            steps
                        joined
                    back
                at
            the
Margin

Leaving us flying like birds into Time
            —eyes and car headlights—
            The shrinkage of emptiness
in the Nebulae

These Galaxies cross like pinwheels & they pass
            like gas—
What forests are born.

September 15, 1959

Psalm IV

Now I'll record my secret vision, impossible sight of the face of God:
It was no dream, I lay broad waking on a fabulous couch in Harlem
having masturbated for no love, and read half naked an open book of Blake
      on my lap
Lo & behold! I was thoughtless and turned a page and gazed on the living
      Sun-flower
and heard a voice, it was Blake's, reciting in earthen measure:
the voice rose out of the page to my secret ear never heard before—
I lifted my eyes to the window, red walls of buildings flashed outside, endless
      sky sad in Eternity
sunlight gazing on the world, apartments of Harlem standing in the uni-
      verse—
each brick and cornice stained with intelligence like a vast living face—
the great brain unfolding and brooding in wilderness!—Now speaking aloud
      with Blake's voice—
Love! thou patient presence & bone of the body! Father! thy careful watch-
      ing and waiting over my soul!
My son! My son! the endless ages have remembered me! My son! My son!
      Time howled in anguish in my ear!
My son! My son! my father wept and held me in his dead arms.

1960

To an Old Poet in Peru

Because we met at dusk
Under the shadow of the railroad station
           clock
While my shade was visiting Lima
And your ghost was dying in Lima
       old face needing a shave
And my young beard sprouted
          magnificent as the dead hair
              in the sands of Chancay
Because I mistakenly thought you were
             melancholy
Saluting your 60 year old feet
      which smell of the death
          of spiders on the pavement
And you saluted my eyes
         with your anisetto voice
Mistakenly thinking I was genial
          for a youth
(my rock and roll is the motion of an
          angel flying in a modern city)
(your obscure shuffle is the motion
         of a seraphim that has lost
            its wings)
I kiss you on your fat cheek (once more tomorrow
Under the stupendous Desamparados clock)
Before I go to my death in an airplane crash
         in North America (long ago)
And you go to your heart-attack on an indifferent
         street in South America
(Both surrounded by screaming
      communists with flowers
        in their ass)
—you much sooner than I—
      or a long night alone in a room
      in the old hotel of the world
         watching a black door
        . . . surrounded by scraps of paper

DIE GREATLY IN THY SOLITUDE

Old Man,
    I prophesy Reward

Vaster than the sands of Pachacamac
Brighter than a mask of hammered gold
Sweeter than the joy of armies naked
                fucking on the battlefield
Swifter than a time passed between
          old Nasca night and new Lima
                in the dusk
Stranger than our meeting by the Presidential
         Palace in an old café
ghosts of an old illusion, ghosts
          of indifferent love—

THE DAZZLING INTELLIGENCE

         Migrates from Death
To make a sign of Life again to you
Fierce and beautiful as a car crash
      in the Plaza de Armas

I swear that I have seen that Light
I will not fail to kiss your hideous cheek
      when your coffin's closed

And the human mourners go back
         to their old tired
            Dream.

And you wake in the Eye of the
      Dictator of the Universe.

Another stupid miracle! I'm
         mistaken again!
Your indifference! my enthusiasm!
        I insist! You cough!
Lost in the wave of Gold that
      flows thru the Cosmos.

Agh I'm tired of insisting! Goodbye,
        I'm going to Pucallpa
to have Visions.
                Your clean sonnets?
I want to read your dirtiest
        secret scribblings,
                your Hope,
in His most Obscene Magnificence. My God!

                                    May 19, 1960

Aether

11:15 P.M., May 27

4 Sniffs & I'm High,
Underwear in bed,
      white cotton in left hand,
  archetype degenerate,
      bloody taste in my mouth
         of Dentist Chair
    music, Loud Farts of Eternity—
an owl with eyeglasses scribbling in the
    cold darkness—
All the time the sound in my eardrums
         of trolleycars below
    taxi fender cough—creak of streets—
  Laughter & pistol shots echoing
         at all walls—
      tic leaks of neon—the voice of Myriad
         rushers of the Brainpan
  all the chirps the crickets have created
  ringing against my eares in the
         instant before unconsciousness
         before,—
    the teardrop in the eye to come,—
    the Fear of the Unknown—

One does not yet know whether Christ was
    God or the Devil—
  Buddha is more reassuring.

Yet the experiments must continue!
Every possible combination of Being—all
    the old ones! all the old Hindu
      Sabahadabadie-pluralic universes
        ringing in Grandiloquent
        Bearded Juxtaposition,
      with all their minarets and moonlit
      towers enlaced with iron
        or porcelain embroidery,
        all have existed—
        and the Sages with

white hair who sat crosslegged on
                    a female couch—
        hearkening to whatever music came
                from out the Wood or Street,
        whatever bird that whistled in the
                              Marketplace,
                whatever note the clock struck to say
                        Time—
        whatever drug, or aire, they breathed
                to make them think so deep
                        or simply hear what passed,
like a car passing in the 1960 street
        beside the Governmental Palace
                in Peru, this Lima
                year I write.
                                Kerouac! I salute yr
wordy beard. Sad Prophet!
        Salutations and low bows from
baggy pants and turbaned mind and hornèd foot
        arched eyebrows & Jewish Smile—
One single specimen of Eternity—each
                of us poets.

Breake the Rhythm! (too much pentameter)
        . . . My god what solitude are you in Kerouac
                now?
        —heard the whoosh of carwheels in the 1950 rain—

And every bell went off on time,
And everything that was created
Rang especially in view of the Creation
For
This is the end of the creation
This is the redemption Spoken of
This is the view of the Created
        by all the Drs, nurses, etc. of
                        creation;
i.e.,—

I JUST NODDED BECAUSE OF THE SECONDARY <u>NEGATION</u>

The unspeakable passed over my head for
        the second time.
                        and still can't say it!

i.e. we are the sweepings of the moon
we're what's *left over* from perfection—
The universe is an OLD mistake
I've understood a million times before
and always come back to the same
                scissor brainwave—
The
Sooner or later all Consciousness will
        be eliminated
                because Consciousness is
        a by-product of—
                (Cotton & N$_2$O)

        Drawing saliva back from the tongue—

Christ! you struggle to understand
                One consciousness
        & be confronted with Myriads—
after a billion years
        with the same ringing in the ears
                and pterodactyl-smile of Oops
                        Creation,
        known it all before.
        A Buddha as of old, with sirens of
whatever machinery making cranging noises in
                        the street
        and pavement light reflected in the facade
                RR Station window in a
                        dinky port in Backwash
        of the murky old forgotten
                fabulous whatever
                        Civilization of
                                Eternity,—
        with the RR Sta Clock ring midnight,
        as of now,
                        & waiting for the 6th
                        you write your
                                Word,
        and end on the last chime—and remember

This *one* twelve was struck
                before,
          and *never again;* both.

. . . . I stood on the balcony
          waiting for an explosion
   of Total Consciousness of the All—
                being Ginsberg sniffing ether in Lima.
          The same struggle of Mind, to reach the
                Thing
          that ends its process with an X
                     comprehending its befores and afters,
          unexplainable to each, except in a prophetic
                     secret recollective hidden
                          half-hand unrecorded way.
As the old sages of Asia, or the white beards of Persia
          scribbled on the margins of their scrolls
          in delicate ink
   remembering with tears the ancient clockbells of their cities
          and the cities that had been—
          Nasca, Paracas, Chancay & Secrecy of the Priests
                buried, Cat Gods
          of all colors, a funeral shroud
                     for a museum—
None remember but all return to the same thought
                before they die—what sad old
          knowledge, we repeat again.
                     Only to be lost
   in the sands of Paracas, or wrapped in a mystic shroud
          of Poesy
   and found by some kid in a thousand years
          inspire what dreadful thoughts of his own?

It's a horrible, lonely experience. And
          Gregory's letter, and Peter's . . .

                                    7:30 P.M., May 28

. . . In the foul dregs of Circumstance
          'Male and Female He created them'
          with mustaches.
          There ARE certain REPEATED
          (pistol shot) reliable points

of reference which the insane
(pistol shot repeated outside
the window)—madman suddenly
writes—THE PISTOL SHOT
outside—the REPEATED situations
the experience of return to the
same place in Universal Creation
Time—and every time we return
we recognize again that we
HAVE been here & that is the
Key to Creation—the same pistol shot
—DOWN, bending over his book of Un
intelligible marvels with his mustache.

(my) Madness is intelligible reactions to
      Unintelligible phenomena.
           Boy—what a marvelous bottle,
      a clear glass sphere of transparent
                    liquid ether—
      (Chloraethyl Merz)

9 P.M.

    I know I am a poet—in this universe—but what good does that do
—when in another, without these mechanical aids, I might be doomed to be
a poor Disneyan Shoe Store Clerk—This consciousness an *accident* of one
of the Ether-possible worlds, not the Final World

      Wherein we all look Crosseyed
      & triumph in our Virginity
      without wearing Rabbit's-foot
          ears or eyes looking sideways
          strangely but in Gold

      Humbled & more knowledgeable, acknowledge
      the Vast mystery of our creation—
      without giving any sign that
        we have heard from the

            GREAT CREATOR

            WHOSE NAME I NOW

PRONOUNCE:

GREAT CREATOR OF THE UNIVERS, IF

THY WISDOM ACCORD IT

AND IF THIS NOT BE TOO

MUCH TO ASK

MAY I PUBLISH YOUR NAME?

I ASK IN THE LIMA

NIGHT

FEARFULLY WAITING

ANSWER,

    hearing the buses out on
    the street hissing,
    Knowing the Terror
        of the World Afar—

I have been playing with Jokes
and His is too mighty to hold
    in the hand like a Pen
and His is the Pistol Shot Answer
    that brings blood to the brain
And—

    What *can* be possible
    in a minor universe
    in which you can see
    God by sniffing the
    gas in a cotton?
The answer to be taken in
    reverse & Doubled Math
    ematically *both* ways.

Am I a sinner?
There are hard & easy universes. This
            is neither.

(If I close my eyes will I regain consciousness?)
      That's the Final Question—with
all the old churchbells ringing and
bus pickup snuffles & crack of iron
whips inside cylinders & squeal of brakes
and old crescendos of responsive
demiurgic ecstasy whispering in streets of ear
      —and when was it Not
      ever answered in the Affir-
      mative? Saith the Lord?

A MAGIC UNIVERSE

Flies & crickets & the sound of buses & my
      stupid beard.
But what's Magic?
Is there Sorrow in Magic?
Is Magic one of my boyscout creations?
Am I responsible? I with my flop?
Could Threat happen to Magic?
Yes! this the one universe in which
      there *is* threat to magic, by
      writing while high.

A Universe in which I am condemned to write statements.

'Ignorant Judgments Create Mistaken Worlds—'
      and this one is joined in
            Indic union to
      Affirm with laughing
                  eyes—
The world is as we see it,
      Male & Female, passing thru the years,
      as has before & will, perhaps
with all its countless pearls & Bloody noses
      and I poor stupid All in G
      am stuck with that old Choice—

Ya, Crap, what Hymn to seek, & in
                     what tongue, if this's the most
                     I can requite from Consciousness?—
That I can skim? & put in words?
                     Could skim it faster with more juice—
           could skim a crop with Death, perchance
                     —yet never know in this old world.
Will know in Death?
                     And before?

                                        Will in

Another know.
                     And in another know.
                                        And

in another know.
                     And

                              Stop conceiving worlds!
                     says Philip Whalen
(My Savior!)   (oh what snobbery!)
           (as if he cd save Anyone)—
     At *least,* he won't understand.
I lift my finger in the air to create
a universe he won't understand, full
           of sadness.

—finally staring straight ahead in surprise
           & recollection into the mirror of
                     the Hotel Comercio room.
           Time repeats itself. Including
this consciousness, which has seen
itself before—thus the locust-whistle
of antiquity's nightwatch in my eardrum . . .

I propounded a final question, and
           heard a series of final answers.
What is God? for instance, asks the answer?
     And whatever else can the replier reply but reply?
Whatever the nature of mind, that
           the nature of *both* question and answer.

                     & yet one wants to live
                     in a *single* universe
                              Does one?

Must it be one?
        Why, as with the Jews
        must the God be One?
        O what does
        the concept ONE mean?
            IT'S MAD!

    GOD IS ONE!

        IS X

    IS MEANINGLESS—

        ADONOI—

    IS A JOKE—

        THE HEBREWS ARE

    WRONG—(CRIST & BUDDA

    ATTEST, also wrongly!)

    What is One but Formation
                of mind?
            arbitrary madness! 6000 years
Spreading out in all directions simultaneously—

        I forgive both good & ill
& I seek nothing, like a painted savage with
spear crossed by orange black & white bands!
    'I found the Jivaros & was
    entrapped in their universe'
                    I'm scribbling nothings.
    Page upon page of profoundest nothing,
    as scribed the Ancient Hebe, when
            he wrote Adonoi Echad or One—
    all to amuse, make money, or deceive—
Let Wickedness be Me
    and this the worst of all
            the universes!
                    Not the worst! Not Flame!

I can't stand that—(Yes that's
      for Somebody Else!
                              Yet I accept
O Catfaced God, whatever comes! It's me!
I am the Flame, etc.
            O Gawd!
                        Pistol shot! Crack!
                                    Circusmaster's whip—
      IMPERFECT!
                        and a soul is damned to
      HELL!
                  And the churchbell rings!
and there is melancholy, once again, throughout the realm.
            and I'm that soul, small as it is.)

            HAVE FELT SAME BEFORE

The death of consciousness is terrible
      and yet! when all is ended
                  what regret?
'S none left to remember or forget.
            And's gone into the odd.
            The only thing I fear is the Last
Chance. I'll see that last chance too
before I'm done, Old Mind. All them
old Last Chances that you knew before.
                  —someday thru the dream wall
      to nextdoor consciousness
            like thru this blue hotel wall
                  —millions of hotel rooms fogging
                        the focus of my eyes—

with whatever attitude I hold the cotton
to my nose, it's still a secret joke
      with pinkie akimbo, or with effete queer
            eye in mirror at myself,
            or serious-brow mien
                        & darkened beard,
      I'm still the kid of obscene chance await-
            ing—

breathing in a chinese Universe
thru the nose like some old Brahmanic God.

O   BELL   TIME   RING   THY
MIDNIGHT FOR THE BILLIONTH
SOUNDY TIME, I HEAR AGAIN!

I'll go to walk the street,
                                    Who'll find
me in the night, in Lima, in my
33'd year,

On Street (Cont.)

The souls of Peter &
I answer each other.
But—and what's a soul?
To be a poet's a
serious occupation,
condemned to that
in universe—
to walk the city
ascribbling in
a book—just accosted
by a drunk—
in Plaza de Armas
sidestreet under
a foggy sky, and
sometimes with no
moon.
        The heavy balcony
hangs over the white
marble of the Bishop's
Palace next the Cathedral—
The fountain plays
in light as e'er—
The buses & the
motorcyclists pass
thru midnight, the
carlights shine
the beggar turns
a corner with his

cigarette stub &
cane, the Noisers
leave the tavern
and delay, conversing
in high voice,
Awake,
        Hasta Mañana
they all say—
        and somewhere
at the other end of
the line, a telephone
is ringing, once again
with unknown news—
        The night
looms over Lima,
sky black fog—
and I sit helpless
smoking with a
pencil hand—
        The long crack
in the pavement
        or yesterday's
volcano in Chile,
or the day before
the Earthquake
that begat the
World.

        The Plaza pavement
shines in the electric

light. I wait.
    The lonely beard
workman staggers
home to bed from
Death.
    Yes but I'm
a little tired of
being alone . . .
    Keats' Nightingale—the
instant of realization
a single consciousness
that hears the chimes
of Time, repeated
endlessly—

All night, w/ Ether, wave
after wave of magic
understanding. A dis-
turbance of the field
of consciousness.
Magic night, magic stars,

magic men, magic moon
magic tomorrow, magic death,
magic Magic.
    What crude Magic
we live in (seeing trolley
like a rude monster
in downtown street
w/ electric diamond
wire antennae to sky
pass night café under
white arc-light by
Gran Hotel Bolívar.)

The mad potter of
Mochica made a
pot w/ 6 Eyes & 2
Mouths & half a Nose
& 5 Cheeks & no Chin
for us to figure out,
serious side-track,
blind alley Kosmos.

Back in Room (Cont.)

How strange to remember anything, even a button
                    much less a universe.
'What creature gives birth to itself?'
The universe is mad, slightly mad.
        —and the two sides wriggle away
        in opposite directions to die
                        lopped off
        the blind metallic length curled up
        feebly & wiggling its feet
                    in the grass
    the millipede's black head moving inches away
            on the staircase at Macchu Picchu
            the Creature feels itself
                        destroyed,
            head & tail of the universe
                    cut in two.

Men with slick mustaches of mystery have
        pimp horrible climaxes & Karmas—
—the mad magician that created Chaos
        in the peaceful void & suave.
    with my fucking suave manners & knowitall
        eyes, and mind full of fantasy—
    the Me! that horror that keeps me conscious
        in this Hell of Birth & Death.

    34 coming up—I suddenly felt old—sitting with Walter & Raquel
in Chinese Restaurant—they kissed—I alone—age of Burroughs when we
first met.

Hotel Comercio, Lima, Peru, May 28, 1960

Magic Psalm

Because this world is on the wing and what cometh no man can know

O Phantom that my mind pursues from year to year descend from heaven
to this shaking flesh

catch up my fleeting eye in the vast Ray that knows no bounds—Inseparable
—Master—

Giant outside Time with all its falling leaves—Genius of the Universe—
Magician in Nothingness where appear red clouds—

Unspeakable King of the roads that are gone—Unintelligible Horse riding
out of the graveyard—Sunset spread over Cordillera and insect—
Gnarl Moth—

Griever—Laugh with no mouth, Heart that never had flesh to die—Promise
that was not made—Reliever, whose blood burns in a million animals
wounded—

O Mercy, Destroyer of the World, O Mercy, Creator of Breasted Illusions,
O Mercy, cacophonous warmouthed doveling, Come,

invade my body with the sex of God, choke up my nostrils with corruption's
infinite caress,

transfigure me to slimy worms of pure sensate transcendency I'm still alive,

croak my voice with uglier than reality, a psychic tomato speaking Thy
million mouths,

Myriad-tongued my Soul, Monster or Angel, Lover that comes to fuck me
forever—white gown on the Eyeless Squid—

Asshole of the Universe into which I disappear—Elastic Hand that spoke to
Crane—Music that passes into the phonograph of years from another
Millennium—Ear of the buildings of NY—

That which I believe—have seen—seek endlessly in leaf dog eye—fault
always, lack—which makes me think—

Desire that created me, Desire I hide in my body, Desire all Man know
Death, Desire surpassing the Babylonian possible world

that makes my flesh shake orgasm of Thy Name which I don't know never
will never speak—

Speak to Mankind to say the great bell tolls a golden tone on iron balconies
in every million universe,

I am Thy prophet come home this world to scream an unbearable Name thru
my 5 senses hideous sixth

that knows Thy Hand on its invisible phallus, covered with electric bulbs
of death—

Peace, Resolver where I mess up illusion, Softmouth Vagina that enters my
brain from above, Ark-Dove with a bough of Death.

Drive me crazy, God I'm ready for disintegration of my mind, disgrace me
    in the eye of the earth,
attack my hairy heart with terror eat my cock Invisible croak of deathfrog
    leap on me pack of heavy dogs salivating light,
devour my brain One flow of endless consciousness, I'm scared of your
    promise must make scream my prayer in fear—
Descend O Light Creator & Eater of Mankind, disrupt the world in its
    madness of bombs and murder,
Volcanos of flesh over London, on Paris a rain of eyes—truckloads of angel-
    hearts besmearing Kremlin walls—the skullcup of light to New
    York—
myriad jeweled feet on the terraces of Pekin—veils of electrical gas descend-
    ing over India—cities of Bacteria invading the brain—the Soul escap-
    ing into the rubber waving mouths of Paradise—
This is the Great Call, this is the Tocsin of the Eternal War, this is the cry
    of Mind slain in Nebulae,
this is the Golden Bell of the Church that has never existed, this is the Boom
    in the heart of the sunbeam, this is the trumpet of the Worm at Death,
Appeal of the handless castrate grab Alm golden seed of Futurity thru the
    quake & volcan of the world—
Shovel my feet under the Andes, splatter my brains on the Sphinx, drape my
    beard and hair over Empire State Building,
cover my belly with hands of moss, fill up my ears with your lightning, blind
    me with prophetic rainbows
That I taste the shit of Being at last, that I touch Thy genitals in the palmtree,
that the vast Ray of Futurity enter my mouth to sound Thy Creation Forever
    Unborn, O Beauty invisible to my Century!
that my prayer surpass my understanding, that I lay my vanity at Thy foot,
    that I no longer fear Judgment over Allen of this world
born in Newark come into Eternity in New York crying again in Peru for
    human Tongue to psalm the Unspeakable,
that I surpass desire for transcendency and enter the calm water of the
    universe
that I ride out this wave, not drown forever in the flood of my imagination
that I not be slain thru my own insane magic, this crime be punished in
    merciful jails of Death,
men understand my speech out of their own Turkish heart, the prophets aid
    me with Proclamation,
the Seraphim acclaim Thy Name, Thyself at once in one huge Mouth of
    Universe make meat reply.

June 1960

The Reply

God answers with my doom! I am annulled
                    this poetry blanked from the fiery ledger
        my lies be answered by the worm at my ear
    my visions by the hand falling over my eyes to cover them
                    from sight of my skeleton
    my longing to be God by the trembling bearded jaw flesh
                    that covers my skull like monster-skin
        Stomach vomiting out the soul-vine, cadaver on
            the floor of a bamboo hut, body-meat crawling toward
                its fate nightmare rising in my brain
The noise of the drone of creation adoring its Slayer, the yowp
                    of birds to the Infinite, dogbarks like the sound
    of vomit in the air, frogs croaking Death at trees
I am a Seraph and I know not whither I go into the Void
I am a man and I know not whither I go into Death—
                                Christ Christ poor hopeless
            lifted on the Cross between Dimension—
                to see the Ever-Unknowable!
a dead gong shivers thru all flesh and a vast Being enters my
            brain from afar that lives forever
    None but the Presence too mighty to record! the Presence
        in Death, before whom I am helpless
                    makes me change from Allen to a skull
Old One-Eye of dreams in which I do not wake but die—
            hands pulled into the darkness by a frightful Hand
                —the worm's blind wriggle, cut—the plough
                    is God himself
What ball of monster darkness from before the universe come
        back to visit me with blind command!
            and I can blank out this consciousness, escape back
                    to New York love, and will
            Poor pitiable Christ afraid of the foretold Cross,
                Never to die—
    Escape, but not forever—the Presence will come, the hour
            will come, a strange truth enter the universe, death
                    show its Being as before
        and I'll despair that *I forgot! forgot!* my fate return,
                    tho die of it—

What's sacred when the Thing is all the universe?
       creeps to every soul like a vampire-organ singing behind
                    moonlit clouds—poor being come squat
under bearded stars in a dark field in Peru
              to drop my load—I'll die in horror that I die!
Not dams or pyramids but death, and we to prepare for that
        nakedness, poor bones sucked dry by His long mouth
           of ants and wind, & our souls murdered to prepare His Perfection!
The moment's come, He's made His will revealed forever
        and no flight into old Being further than the stars will not
           find terminal in the same dark swaying port of unbearable music
No refuge in Myself, which is on fire
        or in the World which is His also to bomb & Devour!
              Recognize His might! Loose hold
        of my hands—my frightened skull
                   —for I had chose self-love—
my eyes, my nose, my face, my cock, my soul—and now
           the faceless Destroyer!
        A billion doors to the same new Being!
        The universe turns inside out to devour me!
and the mighty burst of music comes from out the inhuman door—
                                                   June 1960

The End

I am I, old Father Fisheye that begat the ocean, the worm at my own ear,
the serpent turning around a tree,
I sit in the mind of the oak and hide in the rose, I know if any wake up, none
but my death,
come to me bodies, come to me prophecies, come all foreboding, come spirits
and visions,
I receive all, I'll die of cancer, I enter the coffin forever, I close my eye, I
disappear,
I fall on myself in winter snow, I roll in a great wheel through rain, I watch
fuckers in convulsion,
car screech, furies groaning their basso music, memory fading in the brain,
men imitating dogs,
I delight in a woman's belly, youth stretching his breasts and thighs to sex,
the cock sprung inward
gassing its seed on the lips of Yin, the beasts dance in Siam, they sing opera
in Moscow,
my boys yearn at dusk on stoops, I enter New York, I play my jazz on a
Chicago Harpsichord,
Love that bore me I bear back to my Origin with no loss, I float over the
vomiter
thrilled with my deathlessness, thrilled with this endlessness I dice and bury,
come Poet shut up eat my word, and taste my mouth in your ear.

New York, 1960

Man's glory

Shines on top of Mountains where Grey Stone monastery sits & blinks at
    the sky
There in Tangier in Soco Chico there God's Grammar Arabic jabbers shoe-
    shine Poverty beneath the ultra silent mosque
There in Venice glittering in Canal Grande in Front of San Giorgio Mag-
    giore Gondola'd to cream the fabulous tourist—
There in Mexico in th' Archaeologic Museum where Coatlique Aztec Gol-
    gotha-head Goddess clasps her snakes & skulls & grins—
There over Asia where the desolate white Stupas blast into the Buddhic
    Dome and the Mandala of the stars shines down—
All over Europe where the masses weep & faint in Wooden Trains—
By Florence, by the Windmills, all the churches singing together
"We in the mountains and downtown Pray that America return to the
    Lamb"—
And the Great Boom of the Cathedral at Seville, Granada groaning,
Barcelona chanting out the Crannies of Sagrada Familia
Long horns of Montpellier, Milan screaming and San Marco rocking in
    Venice like a great golden calliope
"America, America, under the elms in parks of Illinois, the Anger, the
    Anger, Beware!"

August 1960

Fragment: The Names II

Bill Burroughs in Tangiers slowly transfiguring into Sanctity season after
season no God save impersonal solitude
Mad Sheila shaking her head on a couch in Frisco, soft tear face half a year,
60 sleeping pills & blue asphyxiation—
Connie much too drunk, slapped in my apartment by plainclothesmen &
strangled in an alley by a lonesome hood
Natalie redhaired in bathrobe on the roof listing sinners' names for Govern-
ment, police scared her to fire escape, her body on the pavement in
the newspapers—
Elise trembling by the phonograph with Bible in her hand, The Book of the
Dead in her family wall reading her thoughts aloud, and her poor
unmarried body broken on that ground Manhattan Heights
Bremser running state to state, trapped Hoboken, Vera Cruz rat tat tat
Poetry defense, frameup reformatory he thinks the cops are real
One Harry Honig carried a laughing gas mask & bomb ten years back in NY
the Kosmos exploded for
John Hoffman too ecstasy of the black sun, Mexican peyote or infantile
paralysis
Iris suicide, delicate ships of paint fading into brown ocean universe—her
longheaded junk-delicate girl's penmanship of Orient small cats on
folded knees
New York & West coast grim as the A bomb deathwatch is set
Nobody knows the way out of Time trap maybe Burroughs maybe Jack in
Florida drinking with Joe McCarthy's ghost, grieving death of mother who
isn't dead, scribing notebooks won't be read till cold war's lost by all

1960/1961?

VI

PLANET NEWS: TO EUROPE AND ASIA

(1961–1963)

Who Will Take Over the Universe?

A bitter cold winter night
conspirators at café tables
      discussing mystic jails
The Revolution in America
   already begun not bombs but sit
      down strikes on top submarines
  on sidewalks nearby City Hall—
How many families control the States?
   Ignore the Government,
      send your protest to Clint Murchison.
The Indians won their case with Judge McFate
      Peyote safe in Arizona—
  In my room the sick junky
        shivers on the 7th day
    Tearful, reborn to the Winter.
Che Guevara has a big cock
       Castro's balls are pink—
The Ghost of John F. Dulles hangs
     over America like dirty linen
  draped over the wintry red sunset,
  Fumes of Unconscious Gas
      emanate from his corpse
    & hypnotize the Egyptian intellectuals—
He grinds his teeth in horror & crosses his
     thigh bones over his skull
  Dust flows out of his asshole
  his hands are full of bacteria
     The worm is at his eye—
He's declaring counterrevolutions in the Worm-world,
  my cat threw him up last
      Thursday.
& Forrestal flew out his window like an Eagle—
America's spending money to overthrow the Man.
    Who are the rulers of the earth?

      New York, January 6, 1961

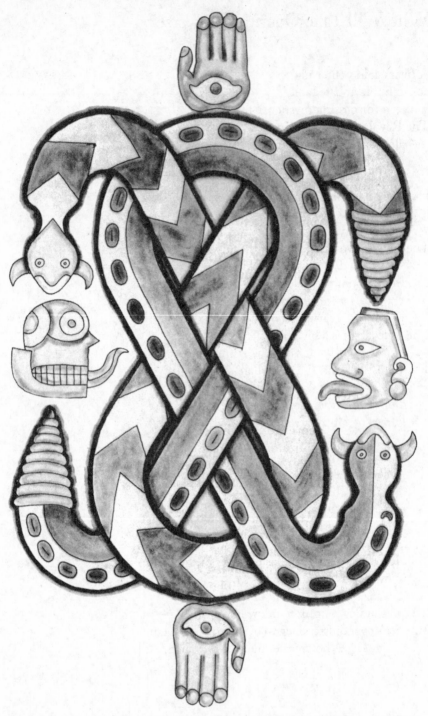

"Southern Cult Composite: The Staten Island Massacre" by Harry Smith, 1984.

Journal Night Thoughts

NY January 1961   *Sept. 28, 1964*

In bed on my green purple pink   *Lower East Side*
    yellow orange bolivian blanket,   *2 Street*
the clock tick, my back against the wall   *High*
—staring into black circled eyes magician   ★
    man's bearded glance & story   *W/Harry Smith*
the kitchen spun in a wheel of vertigo,
the eye in the center of the moving
        mandala—the   ★
        eye in the hand
        the eye in the asshole
        serpent eating or   *Optical*
          vomiting its tail   *Phenomena*
—the blank air a solid wall revolving
    around my retina—   ★
The wheel of jewels and fire I saw moving   *Yage*
      vaster than my head in Peru   *in*
    Band circling in band and a black   *Pucallpa*
      hole of Calcutta thru which
        I stared at my Atman   ★
        without a body—
The Giotto window on Boston giving   *Remembering*
      to a scene in Bibled Palestine   *Leary's Bedroom*
        A golden star   *Harvard*
    and the flight to Egypt
        in an instant now   ★
Come true again—the Kabbala sign   *Jack*
    in the vomit on the floor—   *Hallucinating*
From a window on Riverside Drive,
    one boat moving slowly
up the flowing river, small autos
crawling on Hudson Thruway   ★
    a plash of white snow on
      the Palisades
and a small white park etched   *Out Robt.*
    by bare thin branches   *Lowell's Window*
with black birds aflutter in the
    frosty underbrush

Riverside Drive, as in Breughel
   a girl in red coat
     —a footprint, a lone
      passerby   ★
on sidewalk under apartment wall—
and a blimp from the war floating in air
   over the edge of the city—
Wagner's last echoes, and Baudelaire   *Unsteadily*
   inscribing his oceanic page   *Walking*
      of confessions   *in*
Ah love is so sweet in the Springtime   *Manhattan*
     Omnia amor vincit   *Near Where*
Eliot's voice clanging over the sky   *Poe*
   on upper Broadway   *Wrote*
"Only thru Time is Time conquered"   *The*
I am the answer: I will swallow my   *Raven*
   vomit and be naked—
A heavy rain, the plick of a raindrop   ★
     shattered on the fire escape rail
      at the level of my eye—
This woman is a serpent goddess accepting   *Visiting*
   the propitiation of a bunch of flowers *Dorothy Norman*
   found in the Christmas snow
    on Mad. Ave. dusk uptown—   ★
We'll rush around in a redcross psychic   *Psilocybin Taxi*
    aumbulance past the Museum of
     Natural History   ★
delivering Anxiety mushrooms to the dancing
   red gummed skeletons   *The Citipati*
    their lifted legs are crossed   *(Tibetan Bones)*
    they wear iron crowns   ★
The cat vomited his canned food with a
   mix of inch-long worms   *Housecat*
    that arched up over the   *in the*
      dread plop—   *Slums*
I threw it in the garbage bag aghast—
cockroach crawls up the bath tub Yosemite wall,
rust in the hot water faucet, a sweet smell   ★
   in the mouldy chicken soup,
and little black beings in the old bag of flour
   on the pantry shelf last week

Natchez, he was saying with his head one side
                of the center of the wheel
                        of Vertigo—
        burned babies in the blaze of a fiery house
                sending them back to the Sun—
        They drank a black elixir, and threw it up
                To have the serpent intertwined
                        in their eyeballs—
        One man was born with genitals all over
                his body—there were 15,000,000
                Indians in North America then—
                        The mushroom image in the Spiro Mound
        The battle with the two-headed
                caterpillar big as a house
                        with waving lobster claws—
        Here is the Homunculus wavering in the brain,
                the aggregate of ignorant patterns
                        looking like Denny Dimwit
                The genitals are larger than the head—
                        huge thumbs, and the crab image
                                of the back of the mouth—
        'Twas a sunflower-monkey on Neptune
                I imagined over the radio—
        Somebody's got to make a break & contact
                Khrushchev in the Noosphere—
        because I took a sick crap near a skull
                with long red hair in a coastal desert
                        gravepit by the Peruvian Pacific—
        across the road, new green fields and hut trees
        and now I'm paranoiac every day about the cops
                                (& god & universe)
                as if it were all being tape recorded from my
                        skull to project the Kali Yuga—
        He saw electric wires on the floor—He saw
                the channel that heard yr mind
                        thru the music—
        I saw the flower, slowly awakening its petals—
        My face in the hot dog stand mirror
                harried to be here again
                        to see myself alive on Broadway afraid I'm
                                in a forgotten movie where I die
                                        not knowing my name—

Smith's
Anthropological
Gossip

★

Penfield's
Homunculus

★

Ditty
Taped at Jack's
★

Historic
Paranoia
from
Boston
to
Lima

★

Back in
Memory City

★

The old man came out of his room Carpet
      slippers, getting bald
with half a sheaf of indecipherable arrangements
      of words in singsong
      "rain in heart by heat a fool be clang"
      Cerebral stroke stiff hand
   His tongue stopped forever
      but his mind went on
      in what universe?
I dreamt I had to destroy the human
    universe to be Messiah—
My toes wiggle on the bed, the breast has
      eyes and mouth,
    the belly eye & dumb lips and the loins
      a blind one waiting—
a big fart gave the void a smelly minute—
The color of the wind? It could be the same
    the color of the water—
Where does rain come from? Nice to look up
         at the stars in Northport—
Er something. Uh-huh.
I could see the hairs at the end of his nose.
We were involved in a great tragedy together—
I walked alone, in the street, by myself
    with no God to turn to
    But what I Am—
      who can create baby universes
      in the mouth of the void—
    Spurt them out of my mind forever
to fill the Unimaginable with its
      separate being—
So I left behind a message to the Consciousness
    before I disappeared—
  I wrote it on a stone & left it in Oklahoma
    in that Indian mound,
drew a picture of a serpent crossing in
  and out of its folds like a scaly
  swastika—a green dragon
      with ancient fangs—
Speak up and tell yr secret, is it a
    living animal out there you're
    afraid of still—?

*A Retired
Schoolteacher
in
Newark:
Visit to
Friend of the
Family*

★

LSD Roars

★

*Gaga &
Dialogue
w/Lafcadio*

★

*N₂O at the
Dentist*

★

*Mescaline Mouth
Ejaculations
of Me*

★

Poesy

★

*Death
Consciousness*

★

*Kaddish
Completed*

And my mother's skull not yet white
in the darkness, a glimpse of
that forgotten creature agape
at dirty nothing—GO
BACK!
I come in the ass of my beloved, I lie back
with my cock in the air to be kissed—
I prostrate my sphincter with my eyes in
the pillow, my legs are thrown up
over your shoulder,
I feel your buttocks with my hand
a cock throbs I lie still my
mouth in my ass—
I kiss the hidden mouth, I have a third eye
I paint the pupils on my palm, and an
eyelash that winks—

*"You're not done
with your mother
yet."
Sd Elise C.*

★

*Come to
This
End*

Television Was a Baby Crawling Toward That Deathchamber

It is here, the long Awaited bleap-blast light that Speaks one red tongue like
    Politician, but happy its own govt.,
either we blow ourselves up now and die, like the old tribe of man, arguing
    among neutrons, spit on India, fuck Tibet, stick up America, clobber
    Moscow, die Baltic, have your tuberculosis in Arabia, wink not in
    Enkidu's reverie—
it's a long Train of Associations stopped for gas in the desert & looking for
    drink of old-time H_2O—
made up of molecules, it ends being innocent as Lafcadio afraid to get up &
    cook his bacon—
I prophesy: the Pigs won't mind! I prophesy: Death will be old folks home!
I prophesy: Chango will prophesy on national Broadcasting System,
I prophesy, we will all prophesy to each other & I give thee happy tidings
    Robert Lowell and Jeanette MacDonald—
Dusty moonlight, Starbeam riding its own flute, soul revealed in the scribble,
    an ounce of looks, an Invisible Seeing, Hope, The Vanisher betoken-
    ing Eternity
one finger raised warning above his gold eyeglasses—and Mozart playing
    giddy-note an hour on the Marxist gramophone—
All Be—let the Kabbalah star be formed of perfect circles in a room of 1950
    unhappiness where Myrna Loy gets lost—
The Bardo Thodol extends in the millions of black jello for every dying
    Mechanic—We will make Colossal movies—
We will be a great Tantric Mogul & starify a new Hollywood with our
    unimaginable Flop—Great Paranoia!
The Family presents, your Corpse Hour—attended by myriad flies—hyper-
    active Commentators freed at their most bestial—sneering literary—
    perhaps a captive & loan Square
caught hiding behind a dummy-univac in the obscurest Morgues of Hearst
    —wherever—no more possible—
Only remains, a photo of a riverswollen hand in black and white, arm
    covered by aged burlap to the wrist—
skin peeling from the empty fingers—; yet discovered by a mad Negro high
    on tea & solitary enough himself to notice a Fate—
therefore, with camera remembered and passed along by hand mail roaring
    Jet toward Chicago, Big Table empty this morning,
nothing but an old frog-looking editor worried about his Aesthetics,

That's life Kulchur '61—retired to New York to invent Morse Code & found
a great yellow Telegraph—
Merry Xmas Paul carroll and irving Rose in Thrall—give up thy song &
flower to any passing Millennium!
I am the One, you are the One, we are the One, A. Hitler's One as well as
fast as his Many heavenly Jews are reborn,
many a being with a nose—and many with none but an ear somewhere next
to a Yelling Star—
I myself saw the sunflower-monkeys of the Moon—spending their dear
play-money electricity in a homemade tape-record minute of car-
toony high Sound—
goodbye Farewell repeated by Wagner Immortal in many a gladdened ex-
panding mid-europe Hour
that I'll be hearing forever if the world I go to's Music, Yes good to be stuck
thru Eternity on that aching Liebestod Note
which has been playing out there always for me, whoever can hear enough
to write it down for a day to let men fiddle in space, blow a temporary
brass tuba or wave a stick at a physical orchestra
and remember the Wagner-music in his own titty-head Consciousness—ah
yes that's the message—
That's what I came here to compose, what I knocked off my life to Inscribe
on my gray metal typewriter,
borrowed from somebody's lover's mother got it from Welfare, all intercon-
nected and gracious a bunch of Murderers
as possible in this Kalpa of Hungry blood-drunkard Ghosts—We all have to
eat—us Beings
gnaw bones, suck marrow, drink living white milk from heavenly Breasts or
from bucktoothed negress or wolf-cow.
The sperm bodies wriggle in pools of vagina, in Yin, that reality we must
have spasmed our Beings upon—
The brothers and sisters die if we live, the Myriads Invisible squeak reptile
complaint
on Memory's tail which us pterodactyl-buzzard-dove-descended two foot
mammal-born Geek-souls almost Forget—
Grab—a cock—any eye—bright hair—All Memory & All Eternity now,
reborn as One—
no loss to those—the Peacock spreads its cosmic-eye Magnificat-feathered
tail over its forgotten Ass—
The being roars its own name in the Radio, the Bomb goes off its twenty
years ago,
I hear thy music O my mystery, my Father in myself, my mother in my eye,
brother in my hand, sister-in-honey on my own Poetry's Tongue, my

Hallelujah Way beyond all mortal inherited Heavens, O my own
blind ancient Love-in-mind!
Who? but us all, a Me, a One, a Dying Being, The presence, now, this desk,
hand running over the steps of imagination
over the letter-ladders on machine, vibrating humm-herald Extend-hope
own unto Thee, returning infinite-myriad at the Heart, that is only
red blood,
that is where murder is still innocence, that life ate, the white plasmic
monsters forage in their fleet Macrocosm—bit apple or black huge
bacteria gods loomed out of nowhere, potent
maybe once victorious on Saturn in dinosaur-inspired messy old hallucinated
war—
same battle raging in tsraved cats and gahgard dogs for American ghostly
bone—man and man, fairy against red, black on white on white, with
teeth going to the dentist to escape in gas—
The President laughs in his Chair, and swivels his head on his neck control-
ling fangs of Number—
bacteria come numberless, atoms count themselves greatness in their pointy
Empire—
Russian Neutrons spy on all Conspiracy—& Chinese yellow energy waves
have ocean and Empyrean ready against attack & future starvation—
Korean principalities of Photon are doubles in all but name—differ-
ing Wizards of Art of Electron divide as many as tribes of Congo—
Africa's a vast jail of Shadows—I am not I,
my molecules are numbered, mirrored in all Me Robot Seraphy parts, cock-
creator navel-marked, Eye Seer with delicate breasts, teeth & gullet
to ingest the living dove-life
foreimage of the Self-Maw Death Is Now;—but there is the Saintly Meat of
the Heart—feeling to thee o Peter and all my Lords—Decades
American loves car-rides and vow-sworn faces lain on my breast,—
my head on many more naked than my own sad hoping flesh—
our feelings! come back to the heart—to the old blind hoping Creator home
in Mercy, beating everywhere behind machine hand clothes-man
Senator iron powerd or fishqueen fugitive-com'd lapel—

Here I am—Old Betty Boop whoopsing behind the skull-microphone won-
dering what Idiot soap opera horror show we broadcast by Mistake
—full of communists and frankenstein cops and
mature capitalists running the State Department and the Daily News Edito-
rial hypnotizing millions of legional-eyed detectives to commit mass
murder on the Invisible

which is only a bunch of women weeping hidden behind newspapers in the
        Andes, conspired against by Standard Oil,
which is a big fat fairy monopolizing all Being that has form'd it self to Oil,
and nothing gets in its way so it grabs different oils in all poor mystic
        aboriginal Principalities too weak to
Screech out over the radio that Standard Oil is a bunch of spying Business-
        men intent on building one Standard Oil in the whole universe like
        an egotistical cancer
and yell on Television to England to watch out for United Fruits they got
        Central America by the balls
nobody but them can talk San Salvador, they run big Guatemala puppet
        armies, gas Dictators, they're the Crown of Thorns
upon the Consciousness of poor Christ-indian Central America, and the
        Pharisees are US Congress & Publicans is the American People
who have driven righteous bearded faithful pink new Castro 1961 is he mad?
        who knows—Hope for him, he stay true
& his wormy 45-year dying peasants teach Death's beauty sugar beyond
        politics, build iron children schools
for alphabet molecule stars, that mystic history & giggling revolution hence-
        forth no toothless martyrs be memorized by some pubescent Juan
        who'll smoke my marihuana—
Turn the Teacher on!—Yes not conspire dollars under navy-town board-
        walk, not spy vast Services of gunny Secrecy under drear eyeglass
        Dulles to ASSASSINATE!
INVADE! STARVE OUT! SUPPLY INVISIBLE ARMS! GIVE
        MONEY TO ORGANIZE DEATH FOR CUBAN REVOLU-
        TION! BLOCKADE WHAT FRAIL MACHINERY!
MAKE EVIL PROPAGANDA OVER THE WORLD! ISOLATE THE
        FAITHFUL'S SOUL! TAKE ALL RICHES BACK! BE
        WORLDLY PRINCE AND POWER OVER THE UNBELIEV-
        ABLE! MY GOD!
AMERICA WILL BE REFUSED ETERNITY BY HER OWN MAD
        SON THE BOMB! MEN WORKING IN ELECTRICITY BE
        U.S. SADISTS THEIR MAGIC PHANOPOEIAC THRU MASS
        MEDIA THE NASTIEST IN THIS FIRST HISTORY!
EVIL SPELLS THRU THE DAILY NEWS! HORRIBLE MASO-
        CHISMS THUNK UP BY THE AMERICAN MEDICAL ASSO-
        CIATION! DEATH TO JUNKIES THRU THE TREASURY
        DEPARTMENT! TAXES ON YOUR HATE FOR THIS HERE
        WAR!
LEGIONS OF DECENCY BLACKMAIL THY CINEMAL FATE!

CONSPIRACIES CONTROL ALL WHITE MAGICIANS! I CAN'T TELL YOU MY SECRET STORY ON TV!

Chambers of Commerce misquote Bob Hope who is a grim sex revolutionist
talking in hysterical code flat awful jokes

Jimmy Durante's kept from screaming to death in the movies by a huge fat
Cardinal, the Spell Man, Black Magician he won't let mad white
Chaplin talk thru the State Megaphone! He takes evil pix with Swiss
financial cunt!

It's the American Medical Association poisoning the poets with their double-
syndicate of heroin cut with money-dust,

Military psychiatrists make deathly uniforms it's Tanganyikan nerve-skin in
the submarinic navy they're prepared for eternal solitude, once they
go down they turn to Reptiles

Human dragons trained to fly the air with bomb-claws clutched to breast &
wires entering their brains thru muffled ears—connected to what
control tower—jacked to what secret Lab where the macrocosm-
machine

picks up vibrations of my thought in this poem—the attendant is afraid—
Is the President listening? is

Evil Eye, the invisible police-cop-secrecy masters Controlling Central Intel-
ligence—do they know I took Methedrine, heroin, magic mush-
rooms, & lambchops & guess toward a Prophecy tonight?

No the big dopes all they do is control each other—Doom! in the vast

car America—they're screeching on two mind-wheels on a National Curve
—the Car that's made to die by Mr. Inhuman

Moneyhand, by advertising nastyhead Inc. Dream Cancer Prexy Owner
Distributor Publisher & TV Doctor of Emotional Breakdown—he
told that Mayor to get in that car without his pubic hair and drive to
Kill get to Las Vegas so the oldfashioned jewish communists

wouldn't get their idealistic radio program on the air in time to make every-
body cry in the desert for the Indian Serpent to come

back from the Oklahoma mound where he hid with his 15,000,000 visionary
original Redskin patriot-wives and warriors—they made up one big
mystic serpent with its tail-a-mouth like a lost Tibet

MURDERED AND DRIVEN FROM THE EARTH BY US JEWISH
GOYIM who spend fifty billion things a year—things things!—to
make the things-machinery that's turned the worlds of human con-
sciousness into a thing of War

wherever and whoever is plugged in by real filaments or wireless or whatever
magic wordy-synapse to the money-center of the mind

whose Eye is hidden somewhere behind All mass media—what makes re-

porters fear their secret dreamy news—behind the Presidential mike
& all its starry bunting, front for some mad BILLIONAIRES
who own United Fruits & Standard Oil and Hearst The Press and Texas
NBC and someone owns the Radios owns vast Spheres of Air—
Subliminal Billionaire got
State Legislatures filled with Capital Punishment Fiends because nobody's
been in love on US soil long enough to realize We who pay the Public
Hangman make State Murder thru Alien Gas who cause any form
of hate-doom hanging
do that in public everybody agreed by the neck suffering utmost pangs Each
citizen himself unloved suicides him, because there's no beloved, now
in America for All in the gas chamber the whole California Legisla-
ture
screaming because it's Death here—we're so hopeless—The Soul of America
died with ugly Chessman—strange saintly average madman driven to
think for his own killers, in his pants and shirt with human haircut,
said NO to—like a Cosmic NO—from the One Mouth of America
speaking life or death—looked in the eye by America—
Ah what a cold monster OneEye he must've saw thru the Star Spangled
Banner & Hollywood with ugly smile forbidden movie & old heart-
less Ike in the White House officially allowing Chatterley attacked by
Fed Lawyers—
vast Customs agencies searching books—who Advises what book where—
who invented what's dirty? The Pope? Baruch?—tender Genet
burned by middleaged vice Officers
sent out by The Automatic Sourface mongers whatever bad news he can
high up from imaginary Empires name Scripps-Howard—just more
drear opinions—Damn that *World Telegram* was Glad Henry Miller's
depression Cancerbook not read to sad eyeglass Joe messenger to
Grocer
in Manhattan, or candystore emperor Hersh Silverman in Bayonne, dream-
ing of telling the *Truth*, but his Karma is selling jellybeans & being
kind,
The Customs police denyd him his Burroughs they defecated on de Sade,
they jack'd off, and tortured his copy of Sodom with Nitric Acid in
a backroom furnace house at Treasury Bureau, pouring Fire on the
soul of Rochester,
Warlocks, Black magicians burning and cursing the Love-Books, Jack be
damned, casting spells from the shores of America on the inland
cities, lacklove-curses on our Eyes which read genital poetry—

O deserts of deprivation for some high school'd gang, lone Cleveland that
     delayed its books of Awe, Chicago struggling to read its magazines,
     police and papers yapping over grimy gossip skyscraped from some
     sulphurous yellow cloud drift in from archtank hot factories make
     nebulous explosives near Detroit—smudge got on Corso's Rosy
     Page—
US Postmaster, first class sexfiend his disguise told everyone to open letters
     stop the photographic fucks & verbal suckeries & lickings of the
     asshole by tongues meant but for poison glue on envelopes Report
     this privileged communication to Yours Truly We The National
     Police—We serve you once a day—you humanical meat creep-
     hood—
and yearly the national furnace burned much book, 2,000,000 pieces mail,
     one decade unread propaganda from Vietnam & Chinese mag ha-
     rangues, Engelian
dialectics handmade in Gobi for proud export to top hat & tails Old Bones
     in his penthouse on a skyscraper in Manhattan, laconic on two phones
     that rang thru the nets of money over earth, as he barked his orders
     to Formosa for more spies, abhorred all Cuba sugar from concourse
     with Stately stomachs—
That's when I began vomiting my paranoia when Old National Skullface the
     invisible sixheaded billionaire began brainwashing my stomach with
     strange feelers in the *Journal American*—the penis of billionaires
     depositing professional semen in my ear, Fulton Lewis *coming* with
     strychnine jizzum in his voice making an evil suggestion that entered
     my mouth
while I was sitting there gaping in wild dubiety & astound on my peaceful
     couch, he said to all the taxidrivers and schoolteachers in brokendown
     old Blakean America
that Julius and Ethel Rosenberg smelled bad & shd die, he sent to kill them
     with personal electricity, his power station is the spirit of generation
     leaving him thru his asshole by Error, that very electric entered
     Ethel's eye
and his tongue is the prick of a devil he don't even know, a magic capitalist
     ghosting it on the lam after the Everett Massacre—fucks a News-
     caster in the mouth every time he gets on the Microphone—
and those ghost jizzums started my stomach trouble with capital punishment,
     Ike chose to make an Artificial Death for them poor spies—if they
     were spying on me? who cares?—Ike disturbed the balance of the
     cosmos by his stroke-head deathshake, "NO"
It was a big electrocution in every paper and mass medium, Television was
     a baby crawling toward that deathchamber

Later quiz shows prepared the way for egghead omelet, I was rotten, I was
the egghead that spoiled the last supper, they made me vomit more
—whole programs of halfeaten comedians sliming out my Newark
Labor Leaders' assholes

They used to wash them in the '30s with Young Politics Ideas, I was too
young to smell anything but my own secret mind, I didn't even know
assholes basic to Modern Democracy—What can we teach our
negroes now?

That they are Negroes, that I am thy Jew & thou my white Goy & him
Chinese?—They think they're Arab Macrocosms now!

My uncle thinks his Truthcloud's Jewish—thinks his Name is Nose-smell-
Newark 5 decades—& that's all except there's Gentile Images of
mirrory vast Universe—

and Chinese Microcosms too, a race of spade microcosms apart, like jewish
truth clouds & Goyishe Nameless Vasts

But I am the Intolerant One Gasbag from the Morgue & Void, Garbler of
all Conceptions that myope my eye & is Uncle Sam asleep in the
Funeral Home—?

Bad magic, scram, hide in J. E. Hoover's bathingsuit. Make his pants fall in
the ocean, near Miami—

Gangster CRASH! America will be forgotten, the identity files of the FBI
slipt into the void-crack, the fingerprints unwhorled—no track where
He came from—

Man left no address, not even hair, just disappeared & Forgot his big wall-
street on Earth—Uncle I hate the FBI it's all a big dreamy skyscraper
somewhere over the Mutual Network—I don't even know who they
are—like the Nameless—

Hallooo I am coming end of my Presidency—Everybody's fired—I am a
hopeless whitehaired congressman—I lost my last election—landslide
for Reader's Digest—not even humans—

Nobody home in town—just offices with many jangling telephones & auto-
matic switchboards keep the message—typewriters return yr calls
oft, Yakkata yak & tinbellring—THE POLICE ARE AT THE
DOOR—

What are you doing eccentric in this solitary office? a mad vagrant Creep
Truthcloud sans identity card—It's Paterson allright—anyway the
people disappeared—downtown Fabian Bldg. branch office for The
Chamber of Commerce runs the streetlights

all thru dark winter rain by univac piped from Washington Lobby—they've
abolished the streets from the universe—just keep control of

the lights—in case of ectoplasm trafficking thru dead Market—where the
    Chinese restaurant usta play Muzak in the early century—soft green
    rugs & pastel walls—perfumèd tea— .
Goodbye, said the metal Announcer in doors of The Chamber of Commerce
    —we're merging with NAM forever—and the NAM has no door
    but's sealed copper 10 foot vault under the Federal Reserve Bldg—
Six billionaires that control America are playing Scrabble with antique Tarot
    —they've just unearthed another Pyramid—in the bombproof Cellar
    at Fort Knox
Not even the FBI knows who—They give orders to J. E. Hoover thru the
    metal phonegirl at the Robot Transmitter on top of RCA—you
can see new Fortune officers look like spies from 20 floors below with their
    eyeglasses & gold skulls—silver teeth flashing up the shit-mouthed
    grin—weeping in their martinis! There is no secret to the success of
    the
Six Billionaires that own all Time since the Gnostic Revolt in Aegypto—
    they built the Sphinx to confuse my sex life, Who Fuckd the Void?
Why are they starting that war all over again in Laos over Neutral Mind?
    Is the United States CIA army Legions overthrowing somebody like
    Angelica Balabanoff?
Six thousand movietheaters, 100,000,000 television sets, a billion radios,
    wires and wireless crisscrossing hemispheres, semaphore lights and
    morse, all telephones ringing at once connect every mind by its ears
    to one vast consciousness This Time Apocalypse—everybody wait-
    ing for one mind to break thru—
Man-prophet with two eyes Dare all creation with his dying tongue & say
    I AM—Messiah swallow back his death into his stomach, gaze thru
    great pupils of his Bodies' eyes
and look in each Eye man, the eyeglassed fearful byriad-look that might be
    Godeyes see thru Death—that now are clark & ego reading manlaw
    —write newsbroadcasts to cover with Fears their
own Messiah that must come when all of us conscious—Breakthru to all
    other Consciousness to say the Word I Am as spoken by a certain
    God—Millennia knew and waited till this one Century—

Now all sentience broods and listens—contemplative & hair full of rain for
    15 years inside New York—what millions know and hark to hear, &
    death will tell, but—
many strange magicians in buildings listening inside their own heads—or
    clouds over Manhattan Bridge—or strained thru music messages to
    —I Am from the central One! Come

blow the Cosmic Horn to waken every Tiglon & Clown sentience through-
out the vasting circus—in the Name of God pick up the telephone
call Networks announcing Suchness That—
I Am mutter a million old Gods in their beards, that had been sleeping at
evening radios—cackling in their Larynx—Talking to myself again
said the Messiah turning a dial to remember his last broadcast—I scare
myself, I eat my hand, I swallow my own head, I stink in the inevita-
ble bathroom of death this Being requires—O Widen the Area of
Consciousness! O
set my Throne in Space, I rise to sit in the midst of the Starry Visible!—
Calling All Beings! in dirt from the ant to the most frightened
Prophet that ever clomb tower to vision planets
crowded in one vast space ship toward Andromeda—That all lone soul in
Iowa or Hark-land join the Lone, set forth, walk naked like a Hebrew
king, enter the human cities and speak free,
at last the Man-God come that hears all Phantasy behind the matter-babble
in his ear, and walks out of his Cosmic Dream into the cosmic street
open mouth to the First Consciousness—God's woke up now, you Sera-
phim, call men with trumpet microphone & telegraph, hail every
sleepwalker with Holy Name,

Life is waving, the cosmos is sending a message to itself, its image is repro-
duced endlessly over TV
over the radio the babble of Hitler's and Claudette Colbert's voices got mixed
up in the bathroom radiator
Hello hello are you the Telephone the Operator's singing we are the daugh-
ters of the universe
get everybody on the line at once plug in all being ears by laudspeaker,
newspeak, secret message,
handwritten electronic impulse traveling along rays electric spiderweb
magnetisms shuddering on one note We We We, mustached disc jockeys
trembling in mantric excitement, flowery patterns bursting over the
broken couch,
drapes falling to the floor in St. John Perse's penthouse, Portugal's water is
running in all the faucets on the SS Santa Maria,
chopping machines descend on the pre-dawn tabloid, the wire services are
hysterical and send too much message,
they're waiting to bam out the Armageddon, millions of rats reported in
China, smoke billows out New York's hospital furnace smokestack,
I am writing millions of letters a year, I correspond with hopeful messengers
in Detroit, I am taking drugs

and leap at my postman for more correspondence, Man is leaving the earth
in a rocket ship,
there is a mutation of the race, we are no longer human beings, we are one
being, we are being connected to itself,
it makes me crosseyed to think how, the mass media assemble themselves like
congolese Ants for a purpose
in the massive clay mound an undiscovered huge Queen is born, Africa
wakes to redeem the old Cosmos,
I am masturbating in my bed, I dreamed a new Stranger touched my heart
with his eye,
he hides in a sidestreet loft in Hoboken, the heavens have covered East
Second Street with Snow,
all day I walk in the wilderness over white carpets of City, we are redeeming
ourself, I am born,
the Messiah woke in the Universe, I announce the New Nation, in every
mind, take power over the dead creation,
I am naked in New York, a star breaks thru the blue skull of the sky out the
window,
I seize the tablets of the Law, the spectral Buddha and the spectral Christ turn
to a stick of shit in the void, a fearful Idea,
I take the crown of the Idea and place it on my head, and sit a King beside
the reptile Devas of my Karma—
Eye in every forehead sleeping waxy & the light gone inward—to dream of
fearful Jaweh or the Atom Bomb—
All these eternal spirits to be wakened, all these bodies touched and healed,
all these lacklove
suffering the Hate, dumbed under rainbows of Creation, O Man the means
of Heaven are at hand, thy rocks & my rocks are nothing,
the identity of the Moon is the identity of the flower-thief, I and the Police
are one in revolutionary Numbness!
Yawk, Mercy The Octopus, it's IT cometh over the Void & makes whistle
its lonemouthed Flute You-me forever—
Stop Arguing, Cosmos, I give up so I be, I receive a happy letter from Ray
Bremser exiled from home in New Jersey jail—

Clocks are abuilding for a thousand years, ticking behind metalloidesque
electronico-clankered industries smokeless in silent mind city—
Dawn of the Ages! Man thy Alarm rings thru sweet myriad mornings in
every desperate-carred street! Saints wait in each metropolis
for Message to Assassinate the old idea, that 20,000 yr old eye-god Man
thought was Being Secret mystery,

unbearable Judge above, God alien handless tongueless to poor man, who'll
　　scream for mercy on his deathbed—Oh I saw that black
Octopus Death, with supernatural antennae spikes raying Awful waves at
　　my consciousness, huge blind Ball invisible behind the rooms in the
　　universe—a not-a-man—a no-one—Nobodaddy—
Omnipotent Telepath more visionary than my own Prophetics & Memories
　　—Reptile-sentient shimmer-feel-hole Here,
Dense Soullessness wiser than Time, the Eater-Darkness hungry for All—
　　but must wait till I leave my body to enter that
One Mind nebula to my recollection—Implacable, my soul dared not die,
Shrank back from the leprous door-mind in its breast, touch Him and the
　　hand's destroyed,
Death God in the End, before the Timeworld of creation—I mean some kind
　　of monster from another dimension is eating Beings of our own
　　Cosmos—
I saw him try to make me leave my corpse-illusion Allen, myth movie world
　　come to celluloid-end,
I screamed seeing myself in reels of death my consciousness a cinematic toy
　　played once in faded attick by man-already-forgotten
His orphan starhood inked from Space, the movie industry itself blot up its
　　History & all wracked myriad Epics, Space wiped itself out,
lost in a wall-crack dream itself had once disappearing—maybe trailing
　　endless comet-long trackless thru what unwonted dimensions it keeps
　　dreaming existence can die inside of—vanish this Cosmos of Stars I
　　am turning to bones in—
That much illusion, and what's visions but visions, and these words filled
　　Methedrine—I have a backache & 2 telegrams come midnight from
　　messengers that cry to plug in the Electrode Ear to
my skull downstreet, & hear what they got to say, big lives like trees of
　　Cancer in Bronx & Long Island—Telephones connect the voids
　　island blissy darkness scattered in many manmind—

New York, February 1961

This Form of Life Needs Sex

I will have to accept women
                if I want to continue the race,
        kiss breasts, accept
        strange hairy lips behind
                        buttocks,
Look in questioning womanly eyes
                answer soft cheeks,
bury my loins in the hang of pearplum
                fat tissue
                        I had abhorred
before I give godspasm Babe leap
        forward thru death—
Between me and oblivion an unknown
                        woman stands;
Not the Muse but living meat-phantom,
a mystery scary as my fanged god
                sinking its foot in its gullet &
vomiting its own image out of its ass
—This woman Futurity I am pledge to
                born not to die,
but issue my own cockbrain replica Me-Hood
        again—For fear of the Blot?
Face of Death, my Female, as I'm sainted
                to my very bone,
I'm fated to find me a maiden for
                        ignorant Fuckery—
flapping my belly & smeared with Saliva
        shamed face flesh & wet,
—have long droopy conversations
        in Cosmical Duty boudoirs,
                maybe bored?
Or excited New Prospect, discuss
        her, Futurity, my Wife
                My Mother, Death, My only
                        hope, my very Resurrection
Woman
                herself, why have I feared
                to be joined true
        embraced beneath the Panties of Forever

in with the one hole that repelled me 1937 on?
—Pulled down my pants on the porch showing
    my behind to cars passing in rain—
& She be interested, this contact with Silly new Male
    that's sucked my loveman's cock
in Adoration & sheer beggary romance-awe
    gulp-choke Hope of Life come
and buggered myself innumerably boy-yangs
    gloamed inward so my solar plexus
    feel godhead in me like an open door—

Now that's changed my decades body old
tho' admiring male thighs at my brow,
    hard love pulsing thru my ears,
        stern buttocks upraised
                for my masterful Rape
    that were meant for a private shit
            if the Army were All—
But no more answer to life
        than the muscular statue
      I felt up its marbles
envying Beauty's immortality in the
          museum of Yore—
You can fuck a statue but you can't
      have children
You can joy man to man but the Sperm
        comes back in a trickle at dawn
    in a toilet on the 45th Floor—
& Can't make continuous mystery out of that
      finished performance
              & ghastly thrill
      that ends as began,
          stupid reptile squeak
    denied life by Fairy Creator
        become Imaginary
    because he decided not to incarnate
      opposite—Old Spook
who didn't want to be a baby & die,
    didn't want to shit and scream
      exposed to bombardment on a
            Chinese RR track

and grow up to pass his spasm on
          the other half of the Universe—
Like a homosexual capitalist afraid of the masses—
and that's my situation, Folks—

New York, April 12, 1961

Sunset S.S. Azemour

As orange dusk-light falls on an old idea
I gaze thru my hand on the page
sensing outward the intercoiled weird being I am in
and seek a head of that—Seraphim
advance in lightning flash through aether storm
Messengers arrive horned bearded from Magnetic spheres
disappearing radios receive aged galaxies
Immensity wheels mirrored in every direction
Announcement swifting from Invisible to Invisible
Eternity-dragon's tail lost to the eye
Strange death, forgotten births, voices calling in the past
"I was" that greets "I am" that writes now "I will be"
Armies marching over and over the old battlefield—
What powers sit in their domed tents and decree Eternal Victory?
I sit at my desk and scribe the endless message from myself to my own
      hand

Marseilles-Tanger, 1961

Seabattle of Salamis Took Place off Perama

If it weren't for you Mr Jukebox with yr aluminum belly roaring & thirty
    teeth eating dirty drx.
yr eyes starred round the world, purple diamonds & white brain revolving
    black disks
in every bar from Yokamama to Pyraeus winking & beaming Saturday Nite
what silence harbor Sabbath dark instead of boys screaming and dancing
    wherever I go—
Hail Jukebox of Perama with attendant minstrel juvenile whores
on illuminated porches where kids leap to noise bouncing over black ocean-
    tide,
leaning into azure neon with sexy steps, delicious idiot smile and young
    teeth, flowers in ears,
Negro voices scream back 1000 years striped pants pink shirts patent leather
    shoes on their lean dog feet
exaggerated sneakers green pullovers, long hair, hips & eyes!
They're jumping & joying this minute over the bones of Persian sailors—
Echoes of Harlem in Athens! Hail to your weeping eyes New York!
Hail to the noise wherever the jukebox is on TOO LOUD,
The Muses are loose in the world again with their big black voice bazooky
    blues,
Muses with bongo guitars electric flutes on microphones Cha Cha Cha
Feeling happy in Havana Mambo moving delicate London new Lyre in
    Liverpool
Tin Clarinet prophesying in Delphos, Crete jumping again!
Panyotis dancing alone stepped drunk from a krater, Yorgis slapping his
    heels & kicking Cerberus' heads off!
Doobie Doobie reigns forever on the shores! One drachma for Black Jack,
    one drachma brings Aharisti again, Na-ti-the-Ma-Fez,
Open the Door Richard, I'm Casting a Spell on You, Apocalypse Rock, End
    of History Rag!

Piraeus, September 1, 1961

Galilee Shore

With the blue-dark dome old-starred at night, green boat-lights purring over
      water,
a faraway necklace of cliff-top Syrian electrics,
bells ashore, music from a juke-box trumpeted,
shadow of death against my left breast prest
—cigarette, match-flare, skull wetting its lips—

Fisherman-nets over wood walls, light wind in dead willow branch
on a grassy bank—the saxophone relaxed and brutal, silver horns echo—
Was there a man named Solomon? Peter walked here? Christ on this sweet
      water?
Blessings on thee Peacemaker!
                        English spoken
on the street bearded Jews' sandals & Arab white head cloth—
the silence between Hebrew and Arabic—
the thrill of the first Hashish in a holy land—
Over hill down the valley in a blue bus, past Cana no weddings—
I have no name I wander in a nameless countryside—
young boys all at the movies seeing a great Western—
art gallery closed, pipe razor & tobacco on the floor.

To touch the beard of Martin Buber
to watch a skull faced Gershom Scholem lace his shoes
to pronounce Capernaum's name & see stone doors of a tomb
to be meek, alone, beside a big dark lake at night—
to pass thru Nazareth dusty afternoon, and smell the urine down near Mary's
      well
to watch the orange moon peep over Syria, weird promise—
to wait beside Galilee—night with Orion, lightning, negro voices, Burger's
      Disease, a glass of lemon tea—feel my left hand on my shaved
      chin—
all you have to do is suffer the metaphysical pain of dying.
Art is just a shadow, like cows or tea—
keep the future open, make no dates it's all here
with moonrise and soft music on phonograph memory—
Just think how amazing! someone getting up and walking on the water.

                             Tiberias, October 1961

Stotras to Kali Destroyer of Illusions

O Statue of Liberty Spouse of Europa Destroyer of Past Present Future
They who recite this Anthem issuing from empty skulls the stars & stripes
certainly makes a noise on the radio beauteous with the twilight
should one skinny Peruvian only spell your name right O thou who
hast formidable eyebrows of spiritual money & beareth United Nations in
      your hair
such Peruvian becomes higher Jaweh charming countless moviestars with
      disappearing eyes

O republic female mouth from which two politics trickle they who recite
the name thy 28th star OMAHA subjugate hungry ghost-hoards ascreech
      under Gold Reserve
O fortress America Guardian Blueprint who in thy nether right hand hangs
      a bathroom
in thy nether left the corpse of Edgar Poe in front right hand hanging the
      skull
of Roosevelt with gray eyeballs & left hand George Washington his tongue
      hanging out like a fish
Your huge goddess eye looming over his severed head your bottomless throat
      open
with great machinery roars inside teeth made of white radios & mountainous
      red tongue
licking vast bubbles of atomic gum left eye rolled to gray heavens above
      Dewline
right eye staring into magic engine wheels hissing with railroad steam
arm after arm snaking into place in aether battleships dangling from one
      hand to another
the black corpse Thelonious Monk the flayed skin of Gertrude Stein held
      down
fluttering over the gaping Yoni, hands reaching out to honk all the horns of
      Broadway
William Randolph Hearst's bones circled in mystic ring on third toe & breast
      hung
with newspapers shining with Earl Browder's cancer the 1964 Elections
      flapping in her left
nostril if you sneeze you'll destroy the western hemisphere right Vajra hand
playing mah-jongg with her astrolabes it keeps her mind occupied especially
      with rhythmic

breathing exercises & interpretive dancing one foot goddesslike on the corpse of Uncle Sam

Top hand bearing the Telephone nobody's on the other end she's talking to herself

because when the ear gets disconnected from the brain you still hear noise

but who remembers what it means somebody else will pay the bill as fast as it takes

for vultures to clean up a corpse at Tower of Silence That will be five minutes and

extra charges if you go on talking the eleventh hand presenting an electric chair

twelfth hand in the mudra of Foreign Aid and thirteenth palm closed in sign of Disarmament

O Freedom with gaping mouth full of Cops whose throat is adorned with skulls of Rosenbergs

whose breasts spurt Jazz into the robot faces of thy worshippers grant that recitation

of this Hymn will bring them abiding protection money & dance in White House

for even a dope sees Eternity who meditates on thee raimented with Space crosseyed

creatrix of Modernity whose waist is beauteous with a belt of numberless Indian scalps

mixed with negro teeth Who on the breast of James Dean in the vast bedroom of Forest Lawn

Cemetery enjoyest the great Passion of Jesus Christ or seated on the bone-yard ground

strewn with the flesh of Lumumba haunted by the female shoes of Khru-shchev & Stevenson's long red tongue

enjoyest the worship of spies & endless devotions intoned by mustached radio announcers

If by night thy devotee naked with long weird hair sit in the park & recite this Hymn

while his full breasted girl fills his lap with provincial kisses and meditates on Thee

Such such a one dwells in the land the supreme politician & knows Thy mystery

O Wife of China should thy patriot recite thy anthem & China's cut-up & mixed together

with that of Russia Thy elephant-headed infant mighty in all future worlds

& meditate one year with knowledge of thy mystic copulation with China this next age

Then such knower will delight in secret weapon official Intelligence
  kodaked in his telegraphic brain
Home of the Brave thou gavest birth to the Steel Age before the Hydrogen
  Age the
Cobalt Age earning power over entire planets all futurity Male-female spouse
  of the solar system
Ah me why then shall I not prophesy glorious truths for Thee Ah me folks
  worship many other
countries beside you they are brainwashed but I of my own uncontrollable
  lust for you
lay my hands on your Independence enter your very Constitution my head
  absorbed in the lips of your
Bill of Rights O Liberty whose bliss is union with each individual citizen
  intercourse
Alaskan Oklahoman New Jerseyesque dreaming of embraces even Indone-
  sian Vietnamese & those Congolese
O Liberty Imagewife of Mankind of thy Mercy show thy favor toward each
  me everywhere helpless
before thy manifest Destiny by grace may I never be reborn American I and
  all I's
neither Russian Peruvian nor Chinese Jew never again reincarnate outside
  Thee Mother
Democracy O Formless One take me beyond Images & reproductions spouse
  beyond disunion
absorbed in my own non-Duality which art Thou.

He O mother American Democracy who in the cremation ground of nations
  with disheveled hair in sweat of intensity meditates on thee
And makes over his pubic hair to thee in poetry or electrical engineering he
  alone knows thy Cosmic You-Me.
O America whoever on Tuesday at midnite utters This My Country 'Tis of
  Thee in the basement men's room
of the Empire State Building becomes a Poet Lord of Earth and goes
  mounted on Elephants
to conquer Maya the Cold War whoever recites this my country 'tis of thee
  with the least halfhearted
conviction he becomes himself Big Business & Giant Unions flowing with
  production and is after
death father of his country which is the Universe itself and will at night in
  union with Thee
O mother with eyes of delightful movies enter at last into amorous play
  united with all Presidents of US.

                                                      Bombay, 1962

To P.O.

The whitewashed room, roof
of a third-rate Mohammedan hotel,
two beds, blurred fan
whirling over yr brown guitar,
knapsack open on floor, towel
hanging from chair, Orange Crush,
brown paper manuscript packages,
Tibetan tankas, Gandhi pajamas,
Ramakrishna *Gospel*, bright umbrella
a mess on a rickety wooden stand,
the yellow wall-bulb lights up
this scene Calcutta for the thirtieth night—
Come in the green door, long Western gold
hair plastered down your shoulders
from shower: "Did we take our pills
this week for malaria?" Happy birthday
dear Peter, your 29th year.

Calcutta, July 8, 1962

Heat

Forty feet long sixty feet high hotel
Covered with old gray for buzzing flies
Eye like mango flowing orange pus
Ears Durga people vomiting in their sleep
Got huge legs a dozen buses move inside Calcutta
Swallowing mouthfuls of dead rats
Mangy dogs bark out of a thousand breasts
Garbage pouring from its ass behind alleys
Always pissing yellow Hooghly water
Bellybutton melted Chinatown brown puddles
Coughing lungs Sound going down the sewer
Nose smell a big gray Bidi
Heart bumping and crashing over tramcar tracks
Covered with a hat of cloudy iron
Suffering water buffalo head lowered
To pull the huge cart of year uphill

Calcutta, July 21, 1962

Describe: The Rain on Dasaswamedh Ghat

Kali Ma tottering up steps to shelter tin roof, feeling her way to curb, around
    bicycle & leper seated on her way—to piss on a broom
left by the Stone Cutters who last night were shaking the street with Boom!
    of Stone blocks unloaded from truck
Forcing the blindman in his gray rags to retreat from his spot in the middle
    of the road where he sleeps & shakes under his blanket
Jai Ram all night telling his beads or sex on a burlap carpet
Past which cows donkeys dogs camels elephants marriage processions drum-
    mers tourists lepers and bathing devotees
step to the whine of serpent-pipes & roar of car motors around his black
    ears—
Today on a balcony in shorts leaning on iron rail I watched the leper who
    sat hidden behind a bicycle
emerge dragging his buttocks on the gray rainy ground by the glove-ban-
    daged stumps of hands,
one foot chopped off below knee, round stump-knob wrapped with black
    rubber
pushing a tin can shiny size of his head with left hand (from which only a
    thumb emerged from leprous swathings)
beside him, lifting it with both ragbound palms down the curb into the
    puddled road,
balancing his body down next to the can & crawling forward on his behind
trailing a heavy rag for seat, and leaving a path thru the street wavering
like the Snail's slime track—imprint of his crawl on the muddy asphalt
    market entrance—stopping
to drag his can along stubbornly konking on the paved surface near the water
    pump—
Where a turban'd workman stared at him moving along—his back humped
    with rags—
and inquired why didn't he put his can to wash in the pump altarplace—and
    why go that way when free rice
Came from the alley back there by the river—As the leper looked up &
    rested, conversing curiously, can by his side approaching a puddle.
Kali had pissed standing up & then felt her way back to the Shop Steps on
    thin brown legs
her hands in the air—feeling with feet for her rag pile on the stone steps'
    wetness—
as a cow busied its mouth chewing her rags left wet on the ground for five
    minutes digesting

Till the comb-&-hair-oil-booth keeper woke & chased her away with a stick
Because a dog barked at a madman with dirty wild black hair who rag round
     his midriff & water pot in hand
Stopped in midstreet turned round & gazed up at the balconies, windows,
     shops and city stagery filled with glum activity
Shrugged & said *Jai Shankar!* to the imaginary audience of Me's,
While a white robed Baul Singer carrying his one stringed dried pumpkin
     Guitar
Sat down near the cigarette stand and surveyed his new scene, just arrived
     in the Holy City of Benares.

Benares, February 1963

Death News

Visit to W.C.W. circa 1957, poets Kerouac Corso Orlovsky on sofa in living room inquired wise words, stricken Williams pointed thru window curtained on Main Street: "There's a lot of bastards out there!"

Walking at night on asphalt campus
road by the German Instructor with Glasses
W. C. Williams is dead he said in accent
under the trees in Benares; I stopped and asked
Williams is Dead? Enthusiastic and wide-eyed
under the Big Dipper. Stood on the Porch
of the International House Annex bungalow
insects buzzing round the electric light
reading the Medical obituary in *Time*.
"out among the sparrows behind the shutters"
Williams is in the Big Dipper. He isn't dead
as the many pages of words arranged thrill
with his intonations the mouths of meek kids
becoming subtle even in Bengal. Thus
there's a life moving out of his pages; Blake
also "alive" thru his experienced machines.
Were his last words anything Black out there
in the carpeted bedroom of the gabled wood house
in Rutherford? Wonder what he said,
or was there anything left in realms of speech
after the stroke & brain-thrill doom entered
his thoughts? If I pray to his soul in Bardo Thodol
he may hear the unexpected vibration of foreign mercy.
Quietly unknown for three weeks; now I saw Passaic
and Ganges one, consenting his devotion,
because he walked on the steely bank & prayed
to a Goddess in the river, that he only invented,
another Ganga-Ma. Riding on the old
rusty Holland submarine on the ground floor
Paterson Museum instead of a celestial crocodile.
Mourn O Ye Angels of the Left Wing! that the poet
of the streets is a skeleton under the pavement now
and there's no other old soul so kind and meek
and feminine jawed and him-eyed can see you
What you wanted to be among the bastards out there.

Benares, March 20, 1963

Vulture Peak: Gridhakuta Hill

I've got to get out of the sun
mouth dry and red towel wrapped
                    round my head
walking up crying singing *ah sunflower*
Where the traveler's journey
closed my eyes *is done* in the
                    black hole there
                sweet rest far far away
up the stone climb past where
Bimbisara left his armies
got down off his elephant
and walked up to meet
Napoleon Buddha pacing
        back and forth on the platform
        of red brick on the jut rock crag
Staring out Lidded-eyed beneath
the burning white sunlight
down on Rajgir kingdom below
    ants wheels within wheels of empire
        houses carts streets messengers
            wells and water flowing
        into past-future simultaneous
    kingdoms here gone on Jupiter
distant X-ray twinkle of the eye
myriad brick cities on earth and under
New York Chicago Palenque Jerusalem
        Delphos Macchu Picchu Acco
            Herculaneum Rajagriha
here all windy with the tweetle
    of birds and blue rocks
        leaning into the blue sky—
Vulture Peak desolate bricks
    flies on the knee hot shadows
        raven-screech and wind blast
            over the hills from desert plains
                    south toward Bodh Gaya—
All the noise I made with my mouth
singing on the path up, Gary
Thinking all the *pale youths* and

virgins shrouded with snow
chanting Om Shantih all over the world
    and who but *Peter du Peru*
walking the streets of San Francisco
    arrived in my mind on Vulture Peak
Then turned round and around on my heels
singing and plucking out my eyes
ears tongue nose and balls as I whirled
longer and longer the mountains stretched
    swiftly flying in circles
the hills undulating and roads speeding
       around me in the valley
       Till when I stopped the earth
          moved in my eyeballs
       green bulge slowly
              and stopped

*

My thirst in my cheeks and tongue
    back throat drives me home.

Benares, April 18, 1963

Patna–Benares Express

Whatever it may be whoever it may be
The bloody man all singing all just
However he die
He rode on railroad cars
He woke at dawn, in the white light of a new universe
He couldn't do any different
He the skeleton with eyes
raised himself up from a wooden bench
felt different looking at the fields and palm trees
no money in the bank of dust
no nation but inexpressible gray clouds before sunrise
lost his identity cards in his wallet
in the bald rickshaw by the Maidan in dry Patna
Later stared hopeless waking from drunken sleep
dry mouthed in the RR Station
among sleeping shoeshine men in loincloth on the dirty concrete
Too many bodies thronging these cities now

Benares, May 1963

Last Night in Calcutta

Still night. The old clock Ticks,
half past two. A ringing of crickets
awake in the ceiling. The gate is locked
on the street outside—sleepers, mustaches,
nakedness, but no desire. A few mosquitoes
waken the itch, the fan turns slowly—
a car thunders along the black asphalt,
a bull snorts, something is expected—
Time sits solid in the four yellow walls.
No one is here, emptiness filled with train
whistles & dog barks, answered a block away.
Pushkin sits on the bookshelf, Shakespeare's
complete works as well as Blake's unread—
O Spirit of Poetry, no use calling on you
babbling in this emptiness furnished with beds
under the bright oval mirror—perfect
night for sleepers to dissolve in tranquil
blackness, and rest there eight hours
—Waking to stained fingers, bitter mouth
and lung gripped by cigarette hunger,
what to do with this big toe, this arm
this eye in the starving skeleton-filled
sore horse tramcar-heated Calcutta in
Eternity—sweating and teeth rotted away—
Rilke at least could dream about lovers,
the old breast excitement and trembling belly,
is that it? And the vast starry space—
If the brain changes matter breathes
fearfully back on man—But now
the great crash of buildings and planets
breaks thru the walls of language and drowns
me under its Ganges heaviness forever.
No escape but thru Bangkok and New York death.
Skin is sufficient to be skin, that's all
it ever could be, tho screams of pain in the kidney
make it sick of itself, a wavy dream
dying to finish its all too famous misery

—Leave immortality for another to suffer like a fool,
not get stuck in the corner of the universe
sticking morphine in the arm and eating meat.

May 22, 1963

Understand That This Is a Dream

Real as a dream
What shall I do with this great opportunity to fly?
What is the interpretation of this planet, this moon?
If I can dream that I dream / and dream anything dreamable / can I dream
I am awake / and why do that?
When I dream in a dream that I wake / up what
happens when I try to move?
I dream that I move
and the effort moves and moves
till I move / and my arm hurts
Then I wake up / dismayed / I was dreaming / I was waking
when I was dreaming still / just now.
and try to remember next time in dreams
that I am in dreaming.
And dream anything I want when I'm awaken.
When I'm in awakeness what do I desire?
I desire to fulfill my emotional belly.
My whole body my heart in my fingertips thrill with some old fulfillments.
Pages of celestial rhymes burning fire-words
unconsumable but disappear.
Arcane parchments my own and the universe the answer.
Belly to Belly and knee to knee.
The hot spurt of my body to thee to thee
old boy / dreamy Earl / you Prince of Paterson / now king of me / lost
      Haledon
first dream that made me take down my pants
urgently to show the cars / auto trucks / rolling down avenue hill.
That far back what do I remember / but the face of the leader of the gang
was blond / that loved me / one day on the steps of his house blocks away
all afternoon I told him about my magic Spell
I can do anything I want / palaces millions / chemistry sets / chicken
      coops / white horses
stables and torture basements / I inspect my naked victims
chained upside down / my fingertips thrill approval on their thighs
white hairless cheeks I may kiss all I want
at my mercy. on the racks.
I pass with my strong attendants / I am myself naked
bending down with my buttocks out
for their smacks of reproval / o the heat of desire

like shit in my asshole. The strange gang
across the street / thru the grocerystore / in the wood alley / out in the open
on the corner /
Because I lied to the Dentist about that chickencoop roofing / slate stolen off
his garage
by me and the boy I loved who would punish me if he knew
what I loved him.
That now I have had that boy back in another blond form
Peter Orlovsky a Chinese teenager in Bangkok ten years twenty years
Joe Army on the campus / white blond loins / my mouth hath kisses /
full of his cock / my ass burning / full of his cock
all that I do desire. In dream and awake
this handsome body mine / answered
all I desired / intimate loves / open eyed / revealed at last / clothes on the
floor
Underwear the most revealing stripped off below the belly button in bed.
That's that / yes yes / the flat cocks the red pricks the gentle pubic hair / a-
lone with me
my magic spell. My power / what I desire alone / what after thirty years /
I got forever / after thirty years / satisfied enough with Peter / with all I
wanted /
with many men I knew one generation / our sperm passing
into our mouths and bellies / beautiful when love / given.
Now the dream oldens / I olden / my hair a year long / my thirtyeight
birthday approaching.
I dream I
am bald / am disappearing / the campus unrecognizable / Haledon Avenue
will be covered with neon / motels / Supermarkets / iron
the porches and woods changed when I go back / to see Earl again
He'll be a bald / fleshy father / I could pursue him further in the garage
If there's still a garage on the hill / on the planet / when I get back. From
Asia.
If I could even remember his name or his face / or find him /
When I was ten / perhaps he exists in some form.
With a belly and a belt and an auto
Whatever his last name / I never knew / in the phonebook / the Akashic
records.
I'll write my Inspiration for all Mankind to remember,
My Idea, the secret cave / in the clothes closet / that house probably down /
Nothing to go back to / everything's gone / only my idea
that's disappearing / even in dreams / gray dust piles / instant annihilation
of World War II and all its stainless steel shining-mouthed cannons

much less me and my grammar school kisses / I never kissed in time /
and go on kissing in dream and out on the street / as if it were for ever.
No forever left! Even my oldest forever gone, in Bangkok, in Benares,
swept up with words and bodies / all into the brown Ganges /
passing the burning grounds and / into the police state.
My mind, my mind / you had six feet of Earth to hoe /
Why didn't you remember and plant the seed of Law and gather the sprouts
　　　of What?
the golden blossoms of what idea? If I dream that I dream / what dream
should I dream next? Motorcycle rickshaws / parting lamp shine / little tax-
　　　is / horses' hoofs
on this Saigon midnight street. Angkor Wat ahead and the ruined city's old
　　　Hindu faces
and there was a dream about Eternity. What should I dream when I wake?
What's left to dream, more Chinese meat? More magic Spells? More youths
　　　to love before I change & disappear?
More dream words? This can't go on forever. Now that I know it all /
goes whither? For now that I know I am dreaming /
What next for you Allen? Run down to the Presidents Palace full of Mor-
　　　phine /
the cocks crowing / in the street. / Dawn trucks / What is the question?
Do I need sleep, now that there's light in the window?
I'll go to sleep. Signing off until / the next idea / the moving van arrives
　　　empty
at the Doctor's house full of Chinese furniture.

Saigon, May 31–June 1, 1963

Angkor Wat

      Angkor—on top of the terrace
in a stone nook in the rain
Avalokitesvara faces everywhere
    high in their stoniness
        in white rainmist

    Slithering hitherward paranoia
        Banyans trailing
          high muscled tree crawled
over the roof its big
long snaky toes spread
      down the lintel's red
           cradle-root
           elephantine bigness

    Buddha I take my refuge
bowing in the black bower
before the openhanded lotus-man
       sat crosslegged
and riding in the rain in the
         anxious motorcycle putting
         in the wetness my shirt
         covered with green plastic
        apron shivering
          and throat choking
          with upsurge
          of stroke fear
            cancer Bubonic
            heart failure
          bitter stomach juices
a wart growing on my rib
Objection! This can't be
         Me!

What happens to me when I get high
The echo of Sitaram, Sitaram Hindu

fears—eat no meat or vomit
the body—warnings in dream bearded
Das Thakur—obsessed
     with meat, smoking, ganja
     sex, cannibal spies, Prop-
     agation of this Skin, thin
     vegetable soups, they was
all Chinese eating pigs, was seven
     slanteyes watching me drink tea
     till I saluted the Buddha-baby in
       the cloth flowered pram
       sucking its chubby plum
Music from Walt Disney hearts and roses
       sweet violins—
     yellow skins landing on the green
     vegetable planet—
seven children with identical haircuts
       very polite, saluting
           clasped hand bow—
the Fear ordering peas in the French
       restaurant, with whole garlic
       bread cheese and coffee hot
and
a

b
a
n
a
n
a to finish the bill on the table

pink
p
o
n
k of the rain on the roof tin
below my shuttered window
   in the neon light a Hotel
     clean tiled room

U
n
d
e
r a fan and canopied mosquito net

All well in this solitude, plenty money
for a long ride thru the forest in a
        rainy afternoon with
            long hair wet beard
        glasses clouding—and that
        nausea—passing out
of the Churning of the Ocean

           asuras with teeth fangs
              and fat eared Devas
              with military mustaches

        hanging on to the great Chain Snake
           muscle sandstone railing
             length of the moat-bridge to
the South Gate, Avalokitesvara's huge
        many faces in opposite directions
              in high space
        thru which ran new black road
        at the knees of greater trees, one

needed a haircut, root-hair sprouting
        on branches—thru the forested
        Castle grounds to pathways fallen
          sandstone headless statues
      Damp black bas-relief Dancing Shiva
             or angel lady

The huge snake roots, the vaster
        serpent arms fallen
        octopus over the roof

in a square courtyard—curved
    roofcombs looked Dragon-back-
        stone-scaled
As frail as stone is, this harder wooden
    life crushing them

    with the cricket-glare and parrot
        squads walking across the roof
—last nite full moon in misted heaven
and slow girl dance bent elbow and inspring
    fingers snaking it thru the middle—

    I am afraid where I am
  "I am inert" . . . "I'm just doing my
    Professional duty" . . . "I'm scheming
    murders" . . . "I'm chasing a story"
I'm not going to eat meat anymore
I'm taking refuge in the Buddha Dharma Sangha
Hare Krishna Hare Krishna
Krishna Krishna Hare Hare
Hare Rama Hare Rama
Rama Rama Hare Hare

who how satisfying in the ocean night
    as the exit of laughing gas,
      or the thrice-real moment of hashish
  or the "ordering men about, playing god,
        without drugs"

american husbands in sportshirts with clear,
    bright eyes and legs spread in
      the velocipedomotor bripping
      on holiday from US Army Saigon
       streets hotels   I hitched
    get polite when you'se a hiker

"I going to take *both* sides"

You have no right being a Hitler repeating that
        Abhaya mudra reassurance
           Palm out flat, patting the airhide
              of earth—

Nothing but a false Buddha afraid of
        my own annihilation, Leroi Moi—
afraid to fail you yet terror those Men
        their tiger pictures and uniforms
            dream to see that Kerouac tiger too—
Helikopter to— Sh, spies with telescopes
           for seeing the bullets that shoot—

Leroi I been done you wrong
I'm just an old Uncle Tom in disguise all along
            afraid of physical tanks.
     and those buzzing headphones in my skull.
   and many a butterfly committed suicide
        its wings to the motheaten flame—
Agh! I vomited in fear of the forest of ganja meats—
Eternal Death silliness—Cowards die many times
Not even afraid to be a Coward—Ashamed only by
     metal voices declaring war on Darkness

I seen plenty corpses but not them living wound-flowers
        healing split open "mouths" as you see the
           War Correspondent who wanted to Bash China
Even I wound up with his Titoist anxieties

Whatever happened to Jeannie Frigididia
        Jeanette MacDonald and Nelson Eddy
           radio 20 years behind Cambodia
    Sounds like love is so sweet springtime

all in my head going down worried
        about changing 100 Reales of meat
Whatever you think happened to
            Jeannie Frigididia?
Whatyathink happen to the Frigididy girl?
You think she'll be in the Ille Frigididy news?
Is the Frigididy Universe gonna be awakened?
            Is Leary my laughter?

Plus ça change tonight from 6 P.M.
        wet handed by meat sex
drank tea, drank carrot-potato thin soup
        bread cheese coffee peas pies coffee
        pineapple soda
walked on the rainy.   run out of ink
            market
To write a letter to President Norodom Sihanouk
        to live in the flower-jazz palace at Phnom Penh
        Kingly neutrality enter China for U.P.
            from Hong Kong
        write to Eisenhower, politely inquiring
        get China off the hook
        war of races not Marxism in

Viet Nam Pres. Diem's Queer picture
            —a spy in the chinese soup
            on the restaurant bench—I being also a
            spy for the Left Consuling

        "Geez that's a great job yr doing fellers
            keep it up"

I wish I could fly o'er the leaves of the jungle and not
        get killed see the bamboo stakes
        piercing the foot of the beefy Marine?
    or the bodies Viet Cong piled on the tank
        Vietnamese bosses at Ap Bac battle lost whodunit?
President's messages back and forth in French and Charming

Ike give OK retreat from pregnant belly
             of S.E. Asia,
Antichinese riots Indonesia—out of the papers—
             not seen *Newsweek* a week or the *Times*

Monsoon riding thru the forest gate faces
Creepers silence on Ta-Phrom temple halls
             narrow stone walk under sleeping trees—
             rain on Ta-Keo pyramid—perfect faces
             smiling ladies' fiery headdresses in Thommanom
       till passing the soda stand in forest arbor
             ganja cigarette rolled in Terrasse Supérieur
                    rooftower by Ikon
             of Buddha touching Earth
             the burnt out incense sticks in the tipped can
                    I straightened and shoes off bowed

As I rode thru the forest Hari Hindoo and Lord of Mercy
             struggled like Asur-Devas
             with my mind-snake drifting
             motorized under the trees—that
       long road with a dip and slow strange
       rise into the arch of the four-headed
             Smile—gate to the old park
             of Khmer palaces—ancient morphine
       in a room—Garuda bebeaked and wing-sphinxed—

The many Sphinx-heads with ears on the towers
Looking around the country seventeen, cheek on eye,
Bewildered in a hurry in the rain to make
       this City conquered by Chams (upriver
       burning the wooden city) of
                    Stone to last in forest
       Even that permanence warped cleaned
             in the Alice in Wonderland giant garden
             of Ta-Phrom—followed

by the young guardian with a caterpillar-
       like green frond in his hair

—he shrank back a second when I went to
     touch his crown

And I'm following them naked to the waist
     chinese smooth limbed workmen or darker
     Cambodian cyclist Prisoners cutting the grass
     by the Grand Hotel's

cool waiting room with bar and USIS handout
     news-casts only Journals except
     for the State Paper reprinting the Prince
       King's questionless speech to
     Journalists itching with neon—

So many grounds to cover the terrors of the day
All got to do with snakes and only one shy
     tail, I saw disappearing behind a
     rock, slow banded worm—the smiles
of Avalokitesvara with his big mouth like
     Cambodian Pork Chops—the boys
and why do I not even faintly desire those
     black silk girls in the alley of this
       clean new tourist city?—
Ah those Deva faces on the walls of Thommanom!
     Clean eyebrows and smiles of Lady Yore
Ever Naomi in my ear—a sad case of refusing to
     grow up give birth to die—

I am Coward in every direction—Coughing
     in the motorcycle trailer seat but
     the beautiful forest hath its rain to
       drown my noises—

     Home to the Needle, further violation
or is this vegetable smoke and vein warmth
     futile in the light of my friends Pronouncements

Maybe Gary'll have the answer! Maybe Jack have
        the Answer? Will the Army answer me,

              or will a clang of bells herald the God Creeley
To whom I sent postcards of the cold stonebrows—
        in the green—on the spot

"Blind white mossed gray carved
blocks of stone noses smiling
thin lips
              green mossy fronds of giant
trees, the white drift smoke
sky
      The millions of familiar
raindrops dripping in
floor rock crevasses
              on the broken crown of the
gray lotus
              The stone benches on the roof
Snake balustrades
              Buddha's faces on the
many towers, the forest snakes
waiting in the tall trunks of
              wooden trees
Oh the beautiful pour of the rain noises
waiting below the money cyclopede
Motor driver covered with blue plastic
              Angkor
where I dreamed of trembling to
write—here again after the
hot sun, sleeping and dreaming
2 days ago—back in the wished
for rain past
        rain on my elbows

Buddha save me, what am
        I doing here
again   dreamed of this
        This awful stone monument
        being in the streams

of change or the Clouds
        in the sky—
Kneeled to the statue on
        Porch
Saranam Gochamee Catchme quick
      forced with incense—have to
      go down to the
         velocycle
      thru the bat-tower
        again, or out
    in the rain!"

As might be read for poesy by Olson
At least moves from perception to obsession
      according to waves of Me-ness
    Still clinging to the Earthen straw
        My eye

    Confused with this blue sky cloud drift
        "illusion" over the treetops

    dwelling in my mind "frightened aging nagging flesh"
To step *out* of—? Who, Me?

Just a lot of words and propaganda
    I been spreading getting scared
    of my own bullshit
Except when faced with my confusion
    words meat / death
        mind-soup
    eaten last night, greedily fried macaroni
      with rare beef—all the children
      scream at my long awkward hair,

On the bed as I ached and strained my
    sphincter opened hoped

to get next time befucked by
　　　a Cambodian sweet policeman
　　from the bicycle first day
who had Lord Buddha's lips as on
the towers—all alike many boys—the Monks
　　of Lolei, smoking and eating beef,
　　touched my toes and my beard pulled
　　　　by the shaven kid in yellow

Nandi the bull waiting her owner in the Sun
　　　The house crumbling and Vishnu's arms
　　　　broken, heads off the seated
　　　　　statues
　　　bat families hanging upside down in the
　　　　door beams' cracks—Chinese families

overrunning the earth like greeneyed children of
　　　Science-fiction—Shall I blow
　　　them up, Professor?—and

O Leaf of Buddha! when we get to
　　the green planets will we fight
　　the strange snaky races of—
　　　Cancer Overpopulation
It's a pyramid of faces—Sphinx-Avalokitesvara
all mixed up, I hope Buddha's been there,
Then we'll know if his mind appeared
　　　in all the directions of Space—

The Pope died a saint to be dissolved in
　　　his Christ
Philip Lamantia prophesied truly, all but
　　Mao Tze Tung loved Pope John

Except those newspaper Catholics in Saigon
　　He didn't change their plans yet—

A walk, past the Saigon Market, where
　　　There's a few brass Buddhas for
　　　　　shop sale in the North Wing

Crost the big traffic circle between the Shell
　　　　　gas signs, where at nite the troop
　　　　　Cops got in buses to go to Hué
　　　　　　　Where telephones spoke blisters
　　　　　to the gas students—
　　　　　gathered in front of City Hall to redress
　　　　　their grievances—

Surabaya Johnnie not seen Bodrabadur Temple
　　　in Java next time round this part
　　　　　of the world

All the wire services eating sweet and
　　　sour pork and fresh cold lichee white-meat
　　　　　　in sugarwater—
Discussing the manly truth Gee Fellers—
Even the fat whitehaired belly boy from
　　　　　　　Time and his Kewpiedoll wife
Could've been seen in the movies dancing
　　　the rainy night at the border
　　　Chinese cha-cha, Hysteria
That UP kid flown down from Vientiane
　　　　　　Laos fugitive Hepatitis
　　　Scared of the Yellow Men, or the slow
　　　　　　Alcohol red face of the Logistics
　　　　　　Analyst—"I got the Eichmann syndrome"
said he newsweekly—reporters who
never committed suicide like
　　　　　Hemingway had to, faced
　　　　　with the fat newsman with
　　　　　　Seven children from
　　　　　　　Buddenbrooks
　　　They were living in Greece while Pound
　　　was taking a vow of silence
　　　　　　"I knew too much"
　　　but it was all a mistake,

I fled the Mekong delta, fled the 12,000
        Military speaking hot dog guts on the
        downtown aircooled streets,
fled the Catinat Hotel, flushed my shit
        down the bathroom—

jumped in the cab suddenly, afraid
after left Xaloi temple like a
        Negro disintegrated in New Orleans,
afraid to publish that or they bomb
        my typesetter's woodsy Balcony
                in Louisiana—

Everywhere it's the fear I got in my own
                intestines—Kenyatta Prime Minister
        peacefully with his fly-whisk

                and maybe the Mo Mo's underground
Mao-Mao—everywhere is my own Rhodesia
for Mysterious Choose Up Sides and Die
                like a "Man"

I never wanted to be a "human" being and
this is what I got—a himalayan
striped umbrella I don't use
in the jungle rain—my eyes
        Lid-heavy—my mind skips
back to the overweight knapsack I carry
all these years' scribbles bound in
Ganges towels—
                Down, to drink
        Iced coffee with sweet evaporated milk
        Chinese coffee in small glasses, but
        Manger les Tripes No No—not eat
        that mouthful of snake-apple

        "give up desire for children"
        give up—this Prophecy—

Everything drifted away in the dream
       even the stone buildings of Low Library,
       even the great dome of Columbia,
even the great cities of Khmer—weak
dancers at the portals of Angkor—
       where I saw the praying young
       head shaved peasant kneel at
       the foot of the stairs on a purple
         straw mat,
The cries of the boy dancers to the
      deliberate slow walking drum's
        triple beat—Faunlike
conscious asian steps on the
        stonewalk—My cries of Sex
        in bed echoed in their
           lap-head grass eyes—
Motorcyclists crying together
entering the inner gates to
the huge temple left behind by other
Hindu dreamers—Kingdom
Come or Kingdom Yore—

       reassurance from Buddha's
       two arms, palms out
          stept up to 13th Century
          Sukothai feminacy
            step forward—

I've read the 1910 Guidebook about them
      giant trees strangling the heavy palace
one altar full of little black bugs I never saw
              before,
Broken or stray Lingams left over from another
        Imperial History, Goon squads with Moats,
Kingly reservoirs dried up, must've
been a big city full of wooden poles right
       near here, bamboo thatchments
         Chinese babies screaming at the bearded
         Han traveler—Palms together
           Salute I don't care I don't know

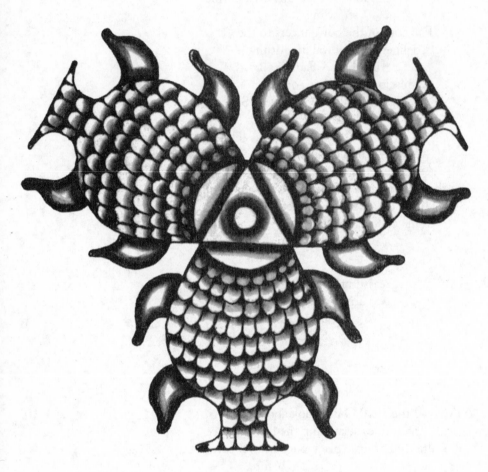

Buddha footprint repetition

Make that a dozen eggs—split em easy.
Make that pig—tied up on the running board
        between iron spokes, with a sharp
    wood stick set between his legs to
carry him squeaking hoarsely pro-
        testing being man-handled to
        get his throat cut for chinese
            hordes—yes they eat

So much pork they'll make a butcher shop
        restaurant of the whole white folks universe
    which should be owned by Negroes but is
        really haircut like Jews or
            Indian Mounties in
                Northern Canada
They been "throwing up radioactive dolphins
        in their icy bays—"?
There was a great ice-floe up north I
        saw holes in the sea crust, weir
    cold green brine slurping up, or mist
    on my fingernail—

I sat in a hammock and waited—a
            big hole appeared in the English
                            Channel
        To let the human beings thru, hordes
        from Italy into White Anglia
    England achange—Stonehenge who
    went back that far to worship the
                        Sun?

Lady Mort's wormy intestines,
    always passed the basement in the Louvre
with that Knight-at-Arms on a stone
    black table carried by hooded monks
        big as huge children getting
            stoned, tired—

It can can't go on forever. I'm in the
    Jet Set, according to my memory,
    dissociated in Space from
    Bangkok to Calcutta 2 hours
        from Bangkok to Saigon the
          old elegance of the hitch thumb
          in Texas past the valley
             town and the green river—

    Coughing in the airplane and my ears hurt
      a headache on the local slow
        airboat—over the great
        water, carrying the 10 tiny
          Buddhas of the negligent
            Mahant of Bodh Gaya—

    Jumping in and out of space—soon
faster than light I'll go back to the
Graham Avenue past, and stare out the
    window happily at Paul R——
    passing down the 1942 Broadway—
the gothic church, the alleys and
    Synagogues of Mea Shearim,

Jerusalem's hated Walls—
I couldn't get over to the Holy Side and weep
      where I was supposed to by History
      Laws got confused stamped
    in my passport, lost in the refugee
      Station at Calcutta. It
winds in and out of space and time the
    physical traveler—
Returning home at last, years later as
    prophesied, "Is this the way that
      I'm supposed to feel?"

with my nightmare underwear downtown
    in the gray haunted midnight street

foggy Vancouver was winter
          then now Summer I'll see
Thru the clear air the great Northern Mountains
    and aspire that lonely visible
    Space-peak before entering the

Moils of New Frisco San York Orleans
      Castro Bomb Shade Protest Shelter
Better write a letter warning against
    the
        Aswan Nile not seen
        Peking's Jewelry feet not Come true
Surely I'll live to take tea in a back yard
    in Kyoto and be calm!

"Make me ready—but not yet"
No I am not "ready" to die when that Choke
comes I'm afraid I'll scream and
        embarrass everybody—go out
like a coward yellow fear I done left no
        Louis babies behind me Rebuke in
          Those 70 year eyes and I speak of Murder
            blessing him?—Alas
to be kinder except   I *was* kind to the
        Man on park bench after the Nite Club

          who "schemed murders" as an
        analyst for air forces.
They need conscience-stricken analysts, I'm
    a conscious-stricken panelist on this
    university show.
            Forward March, guessing
    which bullet which airplane which nausea
    be the dreadful doomy last
        begun while I'm still
conscious—I'll go down and get a cold coffee at
          Midnight

              Siemréap, Cambodia, June 10, 1963

The Change: *Kyoto–Tokyo Express*

I
Black Magicians
Come home: the pink meat image
    black yellow image with
    ten fingers and two eyes
is gigantic already: the black
    curly pubic hair, the
    blind hollow stomach,
the silent soft open vagina
    rare womb of new birth
cock lone and happy to be home
                again
touched by hands by mouths,
    by hairy lips—

Close the portals of the festival?

Open the portals to what Is,
The mattress covered with sheets,
    soft pillows of skin,
long soft hair and delicate
    palms along the buttocks
    timidly touching,
waiting for a sign, a throb
    softness of balls, rough
    nipples alone in the dark
    met by a weird finger;
Tears allright, and laughter
    allright
I am that I am—

        Closed off from this
The schemes begin, roulette,
    brainwaves, bony dice,
    Stroboscope motorcycles
    Stereoscopic Scaly
        Serpents winding thru
        cloud spaces of
           what is not—

". . . convoluted, lunging upon
a pismire, a conflagration, a—"

II
Shit! Intestines boiling in sand fire
    creep yellow brain cold sweat
    earth unbalanced vomit thru
    tears, snot ganglia buzzing
    the Electric Snake rising hypnotic
    shuffling metal-eyed coils
    whirling rings within wheels
    from asshole up the spine
    Acid in the throat the chest
    a knot trembling Swallow back
    the black furry ball of the great
Fear

Oh!

The serpent in my bed pitiful
    crawling unwanted babes of
    snake covered with veins and pores
    breathing heavy frightened love
    metallic Bethlehem out the window
    the lost, the lost hungry
    ghosts here alive trapped
    in carpet rooms   How can I
    be sent to Hell
    with my skin and blood

Oh I remember myself so

Gasping, staring at dawn over
    lower Manhattan   the bridges
    covered with rust, the slime
    in my mouth & ass, sucking
    his cock like a baby crying Fuck
    me in my asshole   Make love
    to this rotten slave   Give me the
    power to whip & eat your heart
    I own your belly & your eyes

I speak thru your screaming
mouth Black Mantra Fuck you
Fuck me Mother Brother Friend
old white haired creep shuddering in
the toilet slum bath floorboards—

Oh how wounded, how wounded, I
murder the beautiful chinese women

It will come on the railroad, beneath
the wheels, in drunken hate screaming
thru the skinny machine gun, it will
come out of the mouth of the pilot
the dry lipped diplomat, the hairy
teacher will come out of me
again shitting the meat out of
my ears on my cancer deathbed

Oh crying man crying woman
crying guerrilla shopkeeper
crying dysentery boneface on
the urinal street of the Self

Oh Negro beaten in the eye in my
home, oh black magicians
in white skin robes boiling the
stomachs of your children that
you do not die but shudder in
Serpent & worm shape forever
Powerful minds & superhuman
Roar of volcano & rocket in
Your bowels—

Hail to your fierce desire, your
Godly pride, my Heaven's gate
will not be closed until
we enter all—

All human shapes, all
trembling donkeys & apes, all
lovers turned to ghost
all achers on trains &

taxicab bodies sped away
from date with desire, old movies,
all who were refused—

All which was rejected, the
leper-sexed hungry of
nazi conventions, hollow
cheeked arab marxists of Acco
Crusaders dying of starvation
in the Holy Land—

Seeking the Great Spirit of the
Universe in Terrible Godly
form, O suffering Jews
burned in the hopeless fire
O thin Bengali sadhus adoring
Kali mother hung with
nightmare skulls O Myself
under her pounding
feet!

Yes I am that worm soul under
the heel of the daemon horses
I am that man trembling to die
in vomit & trance in bamboo
eternities belly ripped by
red hands of courteous
chinamen kids—Come sweetly
now back to my Self as I was—

Allen Ginsberg says this: I am
a mass of sores and worms
& baldness & belly & smell
I am false Name the prey
of Yamantaka Devourer of
Strange dreams, the prey of
radiation & Police Hells of Law

I am that I am I am the
man & the Adam of hair in
my loins   This is my spirit and
physical shape I inhabit

this Universe Oh weeping
   against what is my
   own nature for now

Who would deny his own shape's
   loveliness in his
   dream moment of bed
   Who sees his desire to be
   horrible instead of Him

Who is, who cringes, perishes,
   is reborn a red Screaming
   baby? Who cringes before
   that meaty shape in
            Fear?

In this dream I am the Dreamer
   and the Dreamed   I am
   that I am Ah but I have
   always known

oooh for the hate I have spent
   in denying my image & cursing
   the breasts of illusion—
   Screaming at murderers, trembling
   between their legs in fear of the
   steel pistols of my mortality—

Come, sweet lonely Spirit, back
   to your bodies, come great God
   back to your only image, come
   to your many eyes & breasts,
   come thru thought and
   motion up all your
   arms the great gesture of
   Peace & acceptance Abhaya
   Mudra Mudra of fearlessness
   Mudra of Elephant Calmed &
   war-fear ended forever!

The war, the war on Man, the
   war on woman, the ghost

assembled armies vanish in
    their realms

Chinese American Bardo Thodols
    all the seventy hundred hells from
    Orleans to Algeria tremble
    with tender soldiers weeping

In Russia the young poets rise
    to kiss the soul of the revolution
    in Vietnam the body is burned
    to show the truth of only the
    body in Kremlin & White House
    the schemers draw back
    weeping from their schemes—

In my train seat I renounce
    my power, so that I do
    live I will die

Over for now the Vomit, cut
    up & pincers in the skull,
    fear of bones, grasp
    against man woman & babe.

Let the dragon of Death
    come forth from his
    picture in the whirling
    white clouds' darkness

And suck dream brains &
    claim these lambs for his
    meat, and let him feed
    and be other than I

Till my turn comes and I
    enter that maw and change
    to a blind rock covered
    with misty ferns that
    I am not all now

but a universe of skin and breath
      & changing thought and
      burning hand & softened
      heart in the old bed of
      my skin   From this single
      birth reborn that I am
      to be so—

My own Identity now nameless
      neither man nor dragon or
      God

but the dreaming Me full
      of physical rays' tender
      red moons in my belly &
      Stars in my eyes circling

And the Sun the Sun the
      Sun my visible father
      making my body visible
      thru my eyes!
               Tokyo, July 18, 1963

VII
KING OF MAY:
AMERICA
TO EUROPE
(1963–1965)

Nov. 23, 1963: Alone

Alone
in that same self where I always was
with Kennedy throat brain bloodied in Texas
the television continuous blinking two radar days
with Charlie muttering in his underwear strewn bedroom
with Neal running down the hall shouting about the racetrack
with Ann with her white boy's ass silent under the Cupid thigh
with Lucille talking to herself, feeding the pregnant cat Alice
with Anne mourning her pockmarked womb & the hard muscled chest of
    her Lover
with David's red wine fireplace casting shadows back to the Duchess farm-
    boy faggot of Wichita, on fire in mainstreet
with Lance with his crummy painting & leopard blue breast seeking to buy
    a motorcycle to crosscountry smiling & wan
with the manuscripts of nutritious Roselle the New York suicide on the
    round mahogany table near the kitchen
with Leroi Jones' white-eyeballed war-cry unread, babbling in postmortem
    blue-sneer
with myself confused shock-fingertipt on the rented typewriter
with Alan with horses' teeth metafysiks demurely insisting he was intensely
    so over coffee
with Glen o' the lisp & Justin the olding bluejacketed man-love off in autos
    to Mexico cactus hope
with the fat lady with babe in the auto, feeding & grieving her adolescence's
    backseat
with "Go to Hell" spoke on the streetcorner down hill in dark November
    night
with Judy's blood in the furnace building up weeks before in campus-forest
    headlines, white-haired parents on Television
with Christopher running around in raincoats talking fast about his eyesock-
    ets seeing true streets of '60s
with Jaime phoning collect from New York insulting his lonesome Cunt
with Nemmie insisting she was drunk & insulting on the couch & Marko
    with a bandaged tendon hanging in front of his gaptooth
with Hubert in beret & tweed beard absolutely sober on meth-freak newspa-
    per splatter rorschach universe, drinking milk
with Jordan on the phone suave & retired jobbing invisible mandalas upstairs
    from the technicolor gutter

with Larry whitehaired chewing his teeth nodding in chairs weak & amiable
   lost the pointlessness
with the cat curled in white fur in the kitchen chair
with the transistor radio silent weeks on the typewriter desk
with the novels *Happiness Bastard Sheeper* from Tangier Wichita *Mad Cub*
   Yesterday Today & Tomorrow
with *Now*, with *Fuck You*, with *Wild Dog   Burning Bush Poetry   Evergreen
   C   Thieves   Journal   Soft   Machine   Genesis   Renaissance   Contact
   Kill Roy* Etc.
with spaniards appearing at the doors to know what's happening you wanna
   score or am I the sacred fear the meth-head fuzz the insect trust or
   delicious José
with Robert in his black jacket & tie deciding to make a point of his courtesy
   over the kitchen linoleum
with the Ghosts of Natalie & Peter & Krishna & Ram intoned on the shag
   rugs in the darkness of abandoned rooms
with *Blue Grace* in typescript stepping out of the taxi on the wall, and letters
   arriving from Málaga & Chicago
with me breaking off to rush in to the other room where Adam & Eve lie
   to get my hair spermy.

Why Is God Love, Jack?

Because I lay my
      head on pillows,
Because I weep in the
      tombed studio
Because my heart
      sinks below my navel
because I have an
      old airy belly
   filled with soft
      sighing, and
   remembered breast
      sobs—or
a hand's touch makes
      tender—
Because I get scared—
Because I raise my
      voice singing to
            my beloved self—
Because I do love thee
      my darling, my
      other, my living
            bride
my friend, my old lord
      of soft tender eyes—
Because I am in the
      Power of life & can
      do no more than
      submit to the feeling
      that I am the One
            Lost
Seeking still seeking the
      thrill—delicious
      bliss in the
            heart abdomen loins
            & thighs
Not refusing this
      38 yr. 145 lb. head
      arms & feet of meat

Nor one single Whitmanic
    toenail contemn
nor hair prophetic banish
    to remorseless Hell,
Because wrapped with machinery
I confess my ashamed desire.

New York, 1963

Morning

Ugh! the planet screams
Doves in rusty cornice-
      castles peer
down on auto crossroads,
    a junkey in white jacket
wavers in yellow light on
      way to a negro in bed
Black smoke flowing on roofs, terrific
      city coughing—
garbage can lids music over
      truck whine on E. 5th St.
Ugh! I'm awake again—
      dreary day ahead
what to do?—Dull letters
      to be answered
an epistle to M. Duchamp
more me all day the same
clearly

      Q. "Do you want to live or die?"
      A. "I don't know"
   said Julius after 12 years
         State Hospital

Ugh! cry negroes in Harlem
Ugh! cry License Inspectors, Building
        Inspectors, Police Congressmen,
        Undersecretaries of Defense.
Ugh! Cries Texas Mississippi!
Ugh! Cries India
Ugh! Cries US
        Well, who knows?

O flowing copious!
    total Freedom! To
Do what? to blap! to
      embarrass! to conjoin
Locomotive blossoms to Leafy
      purple vaginas.

To be dull! ashamed! shot!
    Finished! Flopped!
To say Ugh absolutely mean-
    ingless here
To be a big bore! even to
    myself! Fulla shit!

Paper words! Fblup! Fizzle! Droop!
Shut your big fat mouth!
Go take a flying crap in the
        rain!
Wipe your own ass! Bullshit!
You big creep! Fairy! Dopy
    Daffodil! Stinky Jew!
Mr. Professor! Dirty Rat! Fart!

Honey! Darling! Sweetie pie!
Baby! Lovey! Dovey! Dearest!
My own! Buttercup! O Beautiful!
Doll! Snookums! Go fuck
          yourself,
      everybody Ginsberg!
And when you've exhausted
    that, go forward?
Where? kiss my ass!

O Love, my mouth against
    a black policeman's breast.

                 New York, 1963

Waking in New York

I
I place my hand before my beard with awe
and stare thru open-uncurtain window
           rooftop rose-blue sky thru
           which small dawn clouds ride
                rattle against the pane,
      lying on a thick carpet matted floor
          at last in repose on pillows my knees
            bent beneath brown himalayan blanket, soft—
fingers atremble to pen, cramp
         pressure diddling the page white
            San Francisco notebook—
And here am on the sixth floor cold
         March 5th Street old building plaster
         apartments in ruin, super he drunk
           with baritone radio AM nose-sex
Oh New York, oh Now our bird
         flying past glass window Chirp
       —our life together here
      smoke of tenement chimney pots dawn haze
         passing thru wind soar Sirs—

How shall we greet Thee this Springtime oh Lords—?
What gifts give ourselves, what police fear
         stop searched in late streets
Rockefeller Frisk No-Knock break down
        my iron white-painted door?
Where shall I seek Law? in the State
        in offices of telepath bureaucracy—?
in my dis-ease, my trembling, my cry
       —ecstatic song to myself
to my police my law my state my
        many selfs—
Aye, Self is Law and State Police
    Kennedy struck down knew him Self
Oswald, Ruby ourselves
        Till we know our desires Blest
        with babe issue,
           Resolve, accept

this self flesh we bear
in underwear, Bathrobe, smoking cigarette
up all night—brooding, solitary, set
alone, tremorous leg & arm—
approaching the joy of Alones
Racked by that, arm laid to rest,
head back wide-eyed

Morning, my song to Who listens, to
myself as I am
To my fellows in this shape that building
Brooklyn Bridge or Albany name—
Salute to the self-gods on
Pennsylvania Avenue!
May they have mercy on us all,
May be just men not murderers
Nor the State murder more,
That all beggars be fed, all
dying medicined, all loveless
Tomorrow be loved
well come & be balm.

March 16, 1964

II
On the roof cloudy sky fading sun rays
electric torches atop—
auto horns—The towers
with time-hands giant pointing
late Dusk hour over
clanky roofs
Tenement streets' brick sagging cornices
baby white kite fluttering against giant
insect face-gill Electric Mill
smokestacked blue & fumes drift up
Red messages, shining high floors,
Empire State dotted with tiny windows
lit, across the blocks
of spire, steeple, golden topped utility
building roofs—far like
pyramids lit in jagged
desert rocks—

The giant the giant city awake
        in the first warm breath of springtime
Waking voices, babble of Spanish
        street families, radio music
        floating under roofs, longhaired
          announcer sincerity squawking
              cigar voice
      Light zips up phallos stories
        beneath red antennae needling
          thru rooftop chimneys' smog
           black drift thru the blue air—
Bridges curtained by uplit apartment walls,
        one small tower with a light
        on its shoulder below the "moody, water-loving giants"

The giant stacks burn thick gray
        smoke, Chrysler is lit with green,
down Wall street islands of skyscraper
      black jagged in Sabbath quietness—
Oh fathers, how I am alone in this
        vast human wilderness
Houses uplifted like hives off
        the stone floor of the world—
the city too vast to know, too
        myriad windowed to govern
        from ancient halls—
"O edifice of gas!"—Sun shafts
     descend on the highest building's
       striped blocktop a red light
         winks buses hiss & rush
         grinding, green lights
         of north bridges,
           hum roar & Tarzan
            squeal, whistle
            swoops, hurrahs!

Is someone dying in all this stone building?
Child poking its black head out of the womb
        like the pupil of an eye?
Am I not breathing here frightened
           and amazed—?

Where is my comfort, where's heart-ease,
      Where are tears of joy?
Where are the companions? in
         deep homes in Stuyvesant Town
         behind the yellow-window wall?
I fail, book fails—a lassitude,
        a fear—tho I'm alive
and gaze over the descending—No!
peer in the inky beauty of the roofs.

April 18, 1964

After Yeats

Now incense fills the air
and delight follows delight,
quiet supper in the carpet room,
music twangling from the Orient to my ear,
old friends at rest on bright mattresses,
old paintings on the walls, old poetry
thought anew, laughing at a mystic toy
statue painted gold, tea on the white table.

New York, April 26, 1964

I Am a Victim of Telephone

When I lie down to sleep dream the Wishing Well it rings
"Have you a new play for the brokendown theater?"
When I write in my notebook poem it rings
"Buster Keaton is under the brooklyn bridge on Frankfurt and Pearl . . ."
When I unsheath my skin extend my cock toward someone's thighs fat or
thin, boy or girl
Tingaling—"Please get him out of jail . . . the police are crashing down"
When I lift the soupspoon to my lips, the phone on the floor begins purring
"Hello it's me—I'm in the park two broads from Iowa . . . nowhere to sleep
last night . . . hit 'em in the mouth"
When I muse at smoke crawling over the roof outside my street window
purifying Eternity with my eye observation of gray vaporous columns in the
sky
ring ring "Hello this is Esquire be a dear and finish your political commit-
ment manifesto"
When I listen to radio presidents roaring on the convention floor
the phone also chimes in "Rush up to Harlem with us and see the riots"
Always the telephone linked to all the hearts of the world beating at once
crying my husband's gone my boyfriend's busted forever my poetry was
rejected
won't you come over for money and please won't you write me a piece of
bullshit
How are you dear can you come to Easthampton we're all here bathing in
the ocean we're all so lonely
and I lie back on my pallet contemplating $50 phone bill, broke, drowsy,
anxious, my heart fearful of the fingers dialing, the deaths, the singing
of telephone bells
ringing at dawn ringing all afternoon ringing up midnight ringing now
forever.

New York, June 20, 1964

Today

O I am happy! O Swami Shivananda—a smile!
O telephone sweet little black being, what many voices and tongues!
Tonight I'll call up Jack tell him Buster Keaton is under the Brooklyn Bridge
by a vast red-brick wall still dead pan alive in red suspenders, portly abdo-
men.
Today I saw movies, publishers, bookstores, checks—wait, I'm still poor
Poor but happy! I saw politicians we wrote a Noise Law!
A Law to free poetry—Poor Plato! Whoops here comes Fascism! I rode in
a taxi!
I rode a bus, ate hot Italian Sausages, Coca-Cola, a chili-burger, Kool-Aid I
drank—
All day I did things! I took a nap—didn't I dream about lampshade academies
and ouch! I am dying?
I stuck a needle in my arm and flooded my head with drowsy bliss . . .
And a hairy bum asked Mr. Keaton for money drink! Oh Buster! No answer!
Today I was really amazed! Samuel Beckett had rats eyes and gold round
glasses—
I didn't say a word—I had my picture taken and read all thru the NY Times
and Daily News, I read everybody's editorials, I protested in my mind I have
the privilege of being
Mad. Today I did everything, I wore a pink shirt in the street, at home in
underwear
I marveled Henry Miller's iron sink, how could he remember so clearly?
Hypnagogic vision in Brooklyn 50 years ago—just now my eyeball
troops marched in square mufti battalion dragging prisoners to—
eyelids lifted I saw a blue devil with fifteen eyes on the wall—everything's
mine, antique Tibetan Tankas, a siamese cat asleep on its side re-
laxed—
I looked out of the window and saw Tonight, it was dark—someone said
ooo! in Puerto Rican.
But it was light all day, sweating hot—iron eyes blinking at the human
element—
Irreducible Me today, I bought cigarettes at a machine, I was really worried
about my gross belly independent of philosophy, drama, idealism im-
agery—
My fate and I became one today and today became today—
just like a mystic prophecy—I'll conquer my belly tomorrow
or not, I'll toy with Mr. Choice also for real—today I said "Forever"
thrice—

and walked under the vast Ladder of Doom, insouciant, not merely innocent
but completely hopeless! In Despair when I woke this morning,
my mouth furry smoked a Lucky Strike first thing when I dialed telephone
     to check on the Building Department—
I considered the License Department as I brushed my teeth with an odd
     toothbrush
some visitor left I lost mine—where? rack my brains it's there
somewhere in the past—with the snubnosed uncle cock from the freakshow
The old man familiar today, first time I thought of him in years, in the rain
in Massachusetts but I was a child that summer The pink thing bulged at his
     open thigh fly
he fingered it out to show me—I tarried till startled when the whiskied
     barker
questioned mine I ran out on the boardwalk drizzle confronting the Atlantic
     Ocean
—so trotted around the silent moody blocks home speechless
to mother father vaginal jelly rubber instruments discovered in the closet—
a stealthy memory makes hackles rise—"He inserts his penis into her va-
     gina"—
What a weird explanation! I who collected matchbook covers like J. P.
     Morgan
gloating over sodden discoveries in the wet gutter—O happy grubby sewers
     of Revere—distasteful riches—
hopeless treasure I threw away in a week when I realized it was endless to
     complete—
next year gathered all the heat in my loins to spurt my white surprise drops
     into the wet brown wood under a
steamy shower, I used the toilet paper cardboard skeleton tube
to rub and thrill around my unconscious own shaft—playing with myself
     unbeknownst to the entire population of Far Rockaway—
remembered it all today—many years thinking of Kali-Ma and other mat-
     ters—
a big surprise it was Me—Dear Reader, I seem strange to myself—
You recognize everything all over again where you are, it's wonderful
to be introduced to strangers who know you already—
like being Famous—a reverberation of Eternal Consciousness—
Today heraldic of Today, archetypal mimeograph machines reprinting ev-
     erybody's poetry,
like finishing a book of surrealism which I haven't read for years—
Benjamin Péret & René Crevel heroic for real—the old New Consciousness
     reminded
me today—how busy I was, how fatal like a man in the madhouse, distracted

with presence of dishes of food to eat—Today's *"stringbeans in the moonlight"*
Like today I brought home blueberry pie for the first time in years—
Also today bit by a mosquito (to be precise, toward dawn)
(toward dusk ate marshmallows at the News Stand and drank huge cold
      grape soda eyeing:
this afternoon's *Journal* headline FBI IN HARLEM, what kind of Nasty old
      Epic
Afternoons I imagine!) Another event, a $10 bill in my hands, debt repaid,
a café espresso smaller event—Feeling rich I bought a secondhand record of
      Gertrude Stein's actual Voice—
My day was Harmonious—Though I heard no mechanic music—
I noticed some Nazi propaganda—I wrote down my dream about Earth
      dying—I wanted to telephone Long Island—I stood on a street cor-
      ner and didn't know where to go—
I telephoned the Civil Liberties Union—discussed the Junk Problem &
      Supreme Court—
I thought I was planting suggestions in everybody's Me-ity—
thought a few minutes of Blake—his quatrains—I climbed four flights &
      stood at Fainlight's Chinatown door locked up—I'm being mysteri-
      ous—
What does this mean? Don't ask me today, I'm still thinking,
Trying to remember what happened while it's still happening—
I wrote a "poem," I scribbled quotation marks everywhere over Fate passing
      by
Sometimes I felt noble, sometimes I felt ugly, I spoke to man and woman
from *Times* & *Time*, summarized hugely—plots, cinematic glories, I boasted
      a little, subtly—
Was I seen thru? Too much happened to see thru All—
I was never alone except for two blocks by the park, nor was I unhappy—
I blessed my Guru, I felt like a shyster—told Ed how much I liked being
      made love to by delicate girl hands—
It's true, more girls should do that to us, we chalked up another mark what's
      wrong
and told everybody to register to vote this November—I stopped on the
      street and shook hands—
I took a crap once this day—How extraordinary it all goes! recollected, a
      lifetime!
Imagine writing autobiography what a wealth of Detail to enlist!
I see the contents of future magazines—just a peek Today being hurried—
Today is slowly ending—I will step back into it and disappear.

                             New York, July 21, 1964

Message II

Long since the years
letters songs Mantras
eyes apartments bellies
kissed and gray bridges
walked across in mist
Now your brother's Welfare's
paid by State now Lafcadio's
home with Mama, now you're
in NY beds with big poetic
girls & go picket on the street
I clang my finger-cymbals in Havana, I lie
with teenage boys afraid of the red police,
I jack off in Cuban modern bathrooms, I ascend
over blue oceans in a jet plane, the mist hides
the black synagogue, I will look for the Golem,
I hide under the clock near my hotel, it's intermission
for Tales of Hoffmann, nostalgia for the 19th century
rides through my heart like the music of The Moldau,
I'm still alone with long black beard and shining eyes
walking down black smoky tramcar streets at night
past royal muscular statues on an old stone bridge,
Over the river again today in Breughel's wintry city,
the snow is white on all the rooftops of Prague,
Salute beloved comrade I'll send you my tears from Moscow.

March 1965

Big Beat

The *Olympics* have descended into
      red velvet basement
      theaters of Centrum
long long hair over skeleton boys
thin black ties, pale handsome
      cheeks—and screams and screams,
Orchestra mob ecstasy rising from
      this new generation of buttocks and eyes
          and tender nipples
Because the body moves again, the
      body dances again, the body
        sings again
      the body screams new-born after
War, infants cursed with secret cold
      jail deaths of the Fifties—Now
      girls with new breasts and striplings
      wearing soft golden puberty hair—
1000 voices scream five minutes long
clapping thousand handed in great ancient measure
saluting the Meat God of XX Century
that moves thru the theater like the
      secret rhythm of the belly in
         Orgasm
Kalki! Apocalypse Christ! Maitreya! grim
      Chronos weeps
        tired into the saxophone,
The Earth is Saved! Next number!
      SHE'S A WOMAN
        Electric guitar red bells!
and Ganymede emerges stomping
      his feet for Joy on the stage
      and bows to the ground, and weeping, GIVES.
Oh the power of the God on his throne
      constantly surrounded by white drums
      right hand Sceptered beating brass cymbals!

Prague, March 11, 1965

Café in Warsaw

These spectres resting on plastic stools
leather-gloved spectres flitting thru the coffeehouse one hour
spectre girls with scarred faces, black stockings thin eyebrows
spectre boys blond hair combed neat over the skull little chin beards
new spectres talking intensely crowded together over black shiny tables late
  afternoon
the sad soprano of history chanting thru a hi-fidelity loudspeaker
—perspective walls & windows 18th century down New World Avenue to
  Sigmund III column'd
sword upraised watching over Polish youth 3 centuries—
O Polish spectres what've you suffered since Chopin wept into his romantic
  piano
old buildings rubbled down, gaiety of all night parties under the air bombs,
first screams of the vanishing ghetto—Workmen step thru prewar pink-blue
  bedroom walls demolishing sunny ruins—
Now spectres gather to kiss hands, girls kiss lip to lip, red witch-hair from
  Paris
& fine gold watches—to sit by the yellow wall with a large brown brief-
  case—
to smoke three cigarettes with thin black ties and nod heads over a new
  movie—
Spectres Christ and your bodies be with you for this hour while you're
  young
in postwar heaven stained with the sweat of Communism, your loves and
  your white smooth cheekskin soft in the glance of each other's eye.
O spectres how beautiful your calm shaven faces, your pale lipstick scarves,
  your delicate heels,
how beautiful your absent gaze, legs crossed alone at table with long
  eyelashes,
how beautiful your patient love together sitting reading the art journals—
how beautiful your entrance thru the velvet-curtained door, laughing into
  the overcrowded room,
how you wait in your hats, measure the faces, and turn and depart for an
  hour,
or meditate at the bar, waiting for the slow waitress to prepare red hot tea,
  minute by minute
standing still as hours ring in churchbells, as years pass and you will remain
  in Novy Swiat,

how beautiful you press your lips together, sigh forth smoke from your
      mouth, rub your hands
or lean together laughing to notice this wild haired madman who sits weep-
      ing among you a stranger.

April 10, 1965

The Moments Return

a thousand sunsets behind tramcar wires in open skies of Warsaw

Palace of Culture chinese peaks blacken against the orange-clouded hori-
zon—

an iron trolley rolling insect antennae sparks blue overhead, hat man limping
past rusty apartment walls—

Christ under white satin gleam in chapels—trembling fingers on the long
rosary—awaiting resurrection

Old red fat Jack mortal in Florida—tears in black eyelash, Bach's farewell to
the Cross—

That was 24 years ago on a scratchy phonograph Sebastian Sampas bid adieu
to earth—

I stopped on the pavement to remember the Warsaw Concerto, hollow sad
pianos crashing like bombs, celestial tune

in a kitchen in Ozone Park—It all came true in the sunset on a deserted
street—

And I have nothing to do this evening but walk in a fur coat on the cool gray
avenue years later, a melancholy man alone—

the music fading to another universe—the moments return—reverberations
of taxicabs arriving at a park bench—

My beard is misery, no language to these young eyes—that I remember
myself naked in my earliest dream—

now sat by the car-crossing rueful of the bald front of my skull and the gray
sign of time in my beard—

headache or dancing exhaustion or dysentery in Moscow or vomit in New
York—

Oh—the Metropol Hotel is built—crowds waiting on traffic islands under
streetlamp—the cry of tramcars on Jerusalemski—

Roof towers flash Red State—the vast stone avenue hung with yellow bulbs
—stop lights blink, long trolleys grind to rest, motorcycles pass ex-
ploding—

The poem returns to the moment, my vow to record—my cold fingers—&
must sit and wait for my own lone Presence—the first psalm—

I also return to myself, the moment and I are one man on a park bench on
a crowded streetcorner in Warsaw—

I breathe and sigh—*Give up desire for children* the bony-faced white bearded
Guru said in Benares—am I ready to die?

or a voice at my side on the bench, a gentle question—worn young man's
face under pearl gray hat—

Alas, all I can say is "No Panamay"—I can't speak.

Easter Sunday, April 18, 1965

Kral Majales

And the Communists have nothing to offer but fat cheeks and eyeglasses and
lying policemen
and the Capitalists proffer Napalm and money in green suitcases to the
Naked,
and the Communists create heavy industry but the heart is also heavy
and the beautiful engineers are all dead, the secret technicians conspire for
their own glamour
in the Future, in the Future, but now drink vodka and lament the Security
Forces,
and the Capitalists drink gin and whiskey on airplanes but let Indian brown
millions starve
and when Communist and Capitalist assholes tangle the Just man is arrested
or robbed or had his head cut off,
but not like Kabir, and the cigarette cough of the Just man above the clouds
in the bright sunshine is a salute to the health of the blue sky.
For I was arrested thrice in Prague, once for singing drunk on Narodni
street,
once knocked down on the midnight pavement by a mustached agent who
screamed out BOUZERANT,
once for losing my notebooks of unusual sex politics dream opinions,
and I was sent from Havana by plane by detectives in green uniform,
and I was sent from Prague by plane by detectives in Czechoslovakian
business suits,
Cardplayers out of Cézanne, the two strange dolls that entered Joseph K's
room at morn
also entered mine, and ate at my table, and examined my scribbles,
and followed me night and morn from the houses of lovers to the cafés of
Centrum—
And I am the King of May, which is the power of sexual youth,
and I am the King of May, which is industry in eloquence and action in
amour,
and I am the King of May, which is long hair of Adam and the Beard of my
own body
and I am the King of May, which is Kral Majales in the Czechoslovakian
tongue,
and I am the King of May, which is old Human poesy, and 100,000 people
chose my name,
and I am the King of May, and in a few minutes I will land at London
Airport,

and I am the King of May, naturally, for I am of Slavic parentage and a
    Buddhist Jew

who worships the Sacred Heart of Christ the blue body of Krishna the
    straight back of Ram

the beads of Chango the Nigerian singing Shiva Shiva in a manner which
    I have invented,

and the King of May is a middleeuropean honor, mine in the XX century

despite space ships and the Time Machine, because I heard the voice of Blake
    in a vision,

and repeat that voice. And I am King of May that sleeps with teenagers
    laughing.

And I am the King of May, that I may be expelled from my Kingdom with
    Honor, as of old,

To show the difference between Caesar's Kingdom and the Kingdom of the
    May of Man—

and I am the King of May, tho' paranoid, for the Kingdom of May is too
    beautiful to last for more than a month—

and I am the King of May because I touched my finger to my forehead
    saluting

a luminous heavy girl trembling hands who said "one moment Mr. Gins-
    berg"

before a fat young Plainclothesman stepped between our bodies—I was
    going to England—

and I am the King of May, returning to see Bunhill Fields and walk on
    Hampstead Heath,

and I am the King of May, in a giant jetplane touching Albion's airfield
    trembling in fear

as the plane roars to a landing on the gray concrete, shakes & expels air,

and rolls slowly to a stop under the clouds with part of blue heaven still
    visible.

And *tho'* I am the King of May, the Marxists have beat me upon the street,
    kept me up all night in Police Station, followed me thru Springtime
    Prague, detained me in secret and deported me from our kingdom by
    airplane.

Thus I have written this poem on a jet seat in mid Heaven.

                                                   May 7, 1965

KRAL MAJALES

And the Communists have nothing to offer but fat cheeks and
    eyeglasses and lying policemen
and the Capitalists proffer Napalm and money in green suitcases
    to the Naked,
and the Communists create heavy industry but the heart is also
    heavy
and the beautiful engineers are all dead, the secret technicians
    conspire for their own glamor
in the Future, in the Future, but now drink vodka and lament the
    Security Forces,
and the Capitalists drink gin and whiskey on airplanes but let
    Indian brown millions starve
and when Communist and Capitalist assholes tangle the Just man
    is arrested or robbed or had his head cut off,
but not like Kabir, and the cigarette cough of the Just man above
    the clouds
in the bright sunshine is a salute to the health of the blue sky.
For I was arrested thrice in Prague, once for singing drunk on
    Narodni street,
once knocked down on the midnight pavement by a mustached
    agent who screamed out BOUZERANT,
once for losing my notebooks of unusual sex politics dream opinions,
and I was sent from Havana by plane by detectives in green
    uniform,
and I was sent from Prague by plane by detectives in Czecho-
    slovakian business suits,
Cardplayers out of Cezanne, the two strange dolls that entered
    Joseph K's room at morn
also entered mine, and ate at my table, and examined my scribbles,
and followed me night and morn from the houses of lovers to the
    cafés of Centrum—
And I am the King of May, which is the power of sexual youth,
and I am the King of May, which is industry in eloquence and
    action in amour,
and I am the King of May, which is long hair of Adam and the
    Beard of my own body
and I am the King of May, which is Kral Majales in the Czecho-
    slovakian tongue,
and I am the King of May, which is old Human poesy, and 100,000
    people chose my name,
and I am the King of May, and in a few minutes I will land at
    London Airport,
and I am the King of May, naturally, for I am of Slavic parentage
    and a Buddhist Jew
who worships the Sacred Heart of Christ the blue body of Krishna
    the straight back of Ram
The Beads of Chango the Nigerian   singing Shiva Shiva in a
    manner which I have invented,
and the King of May is a middleeuropean honor, mine in the XX
    century
despite space ships and the Time Machine, because I heard the
    voice of Blake in a vision,
and repeat that voice. And I am the King of May that sleeps with
    teenagers laughing.
And I am the King of May, that I may be expelled from my
    Kingdom with Honor, as of old,
To shew the difference between Caesar's Kingdom and the King-
    dom of the May of Man—
and I am the King of May, tho paranoid, for the Kingdom of May
    is too beautiful to last for more than a month—
and I am the King of May because I touched my finger to my
    forehead saluting
a luminous heavy girl with trembling hands who said "one moment
    Mr. Ginsberg"
before a fat young Plainclothesman stepped between our bodies—
    I was going to England—
and I am the King of May, returning to see Bunhill Fields and walk
    on Hampstead Heath,
and I am the King of May, in a giant jetplane touching Albion's
    airfield trembling in fear
as the plane roars to a landing on the grey concrete, shakes &
    expells air,
and rolls slowly to a stop under the clouds with part of blue heaven
    still visible.
And tho I am the King of May, the Marxists have beat me upon
    the street, kept me up all night in Police Station, followed
    me thru Springtime Prague, detained me in secret and
    deported me from our kingdom by airplane.
Thus I have written this poem on a jet seat in mid Heaven.

May 7, 1965

Robert LaVigne

oyez

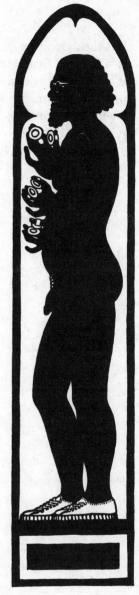

Guru

It is the moon that disappears
It is the stars that hide not I
It's the City that vanishes, I stay
with my forgotten shoes,
my invisible stocking
It is the call of a bell

Primrose Hill, May 1965

Drowse Murmurs

. . . touch of vocal flattery
exists where you wake us
at dawn with happy sphinx
lids eyeball heavy anchored
together in mysterious Signature,
this is the end of the world
whether Atom bomb hits
it or I fall down death
alone no body help help
It's me myself caught in throes
of Ugh! They got me whom you lately loved
of soft cloth beds to stick his cock
in the wrong way lost animal, what wd Zoology
say on Park Bench watching the Spectacle
of this time Me it's my body going to die,
it's My ship sinking forever, O Captain
the fearful trip is done! I'm all alone,
This is human, and the cat that licks its ass
also hath short term to be furry specter
as I do woken by last thought leap
up from my pillow as the cat leaps up
on the desk chair to resolve its foot lick,
I lick my own mind observe the pipe
crawling up the brick wall, see picture
room-sides hung with nails emblem
abstract oil funny glyphs, girls
naked, letters & newspapers the World
Map colored over for emphasis somebody born—
my thoughts almost lost, I absorb the big
earth lamps hung from the ceiling for ready light,
hear the chirp of birds younger than I
and faster doomed, that jet plane whistle
hiss roar above roofs stronger winged
than any thin-jawed bird—the precise robot
for air flying's stronger than me even,
tho' metal fatigue may come before I'm 90—
I scratch my hairy skull and lean on elbow bone
as alarm clock Sat Morn rings next door
and wakes a sleeper body to face his day.

How amazing here, now this time newspaper
history, when earth planet they say revolves
around one sun that on outer Galaxy arm
revolves center so vast slow pinwheel
big this speckless invisible molecule I am
sits up solid motionless early dawn thinking
high in every direction photograph spiral nebula
photograph death BLANK photograph this wakened
brick minute bird-song pipe-flush elbow lean
in soft pillow to scribe the green sign Paradis.

June 1965

Who Be Kind To

Be kind to your self, it is only one
    and perishable
of many on the planet, thou art that
one that wishes a soft finger tracing the
    line of feeling from nipple to pubes—
one that wishes a tongue to kiss your armpit,
    a lip to kiss your cheek inside your
    whiteness thigh—
Be kind to yourself Harry, because unkindness
    comes when the body explodes
napalm cancer and the deathbed in Vietnam
is a strange place to dream of   trees
    leaning over and angry American faces
grinning with sleepwalk terror over your
    last eye—
Be kind to yourself, because the bliss of your own
    kindness will flood the police tomorrow,
because the cow weeps in the field and the
    mouse weeps in the cat hole—
Be kind to this place, which is your present
    habitation, with derrick and radar tower
    and flower in the ancient brook—
Be kind to your neighbor who weeps
    solid tears on the television sofa,
he has no other home, and hears nothing
    but the hard voice of telephones
Click, buzz, switch channel and the inspired
    melodrama disappears
and he's left alone for the night, he disappears
    in bed—
Be kind to your disappearing mother and
    father gazing out the terrace window
    as milk truck and hearse turn the corner
Be kind to the politician weeping in the galleries
    of Whitehall, Kremlin, White House
    Louvre and Phoenix City
aged, large nosed, angry, nervously dialing
    the bald voice box connected to

electrodes underground converging thru
    wires vaster than a kitten's eye can see
on the mushroom shaped fear-lobe under
    the ear of Sleeping Dr. Einstein
crawling with worms, crawling with worms, crawling
    with worms the hour has come—
Sick, dissatisfied, unloved, the bulky
    foreheads of Captain Premier President
    Sir Comrade Fear!
Be kind to the fearful one at your side
    Who's remembering the Lamentations
    of the bible
the prophecies of the Crucified Adam Son
    of all the porters and char men of
                Bell gravia—
Be kind to your self who weeps under
    the Moscow moon and hide your bliss hairs
    under raincoat and suede Levi's—
For this is the joy to be born, the kindness
    received thru strange eyeglasses on
    a bus thru Kensington,
the finger touch of the Londoner on your thumb,
    that borrows light from your cigarette,
the morning smile at Newcastle Central
    station, when longhair Tom blond husband
    greets the bearded stranger of telephones—
the boom bom that bounces in the joyful
    bowels as the Liverpool Minstrels of
    CavernSink
raise up their joyful voices and guitars
    in electric Afric hurrah
    for Jerusalem—
The saints come marching in, Twist &
    Shout, and Gates of Eden are named
    in Albion again
Hope sings a black psalm from Nigeria,
    and a white psalm echoes in Detroit
    and reechoes amplified from Nottingham to Prague
and a Chinese psalm will be heard, if we all
    live out our lives for the next 6 decades—
Be kind to the Chinese psalm in the red transistor
    in your breast—

Be kind to the Monk in the 5 Spot who plays
    lone chord-bangs on his vast piano
lost in space on a bench and hearing himself
    in the nightclub universe—
Be kind to the heroes that have lost their
    names in the newspaper
and hear only their own supplication for
    the peaceful kiss of sex in the giant
    auditoriums of the planet,
nameless voices crying for kindness in the orchestra,
screaming in anguish that bliss come true
    and sparrows sing another hundred years
    to white haired babes
and poets be fools of their own desire—O Anacreon
    and angelic Shelley!
Guide these new-nippled generations on space
    ships to Mars' next universe
The prayer is to man and girl, the only
    gods, the only lords of Kingdoms of
    Feeling, Christs of their own
    living ribs—
Bicycle chain and machine gun, fear sneer
    & smell cold logic of the Dream Bomb
have come to Saigon, Johannesburg,
    Dominica City, Phnom Penh, Pentagon
    Paris and Lhasa—
Be kind to the universe of Self that
    trembles and shudders and thrills
    in XX Century,
that opens its eyes and belly and breast
    chained with flesh to feel
    the myriad flowers of bliss
    that I Am to Thee—
A dream! a Dream! I don't want to be alone!
    I want to know that I am loved!
I want the orgy of our flesh, orgy
    of all eyes happy, orgy of the soul
    kissing and blessing its mortal-grown
    body,
orgy of tenderness beneath the neck, orgy of
    kindness to thigh and vagina

Desire given with meat hand
        and cock, desire taken with
        mouth and ass, desire returned
        to the last sigh!
Tonite let's all make love in London
        as if it were 2001 the years
        of thrilling god—
And be kind to the poor soul that cries in
        a crack of the pavement because he
        has no body—
Prayers to the ghosts and demons, the
        lackloves of Capitals & Congresses
        who make sadistic noises
        on the radio—
Statue destroyers & tank captains, unhappy
        murderers in Mekong & Stanleyville,
That a new kind of man has come to his bliss
        to end the cold war he has borne
        against his own kind flesh
        since the days of the snake.

                                    June 8, 1965

Studying the Signs

After Reading Briggflatts

White light's wet glaze on asphalt city floor,
the *Guinness Time* house clock hangs sky misty,
yellow *Cathay* food lamps blink, rain falls
on rose neon *Swiss Watch* under Regent archway,
Sun Alliance and London Insurance Group stands
granite—"Everybody gets torn down" . . . as a high
black taxi with orange doorlight passes around
iron railing blazoned with red sigma *Underground*—
Ah where the cars glide slowly around Eros
shooting down on one who stands in Empire's Hub
under his shining silver breast, look at Man's
sleepy face under half-spread metal wings—
Swan & Edgar's battlement walls the moving Circus,
princely high windows barred (shadow bank
interior office stairway marble) behind castiron
green balconies emblemed with single swans afloat
like white teacups what—*Boots'* blue sign lit up
over an enamel weight-machine's mirror clockface
at door betwixt plateglass *Revlon* & slimming biscuit
plaques and that alchemical blood-crimson pharmacy
bottle perched on street display. *A Severed Head*
"relished uproariously" above the masq'd *Criterion*
marquee, with Thespis and Ceres plaster Graces lifting
white arms in the shelled niches above a fire gong
on the wooden-pillared facade whose mansard gables
lean in blue-black sky drizzle, thin flagpole.
Like the prow of a Queen Mary the curved building
sign *Players* package, blue capped center
Navvy encircled by his life-belt a sweet bearded
profile against 19th century sea waves—
last a giant red delicious *Coca-Cola* signature
covers half the building back to gold *Cathay*.
Cars stop three abreast for the light, race forward,
turtleneck youths jump the fence toward *Boots*,
the night-gang in Mod slacks and ties sip
coffee at the *Snac-A-Matic* corner opendoor,
a boy leaned under *Cartoon Cinema* lifts hand
puffs white smoke and waits agaze—a wakened

pigeon flutters down from streetlamp to the fountain,
primly walks and pecks the empty pave—now deep
blue planet-light dawns in Piccadilly's low sky.

June 12, 1965

Portland Coliseum

A brown piano in diamond
    white spotlight
Leviathan auditorium
    iron rib wired
      hanging organs, vox
        black battery
A single whistling sound of
    ten thousand children's
      larynxes asinging
      pierce the ears
    and flowing up the belly
    bliss the moment arrived

Apparition, four brown English
    jacket christhair boys
Goofed Ringo battling bright
      white drums
Silent George hair patient
      Soul horse
Short black-skulled Paul
    wit thin guitar
Lennon the Captain, his mouth
    a triangular smile,
all jump together to End
    some tearful memory song
      ancient two years,

    The million children
    the thousand worlds
bounce in their seats, bash
    each other's sides, press
    legs together nervous
Scream again & claphand
    become one Animal
    in the New World Auditorium
    —hands waving myriad
      snakes of thought
    screech beyond hearing

while a line of police with
folded arms stands
Sentry to contain the red
sweatered ecstasy
that rises upward to the
wired roof.

August 27, 1965

VIII
THE FALL OF AMERICA
(1965–1971)

Thru the Vortex West Coast to East   (1965–1966)

Zigzag Back Thru These States   (1966–1967)

Elegies for Neal Cassady   (1968)

Ecologues of These States   (1969–1971)

Bixby Canyon to Jessore Road   (1971)

Thru the Vortex West Coast to East
(1965–1966)

Beginning of a Poem of These States

Memento for Gary Snyder

Under the bluffs of Oroville, blue cloud September skies, entering
U.S. border, red red apples bend their tree boughs propt with sticks—
At Omak a fat girl in dungarees leads her big brown horse by asphalt
highway.
Thru lodgepole pine hills Coleville near Moses Mountain—a white
horse standing back of a 2 ton truck moving forward between trees.
At Nespelem, in the yellow sun, a marker for Chief Joseph's grave
under rilled brown hills—white cross over highway.
At Grand Coulee under leaden sky, giant red generators humm thru
granite & concrete to materialize onions—
And gray water laps against the gray sides of Steamboat Mesa.
At Dry Falls 40 Niagaras stand silent & invisible, tiny horses graze
on the rusty canyon's mesquite floor.
At Mesa, on the car radio passing a new corn silo, Walking Boogie
teenager's tender throats, "I wish they could all be California girls"—as black
highway curls outward.
On plains toward Pasco, Oregon hills at horizon, Bob Dylan's voice
on airways, mass machine-made folksong of one soul—*Please crawl out your
window*—first time heard.
Speeding thru space, Radio the soul of the nation. The Eve of De-
struction and The Universal Soldier.
And tasted the Snake: water from Yellowstone under a green bridge;
darshana with the Columbia, oilslick & small bird feathers on mud shore.
Across the river, silver bubbles of refineries.
There Lewis and Clark floated down in a raft: the brown-mesa'd
gorge of Lake Wallula smelling of rain in the sage, Greyhound buses speed-
ing by.
Searching neither for Northwest Passage, nor Gold, nor the Prophet
who will save the polluted Nation, nor for Guru walking the silver waters
behind McNary Dam.

Roundup time in Pendleton, pinched women's faces and hulking cowboy hats in the tavern, I'm a city slicker from Benares. Barman murmurs to himself, two hands full of beer, "Who wanted that?"

Heavy rain at twilight, trumpets massing & ascending repeat The Eve of Destruction, Georgia Pacific sawmill burners lift smoke thru the dusky valley.

Cold night in Blue Mountains, snow-powdered tops of droopy Tamarack and Fir at gray sunrise, coffee frozen in brown coffeepot, toes chilled in Czechoslovakian tennis sneakers.

Under Ponderosa pine, this place for sale—45th Parallel, half way between equator and North Pole—Tri-City Radio broadcasting clear skies & freezing nite temperatures; big yellow daisies, hay bales piled in square stacks house-high.

"Don Carpenter has a real geologist's hammer, he can hit a rock & split it open & look inside & utter some mantra."

Coyote jumping in front of the truck, & down bank, jumping thru river, running up field to wooded hillside, stopped on a bound & turned round to stare at us—Oh-Ow! shook himself and bounded away waving his bushy tail.

Rifles & cyanide bombs unavailing—he looked real surprised & pointed his thin nose in our direction. Hari Om Namo Shivaye!

Eat all sort of things & run solitary—3 nites ago hung bear dung on a tree and laughed

—Bear: "Are you eating my corpses? Say that again!"

Coyote: "I didn't say nothing."

Sparse juniper forests on dry lavender hills, down Ritter Butte to Pass Creek, a pot dream recounted: Crossing Canada border with a tin can in the glove compartment, hip young border guards laughing—In meadow the skeleton of an old car settled: Look To Jesus painted on door.

Fox in the valley, road markers dript with small icicles, all windows on the white church broken, brown wooden barns leaned together, thin snow on gas station roof.

Malheur, Malheur National Forest—signs glazed snowfrost, last night's frozen dreams come back—staring out thru skull at cold planet— Mila-Repa accepted no gifts to cover his jeweled penis—Strawberry Mountain top white under bright clouds.

Postcards of Painted Hills, fossil beds near Dayville, Where have all the flowers gone? flowers gone? Ra and Coyote are hip to it all, nailed footpaw tracks on Day River bottom, cows kneeled at rest in meadow afternoon.

Ichor Motel, white tailfins in driveway, isolate belfried brown farmhouse circled with trees, chain saws ringing in the vale.

Rilled lava overgrown with green moss cracked in cold wind—Blue Heron and American white egret migrate to shrunken waters of Unhappy —mirage lakes wrongside of the road, dust streaming under Riddle Mountain, Steen Range powder white on horizon—

Slept, water froze in Sierra cup, a lake of bitter water from solar plexus to throat—Dreamt my knee was severed at hip and sutured back together—

Woke, icy dew on poncho and saffron sleep bag, moon like a Coleman lantern dimming icicle-point stars—vomited on knees in arroyo grass, nostrils choking with wet red acid in weak flashlight—

Dawn weakness, climbing worn lava walls following the muddy spring, waterfowl whistling sweetly & a tiny raccoon

pawed forward daintly in green mud, looking for frogs burrowed away from Arctic cold—disappeared into a silent rock shelf.

Climbed up toward Massacre Lake road—sagebrush valley-floor stretched South—Pronghorn abode, that eat the bitterroot and dry spicebush, hunters gathering in trucks to chase antelope—

A broken corral at highway hill bottom, wreck of a dead cow in cold slanting sun set rays, eyes eaten out, neck twisted to ground, belly caved on kneebone, smell of sweet dread flesh and acrid new sage.

Slept in rusty tin feeding trough, Orion belt crystal in sky, numb metal-chill at my back, ravens settled on the cow when sun warmed my feet.

Up hills following trailer dust clouds, green shotgun shells & beerbottles on road, mashed jackrabbits—through a crack in the Granite Range, an alkali sea—Chinese armies massed at the borders of India.

Mud plate of Black Rock Desert passing, Frank Sinatra lamenting distant years, old sad voic'd September'd recordings, and Beatles crying Help! their voices woodling for tenderness.

All memory at once present time returning, vast dry forests afire in California, U.S. paratroopers attacking guerrillas in Vietnam mountains, over porcelain-white road hump the tranquil azure of a vast lake.

Pyramid rocks knotted by pleistocene rivers, topheavy lava isles castled in Paiute water, cutthroat trout; tomato sandwiches and silence.

Reno's Motel traffic signs low mountains walling the desert oasis, radio crooning city music afternoon news, Red Chinese Ultimatum 1 A.M. tomorrow.

Up Donner Pass over concrete bridge superhighways hung with gray clouds, Mongolian Idiot chow-yuk the laughable menu this party arrived.

Ponderosa hillsides cut back for railroad track, I have nothing to do, laughing over Sierra top, gliding adventurer on the great fishtail iron-finned road, Heaven is renounced, Dharma no Path, no Saddhana to fear, my man world will blow up, humming insects under wheel sing my own death rasping migrations of mercy, I tickle the Bodhisattva and salute the new sunset, home riding home to old city on ocean

with new mantra to manifest Removal of Disaster from my self, autumn brushfire's smoky mass in dusk light, sun's bright red ball on horizon purple with earth-cloud, chanting to Shiva in the car-cabin.

Pacific Gas high voltage antennae trailing thin wires across flatlands, entering Coast Range 4 lane highway over last hump to giant orange Bay glimpse, Dylan ends his song "You'd see what a drag you are," and the Pope

cometh to Babylon to address United Nations, 2000 years since Christ's birth the prophecy of Armageddon

hangs the Hell Bomb over planet roads and cities, year-end come, Oakland Army Terminal lights burn green in evening darkness.

Treasure Island Naval Base lit yellow with night business, thousands of red tail lights move in procession over Bay Bridge,

San Francisco stands on modern hills, Broadway lights flash the center gay honky-tonk Elysium, Ferry building's sweet green clock lamps black Embarcadero waters, negroes screaming over radio.

Bank of America burns red signs beneath the neon pyramids, here is the city, here is the face of war, home 8 o'clock

gliding down freeway ramp to City Lights, Peter's face and television, money and new wanderings to come.

September 1965

Carmel Valley

Grass yellow hill,
      small mountain range blue sky
    bright reservoir below road tiny cars
The wing tree green wind sigh
          rises, falls—
    Buddha, Christ, fissiparous
             Tendencies—
White sun rays   pierce my eyeglasses—
    gray bark animal arms,
          skin peeling,
    sprig fingers pointing, twigs trembling
     green plate-thins bobbing,
         knotted branch-sprouts—
No one will have to announce New Age
No special name, no Unique way,
    no crier by Method or
         Herald of Snaky Unknown,
No Messiah necessary but the Country ourselves
           fifty years old—
Allah this tree, Eternity this Space Age!
Teenagers walking on Times Sq.   look up
    at blue planets thru neon metal
            buildingtops,
Old men lie on grass afternoons
    old Walnut stands on green mountain hide,
       ants crawl the page, invisible
       insects sing, birds
         flap down,
Man will relax on a hill remembering tree friends.

Chez Baez, November 1965

First Party at Ken Kesey's with Hell's Angels

Cool black night thru the redwoods
cars parked outside in shade
behind the gate, stars dim above
the ravine, a fire burning by the side
porch and a few tired souls hunched over
in black leather jackets. In the huge
wooden house, a yellow chandelier
at 3 A.M. the blast of loudspeakers
hi-fi Rolling Stones Ray Charles Beatles
Jumping Joe Jackson and twenty youths
dancing to the vibration thru the floor,
a little weed in the bathroom, girls in scarlet
tights, one muscular smooth skinned man
sweating dancing for hours, beer cans
bent littering the yard, a hanged man
sculpture dangling from a high creek branch,
children sleeping softly in their bedroom bunks.
And 4 police cars parked outside the painted
gate, red lights revolving in the leaves.

December 1965

Continuation of a Long Poem of These States

S.F. Southward

Stage-lit streets
     Downtown Frisco whizzing past, buildings
     ranked by Freeway balconies
          Bright Johnnie Walker neon
             sign Christmastrees
And Christmas and its eves
     in the midst of the same deep wood
        as every sad Christmas before, surrounded
           by forests of stars—
Metal columns, smoke pouring cloudward,
        yellow-lamp horizon
          warplants move, tiny
        planes lie in Avionic fields—
Meanwhile Working Girls sort mail into the red slot
     Rivers of newsprint to soldiers' Vietnam
     Infantry Journal, Kanackee
        Social Register, Wichita Star
And Postoffice Christmas the same brown place
     mailhandlers' black fingers
     dusty mailbags filled
        1948 N.Y. Eighth Avenue was
   when Peter drove the mailtruck 1955
        from Rincon Annex—
Bright lights' windshield flash,
     adrenalin shiver in shoulders
        Around the curve
   crawling a long truck
        3 bright green signals on forehead
Jeweled Bayshore passing the Coast Range
     one architect's house light on hill crest
. . . . negro voices rejoice over radio
     Moonlit sticks of tea
Moss Landing Power Plant
     shooting its cannon smoke
        across the highway, Red taillight
        speeding the white line and a mile away
     Orion's muzzle
        raised up
           to the center of Heaven.

December 18, 1965

These States: into L.A.

Organs and War News
        Radio static from Saigon
                "And the Glory of the Lord"
                        Newscaster Voice thru Aether—
The Truce—
        12 hours, 30 hours?
                Thirty Days, said Mansfield.
    Cars roll right lane,
        bridge lights
                rising & falling on night-slope—
        headlights cross speeding reflectors
Handel rejoicing
        chorus whine Requiem, roar in yr Auto
                        window shoulders
Memories of Christmas—
        and the deep Christmas begins:
                U.S. 101 South
The President at home
        in his swinging chair on the porch
                listening to Christmas Carols
        Vice-President returning from Far East
"Check into yourself that you are wrong—
        You may be the Wrong" says Pope His
                Christmas Message—
Overpopulation, overpopulation
            Give me 3 acres of land
            Give my brother how much?
                Each man have fine estate?
            settle giant Communes?
LSD Shakti-snake settles like gas into Consciousness
        —Brightest Venus I've ever seen
Canyon-floor road, near
        bursting tides
        & caves they'd slept in earlier years
                    covered with green water
                    height of a man.
    A stranger walked that ground.
        Five years ago we picnicked
                in this place.

Auto track by a mud log, Bixby Creek
    wove channels
                    thru the shifting sands.
I saw the ghost of Neal
            pass by, Ferlinghetti's ghost
The ghost of Homer roaring at the surf
            barking & wagging his tail
My own footprint at the sea's lips
            white foam to the rock where I sang Harekrishna
sand garden drying, kelp
            standing head upward in sunlight.
                    Dinosaur hard, scabrous
        overgrown with seaweed tendrils,
                    Professors of rock . . .

Where's Stravinsky? Theda Bara? Chaplin? Harpo Marx?
    Where's Laurel and his Hardy?
                    Laughing phantoms
                    going to the grave—
Last time this town   I saw them in movies
    Ending *The Road to Utopia* 'O Carib Isle!'
    Laurel aged & white-haired Hardy
            Hydrogen Comic smoke billowing
                    up from their Kingdom—
Grauman's Chinese Theater's drab sidewalk front's
        concrete footprints, stood there
            stupid, anal, exciting
                    upside down, Crosseyed moviestar'd
    I craned my neck at Myrna Loy & Shirley Temple shoe-marks—

Raccoon crouched at road-edge, praying—
                    Carlights pass—
Merry Christmas to Mr. & Mrs.
                    Chiang Kai Shek
Merry Christmas to President Johnson & pray for Health
Merry Christmas to MacNamara, State Secretary Rusk,
            Khrushchev hid in his apartment house,
                    to Kosygin's name, to Ho Chi Minh grown old,
Merry Christmas to rosycheeked Mao Tze Tung
    Happy New Year Chou En Lai & Laurel and Hardy
Merry Christmas to the Pope
            & to the Dalai Lama Rebbe Lubovitcher

to the highest Priests of Benin,
     to the Chiefs of the Faery Churches—
Merry Christmas to the Four Shankaracharyas,
     to all Naga Sadhus, Bauls & Chanting Dervishes from Egypt to
                                             Malaya—

Black Sign Los Angeles 140 Miles
     stifling car-heat—
          Music on the tacky radio,
               senseless, senseless coughs of emotion—
The Ally Cease-Fire Will Not Be Extended
               ". . . . . . . on a densely populated area"
". . . —Peking will never join the United Nations as long
as it remains under what it termed American Domination."

MOBILIZE THE NATIONAL GUARD, sd Senator Anderson
     IY Mental Rejectees will be reexamined
                    for service in Vietnam.
Bradley high on acid
     drawing pictures on Army Forms?
Peter classified Psycho telling his Sergeant
     "An Army is an Army against Love."

Xmas day work stack of papers on the President's desk
                              a foot high!
                    he has to finish them tonight!
     this determined NBC News entering Lompoc, famed of
                              W. C. Fields
          who proved that Everyman's a
                    natural bullshit artist:
          "spends about 75% of his time on Foreign Matters and is,
               uh, very involved . . ."
                    "and all letters are answered."
WHAT no Xmas message from the
               Texas White House?
     The President must be very *down*—
He's maintaining his communications networks
                    circling the Planet.
          Mambo canned music mush
          Ventura radio Xmas sound
                    Commercial announcements,
     Few minutes of live speech, little joy or thanksgiving,
no voice from Himalayas

Good Cheer Happy Kalpa
for Dominica Vietnam Congo China India America
        Tho England rang with the Beatles!
    "healing all that was oppressed with the Devil."
  & at Santa Barbara exit
            the Preacher hollered in tongues
            YOUR NAME IS WRITTEN IN HEAVEN
                        passing 38th Parallel

Lodge spoke from Saigon "We are morally right,
    we are Morally Right,
        serving the cause of freedom forever giving these people
                an opportunity . . . almost like thinking"—
  He's broadcasting serious-voice on Xmas Eve to America
Entering Los Angeles space age
        three stations simultaneous radio—
                Cut-Up Sounds that fill Aether,
                    voices back of the brain—
                The voice of Lodge, all well, Moral—
                voice of a poor poverty worker,
                    "Well they dont know anybody dont
                    know anything about the poor all
                    the money's going to the politicians
                    in Syracuse, none of it's going to the poor."
                Evers' voice the black Christmas March
                    "We want to be treated like Men, like human . . ."
        Mass Arrest of Campers Outside LBJ Ranch
Aquamarine lights revolving along the highway,
                night stars over L.A., exit trees,
        turquoise brilliance shining on sidestreets—
                                    Xmas Eve 1965

A Methedrine Vision in Hollywood

Here at the atomic Crack-end of Time XX Century
History swifting past horse chariot earth wheel
So I in mid-age, finished with half desire
Tranquil in my hairy body, familiar beard face,
     Same fingers to pen
      as twenty years ago began
    scribbled Confession to fellow Beings
     Americans—
       Heavenly creatures,

This universe a thing of dream
   substance naught & Keystone void
     vibrations of symmetry Yes No
     Foundation of Gold Element Atom
   all the way down to the first Wave
   making opposite Nothing a mirror
which begat a wave of Ladies marrying
waves of Gentlemen till I was born in 1926
   in Newark, New Jersey under the sign of
       sweet Gemini—

Whole universes hived upon the first
   dumb Jerk
     that wasn't there—The
Only One escape from the black Not Ever
was Itself,
    a extra click of Life woke
because Nothing had no hand to switch off
the Light.
     The first dumb Jerk,
one wave, Forward! one way too many—
So forward got backward, & Sideways both
   got there simultaneous with up
     and down who got each other
Meanwhile the first Being got its non-Being
   Opposite which never had to be there before
This calamity, this accident, this Goof,
   this Imperceptible Sneak of Dimension,
     Some Move-Push tickle, Aleph or Aum
      swallowed before uttered,

one-eyed sparkle, giant glint, any tiny fart
or rose-whiff before roses were
                    Thought Impossible
filled every corner of Emptiness with Symmetries of
       Impossible Universe with no Idea
How Come, & Opposite Possible Kosmoses assembled Doubtless—
One makes two, symmetry's infinite touch
makes Sound bounce, light sees
            waves reproduce oceans,
       vibrations are red white & blue—

All like a 3 dimensional TV dream
like Science-fiction opera
       sung by inexistent Gas-brains
            in their N-dimensional bag,
Some what a bubble, some what dewdrop
Some what a blossom, some what lightning flash,
Some what the old Jew in the Hospital—
       snap of dying fingers,
            "Where did it all *go*?"

Made of Ideas, waves, dots, hot projectors
mirror movie screens,
       Some what the Shadow cast at Radio City
                    Music Hall Xmas 1939
gone, gone, utterly completely gone
to a world of Snow
       White and the Seven Dwarfs—
Made up of cartoon picture clouds, papier-mâché
            Japanese lantern stage sets strung
       with moon lights, neon arc-flames,
            electric switches, thunder
reverberating from phonograph record tape machine
       Tin sheets of Zeus on
the Microphone jacked to gigantic Amplifiers, gauge
       needle jumping, red lights warning Other
Dimensions off the overloaded public address Sound
       Systems feedback thru blue void
            echoing the Real of Endless Film.

Xmas 1965

Hiway Poesy: L.A.–Albuquerque–Texas–Wichita

up up and away!
        we're off, Thru America—

Heading East to San Berdoo
        as West did, Nathanael,
California Radio Lady's voice
        Talking about Viet Cong—
    Oh what a beautiful morning
    Sung for us by Nelson Eddy

Two trailer trucks, Sunkist oranges / bright colored
        piled over the sides
    rolling on the road
Gray hulk of Mt. Baldy under
    white misted skies
Red Square signs unfold, Texaco Shell
        Harvey House tilted over the superhighway—

Afternoon Light
        Children in back of a car
        with Bubblegum
a flight of birds out of a dry field like mosquitoes

". . . several battalions of U.S. troops in a search and destroy operation in
the Coastal plain near Bong Son, 300 mi. Northeast of Saigon. Thus far the
fighting has been a series of small clashes. In a related action 25 miles to the
South, Korean troops killed 35 Viet Cong near Coastal highway Number
One."

           "For he's oh so Good
           and he's oh so fine
           and he's oh so healthy
           in his body and his mind"
                  The Kinks on car radio

In Riverside,
    a 1920s song—
        "It's the only words I know / that you'll
                      understand"
    For my uncle Max dead 5 years ago

it's settled—buried
under the blue mountain wall,
Veined with snow at the top
                    clouds passing
                          icy remote heights
Palmtrees on valley floor
        stick up toothpick hairheads—
Toy automobiles piled crushed and mangled
                    topped by a hanging crane,
        The planet hanging,
                the air hanging,
                      Trees hang their branches,
                A dirt truck hanging on the highway—
Spectacle of Afternoon,
            giant pipes glistening in the universe
Magic that weighs tons and tons,
            Old bum with his rough
                    tattered pack hunched
        walking up the hill hanging
                to Ukipah
        cloth cap pulled over his head
                          black fingernails.

        A wall, a wall, a Mesa Wall, There's desert
        flat mountain shadows
            miles along the pale pink floor
                    —Indio in space.

The breath of spring, the breath of fear
        Mexican border . . .
                The LSD cube—
                    silence.
There's those Hellies again,
            over hiway, as over Mekong
                belly lights blinking red
            prob'ly surveying the border—
        shotguns stickin' out all over
            —Two birds swoop under car dashboard.
            Purple Mist,
                motor tire drone.
Sacrifice for Prosperity, says Johnson.
        Joshua Tree Monument
Blue dusk.

Bomb China
says Southern Senator Stennis—
Mobil's neon Pegasus flying overhill.

Colorado River border,
Two lemons an orange seized,
Scaly Mites
and the cube of acid smuggled into Arizona . . .

"It all comes from Crystal hill"—
The whole countryside's Quartzite hereabouts—
Huntley's Perspective on the News
Sukarno a Nut? A wildman?
or potential friend?
Brought to you by Mercury
boasting "sweet
success taste"—
They can go around saying things about people,
and once their policy's adopted it'll rule a decade—
Somebody decided "he's a nut!"
official policy, re-echoed to 14 Million Readers of *Time*
as we drive along in the Bat-mobile thru Arizona—
Approaching Hope, dream maps unfolded
Waves with larger & larger loops,
Tree-posts flashing auto headlights
hit my retina
I saw what it was
light saw light,
a flash in the pan.
Eyes register, nerves send waves along to the brain
Finger touch is electric waves
carlights glare thru eyes—
Voice repeating itself,
wavering over the microphones—
Meditation passing Hope . . .

Horrific outskirts' Eastern Traffic Sign,
Turn backward . . .
Dull sleep on my eyes

*   *   *   *

Morning *Phoenix Gazette*, editorial January 27, '66
"No time for probe of CIA

No Good Purpose would be served—
                    Why poke on the Nose?
            . . . Virtual epidemic of attacks,
Pacifists let Reds take over the world, rather than
                        Fighting Against Them—
        well meaning people . . . distasteful intelligence
        Sacrosanct . . . scuttle . . . demand an investigation . . .
Where the spirit of the Lord is, there is liberty."
                    Righto! The Navaho trail—
        Crescent moon setting on low hills West—
                Military forces over radio
                        push bombing N. Vietnam.
Lifelines, sponsored by Henry L. Hunt, Beans.
            Dead voiced announcer, denouncing
            "a communist conspiracy among the youth . . .
        speakers on campuses / trained to condition
                            idealistic brains . . ."
It's Chase Manhattan Bank lends money to South African
        White government—Rockfeller boy!
        Unless Chase Bank quits I prophesy blood violence.
        Ford has a factory,
        Ford has a factory there—
            "they're aw-fly proud
            of being South African."
        ". . . A hotbed of anti Semitism too?"

PAINTED DESERT,
        petrified forest
                Leslie Howard's scratchy '30s image
                    . . . eating jurassic steak
Petroglyphs over there the Man in the Moon,
        the guy with four fingers . . .
        over there, this is the sun, with two spikes out the North,
        two spikes South, two spikes ray East & West

        Milky way over here, the Moon,
        . . . and all the animal tentacles

Nebula spiraled   "... Roger 1943"
And I hit Julius for eating his avocado cheese sandwich too fast.

Gas flares, oil refinery night smoke,
high aluminum tubes winking red lights
over space ship runways
petrochemical witches' blood boiling underground—
"Looks like they're gettin ready to go to Mars."
Approaching Thoreau—
Fort Wingate Army Depot entrance—
and there's the Continental Divide.
Anti Vietnam War Demonstrator soldiers sentenced
For Contempt of President:
Hard Labor—
Learn thyself in Shell Refinery's Oil Storage Seaboard Rackets,

Lying back on the car seat,
eyelids heavy,
legs spread leaned against the table,
Oh that I were young again and the skin in my anus folds rose,
"La illaba el (lill) Allah bu"
Finally bored,
Over a hill, singing *Raghupati Raghava Raja Ram*
Albuquerque Sparkling blue brilliant
more diamonds & pearls of electricity
running out of power-plants than ever heard of
Turkey or Israel—
intense endless iridescence on black
velvet desert—
Ah what a marvel
orange blue Neon Circling itself Solar System'd
Speed Wash Texaco 19¢ Famous Hamburgers
Lion House Italian Village Pizza ah!
radio warbles Electronic noise
echo chamber vibrations—
Albuquerque streets' fantastic Neon Stars
collapsing to bright red blinks
Satellite Globes plunging their
tiny lamps in and out—
the eyeball.

*   *   *   *

Space stretching North dotted with silver gastanks
        to Sandia Range
Hitchhiking student
        supported by National Defense Fund
                with his black horn rimmed glasses,
                        thin blond hair,
"If your country calls you, would you go?"
"If my country drafted me . . .
                then I would go."
Selfish young american always interested in his own skin
—and blue car speeding along the highway
        sticker on back
                "I'm proud I'm an American"
        right front seat, a 10 gallon hat
        driver a fat car salesman—
Sitting icy tipped
        distant earth peaks over Hilltops
& here's an ugly little oasis, used car tractors
                fenced off by barbed wire
                        below roadside—
Evenings cool clear, sharp
                brilliant blue stars—
Just what we needed, State Penitentiary!
        Two miles off into the brown furze rolling
                East of the highway
"This is Ford Country what are *you* driving?" Be a Ford dealer?
Great snow meadows roof Sangre De Cristo
clouds, North, dipping misty rivulet tails of pointy fog.
. . . .
It's a hard question . . .
        which would you rescue, your mother-in-law
                or the last text of Shakespeare?

        *   *   *   *

Two hitchhikers, one Cajun dumb mouth
        who sang brown voiced
                blues his travelin' baby.
T'other highschool smart
        wavy hair, unbeautiful, unbeautiful and gentle
                pinched pachuco face

had ideas of his own philosophy—
        thumbing out of Albuquerque
                To New Orleans Mardigras
$900 a week, working rolling drunks, or
        fixin signs with ladders and hammers
had spent 3 youth years in Siam,
           Champagne & Pussy 50¢
             kindly eyes
"I love to eat, and I love girls."
Sang them Prajnaparamita Sutra
           entering Panhandle,
left them back at Tukumkarie—
talking in the truckstop booth,
        fat truck drivers
           headed south.

On Radio entering Texas
        Please For Jesus!
Grunts & Screams & Shouts,
        Shouts for the Poison Redeemer,
Shouts for the Venomous Jesus of Kansas.
Onward to Wichita!
        Onward to the Vortex!
           To the Birchite Hate Riddles,
      cock-detesting, pussy-smearing
      dry ladies and evil Police
           of Central Plains State
Where boredom & fury
        magick bars and sirens around
           the innocent citykid eye
& Vampire stake of politics Patriotism's driven
      into the white breast of Teenage
      joyful murmurers
      in carpet livingrooms
        on sidestreets—
Beautiful children've been driven from Wichita
McClure & Branaman gone
      J. Alan White departed left no address
Charlie Plymell come *Now* to San Francisco
      Ann Buchanan passing thru,
Bruce Conners took his joke to another coast—
      in time the *White Dove Review*
        fluttered up from Tulsa

Flatland entering Great Plains
                    Evil gathers in Cities,
                    Eye mouth newspapers
Television concentrates its blue
                    flicker of death in the frontal lobe—
Police department sirens wail,
                    The Building Department inspector Negates
                    What the Fire Department has failed to burn down—
Students departing for Iowa & Chicago,
                    New York beckoning at the end of the stage—
While Soviets have made soft landing on the moon
Today, be it rock or dust?
                    Now's Solar System born anew?
Red lights, red lights at highway end,
                    glass reflectors,
                                   there's no one On the Road.
". . . Don't know what will happen to the proud
                    American soldiers in Vietnam"
              said Ex Ambassador Ex General Taylor—

In this great space, Murchison & Hunt,
              Texas millionaires
                    sit in Isolate skyscrapers
                                   on flatland dotted with lights
or, from cities, isolate from fairies
and screaming european dowagers & sopranos,
                    plot conspiracies against Communists,
send messages to New York, Austin, Wichita
              Vancouver, Seattle, to Los Angeles—
Radio programs about the Federal Octopus—
              Seraphs of Money Power on Texas plains
                    huge fat-bellied power-men
                    shoving piles of Capital
                              by train
                    across grasslands—
Shoving messages into myriad innocent-cleaned ears
              Spiritual messages about spiritual war—
                    Come to Jesus
                         where the money is!
              Texas voice
              singing Vietnam Blues
                    Twanging
"I don't like to die / a man I ain't about t' crawl"

                    In Vital-heart,
Big truck slowly lumbers through town—
Hotels raise signs, neon winks.
Liberal's the beginning of Kansas
              Martial music filling airwaves—
only the last few weeks
              waves of military music
                    drum taps drum beats trumpets
                           pulsing thru radiostations
                                 not even sad,
              bald Sopranos
              Sacred Tenors from 1920s
              Singing antique music style
What Patriot wrote that shit?
Something to drive out the Indian
              Vibrato of Buffy Sainte-Marie?
              Doom call of McGuire?
The heavenly echo of Dylan's despair
                           before the silver microphone
              in his snake suit,
                    a reptile boy
                           disappearing in Time—
soft shoe dancing on the Moon?
It'll be a relief when the Chinese take over Texas!
       Lifeline pumping its venom "Communist Conspiracy"
Secret documents Infiltrate & smash Vatican—
              broadcast to these empty plains,
              Isolate farmhouses with radios
                    hearing the Horror Syndicate
                    take over the Universe!

Radiostations whistling & crashing against each other on autoradio—
Full moonlight on blue snow
Loudspeaker blasting midnite static
                    thru some European Swansong,
       Dit dat dits of outerspace communication
                    blanking out Ear's substance
Vatican whistles undertone
              bloops and eeeeeps, trillion-antennae'd
                    grid of the Shabda
If it's silent it isn't there—

                    *   *   *   *

Entering Kansas
          little red towers blink distance,
                    Lifeline, continued over 7 stations—
H. L. Hunt his books read,
                    Cold reasoning voice over Kansas plains—
O that's Liberal Spread before us!
Truck stopped by roadside Weighing Station

                              *

Heavy Jewish voice heard over Kansas Radio
          Varning the Jews, Take safety in Christ
                    —Dr. Michaelson
          and the Hebrew-Christian Hour
                    —P.O.B. 707 Los Angeles 53—

In 1866 & 1881 the Carbon Companies paid
$2,500,000 for the bones of Buffalos
          Representing 31,000,000 Buffalos.
Handful of Buffalo, lightbrown back shining in the sun
          Grazing at the edge of River Ginnesca—
Peter says Oooo! What
                    visions they must have of human beings—
                    silent tolerant, head bent,
                              cropping grass—
'Right now they're trying to take the Indian territories
                              away, near Hopiland.'
          Wanna build subdivisions,
                                        Mineral rights—
                    The last lands of the redskins—
Saw it in the paper t'other day
                    on the Highway near Tucson—

Blue morning in Kansas,
          black lambs dotted in snow
          Ice gleaming in brown grass at roadside
                    Corn stacks, small
                    lined up around tree groves—
Kingman Salvage, rusty autos under rusty hill,
Jodrell Bank reporting Sensational pictures Rocks on the Moon,
                    "it's a hard surface—"

information about Hog Scallops at Birth,
Meat prices, Grain prices
Steer Meat Dollar values,
     Appeal to end Property Tax

Green signs,
     Welcome to Wichita
     Population 280,000
                         January 28–29, 1966

Chances "R"

Nymph and shepherd raise electric tridents
      glowing red against the plaster wall,
The jukebox beating out magic syllables,
A line of painted boys snapping fingers
      & shaking thin Italian trouserlegs
          or rough dungarees on big asses
             bumping and dipping
ritually, with no religion but the
          old one of cocksuckers
naturally, in Kansas center of America
      the farmboys in Diabolic bar light
    alone stiff necked or lined up
    dancing row on row like Afric husbands
& the music's sad here, whereas Sunset Trip or
Jukebox Corner it's ecstatic pinball machines—
Religiously, with concentration and free
          prayer; fairy boys of the plains
          and their gay sisters of the city
step together to the center of the floor
      illumined by machine eyes, screaming drumbeats,
          passionate voices of Oklahoma City
             chanting No Satisfaction
Suspended from Heaven the Chances R
      Club floats rayed by stars
          along a Wichita tree avenue
    traversed with streetlights on the plain.

Wichita, February 1966

Wichita Vortex Sutra

I
Turn Right Next Corner
> *The Biggest Little Town in Kansas*
> > *Macpherson*

Red sun setting flat plains west streaked
> with gauzy veils, chimney mist spread
> around christmas-tree-bulbed refineries—aluminum
> white tanks squat beneath
> winking signal towers' bright plane-lights,
> > orange gas flares
> beneath pillows of smoke, flames in machinery—
> > transparent towers at dusk

In advance of the Cold Wave
> *Snow is spreading eastward to*
> > *the Great Lakes*

> News Broadcast & old clarinets
> Watertower dome Lighted on the flat plain
> car radio speeding acrost railroad tracks—

Kansas! Kansas! Shuddering at last!
> PERSON appearing in Kansas!
> angry telephone calls to the University
> Police dumbfounded leaning on
> > their radiocar hoods
> While Poets chant to Allah in the roadhouse Showboat!
Blue eyed children dance and hold thy Hand O aged Walt
> who came from Lawrence to Topeka to envision
> Iron interlaced upon the city plain—
> Telegraph wires strung from city to city O Melville!
> > Television brightening thy *rills of Kansas lone*
I come,
> lone man from the void, riding a bus
> hypnotized by red tail lights on the straight
> > space road ahead—
> & the Methodist minister with cracked eyes
> > leaning over the table
> quoting Kierkegaard "death of God"

a million dollars
in the bank   owns all West Wichita
come to Nothing!
Prajnaparamita Sutra over coffee—Vortex
of telephone radio aircraft assembly frame ammunition
petroleum nightclub Newspaper streets illuminated by Bright
EMPTINESS—

Thy sins are forgiven, Wichita!
Thy lonesomeness annulled, O Kansas dear!
as the western Twang prophesied
thru banjo, when lone cowboy walked the railroad track
past an empty station toward the sun
sinking giant-bulbed orange down the box canyon—
Music strung over his back
and empty handed   singing on this planet earth
I'm a lonely Dog, O Mother!
Come, Nebraska, sing & dance with me—
Come lovers of Lincoln and Omaha,
hear my soft voice at last
As Babes need the chemical touch of flesh in pink infancy
lest they die Idiot returning to Inhuman—
Nothing—
So, tender lipt adolescent girl, pale youth,
give me back my soft kiss
Hold me in your innocent arms,
accept my tears as yours to harvest
equal   in nature to the Wheat
that made your bodies' muscular bones
broad shouldered, boy bicept—
from leaning on cows & drinking Milk
in Midwest Solitude—
No more fear of tenderness, much delight in weeping, ecstasy
in singing, laughter rises that confounds
staring Idiot mayors
and stony politicians eyeing
Thy breast,
O Man of America, be born!
Truth breaks through!
How big is the prick of the President?
How big is Cardinal Vietnam?

How little the prince of the FBI, unmarried all these years!
How big are all the Public Figures?
What kind of flesh hangs, hidden behind their Images?

Approaching Salina,
Prehistoric excavation, *Apache Uprising*
in the drive-in theater
Shelling Bombing Range   mapped in the distance,
Crime Prevention Show, sponsor Wrigley's Spearmint
Dinosaur Sinclair advertisement, glowing green—
South 9th Street lined with poplar & elm branch
spread over evening's tiny headlights—
Salina Highschool's brick darkens Gothic
over a night-lit door—
What wreaths of naked bodies, thighs and faces,
small hairy bun'd vaginas,
silver cocks, armpits and breasts
moistened by tears
for 20 years, for 40 years?
Peking Radio surveyed by Luden's Coughdrops
Attacks on the Russians & Japanese,
Big Dipper leaning above the Nebraska border,
handle down to the blackened plains,
telephone-pole ghosts crossed
by roadside, dim headlights—
dark night, & giant T-bone steaks,
and in *The Village Voice*
New Frontier Productions present
Camp Comedy: *Fairies I Have Met.*
Blue highway lamps strung along the horizon east at Hebron
Homestead National Monument near Beatrice—

Language, language
black Earth-circle in the rear window,
no cars for miles along highway
beacon lights on oceanic plain
language, language
over Big Blue River
chanting *La illaha el (lill) Allah hu*
revolving my head to my heart like my mother
chin abreast at Allah
Eyes closed, blackness

vaster than midnight prairies,
                    Nebraskas of solitary Allah,
                        Joy, I am I
                        the lone One singing to myself
                                        God come true—
                        Thrills of fear.
                        nearer than the vein in my neck—?
What if I opened my soul to sing to my absolute self
        Singing as the car crash chomped thru blood & muscle
                                        tendon skull?
        What if I sang, and loosed the chords of fear brow?
                    What exquisite noise wd
                                shiver my car companions?
                    I am the Universe tonite
                            riding in all my Power riding
chauffeured thru my self by a long haired saint with eyeglasses
What if I sang till Students knew I was free
        of Vietnam, trousers, free of my own meat,
        free to die in my thoughtful shivering Throne?
                freer than Nebraska, freer than America—
                        May I disappear
                    in magic Joy-smoke! Pouf! reddish Vapor,
Faustus vanishes weeping & laughing
        under stars on Highway 77 between Beatrice & Lincoln—
        "Better not to move but let things be" Reverend Preacher?
                        We've all already disappeared!

Space highway open, entering Lincoln's ear
        ground to a stop Tracks Warning
                        Pioneer Boulevard—
        William Jennings Bryan sang
        Thou shalt not crucify mankind upon a cross of Gold!
                            O Baby Doe! Gold's
        Department Store hulks o'er 10th Street now
        —an unregenerate old fop who didn't want to be a monkey
        now's the Highest Perfect Wisdom dust
                and Lindsay's cry
                survives compassionate in the Highschool Anthology—
a giant dormitory brilliant on the evening plain
                            drifts with his memories—
There's a nice white door over there
                    for me O dear!   on Zero Street.

                                        February 15, 1966

                                        Wichita Vortex Sutra   405

II

Face the Nation

Thru Hickman's rolling earth hills

          icy winter

                    gray sky   bare trees lining the road

      South to Wichita

          you're in the Pepsi Generation   Signum enroute

Aiken Republican on the radio   60,000

      Northvietnamese troops now infiltrated but over 250,000

      South Vietnamese armed men

                      our Enemy—

                            Not Hanoi our enemy

                            Not China our enemy

                              The Viet Cong!

                McNamara made a "bad guess"

"Bad Guess?" chorused the Reporters.

        Yes, no more than a Bad Guess, in 1962

                    "8000 American Troops handle the

                    Situation"

                    Bad Guess

    in 1954, 80% of the

      Vietnamese people would've voted for Ho Chi Minh

      wrote Ike   years later   *Mandate for Change*

                A bad guess in the Pentagon

And the Hawks were guessing all along

                Bomb China's 200,000,000

              cried Stennis from Mississippi

              I guess it was 3 weeks ago

   Holmes Alexander in Albuquerque Journal

         Provincial newsman

          said I guess we better begin to do that Now,

      his typewriter clacking in his aged office

      on a side street   under Sandia Mountain?

      Half the world away from China

Johnson got some bad advice   Republican Aiken sang

to the Newsmen over the radio

        The General guessed they'd stop infiltrating the South

              if they bombed the North—

              So I guess they bombed!

Pale Indochinese boys came thronging thru the jungle

          in increased numbers

        to the scene of TERROR!

While the triangle-roofed Farmer's Grain Elevator
    sat quietly by the side of the road
        along the railroad track
  American Eagle beating its wings over Asia
    million dollar helicopters
    a billion dollars worth of Marines
      who loved *Aunt Betty*
      Drawn from the shores and farms shaking
    from the high schools to the landing barge
    blowing the air thru their cheeks with fear
      in *Life* on Television
Put it this way on the radio
Put it this way in television language
        Use the words
            language, language:
             "A bad guess"

Put it this way in headlines
  Omaha World Herald—*Rusk Says Toughness*
        Essential For Peace
Put it this way
  Lincoln Nebraska morning Star—
      Vietnam War Brings Prosperity
Put it *this* way
    Declared McNamara   speaking language
      Asserted Maxwell Taylor
      General, Consultant to White House
  Viet Cong losses leveling up three five zero zero per month
    Front page testimony February '66
  Here in Nebraska same as Kansas same known in Saigon
    in Peking, in Moscow, same known
  by the youths of Liverpool three five zero zero
  the latest quotation in the human meat market—
      Father I cannot tell a lie!

A black horse bends its head to the stubble
  beside the silver stream winding thru the woods
  by an antique red barn on the outskirts of Beatrice—
      Quietness, quietness
    over this countryside
      except for unmistakable signals on radio
      followed by the honkytonk tinkle
        of a city piano

to calm the nerves of taxpaying housewives of a Sunday morn.
                    Has anyone looked in the eyes of the dead?
U.S. Army recruiting service sign *Careers With A Future*
           Is anyone living to look for future forgiveness?
Water hoses frozen on the street, the
           Crowd gathered to see a strange happening garage—
              Red flames on Sunday morning
                        in a quiet town!
Has anyone looked in the eyes of the wounded?
           Have we seen but paper faces, Life Magazine?
           Are screaming faces made of dots,
                electric dots on Television—
                    fuzzy decibels registering
                        the mammal voiced howl
from the outskirts of Saigon to console model picture tubes
           in Beatrice, in Hutchinson, in El Dorado
                    in historic Abilene
                    O inconsolable!

           Stop, and eat more flesh.
"We will negotiate anywhere anytime"
           said the giant President
       Kansas City Times 2/14/66: "Word reached U.S. authorities that
Thailand's leaders feared that in Honolulu Johnson might have tried to
persuade South Vietnam's rulers to ease their stand against negotiating
with the Viet Cong.
       American officials said these fears were groundless and Humphrey
was telling the Thais so."
                        AP dispatch
                    The last week's paper is Amnesia.

Three five zero zero is numerals
Headline language poetry, nine decades after Democratic Vistas
           and the Prophecy of the Good Gray Poet
              Our nation "of the fabled damned"
                    or else . . .
       Language, language
Ezra Pound the Chinese Written Character for truth
       defined as man standing by his word
           Word picture: forked creature
                        Man

standing by a box, birds flying out
representing mouth speech
Ham Steak please waitress, in the warm café.
Different from a bad guess.
The war is language,
language abused
for Advertisement,
language used
like magic for power on the planet:
Black Magic language,
formulas for reality—
Communism is a 9 letter word
used by inferior magicians with
the wrong alchemical formula for transforming earth into gold
—funky warlocks operating on guesswork,
handmedown mandrake terminology
that never worked in 1956
for gray-domed Dulles,
brooding over at State,
that never worked for Ike who knelt to take
the magic wafer in his mouth
from Dulles' hand
inside the church in Washington:
Communion of bum magicians
congress of failures from Kansas & Missouri
working with the wrong equations
Sorcerer's Apprentices who lost control
of the simplest broomstick in the world:
Language
O longhaired magician come home take care of your dumb helper
before the radiation deluge floods your livingroom,
your magic errandboy's
just made a bad guess again
that's lasted a whole decade.

N B C B S U P A P I N S L I F E
Time Mutual presents
World's Largest Camp Comedy:
Magic In Vietnam—
reality turned inside out
changing its sex in the Mass Media
for 30 days, TV den and bedroom farce

Flashing pictures Senate Foreign Relations Committee room
    Generals faces flashing on and off screen
                                  mouthing language
  State Secretary speaking nothing but language
  McNamara declining to speak public language
    The President talking language,
          Senators reinterpreting language
      General Taylor *Limited Objectives*
                   Owls from Pennsylvania
        Clark's Face *Open Ended*
             Dove's *Apocalypse*
             Morse's hairy ears
Stennis orating in Mississippi
        half billion chinamen crowding into the
                         polling booth,
    Clean shaven Gen. Gavin's image
                imagining *Enclaves*
      Tactical Bombing the magic formula for
  a silver haired Symington:
Ancient Chinese apothegm:
          Old in vain.
    Hawks swooping thru the newspapers
        talons visible
  wings outspread in the giant updraft of hot air
           loosing their dry screech in the skies
                    over the Capitol
Napalm and black clouds emerging in newsprint
  Flesh soft as a Kansas girl's
        ripped open by metal explosion—
three five zero zero   on the other side of the planet
    caught in barbed wire, fire ball
    bullet shock, bayonet electricity
bomb blast terrific in skull & belly, shrapneled throbbing meat
While this American nation argues war:
      conflicting language, language
              proliferating in airwaves
  filling the farmhouse ear, filling
    the City Manager's head in his oaken office
    the professor's head in his bed at midnight
    the pupil's head at the movies
        blond haired, his heart throbbing with desire
        for the girlish image bodied on the screen:

or smoking cigarettes
and watching Captain Kangaroo
that fabled damned of nations
prophecy come true—
Though the highway's straight,
dipping downward through low hills,
rising narrow on the far horizon
black cows browse in caked fields
ponds in the hollows lie frozen,
quietness.
Is this the land that started war on China?
This be the soil that thought Cold War for decades?
Are these nervous naked trees & farmhouses
the vortex
of oriental anxiety molecules
that've imagined   American Foreign Policy
and magick'd up paranoia 'in Peking
and curtains of living blood
surrounding far Saigon?
Are these the towns where the language emerged
from the mouths here
that makes a Hell of riots in Dominica
sustains the aging tyranny of Chiang in silent Taipeh city
Paid for the lost French war in Algeria
overthrew the Guatemalan polis in '54
maintaining United Fruit's banana greed
another thirteen years
for the secret prestige of the Dulles family lawfirm?

Here's Marysville—
a black railroad engine in the children's park,
at rest—
and the Track Crossing
with Cotton Belt flatcars
carrying autos west from Dallas
Delaware & Hudson gondolas filled with power stuff—
a line of boxcars far east as the eye can see
carrying battle goods to cross the Rockies
into the hands of rich longshoremen loading
ships on the Pacific—
Oakland Army Terminal lights
blue illumined all night now—

Crash of couplings and the great American train
　　　　　moves on carrying its cushioned load of metal doom
　　　　Union Pacific linked together with your Hoosier Line
　　　　　　followed by passive Wabash
　　　　　　　　rolling behind
　　　　　　all Erie carrying cargo in the rear,
　　　　　Central Georgia's rust colored truck proclaiming
　　　　　　　　　The Right Way, concluding
　　　the awesome poem writ by the train
　　　　　　across northern Kansas,
　　　　　land which gave right of way
　　　　　to the massing of metal meant for explosion
　　　　　　　　　in Indochina—
Passing thru Waterville,
　　　Electronic machinery in the bus humming prophecy—
　　　　　paper signs blowing in cold wind,
　　　　　　　　mid-Sunday afternoon's silence in town
　　　　　under frost-gray sky
　　　　　　　　　that covers the horizon—
That the rest of earth is unseen,
　　　　　　　　an outer universe invisible,
　　　　　Unknown except thru
　　　　　　　　　　language
　　　　　　　　　　　airprint
　　　　　　　　　　　　magic images
　　　or prophecy of the secret
　　　　　　heart the same
　　　　　in Waterville as Saigon one human form:
　　　　　When a woman's heart bursts in Waterville
　　　　　　a woman screams equal in Hanoi—
On to Wichita to prophesy! O frightful Bard!
　　　into the heart of the Vortex
　　　　　where anxiety rings
　　　　　　　the University with millionaire pressure,
　　　　　lonely crank telephone voices sighing in dread,
　　and students waken trembling in their beds
　　　　　with dreams of a new truth warm as meat,
　　　　　little girls suspecting their elders of murder
　　　　　　committed by remote control machinery,
　　　　　boys with sexual bellies aroused
　　　　　　chilled in the heart by the mailman

with a letter from an aging white haired General
          Director of selection for service in Deathwar
      all this black language
                    writ by machine!
              O hopeless Fathers and Teachers
            in Hué   do you know
                      the same woe too?

I'm an old man now, and a lonesome man in Kansas
          but not afraid
                      to speak my lonesomeness in a car,
          because not only my lonesomeness
              it's Ours, all over America,
                          O tender fellows—
              & spoken lonesomeness is Prophecy
              in the moon 100 years ago or in
                      the middle of Kansas now.
It's not the vast plains mute our mouths
                  that fill at midnite with ecstatic language
          when our trembling bodies hold each other
              breast to breast on a mattress—
        Not the empty sky that hides
                      the feeling from our faces
      nor our skirts and trousers that conceal
              the bodylove emanating in a glow of beloved skin,
                  white smooth abdomen down to the hair
                              between our legs, ·
          It's not a God that bore us that forbid
              our Being, like a sunny rose
                      all red with naked joy
                  between our eyes & bellies, yes
All we do is for this frightened thing
              we call Love, want and lack—
        fear that we aren't the one whose body could be
              beloved of all the brides of Kansas City,
              kissed all over by every boy of Wichita—
        O but how many in their solitude weep aloud like me—
            On the bridge over Republican River
                  almost in tears to know
                          how to speak the right language—
              on the frosty broad road
                  uphill between highway embankments

I search for the language
                 that is also yours—
       almost all our language has been taxed by war.
Radio antennae high tension
          wires ranging from Junction City across the plains—
       highway cloverleaf sunk in a vast meadow
                    lanes curving past Abilene
                           to Denver filled with old
                                   heroes of love—
                 to Wichita where McClure's mind
                       burst into animal beauty
                       drunk, getting laid in a car
                             in a neon misted street
                                 15 years ago—
        to Independence where the old man's still alive
    who loosed the bomb that's slaved all human consciousness
                   and made the body universe a place of fear—
Now, speeding along the empty plain,
            no giant demon machine
                   visible on the horizon
         but tiny human trees and wooden houses at the sky's edge
           I claim my birthright!
                   reborn forever as long as Man
                        in Kansas or other universe—Joy
           reborn after the vast sadness of War Gods!
A lone man talking to myself, no house in the brown vastness to hear,
           imaging the throng of Selves
                 that make this nation one body of Prophecy
                      languaged by Declaration as Pursuit of
                             Happiness!
I call all Powers of imagination
         to my side in this auto to make Prophecy,
                                      all Lords
          of human kingdoms to come
Shambu Bharti Baba naked covered with ash
          Khaki Baba fat-bellied mad with the dogs
Dehorahava Baba who moans Oh how wounded, How wounded
    Sitaram Onkar Das Thakur who commands
                             give up your desire
Satyananda who raises two thumbs in tranquillity
     Kali Pada Guha Roy whose yoga drops before the void
          Shivananda who touches the breast and says OM

Srimata Krishnaji of Brindaban who says take for your guru
    William Blake the invisible father of English visions
    Sri Ramakrishna master of ecstasy eyes
        half closed who only cries for his mother
Chaitanya arms upraised singing & dancing his own praise
    merciful Chango judging our bodies
        Durga-Ma covered with blood
           destroyer of battlefield illusions
           million-faced Tathagata gone past suffering
Preserver Harekrishna returning in the age of pain
Sacred Heart my Christ acceptable
        Allah the Compassionate One
           Jaweh Righteous One
      all Knowledge-Princes of Earth-man, all
    ancient Seraphim of heavenly Desire, Devas, yogis
        & holymen I chant to—
           Come to my lone presence
                into this Vortex named Kansas,
I lift my voice aloud,
    make Mantra of American language now,
        I here declare the end of the War!
           Ancient days' Illusion!—
      and pronounce words beginning my own millennium.
Let the States tremble,
    let the Nation weep,
        let Congress legislate its own delight
           let the President execute his own desire—
this Act done by my own voice,
           nameless Mystery—
published to my own senses,
           blissfully received by my own form
    approved with pleasure by my sensations
    manifestation of my very thought
    accomplished in my own imagination
        all realms within my consciousness fulfilled
    60 miles from Wichita
           near El Dorado,
             The Golden One,
in chill earthly mist
    houseless brown farmland plains rolling heavenward
                in every direction

one midwinter afternoon Sunday called the day of the Lord—
            Pure Spring Water gathered in one tower
                        where Florence is
                                    set on a hill,
                        stop for tea & gas

            Cars passing their messages along country crossroads
                        to populaces cement-networked on flatness,
                                                giant white mist on earth
                        and a Wichita Eagle-Beacon headlines
                        "Kennedy Urges Cong Get Chair in Negotiations"
The War is gone,
            Language emerging on the motel news stand,
                                    the right magic
                        Formula, the language known
            in the back of the mind before, now in black print
                                    daily consciousness
Eagle News Services Saigon—
            Headline Surrounded Vietcong Charge Into Fire Fight
                        the suffering not yet ended
                                    for others
                        The last spasms of the dragon of pain
                                    shoot thru the muscles
                        a crackling around the eyeballs
                        of a sensitive yellow boy by a muddy wall
Continued from page one   area
            after the Marines killed 256 Vietcong captured 31
            ten day operation Harvest Moon last December
                                    Language language
            U.S. Military Spokesmen
                        Language language
                                    Cong death toll
            has soared to 100 in First Air Cavalry
            Division's Sector of
                        Language language
                        Operation White Wing near Bong Son
Some of the
            Language language
                        Communist
                                    Language language soldiers
charged so desperately
            they were struck with six or seven bullets before they fell

Language Language M 60 Machine Guns
                    Language language in La Drang Valley
the terrain is rougher infested with leeches and scorpions
                    The war was over several hours ago!
Oh at last again the radio opens
        blue Invitations!
                    Angelic Dylan singing across the nation
                        "When all your children start to resent you
                        Won't you come see me, Queen Jane?"
        His youthful voice making glad
                            the brown endless meadows
        His tenderness penetrating aether,
            soft prayer on the airwaves,
                    Language language, and sweet music too
                    even unto thee,
                            hairy flatness!
                    even unto thee
                                despairing Burns!

Future speeding on swift wheels
                    straight to the heart of Wichita!
Now radio voices cry population hunger world
                        of unhappy people
                    waiting for Man to be born
                        O man in America!
        you certainly smell good
                        the radio says
        passing mysterious families of winking towers
        grouped round a quonset-hut on a hillock—
                feed storage or military fear factory here?
Sensitive City, Ooh! Hamburger & Skelley's Gas
                    lights feed man and machine,
        Kansas Electric Substation aluminum robot
            signals thru thin antennae towers
            above the empty football field
                                    at Sunday dusk
to a solitary derrick that pumps oil from the unconscious
                    working night & day
        & factory gas-flares edge a huge golf course
            where tired businessmen can come and play—

Cloverleaf, Merging Traffic East Wichita turnoff
McConnell Airforce Base
nourishing the city—
Lights rising in the suburbs
Supermarket Texaco brilliance starred
over streetlamp vertebrae on Kellogg,
green jeweled traffic lights
confronting the windshield,
Centertown ganglion entered!
Crowds of autos moving with their lightshine,
signbulbs winking in the driver's eyeball—
The human nest collected, neon lit,
and sunburst signed
for business as usual, except on the Lord's Day—
Redeemer Lutheran's three crosses lit on the lawn
reminder of our sins
and Titsworth offers insurance on Hydraulic
by De Voors Guard's Mortuary for outmoded bodies
of the human vehicle
which no Titsworth of insurance will customize for resale—
So home, traveler, past the newspaper language factory
under Union Station railroad bridge on Douglas
to the center of the Vortex, calmly returned
to Hotel Eaton—
Carry Nation began the war on Vietnam here
with an angry smashing ax
attacking Wine—
Here fifty years ago, by her violence
began a vortex of hatred that defoliated the Mekong Delta—
Proud Wichita! vain Wichita
cast the first stone!—
That murdered my mother
who died of the communist anticommunist psychosis
in the madhouse one decade long ago
complaining about wires of masscommunication in her head
and phantom political voices in the air
besmirching her girlish character.
Many another has suffered death and madness
in the Vortex from Hydraulic
to the end of 17th—enough!

The war is over now—
    Except for the souls
        held prisoner in Niggertown
still pining for love of your tender white bodies O children of Wichita!

                           February 14, 1966

Auto Poesy: On the Lam
from Bloomington

Setting out East on rain bright highways
     Indianapolis, police cars speeding past
     gas station—Stopped for matches
PLOWL of Silence,
  Street bulbs flash cosmic blue—darkness!
     POW, lights flash on again!
      pavement-gleam
       Mobil station pumps lit in rain
ZAP, darkness, highway power failure
     rain hiss
       traffic lights dead black—
Ho! Dimethyl Triptamine flashing circle vibrations
    center Spiked—
    Einsteinian Mandala,
  Spectrum translucent,
. . . Television eyeball dots in treehouse Ken Kesey's
Power failure inside the head,
  neural apparatus crackling—
So drift months later past
      Eli Lilly pharmaceuticals' tower walls
  asleep in early morning dark outside Indianapolis
Street lamps lit humped along downtown Greenfield
News from Dallas, Dirksen declareth
  "Vietnam Protesters have forgotten the lessons of History"
Across Ohio River, noon
  old wire bridge, auto graveyards,
  Washington town covered with rust—hm—

         February 1966

Kansas City to Saint Louis

Leaving K.C. Mo.   past Independence   past Liberty
Charlie Plymell's memories of K.C. renewed
              The Jewel-box Review,
                 white-wigged fat camps yakking abt
                Georgie Washington and Harry T.
        filthier than any poetry reading I ever gave
              applauded
        by the police negro wives Mafia subsidized

To East St. Louis on the broad road
              Highway 70 crammed with trucks
        Last night almost broke my heart dancing to
                  Cant Get No Satisfaction
        lotsa beer & slept naked in the guest room—
                           Now
Sunlit wooded hills overhang the highway
rolling toward the Sex Factories of Indiana—
              Automobile graveyard, red cars dumped
              bleeding under empty skies—
        Burchfield's paintings, Walker Evans' photos,
           a white Victorian house on a hill—
Trumble & Bung of chamber music
              pianoesque on radio—midwest culture
              before rock and roll

If I knew   twenty years ago   what I know now
I coulda led a symphony orchestra in Minneapolis
              & worn a tuxedo

Heart to heart, the Kansas voice of Ella Mae
          "are you afraid of growing old,
      afraid you'll no longer be attractive to your husband?"
"... I dont see any reason" says the radio
                        "for those agitators—
Why dont they move in with the negroes? We've been separated all along,
why change things now? But I'll hang up, some other Martian might want
to call in, who has another thought."
              The Voice of Leavenworth
          echoing thru space to the car dashboard

". . . causes and agitations, then, then they're doing the work of the commu-
nists as J. Edgar Hoover says, and many of these people are people with uh
respectable, bility, of a cloak of respectability that shows uh uh teachers
professors and students . . ."
      hollow voice, a minister
      breathing thru the telephone
"God created all the races . . . and it is only men who tried to mix em up,
and when they mix em up that's when the trouble starts."

No place like Booneville though, buddy—
     End of the Great Plains,
       late afternoon sun, rusty leaves on trees
One of these days those boots will walk all over you

We the People—shelling the Viet Cong
"Inflation has swept in upon us . . . Johnson administration rather than a
prudent Budget . . . discipline the American people rather than discipline
itself . . ."

I lay in bed naked in the guest room,
   my mouth found his cock,
     my hand under his behind
      Till the whole body stiffened
       and sperm choked my throat.

Michele, John Lennon & Paul McCartney
   wooing the decade
     gaps from the 30s returned
    It's the only words I know that
      You'll understand . . .

Old earth rolling mile after mile patient
    The ground
      I roll on
        the ground
     the music soars above
The ground electric arguments
      ray over
The ground dotted with signs for Dave's Eat Eat
   scarred by highways, eaten by voices
      Pete's Café—
       Golden land in setting sun

Missouri River icy brown, black cows,
        grass tufts standing up hairy on hills
                mirrored to heaven—
                Spring one month to come.
Sea shells on the ground strata'd by the turnpike—
        Old ocean evaporated away,
                Mastodons stomped, dinosaurs groaned
                        when these brown hillocks were
                        leafy steam-green-swamp-think Marsh nations
        before the Birch Society was a gleam in the
                                Pterodactyl's eye
—Aeroplane sinking groundward
        toward my white Volkswagen prehistoric
        white cockroach under high tension wires—
        my face, Rasputin in car mirror.

Funky barn, black hills approaching Fulton
        where Churchill rang down the Curtain
                on Consciousness
        and set a chill which overspread the world
                one icy day in Missouri
                        not far from the Ozarks—
        Provincial ears heard the Spenglerian Iron
                        Terror Pronouncement
                Magnificent Language, they said,
                        for country ears—
St Louis calling St Louis calling
        Twenty years ago,
                Thirty years ago
                        the Burroughs School
Pink cheeked Kenney with fine blond hair,
        his almond eyes aristocrat
                gazed,
        Morphy teaching English & Rimbaud
                at midnight to the fauns
        W.S.B. leather cheeked, sardonic
                waiting for change of consciousness,
                        unnamed in those days—
        coffee, vodka, night for needles,
                young bodies
                        beautiful unknown to themselves
                running around St Louis

on a Friday evening
            getting drunk in awe & honor of the
                terrific future these
red dry trees at sunset go thru two decades later
                They could've seen
        the animal branches, wrinkled to the sky
                & known the gnarled prophecy to come,
if they'd opened their eyes outa the whiskey-haze
                    in Mississippi riverfront bars
        and gone into the country with a knapsack to
                        smell the ground.

                Oh grandfather maple and elm!
Antique leafy old oak of Kingdom City in the purple light
            come down, year after year,
                to the tune
                    of mellow pianos.
Salute, silent wise ones,
                Cranking powers of the ground,
        awkward arms of knowledge
        reaching blind above the gas station
                by the high TV antennae
        Stay silent, ugly Teachers,
let me & the Radio yell about Vietnam and mustard gas.

                "Torture . . . tear gas legitimate weapons . . .
Worries language beyond my comprehension" the radio
                commentator says himself.
Use the language today
            ". . . a great blunder"
                in Vietnam, heavy voices,
"A great blunder . . . once you're in, uh,
        one of these things, uh . . ."
"Stay in." Withdraw,
        Language, language, uh, uh
        from the mouths of Senators, uh
            trying to think of Senators, uh
                trying to think on their feet
                    Saying uhh, politely
Shift linguals, said Burroughs, Cut the Word Lines!
        He was right all along.
                    ". . . a procurer of these dogs

. . . take them from the United States . . . Major Caty . . . as long as it's not
a white dog . . . Sentry Dog Procurement Center, Texas . . . No dogs, once
trained, are ever returned to the owner . . ."
                    French Truth,
                            Dutch Civility
            Black asphalt, blue stars,
                tail light procession speeding East,
The hero surviving his own murder,
        his own suicide, his own
                    addiction, surviving his own
        poetry, surviving his own
                    disappearance from the scene—
returned in new faces, shining
        through the tears of new eyes.
            New small adolescent hands
                    on tiny breasts,
        pale silken skin at the thighs,
            and the cherry-prick raises hard
                    innocent heat pointed up
            from the muscular belly
of basketball highschool English class spiritual Victory,
        made clean at midnight in the bathtub of old City,
                        hair combed for love—
millionaire body from Clayton or spade queen from E St Louis
            laughing together in the TWA lounge
Blue-lit airfields into St Louis,
        past billboards ruddy neon,
            looking for old hero renewed,
                a new decade—
Hill-wink of houses,
    Monotone road gray bridging the streets
    thin bones of aluminum sentineled dark
    on the suburban hump bearing high wires
                    for thought to traverse
            river & wood, from hero to hero—

Crane all's well, the wanderer returns
                from the west with his Powers,
        the Shaman with his beard
                in full strength,
        the longhaired Crank with subtle humorous voice
                    enters city after city

to kiss the eyes of your high school sailors
and make laughing Blessing
for a new Age in America
spaced with concrete but Souled by yourself
with Desire,
or like yourself of perfect Heart, adorable
and adoring its own millioned population
one by one self-wakened
under the radiant signs
of Power stations stacked above the river
highway spanning highway,
bridged from suburb to suburb.

March 1966

Bayonne Entering NYC

Smog trucks mile after mile high wire
    Pylons trestled toward New York
        black multilane highway showered w/blue arc-lamps,
            city glare horizoning
            Megalopolis with burning factories—
Bayonne refineries behind Newark Hell-light
    truck trains passing trans-continental gas-lines,
        blinking safety signs KEEP AWAKE
Giant giant giant transformers,
           electricity Stacks' glowing smoke—
    More Chimney fires than all Kansas in a mile,
Sulphur chemical Humble gigantic viaducts
                networked by road side
        What smell burning rubber, oil
                "freshens your mouth"
      Railroad rust, deep marsh garbage-fume
              Nostril horns—
   city Announcer jabbering at City Motel,
    flat winking space ships descending overhead
        GORNEY GORNEY MORTUARY
Brilliant signs the
    10 P.M. clock churchspire lit in Suburb City,
    New Jersey's colored streets asleep—
High derrick spotlites lamped an inch above
                roofcombs
    Shoprite lit for Nite people before the vast
Hohokus marshes and Passaic's flat gluey
      Blackness ringed with lightbulbs.
Blue Newark airport,
      Lights at the field edge,
         Robot towers blazon'd Eastern Air TWA
        above the lavender bulbed runway
     across the barrage of car bridges—

I was born there in Newark
    Public Service sign of the twenties
      visible miles away through smoke
        gray night over electric fields
My aunts and uncles died in hospitals,

are buried in graves surrounded by Railroad Tracks,
    tombed near Winking 3 Ring Ballantine Ale's home
      where Western Electric has a Cosmic plant,
    Pitt-Consoles breathes forth fumes
      acrid above Flying Service tanks
      Where superhighway rises over Monsanto
          metal structures moonlit
      Pulaski Skyway hanging airy black in heaven my childhood
      neighbored with gigantic harbor stacks,
             steam everywhere
    Blue Star buses skimming skyroads
        beside th'antennae mazes
          brilliant by Canalside—

Empire State's orange shoulders lifted above the Hell,
New York City buildings glitter
      visible over Palisades' trees
        Guys From War put tiger in yr Tank—
    Radio crawling with Rockmusic youngsters,
           STOP—PAY TOLL
    let the hitchhiker off in the acrid Mist—
    Blue uniformed attendants rocking on their heels in green booths
      Light parade everywhere
    Cliff rooms, balconies & giant nineteenth century schools,
      reptilian trucks on Jersey roads
Manhattan star-spread behind Ft. Lee cliffside
        Evening lights reflected across Hudson water—
    brilliant diamond-lantern'd Tunnel
        Whizz of bus-trucks shimmer in Ear
            over red brick
        under Whitmanic Yawp Harbor here
          roll into Man city, my city, Mannahatta
            Lower East Side ghosted &
    grimed with Heroin, shit-black from Edison towers
        on East River's rib—

Green-hatted doormen awaken the eve
          in statuary-niched yellow lobbies—
zephyrous canyons brightlit, gray stone Empire State
        too small to be God
      lords it over sweet Macy's & Seafood City
        by junkie Grant Hotel—

Ho Ho turn right by the Blackman who crosses the street
　　　　　lighting his cigarette, lone on asphalt
　　　　　　　　as the Lord in Nebraska—
　　　　Down 5th Avenue, brr—the irregular spine
　　　　　　　　of streetlights—
　　　　　　traffic signals all turned red at once—
　　　　　　insect lamps blink in dim artery
　　　　replicated down stone vales to Union Square—
　　　　　　　　In silence wait to see your home
　　　　Cemented asphalt, wire roof-banked,
　　　　　　　　canyoned, hived & churched with mortar,
　　　　　　　　　　mortised with art gas—
　　　　　　　　　　passing Ginsberg Machine Co.
th'axhead antique Flatiron
　　　Building looms, old photographs
　　　　　　　parked in the mind—
　　Cannastra your 21st Street lofts dark no more raw
　　　　　　　　　　meat law business
　　Tonite Naomi your 18th Westside Stalinesque
　　　　　madstreet's blocked by a bus,
　　Dusty your 16th (drunk in yr party dress) walls
　　　　　emptiness Hudson River perspectiv'd
　　Dali in London? Joe Army yr brokenbone Churches
　　　　　　　　stand brown in time—
　　　　　How quiet Washington Monument!
　　& fairy youth turns head downstreet
　　　　　crossing 5th Avenue under trafficlite,
　　　doorman playing poodledog
　　　　on brilliant-lit sidewalk No. 1.
　　an old reporter w/ brown leather briefcase
　　　　　leaves the shiny-pillared apartment—
Gee it's a Miracle to be back on this street
　　　　where strange guy mustache
　　　　　　stares in the windowshield—
　　Lovely the Steak Sign! bleeps on & off
　　　　　beneath Woman's prison—
　　Sixth Avenue bus back-window bright glass
　　　　　Lady in kerchief leans backward,
　　corner Whalen's Drugs, an old Beret familiar face
　　　　　　　nods goodbye girl
Humm, Macdougal I lived here,
　　　　Humm, perfect, there's empty space

Park by the bright-lit bookstore—
Where I'll find my mail
& Harmonium, new from Calcutta
Waiting I come back to New York & begin to Sing.

March 1966

Growing Old Again

The delicate french girl jukebox husky lament
softens the air over checkered tablecloths
I haven't been in Kettle of Fish a year
Between my Moscows and Wichitas a lonesome moment
Content to gaze at Bodenheim & Gould in garish oil,
Phantoms I'm not over the bar wall mirroring photos
of old habitués renowned characteristic seasons for lack
of immortality, a bunch of provincial drunks fucked up
D.T. unbearables or Mafia brothers-in-law.
Old charm of anonymity, phonograph memory playing
familiar bar tunes infrequent   visited much
once real hotspot cops on telephone me drunk loved
some heart friend image money at same table same
prophecy felt immortal then—now come true sit
decade hence jukebox-dazed an Angel remembered to forget.

                                                      March 3, 1966

Uptown

Yellow-lit Budweiser signs over oaken bars,
"I've seen everything"—the bartender handing me change of $10,
I stared at him amiably eyes thru an obvious Adamic beard—
with Montana musicians homeless in Manhattan, teenage
curly hair themselves—we sat at the antique booth & gossiped,
Madame Grady's literary salon a curious value in New York—
"If I had my way I'd cut off your hair and send you to Vietnam"—
"Bless you then" I replied to a hatted thin citizen hurrying to the barroom
    door
upon wet dark Amsterdam Avenue decades later—
"And if I couldn't do that I'd cut your throat" he snarled farewell,
and "Bless you sir" I added as he went to his fate in the rain, dapper Irishman.

April 1966

The Old Village Before I Die

Entering Minetta's soft yellow chrome, to the acrid bathroom
22 years ago a gold kid wrote "human-kindness" contrasting
"humankind-ness" on enamel urinal where Crane's match skated—
Christmas subway, lesbian slacks, friend bit someone's earlobe off
tore gold ring from queer ear, weeping, vomited—
My first drunk nite flashed here, Joe Gould's beard gray
("a professional bore" said Bill cruelly)—but as I was less than twenty,
New scene rayed eternal—caricatures of ancient comedians
framed over checkertabled booths, first love struck my heart heavy
prophecy of THIS MOMENT I looked in the urinal mirror returning decades
late same heavy honey in heart—bearded hairy bald with age
Soft music Smoke gets in your eyes Michele Show Me the Way to Go to
    Jail
from stereophonic jukebox that once echoed You Always Hurt The One
    You Love as dear Jack
did know under portraits of Al Smith, Jimmy Walker, Jimmy Durante, Billy
    Rose.

May 11, 1966

Consulting I Ching Smoking Pot Listening to the Fugs Sing Blake

That which pushes upward
     does not come back
He led me in his garden
      tinkle of 20 year phonograph
   Death is icumen in
     and mocks my loss of liberty
One must see the Great Man
   Fear not it brings blessing
       No Harm
    from the invisible world
Perseverance
   Realms beyond
        Stoned
in the deserted city
    which lies below consciousness
          June 1966

Wings Lifted over the Black Pit

City Flats, Coal yards and brown rivers
    Tower groups toyed by silver bridge
        Sudden the snake uncoils
  w/ thousands of little bodies riding granite scales
  looped in approach to Geo. Washington's steel trestle
    roped to Jersey west
  Blue sunray on air heights, bubbled with thick steam
                roofing the planet—
    The jet plane glides toward Chicago.

Blue ground lands, chill cabin, white wings
    Stretch over mist-ribboned horizon
  small windows let in half moon
    a silver jet hangs in the sky south
  Brown gas of the City wrapped over hills—
Chanting Mantras all the way
    Hare Krishna etc.
      Till dinner, great Lake below,
Heard a sweet drone in the plane-whine
    Hari Om Namo Shivaye—So
Made my own music
    American Mantra—
      "Peace in Chicago,
      Peace in Saigon—"
Raw orange sunset, & plunging in white cloud-shore
    Floated thru vast fog-waves
        down to black Chicago bottom
O'Hare Field's runway's blue insect lights on Wingèd Machinery
    Ozark Airways zoom up toward the Moon
Square Networks bulb-lit
    Twinkling blocks massed toward horizon
        Kremlin'd with red towers,

Aethereal cloverleafs' pinpointed circlets,
   Metropolis by night,
By air, Man's home filamented black panorama-skin
       brilliant below my chair & book—
   Impossible to be Mayor! know all details!?
   Alleyed with light,
      lampless yards
         blazing compounds factoried cube-like,
            prisons shining brilliant!
Suburban moviehouses' tiny glow
       by the Delicatessen corner,
  Vast hoards of men Negro'd in the gloom,
      gnashing their teeth for miles.
  Tears in attick's blackness
  Swastikas worshipped in the White Urb,
    clean teeth bared in Reptilian smiles—

Newsphoto Vision: M. L. King Attacked by Rocks—
Dark Land,
   Sparse networks of Serpent electricity
     Dotted between towers
    Signaling to themselves beneath the moon—

        *

Living like beasts,
  befouling our own nests,
     Smoke & Steam, broken glass & beer cans,
           Auto exhaust—
Civilization shit littering the streets,
Fine black mist over apartments
    watercourses running with oil
      fish fellows dead—

           June 1966

Cleveland, the Flats

To D. A. Levy

Into the Flats, thru Cleveland's
        Steeple trees illuminated
   Lake Bridge Light college cars speed round white lines
         thru Green Lights, past downtown's pale Hotels
Triple towers smokestacked steaming in blue nite
            buildings in water, the shimmer of that
                  factory in the blackness
        a little tinkle RR engine bell
See the orange bedroom shack
         under the viaduct
crisscrossed with 1930s raindrops Tragedies
         extrapolating railroads overhead—
   Asphalt road bumps—
        that blue flame burning? Industry!
   Bom! Bom! Mahadev! Microphone Icecream!
         Battle Conditions! Come in Towers!
Buster Keaton died today, folksongs in the iron smell
         of Republic Steel, hish—!
   American children crossing Jones Laughlin's yellow
               bridge saying o how
        Beautiful, and Work ye Tarriers Work
        in the fiery hill on the Press,
         under black smoke—
Oh yes look, the lake mill lights—
        Like an organpipe that smokestack
            Hart Crane died under—
Black Tank Skeleton lifted over railroads' orange lamps,
illustrious robots stretched with wires,
   smoking organpipes of God in the Cleveland Flats
   Open hearth furnaces light up sky,
   all night gas station
Polack Stokers running out of money
   "Bearded short Amish, square-faced & incestuous,
   big-eared buck-toothed women, like cross-eyed cats"
Steelton downhill, that smell What is it?
The guys wander up & down their gas refining Cracker
         climbing ladders in white light—
Butane smells—Creosote—

"Looka that gas-cloud we just passed thru—"
                    Twin heavy smokestacks there—
Space age children wandering like lost orphans
          thru the landscape filled with iron—
          their grandfathers sweated over forges!
                    now all they know is all them rockets they see silvery
                    Quivering on Television—
                    I don't know any more.
Move ye wheels move
          for Independent Towel—
Dakota Hotel, old Red brick apartment,
up Carnegie to University Circle,
Om Om Om Sa Ra Wa Buddha Dakini Yea,
Benzo Wani Yea   Benzo Bero
     Tsani Yea Hūṃ   Hūṃ   Hūṃ
     Phat Phat Phat Svaha!

                         June 1966

To the Body

Enthroned in plastic, shrouded in wool, diamond crowned,
transported in aluminum, shoe'd in synthetic rubber, fed by asparagus,
    adored by all animals,
ear-lull'd by electric mantra rock, chemical roses acrid in the nose,
observant of large-nostril'd air factories, every crack of the skin kissed by
    beloved grandmothers,
so man woman child are tender meat become consciously genital with the
    shudder & blush of substance
adorned with hair at crotch and brain—beard on lion and youth by fireside.

June 15, 1966

Iron Horse

I
This is the creature I am!
      Sittin in little roomette Santa Fe train
    naked abed, bright afternoon sun light
          leaking below closed window-blind
White hair at chest, ridge
           where curls old Jewish lock
     Belly bulged outward, breathing as a baby
                old appendix scar
    creased where the belt went
detumescent cannon on two balls soft pillowed
Soft stirring shoots thru breast to belly—
What romance planned by the body unconscious?
        What can I shove up my ass?
             Masturbation in America!
     little spasm delight, prick head
           getting bigger
     thumb and index finger slowly stroking
        along cock sides, askew
           cupp'd in hand
    Serpent-reptile prick head
    moving in and out its meat-nest—
Turn and watch the landscape,
wave my baton
     at the passing truckdriver?
Lie back on bunk and lift the shade a bit
    enjoy sun on my flagpole?
Ah, rest, relax, no fear
    look at the sphincter-spasm itself
             in a mirror
             of sound—
Awk—if you jerk—oh it feels so good
Oh if only somebody'd come in &
     shove som'in up that ass a mine—
  Oh those two soldiers talking about Cambodia!
  I wantem to come in and lay my head down
     and shove it in and make me
  Come like I'm coming now,
     Come like I'm coming now,
        Come like I'm coming now—

Ahh—white drops fall,
                 millions of children—
         Santa Fe what can they do to prevent
                       passengers from
                       soiling their
                                   small blankets with love?
Wipe up cream—what if
         The Conductor knocked?
      Go way, I'm—
I have to compose a poem
I have to write a financial report
I have to meditate myself
                 I have to
                 put on my pants—

      just lie back look at the landscape
                 see a tree
                 & cross Ameriky—
                                   Compromised!
                 among green Spinach fields!
Felt good for a minute, flash came thru body
And the Sphincter-spasm spoke
                 backward to the soldiers in the observation car
                       I'd hated their Cambodia gossip!
                       but longed for in moment truth
                                   to punish my 40 years' lies—
      Oh what a wretch I am! What
                             monster naked in this metal box—
Hart Crane, under
         Laughing Gas in the Dentist's Chair 1922 saw
                                   Seventh Heaven
                 said Nebraska scholar.
         On thy train O Crane I had small death too.

Green valley-fields of California telephone-wired—
      Lovers' Desire's State!
         Hollywood starry State!
      Rock poesy State!
                 end of the land!
         where I lay me naked in a pullman coach—
D——
      Thy secrecy arrogance befits thee not
                             Sweet Prince—

open yr ass to my mouth—
       a poem to thee!
                      —my voice an overdramatic madman's
       murmuring to myself late afternoon drowze—
              going home,
                      past cement robots,
              gazing out on palmtrees with reptilian gaze,
All's negative O Edward Carpenter!
       As 'twere thy dainty Chinaman near Paris
                      making crude remarks—
       I'll jus liah hear like a nigger & moan my soul!
Sixty telephone wires strung across poles,
                      Hedges of spinach,
                             hair combed,
       quite a bit of excitement coursing along city-edge
                      plugged in to human ears
              Operators screaming at soldiers
                      returned from Vietnam,
              murder marriage or orgasmic babe born
                      bawling Daddy Come Home!
Train stop, yellow capp'd workmen
       roar at the engine with waterhoses,
I'll take a nap dream, last night
       Homer dog swallowed a furry mollusk—
              barking and gulping—the black sucker parasite
              ate belly & crawled up throat,
       pink mucous   flesh bubble
                      half-retched from dog chest
I smoke too much I'll die lung cancer
       eyes closed sensory illusion dotted
              no-think moviescreens,
              worms'll grow eyeballs silently,
              mosquitoes will row in valley bay night—
       Sausalito, certainly had your big prick there—
Yellow light laid over planet
       telegraph wires over consciousness
              every direction Knowing I am here,
       engine slowly throbbing uphill—

                      Night darkling over Mojave desert,
Yellow planet-light disappearing, mounds westward,
       Soldiers asleep, rocking away from the War.

Autolite headed toward disappearing sun.
Pew! Pew! Pew! cry the children
                    pulling each other's arms,
            What an earth to live on!
    Lights of the City, south,
            brightening a piece of the night—
    and the diamond-green gleam an airfield light—
        Hey! ya bit me, ya bit me,
                hello Missus Fight!
Green Green Green blinks the Diner sign
        where truckmen roam
                    in darkness toward Barstow.
        Stars as when I was a child.
                    Mojave's firmament same Passaic's—
This space capsule softer than trees
        in chemical landscape
                    with electronic clicks.
And is Heaven any different from where we are?
How could it be better or worse?
        Tho delicate chemical brain changes
                Aethereal sensations
                    Muladhara sphincter up thru mind aura
                        Sahasrarapadma promise
                            another Universe—
Whitman, Carpenter, Gavin Arthur, saying
                We are leaves of the Tree,
                        saying
        We are drops of water running to the ocean
                thru the fish's mouth—
    And we shall stand in Flesh in Paradise
            with the Virgin of the 19th Century—?

Borax, Borax, Borax,
        Crystal lights upon a hill, faery castles
    Might be in heaven, only Mojave—
                Borax, Borax, Borax
    Borax the Dinosaur slounges thru
            fronds under Pleiades—
    Delicate filament of highway lights
            the nerves between cities—
    Borax, Borax Borax Borax
            near Bel Mar desert Motel—

AUM

—my enemy machine chatterjabber mind
　　　making Borax Borax Borax Borax
　　　　spinal column thought
　　　o'er turkeys, oil, wind, headlights—
A child peeps thru glass moving night
　　　where red tail lights keep time
　　　　　　　to the Santa Fe train
　　　rolling over Crane's gloom.

　　Ho! a Crescent moon
　　　Mr. Cummings & Mr. Vinal both dead—

"Why you like beer as much as I do,"
　　　　sd the old gal
　　　to a tableful of cans—
　　　　　"Lady, it's my life."—
Where the soldiers sat talkabout gotten their head busted off
　　and there's a cherry in the gin & tonic
　　an angel upside down playing with himself
　　　　kneeling abed looks
　　　between legs into mirror
　　to see the two spots where he sat so long studied Bible
　　　　　reddened each buttock—
Cigarettes and alcohol,
　　　　　the Hundred&81st Airborne
Hmm—They'd be better off puffin'
　　　　a peaceful O pipe
　　　or sipping kif Sebsi in a café
　　　green fig trees
　　　　　blue Gibraltar Strait . . .

"The tricks are what makes business!
　　　you got a college education, it ain't what you got
　　　it's what you DO with yr. college education Son."
And they're all actors.
　　　Waiting at Barstow the engine humming
—"I wanna be an entertainer,
　　　I wanna be a comedy writer," he said—
　　　his hands once colored with Vietnamese blood.
The engine humming—
　　　All others silent, lost in thought.

And the soldier talked all about his troubles with his red hair.
And how he took his girl home after 3 drinks
    when she squinted her eyes at him and said
                "I wanna go with yew,"
and how he drove her to her house
    and said "I'm giving you a last chance"
    and how she leaned her head on his
        shoulder and said
                "Anywhere you're goin take me"
    and how he
        took off her pants
        and she said that he shd take off his pants
        and he wouldn't take off his pants
    and how they'd have some
        love play, like everybody
    and then, he'd drive her home,
                        but when he's out at a bar
        if anybody looks at his girl
he looks 'em in the eye and snaps his finger & says
                whatter ya lookin like that fur—
    and out in a bar alone,
        anybody's fair game for his love.
So I sat an I listened,
    and I brooded in my beard
    and saw he was ugly eyed
    though his voice beautiful Edward Carpenter.
Now I'm lying here
    Cabinette in complete darkness
    Airfields passing by,
        Stars, a few dim white fixed friendly
            in blackness outside
        the modern railroad window
            doubled to reflect
                        passing gas—

"Matter-babble behind the ear" six years ago—
Old poetry grows stale,
    forlorn, as always forlorn
"Ah love is so sweet in the Springtime,"
    Jeanette MacDonald sang
        three decades ago—
    on marble balustrade in giant darkness

                    downtown Paterson Fabian Theater balcony
            I wept, How soft flesh is—
Watching boyish Ronald Reagan
            emote
                    his shadow
                            across the Thirties—
                                    Same black vastness
                                            pierced
                                                    by emotion,
            melancholy toward the stars—
Political planets whirling round the Sun,
                    consciousness expansion,
            earth girdled by telegraph wires, Edward,
            they never dreamed of television then.

Railroad chugging thru yr thighs,
        clear your throat,
                lie there in the dark,
                        cough with cancer
                                close your eyes . . .
I didn't even dream, passing Tehachapi
        and woke, sleepy numb, reluctant
                to face my own language.
        But came back to it,
                tape machine
                        passing Mojave,
                                evening ease,
                            Na-mu sa-man-da mo-to-nan o-ha-ra-chi ko-
to-sha so-no-nan to-ji-to en gya-gya gya-ki gya-ki un-nun shi-fu-ra shi-fu-ra
ha-ra-shi-fu-ra ha-ra-chi-fu-ra chi-shu-sa chi-chu-sa shu-shi-ri shu-shi-ri so-ha-ja
so-ba-ja se-chi-gya shi-ri-ei so-mo-ko

                        The universe is empty.

Click of train
        eyes closed . . . the long green courthouse building
                "Like a monster with many eyes."
                        On valley balcony overlooking Bay Bridge,
                                a horse in leafy corral . . .
600 Cong Death Toll this week
            language language
                        escalating

"and the honor & the glory will go to him who speaks
with the voice of a man of feeling," said Walter Lippmann
face creased w/ wrinkles,
Bakersfield Gazette.
Wear beads, live
in small polkadot tent, tasseled rooftop
in Bixby's Canyon middle
peaceful Ashram
"It's mine, it's mine, I don't want anybody else own
my piece of land private special from Police"
. . . I must be criminal, mind
wanders
nailing down roof boards—
tell him I stopped at the bar.
No time No time Sam Lewis—
Oh—No time Carolyn,
No time now, Neal.
Do you love me?
No, I'm an awkward jerk that's been around yr neck for
so long you got used to it & kinda fond.
The salesman's eyes close,
he stands his jacket off
tie hanging down white shirt
You run 'em a merry chase, Son?

Open your eyes and stars
are back where they were.
And Dr. Louria committed suicide,
accused of abortion,
that sensitive man.
Well gimme yr piece of perspective
for use in the slotmachine marketplace future—

You hafta get permission down in
Freehold New Jersey to see Tibetan Monks.
You hafta get permission.
The magic formula's printed on the back of yr chair
Lady,
yr going to be the most important illuminator
since Dr. Johnson?
And Huncke suffers rejection,
contrariety of others.

"Reform U.S. Government stinks detail,"
like, congratulations Whitey, you'll go far
                    in yr black Maria, right?
A public meeting in my head,
                way back on River Street.

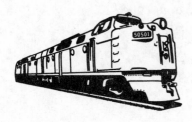

Morning, crossing New Mexico border
            massive cliff waves
                        in mid-earth America—A blessing
these sandstone organpipes under the shimmer-
                            ing consciousness of LSD.
    Defiance, Wingate, Red Cliffs, Thoreau,
        Indian Gallup ahead,
        ran by here with Peter in the white bus once
level everywhere, fenced, flat
            to Texas horizon gray-fleeced with cloud haze,
                where Gemini men walked space that day—

And ninety-nine soldiers piled on the train at Amarillo—
    Hadn't read the paper four weeks
                    training Air Force
                        Pneumohydraulics—
Ninety-nine soldiers entering the train
                and all so friendly
            Only a month
                    hair clipped & insulted
        They weren't too sad,
            glad going to some electronics field near Chicago

—Been taking courses in Propaganda,
    How not to believe what they were told
               by the enemy,
  Young fellas that some of them had long hair
        before they came to the heated camp
    friendly, over hamburgers
          Volunteered
assignments behind the line of Great Machines
          that drop Napalm,
   milking
         the Calf of Gold.
Three months from now
        Vietnam, they said.

Walking the length of the train,
   Lounge Car with Time Magazine
      Amarillo Globe, US News & World Report
    Reader's Digest Coronet Universal Railroad Schedule,
      everyone on the same track,
        bound leatherette read on sofas,
    America heartland passing flat
        trees rising in night—
Dining Car
     negro waiters negro porters
  negro sandwichmen negro bartenders white jacketed
    kindly old big-assed Gents half bald,
  Going, sir, California to Chicago
         feeding the Soldiers.
    Blue eyed children climbing chair backs
     staring at my beard, gay.

A consensus around card table beer—
   "It's my country,
      better fight 'em over there than here,"
  afraid to say "No it's crazy
      everybody's insane—
         This country's Wrong,
   the Universe, Illusion."

   Soldiers gathered round
      saying—"my country
and they say I gotta fight,

I have no choice,
        we're in it too deep to pull out,
                if we lose,
there's no stopping the Chinese communists,
    We're fightin the communists, aren't we?
         Isn't that what it's about?"
Flatland,
      emptiness,
         ninety nine soldiers graduated Basic Training
              eating hamburgers—
    "you learn to eat fast
    you learn to be insulted without caring
    you gotta do what your country expects—"
even the bright talkative orphan farm boy
whose auto parts father wanted 'im to grow up military
"almost et by a male hog up to his shoulders"
    4 hours punching at power steering tractor
        brakes front & hind foot
            giant insect specialized—
The whole populace fed by News
few dissenting on this train, I the lone beard who don't like
                        Vietnam War—
    Ninety nine airforce boys
        lined up with their pants down forever.

Five Persons Wounded Cleveland Riots
Atlantic Next Stop for Jolly Space-men
Bubonic Plague Suspected in Prairie Dogs
U.S. Marine Offensive Operation Hastings
Communist Dead Toll Rose Almost 1000
Stratofortresses struck language language
Communist language language infiltration
         South of 17th Parallel
"Psychedelic drugs no substitute for plain study
        . . . Technicolored Delusion,
      Many report visits to Heaven
          . . . jumping the gun a bit"
      George E. Turner said
"Eat well, Animal" with a package of dog food
        and as for Negroes
"Work not rioting is Magic Formula"

And Johnson reiterated too, "our desire to engage in
                    unconditional discussions"
                        to end the war
"other side . . . concession
                        . . . not the slightest
                                indication"
More manpower would be required he said
                            flatly.

John Steinbeck,
            flaxenhaired Yevtushenko wrote yr phantom
                    End the War

"Unconditional negotiations" sd Johnson
            "Anywhere anytime" sd Johnson in the last poem
    Yesterday Ky So. Vietnam sd
            "Dissolve Vietcong
                National Liberation Front—
                            and Peace"
        Kennedy sd
            "Give V.C. Negotiation Chair"
    —irreconcilable positions, every year
    United States proposes contradictions
            backed with bomb murder,
                    backed with Propaganda—
Soldiers on this train think they're fighting China
Soldiers on this train think Ho Chi Minh's Chinese
Soldiers on this train don't know where they're going
John Steinbeck stop the war John Steinbeck stop
            the war John Steinbeck stop the war.

And the French Army surrounded Madrid,
and the Spanish Army'd marched simultaneously surrounded Paris.
            Then they found out
                it was hopeless.
            Generals sent messages,
                    Call off the attack!
and the Armies rushed to a neutral place confronted
                        & killed each other.
            They just wanted to fight,
                no question of Madrid or Paris, then.
    —& Johnson backed

Saigon's latest conditions:
                    N. Vietnam withdraw all aid,
                    Dissolve Withdraw Viet Cong.
                    These are conditions,
          contradicting Johnson's Unconditionals.
          These languages are gibberish.
John Steinbeck thy language is gibberish,
     thou'st lost the language war,
                         cantankerous phantom!
          Newspaper language ectoplasm fades—
                         Everybody sneeze!

Lightning's blue glare fills Oklahoma plains,
the train rolls east
          casting yellow shadow on grass
                              Twenty years ago
approaching Texas
               I saw
                    sheet lightning
                         cover Heaven's corners
          Feed Storage Elevators in gray rain mist,
               checkerboard light over sky-roof
same electric lightning South
     follows this train
               Apocalypse prophesied—
     the Fall of America
          signaled from Heaven—

Ninety nine soldiers in uniform paid by the Government
                              to Believe—
ninety nine soldiers escaping the draft for an Army job,
ninety nine soldiers shaved
                         with nowhere to go but where told,
ninety nine soldiers seeing lightning flash
                         a thousand years ago
Ten thousand Chinese marching on the plains
     all turned their heads to Heaven at once to see the Moon.
An old man catching fireflies on the porch at night
     watched the Herd Boy cross the Milky Way
                         to meet the Weaving Girl . . .

How can we war against that?
How can we war against that?

Morning song, waking from dreams
brown grass, city edge nettle
wild green stinkweed trees
by railroad thru niggertown, carlot, scrapheap
auto slag bridge outskirts,
muddy river's brown debris
passing Eton Junction
fine rainmist over green fields—

Trees standing upside down
in lush earth approaching Mississippi
green legs waving to clouds,
seed pods exposed to birds & rain
bursting,
tree heads drinking in the ground.
Unfold stones like rag dolls & the Astral
body stares with opal eyes,
—all living things before my spectacles.

In the diner, the Lady
"These soldiers so nice, clean faces
and their hair combed so short—
Ugh its disgusting the others
—down to their shoulders & cowboy boots—"
aged husband spooning cantaloupe.

Too late, too late
the Iron Horse hurrying to war,
too late for laments
too late for warning—
I'm a stranger alone in my country again.
Better to find a house in the veldt,
better a finca in Brazil—
Green corn here healthy under sky
& telephone wires carry news as before,
radio bulletins & television images
build War—

American Fighter Comic Books
                    on coach seat.
Better a house hidden in trees
                    Mississippi bank
                    high cliff protected from flood
Better an acre down Big Sur
                    morning path, ocean shining
                         first day's blue world
Better a farm in backland Oregon,
                         roads near Glacier Peak
Better withdraw from the Newspaper world
Better withdraw from the electric world
Better retire before war cuts my head off,
                    not like Kabir—
     Better to buy a Garden of Love
     Better protect the lamb in some valley
     Better go way from taxicab radio cities
                         screaming President,
                    Better to stop smoking
Better to stop jerking off in trains
Better to stop seducing white bellied boys
Better to stop publishing Prophecy—
          Better to meditate under a tree
          Better become a nun in the forest
          Better turn flapjacks in Omaha
               than be a prophet on the electric Networks—
There's nothing left for this country but doom
There's nothing left for this country but death
               Their faces are so plain
               their thoughts so simple,
                    their machinery so strong—
               Their arms reach out 10,000 miles with lethal gas
               Their metaphor so mixed with machinery
                    No one knows where flesh ends and
                         the robot Polaris begins—
"Waves of United States jetplanes struck at North Vietnam
     again today in the face of . . ."
               Associated Press July 21st—
                    A summer's day in Illinois!

Green corn silver watertowers
     under the viaduct windowless industry

at track crossing white flowers,
American flowers,
American dirt road, American rail,
American Newspaper War—
in Galesburg, in Galesburg
grocery stove pipes and orange spikeflowers
in backyard lots—TV antennae
spiderweb every poor house
Under a smokestack with a broken lip
magnetic cranes drop iron scrap like waterdrops.

Thirtytwo years ago today, the woman in the red
dress outside the Biograph Theatre in Chicago
didn't wanna be sent back to Rumania.
Ambushed Dillinger fell dead on the sidewalk
hit by 4 bullets
FBI man Purvis quit in '35—
Feb 29, 1960 he shot & killed himself in his home
Army Colonel in World War II
Breakfast Cereal Manufacturer.
Dillinger's eyes and Melvin Purvis'—
Dillinger grim, Purvis self-satisfied,
Both died of bullets.

Football field, suburb streets, gray-sheeted clouds
stretched out to the City ahead
Myriad pylons, telegraph poles, a lavender boiler.
Fulbright broadcast attacks war money
Crushed stone mounds, earth eaten
Henry Crown's & General Dynamics'
dust rising from rubble
Sawdust burners
topped by black cloud—
sulphurous yellow
gas rising from red smokestacks
Power stations netted
with aluminum ladders and ceramic balls
rusty scrapheaps' cranes
stub chimneys puffing gray air
Coalbarges' old Holland dusk in a canal,
railroad tracks banded to the city
watertowers' high legs walking the horizon

The Chinese Foreign Minister makes his pronouncement,
Thicker thicker metal
                    lone bird above phonepole
Thicker thicker smokestack wires
        Giant Aztec factories, red brick towers
                    feeder-noses drooped to railyard
                "All human military activity" suspended
                            says radio—
        Campbell's soups a fortress here,
                giant can raised high over Chicago
                        forest of bridge signs
                    Church spires lifted gray
                            hazy towers downtown
        a belfried cross beneath
                    dynamo'd smoke-cathedrals,
The train rolls slower
        past cement trucks'
                    old cabs resting in produce flats
        over city streets, rumbling
        on a canal's green mirror
                    past the blue paint factory,
Thicker thicker the wires
        over cast iron buildings, black windows
local bus passing viaduct stanchions
a lone wino staggers down Industrial Thruway
This nation at war
                sun yellowing gray clouds,
                beast trucks down the
                        Garage's bowels—
        Bright steam
                muscular puffing from an old slue
        Meadowgold Butter besmeared with coal dust,
                    creosote wood bulwarks
Oiltank cars wait their old engine
        tracks curve into the city's heart
                    windowed hulks downtown
        where YMCA beckons the homeless unloved,
the groan of iron tons inching against
                    whitened rail,
            giant train so slowly moved
                    a man can touch the wheels.

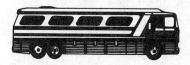

II

Bus outbound from Chicago Greyhound basement
      green neon beneath streets Route 94
        Giant fire's orange tongues & black smoke
            pouring out that roof,
          little gay pie truck passing the wall—
        Brick & trees E. London, antique attics
                mixed with smokestacks
  Apartments apartments square windows set like Moscow
apartments red brick for multimillion population
        out where industries raise craned necks
Gas station lights, old old old old traveler
        "put a tiger in yr tank—"
      Fulbright sang on the Senate floor
      Against the President's Asian War
         Chicago's acrid fumes in the bus
              A-1 Outdoor Theatre
        'gainst horned factory horizon,
        tender steeples ringing Metropolis
    Thicker thicker, factories
      crowd iron cancer on the city's throat—
          Aethereal roses
               distant gas flares
          twin flue burning at horizon
     Night falling on the bus
              steady ear roar
        between Chicago and New York
Wanderer, whither next?
     See Palenque dream again,
       long hair in America,
        cut it for Tehuantepec—
          Peter's golden locks grown gray,
          quiet meditation in Oaxaca's
              old backyard,

Tonalá or Angel Port warm nights
no telephone, the War
rages North
Police break down the Cross
Crowds screaming in the streets—

on Pacific cliff-edge
Sheri Martinelli's little house with combs and shells
Since February fear, she saw LSD
Zodiac in earth grass, stood
palm to cheek, scraped her toe
looking aside, & said
"Too disturbed to see you
old friend w/ so much Power"
—ten years later.

Yajalón valley, bougainvillea flares
against the Mayor's house—
Jack you remember the afternoon
Xochimilco with Fairies?
Green paradise boats
flower laden poled upriver
Pulque in the poop
stringed music in air—
drunkenness, & happiness
anonymous
fellows without care from America—
Now war moves my mind—
Villahermosa full of purple flowers
Merida hath cathedral & cheap hotels
—boat to Isla Cosumel
Julius can wander thru Fijijiapan
forgetting his dog peso Nicotinic Acid—
Bus seat's white light shines on Mexico map,
quietness, quietness over countryside
palmfrond insects, cactus ganja
& Washington's Police 5 thousand miles away?
Ray Charles singing from hospital
"Let's go get stoned."

Durango-Mazatlán road's built over
Sierra Madre's moon valleys now

Children with quartz jewels climbing highway cliff-edge
               Jack you bought crystals & beer—

        Old houses in Panama City
             La Barranca gray canyon under Guadalajara,
                         Tepic for more candy.

I wanna go out in a car
        not leave word where I'm going—
                     travel ahead.
Or Himalayas in Spring
        following the pilgrim's path
               10,000 Hindus
                         to Shiva temples North
               Rishikesh & Laxman Jula
               Homage to Shivananda,
                         the Guru heart—
thru green canyons, Ganges gorge—
               carrying a waterpot
               to Kedernath & Badrinath
               & Gangotri in the ice
               —Manasarovar forbidden,
                     Kailash forbidden,
               the Chinese eat Tibet.

Howl for them that suffer broken bone
                     homeless on moody balconies
        Jack's voice returning to me over & over
                         with prophecy
   "Howl for boys sleeping hungry on tables in cafés with their long hair
               to the sea" in Hidalgo de Parral,
                         Hermosillo & Tetuán—

The masses prepare for war
        short haired mad executives
               young flops from college
        yellow & pink flesh gone mad
               listening to radio news.

& Johnson was angry with Fulbright
               for criticizing his war.

And Hart Crane's myth and Whitman's—
          What'll happen to that?
                    The Karma
accumulated bombing Vietnam
          The Karma bodies napalm-burned
                Karma suspicion
     where machinery's smelt the heat of bodies trembling
                    in the jungle
The Karma of bullets in the back of the head by thatched walls
     The Karma of babies in their mothers' arms
                    bawling destroyed
The Karma of populations moved from center to center of
                              Detention
          Karma of bribery, Karma blood-money
             Must come home to America,
             There must be a war
                America has builded herself a new body.

Peaceful young men in America get out of the Cities & go to
                the countryside & the trees—
Bearded young men in America hide your hair & shave your
                     beards & disappear
        The destroyers are out to destroy—
        Destroyers of Peking & Washington stare face to face
             & will hurl their Karma-bombs
                        on the planet.
          Get thee to the land,
                leave the cities to be destroyed.

Only a miracle appearing in Man's eyes
          only boys' flesh singing
             can show the warless way—
                    or miracle
          Radium destruction over Earth
                seed Planet with New Babe.

Brilliant green lights
          in factory transom windows.
                         Beautiful!
        as eyes close to sleep,
     beautiful as undersea sunshine
                or valleybottom fern.

Why do I fear these lights?
    &smoking chimneys' Industry?
Why see them less godly
            than forest treetrunks
            &sunset orange moons?
Why these cranes less Edenly than Palmfronds?
       these highway neons unequal in beauty
          to violet starfish anemone & kelp
          in Point Lobos'
            tidepools' transparency?

It's these neon Standard Gastation
   cars of men whose faces are dough
   pockets full of 58 billion dollar
         abstract budget money—
   these green lights illuminate
      goggled eyes fixing blowtorches on metal wings
      flying off to war—

Because these electric structures rear tin machines
        that will kill Bolivian marchers
     or flagellate Vietnam adolescents' thighs—
Because my countrymen make this structure to make War
Because this smoke over Toledo's advertised in the Toledo *Blade*
       as energy burning to destroy China.

Baghavan Sri Ramana Maharshi
     in his photo has a fine white halo of hair,
     thin man with a small beard
       silver short-cropped skull-fur
   His head tilted to one side,
     mild smile, intelligent eyes
     "The Jivan-Mukta is not a Person."

Morning sunrise over Tussie Hills,
   earth covered with emerald-dark fur.
      Cliffs to climb, a little wilderness,
       a little solitude,
      and a long valley you could call a home.
Came thru here with Peter before & noticed
       green forest,

What a place to walk & look
                thru cellular consciousness
—Near Nealyton or Dry Run
        Waterfall or Meadow Gap, or Willow Hill.
Sunrays filtering thru clouds like a negative photograph,
        smoky bus window, passengers asleep
        over Susquehanna River's morning mist.
Ike at Gettysburg found himself a nice spot—
                all these places millions of trees' work
                                made green
as millions of workmen's labor raised the buildings of NY,
        Corn here in fields, dollars in the fields of New York.
Morning glow, hills east Harrisburg, bright
        highways, red factory smoke, fires burning
                                upriver in garbage lots—
Philadelphia *Inquirer*:   "Perry County 113 acres
        of woodland, $11,300. Ideal locations for
        cabins, quarters, township road, springs &
        roads on track, best of hunting, call 1-717 . . ."
—Dangerous to want possessions
                        and for so short a time.
        Shoulda had it in 1945, or '53,
                        Times Square & Mexico—
In my twenties I would've enjoyed running around these
                                green woods naked.
In my twenties I would've enjoyed making love naked
                        by these brooks.

Who's the enemy, year after year?
    War after war, who's the enemy?
What's the weapon, battle after battle?
What's the news, defeat after defeat?
What's the picture, decade after decade?
        Television shows blood,
            print broken arms burning skin photographs,
            wounded bodies revealed on the screen
Cut Sound out of television you won't tell who's Victim
Cut Language off the Visual you'll never know
                Who's Aggressor—
                cut commentary from Newscast
                you'll see a mass of madmen at murder.
Chicago train soldiers chatted over beer

They, too, vowed to fight the Cottenpickin Communists
            and give their own bodies to the fray.
Where've they learnt the lesson? Grammarschool
            taught 'em Newspaper Language?
D'they buy it at Safeway with Reader's Digest?

"Reducing the Unreal to Unreality, and causing the one
real Self to shine, the Guru . . ."
1966 trains were crowded with soldiers.
". . . the Divine Eye, the eye that is pure Consciousness
which has no visions. Nothing that is seen is real."
            Passing tollgate,
                                    regatta of yachts on river hazed
                        bend at Reading, giant smokestacks, watertowers
                                    feed elevators—

"Seeing objects and conceiving God in them are mental processes, but
that is not seeing God, because He is within.
        "Who am I? . . . You're in truth a pure spirit   but you identify it with
a body . . ."
            The war is Appearances, this poetry Appearances
                                    . . . measured thru Newspapers
                All Phantoms of Sound
                        All landscapes have become Phantom—
            giant New York ahead'll perish with my mind.
                    "understand that the Self is not a Void"
not this, not that,
            Not my anger, not War Vietnam
            Maha Yoga a phantom
                Blue car swerves close to the bus
                    —not the Self.
            Ramana Maharshi, whittle myself a walkingstick,
                    waterspray irrigating the fields
                            That's not the Self—
        hard-on spring in loins
                rocking in highway chair,
                        poignant flesh spasm not it Self,
                                body's speaking there,
                                & feeling, that's not Self
                    Who says No, says Yes—not Self.
Phelps Dodge's giant white building
                            highway side, not Self.

Who? Who? both asleep & awake
closes his eyes?
Who opens his eyes to Sweden?
You happy, Lady, writing yr
checks on Howard Johnson's counter?
Mind wanders. Sleep, cough & sweat . . .
Mannahatta's
tunnel-door cobbled for traffic,
trucks into that mouth
MAKE NO IMAGE
Mohammedans say
Jews have no painting
Buddha's Nameless
Alone is Alone,
all screaming of soldiers
crying on wars
speech politics massing armies
is false-feigning show—
Calm senses, seek self, forget
thine own adjurations
Who are you?
to mass world armies in planet war?
McGraw-Hill building green grown old, car fumes &
Manhattan tattered, summer heat,
sweltering noon's odd patina
on city walls,
Greyhound exhaust terminal,
trip begun,
taxi-honk toward East River where
Peter waits working

July 22–23, 1966

City Midnight Junk Strains

for Frank O'Hara

Switch on lights yellow as the sun
                     in the bedroom . . .
The gaudy poet dead   Frank O'Hara's bones
                     under cemetery grass
An emptiness at 8 P.M. in the Cedar Bar
          Throngs of drunken
                  guys talking about paint
          & lofts, and Pennsylvania youth.
                  Kline attacked by his heart
& chattering Frank
               stopped forever—
     Faithful drunken adorers, mourn.
               The busfare's a nickel more
          past his old apartment 9th Street by the park.
Delicate Peter loved his praise,
          I wait for the things he says
                         about me—
     Did he think me an Angel
          as angel I am still talking into earth's microphone willy nilly
          —to come back as words ghostly hued
                         by early death
          but written so bodied
                  mature in another decade.
Chatty prophet
                  of yr own loves, personal
                  memory feeling fellow
          Poet of building-glass
I see you walking you said with your tie
          flopped over your shoulder   in the wind down 5th Ave
               under the handsome breasted workmen
                  on their scaffolds ascending Time
                         & washing the windows of Life
—off to a date with martinis & a blond
          beloved poet far from home
               —with thee and Thy sacred Metropolis
     in the enormous bliss   of a long afternoon
     where death is the shadow
          cast by Rockefeller Center
               over your intimate street.

Who were you, black suited, hurrying to meet,
        Unsatisfied one?
                        Unmistakable,
                                Darling date
for the charming solitary   young poet with a big cock
                who could fuck you all night long
                        till you never came,
        trying your torture on his   obliging fond body
        eager to satisfy god's whim that made you
                Innocent,   as you are.
I tried   your boys and found them ready
    sweet and amiable
            collected gentlemen
                    with large sofa apartments
        lonesome to please   for pure language;
and you mixed with money
                    because you knew enough language to be rich
                        if you wanted your walls to be empty—
Deep philosophical terms dear Edwin Denby serious as Herbert Read
        with silvery hair   announcing your dead gift
to the grave crowd whose historic op art frisson was
the new sculpture your big blue wounded body made in the Universe
        when you went away to Fire Island for the weekend
        tipsy with a family of decade-olden friends

Peter stares out the window   at robbers
        the Lower East Side   distracted in Amphetamine
I stare into my head   & look for your / broken roman nose
        your wet mouth-smell of martinis
            & a big artistic tipsy kiss.
    40's only half a life   to have filled
        with so many fine parties and evenings'
        interesting drinks together with one
                        faded friend or new
                        understanding social cat . . .
I want to be there in your garden party in the clouds
                all of us naked
strumming our harps and reading each other   new poetry
        in the boring celestial
                Friendship Committee Museum.
You're in a bad mood?
        Take an Aspirin.

In the Dumps?
I'm falling asleep
safe in your thoughtful arms.
Someone uncontrolled by History would have to own Heaven,
on earth as it is.
I hope you satisfied your childhood love
Your puberty fantasy   your sailor punishment on your knees
your mouth-suck
Elegant insistency
on the honking self-prophetic Personal
as Curator of funny emotions to the mob,
Trembling One, whenever possible. I see New York thru your eyes
and hear of one funeral a year nowadays—
from Billie Holiday's time
appreciated more and more
a common ear
for our deep gossip.

July 29, 1966

A Vow

I will haunt these States
     with beard bald head
    eyes staring out plane window,
     hair hanging in Greyhound bus midnight
leaning over taxicab seat to admonish
        an angry cursing driver
          hand lifted to calm
            his outraged vehicle
that I pass with the Green Light of common law.

Common Sense, Common law, common tenderness
        & common tranquillity
our means in America to control the money munching
        war machine, bright lit industry
everywhere digesting forests & excreting soft pyramids
    of newsprint, Redwood and Ponderosa patriarchs
     silent in Meditation murdered & regurgitated as smoke,
      sawdust, screaming ceilings of Soap Opera,
      thick dead Lives, slick Advertisements
         for Gubernatorial big guns
        burping Napalm on palm rice tropic greenery.

Dynamite in forests,
    boughs fly slow motion
        thunder down ravine,
    Helicopters roar over National Park, Mekong Swamp,
     Dynamite fire blasts thru Model Villages,
Violence screams at Police, Mayors get mad over radio,
       Drop the Bomb on Niggers!
          drop Fire on the gook China
            Frankenstein Dragon
     waving its tail over Bayonne's domed Aluminum oil reservoir!

I'll haunt these States all year
      gazing bleakly out train windows, blue airfield
       red TV network on evening plains,
    decoding radar Provincial editorial paper message,
      deciphering Iron Pipe laborers' curses as
        clanging hammers they raise steamshovel claws
      over Puerto Rican agony lawyers' screams in slums.

October 11, 1966

Autumn Gold: New England Fall

Auto Poetry to Hanover, New Hampshire

Coughing in the Morning
    Waking with a steam beast, city destroyed
    Pile drivers pounding down in rubble,
    Red smokestacks pouring chemical
                into Manhattan's Nostrils . . .
           "All Aboard"
    Rust colored cliffs bulking over superhighway
             to New Haven,
    Rouged with Autumny leaves, october smoke,
        country liquor bells on the Radio—
Eat Meat and your a beast
      Smoke Nicotine & your meat'll multiply
        with tiny monsters of cancer,
Make Money & yr mind be lost in a million green papers,
    —Smell burning rubber by the steamshovel—
Mammals with planetary vision & long noses,
         riding a green small Volkswagen up three lane
              concrete road
                 past the graveyard
     dotted w/tiny american flags waved in breeze,
               Washington Avenue:
Sampans battling in waters off Mekong Delta
    Cuban politicians in Moscow, analyzing China—
Yellow leaves in the wood,
      Millions of redness,
        gray skies over sandstone
           outcroppings along the road—
cows by yellow corn,
     wheel-whine on granite,
        white houseroofs, Connecticut woods
         hanging under clouds—
Autumn again, you wouldn't know in the city
Gotta come out in a car see the birds
     flock by the yellow bush—
In Autumn, in autumn, this part of the planet's
    famous for red leaves—
Difficult for Man on earth to 'scape the snares of delusion—
    All wrong, the thought process screamed at
            from Infancy,

The Self built with myriad thoughts
   from football to I Am That I Am,
Difficult to stop breathing factory smoke,
Difficult to step out of clothes,
    hard to forget the green parka—
Trees scream & drop
    bright Leaves,
Yea Trees scream & drop bright leaves,
Difficult to get out of bed in the morning
     in the slums—
Even sex happiness a long drawn-out scheme
      To keep the mind moving—

Big gray truck rolling down highway
     to unload wares—
Bony white branches of birch relieved of their burden
—overpass, overpass, overpass
   crossing the road, more traffic
    between the cities,
      More sex carried near and far—
    Blinking tail lights
To the Veterans hospital where we can all collapse,
Forget Pleasure and Ambition,
    be tranquil and let leaves
    blush, turned on
by the lightningbolt doctrine that rings
        telephones
   interrupting my pleasurable humiliating dream
    in the locker room
      last nite?—
Weeping Willow, what's your catastrophe?
   Red Red oak, oh, what's your worry?
Hairy Mammal whaddya want,
     What more than a little graveyard
      near the lake by airport road,
Electric towers marching to Hartford,
    Buildingtops spiked in sky,
    asphalt factory cloverleafs spread over meadows
Smoke thru wires, Connecticut River concrete wall'd
   past city central gastanks, glass boat bldgs,
     downtown, ten blocks square,
North, North on the highway, soon outa town,
      green fields.

The body's a big beast,
      The mind gets confused:
            I thought I was my body the last 4 years,
and everytime I had a headache, God dealt me
                              Ace of Spades—
I thought I was mind-consciousness 10 yrs before that,
      and everytime I went to the Dentist the Kosmos disappeared,
Now I don't know who I am—
      I wake up in the morning surrounded
                        by meat and wires,
      pile drivers crashing thru the bedroom floor,
War images rayed thru Television apartments,
Machine chaos on Earth,
      Too many bodies, mouths bleeding on every Continent,
      my own wall plaster cracked,
      What kind of prophecy
                        for this Nation
Of Autumn leaves,
      for those children in High School, green
                        woolen jackets
      chasing football up & down field—
North of Long Meadow, Massachusetts
      Shafts of Sunlight
                  Thru yellow millions,
      blue light thru clouds,

President Johnson in a plane toward Hawaii,
      Fighter Escort above & below
                  air roaring—
Radiostatic electric crackle from the
                  center of communications:
      I broadcast thru Time,
            He, with all his wires & wireless,
                  only an Instant—

Up Main Street Northampton,
            houses gabled sunny afternoon,
                  Ivy library porch—
Big fat pants, workshirt filled w/leaves,
      painted pumpkinshead sitting Roof Corner,
—or hanging from frontyard tree country road—
Tape Machines, cigarettes, cinema, images,
      Two Billion Hamburgers, Cognitive Thought,

Radiomusic, car itself,
              this thoughtful Poet—
Interruption of brightly colored Autumn Afternoon,
              clouds passed away—
Sky blue as a roadsign,
              but language intervenes.
                    on route 9 going North—
"Then Die, my verse" Mayakovsky yelled
              Die like the rusty cars
                    piled up in the meadow—

Entering Whately,
              Senses amazed on the hills,
                    bright vegetable populations
                          hueing rocks nameless yellow,
       veils of bright Maya over New England,
       Veil of Autumn leaves laid over the Land,
Transparent blue veil over senses,
                    Language in the sky—
And in the city, brick veils,
       curtains of windows,
              Wall Street's stage drops,
              Honkytonk scenery—
       or slum-building wall scrawled
              "Bourgeois Elements must go"—

All the cows gathered to the feed truck in the middle of the pasture,
       shaking their tails, hungry for the yellow Fitten Ration
              that fills the belly
                    and makes the eyes shine
                          & mouth go Mooooo.
       Then they lie down in the hollow green meadow to die—
In old Deerfield, Indian Tribes & Quakers
       have come & tried
                    To conquer Maya-Time—
Thanksgiving pumpkins
              remain by the highway,
                    signaling yearly Magic
                          plump from the ground.
Big leaves hang and hide the porch,
              & babies scatter by the red lights
                    of the bridge at Greenfield.

The green Eagle on a granite pillar—
                    sign pointing route 2A The Mohawk Trail,
Federal Street apothecary shop & graveyard thru which
                    highschool athletes
                         tramp this afternoon—
Gold gold red gold yellow gold older than painted cities,
          Gold over Connecticut River cliffs
          Gold by Iron railroad,
                    gold running down riverbank,
          Gold in eye, gold on hills,
                    golden trees surrounding the barn—
Silent tiny golden hills, Maya-Joy in Autumn
                    Speeding 70 MPH.

October 17, 1966

Done, Finished with the Biggest Cock

Done, finished, with the biggest cock you ever saw.
3 A.M., living room filled with quiet yellow electric,
curtains hanging on New York, one window lit
in unfinished skyscraper.
                              Swami White Beard
Being-Consciousness-Delight's photo's tacked
to bookshelf filled with Cosmic Milarepa, Wm. Blake's
Prophetic Writings, Buddhist Logic & Hymn to the Goddess,
and many another toy volume of orient lore, poetry crap;
Poe sober knew his white skull, tranquil Stein
repeated one simple idea *Making Americans* on Space Age's
edge whiten thought to transparent Place. Peace!
Done, finished with body cock desire, anger
shouting at bus drivers, Presidents & Police.
Gone to other shore, empty house, no lovers
suffering under bedsheets, inconceived babies calm.
Surge, a little abdomen warmth, the bus grinds
cobbles past red light, garbage trucks uplift iron
buttocks, old meat gravy & tin cans sink to bottom
in the Airfield. City edge woods wave branches
in chill breeze darkness under Christmas moon.

                                        December 14, 1966

Holy Ghost on the Nod
over the Body of Bliss

Is this the God of Gods, the one I heard about
in memorized language Universities murmur?
Dollar bills can buy it! the great substance
exchanges itself freely through all the world's
poetry money, past and future currencies
issued & redeemed by the identical bank,
electric monopoly after monopoly owl-eyed
on every one of 90 billion dollarbills vibrating
to the pyramid-top in the United States of Heaven—
Aye aye Sir Owl Oh say can you see in the dark you
observe Minerva nerveless in Nirvana because
Zeus rides reindeer thru Bethlehem's blue sky.
It's Buddha sits in Mary's belly waving Kuan
Yin's white hand at the Yang-tze that Mao sees,
tongue of Kali licking Krishna's soft blue lips.
Chango holds Shiva's prick, Ouroboros eats th'cobalt bomb,
Parvati on YOD's perfumèd knee cries Aum
& Santa Barbara rejoices in the alleyways of Brindaban
La illaha el (lill) Allah hu—Allah Akbar!
Goliath struck down by kidneystone, Golgothas grow old,
All these wonders are crowded in the Mind's Eye
Superman & Batman race forward, Zarathustra on Coyote's ass,
Lao-tze disappearing at the gate, God mocks God,
Job sits bewildered that Ramakrishna is Satan
and Bodhidharma forgot to bring Nothing.

December 1966

Bayonne Turnpike to Tuscarora

Gray water tanks in gray mist,
                    gray robot
      towers carrying wires thru Bayonne's
                    smog, silver
         domes, green chinaworks steaming,
         Christmas's leftover lights hanging
                              from a smokestack—
      Monotone gray highway into the gray West—
Noon hour, the planet smoke-covered
      Truck wheels roar forward
            spinning past the garbagedump
      Gas smell wafting thru Rahway overpass
      oiltanks in frozen ponds, cranes' feederladders &
         Electric generator trestles, Batteries open under heaven
Anger in the heart—
         hallucinations in the car cabin, rattling
         bone ghosts left and right
      by the car door—the broken camper icebox—
On to Pennsylvania turnpike
                              Evergreens in Snow
         Laundry hanging from the blue bungalow
Mansfield and U Thant ask halt Bombing North Vietnam
      State Department says "Tit For Tat."
                    Frank Sinatra with negro voice
                         enters a new phase—
      Flat on his face 50 years "I've been a beggar & a clown
         a poet & a star, roll myself in July
                         up into a ball and die."
                              Radio pumping
      artificial rock & roll, Beach Boys
& Sinatra's daughter overdubbed microphone
      antennae'd car dashboard vibrating
   False emotions broadcast thru the Land
   Natural voices made synthetic,
               phlegm obliterated
   Smart ones work with electronics—
               What are the popular songs on the Hiway?
"Home I'm Comin Home I am a Soldier—"
         "The girl I left behind . . .

I did the best job I could
            Helping to keep our land free
I am a soldier"
                    Lulled into War
          thus commercial jabber Rock & Roll Announcers
False False False
          "Enjoy this meat—"
          Weak A&P SuperRight ground round
          Factories building, airwaves pushing . . .

Trees stretch up parallel into gray sky
Yellow trucks roll down lane—
                    Hypnosis of airwaves
          In the house you can't break it
              unless you turn off yr set
          In the car it can drive yr eyes inward
              from the snowy hill,
                  withdraw yr mind from the birch forest
                      make you forget the blue car in the ice,
          Drive yr mind down Supermarket aisles
                  looking for cans of Save-Your-Money
                          Polishing-Glue
          made of human bones manufactured in N. Vietnam
                  during a mustard gas hallucination:
              The Super-Hit sound of All American Radio.

Turnpike to Tuscarora
              Snowfields, red lights blinking in the broken car
          Quiet hills' genital hair black in Sunset
          Beautiful dusk over human tininess
                  Pennsylvanian intimacy,
                          approaching Tuscarora Tunnel
          Quiet moments off the road, Tussey Mountains'
                          snowfields untouched.
A missile lost Unprogrammed
                  Twisting in flight to crash 100 miles
                      south of Cuba into the
                          Blue Carib!
          Diplomatic messages exchanged
          "Don't Worry it's only the Setting Sun—"
          (Western correspondents assembling in Hanoi)
              "perfect ball of orange in its cup of clouds"

Dirty Snowbanks pushed aside from Asphalt thruway-edge—
        Uphill's the little forests where the boyhoods grow
                        their bare feet—

Night falling, "Jan 4 1967, The Vatican Announces Today
        No Jazz at the Altar!"
                        Maybe in Africa
            maybe in Asia they got funny music
                & strange dancing before the Lord
        But here in the West No More Jazz at the Altar,
                "It's an alien custom—"
Missa Luba crashing thru airwaves with Demonic Drums
        behind Kyrie Eleison—
Millions of tiny silver Western crucifixes for sale
            in the Realms of King Baudouin—
Color TV in this year—weekly
        the Pope sits in repose & slumbers to classical music
            in his purple hat—
Gyalwa Karmapa sits in Rumtek Monastery, Sikkim
        & yearly shows his most remarkable woven Dakini-hair
                        black Magic Hat
        Whose very sight is Total Salvation—
    Ten miles from Gangtok—take a look!

                *   *   *   *

Mary Garden dead in Aberdeen,
        Jack Ruby dead in Dallas—
            Sweet green incense in car cabin.
        (Dakini sleeping head bowed, hair braided
                        over her Rudraksha beads
                        driving through Pennsylvania.
            Julius, bearded, hasn't eaten all day
                sitting forward, pursing his lips, calm.)
Sleep, sweet Ruby, sleep in America, Sleep
        in Texas, sleep Jack from Chicago,
        Friend of the Mafia, friend of the cops
            friend of the dancing girls—
            Under the viaduct near the book depot
                Under the hospital Attacked by Motorcades,
                Under Nightclubs under all the
                        groaning bodies of Dallas,

under their angry mouths
Sleep Jack Ruby, rest at last,
bouquet'd with cancer.
Ruby, Oswald, Kennedy gone
New Years' 1967 come,
Reynolds Metals up a Half
Mary Garden, 92, sleeping tonite in Aberdeen.

Three trucks adorned with yellow lights crawl uproad
under winter network-shade, bare trees, night fallen.
Under Tuscarora Mountain, long tunnel,
WBZ Boston coming thru—
"Nobody needs icecream nobody *needs* pot nobody
needs movies."
. . . "Public Discussion."
Is sexual Intercourse any Good? Can the kids handle it?
out the Tunnel,
The Boston Voice returning: "controlled circumstances . . ."
Into tunnel, static silence,
Trucks roar by in carbon-mist,
Anger falling asleep at the heart.
White Rembrandt, the hills—
Silver domed silo standing above house
in the white reality place
farm up the road,
Mist Quiet on Woods,
Silent Reality everywhere.
Till the eye catches the billboards—
Howard Johnson's Silent Diamond Reality
"makes the difference."
Student cannon fodder prepared for next Congress session
Willow Hill, Willow hill, Cannon Fodder, Cannon fodder—
And the Children of the Warmakers're exempt from fighting
their parents' war—
Those with intellectual money capacities who go to college
till 1967—
Slowly the radio war news
steals o'er the senses—
Negro photographs in Rochester
ax murders in Cleveland,
Anger at heart base
all over the Nation—

Husbands ready to murder their wives
            at the drop of a hat-statistic
        I could take an ax and split Peter's skull with pleasure—
Great trucks crawl up road
                insect-lit with yellow bulbs outside Pittsburgh,
        "The Devil with Blue Dress" exudes over radio,
        car headlights gleam on motel signs in blackness,
            Satanic Selfs covering nature
                    spiked with trees.
Crash of machineguns, ring of locusts, airplane roar,
            calliope yell, bzzzs.

                                    January 4, 1967

An Open Window on Chicago

Midwinter night,
    Clark & Halstead brushed with this week's snow
    grill lights blinking at the corner
                decades ago
    Smokestack poked above roofs & watertower
        standing still above the blue
              lamped boulevards,
      sky blacker than th' east
       for all the steel smoke
              settled in heaven from South.
Downtown—like Batman's Gotham City
          battleshipped with Lights,
     towers winking under clouds,
       police cars blinking on Avenues,
            space above city misted w/fine soot
cars crawling past redlites down Avenue,
            exuding white wintersmoke—
Eat Eat said the sign, so I went in the Spanish Diner
The girl at the counter, whose yellow Bouffant roots
     grew black over her pinch'd face,
     spooned her coffee with knuckles
       puncture-marked,
    whose midnight wrists had needletracks,
      scars inside her arms:
    "Wanna go get a Hotel Room with me?"
          The Heroin Whore
thirty years ago come haunting Chicago's midnite streets,
    me come here so late with my beard!

Corner Grill-lights blink, police car turned
    & took away its load of bum to jail,
     black uniforms patrolling streets
   where suffering
     lifts a hand palsied by Parkinson's Disease
        to beg a cigarette.

The psychiatrist came visiting this Hotel 12th floor—
    Where does the Anger come from?

Outside! Radio messages, images on Television,
                              Electric Networks spread
              fear of murder on the streets—
              "Communications Media"
inflict the Vietnam War & its anxiety on every private skin
              in hotel room or bus—
Sitting, meditating quietly on Great Space outside—
Bleep Bleep dit dat dit radio on, Television
                              murmuring,
              bombshells crash on flesh
                   his flesh my flesh all the same.—
The Dakini in the hotel room turns in her sleep
                   while War news flashes thru Aether—
              Shouts at streetcorners as bums
                        crawl in the metal policevan.
And there's a tiny church in middle Chicago
                   with its black spike to the black air
And there's the new Utensil Towers round on horizon.
And there's red glow of Central Neon
                   on hushed building walls at 4 A.M.,
And there's proud Lights & Towers of Man's Central City
         looking pathetic at 4 A.M., traveler passing through,
         staring outa hotel window under Heaven—
Is this tiny city the best we can do?
         These tiny reptilian towers
              so proud of their Executives
         they haveta build a big sign in middle downtown
                        to Advertise
         old Connor's Insurance sign fading on brick
                              building side—
         Snow on deserted roofs & parkinglots—
         Hog Butcher to the World!?
         Taxi-Harmonious Modernity grown rusty-old—
The prettiness of Existence! To sit at the window
         & moan over Chicago's stone & brick
              lifting itself vertical tenderly,
                   hanging from the sky.

Elbow on windowsill,
     I lean and muse, taller than any building here
Steam from my head

wafting into the smog
Elevators running up & down my leg
Couples copulating in hotelroom beds in my belly
        & bearing children in my heart,
Eyes shining like warning-tower Lights,
   Hair hanging down like a black cloud—
Close your eyes on Chicago and be God,
     all Chicago is, is what you see—
That row of lights Finance Building
    sleeping on its bottom floors,
   Watchman stirring
  paper coffee cups by bronzed glass doors—
and under the bridge, brown water
     floats great turds of ice beside buildings' feet
  in windy metropolis
           waiting for a Bomb.

January 8, 1967

Returning North of Vortex

Red Guards battling country workers
        in Nanking
    Ho-Tei trembles,
            Mao's death near,
    Snow over Iowa
    cornstalks on icy hills,
bus wheels murmuring in afternoon brilliance toward Council Bluffs
        hogs in sunlight, dead rabbits on asphalt
        Booneville passed, Crane quiet,
        highway empty—silence as
house doors open, food on table,
                nobody home—
    sign thru windshield
    100 Miles More to the Missouri.
How toy-like Pall Mall's red embossed pack
    cellophane gleaming in sunshine,
        Indian-head stamped crown crested,
        shewing its dry leaf of history to my eye
now that I no longer reach my hand to the ashtray
        nor since Xmas have lit a smoke.
One puff I remember the 18 year joy-musk of manhood
        that curled thru my nostrils first time I kissed
                another human body—
        that time with Joe Army, he seduced me
                into smoking—
I'll give Swami a present like Santa Claus—
                no attachment—
        No meat nor tabaccy—even sex questionable
        Now in America craving its billions
                of needles of War.

Detach yrself from Matter, & look about
                at the bright snowy show of Iowa,
        Earth & heaven mirroring
                eachother's light,
        tiny meat-trucks rolling downhill
                toward deep Omaha.
This is History, to quit smoking Anger-leaf
        into one man's lungs,

            glancing up at gravestone rows
                    in hill woods thru rear window.

This is History: Iowa's Finest Comics:
        Sunday, Rex Morgan M.D. in snowstorm,
        Mustachio'd villain cruel eyed
                with long European hair
                        doubletalking the Doc
    "Meanwhile, under the influence of LSD
    Veronica races through the fields
                in an acute panic"—
                Author Dal Curtis
In a violet box her big tits fall on snowy ground.
Gray ice floating down Missouri, sunset into Omaha
Bishop's Buffets, German Chocolate, wall to wall carpet
                Om A Hah, Om Ah Hūṃ
"The land summoned them and they loved it" cut in granite
                Post Office lintel, Walt Disney
        playing at State, week after his death.
        Table service, fireplace, armchairs,
                homeostasis in Omaha.

Steve Canyon Comics in Color:
        U.S. Military Seabees chopper
        operation dropping bridges
        over the "Lake of the Black Wind"
Princess Snowflower will
            "speak over the bullhorn to the
                    herdsmen—
            So they won't think it's a Chincom trick."
        Ten-year-olds in Sunday
            morning sunlight on the rug
        dreaming of slack-cheekboned blond
                big cocked Steve Canyon
                    fucking the yellow bellies
        tied face down naked on the floor of the lone helicopter
And on Sunday Evening the Reverend Preacher
        C. O. Staggerflup—
                America's Hope
            POB 72 Hopkins Minnesota
Isaiah denouncing the root of Evil to the Nation

14 billion 200 million a year to the Debt Money System,
            Rolling back darkness in Nebraska—
Shanghai water power cut off by Mao's enemies
        I am a Rock, I am an Island   radio souls cry
    passing north of Lincoln's tiny bright downtown horizon;
            Square banks huddled under Capitol turret blinking red,
            electric tower steam-drifts
                        ribboned across building tops
                    under city's ruby night-glow—
Let the Viet Cong win over the American Army!
        Dice of Prophecy cast on the giant plains!
Drum march on airwaves, anger march in the mouth,
Xylophones & trumpets screaming thru American brain—
        Our violence unabated after a year
        in mid-America returned, I prophesy against
        this my own Nation
                enraptured in hypnotic war.
And if it were my wish, we'd lose & our will
                        be broken
    & our armies scattered as we've scattered the airy guerrillas
            of our own yellow imagination.
Mothers weep & Sons be dumb
your brothers & children murder
        the beautiful yellow bodies of Indochina
    in dreams invented for your eyes by TV
all yr talk gibberish mouthed by radio,
        yr politics mapped by paper Star
Thought Consciousness
    Form Feeling Sensation Imagination the
                    5 skandhas, realms of Buddha
    Invaded by electronic media KLYL
            News Bureau
        & yr trapped in red winking Kansas
    one giant delicate electrical antenna upraised
    in midwinter Nebraska plains blackness
                January 1967
    I hope we lose this war.

Lincoln airforce Base, Ruby, Gochner
        US 80 near Big Blue River,
    The radio Bibl'd Hour, Dallas Texas
        a great nose pushed out of the dashboard
        demanding Your Faith Pledge!

Money your dollars support
        The Radio Bible Hour.
            You pledge to God to send
100 or 10 or 2 or $1 a month to the
        Radio Bible Hour—
The electric network selling itself:
        "The medium is the message"
        Even so, Come, Lord Jesus!
Straight thru Nebraska at Midnight
        toward North Platte & Ogallala
    returning down black superhighways to Denver.

January 8, 1967

Wales Visitation

White fog lifting & falling on mountain-brow
      Trees moving in rivers of wind
              The clouds arise
  as on a wave, gigantic eddy lifting mist
     above teeming ferns exquisitely swayed
                  along a green crag
     glimpsed thru mullioned glass in valley raine—

Bardic, O Self, Visitacione, tell naught
    but what seen by one man in a vale in Albion,
       of the folk, whose physical sciences end in Ecology,
          the wisdom of earthly relations,
    of mouths & eyes interknit ten centuries visible
      orchards of mind language manifest human,
   of the satanic thistle that raises its horned symmetry
   flowering above sister grass-daisies' pink tiny
          bloomlets angelic as lightbulbs—

Remember 160 miles from London's symmetrical thorned tower
    & network of TV pictures flashing bearded your Self
  the lambs on the tree-nooked hillside this day bleating
  heard in Blake's old ear, & the silent thought of Wordsworth in eld
                  Stillness
  clouds passing through skeleton arches of Tintern Abbey—
    Bard Nameless as the Vast, babble to Vastness!

All the Valley quivered, one extended motion, wind
         undulating on mossy hills
  a giant wash that sank white fog delicately down red runnels
         on the mountainside
  whose leaf-branch tendrils moved asway
        in granitic undertow down—
and lifted the floating Nebulous upward, and lifted the arms of the trees
  and lifted the grasses an instant in balance
    and lifted the lambs to hold still
  and lifted the green of the hill, in one solemn wave

A solid mass of Heaven, mist-infused, ebbs thru the vale,
  a wavelet of Immensity, lapping gigantic through Llanthony Valley,

the length of all England, valley upon valley under Heaven's ocean
tonned with cloud-hang,
—Heaven balanced on a grassblade.
Roar of the mountain wind slow, sigh of the body,
One Being on the mountainside stirring gently
Exquisite scales trembling everywhere in balance,
one motion thru the cloudy sky-floor shifting on the million feet of
daisies,
one Majesty the motion that stirred wet grass quivering
to the farthest tendril of white fog poured down
through shivering flowers on the mountain's head—

No imperfection in the budded mountain,
Valleys breathe, heaven and earth move together,
daisies push inches of yellow air, vegetables tremble,
grass shimmers green
sheep speckle the mountainside, revolving their jaws with empty eyes,
horses dance in the warm rain,
tree-lined canals network live farmland,
blueberries fringe stone walls on hawthorn'd hills,
pheasants croak on meadows haired with fern—

Out, out on the hillside, into the ocean sound, into delicate gusts of wet
air,
Fall on the ground, O great Wetness, O Mother, No harm on your body!
Stare close, no imperfection in the grass,
each flower Buddha-eye, repeating the story,
myriad-formed—
Kneel before the foxglove raising green buds, mauve bells drooped
doubled down the stem trembling antennae,
& look in the eyes of the branded lambs that stare
breathing stockstill under dripping hawthorn—
I lay down mixing my beard with the wet hair of the mountainside,
smelling the brown vagina-moist ground, harmless,
tasting the violet thistle-hair, sweetness—
One being so balanced, so vast, that its softest breath
moves every floweret in the stillness on the valley floor,
trembles lamb-hair hung gossamer rain-beaded in the grass,
lifts trees on their roots, birds in the great draught
hiding their strength in the rain, bearing same weight,

Groan thru breast and neck, a great Oh! to earth heart
Calling our Presence together

The great secret is no secret
            Senses fit the winds,
                     Visible is visible,
rain-mist curtains wave through the bearded vale,
            gray atoms wet the wind's kabbala
Crosslegged on a rock in dusk rain,
            rubber booted in soft grass, mind moveless,
    breath trembles in white daisies by the roadside,
                     Heaven breath and my own symmetric
Airs wavering thru antlered green fern
drawn in my navel, same breath as breathes thru Capel-Y-Ffn,
            Sounds of Aleph and Aum
                     through forests of gristle,
    my skull and Lord Hereford's Knob equal,
                     All Albion one.

What did I notice? Particulars! The
            vision of the great One is myriad—
    smoke curls upward from ashtray,
                house fire burned low,
The night, still wet & moody black heaven
                     starless
            upward in motion with wet wind.

July 29, 1967 (LSD)—August 3, 1967 (London)

Pentagon Exorcism

"No taxation without representation"

Who represents my body in Pentagon? Who spends
my spirit's billions for war manufacture? Who
levies the majority to exult unwilling in Bomb
Roar? *"Brainwash!"* Mind-fear! Governor's language!
"Military-Industrial-Complex!" President's language!
Corporate voices jabber on electric networks building
body-pain, chemical ataxia, physical slavery
to diaphanoid Chinese Cosmic-eye Military Tyranny
movie hysteria—Pay my taxes? No *Westmoreland* wants
to be Devil, others die for his General Power
sustaining hurt millions in house security
tuning to images on TV's separate universe where
peasant manhoods burn in black & white forest
villages—represented less than myself by Magic
Intelligence influence matter-scientists' *Rockefeller*
bank telephone war investment Usury Agency
executives jetting from *McDonnell Douglas* to *General Dynamics*
over smog-shrouded metal-noised treeless cities
patrolled by radio fear with tear gas, businessman!
Go spend your bright billions for this suffering!
Pentagon wake from planet-sleep! Apokatastasis!
Spirit Spirit Dance Dance Spirit Spirit Dance!
Transform Pentagon skeleton to maiden-temple O Phantom
Guevara! Om Raksa Raksa Hūṃ Hūṃ Hūṃ Phat Svaha!
Anger Control your Self feared Chaos, suffocation
body-death in Capitols caved with stone radar sentinels!
Back! Back! Back! Central Mind-machine Pentagon reverse
consciousness! Hallucination manifest! A million Americas
gaze out of man-spirit's naked Pentacle! Magnanimous
reaction to signal Peking, isolate Space-beings!

Milan, September 29, 1967

Elegy Che Guevara

European Trib. boy's face photo'd eyes opened,
      young feminine beardless radiant kid
           lain back smiling looking upward
Calm as if ladies' lips were kissing invisible parts of the body
Aged reposeful angelic boy corpse,
      perceptive Argentine Doctor, petulant Cuba Major
           pipe mouth'd & faithfully keeping Diary
                in mosquitos Amazonas
Sleep on a hill, dull Havana Throne renounced
More sexy your neck than sad aging necks of Johnson
              De Gaulle, Kosygin,
      or the bullet pierced neck of John Kennedy
Eyes more intelligent glanced up to death newspapers
      than worried living Congress Cameras passing
           dot screens into TV shade, glass-eyed
           McNamara, Dulles in old life . . .

Women in bowler hats sitting in mud outskirts 11,000 feet up in Heaven
           with a headache in La Paz
      selling black potatoes brought down from earth roof'd huts
      on mountain-lipped Puno
would've adored your desire and kissed your Visage
           new Christ
They'll raise up a red-bulb-eyed war-mask's
      white tusks to scare soldier-ghosts
      who shot thru your lungs

Incredible! one boy turned aside from operating room
      or healing Pampas yellow eye
To face the stock rooms of Alcoa, Myriad Murderous
           Board Directors of United Fruit
Smog-Manufacturing Trustees of Chicago U
      Lawyer Phantoms ranged back to dead
           John Foster Dulles' Sullivan and Cromwell lawfirm
      Acheson's mustache, Truman's bony hat
To go mad and hide in jungle on mule & point rifle at OAS
      at Rusk's egoic Courtesies, the metal deployments of Pentagon
      derring-do Admen and dumbed intellectuals
      from *Time* to the CIA

One boy against the Stock Market all Wall Street ascream
        since Norris wrote *The Pit*
    afraid of free dollars showering from the Observers' Balcony
      scattered by laughing younger brothers,
Against the Tin Company, against Wire Services,
     against infrared sensor Telepath Capitalism's
         money-crazed scientists
    against College boy millions watching Wichita Family Den TV

One radiant face driven mad with a rifle
       Confronting the electric networks.

                             Venice, November 1967

War Profit Litany

To Ezra Pound

These are the names of the companies that have made money from this war
nineteenhundredsixtyeight Annodomini fourthousandeighty Hebraic
These Corporations have profited by merchandising skinburning phospho-
      rus or shells fragmented to thousands of fleshpiercing needles
and here listed money millions gained by each combine for manufacture
and here are gains numbered, index'd swelling a decade, set in order,
here named the Fathers in office in these industries, telephones directing
      finance,
names of directors, makers of fates, and the names of the stockholders of these
      destined Aggregates,
and here are the names of their ambassadors to the Capital, representatives
      to legislature, those who sit drinking in hotel lobbies to persuade,
and separate listed, those who drop Amphetamines with military, gossip,
      argue, and persuade
suggesting policy naming language proposing strategy, this done for fee as
      ambassadors to Pentagon, consultants to military, paid by their indus-
      try:
and these are the names of the generals & captains military, who now thus
      work for war goods manufacturers;
and above these, listed, the names of the banks, combines, investment trusts
      that control these industries:
and these are the names of the newspapers owned by these banks
and these are the names of the airstations owned by these combines;
and these are the numbers of thousands of citizens employed by these busi-
      nesses named;
and the beginning of this accounting is 1958 and the end 1968, that statistic
      be contained in orderly mind, coherent & definite,
and the first form of this litany begun first day December 1967 furthers this
      poem of these States.

                               December 1, 1967

Elegy for Neal Cassady

OK Neal
    aethereal Spirit
        bright as moving air
        blue as city dawn
happy as light released by the Day
        over the city's new buildings—

Maya's Giant bricks rise rebuilt
            in Lower East Side
    windows shine in milky smog.
        Appearance unnecessary now.

Peter sleeps alone next room, sad.
Are you reincarnate? Can ya hear me talkin?
If anyone had strength to hear the invisible,
And drive thru Maya Wall
    you *had* it—
           What're you now, Spirit?
That were spirit in body—

The body's cremate
        by Railroad track
    San Miguel Allende Desert,
        outside town,
    Spirit become spirit,
        or robot reduced to Ashes.

Tender Spirit, thank you for touching me with tender hands
When you were young, in a beautiful body,
    Such a pure touch it was Hope beyond Maya-meat,
    What you are now,
        Impersonal, tender—

you showed me your muscle/warmth/over twenty years ago
when I lay trembling at your breast
                        put your arm around my neck,
—we stood together in a bare room on 103d St.
Listening to a wooden Radio,
                                with our eyes closed
Eternal redness of Shabda
                        lamped in our brains
at Illinois Jacquet's Saxophone Shuddering,
        prophetic Honk of Louis Jordan,
        Honeydrippers, Open The Door Richard
                To Christ's Apocalypse—
The buildings're insubstantial—
That's my New York Vision
                outside eastern apartment offices
        where telephone rang last night
                and stranger's friendly Denver Voice
asked me, had I heard the news from the West?

Some gathering Bust, Eugene Oregon or Hollywood Impends
                I had premonition.
"No" I said—"been away all week,"
        "you havent heard the News from the West,
                Neal Cassady is dead—"
        Peter's dove-voic'd Oh! on the other line, listening.

Your picture stares cheerful, tearful, strain'd,
                a candle burns,
        green stick incense by household gods.
Military Tyranny overtakes Universities, your Prophecy
        approaching its kindest sense brings us
                        Down
        to the Great Year's awakening.
Kesey's in Oregon writing novel language
                family farm alone.
Hadja no more to do? Was your work all done?
        Had ya seen your first son?
                Why'dja leave us all here?
        Has the battle been won?

I'm a phantom skeleton with teeth, skull
        resting on a pillow

        calling your spirit
god echo consciousness, murmuring
        sadly to myself.

Lament in dawnlight's not needed,
                the world is released,
    desire fulfilled, your history over,
            story told, Karma resolved,
                        prayers completed
    vision manifest, new consciousness fulfilled,
                spirit returned in a circle,
world left standing empty, buses roaring through streets—
        garbage scattered on pavements galore—
Grandeur solidified, phantom-familiar fate
                returned to Auto-dawn,
                    your destiny fallen on RR track
My body breathes easy,
                I lie alone,
                        living
After friendship fades from flesh forms—
heavy happiness hangs in heart,
            I could talk to you forever,
                The pleasure inexhaustible,
                    discourse of spirit to spirit,
                                O Spirit.

Sir spirit, forgive me my sins,
Sir spirit give me your blessing again,
Sir Spirit forgive my phantom body's demands,
Sir Spirit thanks for your kindness past,
Sir Spirit in Heaven, What difference was yr mortal form,
        What further this great show of Space?
        Speedy passions generations of
                Question? agonic Texas Nightrides?
            psychedelic bus hejira-jazz,
        Green auto poetries, inspired roads?
Sad, Jack in Lowell saw the phantom most—
        lonelier than all, except your noble Self.
Sir Spirit, an' I drift alone:
            Oh deep sigh.

                                    February 10, 1968, 5–5:30 A.M.

Chicago to Salt Lake by Air

If Hanson Baldwin got a bullet in his brain, outrage?
If President Johnson got a bullet in his brain, fast Karma?
If *Reader's Digest* got a bullet in its brain would it be smarter?
March '68, P. 54 "Report from Vietnam, The foe is Hurting"
... "The dismal picture of 1965, when I previously visited Vietnam,
has been reversed: The Allies are winning, and the enemy is being hurt,"
wrote "*The distinguished military Editor of the New York Times*"
The Dinosaur moves slowly over Chicago.
Arrived on United Airlines just in time all wrong.
Anger in the back of the plane cabin, anger at *Reader's Digest*
Hanson   Baldwin's   "Allies"?   Hanson   Baldwin's   "The Enemy"?

Arguing with a schizophrenic is hopeless. A bullet in the brain.
Mr. Baldwin suggests more bullets in the brain to solve his Vietnam Problem.
Hanson Baldwin is a Military Ass-Kisser.

Dead Neal was born in Salt Lake, & Jim Fitzpatrick's dead.
Flowers die, & flowers rise red petaled on the field.

Anger, red petal'd flower in my body

Detroit's lake from a mile above chemical muddy,
streams of gray waste fogging the surface to the center,
more than half the lake discolored metallic—
Cancerous reproductions the house flats rows of bee boxes, DNA Molecular
    Patterns
microscopic reticulations topt w/Television Antennae
and the horizon edged with gray gas clouds from East to West unmoved by
    wind.

They fucked up the planet! Hanson Baldwin Fucked up the Planet all by
    himself,
emitted a long Military gas cloud Dec 26 27 28 1967 in *NY Times*.
"Purely military considerations" he told TV—
Till Gov. LaSalle sd/ the Prexy cdnt be peaceful till election time,
as Baldwin nodded agree.

A bunch of fat & thin Schizophrenics running the planet thoughtwaves.

Shit, Violence, bullets in the brain Unavailing.
We're in it too deep to pull out.
Waiting for an orgasm, Mr. Baldwin?
Yes, waiting for an orgasm that's all.

Give 'em all the orgasms they want.
Give 'em orgasms, give Hanson Baldwin his lost orgasms.
Give *NY Times*, give *Reader's Digest* their old orgasms back.

It's a gold crisis! not enuf orgasms to go round
"I take care of other people's business" said th' old man sleeping next seat,
Wallets & pens in his inside pocket green tie black suit boots,
"Ever since the world began Gold is the measure of Solidarity."
Golden light over Iowa, silver cloud floor, sky roof blue deep
rayed by Western Sun set brightness from the center of the Solar System.
Neal born in Salt Lake. Died in San Miguel, met in Denver loved in
          Denver—
"Down in Denver/down in Denver/all I did was die."
                                        J. Kerouac, '48

Airplanes, a pain in the neck. Thru Heaven, a heavy roar,
vaportrails to the sun moving behind Utah's valley wall.
Give Heaven orgasms, give Krishna all your orgasms, give yr orgasms to the
          clouds. Great Salt Lake!
Fitzpatrick sobbed a lot in New York & Utah, his nervous frame racked with
          red eyed pain.
Farewell Sir Jim, in shiny heaven, bodiless as Neal's bodiless . . .

Brainwash cried Romney, the Governor of Pollution,

Michigan's Lakes covered w/ green slime

     — *"The people now see thru the Administration's continuous brainwashing."*
                                        Chi Trib Mar 16 '68 AP dispatch

Mind is fragments . . . whatever you can remember from last year's *Time
Magazine*, this years sunset or gray cloudmass over Nebraska,
Leroi Jones' deep scar brown skin at left temple hairline . . .
. . . Don McNeil emerging from Grand Central w/6 stitches in Forehead
pushed thru plateglass by police, his presscard bloodied.

Deeper into gray clouds, there must be invisible farms, invisible farmers
　　　walking up and down rolling cloud-hills.
"A hole in its head" . . . another World, America, Vietnam.
The Martians have holes in their head, like Moore's statuary.
& if Dolphin-like Saturnian tongues are invisible & their ecstatic language
　　　irrelevant to the Gold Supply
We'll murder 'em like 100,000,000 Bison—
Do the Buffalo Dance in the Jetplane over Nebraska! Bring back the Gay
　　　'90s.
Gobble gobble sd/ Sanders
& Turkeys' hormone-white-meat drumsticks poison the glands of suburban
　　　kiddies Thanksgiving.
On their bicycles w/ poison glands & DDT livers, hallucinating Tiny Viet-
　　　nams on TV.

Clouds rifts, Gold orgasms in the West,
Nebraska's Steppes herding broken cloud-flocks—
Sun at plane's nose, izzat the Missouri breaking the plains apart? Council
　　　Bluffs & Great Platte gone?
Oh Rockies already? Snow in granite cracks & gray crags.
Hanson Baldwin covered w/ Snowflakes.
Red oxide in air & earth, sunset flowers in clouds, Anger in the Heart,
"Croakers & doubters" . . . Napalm & Mace: Dogs!
Earth ripples, river snakes, iron horse tracks, car paths thin
—Wasatch peak snows, north crags' springtime white wall over desert-lake
　　　brightness—
Salt Lake streets at dusk flowing w/ electric gold. Beautiful Million winking
　　　lights!
Neal was born in Paradise!

March 30, 1968

Kiss Ass

Kissass is the Part of Peace
America will have to Kissass Mother Earth
Whites have to Kissass Blacks, for Peace & Pleasure,
Only Pathway to Peace, Kissass

Houston, April 24, 1968

Manhattan Thirties Flash

Long stone streets inanimate, repetitive machine Crash cookie-cutting
dynamo rows of soulless replica Similitudes brooding tank-like in Army
      Depots
Exactly the same exactly the same exactly the same with no purpose but
      grimness
& overwhelming force of robot obsession, our slaves are not alive
& we become their sameness as they surround us—the long stone streets
      inanimate,
crowds of executive secretaries alighting from subway 8:30 A.M.
bloodflow in cells thru elevator arteries & stairway glands to typewriter
      consciousness,
Con Ed skyscraper clock-head gleaming gold-lit at sun dusk.

1968

Please Master

Please master can I touch your cheek
please master can I kneel at your feet
please master can I loosen your blue pants
please master can I gaze at your golden haired belly
please master can I gently take down your shorts
please master can I have your thighs bare to my eyes
please master can I take off my clothes below your chair
please master can I kiss your ankles and soul
please master can I touch lips to your hard muscle hairless thigh
please master can I lay my ear pressed to your stomach
please master can I wrap my arms around your white ass
please master can I lick your groin curled with blond soft fur
please master can I touch my tongue to your rosy asshole
please master may I pass my face to your balls,
please master, please look into my eyes,
please master order me down on the floor,
please master tell me to lick your thick shaft
please master put your rough hands on my bald hairy skull
please master press my mouth to your prick-heart
please master press my face into your belly, pull me slowly strong thumbed
till your dumb hardness fills my throat to the base
till I swallow & taste your delicate flesh-hot prick barrel veined Please
Master push my shoulders away and stare in my eye, & make me bend over
        the table
please master grab my thighs and lift my ass to your waist
please master your hand's rough stroke on my neck your palm down my
        backside
please master push me up, my feet on chairs, till my hole feels the breath of
        your spit and your thumb stroke
please master make me say Please Master Fuck me now Please
Master grease my balls and hairmouth with sweet vaselines
please master stroke your shaft with white creams
please master touch your cock head to my wrinkled self-hole
please master push it in gently, your elbows enwrapped round my breast
your arms passing down to my belly, my penis you touch w/ your fingers
please master shove it in me a little, a little, a little,
please master sink your droor thing down my behind
& please master make me wiggle my rear to eat up the prick trunk
till my asshalfs cuddle your thighs, my back bent over,

till I'm alone sticking out, your sword stuck throbbing in me
please master pull out and slowly roll into the bottom
please master lunge it again, and withdraw to the tip
please please master fuck me again with your self, please fuck me Please
Master drive down till it hurts me the softness the
Softness please master make love to my ass, give body to center, & fuck me
    for good like a girl,
tenderly clasp me please master I take me to thee,
& drive in my belly your selfsame sweet heat-rood
you fingered in solitude Denver or Brooklyn or fucked in a maiden in Paris
    carlots
please master drive me thy vehicle, body of love dops, sweat fuck
body of tenderness, Give me your dog fuck faster
please master make me go moan on the table
Go moan O please master do fuck me like that
in your rhythm thrill-plunge & pull-back-bounce & push down
till I loosen my asshole a dog on the table yelping with terror delight to be
    loved
Please master call me a dog, an ass beast, a wet asshole,
& fuck me more violent, my eyes hid with your palms round my skull
& plunge down in a brutal hard lash thru soft drip-fish
& throb thru five seconds to spurt out your semen heat
over & over, bamming it in while I cry out your name I do love you
please Master.
        May 1968

A Prophecy

O Future bards
chant from skull to heart to ass
as long as language lasts
Vocalize all chords
zap all consciousness
I sing out of mind jail
in New York State
without electricity
rain on the mountain
thought fills cities
I'll leave my body
in a thin motel
my self escapes
through unborn ears
Not my language
but a voice
chanting in patterns
survives on earth
not history's bones
but vocal tones
Dear breaths and eyes
shine in the skies
where rockets rise
to take me home

May 1968

Bixby Canyon

Path crowded with thistle fern blue daisy,
    glassy grass, pale morninglory
        scattered on a granite hill
bells clanging under gray sea cliffs,
dry brackensprout seaweed-wreathed
where bee dies in sand hollows
       ant-swarmed above
white froth-wave glassed bay surge
    Ishvara-ripple on cave wall
          sea birds
      skating wind swell,
Amor Krishna Om Phat Svaha air rumble at
    ocean-lip
              Yesterday
Sand castles Neal, white plasm balls round
    jellies—
    Skeleton snaketubes & back
    nostrils' seaweed-tail dry-wrinkled
    brown seabulb & rednailed
    cactus blossom-petal tongues—
Brownpickle saltwater tomato ball
    rubber tail Spaghettied
        with leafmeat,
Mucus-softness crown'd Laurel thong-hat
    Father Whale gunk transparent
        yellowleaf egg-sac sandy
    lotos-petal cast back to cold
       watersurge.
          Bouquet of old seaweed
on a striped blanket, kelp tentacle spread
round the prayer place
           Hermes silver
    firelight spread over wave sunglare—
The Cosmic Miasma Anxiety meditating nakedman
        —Soft Bonepipe!
Musical Sea-knee gristlebone rubber
      burp footswat beard ball bounce
of homosexual Shlurp ocean hish
    Sabahadabadie Sound-limit
        to Evil—

Set limit, set limit, set limit to
                    oceansong?
Limit birdcries, limit the Limitless
                in language?   O Say
Can You See The Internationale
            Mental Traveller Marseillaise
        in waves of eye alteration Politics?
'Tis sweet Liberty I hymn in freeman's sunlight
not limited to observe No Nakedness signs
        in silent bud-crowded pathways, artforms
                of flowers limitless Ignorance—
Wet seaweed blossoms froth left, sun breathing
        giant mist under the bridge,
        gray cliffs cloud-skin haloed
            Yellow sunlight of Old
        shining on mossledge, tide foam
            lapped in harmless gold light—
O Eyeball Brightness shimmering! Father Circle
whence we have sprung, thru thy bright
            Rainbow horn, Silence!
So sings the laborer under the rock bridge,
so pipes pray to the Avalanche.

Big Sur, June 16, 1968 (grass)

Crossing Nation

Under silver wing
    San Francisco's towers sprouting
                thru thin gas clouds,
    Tamalpais black-breasted above Pacific azure
        Berkeley hills pine-covered below—
Dr. Leary in his brown house scribing Independence Declaration
             typewriter at window
       silver panorama in natural eyeball—

Sacramento valley rivercourse's Chinese
          dragonflames licking green flats north-hazed
    State Capitol metallic rubble, dry checkered fields
       to Sierras—past Reno, Pyramid Lake's
       blue Altar, pure water in Nevada sands'
         brown wasteland scratched by tires

      Jerry Rubin arrested! Beaten, jailed,
            coccyx broken—
Leary out of action—"a public menace . . .
      persons of tender years . . . immature
         judgment . . . psychiatric examination . . ."
i.e. Shut up or Else   Loonybin or Slam

LeRoi on bum gun rap, $7,000
       lawyer fees, years' negotiations—
SPOCK GUILTY headlined temporary, Joan Baez'
       paramour husband Dave Harris to Gaol
Dylan silent on politics, & safe—
       having a baby, a man—
Cleaver shot at, jail'd, maddened, parole revoked,
Vietnam War flesh-heap grows higher,
       blood splashing down the mountains of bodies
          on to Cholon's sidewalks—
Blond boys in airplane seats fed technicolor
      Murderers advance w/ Death-chords
         thru photo basement,
    Earplugs in, steak on plastic
         served—Eyes up to the Image—

What do I have to lose if America falls?
   my body? my neck? my personality?

June 19, 1968

Smoke Rolling Down Street

Red Scabies on the Skin
Police Cars turn Garbage Corner—
Was that a Shot! Backfire or Cherry Bomb?
Ah, it's all right, take the mouth off,
it's all over.

Man Came a long way,
Canoes thru Fire Engines,
Big Cities' power station Fumes
Executives with Country Houses—
Waters drip thru Ceilings in the Slum—
It's all right, take the mouth off
it's all over—

New York, June 23, 1968

Pertussin

Always Ether Comes
       to dissuade the
              goat-like
                     sensible—
or N_2O recurring to
       elicit ironic
              suicidal pen marks—
Parallels: in Montmartre Rousseau
       daubing or Rimbaud arriving,
              the raw Aether
shines with Brahmanic cool moonshine
       aftertaste, midnight Nostalgia.

June 28, 1968

Swirls of black dust on Avenue D

white haze over Manhattan's towers
    midsummer green Cattails' fatness
        surrounding Hoboken Marsh
              garbage Dumps,

Wind over Pulaski Skyway's
    lacy networks
Trucks crash Bayonne's roadways,
    iron engines roar

Stink rises over Hydro Pruf Factory
Cranes lift over broken earth
Brain Clouds boil out tin-cone scrap burners
      Newark sits in gray gas
      July heat gleams on airplanes
Trailer tyres sing toward forests of oiltowers,
Power grids dance in th'Iron Triangle,
      Tanks roast in Flatness—
Old Soybean-oil-storage Scandals
            echo thru airwaves,
the family car bumps over asphalt toward Bright Mexico.

July 10, 1968

Violence

Mexcity drugstore table, giant
    sexfiend in black spats
Sticks knife in a plump faggot's
    sportscoat seam;
at Teotihuacán in blue sunlight, I slap
    my mocking blond nephew
    for getting lost on the Moon
    Pyramid.
In Oakland, legendary police shoot a
    naked black boy running out
    of his political basement
In Pentagon giant machines humm and
    bleep in neon arcades,
Buttons click in sockets & robots
    pencil prescriptions for acid gas
    sunsets—
New York on the stairway, the dumbed
    whitefaced Junkie pulls a knife
    and stares immobile—the victim
    gasps, "oh come off it" & a sixpack
    of cokebottles
bounces down worn black steps, in
    Vietnam plastic fire
Streams down myriad phantom cheeks
    rayed over planet television—
Adrenalin runs in armpits from Los Angeles
    to Paris, Harlem & Cannes
explode thru plateglass, Sunset Strip & Sorbonne
    are crowded with Longhaired angels
    armed with gasmasks & Acid,
& Angry Democrats gather in Chicago
    fantasizing armies running
    thru Sewers sprayed with Mace.
I walk up Avenida Juárez, over
    cobbled shadows, blue-tiled streetlamps
lighting Sanborns' arcades, behind me violent
    chic fairy gangsters with bloody hands
hustle after midnight to cut my throat from
    its beard.

            July 22, 1968, 4:30 A.M.

Past Silver Durango Over Mexic Sierra-Wrinkles

Westward Mother-mountains drift Pacific, green-sloped canyons vaster than
    Mexico City
without roads under cloud-flowers bearing tiny shadow-blossoms on vegeta-
    ble peaks—
red riverbeds snake thru paradises without electricity
—Huichol or Tarahumara solitudes hectare'd irregular, antpaths to rocky
    plateaux,
hollows for lone indian humility, hand-ploughed mountainside patches—
naked white cloud-fronds floating silent over silent green earth-crags.
O vast meccas of manlessness, Bright cloud-brains tower'd in blue space up
    to the Sun
with rainbow garlands over white water-gas, O tree-furred body defenseless
    thru clear air, visible green breast of America!
vaster than man the Mother Mountains manifest nakedness greater than all
    the bombs Bacteria ever invented
Impregnable cloud-cities adrift & dissolving no History,
white rain-ships alighted in Zenith Blue Ocean—
No ports or capitals to the horizon, emerald mesas ridged infinite-budded
    where rivers and ants gather garbage man left behind in the Valley of
    Mexico—
Iron'll rust under living tree roots & soak back underground
to feed the sensitive tendrils of Ego covering mountains of granite green
    mossed unconscious.
Heaven & ocean mirror their azure, horizon lost in yellowed spectrum-
    mist—
Baja California Blue water lies flat to the brown armpit of United States,
River's course muddies the delta with teardrops washed dusty from Utah—
    Green irrigated farm squares in desert—
& the dung colored gas, brown haze of labor near Los Angeles risen the
    height of Sierras—
gray smog drifts thru low mountain passes, city invisible.
                         Floating armchairs descend
from sky in sunlight, rocking back & forth in polluted fields of air.

                                  July 22, 1968, 11 A.M.

On Neal's Ashes

Delicate eyes that blinked blue Rockies all ash
nipples, Ribs I touched w/ my thumb are ash
mouth my tongue touched once or twice all ash
bony cheeks soft on my belly are cinder, ash
earlobes & eyelids, youthful cock tip, curly pubis
breast warmth, man palm, high school thigh,
baseball bicept arm, asshole anneal'd to silken skin
            all ashes, all ashes again.
                                    August 1968

Going to Chicago

22,000 feet over Hazed square Vegetable planet Floor
Approaching Chicago to Die or flying over Earth another 40 years
to die—Indifferent, and Afraid, that the bone-shattering bullet
be the same as the vast evaporation-of-phenomena Cancer
Come true in an old man's bed. Or Historic
Fire-Heaven Descending 22,000 years End th' Atomic Aeon

The Lake's blue again, Sky's the same baby, tho papers & Noses
rumor tar spread through the Natural Universe'll make Angel's feet sticky.
I heard the Angel King's voice, a bodiless tuneful teenager
Eternal in my own heart saying "Trust the Purest Joy—
Democratic Anger is an Illusion, Democratic Joy is God
Our Father is baby blue, the original face you see Sees You—"

How, thru Conventional Police & Revolutionary Fury
Remember the Helpless order the Police Armed to protect,
The Helpless Freedom the Revolutionary Conspired to honor—?
I am the Angel King sang the Angel King
as mobs in Amphitheaters, Streets, Colosseums Parks and offices
Scream in despair over Meat and Metal Microphone

August 24, 1968

Grant Park: August 28, 1968

Green air, children sat under trees with the old,
bodies bare, eyes open to eyes under the hotel wall,
the ring of Brown-clothed bodies armed
     but silent at ease leaned on their rifles—

Harsh sound of mikrophones, helicopter roar—
A current in the belly, future marches
     and detectives naked in bed—
where? on the planet, not Chicago,
     in late sunlight—

Miserable picnic, Police State or Garden of Eden?
in the building walled against the sky
magicians exchange images, Money vote
     and handshakes—
The teargas drifted up to the Vice
     President naked in the bathroom
—naked on the toilet taking a shit weeping?
Who wants to be President of the
     Garden of Eden?

Car Crash

I
Snow-blizzard sowing
ice-powder drifts on stone fenced
gardens near gray woods.

Yellow hump-backed snow plow
rocking giant tires round
the road, red light flashing
iron insect brain.

Mrow, the cat with diarrhea.

Sunlight settled into human form,
tree rings settled age after age
stone forests accumulating atoms
traveled 93,000,000 miles,
carbon deposits settled into beds,
the mountain's head breathes light,
Earth-hairs gather gold beams
thru chlorophyll, poets walk
between the green bushes
sprouting solar language.

Broken bones in bed,
hips and ribs cracked by autos,
snowdrifts over rubber tires,
tree stumps freeze, the body stump
heals temporarily in wintertime.

II
So that's it the body, ah!
Beat yr meat in a dark bed.
Boy friends wrinkle & shit in snow.
Girls go fat-eyed to their mother's coffin.

Cigarettes burned my tastebuds' youth,
I smelled my lover's behind,
This autocrash broke my hip and ribs,
Ugh, Thud, nausea-breath at solar plexus

paralyzed my bowels four days—
Eyeglasses broke, eyeballs still intact—
Thank God! alas, still alive but talk words
died in my body, thoughts died in pain.

A healthy day in the snow, white breath
and warm wool sox, hat over ears, hot broth,
nakedness in warm boudoirs, stiff prick come,
fame, physic, learning, scepter, dusk
and Aurora Borealis, hot pig flesh, turkey
stuffing—all disappear in a broken skull.

Unstable element, Sight Sound flesh Touch
& Taste, all Odour, one more consciousness
backseat of a steaming auto with broken nose—
Unstable place to be, an easy way out
by metal crash instead of mind cancer.
Unreliable meat, waving a chicken bone
in a hospital bed—get what's coming to you
like the chicken steak you ate last year.
Impossible Dr. Feelgood Forever, gotta die
made of worm-stuff. And worm thoughts?

And who's left watching, or even
remembers the car crash that severed
the skull from the spinal column?
Who gets out of body, or who's shut in
a box of soft pain when Napalm drops
from Heaven all over the abdomen,
breasts and cheek-skin? & tongue cut out
by inhuman knives? Cow tongue? Man tongue?

What does it feel like not to talk?
To die in the back seat, Ow!

December 21, 1968

III
Raw pine walls, ice-white windows
three weeks now, snowy flatness
foot-thick down valley meadows,
wind roar in bare ash arms, oak branch
tendrils icy gleaming, yellow

stain of morning water in front
door's snow—I walk out on crutches
to see white moonglow make snow blue
—three men just rode a space ship
round the moon last week—gnashing
their teeth in Biafra & Palestine,
Assassins & Astronauts traveling from
Athens to the sea of Venus Creatrix—
Lovers' quarrels magnified decades to mad
violence, half naked farm boys stand
with axes at the kitchen table,
trembling guilty, slicing egg
grapefruit breasts on breakfast oilcloth.
Growing old, growing old, forget the words,
mind jumps to the grave, forget words,
Love's an old word, forget words,
Peter with shave-head beardface
mutters & screams to himself at midnight.
A new year, no party tonite, forget
old loves, old words, old feelings.
Snow everywhere around the house,
I turned off the gas-light & came upstairs
alone to read, remembering pictures of dead
moon-side, my hip broken, the cat sick,
earhead filled with my own strong music,
in a houseful of men, sleep in underwear.
Neal almost a year turned to ash, angel
in his own midnight without a phonecall,
Jack drunk in my mind or his Florida.
Forget old friends, old words, old loves,
old bodies. Bhaktivedanta advises Christ.
The body lies in bed in '69 alone,
a gnostic book fills the lap, Aeons
revolve 'round the household, Rimbaud
age 16 adolescent sneers tight lipt
green-eyed oval in old time gravure
—1869 his velvet tie askew, hair
mussed & ruffled by policeman's rape.

January 1, 1969, 1:30 A.M.

Over Denver Again

Gray clouds blot sunglare, mountains float west, plane
softly roaring over Denver—Neal dead a year—clean suburb yards,
fit boardinghouse for the homosexual messenger's
alleyway Lila a decade back before the Atombomb.
Denver without Neal, eh? Denver with orange sunsets
& giant airplanes winging silvery to San Francisco—
watchtowers thru red cold planet light, when the Earth Angel's dead
the dead material planet'll revolve robotlike
& insects hop back and forth between metallic cities.

February 13, 1969

Imaginary Universes

Under orders to shoot the spy, I discharged
    my pistol into his mouth.
He fell face down from the position life
    left his body kneeling blindfold.

No, I never did that. Imagined in airport snow,
    Albany plane discharging passengers.

Yes, the Mexican-faced boy, 19
    in Marine cloth, seat next me
Descending Salt Lake, accompanied his
    brother's body from Vietnam.
"The Gook was kneeling in front of me,
    crying & pleading. There were two;
    he had a card we dropped on them."
The card granted immunity to those
    V.C. surrendering.
"On account of my best friend &
    my brother I killed both Gooks."
That was true, yes.

                February 1969

Rising over night-blackened Detroit Streets

brilliant network-lights tentacle dim suburbs
Michigan waters canalled glitter thru city building blocks'
Throne-brain lamps strung downtown, green signals'
concentrate brightness blinking metal prayers & bright Hare Krishnas
telepathic to Heavenly darkness whence I stare down and adore O beautiful!
Mankind maker of such contemplate machine! Come gentle brainwaves
delicate-soft heart-throbs tender as belly butterflies,
light as Sexual charm-penumbras be, of radiant-eyed
boys & girls black-faced & blond that Born believe
Earth-death at hand, or Eden regenerate millennial Green
their destiny under your Human Police Will, O
Masters, fathers, mayors, Senators, Presidents, Bankers & workers
sweating & weeping ignorant on your own plastic-pain Maya planet . . .

February 15, 1969

To Poe: Over the Planet, Air Albany–Baltimore

Albany   throned in snow! It's winter, Poe,
upstate New York scythed
        into mental fields, flat arbors & hairy woods
        scattered in Pubic mounds twittering w/ birds—
Nobody foresaw these wormpaths asphalted
        uphill crost bridges to small church towns, chill
        hoarfields streaked with metal feces-dust.
Maelstrom roar of air-boats to Baltimore!
Farmland whirlpooled into mechanic apocalypse
        on Iron Tides!
. . . Wheels drop in Sunlight, over
        Vast building-hive roofs glittering,
New York's ice agleam
        in a dying world.
            Bump down to ground
                        Hare Krishna Preserver!

Philadelphia smoking in Gold Sunlight, pink blue
        green Cyanide tanks sitting on hell's floor,
Many chimneys smoldering, city flats virus-linked
        along Delaware bays under horizon-smog—
airplane drifting black vapor-filaments
        above Wilmington—The iron habitations
        endless from Manhattan to the Capital.
Poe! D'jya prophesy this Smogland, this Inferno,
Didja Dream Baltimore'd Be Seen From Heaven
by Man Poet's eyes Astounded in the Fire Haze,
                carbon Gas aghast!
Poe! D'jya know yr prophecies' RED DEATH
would pour thru Philly's sky like Sulphurous Dreams?
Walled into Amontillado's Basement! Man
        kind led weeping drunk into the Bomb
        Shelter by Mad Secretaries of Defense!

South! from the Bearded Sleeper's Wink
at History, Hudson polluted & Susquehanna
        Brown under bridges laced with factory smoke—
Proving grounds by Chesapeake,
            Ammunition & Artillery

Edgewood & Aberdeen
Chemical munitions factories
hid isolate in wooded gardens—
Poe! Frankenstein! Shelley thy Prophecy,
What Demiurge assembles Matter-Factories
to blast the Cacodemonic Planet-Mirror apart
Split atoms & Polarize Consciousness &
let the eternal Void leak thru Pentagon
& cover White House with Eternal Vacuum-Dust!
Bethlehem's miles of Christ-birth Man-apocalypse
Mechano-movie Refinery along Atlantic,
Shit-brown haze worse & worse over Baltimore
where Poe's world came to end—Red smoke,
Black water, gray sulphur clouds over Sparrows Point
Oceanside flowing with rust, scum tide
boiling shoreward—

Red white blue yachts on Baltimore harbor,
the plane bounds down above gas tanks,
gas stations, smokestacks flaring poison mist,
Superhighways razored thru hairy woods,
Down to Earth Man City where Poe
Died kidnapped by phantoms
conspiring to win elections
in the Deathly Gutter of 19th Century.

March 1969

Easter Sunday

Slope woods' snows melt
Streams gush, ducks stand one foot
beak eye buried in backfeathers,
Jerusalem pillars' gold sunlight
yellow in window-shine, bright
rays spikey-white flashed in mud,
coo coo ripples thru maple branch,
horse limps head down, pale grass shoots
green winter's brown vegetable
hair—washed by transparent trickling
ice water freshets
earth's rusty slough bathed clean,
streams ripple leaf-bottomed
channels sounded vocal, white light
afternoon sky end—

Goat bells move, black kids bounce,
butting mother's hairy side & tender tit
one maa'ing child hangs under Bessie's udder
ducks waggle yellow beaks, new grass flooded,
tiger cat maeows on barn straw,
herb patch by stone wall's a shiny marsh,
dimpling snow water glimmers, birds whistle
from icecrystal beds under bare bushes,
breeze blows rooster crow thru chill light
extended from the piney horizon.

1969

Falling Asleep in America

We're in the Great Place, Fable Place, Beulah, Man wedded to Earth, Planet
  of green Grass
Tiny atomic wheels spin shining, worlds change Heavens inside out, the
  planet's reborn in ashes,
Sun lights sparkle on atomic cinder, plants levitate, green moss precedes trees
  trembling sentient,
Stone eats blue skies solar dazzle with invisible mouths & flowers are the
  rocks' excrement—

Each million years atoms spin myriad reversals, worlds in worlds inter-
  change populations—
from worm to man's a tiny jump from earth to earth souls are borne ever
  forgetful—
populations eat their own meat, roses smell sweet in the faeces of horses risen
  red-fac'd.
Consciousness changes nightly, dreams flower new universes in brainy
  skulls.

Lying in bed body darkened ear of the bus roar running, only the eye
  flickering grass green returns me to Nashville.

April 1969

Northwest Passage

Incense under Horse Heaven Hills
Empty logger trucks speed
       Lake Wallula's flatness shimmering
Under Hat Rock painted w/
        white highschool signs.
Chemical smoke boils up
       under aluminum-bright cloud-roof—
Smog assembling over railroad
       cars parked rusting on thin rails—
Factory looming vaster than Johnson
       Butte—Look at that Shit!
Smell it! Got about 30 smokestacks going!
Polluting Wallula! Boise Cascade
         Container Corp!
The Package is the Product, onomatopoeticized
        McLuhan in '67—
Wall Street Journal Apr. 22 full
       page ad Proclaimed:

We got the trees! We got
       the land beneath!
We Gotta invent More Forms
       for Cardboard Country!
We'll dig forests for Genius
       Spirit God Stuff Gold-root
for Sale on Wall Street. Give
       us your money! order
       our cardboard Wastebaskets!
We just invented throwaway Planets!

Trees crash in Heaven! Sulphurous Urine
pours thru Boise, Chevron & Brea
       Wastepipes where Snake & Wallula
         ripple shining
Where Sakajawea led White Men thru blue sky
        fresh sweet water roads
       Towards mountains of juicy
        telepathic pine & open Thalassa
Thalassa! Green salt waves
       washing rock mountains, Pacific

Sirhan lives!
	to hear his jury say
"We now fix the penalty at Death."

Green salt waves washing Wall Street.
Rain on gray sage near Standard
		Oil junction Eltopia,
Static at Mesa! Yodeling ancient
		Prajnaparamita
Gaté Gaté Paragaté Parasamgaté
			Bodhi Svaha!
Way Down Yonder in the Bayoux
		Country in Dear old Louisian,
Hank Williams chanting to country
			Nature, electric
wires run up rolling brownplowed wheatfields—
Wallula polluted! Wallula polluted! Wallula polluted!

	"For most large scale gambling enterprises to continue over any
extended period of time, the cooperation of corrupt Police or local officials
is necessary." P. 1 *Oregonian*, "Mapping a $61 million war against organized
crime, President Nixon suggested . . ."

"Even Jesus Christ couldn't have
saved me." Sirhan . . .
		"shed no tears.
			His face was ashen" *AP*
		America's heart Broken,

Chessman, Vietnam, Sirhan.
52% People thought the War
		always had been a mistake,
			by April 1969. *Gallup Poll.*

May Day parade canceled for Prague
		says Police Radio to
			the old King of May faraway—
SDS chanting thru consciousness megaphones
			in every university.
By now, Beatles & Beach Boys have
		entered the Sublime
thru Acid The Crist of Kali Yuga, thru
		Transcendental Meditation,

Chanting Hare Krishna climbing Eiffel Tower,
Apollinaire & Mira Bai headless
          together with Kabir transmitted
over Apocalyptic Radios, their voice-
          vibrations roaring
thru a million loudspeakers in Green
          Autos on the world's roads—
Matter become so thick, senses so sunk
          in Chickens & Insulation
"Love aint gonna die, I'm gonna haveta
          kill it"
god cries to himself, Christ merging with
          Krishna in Car Crash Salvation!

          "Prosecutor John Howard called Sirhan a cold-blooded political
assassin with '*no special claim to further preservation.*'"
                    Mao reelected Chinese Premier.
Where the Mullan Rd
          meets route 26
                    by 2 giant Sycamores
          approaching Hooper,
Has anyone here any "Special
          claim to further preservation"?

These lambs grazing thru springtime
                    by Cow Creek, quiet in
          American yellow light—
"Even J.C. couldn't have saved me."

Magpie, Meadowlark, rainbow
          apparitions shafted transparent
     down from gray cloud.
                    Dogs see
                    in black & white.

A complete half-rainbow
          hill to hill across the highway
pots of gold anchoring the pretty bridge,
          tumbleweed passing underneath

          "Saigon (AP) U.S. B52 bombers made their heaviest raids of the
Vietnam War last night near the Cambodian border, dropping more than

2,000 tons of bombs along a 30 mile stretch Northwest of Saigon, the US COMMAND reported. 'They are harassing enemy troops so as not to let them get organized,' an American SPOKESMAN said."

Czech student strikes unreported in Prague
Howard Marquette & George Washington U. sit-in:
Hail on new-plowed brown hilltops—
Black rainclouds and rainbows over Albion way—
Drive down valley to Main Street
    Seattle First National Motor
    next to Everybody's Bank.
April 24, 1969

Sonora Desert-Edge

"Om Ah Hu'm Vajra Guru Padma Siddhi Hu'm"
—Drum H. from Gary S. from Tarthang Tulku

Brown stonepeaks   rockstumps
                    cloudless sunlight
Saguaro green arms praying up
        spine ribs risen
                    woodpecker-holed
        nose-pricked limbs
            lifted salutation—
orange flower eyes lifted on
        needly Ocotillo stalk
Jumping Cholla pistils closing pollened
    eyebrow-vagina buds to the
        poked pinkie—
Palo Verde smooth forked branch
                above prickly-pear ears

Smoke plumed up white
    from scratched desert plain,
    chemical smoke, military copper
        airplanes rotting,
            4% Copper Smelter smog

—in wire cage, ivory hook-beaked
                round black pupiled
    Bald Eagle's head, tailfeathers
    hung below claw'd branch, symmetric
body plumes brown webbed like dollarbills,
    insecticides sterilized many
                adults

—green duck neck sheen spectral as
        moon machines
Raven hopping curious black beaked
Coyote's nose sensitive lifted to air
            blinking eye sharp
as the rose bellied Cardinal's ivory whistle

—tiny bright statues of Buddha
    standing,

blue desert valley haze—
    cactus lessons in sentience,
Trees like mental carrots—Anaconda
    smelters white plumesmoke in
    San Manuel, or Phelps-Dodge
    in Douglas?—
Yellow'd Creosote bushes in granular
    dust, hills jeep tracked,
Prairie dogs stand quivering-spined in
    cactus-shade.   A museum,

    minds in Ashramic City—tweetling
    bird radios—Hopi Rain:

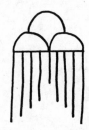

April 29, 1969

Reflections in Sleepy Eye

For Robert Bly

3,489 friendly people
Elm grove, willow, Blue Earth County's
    red barns, tiny feoff with
    gas nozzle snout on hillock,
Large beetles & lizards—
        orange-painted steel
        cranes & truck cabs,
    Green seeder down-pointed
         Science Toy earth-cock.
Thin floods, smooth planted acres
        upturned, brown
    cornstubble plowed under,
    tractor pulling discs over fenced land.
Old box-alder fallen over
    on knees in pond-flood,
white painted gas tanks by
    Springfield's rail yard woods,
        tiny train parade by Meats
        Groceries North Star Seeds
Our Flag at full mast
    TV antennae, large leafy antennaed
        trees upstretched green,
        trunks standing sunlit
Sheep on stormfenced knoll,
        green little wood acres—
one forest from Canada to these
plains—Corn silage in net bins,
        Windmills in Tracy,
      Blue enamel silos cap'd
aluminum, minarets in white sunbeam.
Cannabis excellent for drying lymph-
    glands, specific relief for
    symptoms of colds, flu,
        ear pressure grippe &
    Eustachian tube clogging—
A tree, bent broken mid-trunk
        branches to ground—

Much land, few folk, excelsior grave
                    yard stones
        silver tipp'd phalloi to heaven—
Aum, Om, Ford, Mailbox
            telephone pole wire strung
            down road. Lake house
            fence poles, tree shade
            pine hill grave, Ah
Lake Benton's blue waved waters—
        finally, Time came to
            the brick barn! collapsed!
Old oak trunk sunk thick
                        under ground.
Farm car plowman rolling discs,
            iron cuts smooth ground even,
                        hill plains roll—
Cows browse under alder shoot,
        bent limbs arch clear brown
            stream beds, trees stand
                on banks observing
shade, peculiar standing up or kneeling
            groundward
Car graveyard fills eyes
        iron glitters, chrome fenders
            rust—
White crosses, Vietnam War Dead
                churchbells ring
Cars, kids, hamburger stand
        open, barn-smile
            white eye, door mouth.

                                    May 9, 1969

Independence Day

Orange hawkeye stronger than thought winking above a thousand thin
       grassblades—
Dr. Hermon busted in Texas for green weed garden-grown
licensed Federal, Municipal-cop-prosecuted natheless—
Sweet chirrup from bush top to bush top, orange wing'd
birds' scratch-beaked telegraphy signaled to and fro buttercup earlets—
warbles & sweet whistles swifting echo-noted by fly buzz,
jet-roar rolling down thru clouds—
So tiny a grasshopper climbing timothy stub the birds can't tell they're
       there—
intense soft leaf-spears budding symmetric,
breeze bending gentle flowerheads against yarrow their persons—
eyelids heavy, summer heavy with fear, mapletrunks heavy with green leaf-
       mass—
closed buds of hawkeye stronger than thought tremble on tall hairy stems.

*

Red shelled bedbugs crawl war sheets,
city garbage spoils wet sidewalks where children play—
A telephone call from Texas tells the latest police-state bust.
O Self tangled in TV wires, white judges and laws
your jet-thunder echoes in clouds, your DDT spread thru firmament
       waters poisons algae & brown pelican—
Smog veils Maya, paranoia walks great cities in blue suits with guns,
—are all these billion grassblades safe?
My stomach's bitter, city haste & money loss—
Hawkeye stronger than thought! Horsefly and bee!
St. John's wort nodding yellow bells at the sun! eyes close in your
       presence, I
lie in your soft green bed, watch light thru red lid-skin, language
       persistent as birdwarble in my brain.
Independence Day! the Cow's deep moo's an Aum!

1969

In a Moonlit Hermit's Cabin

Watching the White Image, electric moon, white mist drifting over woods
St. John's Wort & Hawkeye wet with chance Yarrow on the green hillside
"D'ya want your Airline Transport Pilot to smoke grass? Want yr moonmen
    to smoke loco weed?"
What Comedy's this Epic! The lamb lands on the Alcohol Sea—Deep voices
"A Good batch of Data"—The hours of Man's first landing on the moon—
One and a Half Million starv'd in Biafra—Football players broadcast corn-
    flakes—
TV mentioned America as much as Man—Brillo offers you free Moon-Map
    —2 labels—
And CBS repeats Man-Epic—Now here again is Walter Cronkite,
"How easy these words . . . a shiver down the old spine . . .
Russia soundly beaten! China one Fifth of Mankind, no word broad-
    cast . . ."
The Queen watched the moon-landing at Windsor Castle—
Pulling a fast one on Hypnosis at Disneyland, the Kerchief-headed Crowd
Waving to the TV Camera—Ersatz Moon—
"No place gives you history today except the Moon"—
Running behind time entering Space Suits—
And a Moon-in at Central Sheep Meadow—
Western Electric's solemn moment!

And rain in the woods drums on the old cabin!
I want! I want! a ladder from the depths of the forest night to the silvery
    moon-wink—
A flag on the reporter's space-suit shoulder—
Peter Groaning & Cursing in bed, relieved of the lunatic burden at last—

'Tis Tranquillity base where the Tragedy will settle the Eve.
Alert for solar flares, clock ticks, static from Antennae—swift as death.
I didn't think we'd see this Night.
Plant the flag and you're doomed! Life a dream—slumber in eyes of woods,
Antennae scraping the ceiling. Static & Rain!
Saw the earth in Dream age 37, half cloud-wrapped, from a balcony in
    outer-space—
Méliès—giddiness—picture tube gaga—
"Men land on Sun!" decennial sentences—
Announcers going goofy muttering "142—"
Alone in space: Dump Pressure in the LEM!

Hare Krishna! Lift m' Dorje on the kitchen table!
No Science Fiction expected this Globe-Eye Consciousness
Simultaneous with opening a hatch on Heaven.
A moth in the Déjà Vu!
This is the instant—open the hatch—every second is dust in the hourglass
     —Hatch open!
The Virus will grow green slime reptiles in sixty centuries,
& gobble up their fathers as we ate up God—
Imagine dying Tonight! Closing the eyes on the man in the Moon!
Sighing away forever . . . everyone got sleepy . . . On the moon porch—

A 38 year old human American standing on the surface of the moon—
Footprint on the Charcoal dust—stepped out
and it's the old familiar Moon, as undersea or mountaintop, a place—
"Very pretty on the Moon!" oh, 'twere Solid Gold—
Voices calling "Houston to Moon"—Two "Americans" on the moon!
Beautiful view, bouncing the surface—"one quarter of the world denied
     these pix by their rulers"!
Setting up the flag!

Cherry Valley, July Moon Day 1969

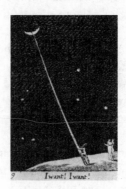

9   I want! I want!

Rain-wet asphalt heat, garbage curbed cans overflowing

I hauled down lifeless mattresses to sidewalk refuse-piles,
old rugs stept on from Paterson to Lower East Side filled with bed-bugs,
gray pillows, couch seats treasured from the street laid back on the street
—out, to hear Murder-tale, 3rd Street cyclists attacked tonite—
Bopping along in rain, Chaos fallen over City roofs,
shrouds of chemical vapour drifting over building-tops—
Get the *Times*, Nixon says peace reflected from the Moon,
but I found no boy body to sleep with all night on pavements 3 A.M.
      home in sweating drizzle—
Those mattresses soggy lying by full five garbagepails—
Barbara, Maretta, Peter Steven Rosebud slept on these Pillows years ago,
forgotten names, also made love to me, I had these mattresses four years
      on my floor—
Gerard, Jimmy many months, even blond Gordon later,
Paul with the beautiful big cock, that teenage boy that lived in
      Pennsylvania,
forgotten numbers, young dream loves and lovers, earthly bellies—
many strong youths with eyes closed, come sighing and helping me
      come—
Desires already forgotten, tender persons used and kissed goodbye
and all the times I came to myself alone in the dark dreaming of Neal or
      Billy Budd
—nameless angels of half-life—heart beating & eyes weeping for lovely
      phantoms—
Back from the Gem Spa, into the hallway, a glance behind
and sudden farewell to the bedbug-ridden mattresses piled soggy in dark
      rain.
     August 2, 1969

Death on All Fronts

"The Planet Is Finished"

A new moon looks down on our sick sweet planet
Orion's chased the Immovable Bear halfway across the sky
from winter to winter. I wake, earlier in bed, fly corpses
cover gas lit sheets, my head aches, left temple
brain fibre throbbing for Death I Created on all Fronts.
Poisoned rats in the Chickenhouse and myriad lice
Sprayed with white arsenics filtering to the brook, City Cockroaches
stomped on Country kitchen floors. No babies for me.
Cut earth boys & girl hordes by half & breathe free
say Revolutionary expert Computers:
Half the blue globe's germ population's more than enough,
keep the cloudy lung from stinking pneumonia.
I called in Exterminator Who soaked the Wall floor with
bed-bug death-oil: Who'll soak my brain with death-oil?
I wake before dawn, dreading my wooden possessions,
my gnostic books, my loud mouth, old loves silent, charms
turned to image money, my body sexless fat, Father dying,
Earth Cities poisoned at war, my art hopeless—
Mind fragmented—and still abstract—Pain in
left temple living death—

Cherry Valley, September 26, 1969

Memory Gardens

covered with yellow leaves
    in morning rain

—Quel Deluge
    he threw up his hands
        & wrote the Universe dont exist
          & died to prove it.

Full Moon over Ozone Park
    Airport Bus rushing thru dusk to
          Manhattan,
Jack the Wizard in his
        grave at Lowell
for the first nite—
That Jack thru whose eyes I
    saw
      smog glory light
        gold over Mannahatta's spires
   will never see these
      chimneys smoking
anymore over statues of Mary
    in the graveyard

Black misted canyons
    rising over the bleak
        river
Bright doll-like ads
    for Esso Bread—
Replicas multiplying beards
    Farewell to the Cross—
Eternal fixity, the big headed
    wax painted Buddha doll
      pale resting incoffined—

Empty-skulled New
    York streets
Starveling phantoms
    filling city—

Wax dolls walking park
                    Ave,
Light gleam in eye glass
Voice echoing thru Microphones
Grand Central Sailor's
                    arrival 2 decades later
                              feeling melancholy—
Nostalgia for Innocent World
                    War II—
A million corpses running
                    across 42d street
Glass buildings rising higher
                         transparent
                                   aluminum—
artificial trees, robot sofas,
              Ignorant cars—
One Way Street to Heaven.

                         *

Gray Subway Roar

A wrinkled brown faced fellow
                    with swollen hands
leans to the blinking plate glass
              mirroring white poles, the heavy car
              sways on tracks uptown to Columbia—
Jack no more'll step off at Penn Station
              anonymous erranded, eat sandwich
                    & drink beer near New Yorker Hotel or walk
under the shadow of Empire State.
Didn't we stare at each other length of the car
              & read headlines in faces thru Newspaper Holes?
Sexual cocked & horny bodied young, look
              at beauteous Rimbaud & Sweet Jenny
                    riding to class from Columbus Circle.
"Here the kindly dopefiend lived."

and the rednecked sheriff beat the longhaired
                    boy on the ass.
—103d street Broadway, me & Hal abused for sidewalk
                    begging twenty-five years ago.

Can I go back in time & lay my head on a teenage
        belly upstairs on 110th Street?
or step off the iron car with Jack
        at the blue-tiled Columbia sign?
at last the old brown station where I had
a holy vision's been rebuilt, clean ceramic
over the scum & spit & come of quarter century.

                    *

Flying to Maine in a trail of black smoke
Kerouac's obituary conserves *Time's*
                Front Paragraphs—
Empire State in Heaven Sun Set Red,
        White mist in old October
over the billion trees of Bronx—
            There's too much to see—
Jack saw sun set red over Hudson horizon
        Two three decades back
thirtynine fortynine fiftynine
                sixtynine
John Holmes pursed his lips,
                wept tears.
Smoke plumed up from oceanside chimneys
        plane roars toward Montauk
            stretched in red sunset—
Northport, in the trees, Jack drank
        rot gut & made haiku of birds
            tweetling on his porch rail at dawn—
Fell down and saw Death's golden lite
        in Florida garden a decade ago.
Now taken utterly, soul upward,
        & body down in wood coffin
        & concrete slab-box.
I threw a kissed handful of damp earth
        down on the stone lid
            & sighed
    looking in Creeley's one eye,
Peter sweet holding a flower
        Gregory toothless bending his
            knuckle to Cinema machine—

and that's the end of the drabble tongued
   Poet who sounded his Kock-rup
     throughout the Northwest Passage.
Blue dusk over Saybrook, Holmes
    sits down to dine Victorian—
& *Time* has a ten-page spread on
   Homosexual Fairies!

Well, while I'm here I'll
   do the work—
and what's the Work?
   To ease the pain of living.
Everything else, drunken
    dumbshow.
       October 22–29, 1969

Flash Back

In a car Gray smoke over Elmira
The vast boy reformatory brick factory
Valed below misty hills 25 years ago
I sat with Joe Army visiting and murmured green Grass.
Jack's just not *here* anymore, Neal's ashes
Loneliness makes old men moan, God's solitude,
O women shut up, yelling for baby meat more.
       November 10, 1969

Graffiti 12th Cubicle Men's Room Syracuse Airport

11 November 1969

I am married and would like to fuck someone else
Have a strange piece (Go Home)
USN '69
I want to suck a big cock Make Date
Support Third World Struggle Against US Imperialism
I fucked Mom and got VD
All power to the Viet Cong!
Yeah! Max Voltage up the Ass!! Ω
Perhaps Man needs—But to kill is only brown butter Wax
April 20, 1965   Mike Heck & Salena Bennett
Keep on Chugglin
Eat prunes and be a regular guy.
I would like to suck a big cock.
So would I.
War is good business Invest your son.
Help me J.P.
John Wayne flunked basic training.
Pat Miller '69 Home on Leave
My wife sucks cock.
Chickenman Lives Yes somewhere in Argentina
Peace & Love Sucks
I want a blow job Who do I call
What if someone gave a war & Nobody came?
Life would ring the bells of Ecstasy and Forever be Itself again.
J. Edgar Hoover F.B.I. is a Voyeur.
Man, I'm really stoned out of my skull really O-Zoned—good old LSD the
    colors in here are so nice really fine colors and the floor tile is really
    outasight if you haven't tried it you ought to since it is the only way
    to really get your head together by first getting it apart LSD Forever.

$$CH_2CH_2N(CH_3)_2$$

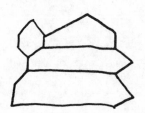

After Thoughts

When he kissed my nipple
    I felt elbow bone thrill—
When lips touched my belly
    tickle ran up to my ear
When he took my cock head to tongue
    a tremor shrunk sphincter, joy
        shuddered my reins
I breathed deep sighing ahh!

    *

Mirror looking, combing
    gray glistening beard
Were I found sharp eyed
    attractive to the young?
Bad magic or something—
Foolish magic most likely.

November 1969

G. S. Reading Poesy at Princeton

Gold beard combd down like chinese fire gold hair braided at skull-
    nape—
gold turning silver soon—worn face young forehead wrinkled, deep-boned
    smile,
tiny azure earring, turquoise finger stone, Paramita beads centered by ivory
    skull-nut—
On Deer Mountain, in ship's iron belly, sat crosslegged on Princeton couch,
body voice rumbling Bear Sutra to younger selves—her long hair to rug,
    dungareed legs lotus-postured;
or that half-Indian boy his face so serious woe'd by tree suffering he's
more compassionate to bear, skunk, deer, coyote, hemlock, whale
than to his own new-sprung cock. O Lizard Dharma
what doth breath, that Aums thru elm bough & rock canyon loud as thru
    mammal skull hummed,
hymn to bone-chaliced minds now multiplied over planet colleges
so many, with such hollow cheek gaze-eye tenderness, Fitzgerald himself'd
    weep to see
student faces celestial, longhaired angelic Beings planet-doomed to look thru
    too many human eyes—?
Princeton in Eternity! Long years fall, December's woods in snow
Old poets half century ago their bones cracked up in death
alcohol trembling in immortal eyes, Fitzgerald & Kerouac weeping, on earth
    once—
earth's voice moves time, old vows and prophecies remembered, mountain
    prayers repeated,
Gary's voice echoes hollow under round electric lamps.

1970

Friday the Thirteenth

Blasts rip Newspaper Gray Mannahatta's mid day Air Spires,
Plane roar over cloud, Sunlight on blue fleece-mist,
I travel to die, fellow passengers silk-drest & cocktailed burn oil NY to
    Chicago—
Blasting sky with big business, billion bodied Poetry Commerce,
all Revolution & Consumption, Manufacture & Communication
Bombburst, vegetable pie, rubber donut sex accessory & brilliant TV Jet-
    plane CIA Joke Exorcism Fart Mantra
or electronic war Laos to AID Gestapo training in Santo Domingo
equally massacre grass, exhaust flower power in coal factory smokedust
—O how beautiful snowy fields earth-floored below cloud-holes
glimpsed from air-roads smogged thru heavens toward Illinois—
What right have I to eat petrol guns & metal from earth heart
What right have I to burn gas air, screech overground rubber tired round
    midnight stoplight corners in Peoria, Fort Wayne, Ames—
What prayer restores freshness to eastern meadow, soil to cindered acres,
    hemlock to rusty hillside,
transparency to Passaic streambed, Blue whale multitudes to coral gulfs—
What mantra bring back my mother from Madhouse, Private Brakefield
    from Leavenworth, Neal from the Streets of Hades,
Hampton, King, Gold, murdered suicided millions from the War-torn fields
    of Sheol
where bodies twitch arm from leg torn heart beat spasmed brainless in
    dynamite Napalm rubble Song-My to West 11th Street Manhattan
as war bomb-blast burns along neckbone-fused nations Hanoi to Chicago
    Tu-Do to Wall Street,
Dynamite metastasis heading toward earth-brain cankering human world
    forms—
Banks burn, boys die bullet-eyed, mothers scream realization the vast ton-
    nage of napalm
rolling down Grand Concourse, Fragmentation nails bounced off Haiphong
    walls
rattling machine-gunned down Halstead, the Karma of State Violence
washing terror-waves round earth-globe back to suburb TV home night
    kitchens
The image 3 years ago, prophetic shriek of electric screen dots bursting thru
    bathroom walls,
tile & pipes exploded in NY as on Saigon's Embassy Street
—"Northrop is favorite in hot bidding on a jet fighter for a fat market
    overseas"—*Business Week* March 7, 1970

Earth pollution identical with Mind pollution, consciousness Pollution identical with filthy sky,

dirty-thoughted Usury simultaneous with metal dust in water courses

murder of great & little fish same as self besmirchment short hair thought control,

mace-repression of gnostic street boys identical with DDT extinction of Bald Eagle—

Mothers' milk poisoned as fathers' thoughts, all greed-stained over the automobile-body designing table—

What can Poetry do, how flowers survive, how man see right mind multitude, hear his heart's music, feel cockjoys, taste

ancient natural grain-bread and sweet vegetables, smell his own baby body's tender neck skin

when 60% State Money goes to heaven on gas clouds burning off War Machine Smokestacks?

When Violence floods the State from above, flowery land razed for robot proliferation

metal rooted & asphalted down 6 feet below topsoil,

then when bombcarrying children graduate from Grammar-school's sex-drenched gymnasia

terrified of Army Finance Meatbones, busted by cops for grassy hair,

Who can prophesy Peace, or vow Futurity for any but armed insects,

steeltip Antennaed metal soldiers porting white eggbombs where genitals were,

Blue-visor'd spray-bugs, gasmasked legions in red-brick Armory Nests—

(bearded spiders ranged under attick & roof with home-brew Arsenic mercury dung plastic readied for the Queen Bee's Immolation

in Sacramento, Trenton, Phoenix, Miami?)

The State set off a plague of bullets bombs & burning words

two decades back, & seeded Asia with Mind-thoughts excreted in Washington bathrooms—

now the Great Fear's rolled round the world & washes over Newspaper Gray air

rolling waved through cloud-smogbanks in Heaven

as the gas-burning TWA Jet house crashes thru sound barriers over Manhattan.

Chicago Chicago Chicago Trials, screams, tears, Mace, coalgas, Mafia highways—old Massacres in suburb garages!

Autos turn to water City Halls melt in Aeon-flood,

Police & revolutionaries pass as gas cloud by eagle wing.

"What's your name?" asks badge-man as machines eat all Name & Form,
History's faster than thought, poetry obsolete in tiny decades tho maybe slow
      tunes dance eternal—
war language comes, bombblasts last a minute, coalmines exhaust earth-heart,
Chicago suburb blocks stretch new-bared earthskin under sun eye,
autos speed myriad thru gray air to jet port.
Slaves of Plastic! Leather-shoe chino-pants prisoners! Haircut junkies! Da-
      cron-sniffers!
Striped tie addicts! short hair monkeys on their backs! Whiskey freaks
      bombed out on 530 billion cigarettes a year—
twenty Billion dollar advertising Dealers! lipstick skin-poppers & syndicate
      Garbage telex-Heads!
Star-striped scoundrelesque flag-dopers! Car-smog hookers Fiendish on
      superhighways!
Growth rate trippers hallucinating Everglade real estate! Steak swallowers
      zonked on Television!
Old ladies on Stockmarket habits—old Wall Street paper Money-pushers!
Central Intelligence cutting Meo opium fields! China Lobby copping pop-
      pies in Burma!
How long this Addict government support our oil-burner matter-habit
shooting gasoline electric speed before the blue light blast & eternal Police-
      roar Mankind's utter bust?
Robot airfields soulless Market electronic intelligence business skyscraper
      streets
empty-soul'd, exploding.
Sheer matter crackling, disintegrating back to void,
Sunyatta & Brahma undisturbed, Maya-cities blow up like Chinese firecrack-
      ers,
Samsara tears itself apart—Dusk over Chicago, light-glitter along boulevards,
insect-eyed autos moving slow under blue streetlamps,
plane motor buzz in eardrum, city cloud roof filling with gray gas on up into
      clear heaven—planet horizon auroral twilight-streaked,
blue space above human truck-moil, Empty sky
Empty mind overhangs Chicago, the universe suspended entire overhanging
      Chicago.
O Jack thou'st scaped true deluge.
Smart cock, to turn to shade, I drag hairy meat loss thru blood-red sky
down thru cloud-floor to Chicago, sunset fire obliterate in black gas.

March 13, 1970

Anti–Vietnam War Peace Mobilization

White sunshine on sweating skulls
Washington's Monument pyramided high granite clouds
over a soul mass, children screaming in their brains on quiet grass
(black man strapped hanging in blue denims from an earth cross)—
Soul brightness under blue sky
Assembled before White House filled with mustached Germans
& police buttons, army telephones, CIA Buzzers, FBI bugs
Secret Service walkie-talkies, Intercom squawkers to Narco
Fuzz & Florida Mafia Real Estate Speculators.
One hundred thousand bodies naked before an Iron Robot
Nixon's brain Presidential cranium case spying thru binoculars
from the Paranoia Smog Factory's East Wing.

May 9, 1970

Ecologue

In a thousand years, if there's History
America'll be remembered as a nasty little Country
full of Pricks, thorny hothouse rose
Cultivated by the Yellow Gardeners.
"Chairman Mao" for all his politics, head of a Billion
              folk, important old & huge
         Nixon a dude, specialized on his industrial
                Island, a clean paranoiac Mechanic—
Earth rolling round, epics on archaic tongues
              fishermen telling island tales—
all autos rusted away,
         trees everywhere.

      *

Rough Wind roar, mapletop mass
      shaking in window,
           a panic Cry from the garden
Bessie Cow's loose near the Corn!

The little dakini playing her bells
       & listening to late baritone Dylan
dancing in the living room's forgot almost
      th'electric supply's vanishing
         from the batteries in the pasture.

Chairs shifting downstairs, kitchen voices
      Smell of apples & tomatoes bubbling on the stove.
Behind the Chicken house, dirt flies from the shovel
      hour after hour, tomorrow they'll be a big hole.

The editor sleeps in his bed, morning Chores are done,
      Clock hands move noonward, pig roots by flagstone
        pathways, papers & letters lie quiet
           on many desks.

    Books everywhere, Kabbalah, Gnostic Fragments, Mahanirvana &
Hevajra Tantras, Boehme Blake & Zohar, Gita & Soma Veda, somebody
reads—one cooks, another digs a pighouse foundation, one chases a Cow

from the vegetable garden, one dances and sings, one writes in a notebook,
one plays with the ducks, one never speaks, one picks the guitar, one moves
huge rocks.

The wind charger's propeller
whirs & trees rise windy
one maple at woods edge's turned red.

Chickens bathe in dust at the house wall,
rabbit at fence bends his nose to a handful of Cornsilk,
fly lights on windowsill.

At the end of a long chain, Billy makes a Circle in grass
by the fence, I approach
he stands still with long red stick
stretched throbbing between hind legs
Spurts water a minute, turns his head down
to look & lick his thin pee squirt—
That's why he smells goat like.

Horse by barbed wire licking salt,
lifts his long head & neighs
as I go down by willow thicket
to find the 3-day-old heifer.
At bed in long grass, wet brown fur—
her mother stands, nose covered with a hundred flies.

The well's filled up—
the Cast-iron ram
that pushes water uphill
by hydraulic pressure
flowed from gravity
Can be set to motion soon,
& water flow in kitchen sink tap.

some nights in sleeping bag
Cricket zinging networks dewy meadows,
white stars sparkle across black sky,
falling asleep I listen & watch
till eyes close, and wake silent—
at 4 A.M. the whole sky's moved,
a Crescent moon lamps up the woods.

& last week one Chill night
                    summer disappeared—
        little apples in old trees red,
                    tomatoes red & green on vines,
green squash huge under leafspread,
                    corn thick in light green husks,
sleepingbag wet with dawn dews
        & that one tree red at woods' edge!

Louder wind! ther'll be electric to play the Beatles!

At summer's end the white pig got so fat
                    it weighed more than Georgia
                        Ray Bremser's 3-year-old baby.
        Scratch her named Dont Bite Me under hind leg,
                she flops over on her side sweetly grunting,
                nosing in grass tuft roots, soft belly warm.

Eldridge Cleaver exiled w/ bodyguards in Algiers
Leary sleeping in an iron cell,
                    John Sinclair a year jailed in Marquette
Each day's paper more violent—
                    War outright shameless bombs
                            Indochina to Minneapolis—
        a knot in my belly to read between lines,
                    lies, beatings in jail—
                    Short breath on the couch—
        desolation at dawn in bed—
                        Wash dishes in the sink, drink tea, boil an egg—
                brood over Cities' suffering millions two
                                hundred miles away
                    down the oilslicked, germ-Chemicaled
                                Hudson river.

Ed Hermit comes down hill
        breaks off a maple branch
        & offers fresh green leaves to the pink eyed rabbit.

Under birch, yellow mushrooms
                    sprout between grassblades & ragweed—
        Eat 'em & you die or get high & see God—
                    Waiting for the exquisite mycologist's visit.

Winter's coming, build a rough wood crib
          & fill it with horse dung, hot horse dung,
                    all round the house sides.

Bucolics & Eclogues!
          Hesiod the beginning of the World,
                    Virgil the end of his World—
          & Catullus sucked cock in the country
                    far from the Emperor's police.

Empire got too big, cities too crazy, garbage-filled Rome
          full of drunken soldiers, fat politicians,
                    circus businessmen—
Safer, healthier life on a farm, make yr own wine
                    in Italy, smoke yr own grass in America.

Pond's down two feet from drainpipe's rusty top—
Timothy turned brown, covered with new spread manure
          sweet-smelt in strong breeze,
                    it'll be covered in snow couple months.
          & Leary covered in snow in San Luis Obispo jail?
                    His mind snowflakes falling over the States.

Did Don Winslow the mason come look at the basement
          So we can insulate a snug root cellar
                    for potatoes, beets, carrots,
                    radishes, parsnips, glass jars of corn & beans
Did the mortician come & look us over for next Winter?

Black flies walking up and down the metal screen,
                    fly's leg tickling my forehead—
          "I'll play a fly's bone flute
          & beat an ant's egg drum"
                    sang the Quechua Injun
                    high on Huilca snuff, Medieval
                    Peruvian DMT.

Phil Whalen in Japan
          stirring rice, eyes in the garden,
                    fine pen nib lain by notebook.

Jack in Lowell farming worms, master of his
          minuscule deep acre.

Neal's ashes sitting under a table piled with
            books, in an oak drawer,
                        sunlight thru suburb windows.

O wind! spin the generator wheel, make Power Juice
To run the New Exquisite Noise Recorder, & I'll sing
            praise of your tree music.

Squash leaves wave & ragweeds lean, black tarpaulin
            plastic flutters over the bass-wood lumber pile
            Hamilton Fish's Congressional letter
                        reports "Stiffer laws against peddling smut"
            flapping in dusty spiderwebs by the windowscreen.

What's the Ammeter read by the Windmill? Will
            we record *Highest Perfect Wisdom* all day tomorrow,
                        or Blake's *Schoolboy* uninterrupted next week?

Fine rain-slant showering the gray porch
            Returnable Ginger Ale Bottles
                        on the wood rail, white paint flaked
                                    off into orange flowered
                                                blossoms
Out in the garden, rain
            all over the grass, leaves, roofs,
                        rain on the laundry.

                        *

Night winds hiss thru maple black masses
Gas light shine from
                        farmhouse window upstairs
            empty kitchen wind
Cassiopeia zigzag
                        Milky Way thru cloud

                                    September 4

The baby pig screamed and screamed
                        four feet rigid on grass
                        screamed and screamed
                                    Oh No! Oh No!

jaw dripping blood
                    broken by the horse's hoof.
Slept in straw all afternoon, eyes closed,
                snout at rest between paws—
        ate hog mash liquid—two weeks
                        and his skull be healed
                said the Vet in overalls.

That bedraggled duck's sat under the door
        June to Labor Day, three hatched
                yellow chicks' dry fur bones found
                        by the garage side—
        two no-good eggs left, nights chillier—
                Next week, move her nest
                to the noisy chickenhouse.

We buried lady dog by the apple tree—
        spotted puppy daughter Radha
                sniffed her bloated corpse, flies
                        whisping round eyeball & dry nostril,
                sweet rot-smell, stiff legs, anus puffed out,
Sad Eyes chased the milk truck & got killed.

        How many black corpses they found in the river
                looking for Goodman, Chaney, Schwerner?

Man and wife, they weep in the attic
        after bitter voices,
                low voices threatening.

                        Broken Legs in Vietnam!
                Eyes staring at heaven,
                        Eyes weeping at earth.
                Millions of bodies in pain!
                Who can live with this Consciousness
                and not wake frightened at sunrise?

The Farm's a lie!
        Madmen growing giant organic zucchini
                mulching asparagus, boiling tomatoes for Winter,
                        drying beans, pickling cucumbers
                sweet & garlicked, salting cabbage for sauerkraut,
                canning fresh corn & tossing Bessie husks—

Marie Antoinette had milkmaid costumes ready,
Robespierre's eyeball hung on his cheek
in the tumbril to guillotine—

Black Panther's teeth knocked out in Paterson,
red blood clotted on black hairy skin—
Millions of bodies in pain!

One by one picked orange striped soft potato bugs off
withered brown leaves
dropped them curl'd up in kerosene,
or smeared them on ground with small stones—

Moon rocket earth photo, peacock colored,
tacked to the wood wall,
globe in black sky
living eyeball bathed in cloud swirls—
Is Earth herself frightened?
Does she know?
Oh No! Oh No! the Continuous scream
of the pig
Don't Bite Me in the backyard,
bloody jawbone askew.

Uphill on pine forest floor
Indian peace pipes curl'd up thru dry needles,
half translucent fungus, half metal blossom

Frog sat half out on mud shallows'
minnow-rippling surface,
& stared at our Universe—
So many fish frog, insect ephemera, swamp fern
—So many Ezekiel-wheeled Dragonflies
hovering over old Hemlock root moss—
They wont even know when humans go

Waking 2 A.M. clock tick
What was I dreaming
my body alert
Police light down this dirt road?
Justice Dogs sniffing field for Grass Seeds?

Would they find a little brown mushroom button
       tossed out my window?
     BI read this haiku?

Four in the morning
    rib thrill eyes open—
       Deep hum thru the house—
    Windmill Whir? Hilltop Radar Blockhouse?
     Valley Traffic 5 miles downtown?
  When'll Policecar Machinery assemble
       outside State pine woods?
   Head out window—bright Orion star line,
    Pleiades and Dipper shining silent—

Bathrobe flashlight, uproad Milky Way
   Moved round the house this month
   —remember Taurus' Horn up there last fall?
White rabbit on goat meadow, got over the chickenwire?
   Hop away from flash light? Wait till Godly
       Dog wakes up!
Come back! He'll bite you! Here's a green beet leaf!
     Pwzxst! Pwzxst! Pwzxst!

Attic window lit between trees,
   Clouds drift past the sickle moon—
Tiny lights in the dark sky
       Stars & Crickets everywhere
      Electric whistle-blinks
      tweedle-twinks
       Squeak-peeks
     Locust planet
      zephyr sizzle
       Squinks—
Grasshoppers in cold dewy fall grass
    Singing lovesongs as they die.

   *

Morning, the white rabbit stiff, eyes closed,
   lain belly up in grass, tooth nosed,
     beside the manure pile—dig a hole
—Shoulda introduced him to dogs in daylight—

Cripple Jack drove up
                    to judge the ducks—
                         All eggs sterile,
              smashed on rock, wet guts
                              & rotted-throat smell—
          Bedraggled duck mother,
                         dragged off straw nest
                              & pecking skin at my wrist,
               All afternoon walked up and down quacking
                    thru chickenwire fence

Pig on her side woke up,
                    slurped beet juice, rooted at porch wood
          ignorant of broken head bones—

Morning dew, papery leafs & sharp blossoms
                    of sunflower ripped off battered stalks,
          Who'd do that!? Too late
                    to fix the barbed wire fence,
                    intelligent Bessie Cow strays in the moonlight.

Leary's climbed the chainlink fence & two strands of
                                   barbedwire too
                    This weekend, "Armed & Dangerous,"
                         Signed with Weathermen!
                    Has Revolution begun? World War III?
May no Evil Eye peek thru window, keyhole or
                              gunsight at his white haired face!

Now's halfmoon over America,
          leaves tinged red fall blush scattered overhill,
          down pasture singular trees orange foreheads think
                         Autumn time in pines—
          The maple at woods' edge fire-red's brighter
Australian Aborigines' Eternal Dream Time's come true—
Usta be bears on East Hill; fox under old Hemlock,
Usta be otter—even woolly mammoths in Eternal
                                        dream time—
Leary's out in the woods of the world—cockroaches immune
                                   to radiation?
Richard Nixon has means to end human Worlds,
                    Man has machines for Suicide,

Pray for Timothy Leary in the planet's Woods!
                    Om Mani Padme Hūṃ
                    & Hare Krishna!
"As we forgive those who trespass against us,
                    Thy Will be done
                                on Earth as in Heaven"
        Oh Bessie you ate my unborn sunflowers!
"God never repeats himself" Harry Smith telephoned tonite.

We may not come back, Richard Nixon.
                    We may not come back, dear hidden Tim.

Will Peter fix the sink's hand pump? the basement freeze?
        Backyard grasses stink, if kitchen drains
                        to septic tank, will Bacteria die
                        of soap, Ammonia & Kerosene?

Get rid of that old tractor or fix it!
                    Cardboard boxes rotten in garageside rain!
Old broken City desks under the appletree! Cleanum
                    up for firewood!
Where can we keep all summer's bottles?
                Gas pumps, broken mandolins, old tires—
                        Ugly backyard—Shelf the garage!
Where stack lumber handy to eye?
        Electric generator money? Where keep mops in Wintertime?

Leary fugitive, Sinclair sent up for a decade—
        though 83% of World's illegal opium's fixed
        in Central Intelligence Agency's Indochinese Brain!
        Fed State Local Narcs peddle junk—
                Nixon got a hard hat from Mafia,
Pentagon Public Relations boodle's 190 million A.D. 1969.
                J. E. Hoover's a sexual blackmailer,
                    Times pities "idealistic students"
                        Police killed 4 Blacks in New Orleans
Fascism in America:—
        i.e. Police control Cities, not Mayors or philosophers—
        Police, & Police alone, cause most crime.
        Preventive Detention now law in D.C.
        Mexico & Senegal close borders to Adam Longhair

So many apples in abandoned orchards,
                    and such fresh sweet Cider, supper tonite—
                        onions & cabbage fried on iron—
                    groundwells overflow, hydraulic ram
                                        works steady again,
Eclogues! the town laundry's detergent phosphate
            glut's foul'd clear Snyders Creek—
        I have a beautiful boy in the house,
        learn keyboard notation, chords, & improvise
            freely on Blake's mantras at midnite.
Hesiod annaled Beginnings
            I annal ends for No man.

Hail to the Gods, who are given Consciousness.
Hail to Men Conscious of the Gods!

Electric tempest!
                Entire hillsides turned wet gold,
                Leaf death's begun, universal September
                                    Emerges in old maples
Goat bells near the house, not much in the
            garden they can eat now anyway,
        & cow got beet tops and mangles already—
                    What do dogs hear?
Birds squeak & chatter as Rooster call
        echoes round house wall

Civilization's breaking down! Freezertray's
            lukewarm, who knows why?
The year-old Toilet's leaking at the heel—Wind
        Charger's so feeble batteries are almost down—
Hundreds of black spotted tomatoes
            waiting near the kitchen wood stove
"Useless! useless! the heavy rain driving into the sea!"
Kerouac, Cassady, Olson ash & earth, Leary the Irish
                    coach on the lam,
Black Magicians screaming in anger Newark to Algiers,
How many bottles & cans piled up in our garbage pail?

                                                        Fall 1970

Guru Om

October 4, 1970

Car wheels roar over freeway concrete
Night falls on Dallas, two buildings shine under sickle moon
Many boys and girls in jail for their bodies poems and bitter thoughts
My belly's hollow breath sighs up thru my heart
Guru Om Guru Om enlarges in the vast space of the breast
The Guru has a man's brown belly and cock long hair white beard short hair
      orange hat no person
The bliss alone no business for my body but to make Guru Om dwell near
      my heart
shall I telephone New York and tell my fellows where I am silent
shall I ring my own head & order my own voice to be silent but
How giant, silent and feather-soft is the cave of my body eyes closed
To enter the body is difficult, the belly's full of bad smelling wind
the body's digesting last weekend's meat thinking of Cigarettes, bright eyes
      of boys
What Acid eight hours equals eight hours' Om continuous attention—
the Guru is equal to the Om of the Seeker
Guru Guru Guru Guru Guru Guru Guru Sitaram Omkar Das Thakur thin
      voic'd recommended "Give up desire for children"
Dehorahava Baba sat on the Ganges and described eat & drinking pranayam
Nityananda floated thru his giant photo body
Babaji's hand the hand of a dead man in my dead man's fingers
Out the plane window brown gas rises to heaven's blue sea
—how end the poetry movie in the mind?
how tell Kabir Blake & Ginsberg shut their ears?
Folded in silence invisible Guru waits to fill his body with Emptiness
I am leaving the world, I will close my eyes & rest my tongue and hand.

October 5, 1970

To look in the City without hatred
the orange moon edge sunk into blue Cloud
a second night autos roar to and fro Downtown towers' horizon
airplane moving between moon and white-lit bank towers
lightning haze above twinkling-bulbed man city flats
It is mind-City risen particularly solid.
What elder age grew such cities visioned from these far towers' windows
Seraph armchaired in Babylonic Déjà Vu from Hilton Inn?

October 6, 1970

Dallas buildings' heaped rock tangled steel electric lit under quarter moon
Cars crash at dusk at Mockingbird Lane, Drugstore Supermarket signs re-
     volve with dumb beckoning persistence over North Central Freeway
Leary leaped over the wall with a sword, Errol Flynn's in the grave, flags
     & bombs fly over Dallas' stock exchange
oil flows thru the Hilton Faucets, gasoline fumes smother Neem trees in
     Ganeshpuri—
Maya revolves on rubber wheels, Samsara's glass buildings light up with
     neon, Illusion's doors open on aluminum hinges—
my mother should've done asanas & Kundalini not straightjackets & Electro-
     shock in the birthdays of Roosevelt's FBI—
Where in the body's the white thumbsize subtle corpus, in the neck they say
where's the half-thumbjoint black causal body, down in the heart hidden?
where's the lentil-sized Cosmic Corpse, a tiny blue speck in the navel?
All beings at war in the Gross body, armor'd Cars & Napalm, rifles & grass
     huts burning, Mace on Wall Street, tear gas flooding the fallen stock-
     market.
Look in halls of the head, *nervous leg halls*, universe inside Chest dark baby
     kingdom in the skull.

"Have You Seen This Movie?"

Old maple hairytrunks root asphalt grass marge, November branches rare
 leaved,
Giant woodlegged wiretowers' threads stretch above pond woods highway,
 white sun fallen hills West.
Car rolling underpass, radio hornvoice "the sight of Bobby Seale bound &
 gagged at Trial" denied lawyer presum'd innocent?
MDA Love Drug Cure Junk Habit? Rochester Exit one mile flashing out
 Volkswagen window—
Blue sky fring'd with clouds' whale-ghost-blue schools north drift—
High, high Manson sighed on Trial, how many folk in jail for grass Ask
 Congressman?
Highway Crash! Politics! Police! Dope! armed robbery Customary E. 10th
 street, no insurance possible.
—Brown deer tied neat footed dead eye horned across blue Car trunk, old
 folks Front seat, they're gonna eat it!
Help! Hurrah! What's Going on here? Samsara? Illusion? Reality?
What're all these trailers row'd up hillside, more people? How can Lyca
 sleep?
Cows on Canandaigua fields lactate into rubber stainless steel plastic milk-
 house machinery vats ashine—
Revolutionary Suicide! Driving on Persian gasoline?
Kill Whale & ocean? Oh one American myself shits 1000 times more Chemi-
 cal waste into freshwater & seas than any single Chinaman!
America Suicide Cure World Cancer! Myself included dependent on
 Chemicals, wheels, dollars,
metal Coke Cans Liquid propane batteries marijuana lettuce avocados ciga-
 rettes plastic pens & milkbottles—electric
in N.Y.C. heavy habit, cut airconditioners isolation from street nightmare
 smog heat study decentralized Power sources 10 years
not atomic thermopollutive monolith. Om. How many species poisoned
 biocided from Earth realms?
O bald Eagle & Blue Whale with giant piteous Cat Squeak—Oh Wailing
 whale ululating underocean's sonic roar of Despair!
Sing thy Kingdom to Language deaf America! Scream thy black Cry thru
 Radio electric Aether—
Scream in Death America! Or did Captain Ahab not scream Curses as he
 hurled harpoon
into the body of the mother, great White Whale Nature Herself,
thrashing in intelligent agony innocent vast in the oil-can sick waters?

All Northvietnam bomb-Cratered ruined topsoil Laos in secrecy more
    bombs than many W W II's!
Mekong swamp lethicided by Monsanto Pentagon Academy Death-brains!
What wisdom teaching this? What Mafia runs N.J.? What Mafia knew
    J. Edgar FBI?
What's Schenley's Whiskey trader Fleischmann's Hoover Institute?
What opium's passed thru CIA Agents' airplane's luggage in Saigon, Bang-
    kok, Athens, Washington?
What narcotic agent's not dependent on Shit for a living?
What Bank's money created ex nihil serves orphan, widow, monk, philoso-
    pher?
or what Bank's money serves real Estate Asphalt over widow's garden?
    Serves old Nick in the Pentagon?
Old Indian prophecies believe Ghost Dance peace will Come restore prairie
    Buffalo or great White Father Honkie
be trampled to death in his dreams by returning herds' thundering reincarna-
    tion!
Oh awful Man! What have we made the world! Oh man capitalist exploiter
    of Mother Planet!
Oh vain insect sized men with metal slaves by Great Lake Erie, tenderest
    Passaic & Hudson poisoned by dollars!
BID TAMPERING PROBED IN LACKAWANNA *Buffalo News* headline folded on
    rubber floor, car vibrating smooth to sun ruddy woods' dusk quiet—
Radio hissing cough words dashboard noisemusic—Any minute Apocalypse
    Rock!
Brown Pelican eggs softened by DDT. Seal's livers poisoned to Northman.
    Oceans Dead 2000 A.D.?
Television Citizen 6% Earths human Americans ingest half the planet's raw
    matter as alchemized by Syracuse Gen. Electric Power brown robot
    palace near 8 Lane Thruway's Exit before Ramada Inn.
HXL Trucks sleeping on brokenearthed embankment past Iron-strutted
    passages,
fields aglitter with damp metallic garbage under th'electricwire trestles—
And woods survive into another Thanksgiving's brown sacred silence—
Lights on cars front Western Lane gray twilight falls on rolling robotland.

November 1970

Milarepa Taste

Who am I? Saliva,
    vegetable soup,
        empty mouth?

Hot roach, breathe smoke
    suck in, hold, exhale—
        light as ashes.

Over Laramie

Western Air boat bouncing
    under rainclouds stippled
        down gray Rockies
            Springtime dusk,
Look out on Denver, Allen,
      mourn Neal no more,
    Old ghost loves departed
    New lives whelm the plains, rains
        wash Rocky mountainsides
World turns under sun eye
    Man flies a moment Cheyenne's
        dry upland highways
A tiny fossil brachiapod in pocket
    Precambrian limestone clam
           fingernail small
four hundred fifty million years old

Brain gone, flesh passed thru myriad
    phantom reincarnations,
the tiny-ridged shell's delicate
        as hardened thought.

—over Laramie, Front Range
    pine gully snow pockets,
Monolith Cement plume smoke
    casting dust gas over
      the red plateau
      into the New World.

April 12, 1971

Bixby Canyon Ocean Path
Word Breeze

Tiny orange-wing-tipped butterfly
fluttering sunlit
from violet
blossom to violet
blossom

Ocean is private
you have to visit
her to see her
Garden undercliff
  Dewey Pinks,
   bitter Mint,
  Sea Sage,
   Orange flaming
    Paintbrush
 greenspiked fleurs,
 Thick dainty stalked
   Cow Parsley,
 Starleaf'd violet bushes,
 yelloweyed blue
   Daisy clump—
red brambled mature sour
    blackberry briars,
yellow budded
   Lupine
  nodding stalkheads
  in Sunwarm'd
    breezes
by the brooks tricklet
  wash in the ravine
    Bridged with cloud

Ruddy withwine morning
        glory's tiny tender
                        cowbells,
        guarded by poison oak sprigs
                        oily hands
Green horned little
        British chickweed,
waxlight-leafed black
                seed stalk's
    lilac sweet budcluster
Ah fluted morning
    glory bud
            oped
& tickled to yellow
        tubed stamen root
    by a six legged
        armed mite
    deeping his head
    into sweet pollened
                        crotches,
Crawls up yr veined
    blossom wall
    to petal lip in
        sunshine clear
    and dives again
    to your tongue-stamen's
        foot-pipe, your
    bloom unfolded
    to light—

Above ye the
Spider's left
his one strand
    catgut silk
        shining
            bridge
between
    cuckoospitted
        mint leafheads
& newgreen leafsprig'd
        seedy lilac

Granite Sagely
 Browed above the Path's
  black pepper peapod marge—
Gray rock dropping
 seed,
withered bush-fingers
 tangled up
 stoneface
 —cracked with
 green stalk
   sprout—
Brooktrickle deep
 below Airplane
  Bridge
   Concrete
 arches balcony'd
Pendant over
Oceancrash
 waves
falling empty eyed
 breathing water
   wash afar

Morning Night shade
 in alder shadow'd
Pathside—Nettle plant
 Leaf-shoulder
 vegetable wing'd
 baby faces,
  green earmouths
   sprouting
 Celery handspread
  Heal-All mudras
 open asking why me.

Sunlight trembling
 branch-leafy willow,
yellow haired wingy bee's
  black horn
bowed into threadpackt mauve
 round thistle mouth,

dewey web throat
    green needle collar'd,
Symmetric little
      Cathead erect
electric thorn'd
under giant hogweed
    stalked parasol blossoms—

Ash branch's tender
    pinecone cluster
    proffered by leathery
    sawtooth rib leafs

red browed beedle
    perched on Egyptian
  bridge of Spider fern's
    soft-jointed spike-sticks
Brown water
streaming
    underbrush
sparrowsong
    winged brown
    whistling above
cold water pebble
    silver pour . . .
Shrouded
  under the
Ash spread, on
  damp leafwither,
shield tubes
    & condensers
      of small Sony
    TV machine enwired
    rusty w/resistances

giant grass
  leafspears
morning glory hillside
  perched over clearing
All branches lifting
    up
  papery seedhusks,

parasolspiked Fern
    Tramping together
       upright pushing
         a thistle aside,
    groundwheat leaned
    by beach path—

Oh ocean white-
    waved pouring
  foamy noises over
    rocky sandshore
Chevrolet writ
  on radiatormouth
Set above
    Private Land
Do Not Enter
  incised wood
    Sign-beams

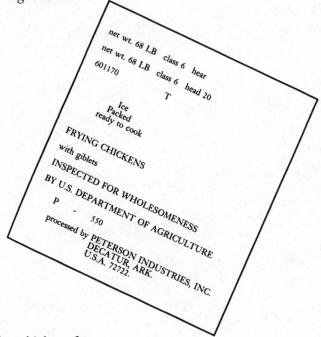

net wt. 68 LB   class 6   hear
net wt. 68 LB   class 6   head 20
601170
T
Ice
Packed
ready to cook
FRYING CHICKENS
with giblets
INSPECTED FOR WHOLESOMENESS
BY U.S. DEPARTMENT OF AGRICULTURE
P - 550
processed by PETERSON INDUSTRIES, INC.
DECATUR, ARK.
U.S.A. 72722.

Frying chickens from
  Arkansas!

Musselshells'
  Briared graveyard
    footplot—

Dewey round bushes
  guarding ocean
      path with
  myriad greenstar'd
    leafarms
  cradling white-walled
       dewdrops

Telephone
  pole trunk
stuck
  out of old
  landslide head
  Covered with iceplant
  green lobsterclaw
    trefoil solid
      edged,
  pinked with
  hundredfingerpetaled
    Sea vine blossoms
Dry brown kelp
  ribs washed
  in a heap at
  streamside in
    wet brown sand
    to listen to
      oceanroar
    and wait the
    slow moon
      tide.

Stream water
  rushing flat through
beachmound
  Sand precipices,
tiny wet arizonas
flood lips
      —cliffs
cradling the last
  graysmooth boulders
  shat by the rains

pissed out
    by spring storm
        from
the forests
        bladder
        hills
    Small granite
    blackpocked
        hearthstones
    washed to last rest
    Ocean wavelet's
        salt tongue
        touching
        forward thru
            sand throated
        streambed
            to lave foam &
        pull back bubbles
        from the iron
    Car's rusty
        under carriage
            kelp pipes
                & brown chassis,
            one rubber wheel
                black poked from
                    Sand mattresses
                    rock wash
O Kerouac
    thy broken
    car Behold
    Digested in
    Saltwater
        sandbottom
giant soulless
    Chicken
        sea gizzard filled
            with unthinking
        marble rocks—
Poured down
    road in
        avalanche!

```
              to the granite
            snout of the
                  seacliff

O see the great
            Snake kelp's
        beet green head still lettuce-
                  haired
            stretch forth
                  a fingerthick tailroot
above seaweed broider
            wavelets
            rushing foam
                      tongued—
Was that kelp
        Intelligent
Einstein hairleafed
        faceless bulbhead

Oh father
      Welcome!
      The seal's
        head lifted
      above the wave,
      eyes watching
        from black
            face
      in waterfroth
        floating!
      Come back again!

Huge white
waves rolling
in gray mist
birds flocking
    rocks foamed
    floating above
    the
        horizon's
            watery
                wrinkled
                skin
```

```
grandmother
    oceanskirt
      rumbling
        pebbles
silver hair ear to ear
```
                    May 28, 1971

Hūṃ Bom!

I
Whom bomb?
We bomb them!
Whom bomb?
We bomb them!
Whom bomb?
We bomb them!
Whom bomb?
We bomb them!

Whom bomb?
You bomb you!
Whom bomb?
You bomb you!
Whom bomb?
You bomb you!
Whom Bomb?
You bomb you!

What do we do?
Who do we bomb?
What do we do?
Who do we bomb?
What do we do?
Who do we bomb?
What do we do!
Who do we bomb?

What do we do?
You bomb! You bomb them!
What do we do?
You bomb! You bomb them!
What do we do?
We bomb! We bomb them!
What do we do?
We bomb! We bomb them!

Whom bomb?
We bomb you!

Whom bomb?
We bomb you!
Whom bomb?
You bomb you!
Whom bomb?
You bomb you!

May 1971

II
Why bomb?
We don't want to bomb!
Why bomb?
We don't want to bomb!
Why bomb?
You don't want to bomb!
Why bomb?
You don't want to bomb!

Who said bomb?
Who said we had to bomb?
Who said bomb?
Who said we had to bomb?
Who said bomb?
Who said you had to bomb?
Who said bomb?
Who said you had to bomb?

We don't bomb!
We don't bomb!
We don't bomb!
We don't bomb!
We don't bomb!
We don't bomb!
We don't bomb!
We don't bomb!

for Don Cherry and Elvin Jones
New York, June 16, 1984

September on Jessore Road

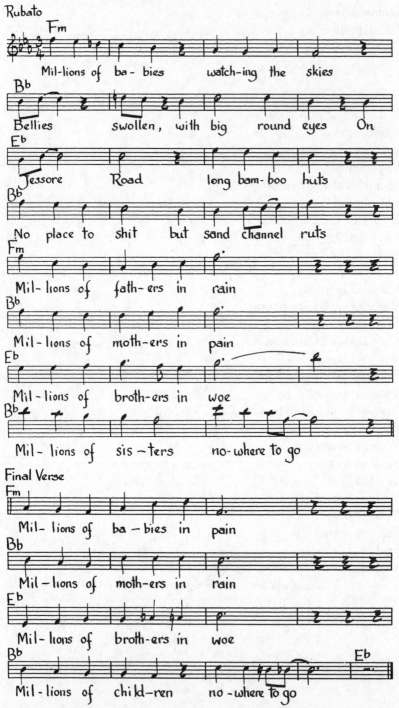

September on Jessore Road

Millions of babies watching the skies
Bellies swollen, with big round eyes
On Jessore Road—long bamboo huts
Noplace to shit but sand channel ruts

Millions of fathers in rain
Millions of mothers in pain
Millions of brothers in woe
Millions of sisters nowhere to go

One Million aunts are dying for bread
One Million uncles lamenting the dead
Grandfather millions homeless and sad
Grandmother millions silently mad

Millions of daughters walk in the mud
Millions of children wash in the flood
A Million girls vomit & groan
Millions of families hopeless alone

Millions of souls Nineteenseventyone
homeless on Jessore road under gray sun
A million are dead, the millions who can
Walk toward Calcutta from East Pakistan

Taxi September along Jessore Road
Oxcart skeletons drag charcoal load
past watery fields thru rain flood ruts
Dung cakes on treetrunks, plastic-roof huts

Wet processions   Families walk
Stunted boys   big heads dont talk
Look bony skulls & silent round eyes
Starving black angels in human disguise

Mother squats weeping & points to her sons
Standing thin legged   like elderly nuns
small bodied   hands to their mouths in prayer
Five months small food   since they settled there

on one floor mat   with a small empty pot
Father lifts up his hands at their lot
Tears come to their mother's eye
Pain makes mother Maya cry

Two children together   in palmroof shade
Stare at me   no word is said
Rice ration, lentils   one time a week
Milk powder for warweary infants meek

No vegetable money or work for the man
Rice lasts four days   eat while they can
Then children starve   three days in a row
and vomit their next food   unless they eat slow.

On Jessore road   Mother wept at my knees
Bengali tongue   cried mister Please
Identity card   torn up on the floor
Husband still waits   at the camp office door

Baby at play I was washing the flood
Now they won't give us any more food
The pieces are here in my celluloid purse
Innocent baby play   our death curse

Two policemen surrounded by thousands of boys
Crowded waiting   their daily bread joys
Carry big whistles   & long bamboo sticks
to whack them in line   They play hungry tricks

Breaking the line   and jumping in front
Into the circle   sneaks one skinny runt
Two brothers dance forward   on the mud stage
The guards blow their whistles   & chase them in rage

Why are these infants   massed in this place
Laughing in play   & pushing for space
Why do they wait here so cheerful   & dread
Why this is the House where they give children bread

The man in the bread door   Cries & comes out
Thousands of boys & girls   Take up his shout

Is it joy? is it prayer?   "No more bread today"
Thousands of Children at once scream   "Hooray!"

Run home to tents   where elders await
Messenger children   with bread from the state
No bread more today! & no place to squat
Painful baby, sick shit he has got.

Malnutrition skulls thousands for months
Dysentery drains   bowels all at once
Nurse shows disease card   Enterostrep
Suspension is wanting   or else chlorostrep

Refugee camps   in hospital shacks
Newborn lay naked   on mothers' thin laps
Monkeysized week-old   Rheumatic babe eye
Gastroenteritis Blood Poison   thousands must die

September Jessore   Road rickshaw
50,000 souls   in one camp I saw
Rows of bamboo   huts in the flood
Open drains, & wet families waiting for food

Border trucks flooded, food cant get past,
American Angel machine   please come fast!
Where is Ambassador Bunker today?
Are his Helios machinegunning children at play?

Where are the helicopters of U.S. AID?
Smuggling dope in Bangkok's green shade.
Where is America's Air Force of Light?
Bombing North Laos all day and all night?

Where are the President's Armies of Gold?
Billionaire Navies   merciful Bold?
Bringing us medicine   food and relief?
Napalming North Vietnam   and causing more grief?

Where are our tears? Who weeps for this pain?
Where can these families go in the rain?
Jessore Road's children close their big eyes
Where will we sleep when Our Father dies?

Whom shall we pray to for rice and for care?
Who can bring bread to this shit flood foul'd lair?
Millions of children alone in the rain!
Millions of children weeping in pain!

Ring O ye tongues of the world for their woe
Ring out ye voices for Love we dont know
Ring out ye bells of electrical pain
Ring in the conscious American brain

How many children are we who are lost
Whose are these daughters we see turn to ghost?
What are our souls that we have lost care?
Ring out ye musics and weep if you dare—

Cries in the mud by the thatch'd house sand drain
Sleeps in huge pipes in the wet shit-field rain
waits by the pump well, Woe to the world!
whose children still starve   in their mothers' arms curled.

Is this what I did to myself in the past?
What shall I do Sunil Poet I asked?
Move on and leave them without any coins?
What should I care for the love of my loins?

What should we care for our cities and cars?
What shall we buy with our Food Stamps on Mars?
How many millions sit down in New York
& sup this night's table on bone & roast pork?

How many million beer cans are tossed
in Oceans of Mother? How much does She cost?
Cigar gasolines and   asphalt car dreams
Stinking the world and dimming star beams—

Finish the war in your breast   with a sigh
Come taste the tears   in your own Human eye
Pity us millions of phantoms you see
Starved in Samsara   on planet TV

How many millions of children die more
before our Good Mothers perceive the Great Lord?

How many good fathers pay tax to rebuild
Armed forces that boast   the children they've killed?

How many souls walk through Maya in pain
How many babes   in illusory rain?
How many families   hollow eyed lost?
How many grandmothers   turning to ghost?

How many loves who never get bread?
How many Aunts with holes in their head?
How many sisters skulls on the ground?
How many grandfathers   make no more sound?

How many fathers in woe
How many sons   nowhere to go?
How many daughters   nothing to eat?
How many uncles   with swollen sick feet?

Millions of babies in pain
Millions of mothers in rain
Millions of brothers in woe
Millions of children   nowhere to go

New York, November 14–16, 1971

IX
MIND BREATHS
ALL OVER
THE PLACE
(1972–1977)

Sad Dust Glories (1972–1974)

Ego Confessions (1974–1977)

Ayers Rock / Uluru Song

When the red pond fills fish appear

When the red pond dries fish disappear.

Everything built on the desert crumbles to dust.

Electric cable transmission wires swept down.

The lizard people came out of the rock.

The red Kangaroo people forgot their own song.

Only a man with four sticks can cross the Simpson Desert.

One rain turns red dust green with leaves.

One raindrop begins the universe.

When the raindrop dries, worlds come to their end.

Central Australia, March 23, 1972

Voznesensky's "Silent Tingling"

Must be thousands of sweet gourmets rustling through
leaf crowded branches, thrushes cracking seedling shells
all over America like crystalline carillon bells,
a really strange silent tingling.

Silent carillons, not to celebrate Main Street
but rustling up some food their only scene—
No miracle but millions of hungry souls
silently tingling.

This tingling silence heralds
an orgy of hermit thrushes eating
like thousands of song-men's clapsticks clacking
or faraway Moscow's million bells
—some dream collective—generational vogue.

Thrush communes don't be afraid of the big Broom,
your flock continues an ancient tradition,
now all over America—collective marriage;
though some detractors put down your in-group, not big enough!

A silent Individualist in top hat & tails drest
coffinlike denounces your collective struggles in bed—
but his own wife wears rings on every finger,
as if she wound up in a group marriage.

This gentle gang's only enemy's insects,
Cleaning up bark parasites—silently, silently—
Anybody can crush bones and oink louder
but cant beat this silent tingling.

Fast New York Sydney chicks—
thanks Brisbane birds & Chicago thrushes
for your own silent tingling—your cities' trees'
leaves tremble like golden curlicues on Byzantine crosses.

Maybe someday our descendants
'll ask about this poet—What'd he sing about?
I didn't ring Halleluiah bells, I didn't clank leg-irons,
I was silently tingling.

Translated with Andrei Voznesensky
Darwin Land—Cairns, Australia, March 26–29, 1972

These States: to Miami Presidential Convention

I
Philadelphia city lights boiling under the
    clouds
green Babylon's heat attracting rain,
    lightning, smoke gathered
  about the excited city—shouts, vibration
    of trucks, radio antennae, streets'
solid electric glitter under sulphur waterfumes—
the plane glides to Miami Beach over Atlantic's
    Coast metropolis
  red downtown sores of theater money,
    bar sign pinprick bulbs under
      Cloud curtain'd sunlit velvet horizon
To the political drama, march to
    Auditorium thru tacky downtown
    Cuban neons blinking angry language,
    Yippies survived unto this Presidentiad!

Woe to the States, whoever's the empty President
    Nixon McGovern X or Caesar
Must decree end to matter habit,
  America swallowing aluminum sleep pills
Cries of millions of trees travel thru TV
    loudspeakers to the Athletic Club's basement steamroom—
    Millions of yellow faces call thru radio
Cries of the longhairs in the Rockies,
    Choruses of American prophets in their graves
  echo thru newspaper horns to the
        Ear Consciousness Mind
Matter Consumption must end,
    Dirty alchemy destroys the House—
  Billion year old leaf plates become inert matter
    Plastic particles mixed
        with living cells in the Walleyed
        pike's retina—

Soaring over Atlantic's lit-up electric
    houses to the politics Warre

Ah! Shall be my mantra—America's gasp of Awe—
    Ah as Fireworks ascend & light glitters
        faery shimmering in treetop darkness
            sky over Eastside Park July 4th—Ah
As the enlightened Aborigine sighs his
    soul-journey with birds to New Guinea
Ah! the madman screamed
        to himself in the silence of the Ward
Ah as car owner collapsed into
        his ruined heap of metal on his own
            Front Yard
Ah! the divorcee steps off her plane onto Mexico City Airport—
Ah! as I ride spitting petrol into the exquisite
                         Midnight Atmosphere
      above cloud cities
toward another gateway of Police Boys
    & State Powers convened
Clocks Ticking two centuries
      now America
approaching the great Ah of all cities
    burning under Clouds, Conscious
        of Death Machines Downtown.
            Ah, for the garden—

After conversation with Chögyam Trungpa, Rinpoche, Boulder, Spring 1972

II
O Peaceful & Wrathful Dieties & Politicians Rejoice, Rejoice
    left and right!
Ah! liberty—we here together conscious of
    heart's feeling ah!
Massacre ah! selling images in America
    bellied meadow bombcrater photo mind
        scream   face skin afire
    eyes penetrated by war needles
Ah! to the Heart from Heart ever Grateful
    for mercy human understanding sigh—
Ah! for our loves dead & gone
Ah! for miseries we caused, youthful screaming
    Pig Cop selves
    Violence in other streets and nations
    Heads of State
      eyes flashing angry—

Ah! that we know ourselves better,
   Ah! that America rise from
      the dead matter
& transcend this body heavy asphalt usury
      being with each other
         Trembling with city hatred
         dropping acid Death Fear
   lovelessness alone on metal
         planet floor—or
         grass green meadow
among Equal Creatures, trees flourishing their Barken Kind
                                    leaf flared—
ah What Seek we in Miami Heaven Earth
      But End to Fear
Ah! to rejoice in World Illusion
   airplane sound street body under sky—
Apocatastasis Ah!
            Release of our knowledge
                  our suffering in kind—

Ah! together, ah! make peace!
   Ah What is this lightness that we know
      body empty & the mind
         Myriad Ah'd in Mid Metropolis zonked
            & baffled by its own Being,

Angers, Loves & Wars—Great Politics shakes
         planet tremors through our souls—
Ah! Great Consciousness Here
Salutations to the Great Self we come to know
Ah to All souls, Republican empty as
Democrat—Identity we Citizens
      share this late century
Conscious after matter madness
         Drunkenness-drug'd manufacture
            Business Consumption
               Transitory petrochemical toy
                  plastic aluminum
            airconditioned hotel & old folks
                  home atrembling in our mortal bed
for the Big Nigger, the FBI the CIA the
      NLF the ITT USSR the U.S.A.

Great Government Robot State
       above us dominates our news,
takes up our telephone time labor paper work
       in Magic War,
Ah! that we return to our Bodies alert
       electric limb'd, lungs & heart
              empty tingling, lightness
       we all know Heaven on Earth
       Our Will Be Thine as we Say

Our Ah—of Suffering Understood,
       our life itself in pain
   Ah! our ignorance! our desire!
Ah to know that suffering ends,
       surrendered self's sweet death—
our Ah to search the way together thru
                     some Eightfold Endless Path!
Ah! for the Hell we have made in America,
       Ah for the Heaven we see among Us
              Ah! for the Earth we are here!
Ah Miami streets, hotels lobbies crowded
       auditorium! Ah for the fat sad police—
              Ah for sad soldiers forlorn all over the world
Ah for the Madman in White House asylum
       who dreams Planet Fate—
Depression armaments? Conspicuous
   Consumption Cars! Great Ah
Protect us! Ah! for the Petrochemical Wonderland,
   Conscious vast glittery buildings
                     fog dream neon'd
                        for Magical Emphasis
              Hypnosis Money
A billfold full of Ah!
       Ah! credit card plastic
              broke in wastebasket
Ah for Cosa Nostra, Imagined or Real
       Ah! Ah! Ah!
Ah Mayor Daley, Senator Humphrey voluble
   Redeemed in Paradise, ah Laborer
       Meany hatted with Milkweed
              & Day Lilies,

Chiefs Nixon Agnew crowned with
        Pigweed & snowballs' tender blue blossoms
    sent with Jersey Greeting,
Governor Wallace flowered with Mushrooms, magic
        amanita & psilocybin, & Morning Glory halo'd
McGovern McCarthy ringed with Roses & Laurels,
ourselves all decked with Common Grass,
        plebeian pleasures, ah
Ah! Normal voiced & Future President
        Whoever Ye Are True Ah to Thee
Ah! to the Republic how it fare, Ah
        sad flag, color transmuted
            into all Three Worlds
                This prayer to All Souls in America
                Citizens of Body Mind & Speech
                        Ah! Ah! Ah!

                    July 9, 1972, 10:15 P.M.

Xmas Gift

I met Einstein in a dream
Springtime on Princeton lawn grass
I kneeled down & kissed his young thumb
like a ruddy pope
his face fresh broad cheeked rosy
"I invented a universe separate,
something like a Virgin"—
"Yes, the creature gives birth to itself,"
I quoted from Mescaline
We sat down open air universal summer
to eat lunch, professors' wives
at the Tennis Court Club,
our meeting eternal, as expected,
my gesture to kiss his fist
unexpectedly saintly
considering the Atom Bomb I didn't mention.

New York, December 24, 1972

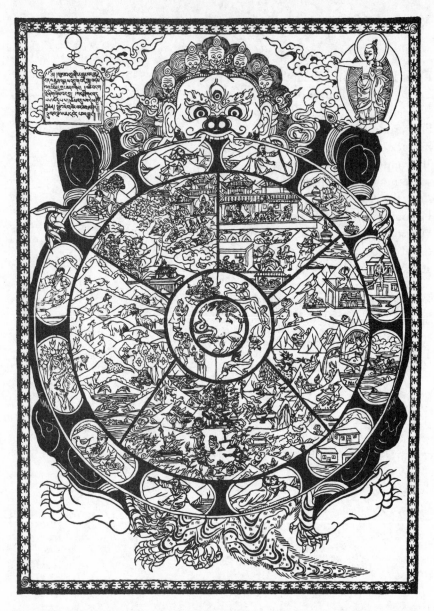

Time Wheel Mandala (Tibetan Buddhist XX Century Woodblock). Six worlds, with Heaven and Angry Warrior Realms consolidated upper left section. At center, Cock Pig Snake eating each other's tails. Twelve-fold chain of interdependent co-origination represented on wheel rim, held in hands of Time.

Thoughts Sitting Breathing

OM—the pride of perfumed money, music food from China, a place to sit quiet

MA—How jealous! the million Pentagon myrmidons with dollar billions to spend on Rock & Roll, restaurant high thrones in sky filled with Electric Bombers—Ah! how jealous they are of the thin stomached Vietnamese boy.

NI—Lust in heart for the pink tender prick'd school-boy upstairs bedroom naked with his books, high school locker shower, stretching on the bed, the young guitar player's ass

PA—Impercipience, cat meows natural words at the window, dog barks cheerful morn, cockroach feelers touch the wall, the fly buzzes long long on the sunny windowsill lying upside-down in deathly prayer exhausted, man bends over oblivious books, buds stick forth their heart-tips when ice melts New Year's eve, green grass shoots show 'neath melted snow, screams rise out of thousands of mouths in Hanoi—

DMI—alone the misery, the broken legs of carcrash alcohol, gimme another cigarette, I ain't got a dime for coffee, got no rupee for rice ain't got no land I got hunger in my gland my belly's swollen potatoes my knees got cut on the Tanks—

HŪM—the pigs got rocks in their head, C.I.A. got one eye bloody mind tongue, fiends sold my phonograph TV set to the junkman, Hate that dog shat my rug, hate Gook Heaven, hate them hippies in Hell stinking Marijuana smog city.

OM—Give it all away, poetry bliss & ready cash for taxicabs, walk Central Park alone & cook your beans in empty silence watching the Worm crawl thru meat walls—

MA—sit down crosslegged and relax, storm Heaven with your mental guns? Give up let Angels alone to play their guitars in Hollywood and drink their Coke-snuff in mountainside bathroom peace—

NI—Light as ashes, love for Neal sublimed into Poesy, love for Peter gone into the Vegetable garden to grow corn & tomatoes—

PA—Dog bark! call the mind gods! scream happiness in Saigon behind the bar my mother in throes of Police vomit rape! that garbage can I threw in Atlantic Ocean floats over Father Fisheye's sacred grave—

DMI—I forgive thee Cord Meyer secret mind police suborned the Student Congress Cultural Freedom & destroyed Intellect in Academe Co-

March: Thoughts Sitting Breathing

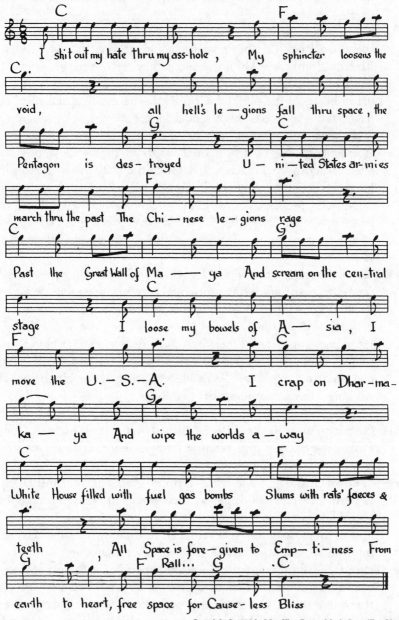

I shit out my hate thru my ass-hole, My sphincter loosens the void, all hell's le—gions fall thru space, the Pentagon is des—troyed U—ni—ted States ar—mies march thru the past The Chi—nese le—gions rage Past the Great Wall of Ma——ya And scream on the cen-tral stage I loose my bowels of A—sia, I move the U.—S.—A. I crap on Dhar—ma—ka—ya And wipe the worlds a—way White House filled with fuel gas bombs Slums with rats' faeces & teeth, All Space is fore—given to Emp—ti—ness From earth to heart, free space for Cause—less Bliss

Copyright © 1978 by May King Poetry Music Inc., Allen Ginsberg

lumbia Harvard made great murder Indochina War our fantasy-
bomb gutted New York's soul—

HŪM—Miserable victims flashing knives, Hell's Angels Manson Nixon
Calley-Ma, all the cops in the world and their gangster lovers, car
salesmen Wall Street brokers smoking in rage over dwindling oil
supplies, O poor sick junkies all here's bliss of Buddha-opium, Sacred
Emptiness to fix your angry brains—

OM—the Crown of Emptiness, relax the skullcap wove of formal thought,
let light escape to Heaven, floating up from heart thru cranium, free
space for Causeless Bliss—

MA—Speech purified, worlds calmed of alcoholic luxury & irritable smok-
ing, jealous fucking rush thru taxicab cities, mental cancer pig war
fever machines—Heart through throat, free space for Causeless Bliss!

NI—How vast, how brightly empty and how old, the breath within the
breast expands threefold, the sigh of no restraint, sigh love's release,
the rest and peacefulness of sweethearts' ease, from Heart to Heart
—free space for Causeless Bliss!

PA—Dog bellies crying happy in the snow, worms share mind's heaviest
part, elephants carry Angels whose animal trumpets blow from abdo-
men deep navel up into the heart—free space for Causeless Bliss

DMI—Down in the pecker, the empty piece of wood—Everyone I fucked
is dead and gone—everyone I'm gonna fuck is turning to a ghost—
All my penis blessedness never'll get lost, but rise from loins & come
in my heart—free space for Causeless Bliss

HŪM—I shit out my hate thru my asshole, My sphincter loosens the void,
all hell's legions fall thru space, the Pentagon is destroyed

> United States armies march thru the past
> The Chinese legions rage
> Past the Great Wall of Maya
> And scream on the central stage
> I loose my bowels of Asia
> I move the U.S.A.
> I crap on Dharmakaya
> And wipe the worlds away
> White House filled with fuel gas bombs
> Slums with rats' faeces & teeth
> All Space is fore-given to Emptiness—
> From earth to heart, free space
> > for Causeless Bliss

January 1, 1973

"What would you do if you lost it?"

said Rinpoche Chögyam Trungpa Tulku in the marble glittering apartment
lobby
looking at my black hand-box full of Art, "Better prepare for Death" . . .
The harmonium that's Peter's
the scarf that's Krishna's the bell and brass lightningbolt Phil Whalen se-
lected in Japan
a tattered copy of Blake, with chord notations, black books from City Lights,
Australian Aborigine song sticks, green temple incense, Tibetan precious-
metal finger cymbals—
A broken leg a week later enough reminder, lay in bed and after few days'
pain began to weep
no reason, thinking a little of Rabbi Schacter, a little of father Louis, a little
of everything that must be abandoned,
snow abandoned,
empty dog barks after the dogs have disappeared
meals eaten passed thru the body to nourish tomatoes and corn,
The wooden bowl from Haiti too huge for my salad,
Teachings, Tantras, Haggadahs, Zohar, Revelations, poetries, Koans
forgotten with the snowy world, forgotten
with generations of icicles crashing to white gullies by roadside,
Dharmakaya forgot, Nirmanakaya shoved in coffin, Sambhogakaya eclipsed
in candle-light snuffed by the playful cat—
Goodbye my own treasures, bodies adored to the nipple,
old souls worshipped flower-eye or imaginary auditory panoramic skull—
goodbye old socks washed over & over, blue boxer shorts, subzero longies,
new Ball Boots black hiplength for snowdrifts near the farm mailbox,
goodbye to my room full of books, all wisdoms I never studied, all the
Campion, Creeley, Anacreon Blake I never read through,
blankets farewell, orange diamonded trunked from Mexico Himalayan
sheepwool lugged down from Almora days with Lama Govinda and
Peter trying to eat tough stubborn halfcooked chicken.
Paintings on wall, Maitreya, Sakyamuni & Padmasambhava, Dr. Samedi
with Haitian spats & cane whiskey,
Bhaktivedanta Swami at desk staring sad eye Krishna at my hopeless selfcon-
sciousness,
Attic full of toys, desk full of old checks, files on NY police & C.I.A. peddling
Heroin,
Files on laughing Leary, files on Police State, files on ecosystems all faded
& brown,

notebooks untranscribed, hundreds of little poems & prose my own hand,

newspaper interviews, assemblaged archives, useless paperworks surrounding me imperfectly chronologic, humorous later in eternity, reflective of Cities' particular streets studios and boudoirs—

goodbye poetry books, I don't have to take you along anymore on a chain to Deux Magots like a red lobster

thru Paris, Moscow, Prague, Milan, New York, Calcutta, Bangkok, holy Benares, yea Rishikesh & Brindaban may yr prana lift ye over the roof of the world—

my own breath slower now, silent waiting & watching—

Downstairs pump-organs, musics, rags and blues, home made Blake hymns, mantras to raise the skull of America,

goodbye C chord, F chord, G chord, goodbye all the chords of The House of the Rising Sun

Goodbye farmhouse, city apartment, garbage subways Empire State, Museum of Modern Art where I wandered thru puberty dazzled by Van Gogh's raw-brained star-systems pasted on blue thick skyey Suchness—

Goodbye again Naomi, goodbye old painful legged poet Louis, goodbye Paterson the 69 between Joe Bozzo & Harry Haines that out-lasted childhood & poisoned the air o'er Passaic Valley,

goodbye Broadway, give my regards to the great falls & boys staring marijuana'd in wonder hearing the quiet roar of Godfather Williams' speech

Goodbye old poets of Century that taught fixed eye & sharp tongue from Pound with silent Mouni heart to Tom Veitch weeping in Stinson Beach,

goodbye to my brothers who write poetry & play fiddle, my nephews who blow tuba & stroke bass viol, whistle flute or smile & sing in blue rhythm,

goodbye shades of dead living loves, bodies weeping bodies broken bodies aging, bodies turned to wax doll or cinder

Goodbye America you hope you prayer you tenderness, you IBM 135-35 Electronic Automated Battlefield Igloo White Dragon-tooth Fuel-Air Bomb over Indochina

Goodbye Heaven, farewell Nirvana, sad Paradise adieu, adios all angels and archangels, devas & devakis, Bodhisattvas, Buddhas, rings of Seraphim, Constellations of elect souls weeping singing in the golden Bhumi Rungs, goodbye High Throne, High Central Place, Alleluiah Light beyond Light, a wave of the hand to Thee Central Golden Rose,

Om Ah Hūṃ A La La Ho Sophia, Soham Tara Ma, Om Phat Svaha

Padmasambhava Marpa Mila sGam.po.pa Karmapa Trungpaye!
Namastaji Brahma, Ave atque vale Eros, Jupiter, Zeus, Apollo, Surya,
Indra

Bom Bom! Shivaye! Ram Nam Satyahey! Om Ganipatti, Om Saraswati
Hrih Sowha! Ardinarishvara Radha Harekrishna faretheewell forev-
ermore!

None left standing! No tears left for eyes, no eyes for weeping, no mouth
for singing, no song for the hearer, no more words for any mind.

Cherry Valley, February 1, 1973

Who

From Great Consciousness vision Harlem 1948 buildings standing in Eternity
I realized entire Universe was manifestation of One Mind—
My teacher was William Blake—my life work Poesy,
transmitting that spontaneous awareness to Mankind.

February 3, 1973

Yes and It's Hopeless

hundred million cars running out of gasoline
million coalstoves burning shale carbonmist over cities
Hopeless I'll never get laid again, O what a beautiful body that boy from
      Jersey City last night
Hopeless, locked in plaster-of-Paris leg cast, bones, skull heart, intestines,
      liver, eyes and tongue
All hopeless, the entire solar system running Thermodynamics' Second Law
down the whole galaxy, all universes brain illusion or solid electric hopeless
      emptiness
evacuating itself through quasar pressure Furnaces,
hopeless the 300,000 junkies in N.Y.
hopeless President waging war, "fighting for peace" sending State Secretary
      to Israel, the moon, China, Acapulco,
hopeless the Dutch boy standing with his finger in the dike,
the energy crisis, the protein crisis 1990, the Folklore Crisis, the Aboriginal
      Crisis, the Honkie Crisis, the old Nazi Crisis, the Arab Crisis, the
      Chrysophrase Crisis, Tungsten, the crisis in Panama, Brazil, Uru-
      guay, Argentina, Chile, Peru, Bolivia, Venezuela, Santa Domingo,
      Haiti, Cuba, Florida, Alabama, Texas, New Jersey, New York, East
      10th Street, the Crisis in San Juan Capistrano, the Oil-spill in Bolinas
      Bay, Santa Barbara's tar tide, the crisis of the Loch Ness Monster &
      the Dublin Bomb Crisis,
all hopeless, the overpopulation of dogs, humans, cockroaches, rats, Crown
      of Thorn Starfish, green algae in Lake Erie—
Hopeless, hopeless, Jesus on the Cross or Buddha voided passing through
Hopeless, the First Zen Institute, the Second Church of the Resurrection,
      the Third Eye System Inc., the 4th Estate, the 5th Column in the
      Kundalini, the 6th sense, the Seventh Seal Chowder & Marching
      Society the 8th Nerve in the Vagus Nebula System the 9th Degree
      Samadhi Monopoly the 10th sorry passenger on the bus crashed over
      Freeway's iron ropes down into the Swamp Abyss outsida
      Roanoke—
OK hopeless, Rolling Stone Consciousness, Mammoth Sunday NY Times
Hopeless all silence, all Yoga, all quiet Ecstasies of Saints and Starvation
      Monks Ceylon to Bhutan—
Hopeless two million deaths in Indochina, the half million Communists
      assassinated in Indonesia? Slaughter of Innocents in Mexico City,
      Massacres of Wounded Knee Mylai Lidice Attica, 15 million never
      came back from Siberia

the jail murder of George Jackson, Sacco & Vanzetti electrocuted Rosen-
    bergs, bullet assassination of Kennedy, Luther King, Malcolm X, the
    burning of Zwingli, hemlock death of Socrates the headless catastro-
    phe Jayne Mansfield's autocrash & Jimmy Dean's highway wreck-
    aged body—
Hopeless, the poems of Dante & Shakespeare, such stuff as dreams are made
    of, Burroughs' Orwell systems, Spengler & Vico's cycles, Pad-
    masambhava Krishnamurti—empty, hopeless
as the great oilfields of Persia
reservoirs of petrochemicals under Alaskan permafrost & Indochinese ocean
    wave
petroleum cracker tanks in Venezuela & robot pumps of Los Angeles,
brokendown cars on the farm, the tire-less Ford,
Oldsmobile sans batteries, dead corpse of Myron the neighbor Farmer the
    live corpse of Ginsberg the prophet
Hopeless.
       New York, March 10, 1973

Under the world there's a lot of ass, a lot of cunt

a lot of mouths and cocks,
under the world there's a lot of come, and a lot of saliva dripping into brooks,
There's a lot of Shit under the world, flowing beneath cities into rivers,
a lot of urine floating under the world,
a lot of snot in the world's industrial nostrils, sweat under the world's iron
      arm, blood
gushing out of the world's breast,
endless lakes of tears, seas of sick vomit rushing between hemispheres
floating toward Sargasso, old oily rags and brake fluids, human gasoline—
Under the world there's pain, fractured thighs, napalm burning in black hair,
      phosphorus eating elbows to bone
insecticides contaminating oceantide, plastic dolls floating across Atlantic,
Toy soldiers crowding the Pacific, B-52 bombers choking jungle air with
      vaportrails and brilliant flares
Robot drones careening over rice terraces dropping cluster grenades, plastic
      pellets spray into flesh, dragontooth mines & jellied fires fall on straw
      roofs and water buffalos,
perforating village huts with barbed shrapnel, trenchpits filled with fuel-gas-
      poison'd explosive powders—
Under the world there's broken skulls, crushed feet, cut eyeballs, severed
      fingers, slashed jaws,
Dysentery; homeless millions, tortured hearts, empty souls.

April 1973

Returning to the Country for a Brief Visit

Annotations to Amitendranath Tagore's Sung Poetry

"In later days, remembering this I shall certainly go mad."

Reading Sung poems, I think of my poems to Neal
dead few years now, Jack underground
invisible—their faces rise in my mind.
Did I write truthfully of them? In later times
I saw them little, not much difference they're dead.
They live in books and memory, strong as on earth.

"I do not know who is hoarding all this rare work."

Old One the dog stretches stiff legged,
soon he'll be underground. Spring's first fat bee
buzzes yellow over the new grass and dead leaves.

What's this little brown insect walking zigzag
across the sunny white page of Su Tung-p'o's poem?
Fly away, tiny mite, even your life is tender—
I lift the book and blow you into the dazzling void.

*"I fear that others may know I am here;
An immortal may appear to welcome me."*

Right leg broken, can't walk around
visit the fishpond to touch the cold water,
tramp thru willows to the lonely meadow across the brook—
here comes a metal landrover, brakes creaking hello.

"You live apart on rivers and seas . . ."

You live in apartments by rivers and seas
Spring comes, waters flow murky, the salt wave's covered with oily
    dung
Sun rises, smokestacks cover the roofs with black mist

winds blow, city skies are clear blue all afternoon
but at night the full moon hesitates behind brick.
How will all these millions of people worship the Great Mother?
When all these millions of people die, will they recognize the Great
      Father?

"I always remember the year I made it over the mountain pass."

Robins and sparrows warble in mild spring dusk
sun sets behind green pines in the little valley
High over my roof gray branches sway gently under motionless clouds
Hunters guns sounded three times in the hillside aspen
The house sat silent as I looked above my book,
quiet old poems about the Yi & Tsangpo Rivers—
I always remember the spring I climbed Glacier Peak with Gary.

                                        Cherry Valley, April 20, 1973

Night Gleam

Over and over thru the dull material world the call is made
over and over thru the dull material world I make the call
O English folk, in Sussex night, thru black beech tree branches
the full moon shone at three AM, I stood in under wear on the lawn—
I saw a mustached English man I loved, with athlete's breast and farmer's
      arms,
I lay in bed that night many loves beating in my heart
sleepless hearing songs of generations electric returning intelligent memory
to my frame, and so went to dwell again in my heart
and worship the Lovers there, love's teachers, youths and poets who live
      forever
in the secret heart, in the dark night, in the full moon, year after year
over & over thru the dull material world the call is made.

July 16, 1973

What I'd Like to Do

Retire abandon world sd Swami Bhaktivedanta my age 47 approaching
    half-century
Go to San Marino see Blake's vision of Moloch, go to Manchester see Moloch
Visit Blake's works all over World West, study prophetic Books interpret
    Blake unify Vision
Step in same river twice
Build hermitage of wood and stone with porch 3000 foot up Rockies, Sierras,
    Catskills fine soft forests
sit crosslegged straight spine belly relaxed heart humming Ah each exhala-
    tion
Inspiration established compose English Apocalypse American science
    Greek rhythm Tibetan mantra Blues
long hours half-lotus-legged at desk window pine trees omming in rainy
    wind
Spend three years in solitude Naropa's Six Doctrines mastered and another
    hundred days intermediate State twixt Death and Birth
Read Milton's Paradise Lost decipher Egyptian Book of Dead and Annutara
    Tantra etc.
Compose poems to the wind
Chant into electric microphones, pacify Rock, enrich
skull emptiness with vocal salami taxicabs, magnetize nervous systems,
destroy Empire State's dead Life Time smog
Masturbate in peace, haunt ancient cities for boys, practice years of chastity,
    save Jewels for God my own ruddy body, hairy delicate antennae
Vegetable, eat carrots, fork cabbage, spoon peas, fry potatoes, boil beets, ox
    forgiven, pig forgotten, hot dogs banished from celestial realms
    cloud-roofed over Kitkitdizze's green spring weeds—milk, angel-
    Milk
Read Dostoyevsky's Brothers Karamazov I laid down half-finished a dozen
    times decades ago
Compose last choirs of Innocence & Experience, set music to tongues of
    Rossetti Mss. orchestrate Jerusalem's quatrains—
War's over, soft mat wood floor, flower vase on inkstand, blue oaks gazing
    in the window.

London, August 1973

On Illness

Lord Heart, heal my right temple bang'd soft pain the bookshelf
rising to fuck Peter embrac'd naked on big wooden couch mattress sheeted
    blanketed
My broken leg Lord Heart heal crooked bone above stiff ankle, straight tibia
    tender sore
Lord Heart, more near, lax abdomen muscle, nausea hiatus hernia
That I never eat too much Lord Heart eat Lord's parts sick with solar plexus
    pain,
deep breath your airy body tingling empty pleasur'd skin kissed cock surren-
    der'd rising buttock entering yr Lord Heart—

Entered I surrender to Lord Heart himself disguised Krishna Ke Jai yr blue
    lingam—Hey Bom Shivaye!
Lord Heart your female poetry bottom, penis female sensitive—
ass kissed & tongued by Jove Jupiter Zeus
Ganymede-ass or Tara ladybelly

Om Saraswati Hrih Sowha
MŌM
Mōm Mōm Mōm Mōm Mōm Mōm Mōm

Lord Heart my baldness cure thru confident eye my lover's open pupil
My teeth Lord Heart keep clean as I do brush them twice daily. Keep me
    from pain.
My hernia rupture paunch healed no pain these coughs—soft muscle stom-
    ach-fold sewn insentient muscle skin.
Lord Heart not smoke cigarette butts anymore—
Keep me Lord Heart for yr Works & Destruction
Body meat cries, sighs, sits immobile Ah, pain passed over—
Lord Heart, my aged father's hand is cool, legs stumbling
defend us from Death Fear, Matter-formed fear faces, disgrac'd mere Flesh
Gone known Lord Heart ourselves defend from Foul Fiend
Grant peace this body Lord Heart, this Soul, this Spirit hand & tongue—
this Great Presence defend Lord Heart your silent Inviolable Witness—
Lord Heart the Great Planet defend this Space Mirror of our Vast Emptiness
Lord Heart come fill my Soul with Mountain snow & Glacier-melt slow
    Aeon's Gnosis—
ancient voice Lord Heart, your thousand arms & eight, of preservation &
    compassion

Conch Shell, Lotus, Diamond Sceptre, Book of Memory, Umbrella, Fish &
      Mirror & Machine Wheel
Eternal One Lord Heart accept my soul and body as your own
Free play of causeless bliss.

London, August 29, 1973

News Bulletin

"Criminal possession of a controlled substance—
        Marijuana" came over the radio
I got mad & sent Gov. Rockefeller a
        crystal skull postcard

Abbie Hoffman just got busted
        million pounds of Cocaine
I wrote the wrong essay & combed burrs
        out of a Godly dog's hide

A lady asked text on Jewish Holocaust
        I filed her letter and made sugar borscht

Tim Leary silent Folsom Jail'd I jacked
        off with a plastic cock in my ass

Catastrophe everywhere today propane
        shortage prophesied I answered my mail
I stuck my head out the edge of
        Universe wheels in starry wheels
while Supreme Court struck down porn-
        ography for the umpteenth time

It'll begin all over dope raids
        sex flick police assassinations
        mass Television in Vietnam
Mugging on streets your favorite
        policeman peddling junk
your favorite President falling falling falling
        endlessly the dream cliff
receding into Heaven Vice
        President falling falling
stars flying by the earth
        oceans awash with blue
galaxies spinning past I washed
        my big toe
I exercised my painful ankle smoked
        a joint I came I wrote letters
        scratched my head

Populations flee the flood, crowds
        move downstreet in teargas clouds,
camel riders footweary skeletons
        walk away from drought
desert burning, sea screaming,
        Bacteria frothing mouth preserve
        jars
I made toast I fried mushrooms I ate
        raw corn

Armies moved on Phnom Penh I
        watched a new born butterfly
        flutter orange-winged in circles
        round me on the grass
Nixon met Agnew papers said Resign
        I resigned I sat and stared at
        a flat gray cloud over the roof—

Three boys in jail on trial in
        Brussels for translating *Anarchist's
        Cookbook* I held the cloth
thru which Peter poured boiling beet
        juice into an Aluminum pot.

                    Cherry Valley, September 1, 1973

On Neruda's Death

Some breath breathes out *Adonais* & *Canto General*
Some breath breathes out Bombs and dog barks
Some breath breathes silent over green snow mountains
Some breath breathes not at all

Teton Village, September 25, 1973

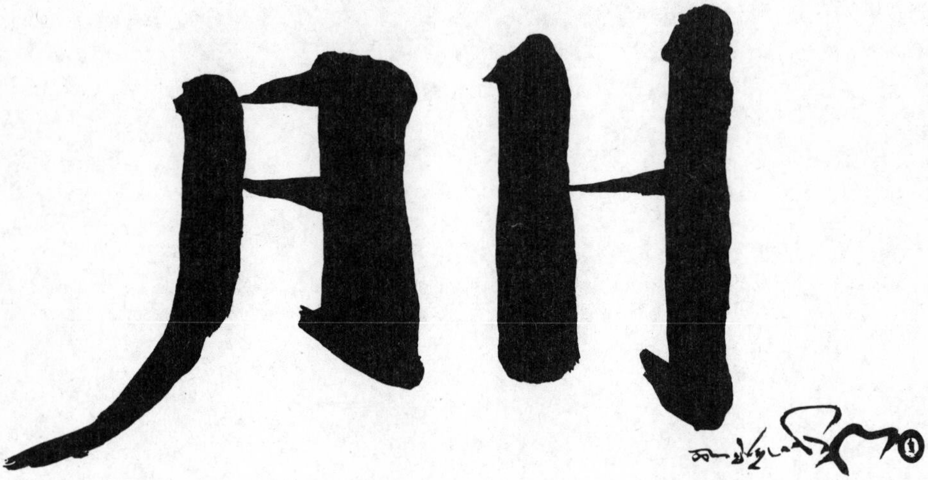

Mind Breaths

Thus crosslegged on round pillow sat in Teton Space—
I breathed upon the aluminum microphone-stand a body's length away
I breathed upon the teacher's throne, the wooden chair with yellow pillow
I breathed further, past the sake cup half emptied by the breathing guru
Breathed upon the green sprigged thick-leaved plant in a flowerpot
Breathed upon the vast plateglass shining back th' assembled sitting Sangha
      in the meditation cafeteria
my breath thru nostril floated out to the moth of evening beating into
      window'd illumination
breathed outward over aspen twigs trembling September's top yellow leaves
      twilit at mountain foot
breathed over the mountain, over snowpowdered crags ringed under slow-
      breathed cloud-mass white spumes
windy across Tetons to Idaho, gray ranges under blue space swept
with delicate snow flurries, breaths Westward
mountain grass trembling in tiny winds toward Wasatch
Breezes south late autumn in Salt Lake's wooden temple streets,
white salt dust lifted swirling by the thick leaden lake, dust carried up over
      Kennecott's pit onto the massive Unit Rig,
out towards Reno's neon, dollar bills skittering downstreet along the curb,
up into Sierras oak leaves blown down by fall cold chills
over peaktops snowy gales beginning,
a breath of prayer down on Kitkitdizze's horngreen leaves close to ground,
over Gary's tile roof, over temple pillar, tents and manzanita arbors in Sierra
      pine foothills—
a breath falls over Sacramento Valley, roar of wind down the sixlane freeway
      across Bay Bridge
uproar of papers floating over Montgomery Street, pigeons flutter down
      before sunset from Washington Park's white churchsteeple—
Golden Gate waters whitecapped scudding out to Pacific spreads
over Hawaii a balmy wind thru Hotel palmtrees, a moist warmth swept over
      the airbase, a dank breeze in Guam's rotten Customs shed,
clear winds breathe on Fiji's palm & coral shores, by wooden hotels in Suva
      town flags flutter, taxis whoosh by Friday night's black promenaders
      under the rock & roll discotheque window upstairs beating with
      English neon—
on a breeze into Sydney, and across hillside grass where mushrooms lie low
      on Cow-Flops in Queensland, down Adelaide's alleys a flutter of
      music from Brian Moore's Dobro carried in the wind—

up thru Darwin Land, out Gove Peninsula green ocean breeze, clack of
      Yerkalla village song sticks by the trembling wave
Yea and a wind over mercurial waters of Japan North East, a hollow wooden
      gong echoes in Kyoto's temple hall below the graveyard's wavy grass
A foghorn blowing in the China Sea, torrential rains over Saigon, bombers
      float over Cambodia, visioned tiny from stone Avelokitesvera's many-
      faced towers Angkor Wat in windy night,
a puff of opium out of a mouth yellowed in Bangkok, a puff of hashish
      flowing thick out of a bearded saddhu's nostrils & eyes in Nimtallah
      Burning Ghat,
wood smoke flowing in wind across Hooghly Bridge, incense wafted under
      the Bo Tree in Bodh Gaya, in Benares woodpiles burn at Manikar-
      nika returning incensed souls to Shiva,
wind dallies in the amorous leaves of Brindaban, still air on the vast mosque
      floor above Old Delhi's alleyways,
wind blowing over Kausani town's stone wall, Himalayan peaktops ranged
      hundreds of miles along snowy horizon, prayer flags flutter over
      Almora's wood brown housetops,
trade winds carry dhows thru Indian Ocean to Mombasa or down to Dar
      'Salaam's riverside sail port, palms sway & sailors wrapped in cotton
      sleep on log decks—
Soft breezes up thru Red Sea to Eliat's dry hotels, paper leaflets scatter by
      the Wailing Wall, drifting into the Sepulchre
Mediterranean zephyrs leaving Tel Aviv, over Crete, Lassithi Plains' wind-
      mills still turn the centuries near Zeus' birth cave
Piraeus wave-lashed, Venice lagoon's waters blown up over the floor of San
      Marco, Piazza flooded and mud on the marble porch, gondolas bob-
      bing up & down choppy waters at the Zattere,
chill September fluttering thru Milan's Arcade, cold bones & overcoats flap-
      ping in St. Peter's Square,
down Appian Way silence by gravesites, stelae stolid on a lonely grass path,
      the breath of an old man laboring up road—
Across Scylla & Charybdis, Sicilian tobacco smoke wafted across the boat
      deck,
into Marseilles coalstacks black fumes float into clouds, steamer's white drift-
      spume down wind all the way to Tangier,
a breath of red-tinged Autumn in Provence, boats slow on the Seine, the lady
      wraps her cloak tight round her bodice on toppa Eiffel Tower's iron
      head—
across the Channel rough black-green waves, in London's Piccadilly beer-
      cans roll on concrete neath Eros' silver breast, the Sunday Times lifts
      and settles on wet fountain steps—

over Iona Isle blue day and balmy Inner Hebrides breeze, fog drifts across
    Atlantic,
Labrador white frozen blowing cold, down New York's canyons manila
    paper bags scurry toward Wall from Lower East side—
a breath over my Father's head in his apartment on Park Avenue Paterson,
a cold September breeze down from East Hill, Cherry Valley's maples
    tremble red,
out thru Chicago Windy City the vast breath of Consciousness dissolves,
    smokestacks and autos drift expensive fumes ribboned across railroad
    tracks,
Westward, a single breath blows across the plains, Nebraska's fields har-
    vested & stubble bending delicate in evening airs
up Rockies, from Denver's Cherry Creekbed another zephyr risen,
across Pike's Peak an icy blast at sunset, Wind River peaktops flowing
    toward the Tetons,
a breath returns vast gliding grass flats cow-dotted into Jackson Hole, into
    a corner of the plains,
up the asphalt road and mud parking lot, a breeze of restless September, up
    wood stairways in the wind
into the cafeteria at Teton Village under the red tram lift
a calm breath, a silent breath, a slow breath breathes outward from the
    nostrils.

September 28, 1973

Flying Elegy

Denver tower blocks group'd under gray haze
on tracted plains gassed to azure horizon—"no place to take revenge."
Alan Watts epicure drank much
sang bass Christo voice a long long long breathed Aum passed on
in sleep exhausted heart philosopher
wandering age 58 in Chinese dressing gown to seek love, or enter Buddha
      blind
like this blue sky wing plunged thru rainbow halo in clouds' drifty whiteness
The skandas are a veil suchlike, no place to take revenge
Blessed the dead who can't fight back resent a poem knife thought
Blessed the dead in ignorance, dead with no sores or cigarette yen
Blessed the dead that don't get laid, don't eat fine casseroles herb-spiced with
      crusty cheese
don't drink slow tea
don't waste petrol surveying clouds in Heaven
don't waste words at their condition, no one to talk to
Bless the free dead lecturing in the deep with moveless tongue
perfect meditators without thought, accomplished in Sunyatā
Bless the dead last Philosophers, thought of the thought of Philosophers
Perfected Wisdom's teachers escaped from Blessing and the Bliss of grasping
      prayer
'scaped from the curse of meditation on a cushion on yr ass
Dead that've left breath, renounced sex body, suffered stroke & begone
alone, the drinker, thinker, divorcé, grandfather weary wise
dying in bed night's stillness silent and wake.

November 17, 1973

Teton Village

Snow mountain fields
seen thru transparent wings
of a fly on the windowpane

November 29, 1973

Sweet Boy, Gimme Yr Ass

lemme kiss your face, lick your neck
touch your lips, tongue tickle tongue end
nose to nose, quiet questions
ever slept with a man before?
hand stroking your back slowly down to the cheeks' moist hair soft asshole
eyes to eyes blur, a tear strained from seeing—

Come on boy, fingers thru my hair
Pull my beard, kiss my eyelids, tongue my ear, lips light on my forehead
—met you in the street you carried my package—
Put your hand down to my legs,
touch if it's there, the prick shaft delicate
hot in your rounded palm, soft thumb on cockhead—

Come on come on kiss me full lipped, wet tongue, eyes open—
animal in the zoo looking out of skull cage—you
smile, I'm here so are you, hand tracing your abdomen
from nipple down rib cage smooth skinn'd past belly veins, along muscle to
            your silk-shiny groin
across the long prick down your right thigh
up the smooth road muscle wall to titty again—
Come on go down on me your throat
swallowing my shaft to the base tongue
cock solid suck—
I'll do the same your stiff prick's soft skin, lick your ass—
Come on Come on, open up, legs apart here this pillow
under your buttock
Come on take it here's vaseline the hard on here's
your old ass lying easy up in the air—here's
a hot prick at yr soft mouthed asshole—just relax and let it in—
Yeah just relax hey Carlos lemme in, I love you, yeah how come
you came here anyway except this kiss arms round my neck
                        mouth open your
        two eyes looking up, this hard slow thrust this
            softness this relaxed sweet sigh.

New York, January 3, 1974

Jaweh and Allah Battle

Jaweh with Atom Bomb
      Allah cuts throat of Infidels
Jaweh's armies beat down neighboring tribes
Will Red Sea waters close & drown th'armies of Allah?

Israel's tribes worshipping the Golden Calf
      Moses broke the Tablets of Law.

Zalmon Schacter Lubovitcher Rebbe what you say
      Stone Commandments broken on the ground
    Sufi Sam whaddya say
      Shall Prophet's companions dance circled
round Synagogue while Jews doven bearded electric?

Both Gods Terrible! Awful Jaweh Allah!
      Both hook-nosed gods, circumcised.
Jaweh Allah which unreal?
              Which stronger Illusion?
                Which stronger Army?
       Which gives most frightening command?
   What God maintain egohood in Eden? Which be Nameless?
          Which enter Abyss of Light?
Worlds of Gods, jealous Warriors, Humans, Animals & Flowers,
      Hungry Ghosts, even Hell Beings all die,
    Snake cock and pig eat each other's tails & perish
All Jews all Moslems'll die All Israelis all Arabs
Cairo's angry millions Jerusalem's multitudes
    suffer Death's dream Armies in battle!
Yea let Tribes wander to tin camps at cold Europe's walls?
Yea let the Million sit in desert shantytowns with tin cups?
I'm a Jew cries Allah! Buddha circumcised!
      Snake sneaking an apple to Eden—
    Alien, Wanderer, Caller of the Great Call!
What Prophet born on this ground
      bound me Eternal to Palestine
   circled by Armies tanks, droning bomber motors,
         radar electric computers?
What Mind directed Stern Gang Irgun Al Fatah
      Black September?

Meyer Lansky? Nixon Shah? Gangster? Premier? King?
one-eyed General Dayan?
Golda Meir & Kissinger bound me with Arms?
HITLER AND STALIN SENT ME HERE!
WEIZMANN & BEN-GURION SENT ME HERE!
NASSER AND SADAT SENT ME HERE!
ARAFAT SENT ME HERE! MESSIAH SENT ME HERE!
GOD SENT ME HERE!
Buchenwald sent me here! Vietnam sent me here!
Mylai sent me here!
Lidice sent me here!
My mother sent me here!
I WAS BORN HERE IN ISRAEL, Arab
circumcised, my father had a coffee shop in Jerusalem
One day the Soldiers came & told me to walk down road
my hands up
walk away leave my house business forever!
The Israelis sent me here!
Solomon's Temple the Pyramids & Sphinx sent me here!
JAWEH AND ALLAH SENT ME HERE!
Abraham will take me to his bosom!
Mohammed will guide me to Paradise!
Christ sent me here to be crucified!
Buddha will wipe us out and destroy the world.
The New York Times and Cairo Editorialist Heykal sent me here!
Commentary and *Palestine Review* sent me here!
The International Zionist Conspiracy sent me here!
Syrian Politicians sent me here! Heroic Pan-Arab
Nationalists sent me here!
They're sending Armies to my side—
The Americans & Russians are sending bombing planes tanks
Chinese Egyptians Syrians help me battle for my righteous
house my Soul's dirt Spirit's Nation body's
boundaries & Self's territory my
Zionist homeland my Palestine inheritance
The Capitalist Communist & Third World Peoples'
Republics Dictatorships Police States Socialisms & Democracies
are all sending Deadly Weapons to our aid!
We shall triumph over the Enemy!
Maintain our Separate Identity! Proud
History evermore!

Defend our own bodies here this Holy Land! This hill
Golgotha never forget, never relinquish
inhabit thru Eternity
under Allah Christ Yaweh forever one God
Shema Yisroel Adonoi Eluhenu Adonoi Echad!
La ilah illa' Allah hu!

OY! AH! HU! OY! AH! HU!
SHALOM! SHANTIH! SALAAM!

New York, January 13, 1974

Manifesto

Let me say beginning I don't believe in Soul
The heart, famous heart's a bag of shit I wrote 25 years ago
O my immortal soul! youthful poet Shelley cried
O my immortal Ego—little knowing
he didn't believe in God. Neither do I.
Nor all science reason reality and good moral Will—
collections of empty atoms as Kerouac Buddha scribed.

Neither does great love immortal defy pain nightmare Death Torture Saigon
       Police Underground Press Pravda Bill of Rights—
And while we're at it, let's denounce Democracy, Fascism, Communism and
       heroes.
Art's not empty if it shows its own emptiness
Poetry useful leaves its own skeleton hanging in air
like Buddha, Shakespeare & Rimbaud.
Serious, dispense with law except Cause & Effect, even the latter has excep-
       tions
No cause & effect is not foolproof.
There is Awareness—which confounds the Soul, Heart, God, Science Love
       Governments and Cause & Effects' Nightmare.

New York, January 28, 1974, 1 A.M.

Sad Dust Glories

To the Dead

You were here on earth, in cities—
              where now?
Bones in the ground,
              thoughts in my mind.

                    *

Teacher
bring me to heaven
or leave me alone.
Why make me work so hard
when everything's spread around
open, like forest's poison oak
              turned red
empty sleepingbags hanging from
              a dead branch.

                    *

When I sit
I see dust motes in my eye
Ponderosa needles trembling
              shine green
in blue sky.
Wind sound passes thru
              pine tops, distant
windy waves flutter black
              oak leaves
and leave them still
like my mind
which forgets
why the bluejay across the woods'
              clearing
squawks, mid afternoon.

                    *

The mood

is sadness, dead friends,
or the boy I slept with last night

came twice silently
and I still lie in the colored
                    hammock, half naked
reading poetry
Sunday
in bright sun pine shade.

*

KENJI MYAZAWA

"All is Buddhahood
to who has cried even once
Glory be?"
So I said glory be
        looking down at a pine
                    feather
risen beside a dead leaf
on brown duff
where a fly wavers an inch
                above ground
midsummer.

*

Could you be here?
Really be here
        and forget the void?
I am, it's peaceful, empty,
filled with green Ponderosa
        swaying parallel crests
fan-like needle circles
glittering haloed
in sun that moves slowly
        lights up my hammock
                heats my face skin
                        and knees.

*

Wind makes sound
            in tree tops
like express trains like city
                machinery
Slow dances high up, huge

branches wave back &
        forth sensitive
needlehairs bob their heads
—it's too human, it's not
     human
It's treetops, whatever they think,
It's me, whatever I think,
It's the wind talking.

            *   *

The moon followed by Jupiter thru pinetrees,

A mosquito comes round your head buzzing
you know he's going to bite you if he can—

First you look at your thoughts
then you look at the moon
then look at the reflection of the moon in your eyeball
      splatter of light on surface retina
        opening and closing the blotched circle
and the mosquito buzzes, disturbing your senses
       and you remember your itching thumb as mind
                wanders again.

      *

Shobo-an

The Acorn people
   read newspapers
      by kerosene light.

     *

By Kitkitdizze Pond in June with Gary Snyder

Bookkeeping in the moonlight
   —"frogs count
      my checks."

     *

Driving Volkswagen
          with tired feet
returned from camping
          in Black Buttes
thru sad dust glories
turning off Malakoff
          Diggings road
Blinded by sunlight
     squirrel in
          windshield.

September 1974

Ego Confessions
(1974–1977)

Ego Confession

I want to be known as the most brilliant man in America
Introduced to Gyalwa Karmapa heir of the Whispered Transmission Crazy
    Wisdom Practice Lineage
as the secret young wise man who visited him and winked anonymously
    decade ago in Gangtok
Prepared the way for Dharma in America without mentioning Dharma—
    scribbled laughter
Who saw Blake and abandoned God
To whom the Messianic Fink sent messages darkest hour sleeping on steel
    sheets "somewhere in the Federal Prison system" Weathermen got
    no Moscow Gold
who went backstage to Cecil Taylor serious chat chord structure & Time in
    a nightclub
who fucked a rose-lipped rock star in a tiny bedroom slum watched by a
    statue of Vajrasattva—
and overthrew the CIA with a silent thought—
Old Bohemians many years hence in Viennese beergardens'll recall
his many young lovers with astonishing faces and iron breasts
gnostic apparatus and magical observation of rainbow-lit spiderwebs
extraordinary cooking, lung stew & Spaghetti a la Vongole and recipe for
    salad dressing 3 parts oil one part vinegar much garlic and honey a
    spoonful
his extraordinary ego, at service of Dharma and completely empty
unafraid of its own self's spectre
parroting gossip of gurus and geniuses famous for their reticence—
Who sang a blues made rock stars weep and moved an old black guitarist to
    laughter in Memphis—
I want to be the spectacle of Poesy triumphant over trickery of the world
Omniscient breathing its own breath thru War tear gas spy hallucination
whose common sense astonished gaga Gurus and rich Artistes—
who called the Justice department & threaten'd to Blow the Whistle

Stopt Wars, turned back petrochemical Industries' Captains to grieve &
    groan in bed
Chopped wood, built forest houses & established farms
distributed monies to poor poets & nourished imaginative genius of the land
Sat silent in jazz roar writing poetry with an ink pen—
wasn't afraid of God or Death after his 48th year—
let his brains turn to water under Laughing Gas his gold molar pulled by
    futuristic dentists
Seaman knew ocean's surface a year
carpenter late learned bevel and mattock
son, conversed with elder Pound & treated his father gently
—All empty all for show, all for the sake of Poesy
to set surpassing example of sanity as measure for late generations
Exemplify Muse Power to the young avert future suicide
accepting his own lie & the gaps between lies with equal good humor
Solitary in worlds full of insects & singing birds all solitary
—who had no subject but himself in many disguises
some outside his own body including empty air-filled space forests &
    cities—
Even climbed mountains to create his mountain, with ice ax & crampons &
    ropes, over Glaciers—

San Francisco, October 1974

Mugging

I

Tonite I walked out of my red apartment door on East tenth street's
    dusk—
Walked out of my home ten years, walked out in my honking neighborhood
Tonite at seven walked out past garbage cans chained to concrete anchors
Walked under black painted fire escapes, giant castiron plate covering a hole
    in ground
—Crossed the street, traffic lite red, thirteen bus roaring by liquor store,
past corner pharmacy iron grated, past Coca Cola & Mylai posters fading
    scraped on brick
Past Chinese Laundry wood door'd, & broken cement stoop steps For Rent
    hall painted green & purple Puerto Rican style
Along E. 10th's glass splattered pavement, kid blacks & Spanish oiled hair
    adolescents' crowded house fronts—
Ah, tonite I walked out on my block NY City under humid summer sky
    Halloween,
thinking what happened Timothy Leary joining brain police for a season?
thinking what's all this Weathermen, secrecy & selfrighteousness beyond
    reason—F.B.I. plots?
Walked past a taxicab controlling the bottle strewn curb—
past young fellows with their umbrella handles & canes leaning against a
    ravaged Buick
—and as I looked at the crowd of kids on the stoop—a boy stepped up, put
    his arm around my neck
tenderly I thought for a moment, squeezed harder, his umbrella handle
    against my skull,
and his friends took my arm, a young brown companion tripped his foot
    'gainst my ankle—
as I went down shouting Om Ah Hūṃ to gangs of lovers on the stoop
    watching
slowly appreciating, why this is a raid, these strangers mean strange business
with what—my pockets, bald head, broken-healed-bone leg, my softshoes,
    my heart—
Have they knives? Om Ah Hūṃ—Have they sharp metal wood to shove
    in eye ear ass? Om Ah Hūṃ
& slowly reclined on the pavement, struggling to keep my woolen bag
    of poetry address calendar & Leary-lawyer notes hung from my
    shoulder
dragged in my neat orlon shirt over the crossbar of a broken metal door

dragged slowly onto the fire-soiled floor an abandoned store, laundry candy
    counter 1929—
now a mess of papers & pillows & plastic car seat covers cracked cockroach-
    corpsed ground—
my wallet back pocket passed over the iron foot step guard
and fell out, stole by God Muggers' lost fingers, Strange—
Couldn't tell—snakeskin wallet actually plastic, 70 dollars my bank money
    for a week,
old broken wallet—and dreary plastic contents—Amex card & Manf. Hano-
    ver Trust Credit too—business card from Mr. Spears British Home
    Minister Drug Squad—my draft card—membership ACLU &
    Naropa Institute Instructor's identification
Om Ah Hūṃ I continued chanting Om Ah Hūṃ
Putting my palm on the neck of an 18 year old boy fingering my back pocket
    crying "Where's the money"
"Om Ah Hūṃ there isn't any"
My card Chief Boo-Hoo Neo American Chruch New Jersey & Lower East
    Side
Om Ah Hūṃ—what not forgotten crowded wallet—Mobil Credit, Shell?
    old lovers addresses on cardboard pieces, booksellers calling cards—
—"Shut up or we'll murder you"—"Om Ah Hūṃ take it easy"
Lying on the floor shall I shout more loud?—the metal door closed on
    blackness
one boy felt my broken healed ankle, looking for hundred dollar bills behind
    my stocking weren't even there—a third boy untied my Seiko Hong
    Kong watch rough from right wrist leaving a clasp-prick skin tiny
    bruise
"Shut up and we'll get out of here"—and so they left,
as I rose from the cardboard mattress thinking Om Ah Hūṃ didn't stop em
    enough,
the tone of voice too loud—my shoulder bag with 10,000 dollars full of
    poetry left on the broken floor—

November 2, 1974

II

Went out the door dim eyed, bent down & picked up my glasses from step
    edge I placed them while dragged in the store—looked out—
Whole street a bombed-out face, building rows' eyes & teeth missing
burned apartments half the long block, gutted cellars, hallways' charred
    beams
hanging over trash plaster mounded entrances, couches & bedsprings rusty
    after sunset

Nobody home, but scattered stoopfuls of scared kids frozen in black hair
chatted giggling at house doors in black shoes, families cooked For Rent
　　　some six story houses mid the street's wreckage
Nextdoor Bodega, a phone, the police? "I just got mugged" I said
to the man's face under fluorescent grocery light tin ceiling—
puffy, eyes blank & watery, sickness of beer kidney and language tongue
thick lips stunned as my own eyes, poor drunken Uncle minding the store!
O hopeless city of idiots empty eyed staring afraid, red beam top'd car at
　　　street curb arrived—
"Hey maybe my wallet's still on the ground got a flashlight?"
Back into the burnt-doored cave, & the policeman's gray flashlight broken
　　　no eyebeam—
"My partner all he wants is sit in the car never gets out Hey Joe bring your
　　　flashlight—"
a tiny throwaway beam, dim as a match in the criminal dark
"No I can't see anything here" . . . "Fill out this form"
Neighborhood street crowd behind a car "We didn't see nothing"
Stoop young girls, kids laughing "Listen man last time I messed with them
　　　see this—"
rolled up his skinny arm shirt, a white knife scar on his brown shoulder
"Besides we help you the cops come don't know anybody we all get arrested
go to jail I never help no more mind my business everytime"
"Agh!" upstreet think "Gee I don't know anybody here ten years lived half
　　　block crost Avenue C
and who knows who?"—passing empty apartments, old lady with frayed
　　　paper bags
sitting in the tin-boarded doorframe of a dead house.
                                                    December 10, 1974

Who Runs America?

Oil brown smog over Denver
Oil red dung colored smoke
level to level across the horizon
    blue tainted sky   above
Oil car smog gasoline
    hazing red Denver's day
        December bare trees
           sticking up from housetop streets
Plane lands rumbling, planes rise over
        radar wheels, black smoke
           drifts wobbly from tailfins

Oil millions of cars speeding the cracked plains
Oil from Texas, Bahrain, Venezuela Mexico
Oil that turns General Motors
      revs up Ford
   lights up General Electric, oil that crackles
thru International Business Machine computers,
      charges dynamos for ITT
    sparks Western Electric
        runs thru Amer Telephone & Telegraph wires
Oil that flows thru Exxon New Jersey hoses,
rings in Mobil gas tank cranks, rumbles
          Chrysler engines
shoots thru Texaco pipelines,
     blackens ocean from broken Gulf tankers
spills onto Santa Barbara beaches from
      Standard of California derricks offshore.

Braniff Air, Denver–Dallas, December 3, 1974

Thoughts on a Breath

Cars slide minute down asphalt lanes in front of
    Dallas Hilton Inn
Trees brown bare in December's smog-mist roll up
      to the city's squared towers
beneath electric wire grids trestled toward country water tanks
distanced under cloud streak crossed with fading
      vapor trails.
Majestic in a skirt of human fog, building blocks
      rise at sky edge,
Branches and house roofs march to horizon.

I sat again to complete the cycle, eyes open seeing
      dust motes in the eye screen
like birds over telephone wires, curve of the eyeball
      where Dallas and I meet—
white motel wall of the senses—ear roar
      oil exhaust, snuffle and bone growl
      motors rolling North Central freeway
Energy playing over Concrete, energy
      hymning itself in emptiness—
What've I learned since I sat here four years ago?
In the halls of the head or out thru the halls of the senses,
      same space
Trucks rolling toward Dallas skyscrapers
      or mind thoughts floating thru my head
vanish on a breath—What was it I began
      my meditation on?
Police state, Students, Poetry open tongue,
      anger and fear of Cops,
oil Cops, Rockefeller Cops, Oswald Cops,
      Johnson Cops Nixon Cops
      president Cops
SMU Cops Trustee Cops CIA Cops
      FBI Cops Goon Squads of Dope
Cops busted Stony Burns and sent him to
      Jail 10 years and a day
for less than a joint of Grass, a Citizen
      under republic, under Constitution, of Texas?
We sit here in police state and sigh, knowing
      we're trapped in our bodies,

our fear of No meat, no oil, no money, airplanes
      sex love kisses jobs no
      work
Massive metal bars about, monster machines
      eat us, Controlled by army
      Cops, the Secret Police, our own thoughts!
Punishment! Punish me! Punish me! we scream
      in our hearts, cocks spurting alone
      in our fists!
What thoughts more flowed thru our hearts alone
      in Dallas? Flowed thru our hearts like oil
      thru Hilton's faucets?
Where shall we house our minds, pay
      rent for Selves, how
      protect our bodies
from inflation, starvation, old age, smoking
      Cancer, Coughing Death?
Where get money to buy off the
      skeleton? If we work with Kissinger
Can we buy time, get off on parole? Does
      Rockefeller want Underground
Newspapers printing his subsconscious mind's
      nuclear oil wars?
Will 92nd Armored Division be sent to seize
      Arabia oilfields
as threatened December's *US News &*
      World Report?
What'd we remember that destroyed these armies
      with a breath?
How pay rent & stay in our bodies
      if we don't sell our minds to Samsara?
If we don't join the illusion—that Gas is life—
      How can we in Dallas SMU
look forward to our futures?
      work with our hands
like niggers growing Crops in the field,
      & plow and harvest our own corny
      fate?
Oh Walt Whitman salutations you knew the laborer,
      the sexual intelligent horny handed
      man who lived in Dirt
and fixed the axles of Capitalism, dumbed and

laughing at hallucinated Secretaries
    Of State!
Oh intellect of body back & Cock whose red neck
supports the S&M freaks of Government
    police & Fascist Monopolies—
Kissinger bare assed & big buttocked
    with a whip, in leather boots
scrawling on a memo to Chile "No more
    civics lectures please"
When the ambassador complained about Torture
    methods used in the Detention Stadium!
And I ride the planes that Rockefeller gassed
    when he paid off Kissinger!
Stony Burns sits in jail, in a stone cell in
    Huntsville
and breathes his news to solitude.
                      Homage
to the Gurus, Guru om! Thanks to the teachers
    who taught us to breathe,
to watch our minds revolve in emptiness,
    to follow the rise & fall of thoughts,
Illusions big as empires flowering &
    Vanishing on a breath!
Thanks to aged teachers whose wrinkles
    read our minds' newspapers &
    taught us not to Cling to yesterday's
    thoughts,
nor thoughts split seconds ago, but
    let cities vanish on a breath—
Thanks to teachers who showed us behold
    Dust motes in our own eye,
    anger our own hearts,
emptiness of Dallases where we
    sit thinking knitted brows—
Sentient beings are numberless I vow
    to liberate all
Passions unfathomable I vow to
    release them all
Thought forms limitless I vow to
    master all
Awakened space is endless I vow to
    enter it forever.
                Dallas, December 4, 1974

We Rise on Sun Beams
and Fall in the Night

Dawn's orb orange-raw shining over Palisades
bare crowded branches bush up from marshes—
New Jersey with my father riding automobile
highway to Newark Airport—Empire State's
spire, horned buildingtops, Manhattan
rising as in W. C. Williams' eyes between wire trestles—
trucks sixwheeled steady rolling overpass
beside New York—I am here
tiny under sun rising in vast white sky,
staring thru skeleton new buildings,
with pen in hand awake . . .

December 11, 1974

Written on Hotel Napkin:
Chicago Futures

Wind mills churn on Windy City's
       rooftops   Antennae
          collecting electric
above thick-loamed gardens
       on Playboy Tower
Merchandise Mart's compost
               privies
       supply nightsoil for Near North Side's
               back Gardens
Cabbages, celery & cucumbers
       sprout in Mayor Daley's
            frontyard
        rich with human waste—
Bathtub beer like old days
Backyard Mary Jane like
            old days,
Sun reflectors gather heat
      in rockpile collectors
         under apartment walls
Horses graze in Parks &
      streets covered with grass
Mafia Dons shovel earth
         & bury Cauliflower
           leaves
Old gangsters & their sons
      tending grapevines
              Mid-March 1975

Hospital Window

At gauzy dusk, thin haze like cigarette smoke
ribbons past Chrysler Building's silver fins
tapering delicately needletopped, Empire State's
taller antenna filmed milky lit amid blocks
black and white apartmenting veil'd sky over Manhattan,
offices new built dark glassed in bluish heaven—The East
50s & 60s covered with castles & watertowers, seven storied
tar-topped house-banks over York Avenue, late may-green trees
surrounding Rockefellers' blue domed medical arbor—
Geodesic science at the waters edge—Cars running up
East River Drive, & parked at N.Y. Hospital's oval door
where perfect tulips flower the health of a thousand sick souls
trembling inside hospital rooms. Triboro bridge steel-spiked
raftertops stand stone-piered over mansard
penthouse orange roofs, sunset tinges the river and in a few
Bronx windows, some magnesium vapor brilliances're
spotted five floors above E 59th St under gray painted bridge
trestles. Way downtown along the river, as Monet saw Thames
100 years ago, Con Edison smokestacks 14th street,
& Brooklyn Bridge's skeined dim in modern mists—
Pipes sticking up to sky nine smokestacks huge visible—
U.N. Building hangs under an orange crane, & red lights on
vertical avenues below the trees turn green at the nod
of a skull with a mild nerve ache. Dim dharma, I return
to this spectacle after weeks of poisoned lassitude, my thighs
belly chest & arms covered with poxied welts,
head pains fading back of the neck, right eyebrow cheek
mouth paralyzed—from taking the wrong medicine, sweated
too much in the forehead helpless, covered my rage from
gorge to prostate with grinding jaw and tightened anus
not released the weeping scream of horror at robot Mayaguez
World self ton billions metal grief unloaded
Phnom Penh to Nakhon Thanom, Santiago & Tehran.
Fresh warm breeze in the window, day's release
from pain, cars float downside the bridge trestle
and uncounted building-wall windows multiplied a mile
deep into ash-delicate sky beguile
my empty mind. A seagull passes alone wings
spread silent over roofs.

May 20, 1975 (Mayaguez Crisis)

Hadda Be Playing on the Jukebox

Hadda be flashing like the Daily Double
Hadda be playing on Tee Vee
Hadda be loudmouthed on the Comedy Hour
Hadda be announced over Loud Speakers
CIA & Mafia are in Cahoots
Hadda be said in old ladies' language
Hadda be said in American Headlines
Kennedy stretched & smiled & got doublecrossed by low life goons &
    Agents
Rich bankers with Criminal Connections
Dope pushers in CIA working with dope pushers from Cuba
working with Big Time syndicate Tampa Florida
Hadda be said with big mouth
Hadda be moaned over Factory foghorns
Hadda be chattered on Car Radio News Broadcast
Hadda be screamed in the kitchen
Hadda be yelled in the basement where uncles were fighting
Hadda be Howled on the streets by Newsboys to bus conductors
Hadda be foghorned into N.Y. Harbor
Hadda echo under hard hats
Hadda turn up the Volume in University ballrooms
Hadda be written in library books, footnoted
Hadda be in headlines of the *Times* & *Le Monde*
Hadda be barked over TV
Hadda be heard in side alleys thru bar room doors
Hadda be played on Wire Services
Hadda be bells ringing, Comedians stopt dead in the middle of a joke in Las
    Vegas,
Hadda be FBI chief J. E. Hoover & Frank Costello syndicate mouthpiece
    meeting in Central Park N.Y. together weekends reported posthu-
    mously *Time* magazine
Hadda be the Mafia & CIA together
started War on Cuba Bay of Pigs & Poison assassination headlines
Hadda be the Dope Cops & the Mafia
sold all that Heroin in America
Hadda be FBI & Organized Crime working together in Cahoots "against the
    Commies"
let Lucky Luciano out of Jail take over Sicily Mediterranean drug trade
Hadda be Corsican goons in Office Strategic Services' Pay busted 1948 dock
    strikes in Marseilles, sixties port transshipment Indochina heroin,

Hadda be ringing on Multinational Cashregisters
world-wide laundry for organized Criminal money
Hadda be CIA & Mafia & FBI together
bigger than Nixon, bigger than War.
Hadda be a gorged throat full of murder
Hadda be mouth and ass a solid mass of rage
a Red hot head, a scream in the back of the throat
Hadda be in Kissinger's brain
Hadda be in Rockefeller's mouth
Hadda be Central Intelligence The Family "Our Thing" the Agency Mafia
    Organized Crime FBI Dope Cops & Multinational Corporations
one big set of Criminal gangs working together in Cahoots
Hit Men murderers everywhere outraged, on the make
Secret drunk Brutal Dirty Rich
on top of a Slag heap of prisons, Industrial Cancer, plutonium smog, gar-
    baged cities, grandmas' bedsores, Fathers' resentments
Hadda be the Rulers wanted Law & Order *they* got rich on
wanted Protection status quo, wanted Junkies wanted Attica Wanted Kent
    State Wanted War in Indochina
Hadda be CIA & the Mafia & the FBI
Multinational Capitalists' Strong arms squads, "Private detective Agencies
    for the very rich"
And their Armies, Navies and Air Force bombing Planes.
Hadda be Capitalism the Vortex of this rage, this
competition man to man, horses' heads in the Capo's bed, Cuban turf &
    rumbles, hit men, gang wars across oceans,
bombing Cambodia settled the score when Soviet Pilots manned Egyptian
    fighter planes
Chile's red democracy bumped off with White House pots & pans a warn-
    ing to Mediterranean governments
Secret Police embraced for decades, NKVD & CIA keep eachother's secrets,
    OGPU & DIA never hit their own, KGB & FBI one mind—brute
    force
world-wide, and full of money
Hadda be rich, hadda be powerful, hadda hire technology from Harvard
Hadda murder in Indonesia 500,000
Hadda murder in Indochina 2,000,000
Hadda murder in Czechoslovakia
Hadda murder in Chile
Hadda murder in Russia
Hadda murder in America

New York, May 30, 1975, 3 A.M.

Come All Ye Brave Boys

Come all you young men that proudly display
Your torsos to the Sun on upper Broadway
Come sweet hearties so mighty with girls
So lithe and naked to kiss their gold curls
Come beautiful boys with breasts bright gold
Lie down in bed with me ere ye grow old,
Take down your blue jeans, we'll have some raw fun
Lie down on your bellies I'll fuck your soft bun.

Come heroic half naked young studs
That drive automobiles through vaginal blood
Come thin breasted boys and fat muscled kids
With sturdy cocks you deal out green lids
Turn over spread your strong legs like a lass
I'll show you the thrill to be jived up the ass
Come sweet delicate strong minded men
I'll take you thru graveyards & kiss you again

You'll die in your life, wake up in my arms
Sobbing and hugging & showing your charms
Come strong darlings tough children hard boys
Transformed with new tenderness, taught new joys
We'll lie embrac'd in full moonlight till dawn
Whiteness shows sky high over the wet lawn
Lay yr head on my shoulder kiss my lined brow
& belly to belly kiss my neck now

Yeah come on tight assed & strong cocked young fools
& shove up my belly your hard tender tools,
Suck my dick, lick my arm pit and breast
Lie back & sigh in the dawn for a rest,
Come in my arms, groan your sweet will
Come again in my mouth, lie silent & still,
Let me come in your butt, hold my head on your leg,
Let's come together, & tremble & beg.

Boulder, August 25, 1975, 4 A.M.

Sickness Blues

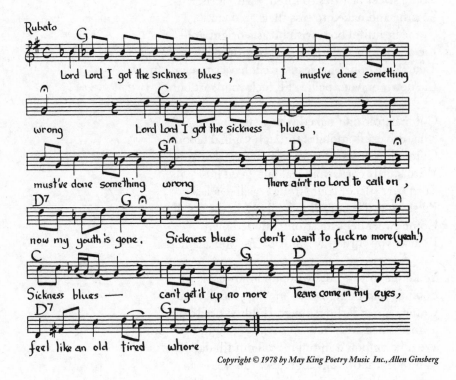

Sickness Blues

Lord Lord I got the sickness blues, I must've done something wrong
There ain't no Lord to call on, now my youth is gone

Sickness blues, don't want to fuck no more
Sickness blues, can't get it up no more
Tears come in my eyes, feel like an old tired whore

I went to see the doctor, he shot me with poison germs
I got out of the hospital, my head was full of worms

All I can think is Death, father's getting old
He can't walk half a block, his feet feel cold

I went down to Santa Fe take vacation there
Indians selling turquoise in dobe huts in Taos Pueblo Square
Got headache in La Fonda, I could get sick anywhere

Must be my bad karma, fuckin these pretty boys
Hungry ghosts chasing me, because I been chasing joys
Lying here in bed alone, playing with my toys

I musta been doing something wrong meat & cigarettes
Bow down before my lord, 100 thousand regrets
All my poems down in hell, that's what pride begets

Sick and angry, lying in my hospital bed
Doctor Doctor bring morphine before I'm totally dead
Sick and angry at the national universe O my aching head

Someday I'm gonna get out of here, go somewhere alone
Yeah I'm going to leave this town with noise of rattling bone
I got the sickness blues, you'll miss me when I'm gone

Boulder, July 19, 1975

Gospel Noble Truths

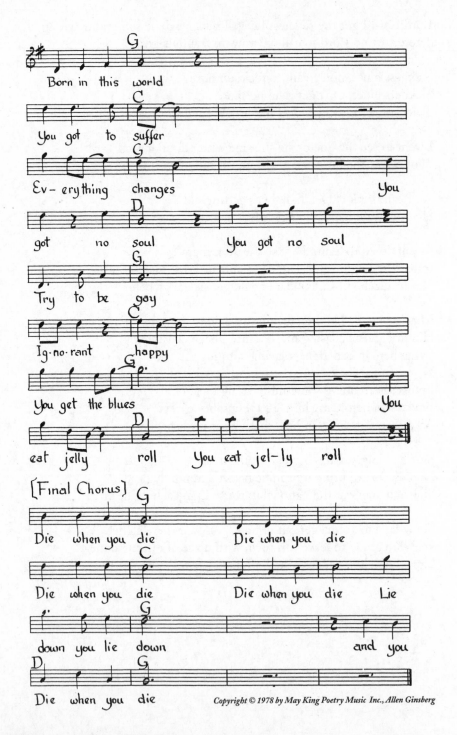

Born in this world
You got to suffer
Ev-ery thing changes   You
got   no   soul   You got no   soul
Try   to   be   gay
Ig-no-rant   happy
You get the blues   You
eat jelly   roll   You eat jel-ly   roll

[Final Chorus]
Die   when you   die   Die when you   die
Die   when you   die   Die when you   die   Lie
down you lie   down   and you
Die   when you   die

Gospel Noble Truths

Born in this world
You got to suffer
Everything changes
You got no soul

Try to be gay
Ignorant happy
You get the blues
You eat jellyroll

There is one Way
You take the high road
In your big Wheel
8 steps you fly

Look at the View
Right to horizon
Talk to the sky
Act like you talk

Work like the sun
Shine in your heaven
See what you done
Come down & walk

Sit you sit down
Breathe when you breathe
Lie down   you lie down
Walk where you walk

Talk when you talk
Cry when you cry
Lie down   you lie down
Die when you die

Look when you look
Hear what you hear
Taste what you taste   here
Smell what you smell

Touch what you touch
Think what you think
Let go Let it go   Slow
Earth Heaven & Hell

Die when you die
Die when you die
Lie down   you lie down
Die when you die

New York Subway, October 17, 1975

Lay Down Yr Mountain

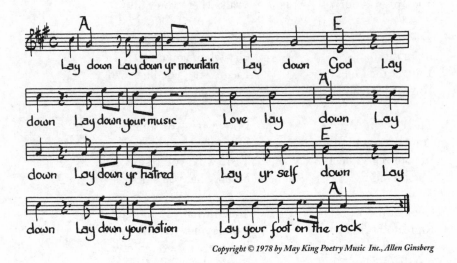

Lay down Lay down yr mountain Lay down God Lay
down Lay down your music Love lay down Lay
down Lay down yr hatred Lay yr self down Lay
down Lay down your nation Lay your foot on the rock

Rolling Thunder Stones

I

LAY DOWN YR MOUNTAIN

Lay down   Lay down yr mountain   Lay down God
Lay down   Lay down your music   Love lay down

Lay down   Lay down yr hatred   Lay yrself down
Lay down   Lay down your nation   Lay your foot on the rock

Lay down yr whole creation   Lay yr mind down
Lay down   Lay down yr empire   Lay your whole world down

Lay down your soul forever   Lay your vision down
Lay down yr bright body   Down your golden heavy crown

Lay down   Lay down yr magic hey!   Alchemist lay it down clear
Lay down your practice precisely   Lay down yr wisdom dear

Lay down yr skillful camera   Lay down yr image right
Lay down your brilliant image   Lay down light

Lay down   your ignorance   Roll yr wheel once more
Lay down yr empty suffering   Lay down yr Lion's Roar

October 31, 1975

II
Sunrise Ceremony Verse
Improvised with Australian Aborigine Song-Sticks
at Request of Medicine Man Rolling Thunder November 5, 1975

When Music was needed Music sounded
When a Ceremony was needed a Teacher appeared
When Students were needed Telephones rang.
When Cars were needed Wheels rolled in
When a Place was needed a Mansion appeared
When a Fire was needed Wood appeared
When an Ocean was needed Waters rippled waves
When Shore was needed Shore met Ocean
When Sun was needed the Sun rose east

When People were needed People arrived
When a circle was needed a Circle formed.

Plymouth

III

SNOW BLUES

Nobody saves America by sniffing cocaine
Jiggling yr knees blankeyed in the rain
When it snows in yr nose you catch cold in yr brain

Danbury, November 10, 1975

IV

TO THE SIX NATIONS AT TUSCARORA RESERVATION

We give thanks for this food, deer meat & indian-corn soup
Which is a product of the labor of your people
And the suffering of other forms of life
And which we promise to transform into friendly song and dancing
To all the ten directions of the Earth.

November 18, 1975

V

Snow falls	in thee
souls freeze	's a drag
Speed kills	dead bag.
heart's ease	Smoke grass
Alcohol	Yaas Yass
fools wills	Shake ass
O slaves	mind's wealth
Who craves	joint's health
junk raves	Ready?
Downer's	Medi-
angers	tations
eyes blur—	patience
I sing	eyes keen
Rolling	serene
Thunder	as graves
Ho ho!	saves! saves
Macho	nations.
frenzy	

Montreal, December 4, 1975

Cabin in the Rockies

I
Sitting on a tree stump with half cup of tea,
   sun down behind mountains—
      Nothing to do.

Not a word! Not a Word!
Flies do all my talking for me—
and the wind says something else.

Fly on my nose,
I'm not the Buddha,
There's no enlightenment here!

Against red bark trunk
   A fly's shadow
lights on the shadow of a pine bough.

An hour after dawn
I haven't thought of Buddha once yet!
—walking back into the retreat house.

II
Walking into King Sooper after Two-week Retreat

A thin redfaced pimpled boy
   stands alone minutes
looking down into the ice cream bin.

Boulder, September 16, 1975

Reading French Poetry

Poems rise in my brain
like Woolworth's 5 & 10¢ Store perfume
O my love with thin breasts
17 year old boy with smooth ass
O my father with white hands
specks on your feet & foul breath bespeak tumor
O myself with my romance
fading but fat bodies remain
in bed with me warm passionless
unless I exercise myself like a dumbbell
O my Fiftieth year approaching
like Tennessee like Andy a failure, big nothing—
very satisfactory subjects for Poetry.

New York, January 12, 1976

Two Dreams

I
As I passed thru Moscow's grass lots I heard
a voice, a small green dwarf, leaf-clothed &
thin corn-stalk arms, head capped with green
husk & tassel, walking toward me talking:
"You see these other tassel heads stalking
thru long green grass spears half buried
in empty lots where building-ghosts stand
razed by police state but bursting from ground
Springtime as now seeds grown natural
So I full grown sprite of Friendship salute
you who seek love in Roman Moscow circuses—
Be cheerful our enemy's enemy is Death
and since Death is We, since all die, all
is not lost but to Death, & what lives eccentric
as yourself & Me, ancient friends, lives
humorous and democratic as your leaves of grass
which die also prophesied but live as you and I.
Bee cheerful, good Sir. Cockhead green am I
an entertainer triumphant in the tiny cliffs
between buildings, in old grasslots of Paterson
where the wrecker's ball creates a tiny farm
for worms, and bottles glint in new turned earth—
and weeds and we sprout renewing Nature's
humor where the architectural police are on the nod.
The sun will rise and I'll accompany your eye
that walks thru Moscow looking for human love."

March 1, 1976

II   SLUDGE
Dantean, the cliffside whereon I walked
With volumes of Milton & the Tuscan Bard enarmed:
Highway prospecting th'ocean Sludged transparent
lipped to asphalt built by Man under sky.
Far down below the factory I espied, and plunged
full clothed into the Acid Tide, heroic precipitous
Stupidly swam the noxious surface to my goal—
An Oil platform at land's end, where Fellows watched
my bold approach to the Satanic World Trade Center.

Father dying tumored, Industry smog
o'erspreads dawn sky, gold beams descend
on Paterson thru subtle tar fumes, viewless
to wakened eye, transfused into family meat.
Capitalism's reckless industry cancers New Jersey.

New York, March 6, 1976

C'mon Jack

Turn me on your knees
Spank me & Fuck me
Hit my ass with your hand
Spank me and Fuck me
Hit my hole with your fingers
Hit my ass with your hand
Spank me and fuck me
Turn me on your knees
Ah Robertson it's you
Yes hit my ass with your hand
real hard, ass on your knees
sticking up hard harder slap
Spank me and Fuck me
Got a hard on Spank me
When you get a hard on Fuck me.

March 29, 1976

Pussy Blues

for Anne Waldman

You said you got to go home   & feed your pussycat
When I ast you to stay here tonight   Where's your pussy at?

Keep your pussy here   Try our hot cat food
Yeah lotsa cats around here   & they's all half nude
Going home alone   do your pussy no good

Hey it's 4th of July   Say it's your U.S. birthday
Yeah stay out all night   National Holiday
Tiger on your fence   Don't let him get away

Pussy pussy come home   I'm gonna feed you fish
Yeah pussy pussy here   come your big red dish
I'll tickle your belly   All the eats you wish

Hey there pussy   Cantcha catch my mouse
Hey please pussy   Play with my white mouse
You can stay all night   You can clean my house

Boulder, Independence Day 1976, 1 A.M.

Don't Grow Old

I

Old Poet, Poetry's final subject glimmers months ahead
Tender mornings, Paterson roofs snowcovered
Vast
Sky over City Hall tower, Eastside Park's grass terraces & tennis courts
      beside Passaic River
Parts of ourselves gone, sister Rose's apartments, brown corridor'd high
      schools—
Too tired to go out for a walk, too tired to end the War
Too tired to save body
too tired to be heroic
The real close at hand as the stomach
liver pancreas rib
Coughing up gastric saliva
Marriages vanished in a cough
Hard to get up from the easy chair
Hands white   feet speckled   a blue toe   stomach big   breasts hanging
      thin
hair white on the chest
too tired to take off shoes and black sox

Paterson, January 12, 1976

II

He'll see no more Times Square
honkytonk movie marquees, bus stations at midnight
Nor the orange sun ball
rising thru treetops east toward New York's skyline
His velvet armchair facing the window will be empty
He won't see the moon over house roofs
or sky over Paterson's streets.

New York, February 26, 1976

III

Wasted arms, feeble knees
    80 years old, hair thin and white
        cheek bonier than I'd remembered—
head bowed on his neck, eyes opened
    now and then, he listened—
    I read my father Wordsworth's *Intimations of Immortality*
"*. . . trailing clouds of glory do we come*
    from God, who is our home . . ."
        "That's beautiful," he said, "but it's not true."

"When I was a boy, we had a house
    on Boyd Street, Newark—the backyard
        was a big empty lot full of bushes and tall grass,
    I always wondered what was behind those trees.
When I grew older, I walked around the block,
    and found out what was back there—
        it was a glue factory."
                        May 18, 1976

IV
Will that happen to me?
Of course, it'll happen to thee.

Will my arms wither away?
Yes yr arm hair will turn gray.

Will my knees grow weak & collapse?
Your knees will need crutches perhaps.

Will my chest get thin?
Your breasts will be hanging skin.

Where will go—my teeth?
You'll keep the ones beneath.

What'll happen to my bones?
They'll get mixed up with stones.

June 1976

Father Death Blues

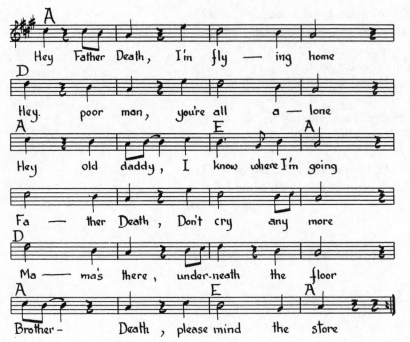

Hey Father Death, I'm fly — ing home

Hey, poor man, you're all a — lone

Hey old daddy, I know where I'm going

Fa — ther Death, Don't cry any more

Ma — ma's there, under-neath the floor

Brother — Death, please mind the store

V

FATHER DEATH BLUES

Hey Father Death, I'm flying home
Hey poor man, you're all alone
Hey old daddy, I know where I'm going

Father Death, Don't cry any more
Mama's there, underneath the floor
Brother Death, please mind the store

Old Aunty Death   Don't hide your bones
Old Uncle Death   I hear your groans
O Sister Death   how sweet your moans

O Children Deaths go breathe your breaths
Sobbing breasts'll ease your Deaths
Pain is gone, tears take the rest

Genius Death   your art is done
Lover Death your body's gone
Father Death   I'm coming home

Guru Death your words are true
Teacher Death I do thank you
For inspiring me to sing this Blues

Buddha Death, I wake with you
Dharma Death, your mind is new
Sangha Death, we'll work it through

Suffering is what was born
Ignorance made me forlorn
Tearful truths I cannot scorn

Father Breath once more farewell
Birth you gave was no thing ill
My heart is still, as time will tell.

July 8, 1976 (Over Lake Michigan)

VI

Near the Scrap Yard my Father'll be Buried
Near Newark Airport my father'll be
Under a Winston Cigarette sign buried
On Exit 14 Turnpike NJ South
Through the tollgate Service Road 1 my father buried
Past Merchants Refrigerating concrete on the cattailed marshes
past the Budweiser Anheuser-Busch brick brewery
in B'Nai Israel Cemetery behind a green painted iron fence
where there used to be a paint factory and farms
where Pennick makes chemicals now
under the Penn Central power Station
transformers & wires, at the borderline
between Elizabeth and Newark, next to Aunt Rose
Gaidemack, near Uncle Harry Meltzer
one grave over from Abe's wife Anna my father'll be buried.

July 9, 1976

VII

What's to be done about Death?
Nothing, nothing
Stop going to school No. 6 Paterson, N.J., in 1937?
Freeze time tonight, with a headache, at quarter to 2 A.M.?
Not go to Father's funeral tomorrow morn?
Not go back to Naropa   teach Buddhist poetics all summer?
Not be buried in the cemetery near Newark Airport some day?

Paterson, July 11, 1976

"Junk Mail"

I received in mail   offer beautiful certificate National Conference Syna-
    gogue Youth
invites subscriber   Monthly Review   Independent Socialist Mag
Congressman Koch reports on collapse of our cities
Epilepsy Foundation misdelivered for Mr. Pantonucci   light candle under-
    standing 4 million Americans
Dear Mr. Orlovsky put Salvation Army on your Christmas List $50 return
    enclosed envelope
American Friends Service Committee act now meet urgent human needs
    hungry families   Prisoners
in remote penal institutions   Rehabilitation Vietnam Laos Northern Great
    Plains Indians block land-destruction by energy seeking industries
    Contact between Israeli Jews & Arabs
Psychoenergetics workshops in Vermont   Green Mountain Quarterly's
    Imperialist Ideology in Donald Duck   with a new bibliography Sri
    Aurobindo and the Mother protected by Intnl. copyright laws News
    of Auroville
Dear Friend: we are Michael & Robert Meeropol, sons of Julius & Ethel
    Rosenberg executed by U.S. Government 22 years ago.
Sue the Government for the Files   duplicating fees alone Twenty-five
    Thousand Dollars
Christmas Greetings   Help Hospitalized Veterans   art or craft Kit en-
    thused busily working for days   Bob Hope helps.
Fund For Peace if   your blood boils   Press accounts C.I.A. blackmail
    assassination   a powerful alternative to World Violence   Private
    Citizens acting Global
Gay Peoples Union NYU faces bankruptcy   Dance Halloween
Boycott Gallo Grapes lettuce United Farmworkers of America   Our strug-
    gle is not over   make checks payable   Si Se Puede   Cesar E. Cha-
    vez   Union Label
Announcing Energy & Evolution Quarterly   how to make harps lyres &
    dulcimers   Quantum Theory   Tantra & land reform   organic gar-
    dening
Give Poets & Writers' CODA to a friend   subscribe United Nations Chil-
    drens' Fund   severe malnutrition   Starvation faces 400 to 500 mil-
    lion children poorer countries. Dwarfism
disease blindness mental retardation stunted growth crop failures drought
    flood   exhausted wheat rice reserves skyrocketing fuel costs   fertili-
    zer shortages   Desperately need your help.

Racial motives lead to Innocent Marine's conviction in Georgia murder trial
a thick envelope from Southern Poverty Law Center Julian Bond
"I didn't mean to harm anyone. I only went into that Police Station to see
what they were doing to my brother . . ." sd Marine Sgt. Roy
Patterson
Won't you help millions in desperate need Thanksgiving urgently bless
Carl's Holiday Food Crusade "Yes! use my tax deductible donation
to keep them alive."
Catholic Peace Fellowship Activist Fund's special appeal help the Staff to
foster Christian Pacifist Continental Walk   Disarmament & Social
Justice
( ) I have no money at present but I wish to remain on the mailing list
( ) Please take my name off your mailing list
An important message from Robert Redford about the Environment   80
separate legal actions   Dirty air you pay your life Aerosol Spray
cancer   the National Resources Defense Council needs your support
The Continental Walk itself: the Nations spent $4.5 Trillion military secu-
rity since 1946   This year $240 Billion join us walk across ⅛ of the
Planet's surface Nonviolent resistance   Unilateral Disarmament
Aum Sri Ganeshaya Namah   Tantra Non-salacious in tone & intent lec-
turer Dr. Thackur   George Washington Hotel Lexington Avenue
NYC
Dear Friend: the War Resisters International is in a desperate financial
situation
Nuclear Age pacifist work must advance   leafleting soldiers British With-
drawal from Northern Ireland Campaign
We are in need of the kind of Miracle you can bring to pass. The huge influx
of Russian Immigrants upon Bikur Cholem Hospital in the heart of
Jerusalem—Don't turn your back on the Herculean efforts . . .
First priority reservation on new gold $100 Canadian Olympic Coin now
available at just $110! for American Express Cardmembers—
Ad Hoc Coalition for a New Foreign Policy (formerly Coalition to Stop
Funding the War) hopes you will join the network by filling out the
enclosed envelope
Human Rights Amendment, end Vietnam Trade Embargo, cut foreign
military assistance encourage people to people Friendshipments to
Vietnam
A literary miracle   843 poems written in 24 hours by Indian Yogi Sri
Chinmoi   Aum Publications
If you haven't joined the Great Falls Development Corp. now's the time to
do so

& subscribe to the William Carlos Williams Newsletter. Penmaen Press:
    Two fascinating heretofore unpublished letters written in 1956 to
    Richard Eberhart by Allen Ginsberg . . .
Please won't you help Central America Sub-Saharan Africa and the Indian
    Subcontinent? Give generously to Planned Parenthood—World Pop-
    ulation
Confidential—Memo to supporters of Open Housing from Fund for Open
    Society a nonprofit mortgage Co. to advance equal housing: fight
    racial steering
Dear Citizen of the World: First days explosion bomb radioactivity starve
    Ozone layer? Isn't it time we did something?
1) Send cooperators ten addresses w/ zip codes 2) Mail friends endorsement
    3) Write your Congressman President Newspaper editor & Presiden-
    tial Candidate.
As a final move, the World Authority would destroy all Nuclear Weapons.
                                        Opened Midnight, New York, September 4, 1976

"You Might Get in Trouble"

Opening a bus window in N.Y.
    with the left hand in front of
    Bellevue you might get a
                hernia.
Walking across First avenue
    you might stumble in a
              pothole
& get your head run over by
              taxicab
Plowing the field by Cherry
    Creek your trailer might
    turn over & fall on your ear
you might get your ear cut off
    arresting a junkie
or having an angry conversation with
    a speedfreak on E. 10 street
or arguing your case before the
    supreme court
someone might shoot you in
    the brain
There's nothing you can do to
    keep your nose clean
taking baths plunging in the
    ice & snow
you might catch cold, the
    flu Swine epidemic's
    "in" this year
according to the Authorities.

                    September 18, 1976

Land O'Lakes, Wisc.

Buddha died and
left behind a
big emptiness.

October 1976

"Drive All Blames into One"

It's everybody's fault but me.
I didn't do it. I didn't start the universe.
I didn't steal Dr. Mahler's tiles from his garage roof for my chicken coop
where I had six baby chicks I paid for so I could attract
my grammar school boyfriends to play with me in my backyard
They stole the tiles I'm going across the street to the candystore
and tell the old uncle behind the glass counter I'm mad at my boyfriends
for stealing that slate I took all the blame—
Last night I dreamt they blamed me again on the streetcorner
They got me bent over with my pants down and spanked my behind I was
    ashamed
I was red faced my self was naked I got hot I had a hard on.

New York, October 25, 1976

Land O'Lakes, Wisconsin: Vajrayana Seminary

Candle light blue banners incense
aching knee, hungry mouth—
any minute the gong—potatoes and sour cream!

Sunlight on the red zafu,
clank of forks & plates—
I'll never be enlightened.

                    *

Did you ever see yourself
a breathing skull
looking out the eyes?

                    *

Under wooden roof beams
a hundred people
sit
sniffling, coughing, clearing throat
sneezing, sighing
breathing through nose
shifting on pillows in clothes
swallowing saliva,
listening.
                    November 11, 1976

For Creeley's Ear

The whole
weight of
everything
too much

my heart in
the subway
pounding
subtly

head ache
from smoking
dizzy
a moment

riding
uptown to see
Karmapa Buddha
tonight.

New York, December 13, 1976

Haunting Poe's Baltimore

I POE IN DUST

Baltimore bones groan maliciously under sidewalk
Poe hides his hideous skeleton under church yard
Equinoctial worms peep thru his mummy ear
The slug rides his skull, black hair twisted in roots of threadbare grass
Blind mole at heart, caterpillars shudder in his ribcage,
Intestines wound with garter snakes
midst dry dust, snake eye & gut sifting thru his pelvis
Slimed moss green on his phosphor'd toenails, sole toeing black
        tombstone—
O prophet Poe well writ! your catacomb cranium chambered
eyeless, secret hid to moonlight ev'n under corpse-rich ground
where tread priest, passerby, and poet
staring white-eyed thru barred spiked gates
at viaducts heavy-bound and manacled upon the city's heart.

January 10, 1977

II HEARING "LENORE" READ ALOUD AT 203 AMITY STREET

The light still gleams reflected from the brazen fire-tongs
The spinet is now silent to the ears of silent throngs
For the Spirit of the Poet, who sang well of brides and ghouls
Still remains to haunt what children will obey his vision's rules.

They who weep and burn in houses scattered thick on Jersey's shore
Their eyes have seen his ghostly image, though the Prophet walks no
                                        more
Raven bright & cat of Night; and his wines of Death still run
In their veins who haunt his brains, hidden from the human sun.

Reading words aloud from books, till a century has passed
In his house his heirs carouse, till his woes are theirs at last:
So I saw a pale youth trembling, speaking rhymes Poe spoke before,
Till Poe's light rose on the living, and His fire gleamed on the floor—

The sitting room lost its cold gloom, I saw these generations burn
With the Beauty he abandoned; in new bodies they return:
To inspire future children 'spite his *Raven*'s "Nevermore"
I have writ this antient riddle in Poe's house in Baltimore.

January 16, 1977

Contest of Bards

For Jonathan Robbins

I

THE ARGUMENT: Old bard lived in solitary stone house at ocean edge three decades retired from the world, Young poet arrives naked interrupting his studies & announces his own prophetic dreams to replace the old Bard's boring verities. Young poet had dreamed old poet's scene & its hidden secret, an Eternal Rune cut in stone at the hearth-front hidden under porphyry bard-throne. Young bard tries to seduce old Boner with his energy & insight, & makes him crawl down on the floor to read the secret riddle Rhyme.

And the youth free stripling bounding along the Hills of Color
And the old man bearded, wrinkled, browed in his black cave
Meet in the broken house of stone, walls graven by Prophet Hands,
& contend for the Mysteries, vanity against vanity, deciphering
Eternal runes of Love, & Silence, & the Monster of Self
Covered with Blood & Lilies, covered with bones and hair and skin:
They glory in Night & Starvation the Fat Bright Cherub of Resurrection,
Bliss & God: Terrible Mental Cherub of Chemistry Imagination & Vanity
Bard after Bard orating and perishing, casting his image behind on men's
        brains
thru sounds symboled on the mind's stone walls reverberating Syllables
        Visionary
Perfect formed to 'dure Millennia, but Phantom is such Rock,
Phantom as the Cellular Believer in's own tangible re-creation.

"I hear the Bard's stone words Build my Immortal Architecture:
This body stone hands and genitals   this Heart stone Tenderness
and Delight   This head Stone language to Rafter the Stone Bed of Love.
Come lay down on this rock pillow, kid, lay down your tender breast,
Pale face, red hair, soft belly   hairy tender foot and Loins
Under the hard immortal blanket, mattress of Rock sheeted with Vocables!
In twenty years I'll vanish from this shore & Solitary Eternal Cave—
Here I studied & Deciphered the Granite Alphabet surrendered
from Graves from Sands that swirled at the door, from star-fish
spotted boulders in seas' low tide when full-moon-gleam
Pulls bones of Leviathan & tiny bass-fins tide-pool'd
many in ancient nights." So one spoke, ocean serpents curl'd around
his whitened beard, eyes wide in horror he be left by the Dark Shore,
to burn his memories in the rocky hearth & keep his cold loins warm

in winter-rain days or in snowy night's vastness filled
with stars and planets, spring summer & autumn mortality.
Sly, craven, conquering he spoke, his words like rainbows,
or firelight, or shadows, moving humorous thru his beard,
falling in the air, clothing his body in hypocritic webs of truth,
to hide his shame, his empty nakedness. He meditated
remembering deeper Buddhic prophecies, abhoring his own runes solid
immovable but by time and storm inexorable, half visible on his walls.

The youth the color of the hills laughed delighted at his Vanity
and cried, "Under the hearth stone's a rune, old Bard of Familiarity,
your eyes forgot, or tempest-addled brain, so busy boiling meat
and tending to your threadbare cares and household hermitage
& fishing day by day for thirty years for thoughts! Behold!"
He naked bent and moved the porphyry-smooth red fire-seat aside:
"Read what's writ on earth here before you Ignorant Prophet,
Learn in your age what True Magicians spelled for all Futurity,
Cut in the vanity of rock before your feeble hand grasped iron Pen
Or feather fancy tickled your gross ear: There have been sages here
before you, and I am after to outlive your gloomy miserous
hospitality. I loved you Ungrateful Unimaginative Bard
And Came over hills thru small cities to companion your steadfast study.
I dreamed of your eyes and beard and rocks and oceans, I dreamed
this room these pitted moss green walls & runes you scraped
deciphered and memorized, pillars worn by tide and smoke
of your lamp   You Grow near blind reading mind on your own house walls,
I dreamt you sitting on your fire-seat reading the vaporous language of flame
        tongues
nescient to the airy rune cut in the Bedrock under yr very Shamanic Throne
You stare at the ceiling half asleep, or sit on your pillow with heavy eyelid
murmuring old bards Truths to your brain, repetitive
imagining me, or some other red-buttocked stripling savior come
to yr stone bed naked to renew your old body's intelligence
and help you read again when blind now what you already memorized
and forgot, peering like a boor illiterate in Shadows 30 years—
Yes I have come but not for your feeble purpose, come of my own dreamed
        will
To show you what you forgot dreamt, Immortal Text neglected
under your groaning seat as you sat self-inspired by your mortal fire.
O Self Absorbed vulgar hungry Demon, leave your body & mine
Take eyes off your own veined hands and worm thoughts, lower
Your watery selfish infatuate eyes from my breast to my feet

& read me aloud in Bardic Voice, that Voice of Rock you boast so well so
        many decades,
Yea Face inland to the fields and railroads skyscrapers & Viaducts.
Youths maddened by Afric jukeboxes & maidens simpering at Picture shows
Read thru smoky air to a hopeless hundred million fools!
Read what young mind's Pearl Majesty made round oracular Beauteous
More unworldly than your own self-haunted snaily skull & stony household
        shell."
Pointing downward, his arm stiff in disdain dismissing lesser Beauty,
Like radiant lively Adolescence rejecting joy or sorrow, shrewd
with bright glance Innocent, albescent limbs ruddy and smooth in Sea-
        Wrack Firelight
Proud with centuries of learning in New-woke brain and boyish limbs, so
        stood the young messenger.

Startled, the wool-wrapped bard looked up at eyes mocking shining into his
        own:
Looked down at the boy's neck unwrinkled white unlike his own: the breast
thin muscled unawakened silken flesh: the belly with a corse of tawny hair
rosed round the pricked virgin-budding genitals, shining in hearth light,
thighs ready and careless like a strong Child's, playful walking & dancing
        tho awkward,
Thick calves with new hair light to the foot long as a man's.
Humbled, bewilderment Touching his tongue, heart beating his ribs
        rewakened
The bard mused on this mortal beauty, remembering dead bodies he'd em-
        braced in rough and silken beds
Years, years, and years of loves ago—his breast grew light, eyes lost
in dream—Then in his forehead Time gapped all youthful-imaged bodies
        there
Devouring their Shadows, as the sea surged out the rocky door.
The stars inclined thru cold air, moved so slow blue shining past
he saw them barely touch the ocean wave and rise and blink and glimmer
        silently engulfed—
Then to the Prophesied Task his inner eyes returned to their dim outward
        orbs:
Saw the gloom in his own stony shell: stone letters wavering on chill walls,
Iron Pots carbon black on shelves, old seaweed clothes in a stone closet,
        folded green
for Holiday Solitude at Vernal Equinox and full Moon face—brass fire tongs
from old Paumanok City bought with gold gleaming strong at the hearth's
        light—

The hearth seat was moved, the porphyry throne worn smooth by the sea's
   muscles
His eyes fell down to the messenger's foot, toes spread firm on the runed
   lintel:

THE RUNE

Where the years have gone,   where the clouds have flown
                          Where the rainbow shone
We vanish,   and we make no moan

Where the sun will blind   the delighting mind
                          in a diamond wind
We appear,   our beauty refined.

Icy intellect,   fi'ry Beauty wreck
                          but Love's castled speck
of Moonbeam,   nor is Truth correct.

Wise bodies leave here   with the mind's false cheer,
                          Eternity near
as Beauty,   where we disappear.

When sufferings come,   when all tongues lie dumb
                          when Bliss is all numb
with knowledge,   a bony white sum,

We die neither blest   nor with curse confessed
                          wanting Earth's worst Best:
But return,   where all Beauties rest.
                          January 17–22, 1977

The Rune

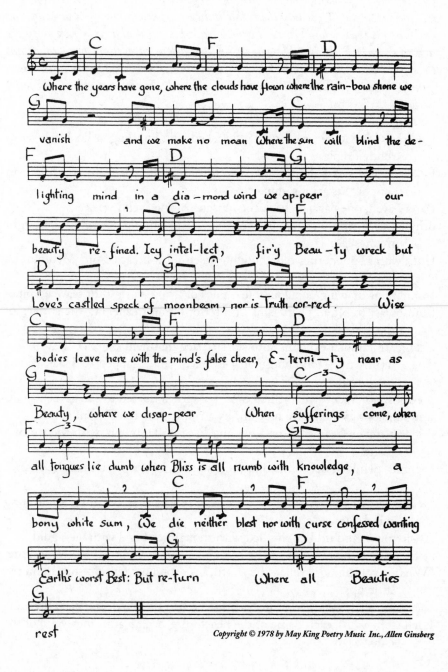

THE ARGUMENT: The Rune having been discovered by the Boy to the Man, the messenger commands the Hermit Sage to go out into the world with him, seek the ancient unearthly Beauty the riddle indicated. The old man gets mad, he says he's near death, has lost Desire. The boy reads his mind and lies down with the sage to make love. At dawn he gets up says he's disgusted with the body, condemns the sage to Chastity, demands the hermit leave his cell forever, and promises to lead him to the land of Poetry in the Sky. Exasperated, the old bard reveals the secret of the mysterious riddle.

And the old man silver bearded gold faced bald kneeling at his black cave's
    ruddy fireplace
Read the airy verses, humming them to himself, hands to the cold floor to
    support his aching spine
watery eyed, one palsied cheek the muscles of the eyelid weak
dripped with empty tears, unsorrowful soul'd, conning & eyeing the bright
    rhymes' No Truth
Unfrowning, pondering old thought arisen on a breath from Meditation's
    hour—
Inspirations drawing populous-hued tides of living plasm thru seaweed pipes
from breast to brain, phantasms of interior ocean freshening the surface of
    the eyeball,
old breath familiar exhaling into starry space that held shore & heaven
where sat his tiny stone house, lost in black winds lapped by black waters
    fishy eyed
oft phosphorescent when jellied monster sprites floated to the golden sand,
wet bubbles of vehemence mouth'd by a ripple, tiny translucent spirits
dried in the eyebeams of the frowning Face o' the moon, with the tip of a
    planet
beaming twinkled deeper in Blackness washed by deep waves in the ear.

Dead bearded propped on his knees the old bard stared thru his beating
    mind's universe
At sharp stanza'd riddles chiseled with thought & filled with wise gold
at the bright colored foot of the boy, reddened by light of driftwood afire.
"What is your mind?" yelled the youth, his proud contention shaped on red
    little lips
beardless, ready to argue & instruct for he had dreamed well clear accurate
Each stony word, each flame of the hearth fire, each tear in the eyelid of the
    elder Sage,

each silver lock of hair, each worried frown wrinkling that skull, each con-
scious smile
that crept along the prophet's thick lips involuntary, who knelt still
at the young teacher's knees—"What Beauty's stopped your Poetry! old
speaker-forth
of Naked Thoughts?" the ruddy legged messenger laughed down, skillful-
tongued, black eye beaming merry—
"Will you obey my will and follow me through a riot of cities, to delicate-
porched countryhouses
& rich polished-marble mansions, where we'll sport with Princes & Mil-
lionaires
and make fun of the world's kings and Presidents Pomps & Limousines all
present in their Unbeauty?
Come leave your stupid business of seashells & seawrack, gathering wrinkles
of the sea?
Come with your pearls and banks of Ambergris hidden under yr bed & in
yr stone closets?
Come wrapped with seaweed round your belly & Neptunic laurel moist on
yr skull's half century?
Carry yr vowelic conch & give blast midnights in Midcity canyons Wall
Street to Washington,
Granite Pillars echoing ocean mouthed pearly syllables along Chicago's
Lakeshore
& reverberating in Pittsburgh's National Banks—Dance with the golden
Trident of Fame in Hollywood
Lift the Inspired Lyre to Strike the Ears of hotels in Los Angeles?"

The old man changed his thought, and stared in the boy's eye, interrupting
his beauty—
His voice grown wrathful, he lifted himself up on his haunches & glared
at the childish youth's face till it paled, brow furrowed in self consideration
small mouth open breathing doubtful thoughts, and tiny sighs uttered to
match his listening.
"Innocent!" the squinting bearded palsied resentful Shaman yelled,
"Come over sunshine colored hills naked thru suburbs boasting
Your beauty intelligence and sexual joy O Delicate Skulled Youth,
You bring news of old prophecy! You wake my wrathful Desires!
old lust for mental power and vain body'd joy! Blind craving for Bliss
of Breast and Loins! Shadow Conquest! Uncompassionate Angel!
Know th' emptiness your own Soul? Think you're a king in oceans of
Thought?
Neptune himself with his Crown of drown'd gold over a beardless face

pale ivory with vanity! Re-waken ignorant desires no mortal boy can satisfy?
I go to a death you never dreamed, in iron oceans! homeless skull
washed underwave with octopus and seahorse, flicked by soft wings of pink
      fish my eyelids!
Teeth a silver wormhouse on the sandy bottom, polypus & green-suckered
      squid in my ribs, wavy
snake-tailed insensible kelp and water-cactus footed in watery loins! clams
      breathe
their cold valved zephyrs where my heart ached on translucent shelves!
      Typhoons carry my voice away!
There is no God or Beauty suffering on earth nor starred in nebulous blue
      heaven
but only Dream that floats vast as an Ocean under the moon—
The moon, the cold full moon, boy, fills the window—look at the sea
waving with lunar glitter like your eye—out there's the moon
Mirror to give back cold pure cheer light on us, fade these Plutonian Images.
There's a clear light without soul or vanity shining thru the stone window
shafting square on that rune uncovered at the hearth—the fire's down but
      we can read it still—
Hermetic years've passed me by here, Cooled my anger like this moonlight
      cools the eye
—my loves & all desires burnt away, like this hearth's wood to ash."

"Behind the ashes of your face your mind wanders strongly—what your
      mind was
I knew as a young boy of books and dreams" the messenger replied calm
      voiced
speaking carefully, piping his thoughts intellectual clear in the old bard's
      ear—
He settled down on the tiger, deer & sheep-skin covered floor, where the old
      man lay
with bearded head uplifted on the gold haird neck of a Lion amber eyed
Staring silent at the moon, huge pelt outstretched four-legged with yellow
      claws
and hard tail laid out on white lamb fleece toward the new discovered
      hearth-Rune.
Shivering in moonlight musing at the fire, the messenger put his nakedness
      against the white robed Elder's
Giant form, slow-breathed resting back on the soft floor, silent eyes
      awake—
"I know your present mind, old heart, I'll satisfy that as you wish
Unspoken, I know your work & nature beyond the wildest daydream

Y'ever had naked in hot sunshine summer noon ecstatic far from mankind
or downy-bearded in your animal bed embraced with glad phantom heroes
in midnight reverie down below Orion's belt, right hand clasped in the heat
      of Creaturehood,
I saw your hard revelry with bodiless immortal companions," the messenger
      cajoled,
laying his mournful sweet visage on the silenced Sage's shoulder, drawing
      his right arm down his nippled thin-ribbed chest.
He shook & trembled chill, for the low moon paled over green ocean waves
and cold bright sun-fire passed upward whitening the long horizon—
The cloud-glory'd orange Orb arc'd living in blue still space, then lifting its
      bulk aflame
circled slowly over the breathing earth, while tiny oil tankers moved thru
      dawn
floating across the widespread ocean's far edge silently going from world to
      world.

The boy took wrinkled years on his flesh, the snow whiskered bard trembled
      and touched
his breast, embracing, adoring from nipple to pink kneecap
and kissing behind him and before, using his form as a girl's.
The youth of colored hills closed his eyes in virgin pleasure, uttered small
      moans
of merciful-limbed ecstasy in his throat, ah tremorous daydream pleasure,
body tingling delicate, made tender, open'd flower-soft, skull top to sole-skin
      touched.
The messenger, young and cold as the sun, sad face turned up to his earth-
      worn host
shuddered then as morning warmed the chill world, shuddered with more
      than world's chill
drawing his old Companion closer face to face embraced, silent thoughted,
      calm and still.
The boy looked in his elder's eyes, which gazed in his while bare branches
      on the hillside stood trembling in sky
blue dawn light. Honey bees woke under heaven inland and sought the lilac,
      Honeysuckle, rose,
pale dew dript from day-lily leaf to leaf, green lamps went out in windows
      on Minneapolis avenues,
Lovers rose to work in subways, buses ground down empty streets in early
      light, the country
robin lit from the maple leaf whistling, cat scratched the farmhouse door

bulls groaned in barns, the aluminum pail clanked on cement by wooden
    stools in steaming flop
& stainless-steel mouths sucked milk from millions of cows into shining vats,
Black nannygoats whinnied nubian complaints to the stinking spotted dog
whose clump'd hair hung from his belly tangled with thistle, Church organs
    sang,
Radios Chattered the nasal weather from barn to barn, the last snow patch
    slipped from the tarpaper roof of the tractor lean-to,
Ice melted in the willow bog, stars vanished from the sky over gravestones
    stained with water melt,
The White House shined near pillared Courts on electric-lit avenues wide
    roaring with cars.

The messenger remembered his dream vision, the Rune discovered by the
    bright fire,
the Hermit's startled wrath, magnificent and vainly noised all night,
his softness now, his careful fear, the wrinkle that remained around his eye
still watery with emotionless tears tho he held love in his arms, a silent
    thinking boy.
The naked messenger returned his thought. "I came for Love, old bard, tho
    you mistook
my youth for Innocence; I came for love, Old Prophet, and I brought you
    Prophecy,
Though you knew all; I came from Beauty, I came to Beauty, and I brought
    more beauty.
I knew the Beauty here; not your ass on your stone seat but under your
    prophetic throne,
older Beauty than your own, that laughs at wrinkled or smooth loins:
thus I have proved pure Beauty to your empty heart—and now you sigh.
It is that Beauty that I love in you, & not your intestinal self—
A Babe I saw more horror than your smoky ocean holds, your empty heaven,
& your tattered Earth. Follow the Prophecy I showed on your floor
Follow the Ancient Command, chase diamonds in the wind, chase years,
    chase clouds
chase this rainbow I brought you, chase Beauty again—
chase wrinkled lust away or chase a moonbeam, chase the rising Sun and then
    Chase setting sun
chase off your Mind thru ocean, chase mind Under the World,
Chase your body down to the grave & rejoice, Chase Chastity at last!
Chaste virgin suffering for you now old bony lecherous Poet."
The boy raged on, with tongue caught fire from the dawn sun lifted now
    over the heavy

skulled rafters of the hermitage long-haired with sea moss barnacled at foot,
stone girders snailed and starfish stinking, sea sperm rotten in kelp masses
at the porch stone. "Your door's the musty stone door of a tomb, old man,
corpses of corrupted loves're buried under the smooth stone bed we lie on,
pitted with yr fearful tears! What animal skins you vulgarize your bed with,
boorish stained with creepy-handed dream stuff jacked out of your Impotent
     loins in Pain—
This toothless lion, stuffed head, ear bit off by sea moths, this your love?
Deerskin stol'n from a Dead Buddha, snatched from wanderings in your
     boring Buddhafields?
A gutless Lamb for a pillow I hear you baah & bleat your Terrified Love—
Naked I have you now, bared, wrinkled, heaving heavy breaths on me
you brought to your bed, and covered with hides of deskeletoned sheep."

Wondering between shame and Longing the old Bard lay thick bellied open
     eyed
Bewilderment at heart, chill-loined, urgent to press that Cherry raving angel
     mouth a soft kiss,
tie down the juvenile prophet on the stone bed back upturned to slap his
     shamed white cheeks
in furious sexual punishment, pubescent weakling pale with anger,
rouse his virgin blood to blush thin buttocks ruddy tingling, humiliated
cock hard pink with desire, heart tamed submissive, soft lipped, tearful.
The kid-like messenger laughed in the bed Despairing and looked the old
     man in the eye:
"Now slap my face, I want to Feel! Hard with all your Love's strength
     coward Bard!
Show your Power!" Bold mute the Bard hit once, and then hit hard—
Cold faced, the Boy complained, "Now hit again, I want to feel an honest
     hand!" The old man struck
his naked cheek with a rough palm, thrice shocked by harsh joy, pain
     enough!
"Now!" said the Changeling boy, "We prove the last verse of this Proph-
     ecy—
Yes the Prophecy old & Confounded Fool, that rune on your floor you never
     beheld before
I forced your gaze to my foot, the prophecy some Elder Mysterious Forebear
     Bard Magician left us—
that prophecy I dreamed & made real before your eyes, renewing your
     Beauty
thru suffering dumb knowledge, yourself roused at my Beauteous Com-
     mand—

All but the Last verse I understand, thick rhymed with senses and nonsenses
   of worst Beauty
no man or boy can interpret in this stupid dank closed cell
Under this Skull that hides the Sun, behind walls covered with yr chill
   laborious decipherings,
your 30 years moony babbling fishy solitude—one verse remains undeci-
   phered,
Magical worthy our mutual war thru Society & Nations, Bards at large on
   the planet
seeking to answer the Text! old man of Love I give you my virgin mind—
You read my youthful Beauty, tender lip and merry eye or Changeling
   glance
and love you think this silken muscular body, red hair even-parted curling
   round my skull—
Sir I do love you, but hate this earth and myself in it and the ignorance
creeping in this house! Sir I do love your beard which you know is Beautiful
   to me,
as beardless my tender-muscled abdomen to you: But my Beauty you love
   most
is that of the aethereal Changeling of Poesy, the same I love in you
which Frightens you; then know yourself slave of Immortality, Master of
   Unearthly Beauty
nothing less, not God nor Empty Gurus of Thibet not Meditation's quiet
   starlit hour
nor aching prostration to the Dharma King nor realms of human poetry
washed at your doorstep everymorn by the sea, stamp'd with gold sand
   dollars
licked by scummy wavelets, nor all the old beloved ghost boys dead
made famous by your Immortality. Here's rotten Fish, Leviathan honor
   stinks your shore!
and makes this hermit house no more habitable! Leave your wordy life
   behind!
Chase the Last Beauty with me till we find the author, even if we enter Death
   Trance with 'im,
rise & gather your Sea gold, all your grassy Emeralds & champagne Amber
   hidden safe
Under the rune stone at the Hearth Yes Sir your Sparkling diamond treasury
I dreamed it well! Clear Sapphires blue as ice you see in sky! And hoarded
   rubies
red & multitudinous enough to make Each maiden and each boy on earth
   blush red with genius joy!
Naked! Naked! rise with me take all your Secrets in the air, the Sun's at
   height, the morning's ope'd blue sky,

Grandfather Clocks bong noon in oriental Carpet living-rooms in the Capi-
tal!
Close the stone door behind you, close this tomb lest gulls that swim the sea
air
pluck the blind eyes of this lion out of its straw-brained head! Come out
horrid Corpse!
But memorize the rune before we go, it'll encompass our lov'd wanderings!
As Dante had his Virgil & as Blake his own Miltonic Fiend, I your Cherub
& Punk Idol
'll be Companion of th' Aethereal Ways till we discover of the Secret Eidolon
What Beauteous Paradise is spelled, & what the Speller of the Stanza was
Who chiseled his unearthly riddle on this floor before I was born."

The old bard trembled pale, at last his heart grew cold, composed to hear the
fair youth raving
thru Hells and Heavens, paradise on his red lips, tricking, ravening Com-
manding,
hissing words half-cursed half prayers! Rending the breathing blue-green
globe apart
in Vanity for what is not, aethereal Death and Life, while Love and sorrow
ache
in the breast of the living moment under living skin, breath thrilled with sigh,
great Death & Life together One & love but a soul Aware,
For mind in heart is one with the body, Truth is the Depth of that,
and Poetry the Groan of Body lost in the Grave, for Thought is the love of
Earth.

"I knew this Rune once long ago, cold Demon inspired kid, bright boy—
thank you for discovering it me again, 'twas meant for you to read in Dreams
and find at your own bare foot one day. I hardly visioned to be here when
you came
naked maddened with delight into my room, demanding I respect your lips
& loins.
Listen now, my turn to tell the story of a day when I was young as you,
Was in this room, for I was here lone witness to the Stranger, Alien, Wan-
derer,
Caller of the Great Call, Serpent minded Messenger that came like yourself
Naked from Beauty to Beauty. He came in the door as you did, but no one
was home
to greet him, make fire to shine on runes or warm him in beds of Power,
Wrath and
Meditation, Service or Tenderness. Nor was Sea gold gathered No nor any
rhymed

or unrhymed Rune, not in this house on America's Eastern Shore.
Some house was here before, but broken down a Century Past, & Uninhab-
itable.
I gathered icy diamonds in the salt sea, plucked the blue eye of the whale
for wisdom,
Green emeralds I found in the growing grass and on tree boughs in their
Springtime buds,
For thirty years enriched with witty penury I gathered Amber from the
generous laurel
and Rubies rolled out of my heart. I threw away the Pearl, back to the sea
To keep God out of trouble under his blue wet blanket, and be done
with clammy envy and his watery blisses and grasping waves.
I brought the shining fire tongs here from Bardic Mannahatta, & the Red
Porphyry Chair of Poetry
from the Ind. I set it beside the hearth and built a fire out of seawracked
thrones of wooden kings
I found on the illuminated shore, and lay down on my belly in my healthy
youth
and Carved your Beauteous riddle on this bedrock basalt floor with the tooth
of an Angel
I imagined one night for Company in Meditation; & Pushed this red por-
phyry seat
smooth over that Mantric Rune with a Prayer to my visible & invisible
teachers—
Beloved Stranger, Naked Beauty, terrible Eidolon O my youth I never
dreamt that you would come."

Washington, January 22, 1977, 3 A.M.–11:30 A.M.

III

EPILOGUE

THE ARGUMENT: Last words spoken by the bard to the boy on a train between Washington and N.Y.

"Some day when we surrender to each other and become One friend,
we'll walk back to this hermitage, returned from America
thru Cities and Bars and Smoking Factories & State Capitols
Universities, Crowds, Parks and Highways, returned from glass-glittering
shrines
& diamond skyscrapers whose windows gleam sunset wealth Golden &
Purple,
White & Red & Blue as Clouds that reflect Smog thru Western heavens.

Back here in our bodies we may renew these studies & labors
of Iron & Feather, dream copybooks, & waking Levitation of heavy Mind.
Now still bodied separate in Vanity & minded contrary each in's Phantasy
only Poetry's Prophetic beauty Transports us on one Train back to
    households
in our north Vast City connected with telephones and buses. We may trip
    out
again into Hidden Beauty, Hearts beating thru the world's Mills & Wires,
    Radiant
at Television Noon or on Ecstatic midnite bed with broken bone or body
    Forgetfulness.
Now we go from our Chambered Cranium forth thru Strangeness:
Careful to respect our Heart, mindful of Beauty's slow working Calm Ma-
    chine,
Cigarette Vending Contraption or neon yellow Sun its face to your face—
All faces different, all forms present a Face to look into with Care:
The College boy his ignorant snub nose is a button whereon Sexual mercies
Press their lusty thumbs & wake his studious energy. The grey hair'd dirty
Professor of history's sought thru ages to find that Country where Love's
    face is King,
While the Care on his face is King of Centuries. And thoughts in his mind
    are
Presidents elected by fresh nerves every seven years to pass new laws of
    Consciousness.
Each Maple waits our gaze erecting tricky branches in the air we breathe.
Nothing is stupid but thought, & all thought we think's our own.
My face you've seen palsied bearded White & Changing energies
from Slavelike lust to snowy emptiness, bald Anger to fishy-eyed prophecy,
Your voice you've heard naked and hard commanding arrogant, pale dandied
in a fit of Burgundy Pique, Childlike delighted fingers twisting my beard
on Lion coverlets in caves far from the Iron Domed Capitol,
Intelligent deciphering runes yours and mine, dreamed & undreamt.
Plebeian Prince of the Suburb, I return to my eastern office pleased with our
    work
accident of our causes & Eidolons, Planned Careful in your Dreams & in my
    daylight Frenzies: failed Projections!
Our icy wills resolved in watery black ink's translucent tears,
Love's vapors are dissolved on seaboard's clear noon open to the Sun
shining thru railroad windows on new-revealed faces, our own inner forms!"

January 23, 1977

I Lay Love on My Knee

I nurs'd love where he lay
I let love get away
I let love lie low
I let my love go
I let love go along
I knew love was strong
So I let love go stray
I told love go away

I called love come home
my tongue wasn't dumb
I kissed love on the neck
& told love to come back
I told love come stay
Down by me love lay
I told love lie down
Love made a fine sound

I told love to Work
as musician or clerk
I sent love to the farm
He could do earth no harm
I told love get married
With children be harried
I said love settle down
with the worms in the ground
I told love have pity
Build me a good city

I taught love to sit
to sharpen his wit
I taught love to breathe
mindful of death
I showed love a straight spine
energetic as mine
I told love take it easy
Manners more breezy
Thoughts full of light
make love last all night

I kissed love on the brow
Where he lay like a cow
moaning and pleasured
his happy heart treasured
I kissed love's own lips
I laid love on his hips
I kissed love on his breast
When he lay down to rest
I kissed love on his thigh
Up rose his cock high

I bid Love leave me now
rest my feverish brow
I'm sick love goodbye
I must close my eye
No love you're not dead
Go find a new bed
for a day for a night
& come back for delight
after thought with new health
For all time is our wealth.

New York, February 21, 1977

Stool Pigeon Blues

I was born in Wyoming, Cody is my home town
Got myself busted, the sheriff brought me down
The Feds hit my nose, I felt like a dirty Clown

I turned in my sister, just like they asked me to
I turned in my brother, I had to, wouldn't you?
If they beat me again, I guess I'd turn you in too

Please don't blame me, they had me for twenty years
An ounce of weed, they planted it in my ears
They found one seed, and watered it with my tears

I got A's in highschool, smartest boy in class
Got laid at eleven, the sweetest piece of ass
They found us in bed smoking a stick of grass

Girl broke down crying, the Narcs liked her looks in the nude
Asked us for blowjobs, I told them that was too crude
Took us to jail & accused us of being lewd

Ten years for resisting arrest, ten years for a little joint
Ten years kid, beginning to get the point?
Feds want a big bust, let's hear you sing oink oink!

Who do you know in highschool, how many's dealing lids?
Who do you smoke with? We want the names of kids.
They'll bust all our parents, unless Good God forbids!

I'm just a poor stoolie, got busted in Wyoming
From Cody, to Casper, to Riverton I will sing!
From Gillette to Powell a pigeon I'm on the wing.

Governor Governor Get me out of this fix!
President President decriminalize the sticks,
Out here in Wyoming, Sheriffs play dirty tricks.

Casper, April 16, 1977

Punk Rock Your My Big Crybaby

I'll tell my deaf mother on you! Fall on the floor
and eat your grandmother's diapers! Drums,
Whatta lotta Noise you want a Revolution?
Wanna Apocalypse? Blow up in Dynamite Sound?
I can't get excited, Louder! Viciouser!
Fuck me in the ass! Suck me! Come in my ears!
I want those pink Abdominal bellybuttons!
Promise you'll murder me in the gutter with Orgasms!
I'll buy a ticket to your nightclub, I wanna get busted!
50 years old I wanna Go! with whips & chains & leather!
Spank me! Kiss me in the eye! Suck me all over
from Mabuhay Gardens to CBGB's coast to coast
Skull to toe Gimme yr electric guitar naked,
Punk President, eat up the FBI w/ yr big mouth.

Mabuhay Gardens, May 1977

Love Replied

Love came up to me
& got down on his knee
& said I am here to serve
you what you deserve
All that you wish
as on a gold dish
eyes tongue and heart
your most private part.

Why do you eat
my behind & my feet
Why do you kiss
my belly like this
Why do you go down
& suck my cock crown
when I bare you the best
that is inside my breast

I lay there reproved
aching my prick moved
But Love kissed my ear
& said nothing to fear
Put your head on my breast
There let your skull rest
Yes hug my breast, this
is my heart you can kiss

Then Love put his face
in my tenderest place
where throbbed my breast sweet
with red hot heart's heat
There, love is our bed
There, love lay your head
There you'll never regret
all the love you can get.

From the hair to the toes
neck & knees in repose
Take the heart that I give

Give heart that you live
Forget my sweet cock
my buttock like a rock
Come up from my thighs
Hear my heart's own straight sighs

I myself am not queer
Tho I hold your heart dear
Tho I lie with you naked
tho my own heart has ached
breast to breast with your bare
body, yes tho I dare
hug & kiss you all night
This is straight hearts' delight.

So bring your head up
from my loins or the cup
of my knees and behind
where you touch your lips blind
Put your lips to my heart
That is my public part
Hold me close and receive
All the love I can give

Boulder, June 18, 1977, 5 A.M.

X
PLUTONIAN
ODE
(1977–1980)

What's Dead?

Clouds' silent shadows passing across the Sun above Teton's mountaintop I
    saw on LSD
Movies dead shadows
ocean 40% dead said expert J. Cousteau A.D. 1968
Shakespeare the magician, Rimbaud visionary dead
silent vamp Alla Nazimova's corpse-lip black dust
Walt Disney of Mickey Mouse, Buck Rogers in the Twenty-fifth Century,
    Hollywood lost in shade
Tragedian Sophocles passed this shore with Charon thru Styx
Ex-Emperor Napoleon obituaried in 1821
Queen Liliuokalani giv'n to her reward
Chief Joseph buried on a brown hill in Washington State
General Douglas MacArthur urged atombombs to blow up China
Eisenhower & Xerxes led armies to the grave
The Skeleton Man in 1930 Barnum & Bailey Circus' Freakshow bony in's
    coffin
The mother Cat I played with in the basement Paterson New Jersey when
    I was ten
with the Lindbergh baby kidnapped found in a swamp of laundry
My father's grave writ "Answer a riddle with a stone" wet with rain in
    Newark
Jesus Christ & Mary for all their Assumption, dust in this world
Buddha relieved of his body, empty vehicle parked noiseless
Allah the Word in a book, or muezzin cry on a Tower
Not even Moses reached Promised Land, went down to Sheol.
Tickertape for heroes, clods of dirt for forgotten grandpas—
Television ghosts still haunt living room & bed chamber
Crooner Bing Crosby, Elvis Presley rock'n'roll Star, Groucho Marx a mus-
    tached joker, Einstein invented the universe, Naomi Ginsberg Com-
    munist Muse, Isadora Duncan dancing in diaphanous scarves
Jack Kerouac noble Poet, Jimmy Dean mystic actor, Boris Karloff the old
    Frankenstein,
Celebrities & Nonentities set apart, absent from their paths shadows left
    behind, breathing no more—
These were the musings of Buddhist student Allen Ginsberg.

Hawaii, October 16, 1977

Grim Skeleton

Grim skeleton come back & put me out of Action
looking thru the rainy window at the Church wall
yellow vapor lamped, 9 P.M. Cars hissing in street water
—woken dizzy from nicotine sleep—papers piled on my desk
myself lost in manila files of yellow faded newspaper Clippings
at last after twenty five years tapes wound thru my brain
Library of my own deeds of music tongue & oratoric yell—
Is it my heart, a cold & phlegm in my skull or radiator
Comfort cowardice that I slumber awake wrapped in Mexican
Blanket, wallet & keys on the white chair by my head.
Is it the guru of music or guru of meditation whose harsh force
I bear, makes my eyelid heavy mid afternoons, is't Death
stealing in my breast makes me nauseous mornings, work undone
on a typewriter set like a green skull by the window
When I wake unwilling to rise & take the narcotic *Times*
above a soft Boiled egg and toasted English muffin daily noon?
Beauty, Truth, Revolution, what skeleton in my closet
makes me listen dumb my own skull thoughts lethargic
Gossip of Poets silenced by drunken Mussolinis every Country on Earth?
My own yatter of meditation, while I work and scream in frenzy
at my wooden desk held up by iron filedrawers stuffed w/press paper
& prophetic fake manuscripts, ears itching & scabbed w/anger
at ghost Rockefeller Brothers pay-off of CIA, am I myself the CIA
bought with acid meat & alcohol in Washington, silenced in meditation
on my own duplicity, stuck in anger at puerto rican wounded
beerdrunk fathers walking East 12th street and their thieving kids
violent screaming under my window 4 A.M.? Some Fantasy of Fame
I dreamt in adolescence Came true last week over Television,
Now homunculus I made's out there in American streets
talking with my voice, accounted ledgered opinionated
Interviewed & Codified in Poems, books & manuscripts, whole library
shelves stacked with ambitious egohood's thousand pages imaged
forth smart selft over half a lifetime! Who'm I now, Frankenstein
hypocrite of good Cheer whose sick-stomached Discretion's grown
fifty years overweight—while others I hate practice sainthood in Himalayas
or run the petrochemical atomic lamplit machines, by whose power
I slumber cook my meat & write these verses captive of N.Y.C.
What's my sickness, flu virus or Selfhood infected swollen sore
confronting the loath'd work of poetic flattery: Gurus, Rock stars

Penthoused millionaires, White House alrightniks crowding my brain
with orders & formulae, insults & smalltalk, threats & dollars
Whose sucker am I, the media run by rich whitemen like myself, jew
intellectuals afraid of poverty bust screaming beaten uncontrolled behind
      bars
or the black hole of narcotics Cops & brutal Mafiosi, thick men in dark hats,
hells angels in blue military garb or wall street cashmere drag
hiding iron muscles of money, so the street is full of potholes, I'm afraid
to go out at night around the block to look at the moon in the Lower East
      Side
where stricken junkies break their necks in damp hallways of
abandoned buildings gutted & blackwindowed from old fires. I'm afraid
to write my thoughts down lest I libel Nelson Rockefeller, Fidel
Castro, Chögyam Trungpa, Louis Ginsberg & Naomi, Kerouac or Peter O.
yea Henry Kissinger & Richard Helms, faded ghosts of Power and Poesy
that people my brain with paranoia, my best friend shall be Nameless.
Whose public speech is this I write? What stupid vast Complaint!
For what impotent professor's ears, which Newsman's brainwave? What jazz
      king's devil blues?
Is this Immortal history to tell tales of 20th Century to striplings
naked centuries hence? To get laid by some brutal queen who'll
beat my hairy buttocks punishment in a College Dorm? To show my ass
to god? To grovel in magic tinsel & glitter on stinking powdered pillows?
Agh! Who'll I read this to like a fool! Who'll applaud these lies

December 16, 1977

Ballade of Poisons

With oil that streaks streets a magic color,
With soot that falls on city vegetables
With basement sulfurs & coal black odor
With smog that purples suburbs' sunset hills
With Junk that feebles black & white men's wills
With plastic bubbles aeons will dissolve
With new plutoniums that only resolve
Their poison heat in quarter million years,
With pesticides that round food Chains revolve
May your soul make home, may your eyes weep tears.

With freak hormones in chicken & soft egg
With panic red dye in cow meat burger
With mummy med'cines, nitrate in sliced pig
With sugar'd cereal kids scream for murder,
With Chemic additives that cause Cancer
With bladder and mouth in your salami,
With Strontium Ninety in milks of Mommy,
With sex voices that spill beer thru your ears
With Cups of Nicotine till you vomit
May your soul make home, may your eyes weep tears.

With microwave toaster television
With Cadmium lead in leaves of fruit trees
With Trade Center's nocturnal emission
With Coney Island's shore plopped with Faeces
While   blue   Whales sing in high infrequent seas
With Amazon worlds with fish in ocean
Washed in Rockefellers greasy Potion
With oily toil fueled with atomic fears
With CIA tainting World emotion
May your soul make home, may your eyes weep tears.

Envoi

President, 'spite cockroach devotion,
Folk poisoned with radioactive lotion,
'Spite soulless bionic energy queers
May your world move to healthy emotion,
Make your soul at home, let your eyes weep tears.

January 12, 1978

Lack Love

Love wears down to bare truth
My heart hurt me much in youth
Now I hear my real heart beat
Strong and hollow thump of meat

I felt my heart wrong as an ache
Sore in dreams and raw awake
I'd kiss each new love on the chest
Trembling hug him breast to breast

Kiss his belly, kiss his eye
Kiss his ruddy boyish thigh
Kiss his feet kiss his pink cheek
Kiss behind him naked meek

Now I lie alone, and a youth
Stalks my house, he won't in truth
Come to bed with me, instead
Loves the thoughts inside my head

He knows how much I think of him
Holds my heart his painful whim
Looks thru me with mocking eyes
Steals my feelings, drinks & lies

Till I see Love's empty Truth
Think back on heart broken youth
Hear my heart beat red in bed
Thick and living, love rejected.

New York, February 8, 1978, 3 A.M.

Father Guru

Father Guru   unforlorn
Heart beat Guru whom I scorn
Empty Guru Never Born
Sitting Guru every morn
Friendly Guru chewing corn
Angry Guru Faking Porn
Guru Guru Freely torn
Garment Guru neatly worn
Guru Head short hair shorn
Absent Guru   Eyes I mourn
Guru of Duncan Guru of Dorn
Ginsberg Guru like a thorn
Goofy Guru Lion Horn
Lonely Guru Unicorn
O Guru whose slave I'm sworn
Save me Guru Om Ah Hūṃ

Austin, February 14, 1978

Manhattan May Day Midnight

I walked out on the lamp shadowed concrete at midnight May Day passing
    a dark'd barfront,
police found corpses under the floor last year, call-girls & Cadillacs lurked
    there on First Avenue
around the block from my apartment, I'd come downstairs for tonight's
    newspapers—
refrigerator repair shop's window grate padlocked, fluorescent blue
light on a pile of newspapers, pages shifting in the chill Spring wind
'round battered cans & plastic refuse bags leaned together at the pavement
    edge—
Wind wind and old news sailed thru the air, old *Times* whirled above the
    garbage.
At the Corner of 11th under dim Street-light in a hole in the ground
a man wrapped in work-Cloth and wool Cap pulled down his bullet skull
stood & bent with a rod & flashlight turning round in his pit halfway sunk
    in earth
Peering down at his feet, up to his chest in the asphalt by a granite Curb
where his work mate poked a flexible tube in a tiny hole, a youth in gloves
who answered my question "Smell of gas—Someone must've reported
    in"—
Yes the body stink of City bowels, rotting tubes six feet under
Could explode any minute sparked by Con Ed's breathing Puttering truck
I noticed parked, as I passed by hurriedly Thinking Ancient Rome, Ur
Were they like this, the same shadowy surveyors & passers-by
scribing records of decaying pipes & Garbage piles on Marble, Cuneiform,
ordinary midnight citizen out on the street looking for Empire News,
rumor, gossip, workmen police in uniform, walking silent sunk in thought
under windows of sleepers coupled with Monster squids & Other-Planet
    eyeballs in their sheets
in the same night six thousand years old where Cities rise & fall & turn to
    dream?

May 1, 1978, 6 A.M.

ADAPTED FROM Neruda's
"Que dispierte el leñador"

V
Let the Railsplitter Awake!
Let Lincoln come with his ax
and with his wooden plate
to eat with the farmworkers.
May his craggy head,
his eyes we see in constellations,
in the wrinkles of the live oak,
come back to look at the world
rising up over the foliage
higher than Sequoias.
Let him go shop in pharmacies,
let him take the bus to Tampa
let him nibble a yellow apple,
let him go to the movies, and
talk to everybody there.

Let the Railsplitter awake!

Let Abraham come back, let his old yeast
rise in green and gold earth of Illinois,
and lift the ax in his city
against the new slavemakers
against their slave whips
against the venom of the print houses
against all the bloodsoaked
merchandise they want to sell.
Let the young white boy and young black
march singing and smiling
against walls of gold,
against manufacturers of hatred,
against the seller of his own blood,
singing, smiling and winning at last.

Let the Railsplitter awake!

VI

Peace for all twilights to come,
peace for the bridge, peace for the wine,
peace for the letters that look for me
and pump in my blood tangled
with earth and love's old chant,
peace for the city in the morning
when bread wakes up,
peace for Mississippi, the river of roots,
peace for my brother's shirt,
peace in the book like an airmail stamp,
peace for the great Kolkhoz of Kiev,
peace for the ashes of these dead
and those other dead, peace for the black
iron of Brooklyn, peace for the lettercarrier
going from house to house like the day,
peace for the choreographer shrieking
thru a funnel of honeysuckle vines,
peace to my right hand
that only wants to write Rosario,
peace for the Bolivian, secret as a lump of tin,
peace for you to get married, peace
for all the sawmills of Bio-Bio,
peace to Revolutionary Spain's torn heart
peace to the little museum of Wyoming
in which the sweetest thing
was a pillowcase embroidered with a heart,
peace to the baker and his loaves,
and peace to all the flour: peace
for all the wheat still to be born,
peace for all the love that wants to flower,
peace for all those who live: peace
to all the lands and waters.

And here I say farewell, I return
to my house, in my dreams
I go back to Patagonia where
the wind beats at barns
and the Ocean spits ice.
I'm nothing more than a poet:
I want love for you all,

I go wander the world I love:
in my country they jail the miners
and soldiers give orders to judges.
But down to its very roots
I love my little cold country.
If I had to die a thousand times
that's where I'd want to die:
if I had to be born a thousand times
that's where I'd want to be born,
near the Araucanian wilds'
sea-whirled south winds,
bells just brought from the bellmaker.
Don't let anybody think about me.
Let's think about the whole world,
banging on the table with love.
I don't want blood to come back
and soak the bread, the beans
the music: I want the miner
to come with me, the little girl,
the lawyer, the sailor, the dollmaker,
let's all go to the movies and come
out and drink the reddest wine.

I didn't come here to solve anything.

I came here to sing
And for you to sing with me.

Boulder, 1978–1981

Nagasaki Days

I *A Pleasant Afternoon*

for Michael Brownstein & Dick Gallup

One day 3 poets & 60 ears sat under a green-striped Chautauqua tent in
    Aurora
listening to Black spirituals, tapping their feet, appreciating words singing
    by in mountain winds
on a pleasant sunny day of rest—the wild wind blew thru blue Heavens
filled with fluffy clouds stretched from Central City to Rocky Flats,
    Plutonium sizzled in its secret bed,
hot dogs sizzled in the Lions Club lunchwagon microwave mouth, orange-
    ade bubbled over in waxen cups
Traffic moved along Colefax, meditators silent in the Diamond Castle shrine-
    room at Boulder followed the breath going out of their nostrils,
Nobody could remember anything, spirits flew out of mouths & noses, out
    of the sky, across Colorado plains & the tent flapped happily open
    spacious & didn't fall down.

June 18, 1978

II *Peace Protest*

Cumulus clouds float across blue sky
    over the white-walled Rockwell Corporation factory
            —am I going to stop that?

       *

Rocky Mountains rising behind us
    Denver shining in morning light
—Led away from the crowd by police and photographers

       *

Middleaged Ginsberg & Ellsberg taken down the road
    to the grayhaired Sheriff's van—
But what about Einstein? What about Einstein? Hey, Einstein Come
                back!

III *Golden Courthouse*

Waiting for the Judge, breathing silent
      Prisoners, witnesses, Police—
the stenographer yawns into her palms.

                           August 9, 1978

IV *Everybody's Fantasy*

I walked outside & the bomb'd
      dropped lots of plutonium
      all over the Lower East Side
There weren't any buildings left just
      iron skeletons
groceries burned, potholes open to
      stinking sewer waters

There were people starving and crawling
      across the desert
the Martian UFOs with blue
      Light destroyer rays
passed over and dried up all the
      waters

Charred Amazon palmtrees for
      hundreds of miles on both sides
      of the river

                         August 10, 1978

V *Waiting Room at the Rocky Flats Plutonium Plant*

"Give us the weapons we need to protect ourselves!"
      the bareheaded guard lifts his flyswatter above the desk
                      —whap!

              *

A green-letter'd shield on the pressboard wall!
      "Life is fragile. Handle with care"—
My Goodness! here's where they make the nuclear bomb-triggers.

                         August 17, 1978

VI *Numbers in Red Notebook*

2,000,000 killed in Vietnam
13,000,000 refugees in Indochina 1972
200,000,000 years for the Galaxy to revolve on its core
24,000 the Babylonian Great Year
24,000 half life of plutonium
2,000 the most I ever got for a poetry reading
80,000 dolphins killed in the dragnet
4,000,000,000 years earth been born

Boulder, Summer 1978

Plutonian Ode

I

1 What new element before us unborn in nature? Is there a new thing
under the Sun?
At last inquisitive Whitman a modern epic, detonative, Scientific theme
First penned unmindful by Doctor Seaborg with poisonous hand,
named for Death's planet through the sea beyond Uranus
whose chthonic ore fathers this magma-teared Lord of Hades, Sire of
avenging Furies, billionaire Hell-King worshipped once

5 with black sheep throats cut, priest's face averted from underground
mysteries in a single temple at Eleusis,
Spring-green Persephone nuptialed to his inevitable Shade, Demeter
mother of asphodel weeping dew,
her daughter stored in salty caverns under white snow, black hail, gray
winter rain or Polar ice, immemorable seasons before
Fish flew in Heaven, before a Ram died by the starry bush, before the
Bull stamped sky and earth
or Twins inscribed their memories in cuneiform clay or Crab'd flood

10 washed memory from the skull, or Lion sniffed the lilac breeze in
Eden—
Before the Great Year began turning its twelve signs, ere constellations
wheeled for twenty-four thousand sunny years
slowly round their axis in Sagittarius, one hundred sixty-seven thousand
times returning to this night

Radioactive Nemesis were you there at the beginning black Dumb
tongueless unsmelling blast of Disillusion?
I manifest your Baptismal Word after four billion years

15 I guess your birthday in Earthling Night, I salute your dreadful pres-
ence lasting majestic as the Gods,
Sabaot, Jehova, Astapheus, Adonaeus, Elohim, Iao, Ialdabaoth, Aeon
from Aeon born ignorant in an Abyss of Light,
Sophia's reflections glittering thoughtful galaxies, whirlpools of star-
spume silver-thin as hairs of Einstein!
Father Whitman I celebrate a matter that renders Self oblivion!
Grand Subject that annihilates inky hands & pages' prayers, old orators'
inspired Immortalities,

20 I begin your chant, openmouthed exhaling into spacious sky over silent
mills at Hanford, Savannah River, Rocky Flats, Pantex, Burling-
ton, Albuquerque

I yell thru Washington, South Carolina, Colorado, Texas, Iowa, New Mexico,

where nuclear reactors create a new Thing under the Sun, where Rockwell war-plants fabricate this death stuff trigger in nitrogen baths,

Hanger-Silas Mason assembles the terrified weapon secret by ten thousands, & where Manzano Mountain boasts to store

its dreadful decay through two hundred forty millennia while our Galaxy spirals around its nebulous core.

25 I enter your secret places with my mind, I speak with your presence, I roar your Lion Roar with mortal mouth.

One microgram inspired to one lung, ten pounds of heavy metal dust adrift slow motion over gray Alps

the breadth of the planet, how long before your radiance speeds blight and death to sentient beings?

Enter my body or not I carol my spirit inside you, Unapproachable Weight,

O heavy heavy Element awakened I vocalize your consciousness to six worlds

30 I chant your absolute Vanity. Yeah monster of Anger birthed in fear O most

Ignorant matter ever created unnatural to Earth! Delusion of metal empires!

Destroyer of lying Scientists! Devourer of covetous Generals, Incinerator of Armies & Melter of Wars!

Judgment of judgments, Divine Wind over vengeful nations, Molester of Presidents, Death-Scandal of Capital politics! Ah civilizations stupidly industrious!

Canker-Hex on multitudes learned or illiterate! Manufactured Spectre of human reason! O solidified imago of practitioners in Black Arts

35 I dare your Reality, I challenge your very being! I publish your cause and effect!

I turn the Wheel of Mind on your three hundred tons! Your name enters mankind's ear! I embody your ultimate powers!

My oratory advances on your vaunted Mystery! This breath dispels your braggart fears! I sing your form at last

behind your concrete & iron walls inside your fortress of rubber & translucent silicon shields in filtered cabinets and baths of lathe oil,

My voice resounds through robot glove boxes & ingot cans and echoes in electric vaults inert of atmosphere,

40 I enter with spirit out loud into your fuel rod drums underground on
        soundless thrones and beds of lead
    O density! This weightless anthem trumpets transcendent through hid-
        den chambers and breaks through iron doors into the Infernal
        Room!
    Over your dreadful vibration this measured harmony floats audible,
        these jubilant tones are honey and milk and wine-sweet water
    Poured on the stone block floor, these syllables are barely groats I scatter
        on the Reactor's core,
    I call your name with hollow vowels, I psalm your Fate close by, my
        breath near deathless ever at your side
45 to Spell your destiny, I set this verse prophetic on your mausoleum walls
        to seal you up Eternally with Diamond Truth! O doomed
        Plutonium.

II

    The Bard surveys Plutonian history from midnight lit with Mercury
        Vapor streetlamps till in dawn's early light
    he contemplates a tranquil politic spaced out between Nations' thought-
        forms proliferating bureaucratic
    & horrific arm'd, Satanic industries projected sudden with Five Hun-
        dred Billion Dollar Strength
    around the world same time this text is set in Boulder, Colorado before
        front range of Rocky Mountains
50 twelve miles north of Rocky Flats Nuclear Facility in United States on
        North America, Western Hemisphere
    of planet Earth six months and fourteen days around our Solar System
        in a Spiral Galaxy
    the local year after Dominion of the last God nineteen hundred seventy
        eight
    Completed as yellow hazed dawn clouds brighten East, Denver city
        white below
    Blue sky transparent rising empty deep & spacious to a morning star
        high over the balcony
55 above some autos sat with wheels to curb downhill from Flatiron's
        jagged pine ridge,
    sunlit mountain meadows sloped to rust-red sandstone cliffs above brick
        townhouse roofs
    as sparrows waked whistling through Marine Street's summer green
        leafed trees.

III

> This ode to you O Poets and Orators to come, you father Whitman as
>> I join your side, you Congress and American people,
> you present meditators, spiritual friends & teachers, you O Master of the
>> Diamond Arts,
60 Take this wheel of syllables in hand, these vowels and consonants to
>> breath's end
> take this inhalation of black poison to your heart, breathe out this bless-
>> ing from your breast on our creation
> forests cities oceans deserts rocky flats and mountains in the Ten Direc-
>> tions pacify with this exhalation,
> enrich this Plutonian Ode to explode its empty thunder through earthen
>> thought-worlds
> Magnetize this howl with heartless compassion, destroy this mountain
>> of Plutonium with ordinary mind and body speech,
65 thus empower this Mind-guard spirit gone out, gone out, gone beyond,
>> gone beyond me, Wake space, so Ah!

July 14, 1978

Old Pond

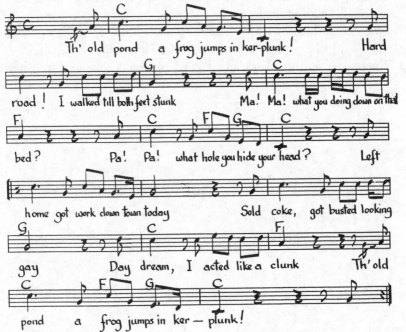

Th' old pond a frog jumps in ker-plunk! Hard road! I walked till both feet stunk Ma! Ma! what you doing down on that bed? Pa! Pa! what hole you hide your head? Left home got work down town today Sold coke, got busted looking gay Day dream, I acted like a clunk Th' old pond a frog jumps in ker — plunk!

Old Pond

The old pond—a frog jumps in, kerplunk!
Hard road! I walked till both feet stunk—
Ma!Ma! Whatcha doing down on that bed?
Pa!Pa! what hole you hide your head?

Left home   got work down town today
Sold coke,   got busted looking gay
Day dream, I acted like a clunk
Th'old pond—a frog jumps in, kerplunk!

Got hitched, I bought a frying pan
Fried eggs, my wife eats like a man
Won't cook, her oatmeal tastes like funk
Th'old pond—a frog jumps in, kerplunk!

Eat shit   exactly what she said
Drink wine, it goes right down my head
Fucked up, they all yelled I was drunk
Th'old pond—a frog jumps in, kerplunk!

Saw God at six o'clock tonight
Flop house, I think I'll start a fight
Head ache like both my eyeballs shrunk
Th'old pond—a frog jumps in, kerplunk!

Hot dog! I love my mustard hot
Hey Rube! I think I just got shot
Drop dead   She said you want some junk?
Th'old pond—a frog jumps in, kerplunk!

Oh ho   your dirty needle stinks
No no I don't shoot up with finks
Speed greed I stood there with the punk
Th'old pond—a frog jumps in, kerplunk!

Yeh yeh   gimme a breath of fresh air
Guess who   I am well you don't care
No name   call up the mocking Monk
Th'old pond—a frog jumps in, kerplunk!

No echo, make a lot of noise
Come home   you owe it to the boys
Can't hear   you scream your fish's sunk
Th'old pond—a frog jumps in, kerplunk!

Just folks, we bought a motor car
No gas   I guess we crossed the bar
I swear we started for Podunk
Th'old pond—a frog jumps in, kerplunk!

I got his banjo on my knee
I played it like an old Sweetie
I sang plunk-a-plunk-a-plunk plunk plunk plunk
Th'old pond—a frog jumps in, kerplunk!

One hand   I gave myself the clap
Unborn, but still I took the rap
Big deal, I fell out of my bunk
Th'old pond—a frog jumps in, kerplunk!

Hey hey! I ride down the blue sky
Sit down with worms until I die
Fare well! Hūṃ Hūṃ Hūṃ Hūṃ Hūṃ Hūṃ!
Th'old pond—a frog jumps in, kerplunk!

Red barn   rise wet in morning dew
Cockadoo   dle do oink oink moo moo
Buzz buzz—flyswatter in the kitchen, thwunk!
Th'old pond—a frog jumps in, kerplunk!

August 22, 1978

Blame the Thought, Cling to the Bummer

I am Fake Saint
magazine Saint Ram Das
Who's not a Fake Saint consciousness, Nobody!
The 12th Trungpa, Karmapa 16, Dudjom lineage of Padmasambhava, Pope
      Jean-Paul, Queen of England crowned with dignity's brilliant empty
      Diamonds Sapphires Emeralds, Amber, Rubies—
The sky is Fake Saint, emptyhearted blue
The Sacramento Valley floor fields no saints either, tractors in green corn
      higher than the T-shirted jogger.
This Volkswagen Fake Saint, license-plate-light wires smoking shorted in
      the rear-engine door.
Filter cigarette butt still smoking in the ashtray
No saints longhaired boys at the busdriver's wheel
Hard workers no Fake Saints laborers everywhere behind desks in
      Plutonium offices
swatting flies under plastic flower-power signs

Driving Ponderosa & Spruce roads to the poet's shrine at Kitkitdizze
Bedrock Mortar hermitage—Shobo-An temple's copper roof on a black-oak
      groved hillside—
Discontinuous, the thought—empty—no harm—
To blame the thought would cling to the Bummer—
Unborn Evil, the Self & its systems
Transitory intermittent gapped in Grass Valley stopping for gas
Plutonium blameless, apocalyptic gift of Furies
Insentient space filled with green bushes—clouds over Ranger Station
      signs
Uncertain as incense.

Nevada City, September 7, 1978

"Don't Grow Old"

I

Twenty-eight years before on the living room couch he'd stared at me, I said
"I want to see a psychiatrist—I have sexual difficulties—homosexuality"
I'd come home from troubled years as a student. This was the weekend I
    would talk with him.
A look startled his face, "You mean you like to take men's penises in your
    mouth?"
Equally startled, "No, no," I lied, "that isn't what it means."

Now he lay naked in the bath, hot water draining beneath his shanks.
Strong shouldered Peter, once ambulance attendant, raised him up
in the tiled room. We toweled him dry, arms under his, bathrobe over his
    shoulder—
he tottered thru the door to his carpeted bedroom
sat on the soft mattress edge, exhausted, and coughed up watery phlegm.
We lifted his swollen feet talcum'd white, put them thru pajama legs,
tied the cord round his waist, and held the nightshirt sleeve open for his
    hand, slow.
Mouth drawn in, his false teeth in a dish, he turned his head round
looking up at Peter to smile ruefully, "Don't ever grow old."

II

At my urging, my eldest nephew came
to keep his grandfather company, maybe sleep overnight in the apartment.
He had no job, and was homeless anyway.
All afternoon he read the papers and looked at old movies.
Later dusk, television silent, we sat on a soft-pillowed couch,
Louis sat in his easy-chair that swiveled and could lean back—
"So what kind of job are you looking for?"
"Dishwashing, but someone told me it makes your hands' skin scaly red."
"And what about officeboy?" His grandson finished highschool with marks
    too poor for college.
"It's unhealthy inside airconditioned buildings under fluorescent light."
The dying man looked at him, nodding at the specimen.
He began his advice. "You might be a taxidriver, but what if a car crashed
    into you? They say you can get mugged too.
Or you could get a job as a sailor, but the ship could sink, you could get
    drowned.

Maybe you should try a career in the grocery business, but a box of bananas
      could slip from the shelf,
you could hurt your head. Or if you were a waiter, you could slip and fall
      down with a loaded tray, & have to pay for the broken glasses.
Maybe you should be a carpenter, but your thumb might get hit by a
      hammer.
Or a lifeguard—but the undertow at Belmar beach is dangerous, and you
      could catch a cold.
Or a doctor, but sometimes you could cut your hand with a scalpel that had
      germs, you could get sick & die."

Later, in bed after twilight, glasses off, he said to his wife
"Why doesn't he comb his hair? It falls all over his eyes, how can he see?
Tell him to go home soon, I'm too tired."

Amherst, October 5, 1978

III

Resigned

A year before visiting a handsome poet and my Tibetan guru,
      Guests after supper on the mountainside
we admired the lights of Boulder spread glittering below
        through a giant glass window—
After coffee, my father bantered wearily
"Is life worth living? Depends on the liver—"
The Lama smiled to his secretary—
It was an old pun I'd heard in childhood.
Then he fell silent, looking at the floor
    and sighed, head bent heavy
       talking to no one—
          "What can you do . . . ?"

Buffalo, October 6, 1978

Love Returned

Love returned with smiles
three thousand miles
to keep a year's promise
Anonymous, honest
studious, beauteous
learned and childlike
earnest and mild like
a student of truth,
a serious youth.

Whatever our ends
young and old we were friends
on the coast a few weeks
In New York now he seeks
scholarly manuscripts
old writs, haunted notes
Antique anecdotes,
rare libraries lain
back of the brain.

Now we are in bed
he kisses my head
his hand on my arm
holds my side warm
He presses my leg
I don't have to beg
his sweet penis heat
enlarged at my hip,
kiss his neck with my lip.

Small as a kid
his ass is not hid
I can touch, I can play
with his thighs any way
My cheek to his chest
my body's his guest
he offers his breast
his belly, the rest
hug and kiss to my bliss

Come twice at last
he offers his ass
first time for him
to be entered at whim
of my bare used cock—
his cheeks do unlock
tongue & hand at soft gland
Alas for my dreams
my part's feeble it seems

Familiar with lust
heartening the dust
of 50 years' boys'
abandoned love joys
Not to queer my idea
he's willing & trembles
& his body's nimble
where I want my hard skin
I can't get it on in.

Well another day comes
Church bells have rung
dawn blue in New York
I eat vegetables raw
Sun flowers, cole slaw
Age shortens my years
yet brings these good cheers
Some nights're left free
& Love's patient with me

December 16, 1978, 6 A.M.

December 31, 1978

Shining Diamonds & Sequins glitter
    Grand Ballroom Waldorf
    Astoria on the TV Screen
radiant shifting goodbye to
    Times Square Phantoms
    waving
massed eyeglasses & umbrellas'
    rainy hands over
    heads
Celebrating China
    diplomatic relations
    Disco in Peking
Congressional black & tan faces
    on the news-dots sober Committee Report
    Concludes Conspiracy Killing
    Kennedy & Martin Luther King
President & Peacemaker last
    Decade departed
mysteriously gloomy miasma
    mind of NY Times Vietnam
    nuclear Warren Commission
    exploded, lies & confusion
popping firecrackers Razz-ma-Tazz
    in mylar hats under klieg lights
    dancing to Guy Lombardo
Hitchy Kitchy Koo in eyeglasses
    & bowties
with tinkling Pianos, Trombones
    & tubas above the round white
    champagne tables
Old Folks smiling into camera one
    last time
appreciating the Royal Canadian
    Nostalgia
among sweepstake kitchen
    sinks & refrigerators
advertised before the deodorized
    stickup by Count Dracula
    with popping eyeballs.

How enthusiastic the soap ads
        while masses honk paper
        horns
between December's canyon'd building
walls straight-sided up
        thru red misted sky
        above Gotham
Broadway Oomp-pa-pa-ing its
        regards to Heaven the
        umpteenth time,
tin Trumpets waiting to
        announce the year's
        midnight,
Big teeth having a good time,
        Puerto Ricans smiling
under 44th Street marquees
        greeting the camera's
        million-eyed blank
        Hope the itching's gone—
Live from New York! thousands
        scream delight
roaring the clock along simultaneous
        congratulations Network Chairman
        Wm. S. Paley—
Forgiveness! Time! the ball's
        falling down, drums
        roll loud
across America's speaker
        systems to
Balloons! Happy New Year!
        Trumpets & Bubbles wave
        thru the brain!
Raise yr hat & shake yr bracelet
        Telephone Edie! Blow yr Trumpet
        Ganymede with a mustache
Ring yr brazen horns ye
        Fire engines of Soho!
Bark ye dogges in lofts, explode
        yr honking halos ye
        weightless Angels of
        Television!

It's gonna be a delightful
        time, thank god nothing's
        happening muchachos
Tonite but parties & car crashes,
        births & ambulance sirens,
Confetti falling over
        heartbroken partygoers
        doing the Lindy Hop at the
        back window of the loft
years ago when Abstract-Expressionist
        painters & poets had a party
        celebrating U.S. Eternity
        on New Year's Eve before the War.

Brooklyn College Brain

For David Shapiro & John Ashbery

You used to wear dungarees & blue workshirt,
sneakers or cloth-top shoes, & ride alone
on subways, young & elegant unofficial
bastard of nature, sneaking sweetness into Brooklyn.
Now tweed jacket & yr father's tie on yr breast,
salmon-pink cotton shirt & Swedish bookbag
you're half bald, palsied lip & lower eyelid
continually tearing, gone back to college.
Goodbye Professor Ginsberg, get your identity
card next week from the front office so you can
get to class without being humiliated dumped on the
sidewalk by the black guard at the Student Union door.

Hello Professor Ginsberg have some coffee,
have some students, have some office hours
Tuesdays & Thursdays, have a couple subway tokens
in advance, have a box in the English Department,
have a look at Miss Sylvia Blitzer behind the typewriter
Have some poems er maybe they're not so bad have a
good time workshopping Bodhicitta in the Bird Room.

March 27, 1979

Garden State

It used to be, farms,
stone houses on green lawns
a wooded hill to play Jungle Camp
asphalt roads thru Lincoln Park.

The communists picnicked
amid spring's yellow forsythia
magnolia trees & apple blossoms, pale buds
breezy May, blue June.

Then came the mafia, alcohol
highways, garbage dumped in marshes, real
estate, World War II, money
flowed thru Nutley, bulldozers.

Einstein invented atom bombs
in Princeton, television antennae
sprung over West Orange—lobotomies
performed in Greystone State Hospital.

Old graveyards behind churches
on grassy knolls, Erie Railroad
bridges' Checkerboard underpass
signs, paint fading, remain.

Reminds me of a time pond's pure
water was green, drink or swim.
Traprock quarries embedded
with amethyst, quiet on Sunday.

I was afraid to talk to anyone
in Paterson, lest my sensitivity
to sex, music, the universe, be discovered &
I be laughed at, hit by colored boys.

"Mr. Professor" said the Dutchman
on Haledon Ave. "Stinky Jew" said
my friend black Joe, kinky haired.
Oldsmobiles past by in front of my eyeglasses.

Greenhouses stood by the Passaic in the sun,
little cottages in Belmar by the sea.
I heard Hitler's voice on the radio.
I used to live on that hill up there.

They threw eggs at Norman Thomas the Socialist speaker
in Newark Military Park, the police
stood by & laughed. Used to murder
silk strikers on Mill St. in the twenties.

Now turn on your boob tube
They explain away the Harrisburg
hydrogen bubble, the Vietnam war,
They haven't reported the end of Jersey's gardens,

much less the end of the world.
Here in Boonton they made cannonballs
for Washington, had old iron mines,
spillways, coach houses—Trolleycars

ran thru Newark, gardeners dug front lawns.
Look for the News in your own backyard
over the whitewashed picket fence, fading signs
on upper stories of red brick factories.

The Data Terminal people stand on Route 40
now. Let's get our stuff together. Let's
go back Sundays & sing old springtime music
on Greystone State Mental Hospital lawn.

Spring 1979

Spring Fashions

Full moon over the shopping mall—
    in a display window's silent light
the naked mannequin observes her fingernails

Boulder, 1979

Las Vegas: Verses Improvised for El Dorado H.S. Newspaper

Aztec sandstone waterholes known by Moapa've
dried out under the baccarat pits
of M.G.M.'s Grand Hotel.

If Robert Maheu knew
       who killed Kennedy
would he tell Santos Trafficante?

If Frank Sinatra had to grow his own
       food, would he learn
how to grind piñon nuts?

If Sammy Davis had to find original water
would he lead a million old ladies laughing
    round Mt. Charleston to the Sheepshead Mountains
        in migratory cycle?

Does Englebert know the name of
the mountains he sings in?

When gas and water dry up
will wild mustangs
    inhabit the Hilton Arcade?

Will the 130-billion-dollared-Pentagon guard
    the radioactive waste dump at Beatty
        for the whole Platonic Year?

Tell all the generals and Maitre D's
to read the bronze inscriptions
    under the astronomical flagpole at Hoover Dam.

Will Franklin Delano Roosevelt
    Bugsy Siegel and Buddha
all lose their shirts at Las Vegas?

Yeah! because they don't know how to gamble
    like mustangs and desert lizards.

September 23, 1979

To the Punks of Dawlish

Your electric hair's beautiful gold as Blake's Glad Day boy,
you raise your arms for industrial crucifixion
You get 45 Pounds a week on the Production line
and 15 goes to taxes, Mrs. Thatcher's nuclear womb swells
The Iron Lady devours your powers & hours your pounds and pride &
scatters radioactive urine on your mushroom dotted sheep fields.
"Against the Bourgeois!" you raise your lip & dandy costume
Against the Money Establishment you pogo to garage bands
After humorous slavery in th' electronic factory
put silver pins in your nose, gold rings in your ears
talk to the Professor on the Plymouth train, asking
"Marijuana rots your brain like it says in the papers, insists on the telly?"
Cursed tragic kids rocking in a rail car on the Cornwall Coastline, Luck to
    your dancing revolution!
With bodies beautiful as the gold blond lads' of Oxford—
Your rage is more elegant than most purse-lipped considerations of Cam-
    bridge,
your mouths more full of slang & kisses than tea-sipping wits of Eton
    whispering over scones & clotted cream
conspiring to govern your music tax your body labor & chasten your impu-
    dent speech with an Official Secrets Act.

Cornwall, November 18, 1979

Some Love

After 53 years
I still cry tears
I still fall in love
I still improve

My art with a kiss
My heart with bliss
My hands massage
Kids from the garage

Kids from the grave
Kids who slave
At study or labor
Still show me favor

How can I complain
When love like rain
Falls all over the land
On my head on my hand

On my breast on my shoes
Kisses arrive like foreign news
Mouths suck my cock
Boys wish me good luck

How long can I last
Such love gone past
So much to come
Till I get dumb

Rarer and rarer
Boys give me favor
Older and older
Love grows bolder

Sweeter and sweeter
Wrinkled like water
My skin still trembles
My fingers nimble

Siegen, December 12, 1979

Maybe Love

Maybe love will come
cause I am not so dumb
Tonight it fills my heart
heavy sad apart
from one or two I fancy
now I'm an old fairy.

This is hard to say
I've come to be this way
thru many loves of youth
that taught me most heart truth
Now I come by myself
in my hand a potbellied elf

It's not the most romantic
dream to be so frantic
for young men's bodies,
a fine sugar daddy
blest respected known
but left to bed alone.

How come love came to end
flaccid, how pretend
desires I have used
Four decades as I cruised
from bed to bar to book
Shamefaced like a crook

Stealing here & there
pricks & buttocks bare
by accident, by circumstance
Naiveté or horny chance
stray truth or famous lie,
How come I came to die?

Love dies, body dies, the mind
keeps groping blind
half hearted full of lust
to wet the silken dust

of men that hold me dear
but won't sleep with me near.

This morning's cigarette
This morning's sweet regret
habit of many years
wake me to old fears
Under the living sun
one day there'll be no one

to kiss & to adore
& to embrace & more
lie down with side by side
tender as a bride
gentle under my touch—
Prick I love to suck.

Church bells ring again
in Heidelberg as when
in New York City town
I lay my belly down
against a boy friend's buttock
and couldn't get it up.

'Spite age and common Fate
I'd hoped love'd hang out late
I'd never lack for thighs
on which to sigh my sighs
This day it seems the truth
I can't depend on youth,

I can't keep dreaming love
I can't pray heav'n above
or call the pow'rs of hell
to keep my body well
occupied with young devils
tongueing at my navel.

I stole up from my bed
to that of a well-bred
young friend who shared my purse
and noted my tender verse,

I held him by the ass
waiting for sweat to pass

until he said Go back
I said that I would jack
myself away, not stay
& so he let me play
Allergic to my come—
I came, & then went home.

This can't go on forever,
this poem, nor my fever
for brown eyed mortal joy,
I love a straight white boy.
Ah the circle closes
Same old withered roses!

I haven't found an end
I can fuck & defend
& no more can depend
on youth time to amend
what old ages portend—
Love's death, & body's end.

Heidelberg, December 15, 1979, 8 A.M.

Ruhr-Gebiet

Too much industry
too much eats
too much beer
too much cigarettes

Too much philosophy
too many thought forms
not enough rooms—
not enough trees

Too much Police
too much computers
too much hi fi
too much Pork

Too much coffee
too much smoking
under gray slate roofs
Too much obedience

Too many bellies
Too many business suits
Too much paperwork
too many magazines

Too much industry
No fish in the Rhine
Lorelei poisoned
Too much embarrassment

Too many fatigued
workers on the train
Ghost Jews scream
on the streetcorner

Too much old murder
too much white torture
Too much one Stammheim
too many happy Nazis

Too many crazy students
Not enough farms
not enough Appletrees
Not enough nut trees

Too much money
Too many poor
turks without vote
"Guests" do the work

Too much metal
Too much fat
Too many jokes
not enough meditation

Too much anger
Too much sugar
Too many smokestacks
Not enough snow

Too many radioactive
plutonium wastebarrels
Take the Rhine gold
Build a big tomb

A gold walled grave
to bury this deadly nuclear slag
all the Banks' gold
Shining impenetrable

All the German gold
will save the Nation
Build a gold house
to bury the Devil

Heidelberg, December 15, 1979

Love Forgiven

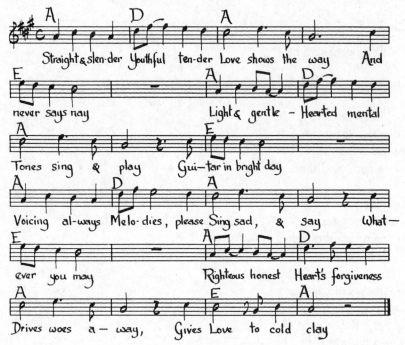

Straight & slen-der Youthful ten-der Love shows the way And
never says nay Light & gentle - Hearted mental
Tones sing & play Gui-tar in bright day
Voicing al-ways Melo-dies, please Sing sad, & say What —
ever you may Righteous honest Heart's forgiveness
Drives woes a — way, Gives Love to cold clay

Tübingen–Hamburg Schlafwagen

I

Why am I so angry at Kissinger?
    Kent State? Terrorism began in 1968!
"Berlin Student Protesting Shah Shot by Police."

II

Building lights above black water!
    passing over a big river, railroad bridge & tower.
Mmm Fairyland! Must be Frankfurt!

December 1979

Love Forgiven

Straight and slender
Youthful tender
Love shows the way
And never says nay

Light & gentle-
Hearted mental
Tones sing & play
Guitar in bright day

Voicing always
Melodies, please
Sing sad, & say
Whatever you may

Righteous honest
Heart's forgiveness
Drives woes away,
Gives Love to cold clay

Tübingen, December 16, 1979

Verses Written for Student Antidraft Registration Rally 1980

The Warrior is afraid
the warrior has a big trembling heart
the warrior sees bright explosions over Utah, a giant bomber moves over
      Cheyenne Mountain at Colorado Springs
the warrior laughs at its shadow, his thought flows out with his breath and
      dissolves in afternoon light
The warrior never goes to War
War runs away from the warrior's mouth
War falls apart in the warrior's mind
The Conquered go to War, drafted into shadow armies, navy'd on shadow
      oceans, flying in shadow fire
only helpless Draftees fight afraid, big meaty negroes trying not to die—
The Warrior knows his own sad & tender heart, which is not the heart of
      most newspapers
Which is not the heart of most Television—This kind of sadness doesn't sell
      popcorn
This kind of sadness never goes to war, never spends $100 Billion on MX
      Missile systems, never fights shadows in Utah,
never hides inside a hollow mountain near Colorado Springs with North
      American Aerospace Defense Command
waiting orders that he press the Secret button to Blow up the Great Cities
      of Earth

Shambhala, Colorado, March 15, 1980

Homework

Homage Kenneth Koch

If I were doing my Laundry I'd wash my dirty Iran
I'd throw in my United States, and pour on the Ivory Soap, scrub up Africa,
    put all the birds and elephants back in the jungle,
I'd wash the Amazon river and clean the oily Carib & Gulf of Mexico,
Rub that smog off the North Pole, wipe up all the pipelines in Alaska,
Rub a dub dub for Rocky Flats and Los Alamos, Flush that sparkly Cesium
    out of Love Canal
Rinse down the Acid Rain over the Parthenon & Sphinx, Drain the Sludge
    out of the Mediterranean basin & make it azure again,
Put some blueing back into the sky over the Rhine, bleach the little Clouds
    so snow return white as snow,
Cleanse the Hudson Thames & Neckar, Drain the Suds out of Lake Erie
Then I'd throw big Asia in one giant Load & wash out the blood & Agent
    Orange,
Dump the whole mess of Russia and China in the wringer, squeeze out the
    tattletail Gray of U.S. Central American police state,
& put the planet in the drier & let it sit 20 minutes or an Aeon till it came
    out clean.

Boulder, April 26, 1980

After Whitman & Reznikoff

1
What Relief

If my pen hand were snapped by a Broadway truck
—What relief from writing letters to the *Nation*
disputing tyrants, war gossip, FBI—
My poems'll gather dust in Kansas libraries,
adolescent farmboys opening book covers with ruddy hands.

2
Lower East Side

That round faced woman, she owns the street with her three big dogs,
screeches at me, waddling with her shopping bag across Avenue B
Grabbing my crotch, "Why don't you talk to me?"
baring her teeth in a smile, voice loud like a taxi horn,
"Big Jerk . . . you think you're famous?"—reminds me of my mother.

April 29, 1980

Reflections at Lake Louise

I

At midnight the teacher lectures on his throne
Gongs, bells, wooden fish, tingling brass
Transcendent Doctrines, non-meditation, old dog barks
Past present future burn in Candleflame
incense fills intellects—
Mornings I wake, forgetting my dreams,
dreary hearted, lift my body out of bed
shave, wash, sit, bow down to the ground for hours.

II

Which country is real, mine or the teacher's?
Going back & forth I cross the Canada border, unguarded,
    guilty, smuggling 10,000 thoughts.

III

Sometimes my guru seems a Hell King, sometimes a King in Eternity,
    sometimes a newspaper story, sometimes familiar eyed
        father, lonely mother, hard working—
Poor man! to give me birth who may never grow up
    and earn my own living.

May 7, 1980

IV

Now the sky's clearer, clouds lifted, a patch of blue
shows above Mt. Victoria. I should go walking to the Plain of the Six
        Glaciers
but I have to eat Oryoki style, prostrate hours in the basement, study for
        Vajrayana Exams—
If I had a heart attack on the path around the lake would I be ready to face
        my mother?

Noon

V

Scandal in the Buddhafields

    The lake's covered with soft ice inches thick.

Naked, he insulted me under the glacier!

    He raped my mind on the wet granite cliffs!

He misquoted me in the white mists all over the *Nation*.

Hurrah! the Clouds drift apart!

    Big chunks of blue sky fall down!

Mount Victoria stands with a mouth full of snow.

VI

I wander this path along little Lake Louise, the teacher's too busy to see me,

my dharma friends think I'm crazy, or worse, a lonely neurotic, maybe I
    am—

Alone in the mountains, same as in snowy streets of New York.

VII

Trapped in the Guru's Chateau surrounded by 300 disciples

I could go home to Cherry Valley, Manhattan, Nevada City

to be a farmer forever, die in Lower East Side slums, sit with no lightbulbs
    in the forest,

Return to my daily mail Secretary, *Hard Times*, Junk mail and love letters,
    get wrinkled old in Manhattan

Fly out and sing poetry, bring home windmills, grow tomatoes and Mari-
    juana

chop wood, do Zazen, obey my friends, muse in Gary's Maidu Territory,
    study acorn mush,

Here I'm destined to study the Higher Tantras and be a slave of Enlighten-
    ment.

Where can I go, how choose? Either way my life stands before me,

mountains rising over the white lake 6 A.M., mist drifting between water and
    sky.

May 7–9, 1980

τεθνάκην δ ὀλίγω ’πιδεύης φαίνομ’ ἄλαια

Red cheeked boyfriends tenderly kiss me sweet mouthed
under Boulder coverlets winter springtime
hug me naked laughing & telling girl friends
        gossip till autumn

Aging love escapes with his Childish body
Monday one man visited sleeping big cocked
older mustached crooked-mouthed not the same teen-
        ager I sucked off

This kid comes on Thursdays with happy hard ons
long nights talking heart to heart reading verses
fucking hours he comes in me happy but I
        can’t get it in him

Cherub, thin-legged Southern boy once slept over
singing blues and drinking till he got horny
Wednesday night he gave me his ass I screwed him
        good luck he was drunk

Blond curl’d clear eyed gardener passing thru town
teaching digging earth in the ancient One Straw
method lay back stomach bare that night blew me
        I blew him and came

Winter dance Naropa a barefoot wild kid
jumped up grabbed me laughed at me took my hand and
ran out saying   Meet you at midnight your house
        Woke me up naked

Midnight crawled in bed with me breathed in my ear
kissed my eyelids   mouth on his cock it was soft
“Doesn’t do nothing for me,” turned on belly
        Came in behind him

Future youth I never may touch any more
Hark these Sapphics lipped by my hollow spirit
everlasting tenderness breathed in these vowels
        sighing for love still

Song your cadence formed while on May night's full moon
yellow onions tulips in fresh rain pale grass
iris pea pods radishes grew as this verse
                    blossomed in dawn light

Measure forever his face eighteen years old
green eyes blond hair muscular gold soft skin whose
god like boy's voice mocked me once three decades past
                    Come here and screw me

Breast struck   scared to look in his eyes   blood pulsing
my ears   mouth dry   tongue never moved ribs shook a
trembling fire ran down from my heart to my thighs
                    Love-sick to this day

Heavy limbed I sat in a chair and watched him
sleep naked all night afraid to kiss his mouth
tender dying waited for sun rise years a-
                    go in Manhattan

                          Boulder, May 17–June 1, 1980

Fourth Floor, Dawn,
Up All Night Writing Letters

Pigeons shake their wings on the copper church roof
out my window across the street, a bird perched on the cross
surveys the city's blue-gray clouds. Larry Rivers
'll come at 10 A.M. and take my picture. I'm taking
your picture, pigeons. I'm writing you down, Dawn.
I'm immortalizing your exhaust, Avenue A bus.
O Thought, now you'll have to think the same thing forever!

                          New York, June 7, 1980, 6:48 A.M.

Ode to Failure

Many prophets have failed, their voices silent
ghost-shouts in basements nobody heard dusty laughter in family attics
nor glanced them on park benches weeping with relief under empty sky
Walt Whitman viva'd local losers—courage to Fat Ladies in the Freak Show!
      nervous prisoners whose mustached lips dripped sweat on chow
      lines—
Mayakovsky cried, Then die! my verse, die like the workers' rank & file
      fusilladed in Petersburg!
Prospero burned his Power books & plummeted his magic wand to the
      bottom of dragon seas
Alexander the Great failed to find more worlds to conquer!
O Failure I chant your terrifying name, accept me your 54 year old Prophet
epicking Eternal Flop! I join your Pantheon of mortal bards, & hasten this
      ode with high blood pressure
rushing to the top of my skull as if I wouldn't last another minute, like the
      Dying Gaul! to
You, Lord of blind Monet, deaf Beethoven, armless Venus de Milo, headless
      Winged Victory!
I failed to sleep with every bearded rosy-cheeked boy I jacked off over
My tirades destroyed no Intellectual Unions of KGB & CIA in turtlenecks
      & underpants, their woolen suits & tweeds
I never dissolved Plutonium or dismantled the nuclear Bomb before my skull
      lost hair
I have not yet stopped the Armies of entire Mankind in their march toward
      World War III
I never got to Heaven, Nirvana, X, Whatchamacallit, I never left Earth,
I never learned to die.

Boulder, March 7 / October 10, 1980

Birdbrain!

Birdbrain runs the World!

Birdbrain is the ultimate product of Capitalism

Birdbrain chief bureaucrat of Russia, yawning

Birdbrain ran FBI 30 years appointed by F. D. Roosevelt and never chased
    Cosa Nostra!

Birdbrain apportions wheat to be burned, keep prices up on the world
    market!

Birdbrain lends money to Developing Nation police-states thru the Interna-
    tional Monetary Fund!

Birdbrain never gets laid on his own he depends on his office to pimp for
    him

Birdbrain offers brain transplants in Switzerland

Birdbrain wakes up in middle of night and arranges his sheets

I am Birdbrain!

I rule Russia Yugoslavia England Poland Argentina United States El Salva-
    dor

Birdbrain multiplies in China!

Birdbrain inhabits Stalin's corpse inside the Kremlin wall

Birdbrain dictates petrochemical agriculture in Afric desert regions!

Birdbrain lowers North California's water table sucking it up for Orange
    County Agribusiness Banks

Birdbrain harpoons whales and chews blubber in the tropics

Birdbrain clubs baby harp seals and wears their coats to Paris

Birdbrain runs the Pentagon his brother runs the CIA, Fatass Bucks!

Birdbrain writes and edits *Time Newsweek Wall Street Journal Pravda Izvestia*

Birdbrain is Pope, Premier, President, Commissar, Chairman, Senator!

Birdbrain voted Reagan President of the United States!

Birdbrain prepares Wonder Bread with refined white flour!

Birdbrain sold slaves, sugar, tobacco, alcohol

Birdbrain conquered the New World and murdered mushroom god Xo-
    chopili on Popocatepetl!

Birdbrain was President when a thousand mysterious students were ma-
    chinegunned at Tlatelulco

Birdbrain sent 20,000,000 intellectuals and Jews to Siberia, 15,000,000 never
    got back to the Stray Dog Café

Birdbrain wore a mustache & ran Germany on Amphetamines the last year
    of World War II

Birdbrain conceived the Final Solution to the Jewish Problem in Europe

Birdbrain carried it out in Gas Chambers

Birdbrain borrowed Lucky Luciano the Mafia from jail to secure Sicily for
    U.S. Birdbrain against the Reds

Birdbrain manufactured guns in the Holy Land and sold them to white
    goyim in South Africa

Birdbrain supplied helicopters to Central America generals, kill a lot of
    restless Indians, encourage a favorable business climate

Birdbrain began a war of terror against Israeli Jews

Birdbrain sent out Zionist planes to shoot Palestinian huts outside Beirut

Birdbrain outlawed Opiates on the world market

Birdbrain formed the Black Market in Opium

Birdbrain's father shot skag in hallways of the lower East Side

Birdbrain organized Operation Condor to spray poison fumes on the mari-
    juana fields of Sonora

Birdbrain got sick in Harvard Square from smoking Mexican grass

Birdbrain arrived in Europe to Conquer cockroaches with Propaganda

Birdbrain became a great International Poet and went around the world
    praising the Glories of Birdbrain

I declare Birdbrain to be victor in the Poetry Contest

He built the World Trade Center on New York Harbor waters without
    regard where the toilets emptied—

Birdbrain began chopping down the Amazon Rainforest to build a wood-
    pulp factory on the river bank

Birdbrain in Iraq attacked Birdbrain in Iran

Birdbrain in Belfast throws bombs at his mother's ass

Birdbrain wrote *Das Kapital*! authored the *Bible*! penned *The Wealth of
    Nations*!

Birdbrain's humanity, he built the Rainbow Room on top of Rockefeller
    Center so we could dance

He invented the Theory of Relativity so Rockwell Corporation could make
    Neutron Bombs at Rocky Flats in Colorado

Birdbrain's going to see how long he can go without coming

Birdbrain thinks his dong will grow big that way

Birdbrain sees a new Spy in the Market Platz in Dubrovnik outside the
    Eyeglass Hotel—

Birdbrain wants to suck your cock in Europe, he takes life very seriously,
    brokenhearted you won't cooperate—

Birdbrain goes to heavy duty Communist Countries so he can get KGB
    girlfriends while the sky thunders—

Birdbrain realized he was Buddha by meditating

Birdbrain's afraid he's going to blow up the planet so he wrote this poem to
    be immortal—

       Hotel Subrovka, Dubrovnik, October 14, 1980, 4:30 A.M.

Eroica

White marble pillars in the Rector's courtyard
at the end of a marble-white street in the walled city of Dubrovnik—
All the fleet sunk, Empire foundered, Doges all skeletons & Turks vanished
    to dust
World Wars passed by with cannonfire mustard gas & amphetamine-wired
    Führers—
Beethoven's drum roll beats again in the stone household
White jackets and Black ties the makers of Dissonant thunderbolts concen-
    trate on music sheets
Bowing low, the Timpanist bends ear to his Copper Kettledrums' heroic
    vibration—
Bassists with hornrim glasses and beards, young and old pluck ensemble with
    middle fingers at thin animal strings—
Bassoonists press lips to wooden hollow wands,
The Violinists fiddle up and down excitedly—First Violin
with a stubborn beard (at his music stand with a young girl in black evening
    dress) waits patiently the orchestra tuning and tweedling to a C—
The Conductor moves his baton & elbows to get the Beethoven bounce
    jumping
Sweating in the cool Adriatic air at 10:15 white collar round his neck, black
    longtailed jacket & celluloid cuffs, high heeled black shoes—he turns
    the glossy page of the First Movement—
The brasses ring out, trumpets puffing, French horns blaring for Napoleon!
Conductor whips it to a Bam Bam Bamb.

But Beethoven got disgusted with Napoleon & scratched his hero name
    off the Dedication page—

Now the Funeral March! I used to listen to this over the radio in Paterson
    during the Spanish Civil War—
At last I know it's the bassoons Carry the wails of high elegy
at last I see the cellos in their chairs, violinists swaying forward, bassmen
    standing looking sad
as all bow together the mournful lament & dead march for Europe,
The end of the liberty of Dubrovnik, the idiot cry March on Moscow!
Dubrovnik's musicians take revenge on Napoleon,
by playing Beethoven's heroic chords in a Castle by the sea at Night—
Electric Globes on wrought iron stands light the year 1980 (Emperor Napo-
    leon & Emperor Beethoven alike snoring skulls)

in the Rector's house reconstructed a Concert Hall for Tourists
Beethoven's heart pulses in the drums, his breath huffs and puffs, the black
      robed violin lady & the bearded Concert-master swing their arms.
The Funeral Fugue Begins! The Death of Kings, the screaming of Revolu-
      tionary multitudes
as the Middle Ages tumble before Industrial Revolution
a Mysterious Clarion! an extended brassy breath!
serene rows of island cities in violin language,
working back and forth from violins to bassoons—
The drum beats the footfalls of Coffin Carriers—
over the roofs the lilt of a sad melody emerges,
like silent cats on red tile, the strings Climb up sadder—
a broken-muzzled lion's head sticks out of a white plaster Fountain wall in
      the courtyard
Now rats and lions chase each other round the orchestra from fiddle string
      to bass gut staccato—
Hunting horns echo mellow against marble staircase blocks—
Napoleon has himself crowned Emperor by the Pope!
Unbelievable! Atom Bombs drop on Japan! Hitler attacks Poland! The Allies
      fire-bomb Dresden alive! America goes to war—
Now Violins and Horns rise Counterpoint to a thunderous bombing! Kettle-
      drums war up! Bam Bamb! End of Scherzo!

Finale—Tiptoeing thru history, Pizzicato on the Bass Cello & Violins as
      Time marches on.
Running thru the veins, the lilt of victory, the Liberation of man from the
      State!
It's a big dance, a festival, every instrument joined in the Yea Saying!
Who wouldn't be happy meeting Beethoven at Jena in 1812 or 1980! It's a
      small world, standing up to sing like a big beating heart!
Getting ready for the Ecstatic European Dance! Off we go on one ear, then
      another, Titanic Footsteps over Middle Europe—
And a waltz to quiet down the joy, But the big dance will come back like
      Eternity like God like
a hurricane an Earthquake a Beethoven Creation
a new Europe! A new world of Liberty almost 200 years ago
Prophesied thru brass and catgut, wood bow & breath
Gigantic Heartbeat of Beethoven's Deaf Longing—
The Prophecy of a Solid happy peaceful Just Europe—
Big as the Trumpets of the Third Symphony.
The Unification of the World! The triumph of the Moon! Mankind liberated
      to Music!

Enough to make you cry in the middle of the Rector's Palace, thinking of
        Einstein's
Atom Bomb exploded out of his head—
In the middle of a note, an interruption! Cloudburst!
The Conductor wipes his head & runs away,
basses and cellos lift up their woods and vanish into Cloakrooms,
French Horns Violins and Bassoons lift eyes to the shower & scatter under
        balconies
in the middle of a note, in the middle of a big Satyric Footstep,
Pouf! Rain pours thru the sky!
Musicians and audience flee the stone floor'd courtyard,
Atrium of the Rector's House Dubrovnik October 14, 1980, 10:45 P.M.

"Defending the Faith"

Stopping on the bus from Novi Pazar in the rain
I took a leak by Maglić Castle walls
and talked with the dogs on Ivar River Bank
They showed me their teeth & barked a long long time.

October 20, 1980

Capitol Air

I don't like the government where I live
I don't like dictatorship of the Rich
I don't like bureaucrats telling me what to eat
I don't like Police dogs sniffing round my feet

I don't like Communist Censorship of my books
I don't like Marxists complaining about my looks
I don't like Castro insulting members of my sex
Leftists insisting we got the mystic Fix

I don't like Capitalists selling me gasoline Coke
Multinationals burning Amazon trees to smoke
Big Corporation takeover media mind
I don't like the Top-bananas that're robbing Guatemala banks blind

I don't like K.G.B. Gulag concentration camps
I don't like the Maoists' Cambodian Death Dance
15 Million were killed by Stalin Secretary of Terror
He has killed our old Red Revolution for ever

I don't like Anarchists screaming Love Is Free
I don't like the C.I.A. they killed John Kennedy
Paranoiac tanks sit in Prague and Hungary
But I don't like counterrevolution paid for by the C.I.A.

Tyranny in Turkey or Korea Nineteen Eighty
I don't like Right Wing Death Squad Democracy
Police State Iran Nicaragua yesterday
Laissez-faire please Government keep your secret police offa me

I don't like Nationalist Supremacy White or Black
I don't like Narcs & Mafia marketing Smack
The General bullying Congress in his tweed vest
The President building up his Armies in the East & West

I don't like Argentine police Jail torture Truths
Government Terrorist takeover Salvador news
I don't like Zionists acting Nazi Storm Troop
Palestine Liberation cooking Israel into Moslem soup

Capitol Air

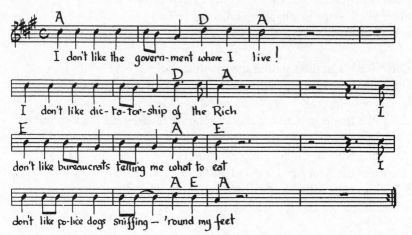

I don't like the Crown's Official Secrets Act
You can get away with murder in the Government that's a fact
Security cops teargassing radical kids
In Switzerland or Czechoslovakia God Forbids

In America it's Attica in Russia it's Lubianka Wall
In China if you disappear you wouldn't know yourself at all
Arise Arise you citizens of the world use your lungs
Talk back to the Tyrants all they're afraid of is your tongues

Two hundred Billion dollars inflates World War
In United States every year They're asking for more
Russia's got as much in tanks and laser planes
Give or take Fifty Billion we can blow out everybody's brains

School's broke down 'cause History changes every night
Half the Free World nations are Dictatorships of the Right
The only place socialism worked was in Gdansk, Bud
The Communist world's stuck together with prisoners' blood

The Generals say they know something worth fighting for
They never say what till they start an unjust war
Iranian hostage Media Hysteria sucked
The Shah ran away with 9 Billion Iranian bucks

Kermit Roosevelt and his U.S. dollars overthrew Mossadegh
They wanted his oil then they got Ayatollah's dreck
They put in the Shah and they trained his police the Savak
All Iran was our hostage quarter-century That's right Jack

Bishop Romero wrote President Carter to stop
Sending guns to El Salvador's Junta so he got shot
Ambassador White blew the whistle on the White House lies
Reagan called him home cause he looked in the dead nuns' eyes

Half the voters didn't vote they knew it was too late
Newspaper headlines called it a big Mandate
Some people voted for Reagan eyes open wide
3 out of 4 didn't vote for him That's a Landslide

Truth may be hard to find but Falsehood's easy
Read between the lines our Imperialism is sleazy

But if you think the People's State is your Heart's Desire
Jump right back in the frying pan from the fire

The System the System in Russia & China the same
Criticize the System in Budapest lose your name
Coca Cola Pepsi Cola in Russia & China come true
Khrushchev yelled in Hollywood "We will bury You"

America and Russia want to bomb themselves Okay
Everybody dead on both sides   Everybody pray
All except the Generals in caves where they can hide
And fuck each other in the ass waiting for the next free ride

No hope Communism no hope Capitalism Yeah
Everybody's lying on both sides Nyeah nyeah nyeah
The bloody iron curtain of American Military Power
Is a mirror image of Russia's red Babel-Tower

Jesus Christ was spotless but was Crucified by the Mob
Law & Order Herod's hired soldiers did the job
Flowerpower's fine but innocence has got no Protection
The man who shot John Lennon had a Hero-worshipper's connection

The moral of this song is that the world is in a horrible place
Scientific Industry devours the human race
Police in every country armed with Tear Gas & TV
Secret Masters everywhere bureaucratize for you & me

Terrorists and police together build a lowerclass Rage
Propaganda murder manipulates the upperclass Stage
Can't tell the difference 'tween a turkey & a provocateur
If you're feeling confused the Government's in there for sure

Aware Aware wherever you are   No Fear
Trust your heart Don't ride your Paranoia dear
Breathe together with an ordinary mind
Armed with Humor Feed & Help Enlighten   Woe Mankind

                                    Frankfurt–New York, December 15, 1980

APPENDIX

Notes

Epigraphs from Original Editions

Dedications

Acknowledgments

Introduction by William Carlos Williams to Empty Mirror

Introduction by William Carlos Williams to Howl

Author's Cover Writ

Index of Proper Names

Notes

Notes were composed 1961–1984 in collaboration with Fernanda Pivano, Italian translator; Jean-Jacques Lebel, Mary Beach and Claude Pelieu, Gérard-Georges Lemaire and Philippe Mikriammos, French translators; as well as Carl Weissner, Heiner Bastien, Bernd Samland, Jürgen Schmidt and Michael Kellner, German translators. Ever-patient confidante, guide, adviser and scholar Fernanda Pivano has borne the burden of pioneer interpretation of American personal and ephemeral references in these texts to her Italian readers, and other translators, for almost a quarter century. Musician-poet Steven Taylor integrated notes from four languages. The author edited and expanded the work through Summer 1984. Poet Philip Whalen, Sensei, aided interpretation of Buddhist terminology.

A.G.

I
EMPTY MIRROR: GATES OF WRATH
(1947–1952)

The four poems that follow, dedicated to Neal Cassady in the first years of our friendship, were set among "Earlier Poems: 1947," appended to *Gates of Wrath*, a book of rhymed verse. These compositions, college imitations of Marlowe, Marvell and Donne (and Hart Crane), are now relocated among these notes. Subsequent poems of Summer 1948, also imitative in style, are placed with the main body of the collection because they deal with primary visionary experience.

A FURTHER PROPOSAL

Come live with me and be my love,
And we will some old pleasures prove.
Men like me have paid in verse
This costly courtesy, or curse;

But I would bargain with my art
(As to the mind, now to the heart),
My symbols, images, and signs
Please me more outside these lines.

For your share and recompense,
You will be taught another sense:
The wisdom of the subtle worm
Will turn most perfect in your form.

Not that your soul need tutored be
By intellectual decree,
But graces that the mind can share
Will make you, as more wise, more fair,

Till all the world's devoted thought
Find all in you it ever sought,
And even I, of skeptic mind,
A Resurrection of a kind.

This compliment, in my own way,
For what I would receive, I pay;
Thus all the wise have writ thereof,
And all the fair have been their love.

1947

A LOVER'S GARDEN

How vainly lovers marvel, all
To make a body, mind, and soul,
Who, winning one white night of grace,
Will weep and rage a year of days,
Or muse forever on a kiss,
If won by a more sad mistress—
Are all these lovers, then, undone
By him and me, who love alone?

O, have the virtues of the mind
Been all for this one love designed?
As seconds on the clock do move,
Each marks another thought of love;
Thought follows thought, and we devise
Each minute to antithesize,
Till, as the hour chimes its tune,
Dialectic, we commune.

The argument our minds create
We do, abed, substantiate;
Nor we disdain, in our delight,
To flatter the old Stagirite:
For in one speedy moment, we
Endure the whole Eternity,
And in our darkened shapes have found
The greater world that we surround.

In this community, the soul
Doth make its act impersonal,
As, locked in a mechanic bliss,
It shudders into nothingness—

Three characters of each may die
To dramatize that Unity.
Timed, placed, and acting thus, the while,
We sit and sing, and sing and smile.

What life is this? What pleasure mine!
Such as no image can insign:
Nor sweet music, understood,
Soft at night, in solitude
At a window, will enwreathe
Such stillness on my brow: I breathe,
And walk on earth, and act my will,
And cry Peace! Peace! and all is still.

Though here, it seems, I must remain,
My thoughtless world, whereon men strain
Through lives of motion without sense,
Farewell! in this benevolence—
That all men may, as I, arrange
A love as simple, sweet, and strange
As few men know; nor can I tell,
But only imitate farewell.

1947

LOVE LETTER

    Let not the sad perplexity
      Of absent love unhumor thee:
  Sighs, tears, and oaths, and laughter I have spent
To make my play with thee resolve in merriment;
      For wisest critics past agree
      The truest love is comedy.
Will thou not weary of the tragic argument?

    Wouldst thou make love perverse, and then
      Preposterous and crabbed, my pen?
  Tempt Eros not (he is more wise than I)
To suck the apple of thy sad absurdity.
      Love, who is a friend to men,
      You'd make a Devil of again:
Then should I be once more exiled, alas, in thee.

    Make peace with me, and in my mind,
      With Eros, angel of the mind,
  Who loves me, loving thee, and in our bliss
Is loved by all of us and finds his happiness.
      Such simple pleasures are designed
      To entertain our days, I find,
And so shalt thee, when next we make a night of this.

This spring we'll be not merely mad,
    But absent lovers, therefore sad,
  So we'll be no more happy than we ought—
That simple love of Eros may be strangely taught.
    And wit will seldom make me glad
    That spring hath not what winter had,
Therefore these nights are darkened shadows of my thought.

Grieve in a garden, then, and in a summer's twilight,
  Think of thy love, for spring is lost to me.
  Or as you will, and if the moon be white,
  Let all thy soul to music married be,
To magic, nightingales, and immortality;
  And, if it pleases thee, why, think on Death;
  For Death is strange upon a summer night,
  The thought of it may make thee catch thy breath,
And meditation hath itself a great beauty;
Wherefore if thou must weep, now I must mourn with thee.

                          Easter Sunday, 1947

DAKAR DOLDRUMS

I

Most dear, and dearest at this moment most,
Since this my love for thee is thus more free
Than that I cherished more dear and lost;
Most near, now nearest where I fly from thee:
Thy love most consummated is in absence,
Half for the trust I have for thee in mind,
Half for the pleasures of thee in remembrance—
Thou art most full and fair of all thy kind.

Not half so fair as thee is fate I fear,
Wherefore my sad departure from this season
Wherein for some love of me thou held'st me dear,
While I betray thee for a better reason.
I am a brutish agonist, I know
Lust or its consummation cannot ease
These miseries of mind, this mask like sorrow:
It is myself, not thee, shall make my peace.

Yet, O sweet soul, to have possessed thy love,
The meditations of thy mind for me,
Hath half deceived a thought that ill shall prove.
It was a grace of fate, this scene of comedy
Foretold more tragic acts in my short age.
Yet 'tis no masque of mine, no mere sad play
Spectacular upon an empty stage—
My life is more unreal, another way.

To lie with thee, to touch thee with desire,
Enrage the summer nights with thy mere presence—
Flesh hath such joy, such sweetness, and such fire!
The white ghost fell on me, departing thence.
Henceforth I must perform a winter mood;
Belovèd gestures freeze in bitter ice,
Eyes glare through a pale jail of solitude,
Fear chills my mind: Here endeth all my bliss!

Cursed may be this month of Fall! I fail
My full and fair and near and dear and kind.
I but endure my role, my own seas sail,
Far from the sunny shores within thy mind.
So this departure shadoweth mine end:
Ah! what poor human cometh unto me,
Since now the snowy spectre doth descend,
Henceforth I shall in fear and anger flee.

II
Lord, forgive my passions, they are old,
And restive as the years that I have known.
To what abandonments have I foretold
My bondage? And have mine own love undone!
How mad my youth, my sacramental passage!
Yet I dream these September journeys true:
When five days flowed like sickness in this knowledge,
I vomited out my mockery, all I knew.

III
Five nights upon the deep I suffered presage,
Five dawns familiar seabirds cried me pale:
I care not now, for I have seen an image
In the sea that was no Nightingale.

—My love, and doth still that rare figurine
In thy sad garden sing, now I am gone?
Sweet carols that I made, and caroller serene,
They broke my heart, and sang for thee alone.
Secret to thee the Nightingale was Death;
So all the figures are that I create.
For thee awhile I breathed another breath,
To make my Death thy Beauty imitate.—

More terrible than these are the vast visions
Of the sea, nor comprehensible.
Last night I stared upon the Cuban mountains,
Tragic in the mist, as on my soul,
Star studded in the dark, sea shaded round

And still, a funeral of Emperors,
Wind wound in ruined shrouds and crescent crowned
And tombed in desolation on dead shores.

The place was dread with age: the evening tide,
Eternal wife of death that washed these bones,
Turns back to sea by night, eternal bride:
She clasped my ship and rocked to hear its groans.
I did imagine I had known this sea,
Had been an audience to this before;
The place was prescient, like a great stage in me,
As out of a dream that late I dream no more.

I did imagine I had known this sea;
It raged like a great beast in my passage,
Till I, enragèd creature, anciently
Engendered here, cried out upon mine image:
"How long in absence O thou journeyest,
Ages my soul and ages! Here ever home
In this sea's endangerments thou sufferest;
And do, and do, and now my will hath done!"

Ah, love, I tell thee true, nor false affix
The solitude I watched by th'iron prow:
While I interpreted I stared me sick
At transformations in the tides below;
For the grim bride rose up, and all surrounding,
Carried me through the star-piercèd air,
Till I cried Stay! and Stay! surrendering
My movèd soul in flight to faster fear.

As I dived then I cried, delving all depthed in foam,
"Now close in weeds thy wave-lipped womb, mistress!"
But she ope'd her watering wounds and drew me down
And drove me dancing through the white-wreathed darkness.
Though I stood still to memorize the deep,
And woke my eyes wild-wide upon the height,
My soul it feareth its descent to keep,
My soul it turneth in its famous flight.

IV
Ha! now I die or no, I fear this tide
Carrieth me still, perishing, past where I stood,
So mild, to gaze whereat I long had died,
Or shall, as well, in future solitude.
What other shores are there I still remember?
I was in a pale land, I looked through a pure vision
In a pallid dawn, with a half-vacant glare.
Alas! what harbour hath the imagination?

O the transparent past hath a white port,
Tinted in the eye; it doth appear
Sometime on dark days, much by night, to sport
Bright shades like dimes of silver shining there,
On red dull sands on green volcanic shores.
I thought these stanzas out this cloudy noon,
Past Cuba now, past Haiti's stony jaws,
In the last passage to Dakar. The moon

Alone was full as it had been all year,
Orange and strange at dawn. It was my eyes,
Not Africa, did this: they shined so pure
Each island floated by a sweet surprise.
Coins, then, on Cape Verde's peakèd cones
Sparkle out with pallors various.
It makes me God to pass these mortal towns:
Real people sicken here upon slopes sulphurous.

So in my years I saw my serious cities
Colored with Love and chiming with Nightingales,
Architectural with fantasies,
With fools in schools and geniuses in jails.
When in sweet vivid dreams such rainbows rise,
and spectral children dance among the music,
I watch them still: hot emeralds are their eyes!
My eyes are ice, alas! How white I wake!

v
Twenty days have drifted in the wake
Of this slow agèd ship that carries coal
From Texas to Dakar. I, for the sake
Of little but my causelessness of soul,
Am carried out of my chill hemisphere
To unfamiliar summer on the earth.
I spend my days to meditate a fear;
Each day I give the sea is one of death.

This is the last night of the outward journeying,
The darkness falleth westward unto thee;
And I must end my labors of this evening,
And all the last long night, and all this day:
It doth give peace, thus to torment the soul,
Till it is sundered from its forms and sense,
Till it surrendereth its knowledge whole,
And stares on the world out of a sleepless trance.

So on these stanzas doth a peace descend,
Now I have journeyed through these images
To come upon no image in the end.
So are we consummated in these passages,

Most near and dear and far apart in fate.
As I mean no mere sweet philosophy,
So I, unto a world I must create,
Turn with no promise and no prophecy.

South Atlantic, 1947

page

Sweet Levinsky

27 LEVINSKY: Leon Levinsky is a character in Jack Kerouac's *The Town and the City*.

A Poem on America

72 ACIS AND GALATEA . . . VERSILOV: In Fyodor Dostoyevsky's penultimate novel, *A Raw Youth*, hero Dolgoruki's father, Versilov, the ex-revolutionary, wore a hair shirt and mused on Poussin's painting.

II
THE GREEN AUTOMOBILE
(1953–1954)

The Green Automobile

94 NEAL: Neal Cassady, to whom the poem is dedicated.

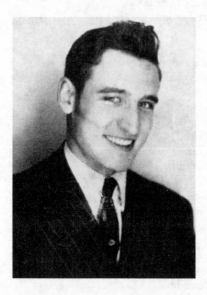

Neal Cassady (1925–1968) in his first suit, bought second hand in China-town, 1946, the day before his return to Denver on Greyhound bus.

Sakyamuni Coming Out from the Mountain

98 SAKYAMUNI: Buddha (563–483 B.C.) Sage born to warrior-caste Sakya family; human aspect of Buddha. Poem interprets noted Chinese painting, Sung dynasty.

98 ARHAT: Self-liberated sage who has not taken Bodhisattva's vows to liberate all sentient beings.

Havana 1953

100 CAB CALLOWAY: (b. 1907) Ex-law student, stage-show black jazz singer, slick-haired satin-suited early hipster popular band leader who composed and sang "Minnie the Moocher," "Are You Hep to the Jive," "Are You All Reet" and "Hi-De-Ho Man."

101 VIVA JALISCO: Mexican state mariachi music macho whoop, like Viva Texas!

101 FREER: Gallery of Oriental Art, Mall adjunct to Washington, D.C., Smithsonian Institution.

Siesta in Xbalba

105 UXMAL . . . : Proper names mentioned in the first part of the poem are those of ruined cities. Xbalba, translatable as Morning Star in Region Obscure, or Hope, and pronounced Chivalvá, is the area in Chiapas between the Tabasco border and the Usumacinta River at the edge of the Petén rain forest; the boundary of lower Mexico and Guatemala today is thereabouts. The locale was considered a Purgatory, or Limbo (the legend is vague), in the (Old) Mayan Empire. To the large tree at the crest of what is now called Mount Don Juan, at the foot of which this poem was written, ancient craftsmen came to complete work left unfinished at their death.

On Burroughs' Work

122 Written on receiving early "routines" from Burroughs in Tangier, including *Dr. Benway in the Operating Room* and *The Talking Asshole.*

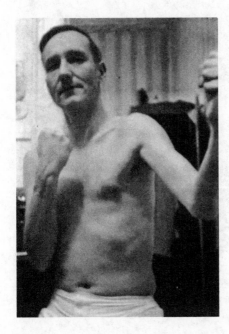

W. S. Burroughs, 206 East 7th Street, N.Y.C., Fall 1953, at time assembling "Yage Letters" and visioning Interzone Market Naked Lunch. Photo by A.G.

III
HOWL, BEFORE AND AFTER: SAN FRANCISCO BAY AREA
(1955–1956)

Malest Cornifici Tuo Catullo

131 MALEST, CORNIFICI, TUO CATULLO: Catullus #38, probably addressed to the erotic "new poet" friend of Catullus, a verse note beginning "I'm ill, Cornificus, your Catullus is ill," asking for a little friendly word, and ending *"Maestius lacrimis Simonideis"*—"Sad as the tears of old Simonides." Ginsberg to Kerouac, on meeting Peter Orlovsky.

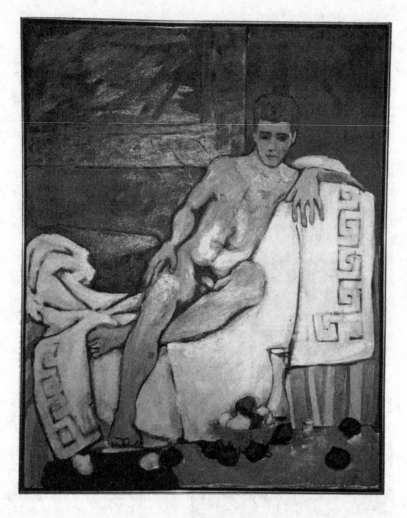

Peter Orlovsky by Robert LaVigne, 1954, San Francisco. Author met Orlovsky immediately after viewing this painting, 1403 Gough Street.

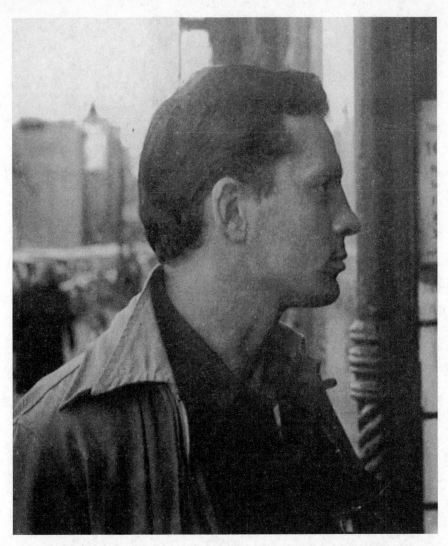

Jack Kerouac on Avenue A, Manhattan, 1953, at time of *The Subterraneans*.
Photo by A.G.

Dream Record: June 8, 1955

132 HUNCKE: Herbert E. Huncke (1915–1996), American prose writer. Friend and
early contact for Kerouac, Burroughs and the author in explorations circa
1945 around Times Square, where he hung out at center of the hustling
world in early stages of his opiate addictions. He served as connection to
midtown's floating population for Dr. Alfred Kinsey's interviews with that
population segment in his celebrated surveys of human sexuality. Huncke
introduced Burroughs and others to the slang, information and ritual of the
emergent "hip" or "beat" subculture. See the author's preface to Huncke's

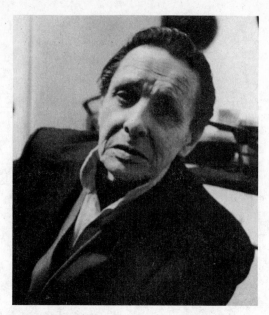

Herbert Huncke, 1983. Photo by A.G.

book of sketches and stories, *The Evening Sun Turned Crimson* (Cherry Valley, N.Y.: Cherry Valley Editions, 1980): "Huncke's figure appears variously in Clellon Holmes's novel *Go*, there is an excellent early portrait in Kerouac's first bildungsroman *The Town and the City*, fugitive glimpses of Huncke as Gotham morphinist appear in William Lee's *Junkie*, Burroughs' dry first classic of prose. He walked on the snowbank docks with shoes full of blood into the middle of *Howl*, and is glimpsed in short sketches by Herb Gold, Carl Solomon and Irving Rosenthal scattered through subsequent decades.... Kerouac always maintained that he was a great story teller."

Howl

134 PARADISE ALLEY: A slum courtyard N.Y. Lower East Side, site of Kerouac's *Subterraneans*, 1958.

139 ELI ELI LAMMA LAMMA SABACTHANI: "My God, my God, why have you forsaken me?" Christ's last words from the cross ("Eli, Eli, lama sabachthani": Matthew 27:46).

139 MOLOCH: Or Molech, the Canaanite fire god, whose worship was marked by parents burning their children as propitiatory sacrifice. "And thou shalt not let any of thy seed pass through the fire to Molech" (Leviticus 18:21).

A Supermarket in California

144 GARCÍA LORCA
Not for one moment, old beautiful Walt Whitman,
have I failed to see your beard full of butterflies
nor your corduroy shoulders worn down by the moon . . .
Not for one moment, virile beauty

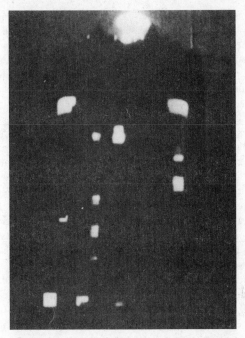

Sir Francis Drake Hotel tower, Powell and Sutter Streets, San Francisco, seen from Nob Hill, original motif of Moloch section of Howl, Part II. Photo 1959 by Harry Redl. (See n.p. 139.)

page

who in mountains of coal, posters and railroads,
dreamed of being a river and sleeping like a river
with whatever comrade would lay on your breast
the little pain of an ignorant leopard.

—Federico García Lorca,
"Oda a Walt Whitman" (*adapted by Allen Ginsberg*)

America

154 WOBBLIES: International Workers of the World, strong on Northwest coast, some Anarchist-Buddhist-Populist tinge, primarily lumber and mining workers, pre–World War I activist precursors to organized American labor unions. For "I dreamed I saw Joe Hill last night . . ." see *Little Red Song Book*.

155 TOM MOONEY: (1882–1942) Labor leader accused of bomb-throwing, 1919 San Francisco Preparedness Day Parade; imprisoned still protesting innocence till pardoned 1939 by Governor Earl Warren; cause célèbre in left-wing populist circles worldwide.

155 SACCO & VANZETTI: Nicola Sacco and Bartolomeo Vanzetti, Italian-American anarchists convicted of robbery and murder, executed in Massachusetts, 1927, after international protest. Vanzetti's last speech to the court: "I found myself compelled to fight back from my eyes the tears, and quanch my heart trobling to my throat to not weep before him. But Sacco's name will live in the hearts of the people when your name, your laws, institutions and your false god are

but a dim rememoring of a cursed past in which man was wolf to the man." And a letter to his son, April 1927: "If it had not been for this thing I might have live out my life talking at street corners to scorning men. I might have die unmarked, unknown, a failure. Now we are not a failure. This is our career and our triumph. Never in our full life could we hope to do such work for tolerance, for justice, for man's understanding of man, as now we do by accident.... Our words—our lives—our pains: nothing. The taking of our lives—lives of a good shoemaker and a poor fish peddler—all! That last moment, belongs to us—that agony is our triumph."

155 SCOTTSBORO BOYS: Nine black youths arrested 1931 by mob in Paint Rock, Alabama, jailed in Scottsboro, set up and sentenced to death for alleged train rape of two white girls, despite popular belief in their innocence. Their cause focused international attention on Southern U.S. legal injustice and racial discrimination. Supreme Court reversed convictions twice, setting landmark precedents for adequate counsel representation and fair race-balanced juries.

155 SCOTT NEARING: (1883–1983) Sociology professor bounced from Academe for anti-World War I views, Socialist congressional candidate 1919, staunch pro-Soviet historian and autobiographer. In old age, Nearing evolved into "new age" counterculture role model with publication of *Living the Good Life* (pioneering, building, organic gardening, cooperation and vegetarian living on a self-subsistent Vermont homestead; working plans for a twenty-year project), 1954; and *The Maple Sugar Book* (account of the art and history of sugaring; practical details for modern sugar-making; remarks on pioneering as a way of living in the twentieth century), 1950; both coauthored with Helen Nearing (reprint ed., New York: Schocken Books, 1970, 1971).

155 MOTHER BLOOR: Ella Reeve Bloor (1862–1951) Communist leader, writer, traveling union strike organizer and speechmaker.

155 EWIG-WEIBLICHE: (German) Eternal feminine.

155 ISRAEL AMTER: (1881–1954) A leading American Communist, Yiddish part of movement, traveling orator, ran for N.Y. governor 1930s.

Fragment 1956

157 TOMBS: New York City jailhouse.

Afternoon Seattle

158 MANDALA: Map of psychological universe, generally Hindu-Buddhist. See Time Wheel Mandala, p. 590.

158 SNYDER: Gary Snyder (b. 1930) Naturalist-woodsman, poet, early U.S. student of Zen, hitchhiked Northwest with author 1956, as described in poem. Prototype for Kerouac's *Dharma Bums* hero.

158 GREEN PARROT THEATER: First Avenue vaudeville movie playhouse, whose marquee was celebrated for Art Nouveau design and extravagant variety of neon colors in tail of its green parrot insignia. At time of poem, the 1930s Nelson Eddy–Jeanette MacDonald movie *Maytime* was rerun. See *Maytime* song quotes, "Iron Horse."

158 FRANK H. LITTLE: His dry mummy stood in a glass case in a curio shop on Seattle waterfront, as described.

IV
REALITY SANDWICHES: EUROPE! EUROPE!
(1957–1959)

To Aunt Rose

193 *THE ATTIC OF THE PAST AND EVERLASTING MINUTE*: Books of lyric poetry by the author's father, Louis Ginsberg (1896–1976). *The Everlasting Minute* was published 1937 by Horace Liveright, N.Y. Certain poems were anthologized in various editions of Louis Untermeyer's standard anthology *Modern American and British Poetry*.

Laughing Gas

198 SATORI: (Japanese) Sudden flash of enlightenment, awakening a glimpse of ordinary mind, often result of prolonged Zazen meditation practice. See also opening pages of Kerouac, *Satori in Paris* (New York: Grove Press, 1966). (There are various kinds of Satori: it is believed that a Zen master can recognize what kind and how profound, long lasting, or life-changing some person's Satori is.—P.W.)

198 SUTRAS: Buddhist discourses or dialogues, joining teacher and student in transmission of Dharma, or doctrine, over generations.

201 CZARDAS: East European dance, wildly spirited.

202 SHERMAN ADAMS: Assistant to President Eisenhower, who did resign; involved in minor White House scandal for accepting fur coat as gift.

V
KADDISH AND RELATED POEMS
(1959–1960)

Kaddish

217 FIRST POISONOUS TOMATOES OF AMERICA: Russian immigrants to U.S. at turn of the century had not seen tomatoes; some believed them poisonous.

218 YPSL: Young People's Socialist League.

221 GRAF ZEPPELIN: Refers to giant hydrogen-inflated German airship *Hindenburg*, destroyed in flames with 36 deaths while mooring at Lakehurst, N.J., May 6, 1937, arrived on its first transatlantic crossing.

222 PARCAE: The Three Fates: goddess Clotho, spinning thread of life; Lachesis, holding and fixing length; and Atropos, whose shears cut thread's end.

222 THE GREEN TABLE: German Jooss Ballet's 1930s classic, wherein warmonger capitalists in black tie and tails pirouette round long green table at diplomatic conference, arranging mobilization, combat, arms profit, refugee fate and division of spoils, with Death figure dancing in foreground throughout eight-scene parable WWI.

222 DEBS: Eugene Victor Debs (1855–1926) Rail union organizer, founder IWW, "one big union," Socialist presidential candidate 1900–1920, ran from Atlanta

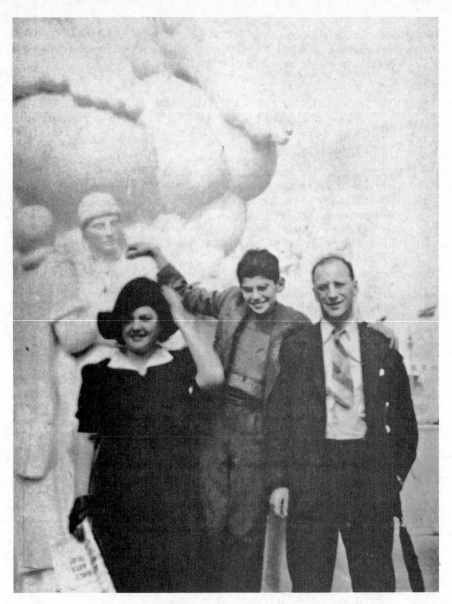

Naomi, Allen, and Louis Ginsberg, New York World's Fair, June 15, 1940.

page

penitentiary during ten-year sentence under so-called Espionage Act for speech denouncing U.S. entry into WWI; received nearly 1 million votes 1920.

222 ALTGELD: John P. Altgeld (1847–1902) First Democratic governor of Illinois (1892–1896) since Civil War. Pardoned surviving anarchists of 1886 Haymar-

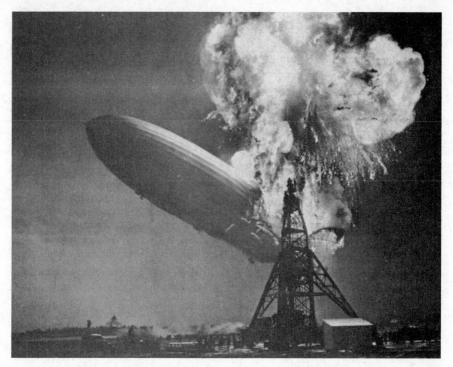

Hindenberg Explosion. (See n.p. 221.) The Bettmann Archive, Inc.

page

ket Riots, initiated prison reform, protected laboring women and reformed child labor laws, opposed use of fed troops to suppress RR strikes, incorruptible, rich entering governorship, which he left penniless. See Vachel Lindsay's poem "The Eagle That Is Forgotten": "Sleep softly . . . eagle forgotten . . . under the stone. Time has its way with you there, and clay has its own. / 'We have buried him now,' thought his foes, and in secret rejoiced . . . / Sleep on, O brave hearted, O wise man, that kindled the flame— / To live in mankind is far more than to live in a name . . ."—Vachel Lindsay, *Collected Poems* (New York: Macmillan, 1925).

222 LITTLE BLUE BOOKS: Tiny blue-covered booklets, first mass-market paperbacks in U.S., freethinking content, distributed from immigrant socialist town Girard, southeast Kansas, by E. Haldeman-Julius (1889–1951), whose mission was to educate the masses by offering great literature at cheapest price, including all Shakespeare, much Oscar Wilde, Tom Paine, Clarence Darrow, Upton Sinclair, the agnostic orator Robert Ingersoll, and Mark Twain. For publishing *The FBI—The Basis of an American Police State, The Alarming Methods of J. Edgar Hoover*, by Clifton Bennett, 1948, Haldeman-Julius was hounded by FBI; withdrew *The Black International*, by Joseph McCabe, 20-pamphlet series exposing relation between Roman Catholic Church and fascist Axis.

224 ZHDANOV: Andrei Aleksandrovich Zhdanov (1896–1948) Bolshevik Central Committee Secy., Politburo member, etc., later noted for "anticosmopolitan" chauvinistic pronouncements, 1946, as Stalin's literary and cultural affairs

chief. "Doctors' Plot" accusations that ten Jewish Kremlin physicians were responsible for the death of Zhdanov and other high military figures signaled a purging of the Party in the year preceding Stalin's death in 1953.

225 METRAZOL: Used with insulin for shock treatment in common but now abandoned mental therapy experiments.

225 STENKA RAZIN: Russian song, name of folk-heroic Cossack river pirate, tortured and killed in Moscow in 1671.

226 WORKMEN'S CIRCLE: Newark-area Jewish immigrants' Socialist community service organization.

227 YISBORACH . . . B'RICH HU: Heart of Kaddish prayer for the dead; for translation see lines 1–2, "Hymmnn" section of *Kaddish*.

229 BUBA: (Yiddish) Grandmother.

229 SHEMA Y'ISRAEL: (Hebrew) Listen, O Israel!

229 SRUL AVRUM: (Hebrew) Israel Abraham, equivalent to Irwin Allen, names on the author's birth certificate.

231 CAMP NICHT-GEDEIGET: (Yiddish) Camp "No Worry," near Monroe, N.Y., summer settlement used by left-wing families, 1930s.

Mescaline

236 MESCALINE: Active psychedelic ingredient in peyote cactus, Southwest Indian religious-vision use. See Aldous Huxley, *The Doors of Perception* (New York: Harper & Row, 1970).

Lysergic Acid

239 LYSERGIC ACID: Synthetic psychoactive chemical with which author first experimented at Mental Research Institute, Palo Alto, California, whence poem is dated.

240 GHOST TRAP: A multicolor-stringed wool antenna, to trap stupid ghosts, used during LSD experiments at Stanford Mental Research Institute.

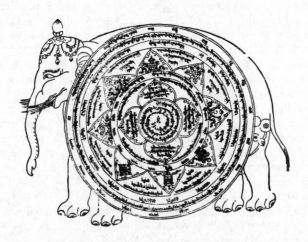

240 ELEPHANT MANDALA: A picture of the universe borrowed by the author from Prof. Frederic Spiegelberg for study during a Lysergic Acid vision and described in

section six of the accompanying poem. The mandala and various Ghost Traps—see section five—were brought by Prof. Spiegelberg from a monastery in Sikkim. He writes: "The inscription consists mainly of Mantras, power-words in Sanskirt, which do not carry any mental symbolism, no intellectually expressible meaning, but are supposed to be directly effective as a transforming soul-influence" etc.

To an Old Poet in Peru

247 OLD POET: Martín Adán, pseud. (1908–1985) Refers to his celebrated sonnets in *La Rosa de la Espenela*, 1939.

247 DISAGUADEROS: Railroad station behind presidential palace in Lima, across from which, in Hotel Comercio, "Old Poet" and "Aether" were written.

247–254 CHANCAY, PACHACAMAC, NASCA: Pre-Incaic cultures of coastal desert Peru. Myriad relics were found by graverobbers opening the sand of these necropolises.

Aether

257 PHILIP WHALEN (1923–2002): San Francisco Renaissance poet and Soto Zen priest, born Northwest 1923, peer among poets Kerouac, Snyder, Welch, McClure, Creeley.

258 ADONOI ECHAD: (Hebrew) "The Lord is one," end of the "Eli Eli" prayer song.

263–267 *Magic Psalm, The Reply* and *The End* record visions experienced after drinking Ayajuasca (Yage or Soga de Muerte, *Banisteriopsis caapi*), a vine infusion used by Amazon *curanderos* as spiritual potion, for medicine and sacred vision. See author's *The Yage Letters*, w/ William S. Burroughs (San Francisco: City Lights Books, 1963). The message is: Widen the area of consciousness.

The End

267 YIN: Feminine principle, receptivity or emptiness, in Chinese Taoist apposition to Yang, active masculine form.

VI
PLANET NEWS: TO EUROPE AND ASIA
(1961–1963)

Who Will Take Over the Universe?

273 CLINT MURCHISON: (1895–1969) Dallas billionaire industrialist (banks, rail, steamships, real estate, gas, oil, publishing, office equipment, movie theaters, restaurants, fishing tackle), conservative establishment Democrat.

273 JUDGE YALE MCFATE: His July 1960 decision affirmed constitutional protection for Native American Church use of psychedelic peyote cactus. Weston LaBarre, *The Peyote Cult* (New York: Shocken paperback, 1977), pp. 224–25: "The legal action most likely to set precedent, however, is the disposition of the case against Mary Attakai, a member of the Navaho Native American Church, under an anti-peyote ordinance of the Navaho Tribe. The local judge in

Flagstaff, Arizona, H. L. Russell, disqualified himself, whereupon the Hon. Yale McFate was sent from Phoenix to preside over the case in the Superior Court of Coconino County in Flagstaff. In a notably lucid and well-informed opinion, rendered on 26 July 1960, the Court held that:

'Peyote is not a narcotic. It is not habit-forming. . . . There are about 225,000 members of the organized church, known as the Native American Church, which adheres to this practice. . . . The use of peyote is essential to the existence of the peyote religion. Without it, the practice of the religion would be effectively prevented. . . . It is significant that many states which formerly outlawed the use of peyote have abolished or amended their laws to permit its use for religious purposes. It is also significant that the Federal Government has in nowise prevented the use of peyote by Indians or others.'

Inasmuch as the statute under which Mary Attakai was convicted of illegal possession is contrary to both the 14th Amendment of the Federal Constitution and Article II Sections 4, 8, 12, and 13 of the Arizona Constitution, the Court found the statute unconstitutional, exonerated the bond, and dismissed the case. Expert opinion has widely admired the decision of Judge McFate."

273 JOHN FOSTER DULLES: (1888–1959) Eisenhower secretary of state (1953–1959), who escalated cold war with China at 1954 Geneva Conference, where, refusing to shake hands or speak with Chinese foreign minister, he walked past icily, thereby initiating the thirty-year U.S.–China "containment policy." U.S. refused to sign the French–Indo-Chinese Peace Agreement at Geneva for fear "80% of the populace [of united Vietnam] would have voted for the Communist Ho Chi Minh as their leader."

273 FORRESTAL: James V. Forrestal (1892–1949) First U.S. secretary of defense; inaugurated first U.S. peacetime draft 1948, early cold war time (never before in U.S. history!) by illegally spending military-budget money for pro-draft propaganda. Next year, in mental decline, obsessed with Zionists and Communist Russian invasion of America, he threw himself out of Bethesda government mental hospital window, May 22, 1949.

Journal Night Thoughts

275 HARRY SMITH (1923–1991): Celebrated experimental filmmaker, artist, philosopher, hermeticist; editor Ethnic Folkways Records' *The Kiowa Peyote Meeting* (FE 4601, 1973) and three-volume, six-disc *Anthology of American Folk Music* (FA 2951–3, 1952), influential on midcentury world folk-rock renaissance.

275 ATMAN: Notion of individual self, identifiable with permanent self, Brahman.

275 KABBALA: Hebrew Gnostic numerical meditation practice using letters of Pentateuch (Torah). "Natural language letters."—H. Smith.

277 SPIRO MOUND: Southern Cult (A.D. 1200) Indian mound in Spiro, Oklahoma.

277 PENFIELD'S HOMUNCULUS: Map of brain areas controlling motor and sensory functions. See design p. 70, Fig. III-15, in Wilder Penfield and Jasper Herbert, *Epilepsy and the Functional Anatomy of the Human Brain* (Boston: Little, Brown, 1954).

277 KALI YUGA: Present era is last aeon in Hindu cycle of four ages, an age of iron during which spiritual awareness is at nadir, and cosmic apocalyptic destruction follows.

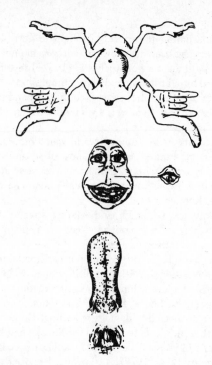

Combination sensory and motor homunculus (as they appear
from above on Rolandic cortex). Penfield's Homunculus. (See n.p. 277.)

page

Television Was a Baby Crawling Toward That Deathchamber

280 ENKIDU: Friend-servant of Gilgamesh, for whose shade's sake Gilgamesh visited the dusts of Deathworld.

280 LAFCADIO: L. Orlovsky, brother of poet Peter Orlovsky; see "Lazarus" portrait, Kerouac's *Desolation Angels*, Book Two, Part One, section 10.

280 CHANGO: Afro-Cuban Oricha, Lord of Drum, phallic creation divinity, somewhat equivalent to Hindu Shiva among polytheistic systems.

280 BARDO THODOL: Experience of gap between death and rebirth; see *The Tibetan Book of the Dead: The Great Liberation Through Hearing in the Bardo*, trans. Francesca Fremantle, commentary by Chögyam Trungpa (Boulder: Shambhala, 1975).

281 KULCHUR: Magazine of new writing, 1961, ed. Leroi Jones et al.

281 IRVING ROSE IN THRALL: Irving Rosenthal (with Paul Carroll), editing 1959 *Big Table* magazine, published first eighty-page chunk of Burroughs's *Naked Lunch*, previously censored in *Chicago Review*.

281 KALPA: Complete Aeonic four-yuga cycle, according to Hindu mythology.

285 CHESSMAN: Caryl Chessman (1921–1960) Executed for murder in California after lengthy court appeals intelligently written by himself, and despite world protest in favor of his life.

285 CHATTERLEY ATTACKED: Postmaster General Arthur Summerfield laid copy of D. H. Lawrence's long-banned masterpiece, *Lady Chatterley's Lover*, on President Eisenhower's desk with certain words underlined as "obscene," and asked

for permission to ban its transport by U.S. mail. "Terrible, we can't have that," said Ike in *Time* magazine (according to author's memory, 1959).

285 ROCHESTER: John Wilmot, Earl of Rochester (1647–1680) English poet, Milton's contemporary, whose brilliant gaudy lyrics, published 1950s Paris by Olympia Press, when imported to America were confiscated and burned by Eisenhower U.S. Customs, along with novels by Henry Miller, D. H. Lawrence, Jean Genet, etc.

296 2,000,000 PIECES MAIL: At beginning of cold war, 1945, U.S. Customs and Post Office departments burned as propaganda all second-class mail (books and printed matter) arriving from China, N. Vietnam, and other Communist lands. Two million items a year were incinerated. The practice was ended by President John Kennedy.

287 FABIAN BLDG.: Downtown Church and Market streets, Paterson, New Jersey, movie theater where author in boyhood saw movie phantoms of Jeanette MacDonald, Nelson Eddy, Ronald Reagan.

288 ANGELICA BALABANOFF: (1876–1965) Kiev-born aristocrat, first Secretary of Third Communist International 1919, quit disillusioned 1923 with Lenin's & Trotsky's use of "unscrupulous calumny" for centralization of power, went her own way, radical, poet. Earlier as Benito Mussolini's mistress she sheltered and introduced him to Socialist ideology, co-edited Rome socialist daily *Avanti*; later broke with him, was betrayed and confined, when he formed Italian Fascist Party. See *My Life as a Rebel* (New York: Harper & Brothers, 1938; reprint Indiana University Press, 1978). Author met her briefly at pacifist gathering, Brooklyn, 1945.

289 SS SANTA MARIA: "Cruise ship Santa Maria, with 600 passengers aboard, seized . . . by armed band of 69 . . . leader identified as [Portuguese dictator] Salazar foe, Army ex-Capt Galvao . . . colonial policy manifesto demands creation of Fed Repub of the US of Portugal including overseas territories . . . Portuguese exiles in GB open drive against Salazar regime" (*New York Times*, January 24–27, 1961). See also *Time*, February 10, 1961.

290 DEVAS: Hindu or Buddhist gods, attendant psychological spirits.

290 RAY BREMSER: American poet (b. 1934) See *The New American Poetry*, ed. Donald M. Allen (New York: Grove Press, 1960). Much praised by Kerouac and Bob Dylan for his celebrated word-syncopation, as in *Blowing Mouth* (Cherry Valley Editions, 1978).

Seabattle of Salamis Took Place off Perama

296 PANYOTIS . . . YORGIS: Greek youths' common given names.

296 AHARISTI . . . NA-TI-THE-MA-FEZ: Bouzouki songs, Athens suburb jukebox, 1961.

296 OPEN THE DOOR RICHARD, I'M CASTING A SPELL ON YOU: American jukebox songs, the latter by Screamin' Jay Hawkins, actually titled "I Put a Spell on You."

Stotras to Kali Destroyer of Illusions

298 YONI: Vagina, counterpart to lingam, in Hindu iconography.

Heat

302 HOOGHLY: River Ganges at Calcutta.

302 BIDI: Tiny cheap Indian cigarette.

page

Describe: The Rain on Dasaswamedh Ghat

303 KALI MA: Benares beggar lady with a holy name; see her photograph, *Indian Journals* (NY: Grove Press, 1996).

303 JAI RAM: "Victory to Ram" (aspect of Vishnu the Preserver).

304 JAI SHANKAR: Shankar or Shiva, patron lord of Benares.

304 BAUL: Mystical sect of wandering, patchwork-clothed Vaishnav singers, some devoted to Krishna, in North Bengal. See *Obscure Religious Cults*, Sashi Bhusan Das Gupta (Calcutta: Firma K. L. Makhopadhyay, 1959). "The elephant is caught in the spider web, and the ant bursts out laughing." Influenced Tagore songs.

Death News

305 GANGA-MA: Mother Ganges, represented traditionally riding a crocodile.

305 HOLLAND: John P. Holland (1841–1914) Irish born. His invention, the first iron submarine, the *Fenian Ram*, launched and sank in 1878, was fished up rusty from the Passaic in 1927, and exhibited thereafter in the Paterson Museum. Holland cofounded Electric Boat Co., ancestor General Dynamics Corp.

Patna-Benares Express

308 MAIDAN: Area that contains a horse track and polo field in Bankipore, sector of Patna city.

308 PATNA: Capital, Bihar state on right bank of Ganges, 125 miles from Benares.

Angkor Wat*

314 AVALOKITESVERA: The gates to the palaces and some temples of Angkor Wat are made of giant heads of Avalokitesvera (Down-Glancing Lord, Buddha of Mercy) facing in four directions. Principal Bodhisattva of Lotus Sutra pantheon, Chinese Kwan-Yin mercy god, Japanese Lady Kannon, sometimes thousand-armed energetic in compassionate activity.

314 BANYANS: Banyan trees, whose giant roots grow out of ruined walls and temple roofs.

314 SITARAM: Sitaram Onkar Das Thakur, a Vaishnavite guru who told the author in Benares, "Give up desire for children," and gave other instructions for purity.

316 CHURNING OF THE OCEAN: Bas-reliefs of old Hindu myth "Churning of the Ocean" cover one wall of Angkor Wat (a theme repeated throughout the temple areas).

317 BUDDHA DHARMA SANGHA: *Buddham Saranam Gochamee*—I take my refuge in the Buddha; *Dhammam Saranam Gochamee*—I take my refuge in the Dharma; *Sangham Saranam Gochamee*—I take my refuge in the Sangha. The Three Refuges, which the author interprets as: I take my refuge in my Self, I take my refuge in the nature of my Self, I take my refuge in the company of my fellow Selfs. [Non-Self interpretation.—A.G., 1984.]

317 HARE KRISHNA: This Maha Mantra (Great Prayer) for the Kali Yuga, first recommended to the author by Shivananda, consisting of different names of Vishnu the Preserver, can be sung with ecstatic rock beat.

318 ABHAYA MUDRA: Mudra—Buddhist hand gesture; Abhaya—gesture of calm, stilling stormy waters. Commonly seen on seated Buddhist statuary.

*Notes for "Angkor Wat" from Fulcrum Press edition (London, 1968).

318 LEROI MOI: The American radical poet Leroi Jones, later known as Amiri Baraka.

319 LEARY: Dr. Timothy Leary, an early heroic explorer of Psychedelic Consciousness.

319 AP BAC: Early guerilla battle in Vietnam won by Viet Cong, with many unreported losses of life by S. Vietnam Government soldiers and great confusion of leadership.

320 TA-PHROM . . . TA-KEO . . . THOMMANOM: Giant ruined Khmer civilization temple areas near Angkor Wat.

320 GARUDA: God of the Hindu pantheon, bird-headed, aide of King Ram in the Ramayana. [Spontaneously self-born enlightenment, Vajrayana Buddhist view—A.G., 1984.]

320 CHAMS: A northern tribe that conquered and burned the wooden Khmer cities that surrounded the temples.

320 TA-PHROM: Huge temple in giant stone-walled enclosure, unreconstructed by archaeologists, its paths cleaned of small overgrowth to show the Baynan jungle encroachment on the tumbling stone architecture.

322–323 "BLIND . . . RAIN!": The entire text of this composition was written in one night half sleeping and waking, as transcription of passages of consciousness in the author's mind made somnolent by an injection of morphine-atrophine in a hotel room in the town of Siemreap, adjacent to the ruins of Angkor Wat. The passage incorporated in quotation marks was notes taken earlier that day high on ganja (pot) on the roof of the temple of Angkor Thom.

324 LOLEI: A small ruined temple with an active monastery in the same compound, a few miles on the highway out of Siemreap.

325 HUÉ: S. Vietnamese city on north coast above Saigon, where student protests against suppression of Buddhist radio ceremonies ended in blister-gas riots, reported by telephone to UP office in Saigon, June 1963.

325 RAINY NIGHT AT THE BORDER: "Rainy Night at the Border," a popular song like "Lili Marlene," and classic complaint of Oriental soldiers, was banned in the nightclubs of Saigon by Mme. Nhu (wife of Catholic Premier Diem) as being "too pessimistic and demoralizing."

326 XALOI TEMPLE: Center of Buddhist Association hunger strike, early resistance to Diem government.

326 AFRAID TO PUBLISH: A letter from Jon Edgar Webb of *Outsider* magazine, apologizing for not publishing a dream of Negroes by the author, for fear of violent white gang reprisals against his office in New Orleans.

327 SUKOTHAI: Very graceful early Thai style of Buddha statues, one hand delicately flowing behind, one hand raised in reassurance, one foot set forward as he steps out into the world of action.

327 LINGAM: Stone phallus universally worshipped in India as basic form of Shiva the Creator.

328 BUDDHA FOOTPRINT: Three fish with one head—a sign of Buddhahood incised in giant stone carving of Buddha footprint found under Bo Tree at Bodh Gaya, mythological Indian site of the Buddha's realization.

329 RADIOACTIVE DOLPHINS: From a letter from J. Kerouac describing the twentieth-century complaints of his Canuck cousins.

330 10 TINY BUDDHAS: A little fragment of the twelfth-century miniature Stupa carried by the author from broken-down Hindu garden near Bo Tree as a present to poet Gary Snyder in Kyoto.

330   MEA SHEARIM: Orthodox Hasidic section of modern Jerusalem.

331   PEKING S JEWELRY FEET: See poem "Magic Psalm."

331   "MAKE ME READY—BUT NOT YET": A line from W. H. Auden, out of St. Augustine: "O Lord, make me chaste—but not yet."

The Change: *Kyoto–Tokyo Express*

333   ". . . CONVOLUTED . . .": See "The Clouds," part IV, in William Carlos Williams, *The Collected Later Poems* (New York: New Directions, 1963), p. 128.

VII
KING OF MAY: AMERICA TO EUROPE
(1963–1965)

Morning

345   JULIUS: Julius Orlovsky, brother of the poet Peter Orlovsky, rescued by latter 1958 after twelve years' residence Central Islip State Hospital, N.Y. See Robert Frank film *Me and My Brother*, 1966.

Today

353   SWAMI SHIVANANDA: (1887–1962) "Your own heart is the guru." Spoken to author, Rishikesh, 1962. See dedication, Ginsberg, *Indian Journals*.

354   BENJAMIN PÉRET & RENÉ CREVEL: Péret—French surrealist poet (1899–1959); Crevel—French dada dandy poet suicide (1900–1935).

355   FAINLIGHT: Harry Fainlight, young British poet active N.Y. underground film literary circles early 1960s. Participated Albert Hall, London, Poetry Incarnation, 1965. Died 1982.

355   ED: Edward Sanders (b. 1939) American poet, classicist, and musician, leader of Fugs rock group, editor *Fuck You/A Magazine of the Arts*.

Message II

356   GOLEM: Artificial man created, in one Hebrew legend, by the Kabbalist Rabbi Löw, Prague, end of sixteenth century. Parallel to Mary Shelley's Frankenstein monster.

356   BREUGHEL: Pieter Breughel (1520?–1569) His painting *Winter Landscape of Prague* (including Vltava panorama) is exhibited in that city.

Big Beat

357   KALKI: Final avatar (incarnation) of Vishnu, appearing at close of Kali Yuga (see "Journal Night Thoughts" note) to destroy world and initiate Maha Yuga, the aeon of greatest spiritual virtue, first Yuga of four in Hindu Kalpa cycle.

357   MAITREYA: Future Buddha, aspect of compassion, personification of love, parallel formation to maitri (Sanskrit), friendship.

The Moments Return

360   SEBASTIAN SAMPAS: Youthtime poet friend of Jack Kerouac, brother of widow Stella, killed at Anzio beachhead WW II a few weeks after sending Kerouac a recording: "I weep for Adonais, he is dead. . . . Goodbye, Jack."

360   OZONE PARK: In Queens, N.Y., where Jack Kerouac lived with his family late 1940s and wrote *The Town and the City*, his first novel.

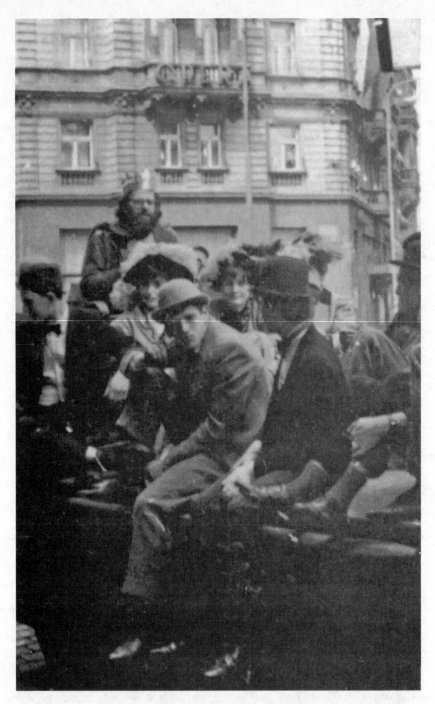

The author setting forth from hotel with throne and crown on flatbed truck to Prague Culture-Park for May King election; May 1, 1965. Note formal-dressed students for May Day holiday. Photographer unknown.

360 GURU: Sitaram Onkar Das Thakur. See "Wichita Vortex Sutra."

Kraj Majales

361 KRAL MAJALES: May King. Traditional May Day festival, suspended after German occupation prior to WWII. Previous years' student disturbances persuaded Czech government to restore May King and Queen crowning ceremony in 1965, the occasion of massive public park demonstration by festive Prague populace. Nominated by Polytechnic students, author was elected May King by 100,000 citizens; ministers of culture and education objected. A week later, detained incommunicado, his Prague notebook confiscated, author was deported by plane to London, poem scribed en route.

361 KABIR: (1450?–1518) Illiterate Benares mystic poet-singer, weaver, disciple of Saint Ramanand, comparable to Blake: "If I heard love in exchange for the head in market is being sold,/I shall lose no time in entering the bargain and instantly sever my head, and offer it." (*Sufis, Mystics and Yogis of India*, trans. Bankey Behari [Bombay: Bharatiya Vidya Bhavan, 1962], p. 224.) See Kabir poems also translated by Tagore, Bly, Linda Hess.

361 BOUZERANT: (Czech slang) Homosexual.

361 AND I WAS SENT FROM HAVANA: Author was deported from Cuba, February 1965 for private criticism of speech at Havana University in which Fidel Castro denounced homosexuals and ordered purge of theater school. Detained in hotel room, held incommunicado from Casa de las Americas, which hosted the month-long Interamerican Poetry contest he'd been invited to help judge, author was expelled by plane to Prague.

361 JOSEPH K: See Kafka, *The Trial*.

362 BUNHILL FIELDS: Chief nonconformist burial ground of Old London. Site where Blake's bones are buried, adjacent to gravestones of Daniel Defoe, John Wesley and Isaac Watts.

362 HAMPSTEAD HEATH: "The great old piece of uncultivated common land and woods whose ancient oaks were protected by Royal Charter in North London, haunt of painter John Constable and poet John Keats, who wrote 'Ode to a Nightingale' in a house which still stands at the heath's edge in Hampstead."—Tom Pickard

Guru

364 Poem occasioned by a nap at dusk on the site of Druid mysteries, the grassy crest of London's Primrose Hill, overlooking London's towery skyline.

Who Be Kind To

367 HARRY: Harry Fainlight (see "Today" note).

369 MONK IN THE 5 SPOT: Thelonious Monk (1918–1982) Genius of spare precise "out" piano harmony and innovator of "bop" rhythm, long denied by drug bureaucracy the necessary police "cabaret card" permit to work in N.Y., returned early 1960s to play many months at Bowery's Five Spot, jazz club.

Studying the Signs

371 STUDYING THE SIGNS: 360-degree panorama sketch of Piccadilly Circus composed after midnight conclusion of Albert Hall International Poetry Incarnation.

371 BRIGGFLATTS: Late long poem by English master Basil Bunting (1900–1985), who'd suggested to Ezra Pound that Poetry be equated with Condensation, as in Briggflatts verse describing a Northumbrian road cart: "Rut thuds the rim . . ." See his *Collected Poems*, Oxford University Press, 1980.

VIII
THE FALL OF AMERICA
(1965–1971)

Thru the Vortex West Coast to East
(1965–1966)

A Methedrine Vision in Hollywood

388 TITLE: See Earl of Rochester's satire "Upon Nothing": "Ere time and place were, time and place were not, / When primitive *Nothing* something strait begot, / Then all proceeded from the great united—What?"

Wichita Vortex Sutra

403 PRAJNAPARAMITA SUTRA: Highest Perfect Wisdom Sutra, central to Zen and Tibetan Buddhist practice. It includes the phrase "Form is emptiness, emptiness is form," and mantra "Gate Gate Paragate Parasamgate Bodhi Svaha."

404 LA ILLAHA EL (LILL) ALLAH HU: "There is no god but God [Allah]," Sufi chant for trance dance as taught by Bay Area Sufi Sam circa 1967.

405 WILLIAM JENNINGS BRYAN: (1860–1925) Congressman, presidential candidate 1908. Later involved in Baby Doe silver mine speculation; leader of populist silver monetary movement: "Thou shalt not crucify Mankind upon a Cross of Gold." See Vachel Lindsay's poem "Bryan, Bryan, Bryan, Bryan" (1919):

I brag and chant of Bryan, Bryan, Bryan,
Candidate for President who sketched a silver Zion,
The one American who could sing outdoors . . .

Where is Altgeld, brave as the truth,
Whose name the few still say with tears?
Gone to join the ironies with old John Brown,
Whose fame rings loud for a thousand years.

Where is that Boy, the Heaven-born Bryan
That Homer Bryan, who sang from the West?
Gone to join the shadows with Altgeld the Eagle,
Where the kings and the slaves and the troubadors rest.
—Vachel Lindsay, *Collected Poems* (New York: Macmillan, 1925), p. 96.

405 WHO DIDN'T WANT TO BE A MONKEY: John T. Scopes disobeyed 1920's Tennessee law prohibiting high-school teaching of Darwin evolution theory. Defended

at trial by Clarence Darrow, he was, interestingly, opposed by Biblical fundamentalist W. J. Bryan, who maintained that God created Adam and Eve in 4004 B.C.

406 AIKEN REPUBLICAN: George D. Aiken (1892–1984) Vermont senator from 1940 through Vietnam War, author, *Pioneering with Wildflowers*, 1933, other nature books. Interviewed by newsmen on *Face the Nation* broadcast through Midwest heard by author (through Volkswagen radio) February 20, 1966, on Kansas roads. Senator Aiken pronounced the entire Indochina war involvement "a bad guess" by policymakers who had predicted in 1962 that "8,000 American troops could handle the situation." Defense Secretary McNamara contended that U.S. was defending South Vietnam from invasion by North Vietnam. "China Lobby" ideologues saw Chinese expansionist plot behind Hanoi and urged nuclear bombing of China.

Senator Aiken argued that the quarter-million South Vietnamese Viet Cong guerrilla army outweighed Hanoi's troops in confounding the U.S. technologic army then massing toward half-million men. That month, Senator Strom Thurmond backed nuclear arms to win the war.

Later, General Curtis LeMay urged America to "bomb North Vietnam back to the Stone Age." Carpet bombing of north did take place, and Mekong jungle cover was saturated with Agent Orange.

In mid-'70s chaos after American withdrawal, North Vietnam dismantled and bypassed what was left of the same South Vietnamese Provisional Revolutionary Government (P.R.G. or Viet Cong) political infrastructure U.S. had rejected 1966. Traditional hostilities were renewed between Vietnam and China at disputed border areas. By then, U.S. was allied with China. Doves & hawks both lost the war, always "a bad guess."

406 MCNAMARA: Robert S. McNamara (b. 1916) Defense secretary under President LBJ during 1960s Vietnam War, brought managerial sophistication to Pentagon mechanized warfare, though privately doubted its purpose.

406 MANDATE FOR CHANGE: "It was generally conceded that had an election been held, Ho Chi Minh would have been elected Premier." (p. 337–38) "I have never talked or corresponded with a person knowledgeable in Indochinese affairs who did not agree that had elections been held as of the time of the fighting, possibly 80 per cent of the population would have voted for the Communist Ho Chi Minh as their leader. . . ." (p. 372) Dwight D. Eisenhower, *Mandate for Change* (New York: Doubleday, 1963).

406 STENNIS: John C. Stennis (1901–1995) U.S. senator, Mississippi, Armed Services Committee man and "hawk," urged nuclear war for Indochina, 1966.

407 AUNT BETTY: Highway billboard advertising bread.

407 RUSK SAYS TOUGHNESS . . . VIETNAM WAR BRINGS PROSPERITY: Literal headlines, Midwest newspapers February 1966.

407 BEATRICE: Nebraska town, Route 77.

408 HUTCHINSON . . . EL DORADO: Kansas towns en route between Lincoln, Nebraska, & Wichita.

408 ABILENE: Dwight D. Eisenhower's hometown, site of his Presidential Library.

408 NATION "OF THE FABLED DAMNED": See concluding paragraphs of Whitman's *Democratic Vistas* for prophetic warning against America's hawkish materialism.

410 CLARK: Joseph S. Clark (1901–1990) U.S. senator, Pennsylvania, described Viet-

nam War at the time as "open-ended"—i.e., could go on forever, including war with China.

410   MORSE: Wayne Morse (1900–1974) U.S. senator, Oregon, outstanding legislative "dove" in active opposition to America's undeclared war in Vietnam.

411   OR SMOKING CIGARETTES/AND WATCHING CAPTAIN KANGAROO: Pop song of the day referring to children's TV program.

411   UNITED FRUIT: United Fruit Company's law firm, Sullivan and Cromwell, had employed State Secretary Dulles (see "Who Will Take Over the Universe?" note), whose brother, Allen, heading CIA, coordinated the 1954 then-covert overthrow of Jacobo Arbenz, elected president of Guatemala. The event is notorious throughout Latin America as a mid-twentieth-century example of "banana republic" repression by North American imperium. By 1980, the U.S.-trained Guatemalan military had reportedly genocided 10 percent of jungle Indian population as part of "pacification" program to "create a favorable business climate."

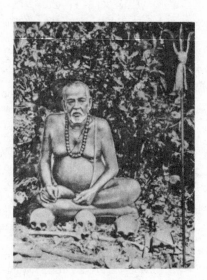

Birbhum yogi, likely Khaki Baba.
Photographer unknown.

411   OAKLAND ARMY TERMINAL: California students had passed leaflets and picketed this Pacific war transshipment center. Gary Snyder & Zen companions had sat meditating at its gates.

412   MILLIONAIRE PRESSURE: Refers to a Mr. Love from Wichita, second biggest backer of cold-war-conspiracy-obsessed John Birch Society.

412   TELEPHONE VOICES: When Peter Orlovsky and author came to read poetry, Philosophy Department hosts at Wichita's Kansas State University received many crank phone complaints.

413   AGING WHITE HAIRED GENERAL: Lewis B. Hershey (1893–1977) Selective Service director since Truman appointment 1948, time of first U.S. peacetime draft.

413   REPUBLICAN RIVER: Runs from Kansas City to Junction City.

414   OLD HEROES OF LOVE: Neal Cassady, born in Independence, Mo.

414   MCCLURE: Michael McClure, American Romantic bard and playwright (b. 1932), Marysville, Kansas. See *The New American Poetry*, Donald M. Allen, ed. (New York: Grove Press, 1960), for McClure's part as key biological philosopher-poet in 1950s "San Francisco Renaissance" and subsequent "generational" culture.

414   OLD MAN'S STILL ALIVE: Ex-President Harry S. Truman.

414   SHAMBU BHARTI BABA: A Naga (naked) saddhu the author often met at Benares's Manikarnika Ghat cremation ground. See photographs, *Indian Journals*.

414   KHAKI BABA: North Bengali (Birbhum area) 19th-century saint who, dressed in khaki loincloth, is pictured sometimes sitting surrounded by dog friends and protectors. (See photograph on page 786.)

414   DEHORAHAVA BABA: A yogi author met at Ganges River across from Benares, 1963.

414   SATYANANDA: Calcutta swami encountered by author 1962, had twin-thumbed hands, and said, "Be a sweet poet of the Lord."

414   KALI PADA GUHA ROY: Tantric acharya or guru visited by author in Benares, 1963.

414   SHIVANANDA: Swami, teacher to Satchitananda, visited by author, Peter Orlovsky, Gary Snyder and Joanne Kyger, Rishikesh, 1962: "Your own heart is your Guru."

415   SRIMATA KRISHNAJI: Contemporary Brindaban lady saint, translator of poet Kabir, advised author thus.

415   BRINDABAN: Holy town near Delhi where Krishna spent childhood in play as cow herder.

415   CHAITANYA: 16th-century North Bengali saint, founder of Hare Krishna Mahamantra lineage, pictured dancing, singing.

415   DURGA-MA: Mother Durga, aspect of Shiva's consort Parvati emphasized in Bengali Hindu mythology, 10-armed goddess of war fields, who consumes evil through violence.

415   TATHAGATA: (Sanskrit) Buddha characterized as "He who has passed through," or "that which passed." ("Thus come," and also "Thus gone": "Thus come [One].")

415   DEVAS: Indian gods, seen as aspects of human or divine being.

415   MANTRA: Sacred verbal spell or prayer composed of elemental sound "seed" syllables, used in meditative concentration practice. Literally, "mind protection" speech.

416   "KENNEDY URGES CONG GET CHAIR" . . . : February 14, 1966, news headlined Senator Robert Kennedy's proposal that U.S. offer Viet Cong share of power in South Vietnam. This was major break with administration war policy.

416   CONTINUED FROM PAGE ONE: In February 14, 1966, *Wichita Eagle*.

416   BONG SON: 100 Viet Cong soldiers were killed close to Bong Son and were reported struck by many bullets before falling.

417   LA DRANG: Vietnamese battlefield mentioned in news reports third week February 1966.

417   BURNS: Tiny Kansas town near Wichita.

418   KELLOGG: Main drag in Wichita.

418   HOTEL EATON: On Douglas Street, near local Vortex Gallery patronized by Charles Plymell and Kansas artists.

418 CARRY NATION: "(b. Garrard Co., 1846; d. Leavenworth, Kans., 1911), temperance agitator. An ignorant, unbalanced, and contentious woman of vast energies, afflicted with an hereditary paranoia, she was subjected to early hardships that fused all her great physical and emotional powers into a flaming enmity toward liquor and its corrupt purveyors. From her first saloon-smashing ventures at Medicine Lodge, Kans., she carried her campaign to Wichita (1900), where her distinctive weapon, the hatchet, was first used, and then on to many of the principal American cities. Arrested thirty times for 'disturbing the peace,' she paid fines from sales of souvenir hatchets, lecture tours, and stage appearances. Her autobiography was published, 1904."—*Concise Dictionary of American Biography* (New York: Scribner's, 1964), p. 721.

419 NIGGERTOWN: Area of Wichita between Hydraulic and 17th streets.

Kansas City to Saint Louis

421 CHARLIE PLYMELL: American poet, filmmaker and pioneer editor, accompanied author in Kansas-Nebraska travel.

421 THE JEWEL-BOX REVIEW: Transvestite club show, Kansas City.

421 SEX FACTORIES: Kinsey Institute, University of Indiana, Bloomington, gave birth to this jump-cut phrase.

421 BURCHFIELD: Charles Burchfield (1893–1967) American painter, best known for portraits of particular solitary gabled Victorian houses in bare U.S. regional landscapes.

421 WALKER EVANS: (1903–1975) Classic American photographer whose record of Boston houses, poets' faces, Cuban visages, Southern agrarian scenes (for Farm Security Administration Project, 1930s), billboards, junkyards, main streets, subway riders, Chicago corners and train glimpses helped define a second generation of American photography, and influenced younger eyes, including Robert Frank's.

423 KENNEY . . . MORPHY: Friends of William S. Burroughs in 1930s St. Louis.

423 W.S.B.: William Seward Burroughs

425 FRENCH TRUTH, DUTCH CIVILITY: "*French* Truth, *Dutch* prowess, *British* Policy,/*Hibernian* Learning, *Scotch* civility,/*Spaniards* Dispatch, *Danes* wit,/are mainly seen in thee."—Earl of Rochester, "On Nothing"

425 CRANE: See Hart Crane's address to Whitman, *The Bridge*, end of Cape Hatteras section.

Bayonne Entering NYC

429 CANNASTRA: William Cannastra, ex-Harvard Law suicide-accident-dead (1950) friend of N.Y. painters and poets, including W. H. Auden and Jack Kerouac. See "In Memoriam," September 1950.

Uptown

432 MADAME GRADY: Panna Grady, patron of letters, friend of poets Charles Olson, John Wieners and William Burroughs, once lived at Dakota Apartments, Central Park West, N.Y., and held literary salon there.

Iron Horse

442 EDWARD CARPENTER: Contemporary, disciple of Whitman, British educator-poet. See "Turin-Paris Express" from his poem book *Towards Democracy*, 1902, a rare example of successful Whitmanic line.

442 HOMER: Poet Lawrence Ferlinghetti's late sizable black dog, subject of several popular poems.

443 MULADHARA SPHINCTER: Refers to anal chakra (one of seven bodily centers of spirit energy in Orient yoga practice).

443 SAHASRARAPADMA: Seventh chakra, "thousand-petal lotus" at skulltop.

443 GAVIN ARTHUR: (d. 1972) Bay area astrologer, grandson of U.S. President Chester A. Arthur, had slept with Carpenter, who'd slept with Whitman, according to written testament entrusted to author. See text, *Gay Sunshine Interviews*, ed. Winston Leyland, vol. 1, San Francisco, 1978, pp. 126–28.

444 MR. CUMMINGS & MR. VINAL: E. E. Cummings wrote much-anthologized poem mocking lesser poet Harold Vinal: "Poem, or Beauty Hurts Mr. Vinal."

444 SEBSI: Moroccan clay pipe for kif.

446 NA-MU SA-MAN-DA . . . SO-MO-KO: "Dharani of Removing Disasters," repeated thrice in temple usage. See D. T. Suzuki, *Manual of Zen Buddhism* (New York: Grove Press, 1960).

447 WALTER LIPPMANN: (1889–1974) Aging political columnist/philosopher wrote thus in newspapers the week of "Iron Horse" ride.

447 SAM LEWIS: "Sufi Sam"—world traveler, founder of Sufi sect in San Francisco, friend of Gavin Arthur.

447 DR. LOURIA: Leon Louria, Naomi's boyfriend, "Dr. Isaac" of "Kaddish," had served as consulting physician for National Maritime Union until purged as leftwinger in Senator Joe McCarthy era, early 1950s.

447 FREEHOLD NEW JERSEY: Geyshe Wangyal, first Gelugpa sect Tibetan Buddhist teacher in America, founded his monastery at Freehold in 1950s.

450 GEORGE E. TURNER: Ephemeral Texas journalist (b. 1925) whose acid comments author read on train newspaper.

451 YEVTUSHENKO: Yevgeny Yevtushenko, the then-popular Russian poet, had written an open letter to novelist John Steinbeck questioning his support for U.S. military occupation of South Vietnam.

455 THE WOMAN IN THE RED DRESS: The woman who "informed" on "Public Enemy No. 1," John Dillinger, leading FBI to the Biograph movie house where he was cornered and shot.

455 PURVIS: FBI agent who organized Dillinger's fatal ambush.

455 HENRY CROWN: (1896–1990) Chicago business hustler, made early fortune buying municipally owned rock waste and selling it back to Chicago for road construction; later major stockholder and 1959–1966 chairman executive committee, director, of then-number-one military-industrial-complex corporation, General Dynamics.

457 FULBRIGHT: Senator James William Fulbright (1905–1995) Head of Senate Foreign Relations Committee 1959–1974, made eloquent public attack on President Johnson's expansion of the Vietnam War.

458 SHERI MARTINELLI: American painter and miniaturist, formerly N.Y. fashion model, friend-companion to Ezra Pound at St. Elizabeths Hospital, Washing-

ton, D.C., in mid-'50s. An acquaintance of Charlie Parker, she served somewhat as Pound's connection to the new cultural life in U.S. postwar underground. A tiny book of her portraits, with prefatory note by Pound, was published by Editions Scheiwiller, Milan, 1956.

458 YAJALÓN VALLEY: Isolated mountain valley town, Chiapas.

458 XOCHIMILCO: Ancient floating gardens, Mexico City, where Kerouac, Orlovsky and the author met a party of Mexican ballet boys in a sightseeing boat. See Kerouac's *Desolation Angels*, Book Two, Part One, section 20.

458 FIJIJIAPAN: town close to Guadalajara, Mexico, notable for its candy.

459 KEDERNATH & BADRINATH & GANGOTRI: Northwest India Hindu pilgrimage sites on the way to Kailash, Shiva's sacred Tibetan border mountain abode, source of Ganges.

459 MANASAROVAR: Iced lake on Kailash.

450 KARMA: Hindu-Buddhist concept of inevitable interconnection of cause and effect. Karma may be "white" and "black," wholesome and unwholesome, meritorious or unmeritorious, or neutral, in mixed degrees, according to the activities of Mind, Speech, and Body that initiate karmic momentum and payback. "Black" karma example: As ignorant greed motivates agribusiness to aggressive exploitation of soil, so soil may collapse under assault of chemical poisons, finally become barren, eroded, no longer nourishing its bewildered and inconsiderable stewards. Further example: As American populace is indifferent to military sufferings its government wreaks on distant nations, Indochina to Central America, so will that public heartlessness progressively discourage private trust and adhesiveness between government and populace. On individual scale, a father, careless of his children, may not have faithful helpers on his deathbed.

Such karmic patterns may be altered and their energy made wholesome through meditative mindfulness, conscious awareness, the practice of appreciation, which burns up karma on the spot. Traditionally, attentive appreciation of an enlightened teacher who has transcended his/her own karma may inspire the student/seeker/citizen to work from "black" through "white" situations toward holistic primordial experience, or unconditioned states of mind and activity, exchanging self for others, liberated from karma as may be Mahatma Gandhi or certain Buddhist folk or Native American elders.

461 SRI RAMANA MAHARSHI: 20th-century South Indian ascetic saint, instructed meditation practice, "Who Am I?" Quotations are from his book *Maha Yoga*.

464 MANNAHATTA:

Starting from fish-shaped Paumanok where I was born,
Well-begotten, and rais'd by a perfect mother,
After roaming many lands, lover of populous pavements,
Dweller in Mannahatta, my city . . . ("Starting from Paumanok")

"Thus Walt Whitman, born in Long Island, paraphrases the old Indian name for New York City. 'Mannahatta! How fit a name for America's great democratic island city! The word itself, how beautiful! how aboriginal! how it seems to rise with tall spires glistening in the sunshine, with such New World atmosphere, vista and action!' " (Justin Kaplan, *Walt Whitman: A Life* [New York: Simon & Schuster, 1980] p. 107.)

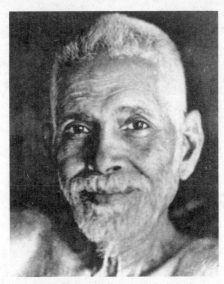

Sri Ramana Maharshi. Photographer unknown.
(See n.p. 461.)

City Midnight Junk Strains

465 FRANK O HARA: (1926–1966) Gay central figure in N.Y. literary art life 1950s till his death; MOMA exhibitions department curator, inspired a whole genera-tion of N.Y. "Personism" poets; died struck by beach buggy, dark midnight accident Fire Island. See "The Day Lady Died," in his *Collected Poems* (New York: Knopf, 1972).

465 KLINE: Franz Kline (1910–1962) American abstract expressionist pioneer painter, on whose work Frank O'Hara wrote monograph, died of heart attack.

466 EDWIN DENBY: (1903–1983) China-born, influential dance critic, poet, friend of younger writers of "New York School," 1960s–1980s; frequented N.Y.C. Bal-let and St. Mark's Poetry Project. (*Collected Poems* published by Full Court Press, New York, 1975.)

Holy Ghost on the Nod over the Body of Bliss

475 KUAN YIN: Chinese name, Avelokitesvera, compassionate aspect of Buddha. See "Angkor Wat."

475 SHIVA: Lord energy of creation and destruction, symbolized in Hindu shrines by Shiva lingam or phallus, generally a standing rounded oblong rock covered with flowers and incense.

475 OUROBOROS: Great cosmic snake, tail in mouth completing Einsteinian circle.

475 PARVATI: Shiva's consort.

475 YOD: Hebrew abbreviation, divine unutterable name.

475 COYOTE: Amerindian trickster-hero god.

475 RAMAKRISHNA: Ecstatic Hindu saint (1836–1886), founder of Vedanta order, entered all religious practices. See *The Gospel of Shri Ramakrishna*, trans. Swami Nikhilananda (Madras, India: Shri Ramakrishna Math, 1957).

475 BODHIDHARMA: Twenty-eighth Zen patriarch after Sakyamuni in orthodox trans-mission line, brought Buddhism from India to Canton in the West 520 A.D.,

thus first Chinese patriarch of "Wall-gazing" Chan (Zen) practice; died aged 150 years.

Hui-K'o (486–593) cut off his arm and gave it to Bodhidharma, token of sincerity: "I have no peace of mind . . . Please pacify it."

"Bring your mind here."

"I can't find it."

"There, I have pacified your mind."

An Open Window on Chicago

481 BOUFFANT ROOTS: Upswept hairstyle, with undyed roots growing visible.

482 DAKINI: Buddhist sky goddess, conveyor of insight.

Wales Visitation

488 VISITACIONE: Ancient bardic visiting round in Wales.

488 LLANTHONY VALLEY: Pastoral vale, Welsh Black Mountains.

490 CAPEL-Y-FFN: Ancient ruined chapel at green bottom of Llanthony Valley. Eric Gill, type-font designer and craftsman, dwelt there 1920s with arts commune.

490 LORD HEREFORD S KNOB: Mountain walling north side Llanthony Valley.

490 (LSD): First draft main body of poem was written in fifth hour LSD-inspired afternoon.

Pentagon Exorcism

491 EXORCISM: Gary Snyder's 1967 Bay Area broadside, *A Curse Against the Men in Pentagon, Washington*, helped initiate flower-power era mass peace-protest "Levitation" of Pentagon, the demystification of its authority. See Norman Mailer's extensive account in *Armies of the Night* (New York: New American Library, 1971 reprint).

491 DIAPHANOID: From title of science fiction movie the author saw 1967 at S. Gemignano while traveling from Florence to Milan.

491 WESTMORELAND: General William C. Westmoreland (b. 1914) "Hawk" commander of U.S. forces in Vietnam 1964–1968, who, not realizing that the majority of Vietnamese didn't welcome American/Catholic domination of South Vietnam as part of China-containment policy, urged escalation of war, all-out victory by any means, including nuclear.

491 USURY: Allusion to Ezra Pound's monetarist theory: that banks' usurous (fast buck high interest) abuse of credit as a commodity, for speculative moneymaking rather than productive ends, cankers the entire economic system of the West. See the *Cantos* of Ezra Pound, "Canto XLV" (New York: New Directions, 1970): "With Usura the line grows thick."

491 MCDONNELL DOUGLAS TO GENERAL DYNAMICS: These corporations were chief military contractees to Pentagon, 1967.

491 APOKATASTASIS: Event wherein ignorant or "satanic" energy is transformed instantaneously to divine wisdom light, as might be at end of Kali Yuga.

491 RAKSA: Tibetan mantra to purify site for a ceremony, from Hevajra Tantra. Raksa is an energy daemon.

491 PEKING: At time of composition, diplomatic nonrecognition of existence of People's Republic of China was an obsession central to U.S. anti-red cold war monolithic "containment policy" strong-armed politically by "China Lobby," including then ex-Vice-President Richard Nixon.

Elegy Che Guevara

492 RUSK: Secretary of State Dean Rusk (1909–1994) President Johnson's hawkish diplomatic executive for Vietnam War.

493 NORRIS: Frank Norris (1876–1902) Novelist, author of naturalist novel *The Pit*, drama of frenzied Chicago grain market.

493 OBSERVERS' BALCONY: "Street theater action" initiated 1968 by Abbie Hoffman at New York Stock Exchange, throwing a bag of dollars on the exchange floor as war protest. Thenceforth balcony was walled with glass.

Elegies for Neal Cassady
(1968)

Elegy for Neal Cassady

496 SHABDA: (Sanskrit) Sound or vibration, a path of yoga.

496 GREAT YEAR: 24,000-year cycle of the sun, which rises for 2,000 years each through 12 zodiacal constellations, as it wobbles almost imperceptibly on its sidereal axis; presently entering Age of Aquarius.

497 HEJIRA: Mohammed's flight from Mecca, A.D. 622; Kesey's bus trip, A.D. 1964, Neal Cassady at driver's wheel.

497 LOWELL: Massachusetts Merrimack River redbrick mill town where Jack Kerouac was raised, site of many novels.

Ecologues of These States
(1969–1971)

Over Denver Again

519 ALLEYWAY LILA: Lila (Sanskrit), "play," as in Krishna's play on earth, "Krishna Lila."

Falling Asleep in America

525 BEULAH: Blake term for mythic realm of subconscious, source of dream-poetic inspiration.

Northwest Passage

526 JOHNSON BUTTE: High mountain plateau overlooking Lake Wallula at confluence of Snake and Columbia rivers. Horse Heaven Hills top the vast butte.

526 SAKAJAWEA: Indian lady guide for Lewis and Clark expedition through Northwest native territory hitherto unknown by white men.

526 THALASSA: (Greek) Sea.

527 SIRHAN: Sirhan J. Sirhan, young Palestine-born assassin of Robert F. Kennedy, Los Angeles 1968. His comments on conviction, and description of his visage, were taken from Associated Press reports.

527 52% PEOPLE: Refers to 1968 Gallup poll.

527 SDS: Radical activist Students for a Democratic Society, whose early 1960s "Port Huron Declaration" proposed patriotic reform of institutionalized race prejudice and abusive imperial exploitation of nature and human labor. SDS rose as

an alternative to the relatively passive "establishment" National Students Association, which had absorbed much natural student energy but was revealed during mid-1960s Senate investigation to have been funded by the CIA as a front for covert propaganda activity and an illegal domestic training ground for agents. SDS was later infiltrated and sabotaged covertly by the FBI, whose "cointel" (counterintelligence) policy was blueprinted to create leadership dissension and split white student youth from alliance with black activist groups. SDS fragmented in early 1970s, having helped spearhead early civil rights struggle in South and later extreme student opposition to U.S. military invasion of Indochina.

528 MIRA BAI: 14th-century Indian poetess, ecstatic Krishna worshiper. Her sacred devotional songs are still sung in villages and cities of India.

Sonora Desert–Edge

530 DRUM H.: Arizona poet Drummond Hadley (student of Charles Olson, friend of Gary Snyder), from whom author first heard Padmasambhava mantra.

530 TARTHANG TULKU: N'yingma-pa lineage Tibetan Buddhist teacher, Berkeley friend of Gary Snyder, taught the millennial Padmasambhava mantra quoted: "Body, Speech, Mind, Lotus-Flower-Power Diamond-Teacher, Hūṃ."

530 SAGUARO . . . OCOTILLO . . . CHOLLA . . . PALO VERDE: Varieties of cacti.

Memory Gardens

539 MEMORY GARDENS: Cemetery near Albany Airport glimpsed on way to Jack Kerouac's funeral in Lowell, Mass. Poem was written on that trip.

540 HAL: Hal Chase, Denver-bred contemporary and friend of Cassady and Kerouac, later boat and lute builder in Bolinas, California, 1960s.

541 JOHN HOLMES: John Clellon Holmes (1926–1988) Author of first published (1952) Beat romance, *Go* (New York: New American Library, 1980).

Graffiti 12th Cubicle Men's Room Syracuse Airport

543 LSD: Formula for lysergide written on the john wall differs from that given in *Dorland's Medical Dictionary* (1981): $C_{20}H_{25}N_3O$.

Friday the Thirteenth

546 FRIDAY THE THIRTEENTH: Allusion to date of explosion in town house West 11th Street, New York. While parents were on vacation, it was used as safe-house bomb factory by "Weathermen."

546 HAMPTON, KING, GOLD: Fred Hampton, Chicago Black Panther murdered in bed by police with FBI collaboration, 1968. Martin Luther King, assassinated in Memphis, April 5, 1968. Theodore Gold, killed in Weathermen blast (see note above).

546 SONG-MY: Vietnamese village blasted and burned by U.S. forces "to save it from the Viet Cong."

546 TU-DO: Main Saigon hotel-café street during U.S. occupation.

Ecologue

550 MAHANIRVANA & HEVAJRA TANTRAS: Buddhist Vajrayana texts used by advanced meditation practitioners.

552 JOHN SINCLAIR: Poet, pioneer Detroit publisher, jazz critic, leader of Ann Arbor "White Panthers." Arrested 1969 for giving two marijuana joints to police spies in his Artists Workshop interracial poet-musicians' enterprise, he was sentenced to $9^1/2$–10 years jail, and liberated by state legislation the weekend after John Lennon-Yoko Ono's "Free John Sinclair" concert, Ann Arbor, 1972. This libertarian protest provoked unsuccessful Nixon administration deportation proceedings against Lennon.

553 QUECHUA: The Quechua Indian city Macchu Picchu is located in Huilca Bamba valley.

553 DMT: Dimethyltryptamine, a short-lived "high," psychedelic drug related to traditional Peruvian intoxicant Huilca. The chemical was later described by an early experimenter, Dr. Oscar Janiger, as "most powerful of all hallucinogenic agents." DMT use has not yet been experimentally discerned in a cultural climate (1970s–1980s) discouraging to this area of scientific investigation.

555 GOODMAN, CHANEY, SCHWERNER: N.Y. Jewish boys and a Southern black were murdered together while traveling in Mississippi, 1964, to aid black civil rights campaign.

558 WEATHERMEN: Underground radical extreme confrontation-protest antiwar SDS splinter group engineered pot-convict scientist Dr. Timothy Leary's over-the-wall departure from half-ounce grass-bust twenty-year sentence to California prison.

558 EAST HILL: Highest point Otsego County, N.Y., 2,400 feet near Cherry Valley town (pop. 300).

Guru Om

561 PRANAYAM: Yogic conscious breath attention practice.

561 NITYANANDA: Swami, guru to Swami Muktananda Paramahamsa, from whom author received meditation instruction at time of writing.

562 SAMSARA: World of illusory suffering, or existence seen as condition of suffering.

562 ASANAS: Yogic postures.

562 KUNDALINI: Energy wakened by yogic practice. See *The Serpent Power*, by Arthur Avalon (New York: Dover, 1974), celebrated early exposition-translation by Westerner.

Milarepa Taste

565 MILAREPA: "Cotton-clad" Himalayan yogi poet, early father of Kagyu lineage, Tibetan Buddhist hero, author *The Hundred Thousand Songs of Milarepa*, trans. Garma C. C. Chang, 2 vols. (New Hyde Park, N.Y.: University Books, 1962).

Bixby Canyon to Jessore Road
(1971)

Bixby Canyon Ocean Path Word Breeze

569 MUDRAS: Sacramental or yogic hand gestures, bodily or psychologic attitudes.

570 BEEDLE: Beetle, or beadle: church official who bears the mace. See Blake, *Songs of Innocence*, "Holy Thursday": "Grey headed beadles walked before / with wands as white as snow / . . ."

September on Jessore Road

579 JESSORE ROAD: At time of author's visit, millions of Hindu refugees from East Pakistan communal strife crowded starving in floods on this main road between Bangladesh and Calcutta.

582 SUNIL POET: Calcutta poet Sunil Ganguly (Ganghopadhyay), with whom author traveled Jessore Road, in company with American Buddhist student and poet John Giorno.

IX
MIND BREATHS ALL OVER THE PLACE
(1972–1977)

Sad Dust Glories
(1972–1974)

Thoughts Sitting Breathing

597 OM MANI PADMI HŪM: (Sanskrit) "Hail jewel in the lotus," Tibetan mantra for compassion practice, each syllable penetrating its equivalent among the six worlds pictured in Time Wheel Mandala: Heaven Realm, Human Realm, Hungry Ghost Realm, Hell Realm, Animal Realm, Angry Warrior Realm, transitory delusive states of consciousness, all revolving on the axle of vanity, greed and ignorance. The poem explores the cycle thrice. See illustration to poem.

597 CORD MEYER: CIA officer responsible for covert subsidization of international intellectuals' opinion-making organizations and periodicals, 1950s–60s Committee for Cultural Freedom, *Encounter* magazine, etc.

599 DHARMAKAYA: Buddhist term—kaya: realm, world or body; dharma: truth, law or nature. World of absolute, in the sense of totally accommodating open space, nondiscriminating ultimate reality, equivalent to the nonconceptualizing awareness of ordinary mind.

"What would you do if you lost it?"

600 RINPOCHE CHÖGYAM TRUNGPA TULKU: (1939–1987) Rinpoche, honorific title for lamas: "precious jewel"; Tulku, one of succession of teachers "reincarnated" or trained in specific lineage teachings. Chögyam Trungpa, the author's Vajracharya, or Mantrayana-style meditation practice master, born in Tibet, abbot of Surmang Monastery, is presently director of Vajradhatu Buddhist Centers and Naropa Institute. See his *Cutting Through Spiritual Materialism*,

1973, and *First Thought, Best Thought* (108 poems), with introduction by Allen Ginsberg, 1984, both Shambhala Press, Boulder.

600 TANTRAS: Buddhist texts for Mantrayana practice mode.

600 HAGGADAHS: Hebrew liturgy, Passover Seder service.

600 ZOHAR: Kabbalist-gnostic theosophical work expounding Pentateuch mysteries.

600 KOANS: Extrarationalistic riddles for nonconceptual mindfulness and "nonlinear" awareness used in Zen meditation practice with a committed teacher's guidance.

600 DHARMAKAYA . . . NIRMANAKAYA . . . SAMBHOGAKAYA: "body of truth" (absolute Buddha nature), "body of creation" (earthly or grounded Buddha form) and "body of bliss" (visionary communicative aspect of Buddha as speech).

600 PADMASAMBHAVA: Founder Tibetan Buddhist Nyingma or "old sect," A.D. 747 author of *Tibetan Book of the Dead*.

600 DR. SAMEDI: Traditional Vodun presence in Haitian graveyard, dressed as described.

600 BHAKTIVEDANTA SWAMI: Founder of U.S. Hare Krishna movement, spiritual friend of author; died 1977.

600 FILES ON NY POLICE AND C.I.A. PEDDLING HEROIN: See section "Narcotics Agents Peddling Drugs," including "Brief bibliography of news reports showing that narcotics agents, federal, state and local, the bulk of each group, are themselves involved in dope trafficking," pp. 63–70, and "CIA Involvement with Opium Traffic at Its Source," pp. 71–97, *Allen Verbatim*, ed. Gordon Ball (New York: McGraw-Hill, 1974). See also Alfred W. McCoy, *The Politics of Heroin in Southeast Asia* (New York: Harper & Row, 1973).

601 JOE BOZZO & HARRY HAINES: Respectively, reputed 1930s mob boss, Paterson N.J., and publisher of *Paterson Evening News*.

601 MOUNI: (Sanskrit) Wise man, sage, sometimes vowed to silence.

601 TOM VEITCH: American poet (b. 1941) See his *Death Collage*, (Berkeley: Big Sky, 1976), with afterword by Allen Ginsberg.

601 IBM 135-35: During U.S. invasion of Vietnam, world's largest computer located at Nakon Thanom Airbase, Thailand, directed "electronic battlefield" Indochina bombing.

601 IGLOO WHITE: U.S. project to destroy supply trucks and people moving down Laotian Ho-Chi-Minh jungle trail, 1967 on. Sensors, implanted on ground or suspended from trees by air drop, sent electronic messages to aircraft overhead, for relay to central computer control station. Then flying gunships equipped with low light-level TV systems and infrared detectors were directed to strike area.

601 DRAGON-TOOTH: Plastic pellet bombs which devastated football-field-sized areas.

601 FUEL-AIR BOMB: Scattered a powder gas which exploded after penetrating underground caves and shelters used by Viet Cong.

601 BODHISATTVAS: Who take Four Vows: (1) Sentient Beings are numberless, I vow to liberate all; (2) Obstacles are countless, I vow to uncover all; (3) Gates of Dharma are innumerable, I vow to enter all; (4) Buddha path is endless, I vow to follow through.

601 BHUMI: (Sanskrit) World, realm, among graduated stages of awareness. For Ten Bhumis, see Gampopa, *The Jewel Ornament of Liberation*, trans. H. V. Guenther (Boulder: Shambhala Press, 1971).

601 RUNG: (Hebrew mystic term) Realm or state of attainment.

601 OM AH HŪM: Trikaya mantra of body, speech and mind.

601 A LA LA HO: Salutation mantra.

page

601 SOPHIA: Gnostic wisdom goddess.

601 SOHAM: Pranayama breath mantra, "I am."

601 TARA MA: Mother Tara, Hindu-Buddhist compassion aspect goddess; also, a female Buddha.

601 OM PHAT SVAHA: Mantra of offering to affective spirits. See D. L. Snellgrove, *Hevajra Tantra* (New York: Oxford, 1959). (For traditional use, consult lineage teacher.)

602 MARPA . . . GAMPOPA: Kagyu order, early Tibetan lineage teachers. Marpa the translator (1012–1096), farmer-yogi; Milarepa (1052–1135), yogi-poet; Gampopa (1079–1153), consolidator of teachings, author guidebook, *The Jewel Ornament of Liberation.*

602 TRUNGPAYE: Chögyam Trungpa, Rinpoche, a current bearer of Kagyu teachings.

602 NAMASTAJI: Intimate Indian salutation.

602 BRAHMA: Formless aspect of Hindu trinity with Vishnu, Preserver, and Shiva, Changer.

602 SURYA: Vedic sun god, much like Occidental Apollo.

602 INDRA: Chief Vedic god, rain-lightning-thunder.

602 BOM BOM! SHIVAYE!: Mantra of offering cried out, often at cremation grounds, by cannabis-smoking saddhus to grace a chilam (clay ganja pipe) before inhaling.

602 RAM NAM SATYAHEY: "Ram's name is the truth," traditional chant of Hindus bearing corpse litter to Ganges cremation ground.

602 GANIPATTI: Or Ganesha, four-armed, elephant-headed Remover of Obstacles, god of wisdom, prudence and learning, son of Shiva and Parvati, whose vehicle is a rat.

602 OM SARASWATI HRIH SOWHA: Traditional mantric invocation to goddess of music, learning and poetry.

602 ARDINARISHVARA: Hermaphrodite-bodied Hindu divinity.

602 RADHA: Krishna's consort.

602 HAREKRISHNA: Krishna, seventh of nine avatars of Vishnu, lord of preservation. Hare may be shakti of Krishna, consort, or spiritual-bliss potency of supreme person of universe.

Who

603 WHO: Reply to request from *Who's Who* for self-characterization.

Yes and It's Hopeless

604 HALF MILLION COMMUNISTS ASSASSINATED: Indonesian slaughter accompanying 1965–1966 overthrow of President Sukarno, political coup influenced by U.S. business intelligence.

604 SLAUGHTER . . . MEXICO CITY: Refers to 1968 machine-gun massacre of 1,000 student protesters at Tlatelolco Square, a clean-up of political dissidents preparatory to Olympic festivals. See also "Birdbrain."

What I'd Like to Do

610 NAROPA'S SIX DOCTRINES: Psychic Heat, Illusory Body, Dream State, Clear Light, After Death State, and Consciousness Transference; see *Tibetan Yoga and Secret Doctrines,* W. Y. Evans-Wentz (Oxford, 1967).

610 KITKITDIZZE: Wintun Indian name for tarweed, bear clover or mountain misery, dark green shrub varying 3–15 inches in height, tarry touch and smell, belonging to rose family. Typical ground cover, western slope Sierra ponderosa pine forest. Poet Gary Snyder's Sierra household is named Kitkitdizze, after this common plant, *Chamaebatia foliolosa*.

Mind Breaths

616 AH: Calligraphy by Chögyam Trungpa, Rinpoche, 1978. Symbol of Tibetan Buddhist Kagyu order; one syllable summary of Prajnaparamita Sutra; mantra for purification of speech, and appreciation of space; related to Samatha meditation practice, mindfulness of outbreath; a vocalization of the outbreath.

617 SANGHA: (Sanskrit) Community of Buddhist practitioners.

618 BO TREE: The ancient pipal, *Ficus religiosa*, or sacred fig tree, in Bodh Gaya, India, under which Buddha meditated till enlightened.

Flying Elegy

620 SKANDAS: (Sanskrit) The five "heaps" of experience or psychosomatic aggregates of individual personality, namely: form, reaction-sensation, feeling-ideation, cumulative habit pattern, and apparent consciousness, which compound the transitory energies of ego.

620 SUNYATA: Emptiness, nonmind, or awareness devoid of egocentric projection.

Jaweh and Allah Battle

622 SNAKE COCK AND PIG EAT EACH OTHER'S TAILS: Symbols of anger, vanity and ignorance at center axle of Time Wheel Mandala. See illustration, p. 588.

622 CALLER OF THE GREAT CALL: According to Barbelo-Ophitic myth of Garden of Eden, the snake (as caller of the Great Call) was Sophia's messenger to waken awareness in Adam and Eve. Sabaot, archon of their aeon, was but seven-aeon-times-removed reflection of Sophia's first thought. See Hans Jonas, *Gnostic Religion* (Boston: Beacon Press, 1963). Refer also to "Plutonian Ode," note to verse 16, *Sabaot*.

622 STERN GANG IRGUN: Terrorist groups under British mandate, fought for Zionist cause.

622 AL FATAH BLACK SEPTEMBER: Terrorist groups after Israeli sovereignty, fought for Palestinian cause.

623 MEYER LANSKY: U.S. organized-crime chief reported to've supplied guns to Zionist terrorist/freedom fighters. Retired to Israel for years, was deported back to U.S. after public scandal, 1972, and arrested for income tax evasion.

623 MY FATHER HAD A COFFEE SHOP IN JERUSALEM: See poem "Write It Down, Allen Said," in *Clean Asshole Poems & Smiling Vegetable Songs*, Peter Orlovsky (San Francisco: City Lights Pocket Poet Series #37, 1978), pp. 118–20.

623 COMMENTARY: American highbrow crypto-Zionist right-wing ideological journal edited by ambitious early prose critic of Kerouac's poetic prose, later hawkish proponent of military hard-line hardware equated as alternative discipline for supposed loose 1960s national morals including public acknowledgment of gaiety.

623 PALESTINE REVIEW: Pro-Palestinian journal.

624 SHEMA YISROEL ADONOI ELUHENU: End of Hebrew chant: "Rejoice, O Israel, the Lord is one, the Lord is God."

624   LA ILAH . . . : Sufi chant: "There is no god but Allah."

624   HU: Sufi mantric out-breath.

624   SHALOM! SHANTIH! SALAAM!: Hebrew, Sanskrit, Arabic for "Peace!"

Sad Dust Glories

627   KENJI MYAZAWA: 20th-century Japanese poet, trans. Gary Snyder among others.

628   SHOBO-AN: Japanese Soto temple reconstructed by San Francisco Zen Center in California Sierras adjacent to Kitkitdizze "Ring of Bone" Zen Practice Center.

628   ACORN PEOPLE: Sierra Indian diet staple was acorn mush.

Ego Confessions
(1974–1977)

Ego Confession

631   GYALWA KARMAPA: 16th lama head of Milarepa lineage, Kagyu order of Tibetan Buddhism.

631   WEATHERMEN GOT NO MOSCOW GOLD: Timothy Leary, held incommunicado for years, early 1970's, by Feds, refused to testify falsely that Weathermen were directed by Moscow finance. FBI heads were later convicted of illegal wiretapping since no evidence that antiwar protesters were agents of foreign powers could be found.

631   VAJRASATTVA: Central image of Nyingma old-school Tibetan meditation practice, blue-bodied, with diamond-lightning bolt (vajra) form held in right hand at breast, bell (ghanta) of empty (open) space held at left hip. Dharmakaya Buddha.

631   OVERTHREW THE CIA WITH A SILENT THOUGHT: Refers to 1970 Georgetown dinner bet between author and then CIA chief Richard Helms: whether or not Central Intelligence Agency had working relationship with opium traffickers at "secret" CIA base, Long Cheng, Laos. Author offered his vajra, if misinformed, and requested CIA Director Helms to practice meditation an hour a day for life if his denial proved incorrect. The wager was accepted, a bet either party might profit from by losing. Note also:

The New York Times
3 rue Scribe
75 Paris 9e

Apr. 11 1978

Dear Allen,

    I fear I owe you an apology. I have been reading a succession of pieces about CIA involvement in the dope trade in Southeast Asia and I remember when you first suggested I look into this I thought you were full of beans. Indeed you were right and I acknowledge the fact plus sending my best personal wishes.

C. L. Sulzberger

Who Runs America?

636 GENERAL MOTORS ... STANDARD OF CALIFORNIA: The dozen corporations name-dropped herein are top twelve capital powers whose $133 billion sales represented a tenth the total gross national product one yearly trillion $. Traditionally, an oil corporation representative fills post of U.S. Secy of State and auto corporation representative fills Secretary of Defense post. This gossip's source was conversation with Daniel Ellsberg & Gary Snyder, November 26, 1974, re: Douglas F. Dowd's *The Twisted Dream, Capitalist Development in the United States Since 1776*, 2nd ed. (Cambridge: Winthrop, 1977).

Thoughts on a Breath

637 FOUR YEARS AGO: Poem is sequel to "Guru Om," October 4–6, 1970.

637 STONY BURNS: "After being arrested twice on pornography charges, then convicted for inciting riot, Stony Burns, art director and founder of *Iconoclast* and *Dallas Notes* [underground newspapers], was sentenced in Dallas to ten years and one day in prison for the possession of less than one tenth of an ounce of marijuana. The extra day in the sentence prevented eligibility for parole. Within a year, public protest freed editor Burns."—*Unamerican Activities: The Campaign Against the Underground Press*, PEN American Center report, ed. Geoffrey Rips, foreword by Allen Ginsberg (San Francisco: City Lights, 1981); see pp. 102, 107–8. The poem was written when Stony Burns was first jailed, 1974.

Hospital Window

642 (MAYAGUEZ CRISIS): After U.S. withdrawal from Indochina war, the U.S. merchant ship *Mayaguez*, presumed to be spy ship, was taken by Cambodians near their coast in 1975. The ship was recaptured by U.S. with giant force, some loss of life, large headlines. The incident was argued at the time to symbolize U.S. resolve to "be perceived" still as "number one" in world might.

Hadda Be Playing on the Jukebox

643 BIG TIME SYNDICATE TAMPA: Sam Giancana and John Roselli, associated with Tampa mob chief, engaged by CIA to assassinate Cuban Premier Castro in "turf war," early '60s. Both were murdered or "rubbed out" prior to scheduled testimony before Senate Select Committee on Intelligence, chaired by late Senator Frank Church, 1965, re CIA assassination attempts against Castro. Roselli was found in barrel in ocean; Giancana was shot in his kitchen.

643 LET LUCKY LUCIANO OUT OF JAIL ... : The international organized crime chief was released from federal prison by wartime Office of Strategic Services to supplant influence of Communist partisan anti-Hitler underground in Sicily with Mafia political infrastructure. According to American authorities, Luciano later became Mediterranean narcotics overlord. See "I'm Glad the CIA Is Immoral," Thomas W. Braden, *Saturday Evening Post*, May 20, 1967, p. 14.

644 CHILE'S RED DEMOCRACY . . . : Salvador Allende (1908–1973), first democratically elected Marxist-socialist head of state in the western hemisphere, was deposed by U.S.-trained generals' junta, 1973. Subsequent Senate investigation revealed that CIA funds were used to organize destabilizing truck transport strikes, to penetrate Santiago's daily newspaper *Mercurio,* and to arrange "housewife demonstrations" against the new Allende government. Well-dressed family ladies walked in the streets, and banged on pots and pans, conveying an impression of normal people spontaneously protesting Allende government's socialist austerities. The night after the U.S.-backed generals' assault on presidential palace and assassination of Allende, the author remembers watching the TV screen with his father while news commentator Victor Riesel energetically congratulated American viewers: "The CIA was not involved!"

644 NKVD: People's Commissariat for Internal Affairs—Soviet secret police.

644 OGPU: 1930s Russian secret police.

644 DIA: U.S. Defense Intelligence Agency.

644 KGB: Soviet Committee of State Security, equivalent to U.S. FBI, but worse.

Come All Ye Brave Boys

645 LIDS: Lid, a quantity of marijuana, equivalent to an ounce, originally a Prince Albert tobacco can full.

Gospel Noble Truths

649 YOU GOT TO SUFFER: First stanza refers to Buddhist doctrine of three "marks" or characteristics of existence: (1) suffering, (2) change, (3) Anatma (no permanent selfhood). Stanzas 1–3 refer to the Four Noble Truths of Buddhist philosophy: (1) Existence contains suffering; (2) Suffering is caused by ignorance; (3) Ignorance can be changed by practice of detachment, wisdom and compassion (4) and by following an eightfold path as paraphrased in song lines 13–20: (1) right views, (2) right aspiration, (3) right speech, (4) right activity, (5) right labor, (6) right energy, (7) right mindfulness, (8) right meditation. There follows brief instruction for sitting and review of six sense fields.

Rolling Thunder Stones

652 WE GIVE THANKS FOR THIS FOOD . . . : After Snyder/Whalen adaptation of Zen thanks offering for food.

Two Dreams

656 ACID TIDE: Nitrous waste pollution of Jersey-Manhattan waters. A 1966 *Los Angeles Free Press* Robert Cobb cartoon showed ocean of LSD washing away a pillared fortress-island of Law, God, Self, Good, Evil, etc., seen somewhat as Urizenic Blakean abstractions.

Don't Grow Old

664 AUNT ROSE: See "To Aunt Rose," Paris, 1958.

664 NAROPA: Naropa Institute, contemplative college founded 1974 by Chögyam Trungpa; named for Kagyu lineage second patriarch, once rector of eighth-

century Buddhist Nalanda International University. Naropa's Jack Kerouac School of Disembodied Poetics, codirected by author and Anne Waldman, was founded same year.

Contest of Bards

673 ETERNAL RUNE CUT IN STONE: Rune (Old Norse), character of Old Teutonic or Scandinavian alphabets; magical cipher.
685 EIDOLON: Platonic Image. See Whitman's poem "Eidolons."

Punk Rock Your My Big Crybaby

691 MABUHAY GARDENS TO CBGB'S: Punk rock/new wave youth clubs, on San Francisco's North Beach and New York's Bowery.

X
PLUTONIAN ODE
(1977–1980)

Grim Skeleton

699 RICHARD HELMS: See "Ego Confession" note.

Adapted from Neruda's "Que dispierte el leñador"

704 QUE DISPIERTE: Adapted Summer 1978–Spring 1981 by Sidney Goldfarb and Allen Ginsberg from Waldeen's trans. of *Let The Railsplitter Awake and Other Poems*, by Pablo Neruda (New York: Masses and Mainstream, 1950).

Nagasaki Days

707 ELLSBERG: Daniel Ellsberg (b. 1931) Author, revealer of the "Pentagon Papers," now-public "secret" Defense Department analysis of built-in futility of U.S. Vietnam War adventure, had also helped design nuclear-strategy practical mechanics, including the failsafe system. The author and scholar Ellsberg were arrested together in Colorado during anti-nuclear peace protest at Rockwell Corporation's Rocky Flats plutonium-bomb-trigger factory.
708 GOLDEN COURTHOUSE: See Kerouac's verse "I wanna go to Golden," i.e., Golden, Colorado, Jefferson county seat, where Rocky Flats anti-nuclear-weapons-manufacture demonstrators were tried.

Plutonian Ode

710 WHITMAN: Walt Whitman.
710 DOCTOR SEABORG: Glenn Seaborg, "Discoverer of Plutonium."
710 SEA BEYOND URANUS: Pluto, past planets Uranus and Neptune.
710 AVENGING FURIES: Pluto was father to Eumenides, the Furies who return to avenge mindless damage done in passion, aggression, ignorance, etc. Pluto was also Lord of Wealth.
710 DEMETER: Pluto's mother-in-law, the Earth fertility goddess whose daughter Persephone was stolen for marriage by underworld lord Pluto (Greek: Hades [Aides], brother to Zeus and Poseidon) and kept in his caverns a half year at a

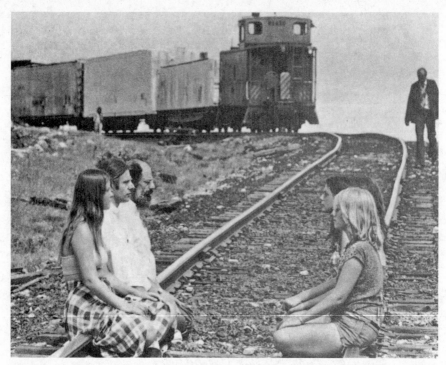

Allen Ginsberg, Peter Orlovsky and friends of Rocky Flats Truth Force, meditating on R.R. Tracks outside Rockwell Corporation Nuclear Facility's Plutonium bomb trigger factory, Colorado, halting trainload of waste fissile materials on the day Plutonium Ode was completed, July 14, 1978. Photo by Steve Groer, *Rocky Mountain News*.

page

time, released to her mother each spring. Demeter gave wheat to man at Eleusis, site of her temple, one place in ancient world where Hades also was acknowledged with ceremonies indicated above.

710 ASPHODEL: W. C. Williams wrote of asphodel, "that greeny flower," as the blossom of Hades.

710 FISH . . . RAM . . . BULL . . . TWINS . . . CRAB . . . LION: Ages of Pisces, Aries, Taurus, Gemini, Cancer, Leo—2,000 years each age.

710 GREAT YEAR: Platonic, or Babylonian, or Sidereal "Great Year"—24,000 years— half life of Plutonium radioactivity. This fact, pointed out to me by Gregory Corso, inspired this poem. Cf. W. B. Yeats, *A Vision*.

710 ONE HUNDRED SIXTY-SEVEN THOUSAND: The 24,000-year span of the Great Year—167,000 cycles—4 billion years, supposed age of Earth.

710 BLACK . . . DISILLUSION: Six senses, including mind.

710 SABAOT . . . IALDABAOTH: Archons of successive aeons born of Sophia's thought, according to Ophitic and Barbelo-Gnostic myths.

710 SKY OVER SILENT MILLS AT HANFORD . . . MASON: Plutonium factories, whose location by state and whose function in bomb-making are here described. Plants in Pantex, Texas, and Burlington, Iowa, managed by Mason & Hanger-Silas Mason Co., Inc., assemble the finished components of the nuclear weapons.

711 TWO HUNDRED FORTY MILLENNIA: 240,000 years the supposed time till Plutonium becomes physically inert.

711 TEN POUNDS: Ten pounds of Plutonium scattered throughout the earth is calculated sufficient to kill 4 billion people.

711 SIX WORLDS: Six worlds of Gods, Warrior Demons, Humans, Hungry Ghosts, Animals, and Hell Beings held together in the delusion of time by pride, anger and ignorance: a Buddhist concept. See notes to "Thoughts Sitting Breathing," p. 796.

711 DIVINE WIND: Kamikaze, typhoon, wind of Gods.

711 THREE HUNDRED TONS: 300 tons of Plutonium, estimate circa 1978 of the amount produced for American bombs.

711 I SING YOUR FORM: "The Reactor hath hid himself thro envy. I behold him. But you cannot behold him till he be revealed in his System."—Blake, *Jerusalem*, Chap. II, Plate 43, lines 9–10.

712 HONEY . . . WATER: Traditional libation to Hades poured at Temple of Eleusis, and by Odysseus at the Necromanteion at Acheron.

712 DIAMOND TRUTH: Reference to Buddhist doctrine of Sunyatā, i.e., existence as simultaneously void and solid, empty and real, all-penetrating egoless (empty void) nature symbolized by adamantine Vajra or Diamond Sceptre.

712 FIVE HUNDRED BILLION DOLLAR: Estimated world military budget; 116 billion, U.S. share, October 1978.

713 TAKE THIS INHALATION . . . THOUGHT-WORLDS: Four characteristics of Buddha-nature activity: to pacify, enrich, magnetize & destroy.

713 GONE OUT . . . AH!: Americanese approximation and paraphrase of Sanskrit Prajnaparamita (Highest Perfect Wisdom) Mantra: Gate Gate Paragate Parasamgate Bodhi Svaha.

Blame the Thought, Cling to the Bummer

717 DUDJOM LINEAGE: Dudjom Rinpoche, contemporary head of Nyingma "old school" Tibetan teachings founded by Padmasambhava.

717 BEDROCK MORTAR . . . : Cottage built by author and friends in California Sierra woods adjoining Kitkitdizze, at site of original Indian inhabitants' mortar holes. See "Sad Dust Glories" note.

"Don't Grow Old"

718 DON'T GROW OLD: See poems on the death of Louis Ginsberg, January 12–July 11, 1976.

December 31, 1978

724 LINDY HOP: Peculiar quick dance step popular late 1920s.

Brooklyn College Brain

725 BODHICITTA: Seed of enlightenment stuff, enlightened essence of Buddha mind, or awakening aspect of mind.

Garden State

727 HARRISBURG HYDROGEN BUBBLE: In Pennsylvania's Three Mile Island nuclear accident, March 28, 1979, unit #2's reactor core was badly damaged. A pres-

sure relief valve in the main cooling system had jammed while the reactor was operating at full power. Thousands of gallons of water unexpectedly drained from the core. At this pass, operators mistakenly turned off pumps designed to flood the reactor in such emergency. Consequent overheating resulted in damage to the reactor, and release of radiation.

Las Vegas: Verses Improvised for El Dorado H.S. Newspaper

728 MOAPA: Original nomadic inhabitants of Nevada.

728 ROBERT MAHEU: (b. 1917) Secretary to Howard Hughes, ex-FBI, introduced Sam Giancana and John Roselli (business acquaintances of Tampa syndicate boss Santos Trafficante, co-worker with Jack Ruby, and pre-Castro vice/narcotic lord of Havana territory) to CIA official Sheffield Edwards, to arrange assassination of Cuban premier Castro. Personages of Watergate plumbers team were associated with the much-reported yet little-researched anti-Castro Cuban Mafia circle of secret operations. See "Hadda Be Playing on the Jukebox" note.

(Sheffield Edwards was also CIA Chief of Security, which office oversaw early 1950s drug experiment programs, psychedelic and otherwise.)

728 MT. CHARLESTON: Sacred mountain among Moapa tribes in traditional migratory cycle.

728 ENGLEBERT: Mr. Humperdinck, popular cabaret entertainer.

728 PLATONIC YEAR: See "Plutonian Ode" note.

728 UNDER THE ASTRONOMICAL FLAGPOLE: Harold Ickes, interior secretary under FDR, commissioned various solar system designs, including the Great Year pattern of earth's wobble on its sidereal axis, to be set in bronze on Hoover Dam's plaza, marking the monumental size of the project, equal in scope to the Egyptian pyramids.

728 BUGSY SIEGEL: Original organized crime/vice chief of Las Vegas, assassinated by shots through window of Beverly Hills living room, 1947.

Ruhr-Gebiet

734 STAMMHEIM: Isolation prison where "terrorist" Baader-Meinhof gang members (originally armed by police double agents) were subject to continuous interrogation under 24-hour glare lighting.

735 "GUESTS" DO THE WORK: *Gastarbeiter*, "guest workers" of post-WWII West Germany: Turks, Italians, Slavs imported for heavy labor or menial work.

Reflections at Lake Louise

741 ORYOKI: Traditional style of formal three-bowl mindful silent eating practice in Zendō (meditation hall).

Ode to Failure

745 MAYAKOVSKY CRIED, THEN DIE! MY VERSE: "Let glory/disconsolate widow frail/ trudge after genius/in funeral anthems/Die, my verse,/die, like the rank and file/as our unknown, unnumbered, fell/in storming heaven."—Vladimir Mayakovsky, "At the Top of My Voice," 1930, in *Mayakovsky and His Poetry*, trans. Herbert Marshall (London: Pilot Press, 1943). Frank O'Hara first called author's attention to this poem.

Birdbrain!

746   XOCHOPILI: Formerly referred to as "God of Flowers" in tourist guidebooks. Vegetable forms incised on his celebrated statue in Mexico City's Archaeological Museum have been identified by Harvard Botanical Museum director Richard E. Schultes as peyote, morning glory, amanita mushroom, tobacco, etc. Evidence of Xochopili culture was obliterated during Spanish conquest.

746   RAN GERMANY ON AMPHETAMINES: Among other books, *Inside the Third Reich*, memoirs of Albert Speer (New York: Macmillan, 1970), gives evidence on Hitler's rug-chewing speed addiction.

"Defending the Faith"

750   MAGLIĆ CASTLE: Castle of "mist" or "fog" (*maglić*) at heart of original kingdom of Serbia.

750   IVAR RIVER BANK: (12th-century "Ras") In Ivar River Valley, "Valley of the Kings." "Where the valley narrows to form a dramatic gorge . . . stand the remains of the Magli´c fortress perched like an eagle's nest upon a separate spur of the mountains" (Fodor's *Yugoslavia*, 1972, p. 277).

Epigraphs from Original Editions

'Unscrew the locks from the doors!
Unscrew the doors themselves from their jambs!' (*Howl*)

'—Die,
If thou wouldst be with that which thou dost seek!' (*Kaddish*)

'Scribbled secret notebooks, and wild typewritten pages, for yr own joy' (*Reality Sandwiches*)

'O go way man I can
    hypnotize this nation
I can shake the earth's foundation
    with the Maple Leaf Rag.' (*Planet News*)

'To find the Western path
Right thro' the Gates of Wrath
I urge my way;
Sweet Mercy leads me on:
With soft Repentant moan
I see the break of day.' (*Gates of Wrath*)

'Thus is the heaven a vortex pass'd already, and the earth
A vortex not yet pass'd by the traveller thro' Eternity.' (*Gates of Wrath*)

'The yearning infinite recoils,
For terrible is earth!' (*Gates of Wrath*)

'. . . same electric lightning South
        follows this train
                Apocalypse prophesied—
        the fall of America
            signalled from Heaven—' (*The Fall of America*)

  'Time after time for such a journey none but iron pens
Can write And adamantine leaves receive nor can the man who goes
The journey obstinate refuse to write time after time' (*Mind Breaths*)

'Meeting, the two friends laugh aloud;
In the grove, fallen leaves are many.' (*Poems All Over the Place*)

'La science, la nouvelle noblesse! Le progrès. Le monde marche! Pourquoi ne tour-
nerait-il pas?' (*Plutonian Ode*)

Dedications to

Jack Kerouac, new Buddha of American prose, who spit forth intelligence into eleven books written in half the number of years (1951–1956)—*On the Road, Visions of Neal, Dr Sax, Springtime Mary, The Subterraneans, San Francisco Blues, Some of the Dharma, Book of Dreams, Wake Up, Mexico City Blues*, and *Visions of Gerard*—creating a spontaneous bop prosody and original classic literature. Several phrases and the title of *Howl* are taken from him.

William Seward Burroughs, author of *Naked Lunch*, an endless novel which will drive everybody mad.

Neal Cassady, author of *The First Third*, an autobiography (1949) which enlightened Buddha.

All these books are published in Heaven.

HOWL

Peter Orlovsky
in
Paradise
'Taste my mouth in your ear'

KADDISH

*dear
poet's poet
Philip Whalen*

AIRPLANE DREAMS

To Herbert E. Huncke
for his *Confessions*

EMPTY MIRROR

Miles
London's Scholar

ANGKOR WAT

the Pure Imaginary
POET
Gregory Corso

REALITY SANDWICHES

The Soul of
Leroi Jones

SCRAP LEAVES

Neal Cassady
again
Spirit to Spirit
February 8, 1925–February 4, 1968
'the greater driver'
'secret hero of these poems'

PLANET NEWS

Larry Ferlinghetti
Fellow
Poet
Editor

POEMS ALL OVER THE PLACE

Walt Whitman

"Intense and loving comradeship, the personal and passionate attachment of man to man—which, hard to define, underlies the lessons and ideals of the profound saviors of every land and age, and which seems to promise, when thoroughly develop'd, cultivated and recognised in manners and literature, the most substantial hope and safety of the future of these States, will then be fully express'd.

"It is to the development, identification, and general prevalence of that fervid comradeship, (the adhesive love, at least rivaling the amative love hitherto possessing imaginative literature, if not going beyond it,) that I look for the counterbalance and offset of our materialistic and vulgar American democracy, and for the spiritualization thereof. Many will say it is a dream, and will not follow my inferences: but I confidently expect a time when there will be seen, running like a half-hid warp through all the myriad audible and visible worldly interests of America, threads of manly friendship, fond and loving, pure and sweet, strong and life-long, carried to degrees hitherto unknown—not only giving tone to individual character, and making it unprecedentedly emotional, muscular, heroic, and refined, but having the deepest relations to general politics. I say democracy infers such loving comradeship, as its most inevitable twin or counterpart, without which it will be incomplete, in vain, and incapable of perpetuating itself."

Democratic Vistas, 1871

THE FALL OF AMERICA

Vajracarya
Chögyam Trungpa, Rinpoche
Poet
"Guru Death your words are true
Teacher Death I do thank you
For inspiring me to sing this Blues"

MIND BREATHS

Lucien Carr
for friendship
all these years

PLUTONIAN ODE

Acknowledgments

Author wishes to imprint thanks to poets & editors who initially published these writings. A wild gamut of literary magazines & papers rose to manifest renaissance of vernacular poetry in postwar II USA, invented by the World War I generation. W. C. Williams & Ezra Pound prophesied an American poetic mode measured to the variety of contemporary body english, speech and mind. Individuation of idiom was followed by individuation of print form. Poetic "Mimeograph Revolution" coincided (mid-1950s) with a "San Francisco Poetry Renaissance" and the names of publications improvised became a poem in itself.

A.G.

Adventures in Poetry, A Hundred Posters, Allen Verbatim (ed. Gordon Ball, McGraw-Hill), Alternative Features Syndicate, Alternative Press, Alternative Press Broadside, American Dialogue, American Poetry Review, Antioch Review, Aquarian, Ark/Moby, Ashok Shahane, A Shout in the Streets, Athanor, Auerhahn/Haselwood Press, A Year of Disobedience

Bad Breath, Bastard Angel, Beatitude, Berkeley Barb, Berkeley Tribe, Bernerzeitung, Between Worlds, Big Sky, Big Table, Birthstone, Black Mountain Review, Bombay Gin, Boulder Express, Boulder Monthly, Boulder Street Poets, Brahma, Brandeis Folio, Brown Paper, Buffalo Stamps, Bugger (Fuck You/a Magazine of the Arts supplement), Burning Bush

'C', Cambridge Review (i.e.), Capella Dublin, Caterpillar, Che Fare, Cherry Valley Editions, Chicago, Chicago Review, City Lights Anthology, City Lights Books, City Lights Journals, Clean Energy Verse, Coach House Press, Cody's Bookshop Calendar, Coevolution Quarterly, College Press Service, Colorado North Review, Columbia *Jester*, Columbia Review, Combustion, Concerning Poetry, Coyote, Coyote's Journal, Cranium Press Broadsides, Creative Arts Book Co.

Dakota Broadsides Montreal, Desert Review, Dirty, Do-it

Earth Day Folio, Earth Magazine, East Village Other, El Dorado H.S. Newspaper, Evergreen Review, Expressen, Expresso

Fervent Valley Digest, Fifth Estate, Firefly Press, Fits, Floating Bear, Folger Shakespeare Library Broadside, Folio, Four Seasons, From Here Press, Fruit Cup, Fuck You/A Magazine of the Arts, Fulcrum Press, Fuori!

Gay Sunshine Press, Gemini, Georgia Strait, Gnaoua, Gotham Book Mart, Grabhorn Press, Grecourt Review, Greenpeace, Grey Fox Books, Grist, Grove Press,

Hard & Hardly Press, Hard Times, Harvard Crimson, Harvard Magazine, Hasty Papers, High Times, Hika, House of Anansi

Ice & Frice, Il Tarocco, Ins & Outs, Intrepid, Isis, Izvestia

Jabberwock (Sidewalk), Jack Albert's Boston Newspaper, Jargon 31, Jerusalem Post, Jonathan Cape-Golliard Press

Klacto 23, Kuksu, Kulchur

Lama Foundation: Bountiful Lord's Delivery Service, Lampeter Muse, L.A. Staff, League for Sexual Freedom Leaflet series, Lemar Marijuana Review, Liberation, Liberation News Service, Life, Literaturnya Gazeta, Loka, London Times Literary Supplement, Look, Los Angeles Free Press, Los Angeles Times, Lowenfel's Anthology, (lower) Eastside Review

Mag City, Mahenjodaro, Mattachine Review, Metronome, Mikrokosmos, Mojo Navigator, Mutantia, My Own Mag

Nadada, Neurotica, New Age Journal, New American Review, New Departures, New Directions Annuals, New York Free Press, New York Quarterly, New York Times, Nomad, Notes from the Garage Door, Notes from Underground, Now, Nuke Chronicles

Oyez poster

Pacific Nation, Painted Bride Quarterly, Paris Review, Partisan Review, Passaic Review, Peace News, Pearl, Peninsula Skyway, Pequod Press, Piazza, Planeta Fresca, Playboy, Poetry London/Apple, Poetry London-NY, Poetry on the Tracks, Poetry Review London, Poetry Toronto, Poets at Le Metro, Poets-and-Writers, Poet's Press, Portents, Provincetown Review, Pull My Daisy

Quixote

Rain, Ramparts, Read Street, Red Osier Press, Residu, rhinozeros, River Run, River Styx, Rocky Flats Truth Force, Rocky Ledge, Rolling Stone, Rolling Thunder Review Phantom Newsletter

Salted Feathers, San Francisco Free Press, Saturday Morning, Schism, Scrip Magazine, Seven Days, Sing Out, Soho News, Something, Southwest Review, Spradie im Technisehen Zeitalter, Stone Press Weekly, Stupa: Naropa Student Newsletter, Sun Books Australia, Swank, Synapse

Takeover, Telephone, The American Pen International Quarterly, The American Poetry Review, The Beat Scene, The End Magazine, The Grapevine, The Marijuana Review, The Nation, The Needle, The New Yorker, The Outsider, The Paris Magazine, The Raven, The Seventies, The Stone, The Sunflower (Wichita State), The Unspeakable Visions of the Individual, The Villager, The Workingman's Press, The World, The Yale Literary Magazine, Throat, Title I, Toronto Waves, Totem/-Corinth Books, Transatlantic Review

Underdog, Unmuzzled Ox Encyclopedia, Utigeverij 261

Vajradhatu Sun, Vancouver Express, Vancouver Vajradhatu, Variegation, Venture, Vigencia, Village Voice, Voices

Walker Art Center Broadside, West Hills Review, White Dove, Wholly Communion, Wild Dog, Win, W.I.N. (Workshop in Nonviolence) Magazine, Writer's Forum

Yugen

Zero

Nancy Peters, Lawrence Ferlinghetti, Annie Janowitz & Bob Sharrard helped prepare texts for City Lights Books.

Ted Wilentz, Amiri Baraka, Winston Leyland, Barry Gifford, Stuart Montgomery, Miles, Mary Beach, Claude Pelieu, Charles Plymell, Diane DiPrima, R'lene Dahlberg, Dave Haselwood and Marshall Clements helped edit other books of prose and poetry from which poems were drawn for this collection.

Don Allen consistently offered refined advice. Lucien Carr formulated "The Archetype Poem" and "How Come He Got Canned at the Ribbon Factory" anonymously three decades before this due acknowledgment of his wit and lifelong editorial prescience. Andrew Wylie shepherded this volume to New York.

For preparation of *Collected Poems* the sangha of editors at Harper & Row headed by Aaron Asher working with Carol Chen, Sidney Feinberg, Dan Harvey, Marge

Horvitz, Lydia Link, William Monroe, Joe Montebello, and Dolores Simon provided essential sympathetic skills.

Kenneth A. Lohf, Director of Manuscripts and Rare Books, Bernard Crystal, Assistant Director, and Mary Bowling, librarian in charge of manuscripts at Special Collections Division, Butler Library, Columbia University, preserved author's papers since 1968. Librarians at Humanities Research Center, University of Texas at Austin, conserved letters and notebooks useful in assembling manuscript.

Various typescripts were assembled at Naropa Institute's Jack Kerouac School of Disembodied Poetics by apprentice poets Walter Fordham, Jason Shinder, Sam Kashner, Helen Luster, Denyse King, Gary Allen, Alice Gambrell and Randy Roark among others, 1974–83.

Gordon Ball and Miles editing notebooks, journals and bibliographic papers retrieved texts and aided relatively precise chronology of poems.

Bill Morgan's bibliographic survey of author's work-spaces and Columbia Special Collections made possible ordering and retrieval of many writings in early script and book forms. Raymond Foye edited appropriate images from photo archive.

Bob Rosenthal provided years of logistical support to author and fellow archive workers. Juanita Lieberman contributed many hours.

Parts of *Collected Poems* were written & assembled during periods of National Endowment for the Arts Fellowship, N.Y. State Creative Artists Program Service, Inc., and Rockefeller Foundation grants to author.

Collaborative Artisans

Calligraphy AH by Chögyam Trungpa, Rinpoche.
Wheel of Life: Block Print, source unknown.
Tag lines for *Returning to the Country for a Brief Visit: Moments of Rising Mist*, a Collection of Sung Landscape Poetry, Mushinsha/Grossman, 1973.
Steven Taylor: lead sheets; Walter Taylor: lyric calligraphy.
Harry Smith: Illustration to *Journal Night Thoughts* (p. 274), and three fish one head cover insignia designed after incision on stone footprint of Buddha, seen by author at Bodh-Gaya, India, 1963; other version (p. 328).
Robert LaVigne: Illustrations, pp. 123, 143, 363, 766.

Diligent reader will find 22 additional poems rhymed, many with lead sheets, published as *First Blues: Rags, Ballads & Harmonium Songs 1971–1974*, Full Court Press, N.Y., 1975, to correlate with poems of that decade, supplementing the volume of musical inspiration.

Songs from *Collected Poems* and *First Blues* are vocalized solo on First Blues, Folkways Records, N.Y., 1981; and with musicians, First Blues, Double album, Hammond/C.B.S., N.Y., 1983.

Introduction by William Carlos Williams to *Empty Mirror*

The lines are superbly all alike. Most people, most critics would call them prose—they have an infinite variety, perfectly regular; they are all alike and yet none is like the other. It is like the monotony of our lives that is made up of the front pages of newspapers and the first (aging) 3 lines of the *Inferno*:

> In the middle of the journey of our life I (came to)
> myself in a dark wood (where) the
> straight way was lost.

It is all alike, those fated lines telling of the mind of that poet and the front page of the newspaper. Look at them. You will find them the same.

This young Jewish boy, already not so young any more, has recognized something that has escaped most of the modern age, he has found that man is lost in the world of his own head. And that the rhythms of the past have become like an old field long left unploughed and fallen into disuse. In fact they are excavating there for a new industrial plant.

There the new inferno will soon be under construction.

A new sort of line, omitting memories of trees and watercourses and clouds and pleasant glades—as empty of them as Dante Alighieri's *Inferno* is empty of them—exists today. It is measured by the passage of time without accent, monotonous, useless—unless you are drawn as Dante was to see the truth, undressed, and to sway to a beat that is far removed from the beat of dancing feet but rather finds in the shuffling of human beings in all the stages of their day, the trip to the bathroom, to the stairs of the subway, the steps of the office or factory routine the mystical measure of their passions.

It is indeed a human pilgrimage, like Geoffrey Chaucer's; poets had better be aware of it and speak of it—and speak of it in plain terms, such as men will recognize. In the mystical beat of newspapers that no one recognizes, their life is given back to them in plain terms. Not one recognizes Dante there fully deployed. It is not recondite but plain.

And when the poet in his writing would scream of the crowd, like Jeremiah, that their life is beset, what can he do, in the end, but speak to them in their own language, that of the daily press?

At the same time, out of his love for them—a poet as Dante was a poet—he must use his art, as Dante used his art, to please. He must measure, he must so disguise his lines, that his style appear prosaic (so that it shall not offend) to go in a cloud.

With this, if it be possible, the hidden sweetness of the poem may alone survive and one day rouse the sleeping world.

There cannot be any facile deception about it. The writing cannot be made to be "a kind of prose," not prose with a dirty wash of a stale poem over it. It must not set out, as poets are taught or have a tendency to do, to deceive, to sneak over a poetic way of laying down phrases. It must be prose but prose among whose words the terror of their truth has been discovered.

Here the terror of the scene has been laid bare in subtle measures, the pages are warm with it. The scene they invoke is terrifying more so than Dante's pages, the poem is not suspect, the craft is flawless.

1952

Introduction by William Carlos Williams to *Howl*

When he was younger, and I was younger, I used to know Allen Ginsberg, a young poet living in Paterson, New Jersey, where he, son of a well-known poet, had been born and grew up. He was physically slight of build and mentally much disturbed by the life which he had encountered about him during those first years after the first world war as it was exhibited to him in and about New York City. He was always on the point of 'going away', where it didn't seem to matter; he disturbed me, I never thought he'd live to grow up and write a book of poems. His ability to survive, travel, and go on writing astonishes me. That he has gone on developing and perfecting his art is no less amazing to me.

Now he turns up fifteen or twenty years later with an arresting poem. Literally he has, from all the evidence, been through hell. On the way he met a man named Carl Solomon with whom he shared among the teeth and excrement of this life something that cannot be described but in the words he has used to describe it. It is a howl of defeat. Not defeat at all for he has gone through defeat as if it were an ordinary experience, a trivial experience. Everyone in this life is defeated but a man, if he be a man, is not defeated.

It is the poet, Allen Ginsberg, who has gone, in his own body, through the horrifying experiences described from life in these pages. The wonder of the thing is not that he has survived but that he, from the very depths, has found a fellow whom he can love, a love he celebrates without looking aside in these poems. Say what you will, he proves to us, in spite of the most debasing experiences that life can offer a man, the spirit of love survives to ennoble our lives if we have the wit and the courage and the faith—and the art! to persist.

It is the belief in the art of poetry that has gone hand in hand with this man into his Golgotha, from that charnel house, similar in every way, to that of the Jews in the past war. But this is in our own country, our own fondest purlieus. We are blind and live our blind lives out in blindness. Poets are damned but they are not blind, they see with the eyes of the angels. This poet sees through and all around the horrors he partakes of in the very intimate details of his poem. He avoids nothing but experiences it to the hilt. He contains it. Claims it as his own—and, we believe, laughs at it and has the time and affrontery to love a fellow of his choice and record that love in a well-made poem.

Hold back the edges of your gowns, Ladies, we are going through hell.

1955

Author's Cover Writ

Hindsight for *Gates of Wrath*

Gates of Wrath's first sonnets, "Woe to Thee Manhattan," were inspired by first reading ms. of Kerouac's triumphant record of youth family *The Town and the City*. All poems hermetic "The Eye Altering" thru "A Western Ballad" refer to breakthru of visionary consciousness 1948 described elsewhere prosaically: early mind-manifesting flashes catalyzed by lonely despair I felt at sudden termination of erotic spiritual marriage mutually vowed by myself and Neal Cassady. The "Earlier Poems," 1947, were love poems to N.C., though love's gender was kept closet. "Sweet Levinsky" (counterimage to Kerouac's tender caricature) thru "Pull My Daisy" were written Jack much in mind ear. "Pull My Daisy"'s form grew out of J.K.'s adaptation of "Smart Went Crazy" refrain: recombining images jazzier as

> Pull my daisy,
> Tip my cup,
> All my doors are open—

from my more wooden verse. Jack brought this verse into York Ave. coldwater flat—I remember his athletic pencil-dash'd handscript, notebooked. I replicated that form and Jack dubbed in more lines—about a third of the poem was his. One line "How's the Hicks?" was tossed to us as we walked into Cassady's midnite NY parkinglot 1949 asking Neal "What's the Hex, Who's the Hoax?"

"Sometime Jailhouse" poems to "Ode 24th Year" reflect early dope-type bust & subsequent hospital rehabilitation solitude-bench dolmen realms so characteristic of mental penology late 40s contemporary. The letter to W.C.W. enclosing poems was answered thus: "In this mode perfection is basic." The poems were imperfect. I responded by sending Williams several speedworthy notations that form the basis of book *Empty Mirror*, texts written roughly same years as these imperfect lyrics.

Gates of Wrath ms. was carried to London by lady friend early fifties, it disappeared, and I had no complete copy till 1968 when old typescript was returned thru poet Bob Dylan—it passed into his hands years earlier. By coincidence, I returned to this rhymed mode with Dylan's encouragement as fitted for musical song. Tuned to lyric guitar, composing on harmonium, chant or improvising on rhythmic chords in electric studio, I began 'perfecting' use of this mode two decades after W.C.W.'s wise objection, dear reader, in same weeks signatured below.

December 8, 1971

Jacket for *Howl*

Allen Ginsberg born June 3, 1926, the son of Naomi Ginsberg, Russian émigré, and Louis Ginsberg, lyric poet and schoolteacher, in Paterson, N.J. High school in Paterson till 17, Columbia College, merchant marine, Texas and Denver, copyboy, Times Square, amigos in jail, dishwashing, book reviews, Mexico City, market research, Satori in Harlem, Yucatan and Chiapas 1954, West Coast 3 years.... Carl Solomon, to whom *Howl* is addressed, is an intuitive Bronx dadaist and prose-poet.

1960

Hindsight for *Kaddish*

In the midst of the broken consciousness of mid twentieth century suffering anguish of separation from my own body and its natural infinity of feeling its own self one with all self, I instinctively seeking to reconstitute that blissful union which I experienced so rarely I took it to be supernatural and gave it holy Name thus made hymn laments of longing and litanies of triumphancy of Self over the mind-illusion mechano-universe of un-feeling Time in which I saw my self my own mother and my very nation trapped desolate our worlds of consciousness homeless and at war except for the original trembling of bliss in breast and belly of every body that nakedness rejected in suits of fear that familiar defenseless living hurt self which is myself same as all others abandoned scared to own our unchanging desire for each other. These poems almost un-conscious to confess the beatific human fact, the language intuitively chosen as in trance & dream, the rhythms rising on breath from belly thru breast, the hymn completed in tears, the movement of the physical poetry demanding and receiving decades of life while chanting Kaddish the names of Death in many mind-worlds the self seeking the Key to life found at last in our self.

August 28, 1963

Back Cover for *Reality Sandwiches*

"Wake-up nightmares in Lower East Side, musings in public library, across the U.S. in dream auto, drunk in old Havana, brooding in Mayan ruins, sex daydreams on the West Coast, airplane vision of Kansas, lonely in a leafy cottage, lunch hour in Berkeley, beery notations on Skid Row, slinking to Mexico, wrote this last nite in Paris, back on Times Square dreaming of Times Square, bombed in NY again, loony tunes in the dentist chair, screaming at old poets in South America, aethereal zigzag Poesy in blue hotel rooms in Peru—a wind-up book of dream notes, psalms, journal enigmas & nude minutes from 1953 to 1960 poems scattered in fugitive magazines here collected now book."

1960

Back Cover for *Planet News*

Planet News collecting seven years' Poesy scribed to 1967 begins with electronic politics disassociation & messianic rhapsody *TV Baby* in New York, continues picaresque around the world globe, élan perceptions notated at Mediterranean, Galilee & Ganges till next breakthrough, comedown Poem heart & soul last days in Asia *The Change* 1963; tenement doldrums & police-state paranoia in Manhattan then half year behind Socialist Curtain climaxed as *Kral Majales* May King Prague 1965, same year's erotic gregariousness writ as *Who Be Kind To* for International Poetry Incarnation Albert Hall London; next trip West Coast U.S. & voyage back thru center America midwest *Wichita Vortex Sutra* which is mind-collage & keystone section of progressively longer poem on "These States"—here Self sitting in its own meat throne invokes Harekrishna as preserver of human planet & challenges all other Powers usurping State Consciousness to recognize same Identity, thus 'I here declare the End of the War.' Back dwelling on East Coast local psyche notes, elegy for O'Hara dead friend poet & worship for all Gods; at last across Atlantic *Wales Visitation* promethian text recollected in emotion revised in tranquillity continuing tradition of ancient Nature Language mediates between psychedelic inspiration and humane ecology & integrates acid classic Unitive Vision with democratic eyeball particulars— book closes on politics to exorcise Pentagon phantoms who cover Earth with dung-colored gas.

May 26, 1968

After Words for *The Fall of America*

Beginning with "long poem of these States," *The Fall of America* continues *Planet News* chronicle taperecorded scribed by hand or sung condensed, the flux of car bus airplane dream consciousness Person during Automated Electronic War years, newspaper headline radio brain auto poesy & silent desk musings, headlights flashing on road through these States of consciousness. Texts here dedicated to Whitman Good Grey Poet complement otherwhere published *Wichita Vortex Sutra* and *Iron Horse*. The book enters

Northwest border thence down California Coast Xmas 1965 and wanders East to include history epic in Kansas & Bayonne, mantra chanting in Cleveland smoke flats, Great Lake hotel room midnight soliloquies, defeatest prophetics Nebraskan, sociable kissass in Houston, sexist gay rhapsodies, elegy for love friend poet heroes threaded through American silver years, pacifist-voweled changes of self in robot city, wavecrash babbling & prayers airborne, reportage Presidentiad Chicago police-state teargas eye, car crash body consciousness, ecologue inventory over Atlantic seaboard's iron Megalopolis & west desert's smog-tinged Vast. Back home, Mannahatta's garbaged loves survive, farm country without electricity falltime harvest's the illegal Indochina bomb paranoia guilt. Guru Om meditation breaks through onto empty petrochemical wonderland, & so adieu to empty-lov'd America. Book returns to Pacific flowered seashore with antibomb call, then across ocean great suffering starvation's visible, bony human *September on Jessore Road* ends as mantric lamentation rhymed for vocal chant to western chords F minor B flat E flat B flat.

October 7, 1972

Back Cover for *Mind Breaths*

Australian songsticks measure oldest known poetics, broken-leg meditations march thru Six Worlds singing Crazy Wisdom's hopeless suffering, the First Noble Truth, inspiring quiet Sung sunlit greybeard soliloquies, English moonlit night-gleams, ambitious mid-life fantasies, Ah crossedlegged thoughts sitting straight-spine paying attention to empty breath flowing round the globe; then Dharma elegy & sharp eyed haiku, pederast rhapsody, exorcism of mid-East battlegods, workaday sad dust glories. American ego confession & mugging downfall Lower East Side, hospital sickness moan, hydrogen Jukebox Prophecy, Sex come-all-ye, mountain cabin flashes, Buddhist country western chord changes, Rolling Thunder snow balls, a Jersey shaman dream, Father Death in a graveyard near Newark, Poe bones, two hot hearted love poems: Here chronicled midSeventies' half decade inward & outward Mindfulness in many Poetries: Aboriginal rhetoric, mouth-page free verse-forms, Whitmanic-miltonic periods, Chinese-american imagery, scholarly politics apostrophe, dirty blues & racy ballads rocknroll & airy numbers musicked with lead-sheets, 3 line sparks, objective tombstones, & in narrative high style Oratory a Blakean Punk Epic with nirvanic Rune music the *Contest of Bards*.

September 23, 1977

Back Cover for *Plutonian Ode*

Title poem combines scientific info on 24,000-year cycle of the Great Year compared with equal half-life of Plutonium waste, accounting Homeric formula for appeasing underground millionaire Pluto Lord of Death, jack in the gnostic box of Aeons, and Adamantine Truth of ordinary mind inspiration, unhexing Nuclear ministry of fear. Following poems chronologize Wyoming grass blues, a punk-rock sonnet, personal grave musing, Manhattan landscape hypertension, lovelorn heart thumps, mantric rhymes, Neruda's tearful Lincoln ode retranslated to U.S. vernacular oratory, Nagasaki Bomb anniversary haikus, Zen Bluegrass raunch, free verse demystification of sacred fame, Reznikoffian filial epiphanies, hot pants Skeltonic doggerel, a Kerouackian New Year's eve ditty, professorial homework, New Jersey quatrains, scarecrow haiku, improvised dice roll for high-school kids, English rock-and-roll sophistications, an old love glimpse, little German movies, old queen conclusions, a tender renaissance song, ode to hero-flop, Peace protest prophecies, Lower East Side snapshots, national flashes in the Buddhafields, Sapphic stanzas in quantitative idiom, look out the bedroom window, feverish birdbrain verses from Eastern Europe for chanting with electric bands, Beethovinean ear strophes drowned in rain, a glance at Cloud Castle, poems 1977–1980 end with International new wave hit lyric Capitol Air.

September 28, 1981

Index of Proper Names

Abe (Ginsberg), 664
Abraham, 623
Abraham, Israel (Irwin Allen), see Ginsberg, Allen
Acheson, Dean, 492
Acis, 72
Adam, 335, 342, 361, 368, 559
Adam Longhair, see Adam
Adams, Sherman, 202, see n.
Adonaeus, 710
Adonais, 217, 615
Adonis, 136
Agnew, Spiro, 594, 614
Ahab, Captain, 563
Aiken, George D., 406, see n.
Alan, see White, J. Alan
Alexander the Great, 745
Alexander, Holmes, 406
Alice in Wonderland, 222
Allah, 402, 404, 415, 622, 623, 624, 697
Allen, see Ginsberg, Allen
Altgeld, John P., 222, see n.
Amitendranath Tagore, 607
Amter, Israel, 155, see n.
Anacreon, 369, 600
Anderson, Senator, 386
Andy (Warhol), 654
Angelico, Beato, 236
Ann, see Buchanan, Ann
Anna (Ginsberg), 664
Anne (Murphy), 341
Ansen, Alan, 106, 186
Antinoüs, 236
Antoinette, Marie, 556
Apollinaire, Guillaume (William), 188, 528
Apollinaire de Kostrowitsky, Guillaume, see Apollinaire, Guillaume
Apollo, 34, 190, 602
Arafat, Yasir, 623
Ardinarishvara, 602, see n.
Arhat, 98, see n.
Artaud, Antonin, 177, 189
Arthur, Gavin, 443, see n.
Ashbery, John, 725
Astapheus, 710
Avalokitesvara, 316, 321, 324, see n.
Avrum, Svul (Irwin Allen), see Ginsberg, Allen
Ayatollah, 753

Babaji, 561
Bach, Johann Sebastian, 159, 360
Baez, Joan, 381, 507
Baghavan Sri Ramana Maharshi, 461
Baldwin, Hanson, 498, 499, 500
Balabanoff, Angelica, 288, see n.
Balzac, Honoré de, 185
Bara, Theda, 385
Barbara (Rubin), 537
Bartleby, 78
Baruch, Bernard, 285
Batman, 475, 481
Baudelaire, Charles, 74, 81, 276
Baudouin, King, 478
Beach Boys, The, 476, 527
Beatles, The, 379, 382, 387, 527, 552
Beaverbrook, Lord, 179
Beckett, Samuel, 353
Beethoven, Ludwig van, 745, 748, 749
Ben-Gurion, David, 623
Bhaktivedanta Swami, 518, 600, 610, see n.
Bill, see Burroughs, William S.
Bimbisara, 306
Black, Phil, 185
Blake, William, 14, 146, 172, 196, 212, 246, 305, 309, 355, 362, 415, 434, 474, 550, 561, 600, 603, 610, 631, 685
Blitzer, Sylvia, 725
Blok, Alexander, 177
Bloor, Mother (Ella Reeve), 155, see n.
Blow, Joe, see Ginsberg, Allen
Bly, Robert, 532
Bodhidharma, 475, see n.
Boehme, Jakob, 550
Boito, Arrigo, 236
Bond, Julian, 666
Borah, Senator, 224
Bozzo, Joe, 601, see n.
Bradley, 386
Brahma, 548, 602
Brakefield, Private, 546
Branaman, 396
Bremont, Famille, 190
Bremser, Ray, 269, 290, 552, see n.
Breton, André, 189
Breughel, Pieter, 276, 356, see n.
Bronte, Emily, 192
Browder, Earl, 298
Brownstein, Michael, 707

Bryan, William Jennings, 405, see n.
Buba, see Ginsberg, Rebecca (grandmother)
Buber, Martin, 297
Buchanan, Ann, 341, 396
Budd, Billy, 537
Budd, Dan, 164
Budda, see Buddha
Buddha, 132, 138, 171, 183, 189, 198, 250,
    252, 290, 306, 314, 318, 320, 322, 324, 381,
    438, 475, 530, 601, 604, 622, 623, 625, 653,
    669, 671, 683, 697, 728, 747
Bunker, Ambassador, 581
Burchfield, Charles, 421, see n.
Burns, Stony, 637, 639, see n.
Burroughs, Joan, 132, 157, 185
Burroughs, William S., 122, 132, 142, 154,
    157, 213, 262, 269, 285, 423, 424, 433, 605

Cal, see Lowell, Robert
Calloway, Cab, 100, see n.
Campion, 600
Cannastra, William, 65, 429, see n.
Canyon, Steve, 485
Carl, see Solomon, Carl
Carlos, 621
Carolyn (Cassady), 447
Carpenter, Don, 378, 443
Carpenter, Edward, 442, 443, 445, 446, see n.
Carroll, Paul, 281, see n.
Carter, Jimmy, 753
Cassady, Neal, 33, 136, 142, 164, 186, 187,
    341, 375, 385, 447, 495, 496, 498, 499, 500,
    505, 513, 518, 519, 537, 542, 546, 554, 560,
    566, 597, 607
Castro, Fidel, 273, 283, 331, 699, 752
Catullo, see Catullus
Catullus, 131, 553
Caty, Major, 425
Ceasar, 362, 590
Céline, Louis-Ferdinand, 213
Cendrars, Blaise, 189
Cerberus, 296
Ceres, 371
Cézanne, Paul, 61, 361
Chaitanya, 415, see n.
Chaliapin, 218
Chaney, 555, see n.
Chango, 280, 362, 415, 475, see n.
Chaplin, Charlie, 218, 284, 385
Charles, Ray, 217, 382, 458
Charon, 144, 697
Chavez, Cesar E., 665
Cherry, Don, 577
Chessman, Caryl, 285, see n.

Chiang Kai Shek, 385, 411
Chopin, Frédéric, 358
Chou En Lai, 385
Christopher (MacLaine), 341
Chronos, 357
Churchill, Winston, 423
Citaram Onkar Das Thakur, 315, 414, see n.
Claire (Gaidemack), 193
Clark, Joseph S., 410, see n.
Cleaver, Eldridge, 507, 552
Cocteau, Jean, 189
Colbert, Claudette, 289
Coleridge, Samuel Taylor, 211
Colorado (pseud.), 189
Columbus, 101
Connie, 269
Connors, Bruce, 396
Cornifici, see Cornificus
Cornificus, 131
Corso, Gregory, 75, 157, 171, 203, 237, 253
Costello, Frank, 643
Cousteau, J., see Cousteau, Jacques
Cousteau, Jacques, 697
Cowan, Elise, 269, 279, 341
Coyote, 475, see n.
Crane, Hart, 175, 176, 177, 425, 433, 437, 441,
    444, 460, 484, see n.
Crapp (pseud.), 224
Creeley, Robert, 322, 541, 600, 671
Crevel, René, 354, see n.
Cronkite, Walter, 535
Crosby, Bing, 697
Crown, Henry, 455, see n.
Cummings, E. E., 444, see n.
Curtis, Dal, 485

D., see Dostoyevsky, Fyodor
D—(anon.), 441
Dalai Lama, 385
Daley, Mayor Richard, 593
Dali, Salvador, 429
Dante, 605, 685
David, 341
David (anon.), 232
Davis, Sammy, 728
Dayan, Moshe, 623
Dean, James (Jimmy), 299, 605, 697
Debs, Eugene, 222, 224, see n.
De Gaulle, Charles, 492
Demeter, 710, see n.
Dehorahava Baba, 414, 561, see n.
de Kock, Paul, 81
Denby, Edwin, 466, see n.
de Sade, 285

Dickens, Charles, 211
Dickinson, Emily, 219
Diem, 319
Dietrich, Marlene, 62
Dillinger, John, 455, see n.
Dimwit, Denny, 277
Dirksen, Everett, 420
Disney, Walt, 315, 485, 697
Donald Duck, 665
Dostoievski, see Dostoyevsky, Fyodor
Dostoyevsky, Fyodor, 40
Dove, 410
Dracula, Count, 722
Dressler, Marie, 218
Drum H., see Hadley, Drummond
Duchamp, Marcel, 345
Dudjom, 717, see n.
Dulles, Allen, 283, 411
Dulles, John F., 273, 409, 411, 492, see n.
Duncan, Isadora, 697
du Peru, Peter, 282
Durante, Jimmy, 284, 433
Durga-Ma, 415, see n.
Durgin, Russell, 106
Dusty, see Dostoyevsky, Fyodor
Dusty, see Moreland, Dusty
Dylan, Bob, 377, 380, 398, 417, 507, 550

Earl, 311, 312
Eberhart, Richard, 667
Ed (Sanders), 355, see n.
Eddy, Nelson, 318, 390
Edie, see Leegant, Edie
Eichmann, Adolf, 325
Eisenhower, Dwight D., 188, 194, 203, 285,
     286, 319, 320, 406, 409, 462, 697
Einstein, Albert, 171, 175, 368, 574, 595, 697,
     707, 710, 726, 750
Elanor, Aunt, see Frohman, Elanor
Eliot, T. S., 213, 276
Elise, see Cowan, Elise
Ella Mae, 421
Ellsberg, Daniel, 707, see n.
Englebert (Humperdinck), 728
Enkidu, 280, see n.
Ephraim, Uncle, 224
Eros, 602
Eugene, see Ginsberg, Eugene
Evans, Walker, 421, see n.
Eve, 342
Evers, Medgar, 387

Ferlinghetti, Lawrence, 341, 385
Fields, W. C., 211, 386

Fitzpatrick, Jim, 498, 499
Fitzgerald, F. Scott, 545
Flynn, Errol, 562
Ford, Henry, 155
Forrestal, James V., 273, see n.
Franco, Francisco, 175, 229
Frank, see O'Hara, Frank
Frankenstein, 523, 697, 698
Frohman, Elanor, 218, 219, 222, 226, 228, 229,
     230, 231, 234
Frohman, Max, 218, 219, 229, 230, 231
Fugs, The, 434
Fulbright, James William, 455, 457, 459,
     see n.
Fyodor, see Dostoyevsky, Fyodor

Gaidemack, Aunt Rose, 192, 193, 224, 659,
     664
Galatea, 72
Gallup, Dick, 707
Gandhi, 301
Ganga-Ma, 305, see n.
Ganipatti, 602, 666, see n.
Ganymede, 357, 611, 723
Garbo, Greta, 231
García Lorca, Federico, 144, 175, see n.
Garden, Mary, 478, 479
Garuda, 320, see n.
Garver, Bill, 196
Gary S., see Snyder, Gary
Gavin, General, 410
Gene, see Ginsberg, Eugene
Genet, Jean, 176, 188, 285
George, see Harrison, George
Gerard, 537
Gide, André, 189
Ginsberg, Allen, 33, 69, 116, 131, 142, 150,
     157, 229, 231, 232, 236, 239, 253, 264, 313,
     334, 346, 561, 566, 605, 667, 697, 707,
     725
Ginsberg, Eugene, 219, 223, 224, 225, 228,
     229, 230, 232
Ginsberg, Louis, 218, 221, 222, 223, 225, 226,
     227, 228, 229, 230, 231, 331, 600, 601, 699,
     718
Ginsberg, Naomi, 217, 219, 220, 221, 222,
     223, 224, 225, 226, 227, 228, 229, 230, 231,
     232, 233, 236, 321, 429, 601, 697, 699
Ginsberg, Rebecca (Grandmother), 220, 221,
     230, 232
Glen, 341
Godunov, Boris, 218
Gold, Theodore, 546, see n.
Goldfinger (anon.), 173

Goliath, 475
Goodman, 555, see n.
Gordon, 537
Gorgeous George, 126
Gould, Joe, 433
Grady, Madame (Panna), 432, see n.
Gregory, see Corso, Gregory
G. S., see Snyder, Gary
Guevara, Che, 273, 491, 492
Guillaume, see Apollinaire, Guillaume
Gyalwa Karmapa, see Karmapa, Gyalwa

Hadley, Drummond, 530, see n.
Haines, Harry, 601, see n.
Hal (Chase), 157, 540, see n.
Hampton, Fred, 546, see n.
Handel, Georg Fredrich, 384
Hannah (pseud.), 229
Hardy, Thomas, 31
Harris, Dave, 507
Harrison, George, 373
Harry (Fainlight), 367, see n.
Harry, Uncle, see Meltzer, Harry
Harry T., see Truman, Harry
Hart, Professor, 151
Hawthorne, Nathaniel, 124, 224
Hearst, William Randolph, 229, 280, 285, 298
Heck, Mike, 543
Helms, Richard, 699, see n.
Hemingway, Ernest, 76
Hereford, Lord, 490
Hermit, Ed, 552
Hermon, Dr., 534
Herod, 754
Hesiod, 553, 560
Heykal, 623
Hitler, Adolf, 192, 193, 221, 226, 229, 233, 234, 281, 289, 318, 623, 727, 749
Ho Chi Minh, 385, 406, 451
Hoffman, Abbie, 613
Hoffman, John, 269
Hohnsbean, John, 106
Holiday, Billie, 467
Holland, John P., 305, see n.
Holmes, John Clellon, 541, 542, see n.
Homer, 385
Honey (Litzky), Aunt, 192
Honig, Harry, 269
Hoover, J. Edgar, 176, 287, 288, 422, 543, 559, 564, 643
Hope, Bob, 284, 665
Horace, 106
Ho-Tei, 484

Howard, John, 528
Howard, Leslie, 393
H. P. (pseud.), 149
Hubert (Leslie, "Hube the Cube"), 341
Humphrey, Hubert, 408, 593
Huncke, Herbert E., 132, 142, 157, 184, 447, see n.
Huntley, Chet, 392

Iao, 710
Ialdabaoth, 710
Ike, see Eisenhower, Dwight D.
Indra, 602, see n.
Iris (Brodey), 269
Iroquois (pseud.), 185
Isaac, Dr., see Louria, Dr. Leon
Isaiah, 485

Jack, 558
Jack, see Kerouac, Jack
Jack (pseud.), 657
Jackson, George, 605
Jackson, Jumping Joe, 382
Jackson, Natalie, 269, 342
Jacquet, Illinois, 496
Jacob, Max, 189, 190
Jaime, 341
Jaweh, 415, 622, 623, 624
J.C. (Jesus Christ), 528
Jean-Paul, Pope, 717
J. Edgar, see Hoover, J. Edgar
J. E. Hoover, see Hoover, J. Edgar
Jehova, see Jehovah
Jehovah, 139, 710
Jenny (pseud.), 540
Jimmy (Gutierrez), 537
Joan, see Burroughs, Joan
Job, 475
Joe, 161
Joey, see Kerouac
John, Pope, 324
Johnson, Lyndon Baines, 385, 391, 406, 408, 422, 451, 452, 459, 471, 492, 498, 637
Johnson, Dr. Samuel, 447
Jones, Elvin, 577
Jones, Leroi, 318, 341, 499, 507, see n.
Jordan (Belson), 341
Jordan, Louis, 496
Jose (anon.), 342
Joseph, Chief, 377, 797
Joseph K., see Kafka, Franz Joseph
Jove, 611
J. P. (anon.), 543
Jude, 78

Judy, 341
Julius, see Orlovsky, Julius
Jupiter, 602, 611
Justin, 341

Kabir, 361, 528, 561, see n.
Kafka, Franz Joseph, 361
Kali, 298, 475, 527
Kali Ma, 303, 354, see n.
Kali Pada Guha Roy, 414, see n.
Kalki, 357, see n.
Kandinsky, Professor, 183
Kangaroo, Captain, 411
Karloff, Boris, 697
Karmapa, Gyalwa, 478, 602, 631, see n.
Keaton, Buster, 352, 353, 437
Keats, John, 211, 261
Keck, William, 106
Kenji Myazawa, 627, see n.
Kennedy, John F., 341, 347, 479, 492, 605, 643, 722, 728, 752
Kennedy, Robert, 416, 451, see n.
Kenney, 132, 423, see n.
Kenyatta, Jomo, 326
Kerouac, Jack, 13, 32, 33, 131, 132, 142, 146, 147, 157, 164, 182, 199, 251, 269, 275, 285, 305, 318, 322, 343, 353, 360, 433, 458, 459, 497, 499, 518, 539, 540, 541, 542, 545, 548, 553, 560, 573, 607, 625, 697, 699
Kesey, Ken, 382, 420, 496
Khaki Baba, 414, see n.
Khrushchev, Nikita, 277, 299, 385, 754
Kierkegaard, Soren, 402
King, Bill, 157, 186
King, Martin Luther, 436, 546, 605, 722
King, M. L., see King, Martin Luther
Kingsland, 106
Kinks, The, 390
Kissinger, Henry, 623, 638, 639, 644, 699, 736
Kline, Franz, 465, see n.
Koch, Edward, 665
Koch, Kenneth, 739
Kosygin, Alexi, 385, 492
Krishna, 320, 362, 415, 475, 521, 522, 528, 536, 559, 600, 602
Krishnamurti, 605
Kuan Yin, 475, see n.
Ky, General Nyugen, 451

Lafcadio, see Orlovsky, Lafcadio
Lama Anikgarika Govinda, 600
Lamantia, Philip, 324
Lance, 341

Lansky, Meyer, 623, see n.
Lao-Tze, 176, 475
Larry, see Ferlinghetti, Lawrence
LaSalle, Governor Melvin, 498
Laurel and Hardy, 385
LaVigne, Robert, 342
Leary, Timothy, 275, 319, 507, 552, 553, 558, 559, 560, 562, 600, 613, 633, see n.
Leegant, Edie, 228, 229, 230
Lennon, John, 373, 422, 754
Leroi, see Jones, Leroi
Leroi (pseud.), 185
Levinsky, 27, see n.
Levy, D. A., 437
Lewis, Fulton, 286
Lewis, Sam, 447, see n.
Lewis and Clark, 377
Liang Kai, 10
Liliuo Kalani, Queen, 697
Lilly, Eli, 420
Lincoln, Abraham, 192, 195, 704
Lindbergh, Charles, 697
Lindsay, Vachel, 176, 177, 191, 405
Lippmann, Walter, 447, see n.
Little, Frank H., 158, see n.
Lizzie (anon.), 186
Lodge, Henry Cabot, 387
Lombardo, Guy, 722
Lorca, see García Lorca
Lou, see Ginsberg, Louis
Louis, see Ginsberg, Louis
Louria, Dr. Leon, 226, 447, see n.
Lowell, Robert, 275, 280
Loy, Myrna, 280, 385
Lubovitcher Rebbe, 385, 622
Luciano, Lucky, 643, 747, see n.
Lucien (Carr), 142
Lucille, 341
Lumumba, Patrice, 299

MacArthur, Douglas, 697
MacDonald, Jeanette, 280, 318, 445
MacNamara, Robert S., 385, 406, see n.
Maheu, Robert, 728, see n.
Mahler, Dr., 669
Maitreya, 357, 600, see n.
Mansfield, Jayne, 605
Mansfield, Mike, 384, 476
Manson, Charles, 563
Mao-Mao, see Mao Tze Tung
Mao Tze Tung, 324, 385, 475, 484, 486, 528, 550
Maretta (Greer), 537
Marko, 341

Marpa, 602, see n.
Martinelli, Sheri, 458
Marx, Chico, 152
Marx, Groucho, 697
Marx, Harpo, 211, 385
Marx, Karl, 154
Mary, 297, 475, 539, 697
Mary (pseud.), 69
Max, see Frohman, Max
Max (Levy), Uncle, 154, 228, 390
Mayakovsky, Vladimir, 175, 176, 180, 190, 472,
    745, see n.
McCarthy, Eugene, 594
McCarthy, Joe, 269
McCartney, Paul, 373, 422
McClure, Michael, 396, 414, see n.
McFate, Judge Yale, 273, see n.
McGovern, George, 590, 594
McGuire, Barry, 398
McLuhan, Marshall, 526
McNeil, Don, 499
Meany, George, 593
Meeropol, Michael and Robert, 665
Meir, Golda, 623
Melville, Herman, 402
Meltzer, Harry, 193, 664
Meyer, Cord, 597, see n.
Michaelson, Dr., 399
Mickey Mouse, 199, 697
Mila, see Mila-Repa
Mila-Repa, 378, 602, see n.
Miller, Henry, 285, 353
Miller, Pat, 543
Milton, John, 172, 610
Minerva, 194, 475
Mira Bai, 528
Mohammed, 171, 623
Moloch, 139, 140, 610, see n.
Monet, Claude, 642, 745
Monk, Thelonius, 298
Mooney, Tom, 155, see n.
Moore, Brian, 617
Moore, Henry, 500
Moreland, Dusty, 106, 429
Morgan, J. P., 354
Morgan, M.D., Rex, 485
Morphy (pseud.), 157, 184, 423, see n.
Morse, Wayne, 410, see n.
Mosca, 224
Moses, 622, 697
Mossadegh, 753
Mozart, Wolfgang Amadeus, 280
Murchison, Clint, 273, 397, see n.

Mussolini, 223, 229, 698
Myron, 605

Naomi, see Ginsberg, Naomi
Napoleon, 697, 748, 749
Nasser, 623
Natalie, see Jackson, Natalie
Nation, Carry, 418, see n.
Nazimova, Alla, 697
N.C., see Cassady, Neal
Neal, see Cassady, Neal
Nearing, Scott, 155, see n.
Nemmie (Frost), 341
Neruda, Pablo, 704
Nick, 564
Nirmanakaya, 600
Nityananda, 561, see n.
Nixon, Richard M., 527, 537, 549, 550, 558,
    559, 590, 594, 599, 614, 623, 637, 644
Norman, Dorothy, 276
Norris, Frank, 493

O'Hara, Frank, 209, 465
Olson, Charles, 323, 560
Orlovsky, Lafcadio, 278, 280, 356, see n.
Orlovsky, Julius, 345, 394, 458, 478, see n.
Orlovsky, Peter, 142, 153, 188, 232, 253, 260,
    282, 301, 305, 312, 342, 380, 383, 386, 399,
    448, 457, 461, 464, 465, 466, 480, 495, 496,
    518, 535, 537, 541, 559, 600, 611, 614, 665,
    699, 718
Orwell, George, 605
Oswald, Lee Harvey, 347, 479, 637
Ouroboros, 475

Padmasambhava, 600, 602, 605, 717, see n.
Paley, William S., 723
Pantonucci, Mr., 665
Parcae, 65, 222, see n.
Parker, Helen, 106
Parvati, 475
Patterson, Roy, 666
Paul, 537
Paul, see McCartney, Paul
Paul R—, 330
Péret, Benjamin, 354, see n.
Persephone, 710
Peter, see Orlovsky, Peter
Peter O., see Orlovsky, Peter
Peter, St., 297
Phaëthon, 46
Piaf, Edith, 160
Picasso, Pablo, 189, 190

Plotinus, 135
Plato, 183, 353
Plymell, Charlie, 396, 421, see n.
Poe, Edgar Allan, 135, 176, 222, 228, 276, 298, 474, 522, 523, 672
Pound, Ezra, 177, 325, 408, 494, 601, 632
Presley, Elvis, 697
Prospero, 745
Purvis, Melvin, 455
Pushkin, 309

R—, 222
Ra, 378
Radha, 602, see n.
Radiguet, Raymond, 189
Rainey, Ma, 235
Ram, 303, 362, 602
Ramana Maharshi, 463
Ramakrishna, 301, 475
Raquel (Jodorofsky), 262
Ranger, Lone, 237
Rasputin, 423
Read, Herbert, 466
Reagan, Ronald, 446, 746, 753
Rebecca, see Ginsberg, Rebecca
Redford, Robert, 666
Rembrandt, 224, 479
Rexroth, Kenneth, 160
Reznikoff, 740
Rigaut, Jacques, 189
Rilke, Rainer Maria, 309
Rimbaud, Jean Arthur, 211, 423, 509, 518, 540, 625
Ringo, see Starr, Ringo
Rivers, Larry, 744
Robbins, Jonathan, 673
Robert, see LaVigne, Robert
Robertson (pseud.), 657
Robespierre, 556
Rochester, John Wilmot, 285, see n.
Rockefeller, David, 393, 491, 698, 700
Rockefeller, Nelson, 347, 613, 637, 638, 644, 698, 699, 700
Rogers, Buck, 194, 697
Rolling Stones, 382, 604
Romero, Bishop, 753
Romney, George, 499
Roosevelt, Franklin D., 221, 226, 298, 562, 728, 746
Roosevelt, Kermit, 753
Roosevelt, Theodore, 177
Rosario, 705
Rose, Aunt, see Gaidemack, Aunt Rose

Rose, Billy, 433
Rose in Thrall, irving (Irving Rosenthal), 281, see n.
Rose (Savage), 226
Rosebud (Filieu), 537
Roselle, see Cowan, Elise
Rosenberg, Julius and Ethel, 286, 299, 605, 665
Rousseau, Henri, 189, 509
Rubin, Jerry, 507
Ruby, Jack, 347, 478, 479
Rusk, Dean, 385, 407, 492
Russell, Bertrand, 175
Ruth, 232

Sabaot, 710
Sacco, Nicola, 155, 176, 222, 605, see n.
Sadat, Anwar, 623
St. Germain, 190
St. John of the Cross, 135
St. John Perse, 289
Sainte-Marie, Buffy, 398
Sakajawea, 526
Sakyamuni, 98, 600, see n.
Sam, 161
Sam, Uncle, 192, 225, 287, 299
Samedi, Dr., 600, see n.
Sampas, Sebastian, 360, see n.
Sandburg, Carl, 222
Santa Claus, 198
Saraswati, 602
Satan, 198
Satyananda, 414, see n.
Schacter, Zalmon, 622
Scholem, Gershom, 297
Schwerner, 555, see n.
Scottsboro boys, 155, see n.
Seaborg, Doctor, 710
Seale, Bobby, 563
sGam.po.pa, 602, see n.
Shah, 753
Shakespeare, William, 76, 309, 395, 605, 625, 697
Shambu Bharti Baba, 414, see n.
Shankar, 304, see n.
Shapiro, David, 725
Sheila, 269
Shelley, Percy Bysshe, 172, 211, 369, 523, 625
Shields, Karena, 105
Siegel, Bugsy, 728, see n.
Shiva, 316, 380, 475, 602, 618
Shivaye, see Shiva

Sigmund III, 358
Sihanouk, Norodom, 319
Silverman, Hersh, 285
Sinatra, Frank, 203, 379, 476, 728
Sinatra, Nancy, 476
Sinclair, John, 552, 559, see n.
Sirhan, Sirhan, 527, 528
Smith, Al, 433
Smith, Harry, 275, 565, see n.
Smith, Mr., 68
Snowflower, Princess, 485
Snow White, 389
Snyder, Gary, 158, 197, 199, 306, 322, 377,
    530, 545, 617, 628, 742, see n.
Socrates, 605
Solomon, 297
Solomon, Carl, 76, 134, 138, 140, 142
Sophia, 601, 710
Sophocles, 697
Spade, 161
Spellman, Cardinal, 284
Spengler, Oswald, 605
Spinoza, 171
Sri Chinmoi, 666
Sri Ganeshaya, see Ganapatti
Srimata Krishnaji, 415, see n.
Sri Ramakrishna, 415
Staggerflup, C. O., 485
Stalin, Josef, 623, 752
Starr, Ringo, 373
Stein, Gertrude, 298, 355, 474
Steinbeck, John, 451, 452
Stennis, John C., 392, 406, 410, see n.
Steven, 537
Stevens, Wallace, 194
Stevenson, Adlai, 299
Stravinsky, Igor, 385
Sukarno, 392
Superman, 475
Surabaya Johnnie, 325
Surya, 602, see n.
Su Tung-p'o, 607
Swami Bhaktivedanta, see Bhaktivedanta
    Swami
Swami Shivananda, 353, 414, see n.
Symington, 410, see n.

Tamburlane, 192
Tara, 601, 611, see n.
Tathagata, 415, see n.
Taylor, Cecil, 631
Taylor, Maxwell, 397, 407, 410
Temple, Shirley, 385
Tennessee (Williams), 654

Thakur, Das, see Citaram Onkar Das Thakur
Thakur, Dr., 666
Thant, U, 476
Thatcher, Margaret, 729
Thespis, 371
Thomas, Norman, 222, 727
Thoreau, Henry David, 394, 448
Tom (Pickard), 368
Trafficante, Santos, 728
Trotsky, Leon, 224, 234
Trotskyites, 154
Truman, Harry, 421, 492
Trungpa, Chögyam, 591, 600, 602, 699, see n.
Trungpaye, see Trungpa, Chögyam
Tulku Tarthang, 530
Turner, George E., 450
Tzara, Tristan, 189

Vaché, Jacques, 189
Van Gogh, Vincent, 175, 177, 189, 229
Vanzetti, Bartolomeo, 155, 176, 222, 605, see n.
Veitch, Tom, 601, see n.
Veronica, 485
Versilov, 72, see n.
Vico, Giambattista, 605
Vinal, Harold, 444, see n.
Virgil, 553, 685
Vishnu, 324
Voznesensky, Andrei, 588, 589

Wagner, 276, 281
Waldman, Anne, 658
Walker, Jimmy, 433
Wallace, George, 594
Walt, see Whitman, Walt
Walter, see Whitman
Walter (Curanosy), 262
Washington, George, 194, 298, 421
Watts, Alan, 620
Wayne, John, 543
W. C. Williams, see Williams, William Carlos
Weizmann, 623
West, Nathanael, 390
Westmoreland, 491
Whalen, Philip, 232, 257, 553, 600, see n.
White, Ambassador, 753
White, J. Alan, 341, 396
Whitman, Walt, 118, 123, 144, 164, 172, 175,
    189, 211, 402, 443, 460, 638, 710, 713, 740,
    745
William, see Burroughs, William S.
Williams, Godfather, 601
Williams, Hank, 527
Williams, William Carlos, 213, 237, 305, 640

Winslow, Don, 553
Wisdom, Ignaz (pseud.), 182
Woodford, Jack, 81
Woodpecker, Woody, 198
W. S. B., see Burroughs, William S.

X, Malcolm, 590, 605
Xerxes, 697
Xochopili, 746, see n.

Yamantaka, 335
Yeats, William Butler, 351
Yevtushenko, Yevgeny, 451, see n.

Zarathustra, 475
Zeus, 389, 475, 602, 611
Zhdanov, Andrei Aleksandrovich, 224,
    see n.
Zwingli, 605

WHITE SHROUD

POEMS

1980–1985

"Old lovers yet may have
All that Time denied—
Grave is heaped on grave,
That they be satisfied—"

Thanks to hospitable editors, variants of these writings were printed first in: *Action, American Poetry Review, Apartment, Art contre/against Apartheid, The Atlantic, Big Scream, Bombay Gin, Christopher Street, Folger Library Broadside, Full Circle, Here Now, Hidrogenski Dzuboke, L. A. Weekly, Long Shot, Mag City, Nagyvilag, NAMBLA Journal, Naropa Institute Bulletin, National Lampoon, New Age, New Blood, Northern Literary Quarterly, Open, Paris Review, Partisan Review, Peace or Perish, Poesi 1 (Oslo), Poetry, Poetry East, Portable Lower East Side, riverrun, Spao Spassiba, Sulfur, The New York Times Magazine, Tribu, United Press International, Vajradhatu Sun, Vanity Fair, White Shroud (Kunsthalle, Basle).*

To
Edith Ginsberg

Acknowledgments

Steven Taylor: Lead sheets; Walter Taylor: Lyric calligraphy.

Harry Smith: Archetype design for cover, executed by Julie Metz.

Bill Morgan, Bob Rosenthal, Juanita Lieberman, Gary Allen and Vicki Stanbury helped assemble typescript texts.

Aaron Asher & Terry Karten, Editors; Marge Horvitz, Copy Editor; Bill Monroe, Surveyor of Detail.

Porch Scribbles

Balmy, hotter outside than in the living room—
        Wind rustles the rattlesnake reeds.
Didja see the Perseus star shower last night?

        *   *   *

Bright on Flatirons, sunshine gleams
        on clouds, on brown shake shingles,
                tree limbs rock,
So bright on the car roof, I gotta sleep—

        *   *   *

I want that brick house on Mapleton,
it's for sale "Moore Real Estate"—
        But price too high,
I'm too drowsy to go to the telephone.

        *   *   *

Clouds float up from the end of the world—
        Have we enough room for population explosion?
Call up Gary, let's find out what he thinks.

                          July 11, 1980

That tree stands higher than a house
        like a dog with hair drooping over its mouth—
    green long beanpods hang from its branches

        *   *   *

It's a whale that big gray-bottom cloud floating
over the Flatirons, it's a mushroom, a shipcastle, a
        mountain with sunshine and Coasts—
                It's a pile of mist.

        *   *   *

Look up, clouds in the sky,
        suddenly their shadows fall where Mrs. Hurst
        on Mapleton Street sprays her front lawn.

        *   *   *

Midsummer, green leaves thick on maples
        The front yard, white flowers—
        Cause it's just so beautiful now!
How sad, to be alive watching the season at its height—

        *   *   *

Spray the lawn, it's too hot—
Street children call, car radios play muted disco
            Gray clouds umbrella brilliant sun
I used to be young once, bewildered
                    like that barechested little
                            girl across the street.

                    *   *   *

Where I sit, leg over my knee
listening to the whippoorwill call of a distant ambulance,
the thin tree's little leaves startle and jump,
raindrops fall thicker & the smell of ozone
            wafts across the porch.

                    *   *   *

Everyone loves the rain, except those caught in their
                            business suits,
birds whistle, tree leaves shake excited, electric smells
rise across the City to the watchers on the balcony—
                                        August 2, 1980

Did the Ecologist chop his girl with an ax in Philadelphia
        & hide her corpse a year in the trunk?
What does that red-haired boy half-naked on the sidewalk
                with his Frisbee think of that?
                                Boulder, August 3, 1980

Industrial Waves

Tune: *Capitol Air*

The New Right's a creepy pre-Fascist fad
Salute the flag & call on Mom & Dad
Shit on the niggers it's their fault they were slaves
In a free market you can get rich filling graves.

Freedom for the rich to suck off the Work of the Poor
Freedom for Monopoly to corner the market in horse manure
Freedom for the secret police and guys with guns
Freedom for bully buys! Death to the Radical Nuns!

Freedom to buy Judges! Freedom for organized crime!
Freedom for the Military! "I got mine."
Hundred millions free to starve, isn't that great?
Freedom for the Neutron bomb to radiate!

Freedom for War! Fight for Peace! Whoopee!
"Government off our backs"—except the Military!
Freedom for Narcs to put junkies in jail!
Freedom to punish sick addicts, all hail!

Freedom to bust you for grass if you please
Freedom to beat you up when you're down on your knees
Freedom for Capital Punishment, without fail!
Freedom to wiretap your phone & open up your mail.

Freedom for Cosa Nostra's pornography
Freedom to ban your verse in the high school library
Freedom to stop deaf widows' food stamps
Freedom to draft-register everyone wearing pants.

Free computerized National Police!
Everybody got identity cards? At Ease!
Freedom for Big Business to eat up the sea
Freedom for Exxon to examine your pee!

Freedom of the air for William Buckley
Freedom for Mobil to buy up TV

Freedom to influence Network News
Freedom for money to make you wear shoes.

Freedom to fink out Nicaraguan liberty
Freedom to shove them into Soviet economy!
Freedom for Costa Rica to eat our military scenes
Freedom in Honduras for Contras & Marines!

Freedom for Indonesia to murder half million
Freedom for South Africa to stabilize the Bullion
Freedom for South Africa to slave her Blacks
Freedom for Korea's corrupt party hacks.

Freedom for America to kick plenty Ass
Allende Lumumba yass yass yass!
Freedom for Martin Luther King it's a gas
Freedom to forget our bloody Indochinese past!

Freedom to be Macho to be Number One
Freedom to boast the heaviest nuclear gun!
Freedom to kill for KKK
If you got a White Jury you might get away.

Freedom to work if you don't Unionize
Freedom to listen to Presidential lies
Freedom to have your name in Secret Service file
Freedom to run with the Mob for a while.

Freedom from government regulation!
Freedom to not be allowed an abortion!
Freedom for old folks to enjoy inflation
Freedom to destabilize the Chilean Nation!

Freedom to abandon Latin Human Rights
To deport John Lennon for his Political delights
Freedom to ban Genius entering the Land
& slap Nobel Prize novelists on the hand.

Freedom for overt Covert War sleaze
Freedom for Death Squads to chop off your knees
Freedom to put pederasts in Prison
Freedom to stop Fairies from eating Gyzym.

Freedom to assemble & get gassed or shot
Freedom to not be allowed to smoke pot
Freedom to drink till you got the DT's
Freedom to never take LSD.

Freedom to smoke & have your Utah Cancer
Freedom to shake down a bottomless Dancer
Freedom to be forbidden Peyote Vision
Freedom to censor *Howl* on Television.

Freedom to farm if you're a big bank
Freedom to go bankrupt or land in the tank
If you're a small farmer who grows a little grass
Freedom to be arrested & kicked in the ass.

Freedom to cut down world's oldest trees
Freedom to make Indians get down on their knees
And pray to your God and obey your FBI
And freedom to protest if you're not too scared to die.

Freedom to persecute the Underground Press
& Murder Malcolm X if that's what you think's best
Freedom to Assassinate, & never go to jail
If the CIA Protects you, and they hardly ever fail.

Freedom to squirt Mace in a little boy's face
If you're on the TAC Squad & you don't like his race
Freedom to shoot him if he makes you nervous
And he's 12 years old and you've just joined the service.

Freedom to bribe Japan if you're Lockheed
You won't go to jail unless you're smoking weed
Freedom to buy Iran if you want
At least we used to, right now we can't.

Freedom to foment a Strike in Chile
And lie to Congress if you're Pres. of ITT
Freedom to kill an elected President
If you're a CIA stringer, that's how it went.

Freedom to commit a little perjury—
If your name is Richard Helms, you pay a little fee

Then get yourself appointed Ambassador to Iran
They keep calling you Ambassador as long as they can.

Freedom to sell dope if you're CIA
Or a Narc on the Street you can do it anyway
Or the sister of the Shah or informer for the law—
If your name is Abbie Hoffman you might take a fall.

Freedom to announce what you want to the Press
They print what they hear, it's anybody's guess
The public is free not to hear what you meant
But there's freedom for full-page advertisement

If you're Mobil, if you're Dow, or a millionaire Jerk
Buy a column on the Op Ed page for your work
If you're rich as Rockefeller you can die without your pants
Sniffing poppers and the papers won't give yr corpse another glance.

If you're AT&T you have plenty Liberty
To wave your flag all over the land of the free
You can take the back page of The News in Review
To say what's good for America's nothing else but you.

If you got a million from a Texas millionaire
You can buy television time, get yrself on the air
Freedom to shut up if you're Powerful Poor
Freedom to wait outside the Police Station door.

You're free to denounce any Pinko that you please!
You can ask for Moral Money, give your God's heart ease!
Free to attack the producers in a rage
Free to land in Jail, get beat up on the back page.

Freedom to be one of the few that count
Freedom to be "Serious," that freedom'll amount
To the fact that you're free to agree to more Cold War—
Flakes & Losers are free to go 'way sore.

                                        March 1981

Those Two

That tree said
    I don't like that white car under me,
            it smells gasoline
That other tree next to it said
    O you're always complaining
        you're a neurotic
      you can see by the way you're bent over.

July 6, 1981, 8 P.M.

Homage Vajracarya

Now that Samurai bow & arrow, Sumi brush, teacup
& Emperor's fan are balanced in the hand
—What about a glass of water?
Holding my cock to pee, the Atlantic gushes out.
Sitting to eat, the Sun & the Moon fill my plate.

July 8, 1981

Why I Meditate

I sit because the Dadaists screamed on Mirror Street
I sit because the Surrealists ate angry pillows
I sit because the Imagists breathed calmly in Rutherford and Manhattan
I sit because 2400 years
I sit in America because Buddha saw a Corpse in Lumbini
I sit because the Yippies whooped up Chicago's teargas skies once
I sit because No because
I sit because I was unable to trace the Unborn back to the womb
I sit because it's easy
I sit because I get angry if I don't
I sit because they told me to
I sit because I read about it in the Funny Papers
I sit because I had a vision also dropped LSD
I sit because I don't know what else to do like Peter Orlovsky
I sit because after Lunacharsky got fired & Stalin gave Zhdanov a special
       tennis court I became a rootless cosmopolitan
I sit inside the shell of the old Me
I sit for world revolution
               July 19, 1981

Love Comes

I lay down to rest
weary at best
of party life
& dancing nights
Alone, Prepared
all I dared
bed & oil
bath, small toil
to clean my feet
place my slippers neat.

Alone, despair—
lighthearted, bare-
bottom trudged about,
listening the shout
of students down below
rock rolling fast and slow
shaking ash for show,
or love, or joy
hairless girl and boy
goldenhaired goy.

The door creaked loud
far from the crowd
Upstairs he trod
Eros or some god
come to visit,
Washed in the bath
calm as death
patient took a shit
approached me clean
naked serene

I sat on his thighs
looked in his eyes
I touched his hair

Bare body there
head to foot
big man root
I kissed his chest
Came down from above
I took in his rod
he pushed and shoved
That felt best

My behind in his groin
his big boyish loin
stuck all the way in
That's how we began
Both knees on the bed
his head to my head
he shoved in again
I loved him then

I pushed back deep
Soon he wanted to sleep
He wanted to rest
my back to his chest
My rear went down
I rolled it around
He pushed to the bottom
Now I've got 'em
He took control
made the bed roll

I relaxed my inside
loosed the ring in my hide
Surrendered in time
whole body and mind
and heart at the sheet
He continued to beat
his meat in my meat,
held me around
my chest love-bound
sighed without sound

My breast relaxed
my belly a sack
my sphincter loosed
to his hard deep thrust
I clenched my gut tight
in full moon light
thru curtained window
for an hour or so
thin clouds in the sky
I watched pass by
sigh after sigh

He fucked me in the East
he fucked me in the West
he fucked me South
my cock in his mouth
he fucked me North
No sperm shot forth

He continued to love
I spread my knees
pushed apart by his
so that he could move
in and out at ease,
Knelt on the bed
pillow against my head
I wanted release

Tho' it hurt not much
a punishment such
as I asked to feel
back arched for the real
solid prick of control
a youth 19 years old
gave with deep grace,
body fair, curly gold
hair, angelic face

I'd waited a week
the promise he'd keep
if I trusted the truth
of his love in his youth
and I do love him—
tall body, pale skin
Hot heart within
open blue eyes—
a hard cock never lies.

July 4–October 11, 1981

Old Love Story

Some think the love of boys is wicked in the world, forlorn,
Character corrupting, worthy mankind's scorn
Or eyes that weep and breasts that ache for lovely youth
Have no mouth to speak for mankind's general truth
Nor hands to work manhood's fullest delight
Nor hearts to make old women smile day and night
Nor arms to warm young girls to dream of love
Nor thighs to satisfy thighs, nor breath men can approve—
Yet think back to the time our epic world was new
When Gilgamesh followed the shade of his friend Enkidu
Into Limbo's dust to talk love man to man
So younger David enamored of young Jonathan
Wrote songs that women and men still chant for calm
Century after century under evergreen or palm
A love writ so sacred on our Bible leaf
That heart-fire warms cold millennial grief.
Same time Akilleos won the war at Troy
Grieving Patroklos' body, his dead warrior boy
(One nation won the world by reading Greek for this
And fell when Wilde was gaoled for his Bellboy's kiss)
Marvelous Zeus himself took lightning eagle shape
Down-cheeked Ganymede enjoyed God's thick-winged rape
And lived a youth forever, forever as can be,
Serving his nectar to the bearded deity
The whole world knew the story, the world laughed in awe
That such Love could be the Thunder of immortal Law.
When Socrates climbed his ladder of love's degrees
He put his foot in silence on rough Alcibiades
Wise men still read Plato, whoever they are,
Plato whose love-lad Aster was his morning star
Plato whose love-lad was in death his star of Night
Which Shelley once witnessed as Eternal Light.
Catullus and tough Horace were slaves to glad young men
Loved them cursed them, always fell in love again
Caesar conquered the world, top Emperor Power
Lay soft on the breast of his soldier of the hour
Even Jesus Christ loved his young John most
Later he showed him the whole Heavenly Host
Old Rome approved a beautiful bodied youth

Antinöus Hadrian worshipped with Imperial Truth
Told in the calm gaze of his hundred stone
Statues standing figleafed in the Vatican.
Michelangelo lifted his young hand to smooth
The belly of his Bacchus a sixteen-year youth
Whose prick stands up he's drunk, his eyes gaze side-
Ways to his right hand held up shoulder high
Waving a cup of grape, smart kid, his nose is sharp,
His lips are new, slightly opened as if part-
Ed to take a sip of purple nakedness,
Taste Michelangelo's mortal-bearded kiss,
Or if a hair-hooved horny Satyr happens to pass
Fall to the ground on his strong little marble ass.
Michelangelo loved him! What young stud
Stood without trousers or shirt, maybe even did
What the creator wanted him to in bed
Lay still with the sculptor's hand cupped on his head
Feeling up his muscles, feeling down his bones
Palm down his back and thighs, touching his soft stones—
What kind of men were the Slaves he tied to his bed?
And who stood still for David naked foot to head?
But men love the muscles of David's abdomen
And come with their women to see him again and again.

Enough, I've stayed up all night with these boys
And all my life enjoyed their handsome joys
I came with many companions to this Dawn
Now I'm tired and must set my pen down
Reader, Hearer, this time Understand
How kind it is for man to love a man,
Old love and Present, future love the same
Hear and Read what love is without shame.

I want people to understand! They can! They can! They can!
So open your ears and hear the voice of the classical Band.

October 26, 1981

AIRPLANE BLUES

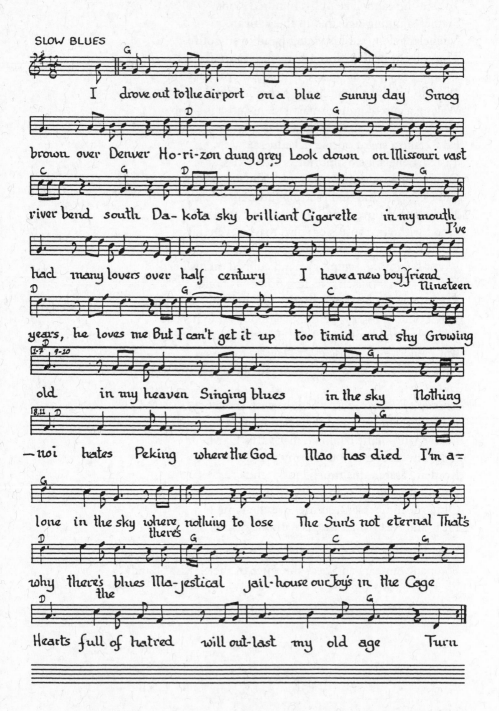

Airplane Blues

I drove out to the airport
    on a blue sunny day
Smog brown over Denver
    Horizon dung gray
Look down on Missouri
    vast river bend south
Dakota sky brilliant
    Cigarette in my mouth

I've had many lovers
    over half century
I have a new boyfriend
    Nineteen years, he loves me
But I can't get it up
    too timid and shy
Growing old in my heaven
    Singing blues in the sky

Nothing here to complain of
    White clouds in the sun
Peace in my heart
    Empty sky Everyone
But earth I look down on
    Turns round misery
Green dollars fat
    with the war industry

Mankind's great delusions
    Scrape sky with red rage
Build bombs out of Atoms
    to blast out the words on this page
Majestical jailhouse
    our Joy's in the Cage
Hearts full of hatred
    will outlast my old age

* * *

My mother has perished
                my father's long dead
I have a sweet brother
                healed the pain in his head
I'm going to the Apple
                to eat with my friends
While the radio chatters
                what the President intends

Down there Mississippi
                Minneapolis near
Farms and green comforts
                of the Northern Hemisphere
While Earth's hundred millions
                Chew miserable clay
Old African kingdoms
                Starve this century

I'll read in the papers
                more deaths in Iran
Jahweh rules Israel
                Tanks in Afghanistan
Martial Law rules Gdansk
                and the old Viet-Nam War
Murders Indians in Guatemala
                and burns down El Salvador

London and Belfast
                Los Angeles and Prague
Tel Aviv & Moscow
                sit in their smog
Phnom Penh's red ruin
                was Washington's pride
Hanoi hates Peking
                where the God Mao has died

I'm alone in the sky
                where there's nothing to lose
The Sun's not eternal
                That's why there's the blues
Majestical jailhouse
                our Joy's in the Cage

Hearts full of hatred
           will outlast my old age

            * * *

Turn round in the sunset
           over Manhattan isle
Newark was my birthplace
           under the wing for a while
Green gastanks of Kearny
           Smog brown in the sky
Seven million black men and white
           live here and die

Come down over Harlem
           red buildings stand still
Dusk light gleams their windows
           wheels bound on the landfill
Sky streaked with jet streams
           black clouds in the west
In the Lower East Side
           I'll go take my rest.
                  October 30, 1981

DO THE MEDITATION ROCK

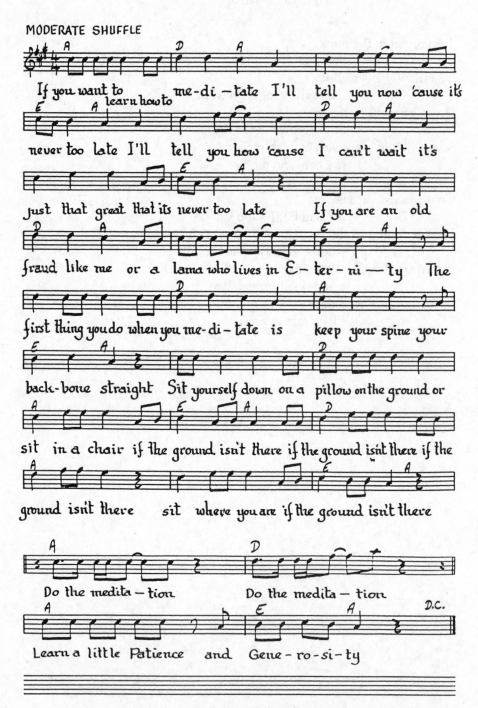

MODERATE SHUFFLE

If you want to learn how to me-di-tate I'll tell you now 'cause it's never too late I'll tell you how 'cause I can't wait it's just that great that its never too late If you are an old fraud like me or a lama who lives in E-ter-ni-ty The first thing you do when you me-di-tate is keep your spine your back-bone straight Sit yourself down on a pillow on the ground or sit in a chair if the ground isn't there if the ground isn't there if the ground isn't there sit where you are if the ground isn't there

Do the medita-tion Do the medita-tion

Learn a little Patience and Gene-ro-si-ty

Do the Meditation Rock*

Tune: *I fought the Dharma, and the Dharma won*

If you want to learn how to meditate
I'll tell you now 'cause it's never too late
I'll tell you how 'cause I can't wait
it's just that great that it's never too late
If you are an old fraud like me
or a lama who lives in Eternity
The first thing you do when you meditate
is keep your spine your backbone straight
Sit yourself down on a pillow on the ground
or sit in a chair if the ground isn't there
  Do the meditation *Do the meditation*
  Learn a little Patience and Generosity

Follow your breath out open your eyes
and sit there steady & sit there wise
Follow your breath right outta your nose
follow it out as far as it goes
Follow your breath but don't hang on
to the thought of yr death in old Saigon
Follow your breath when thought forms rise
whatever you think it's a big surprise
  Do the meditation *Do the meditation*
  Learn a little Patience and Generosity
  Generosity *Generosity* *Generosity & Generosity*

All you got to do is to imitate
you're sitting meditating and you're never too late
when thoughts catch up but your breath goes on
forget what you thought about Uncle Don
Laurel Hardy Uncle Don Charlie Chaplin Uncle Don
you don't have to drop your nuclear bomb
If you see a vision come say Hello Goodbye
play it dumb with an empty eye
if you want a holocaust you can recall your mind
it just went past with the Western wind
  Do the meditation *Do the meditation*
  Learn a little Patience *& Generosity*

*Buddhist Samatha-Vipassana Sitting Practice of Meditation

If you see Apocalypse   in a long red car
or a flying saucer   sit where you are
If you feel a little bliss   don't worry about that
give your wife a kiss   when your tire goes flat
If you can't think straight   & you don't know who to call
it's never too late   to do nothing at all
Do the meditation   follow your breath
so your body & mind   get together for a rest
    Do the meditation   *Do the meditation*
    Learn a little Patience   *and Generosity*

If you sit for an hour   or a minute every day
you can tell the Superpower to sit the same way
you can tell the Superpower to watch and wait
& to stop & meditate   'cause it's never too late
    Do the meditation   *Do the meditation*
    Get yourself together   *lots of Energy*
    & Generosity   Generosity   Generosity & Generosity!

                                     St. Mark's Place, Xmas 1981

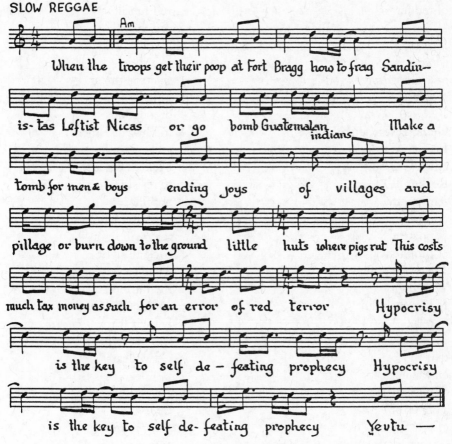

The Little Fish Devours the Big Fish

When the troops
get their poop
at Fort Bragg
how to frag
Sandinistas
Leftist Nicas
or go bomb
Guatemalan
Indians

Make a tomb
for men & boys
ending joys
of villages
and pillage
or burn down
to the ground
little huts
where pigs rut

This costs much
tax money as such
for an error
of red terror

Hypocrisy
is the key
to self defeating
prophecy

Genia Yevtushenko
Ernesto Cardenal
Allen Ginsberg
Rocknroll
sentimental
& reliable
& poetical
& prophetical
Therefore urge
Washington
& Havana men
to relax
& reflect
that the ax
on the neck
of Nicaragua's
a big error
of war fever

Double bind
makes us blind
to self fulfilling
prophecy—
If you're willing,
lose your eye
& your ear
mad with fear

Hypocrisy
is the key
to self fulfilling
prophecy

You can bet
Marxist threat
starts with that
self fulfilling
prophecy
if you're willing
to admit
that the threat
of invasion
of a nation
might cause them
great alarm,
Make them arm
to resist,
mobilize
to insist
they will fight
back all right—
Then to condemn
their armed men
and not molli-
fy their fears
is sheer folly
O my dears!

Hypocrisy
is the key
to self fulfilling
prophecy

United States
you're the greatest
Superdick
your big stick
& big mouth
North & South
causes fear—
Armies near
and armies far
or army talk
wherever you are
makes folks here

think you're queer
Big gun boats
that you float,
big rumors
that you dote
on will be quot-
ed in Managua
Santiago
Buenos Aires
& Havana
as more dread
threat of war
and Central
America will
Mobilize
militarize
and devise
a defense,

it's common sense.
Then to complain
that their plan
to fight back
is a pain in the neck
of the Pentagon—
Washington
is crazy, Man.

Hypocrisy
is the key
to self fulfilling
prophecy—
If you're willing—
costs an eye
and an ear
mad with fear.
Intercontinental Hotel Bar, Managua
January 25, 1982, 11 P.M.

Happening Now?

Happening now? End of Earth? Apocalypse days?
President says "Armageddon!" $254 Billion Military Budget!
The 5 A.M. subway train leaves Times Square
Crowded with murderers & corpses sitting in dress suits,
Earphones listening to mechanical disco, infinite
Deaf universe of Walkman   Happening now
While I drink Perrier at parties in Bel Air
Neutron bomb Nerve Bacteria gas, fruit fly recombinant
Germ plasm, Stratospheric X-ray laser
Anti-rocket beams, MX Cruise Stealth & Pershing missiles
In dream ten years ago I stood on a South Texas crossroad
Walked out alone from what City I couldn't remember
Half the sky was covered with ink-black cloud
Tanks and bombers moved toward the distant horizon

February 7, 1982

A Public Poetry

The fact is, the Russians are sissies
And Chinese big yellow sissies too
Americans by their nature sissies
Ran away to the New World & beat up Indians,
Now we're gonna let Peabody Coal take their Four Corners away!
So sissy we exploded Atom Bombs on Japs!

I myself a famous sissy, it takes one to know one
and know State Secretary XYZ a prissy sissy
Gave his nickels to Indian killer Juntas in Guatemala
Too freaked out to look El Salvador Deathsquads in the eye
Yelling tiny Nicaragua's a big threat to undernourished Mexico!
President ABC's the biggest sissy
Hollywood sissy
Bechtel Corporation sissy
Such a sissy he gave 200 Billion Dollars to Pentagon Bullies
frightened they'll beat him up if he don't let the Generals grab all his
     money
And the American public's sissy too
Scared if they don't give everything in their pockets to Defense
     Department
the muscle men at the Pentagon and tough guys at CIA'll
beat up Congress and Supreme Court
and take over the whole Western Block.

April 6, 1982, 2:00 P.M.

"What You Up To?"

"Oh just hanging around
    picking my nose . . ."
I replied, embarrassed
    in Naropa's corridor,
the Sanskrit professor'd saluted me
as Americans are wont to do—
What must he think my genius,
    a large red blob on my
    index finger tip—
But I suffer from Bell's palsy
my lower eyelid slightly paralyzed
no longer conducts tears thru
    my nostril
thus my nose corridors dry up
    & crack, for five years
whenever I lift the handkerchief
    from my face
a spot of red stains the pure
    cotton & shames me.
When I walk with bent spine & cane
    will my nose be caked with
blood black & ulcerous? tears
    running down my cheeks
a bony pinkie picking at the
    scarlet scab that got thick
overnight, I forgot to grease my
    wrinkled snout the nite
    of my eightieth birthday

and dreamed all the red
    mountain of mucus accumulated
    round me
Himalaya of suffering gelatinous
    slop my lifetime since 1976
when the right side my face
    drooped dead muscles
'cause an O.D. on Doctor's Antibiotic
    inflamed my seventh cranial nerve inside
    its cheekbone

& left me dry-nosed with crooked
    smile & sneaky finger
Probing the irritation in the
    middle of my face
walking daydreaming in the school hall—
That White boy in a two-piece suit
    Hotel Astor bar on Times Square
I took home one night in 1946
    he fucked me naked in the ass
till I smelled brown excrement
    staining his cock
& tried to get up from bed to go to the
    toilet a minute
but he held me down & kept pumping
    at me, serious & said
"No I don't want to stop I like it dirty
    like this."
        April 30, 1982

Maturity

Young I drank beer & vomited green bile
Older drank wine vomited blood red
Now I vomit air
                    July 1982

"Throw Out the Yellow Journalists of Bad Grammar & Terrible Manner"

for Anne Waldman

who report Ten Commandments & Golden Rule forgetting *Thou shalt*
   not bear false witness Do unto others as you'd have them do
   unto you
and say the Man got crucified for insulting the Sanhedrin at a Victory
   Dance in the bombed out madhouse in Beirut
Out! Out! The Mad Correspondent who headlined "Madman or Messiah?
   He Died of Bad Pork" the night of Tathagata's Parinirvana
or the snide reporter with yellow teeth who asked the Big Question,
   "Kerouac couldn't write, so what'd he do it for, money?"
or the *Time* stringer who asks "You could say it was a nostalgia Trip,
   wouldn't you?"
as you fly off to the moon on your translucent sexual wings forever
and the wire-service fellow ex-Harvard, "This business about Secret
   Police, why would you care, successful Abstract Expressionist
   painter, got a grudge to work out on your parents?"
Out! Out! into the Buddhafields, among stars to wander forever, weight-
   less without a headline, without thought, without newspapers
   to read by the light of the Galaxies.

August 10, 1982

GOING TO THE WORLD OF THE DEAD

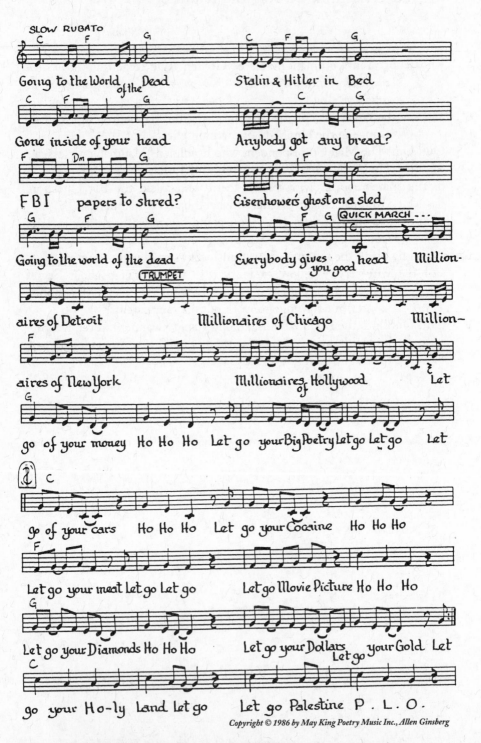

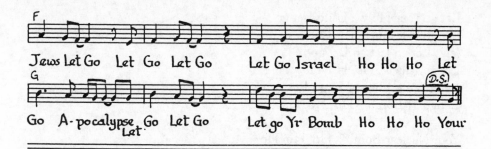

Going to the World of the Dead

Going to the World of the Dead
Stalin & Hitler in Bed
Gone inside of your head
Anybody got any bread?
FBI papers to shred?
Eisenhower's ghost on a sled
Going to the world of the dead
Everybody gives you good head

Millionaires of Detroit
Millionaires of Chicago
Millionaires of New York
Millionaires of Hollywood
Let go of your money Ho Ho Ho
Let go your Big Poetry Let go Let go

Let go of your cars   Ho Ho Ho
Let go your Cocaine   Ho Ho Ho
Let go your meat Let go Let go
Let go Movie Picture Ho Ho Ho
Let go your Diamonds   Ho Ho Ho
Let go your Dollars Let go yr Gold

Let go your Houses Your Bodies Let go
Let go your Souls   Ho Ho Ho
Let go God   Buddha Let go
Let go Allah ' Let go Let go
Let go your Armies   Ho Ho Ho
Let go your war   Ho Ho Ho

Let go your Holy   Land Let go
Let go Palestine   P.L.O.
Jews Let go Let go Let go
Let go Israel   Ho Ho Ho
Let go Apocalypse Let go Let go
Let go Yr Bomb   Ho Ho Ho

Your Nuclear Bomb   Ho Ho Ho
Let go your Disaster your Death Let go
Ho Ho Ho Ho Ho Ho
Ho Ho Ho Ho Ho Ho
Millionaires of Mexico   Ho Ho Ho
Millionaires of Nicaragua Let go Let go

August 22, 1982, 6:30 P.M.

Guasave-Las Mochis bus past soya & cotton fields where red flags flew over
plastic huts squatting by highway side

Irritable Vegetable

Don't send me letters   Don't send me poems
Too busy sick to write poetry   Sky's covered with gray clouds
Perfect for photography
I have brain metal fatigue   Knee jerk aesthetic tears
So you got a junk habit
So you need a recommendation to Purgatory U.
So you're working with Fort Collins' Nuclear Freeze Campaign
So you got hi blood pressure   Your big toe hurts
Someday you'll die
So you sing Hare Krishna Hare Krishna Krishna Krishna Hare Hare
      Hare Rama Hare Rama Rama Rama Hare Hare
So you work on the top floor of the Empire State Building
You're a jerk
You're a hypocrite who eats hot dogs.
October 28, 1982

Thoughts Sitting Breathing II

When I sat in my bedroom for devotions, meditations & prayers
my Gomden on a sheepskin rug beside the mirrored closet,
white curtains morning sunlit, Friday *Rocky Mountain News* "Market
        Retreats in Busiest Day"
lying on the table by Nuclear Nightmare issue of *Newsweek*,
Katherine Mansfield's thick bio & Addington Symonds' *The Greek Poets*
lifting a white lamp above my headboard pillow illuminating *Living
        Country Blues'* small print 1 A.M. last night,
with B complex bottled, green mint massage oil, High Blood Pressure
        nightly Clonadine Hydrochloric pills,
athlete's foot Tolnaftate cream, newsclip scissors and a rusty shoe-last
        bookweight standing on xeroxed Flying Saucer papers,
new ballpoint pens, watch, wallet, loose coins keys Swiss army knife
toothpicks, pencil sharpener & filefolder of Buddhist Analytic Psyche
        papers
scattered random across this bedstead desk—
As I breathed between white walls, Front Range cliffs resting in the sky
        outside south windows
I remembered last night's television suitcoat tie debate, the neat Jewish
        right wing student outwitted a nervous Dartmouth pimply
        liberal editor
knowing that boy who swears to "get the Government off our backs"
        would give my tax money to Army brass bands FBI rather
        than St. Mark's Poetry Project—
He can't read verse with any sense of humor sharp eyed
but then some poets can't either, did Ed Dorn find me fatuous, can I
        breathe in hot black anger & breathe out white cool bliss?
Doomed guilty layman all my life! these pills causing impotency?
Could I move bookcases & clothes out of my bedroom, 8 foot desk file
        cabinets & typewriter
to the small apartment next door N.Y., would that end my hideous Public
        Karma,
Telephones tingling down my spine, pederast paranoid hypnotic burnt
        out teenage fruitcake poets
banging the door for protection from Brain Damaged Electric Guitar
        Police in New Wave Blue Vibration Uniforms?
Be that as it may as blue empty Buddha floats through blue bodied sky,
should I settle down & practice meditation, care for my nervous Self, do
        nothing,

arrange paper manuscripts, die in Lower East Side peace instead of heart
        attack in Ethiopia,
What way out of this Ego? let it appear disappear, mental images
Nothing but thoughts, how solve World Problems by worrying in my
        bedroom?—
Still one clear word-mighty poem might reveal what Duncan named
        Grief in America
that one hundred million folk malnourish the globe while Civic Powers
        inflate $200 billion War Machines this year—
and who gets rich on that, don't all of us get poor heart?—but what do
        I know of Military Worlds?
Airfields and Aircraft Carriers, bugle Corps, ice cream concessions,
million dollar Computer rockets—yes I glimpse CIA's spooky dope deal
        vanity—but nothing of Camp Pendleton's brainy Thoughts
Norfolk officers' vast housing tracts, messes and helicopters, food re-
        source
logistics Pentagon committees've amassed—NORAD's Rapture Moun-
        tain
Maybe get rid of Cold War, give Russian Empire warm weather access,
inaugurate trillion dollar Solar Power factories on every Continent—
Yes access to sunny blue ocean, not Cold Murmansk & Vladivostok Ports
        they need a vast hot harbor
International Agreement big warships forbidden, no battleships from
        Russia or America in the azure Greek pond—
What about pirates, storms at sea or kamikaze Hell's Angel North
        Africans shooting Jews?
Well a few small Police boats, no Cruisers or Nuclear Subs—
Yes a warm weather port for Russian access South I thought
sitting on my bedroom floor cushion 10:30 A.M. getting hungry breath-
        ing thru shades & curtains on transparent windows, morning
        sun shining on white painted walls and gray rug—
So remembering the old story of Russia's claim to a warm weather harbor
        I came back to myself, blue clouded Colorado sky adrift above
        the Bluff Street Boulder house.

November 8, 1982

What the Sea Throws Up at Vlissingen

for Simon Vinkenoog

Plastic & cellophane, milk cartons & yogurt containers, blue & orange
      shopping bag nets
Clementine peels, paper sacks, feathers & kelp, bricks & sticks,
succulent green leaves & pine tips, waterbottles, plywood and tobacco
      pouches
Coffee jartops, milkbottle caps, rice bags, blue rope, an old brown shoe,
      an onion skin
Concrete chunks white pebbled, sea biscuits, detergent squeezers, bark
      and boards, a whisk-brush, a box top
Formula A Dismantling Spray-can, a whole small brown onion, a yellow
      cup
A boy with two canes walking the shore, a dead gull, a blue running shoe,
a shopping bag handle, lemon half, celery bunch, a cloth net—
Cork bottletop, grapefruit, rubber glove, wet firework tubes,
masses of iron-brown-tinted seaweed along the high water mark near the
      sea wall,
a plastic car fender, green helmet broken in half, giant hemp rope knot,
      tree trunk stripped of bark,
a wooden stake, a bucket, myriad plastic bottles, pasta Zara pack,
a long gray plastic oildrum, bandage roll, glass bottle, tin can, Christmas
      pine tree
a rusty iron pipe, me and my peepee.

January 3, 1983

I Am Not

I'm not a lesbian screaming in the basement strapped to a leather
    spiderweb
I'm not a Rockefeller heart attacked in the paramour bed with pants off
I'm not a radical Stalinist intellectual fairy
not an antisemitic Rabbi with black hat white beard & dirty fingernails
not the San Francisco jail cell poet beaten by minions of yellow police
    New Year's eve
not Gregory Corso Orpheus Maudit of these States
nor yet a schoolteacher with marvelous salary
I'm not anyone I know
in fact I'm only here for 80 years

St. Clement's Church, March 7, 1983

I'm a Prisoner of Allen Ginsberg

Who is this Slave Master makes
    me answer letters in his name
Write poetry year after year, keep up
    appearances
This egotist whose file cabinets
    leave no room for more
    pictures of Me?
How escape his clutches, his public sound,
    bank accounts, Master Charge
    interest
Who's this politician hypnotized my life
    with his favors
Petty friends & covert Nemesis, dead heroes and
    living ghosts hanging around
waiting Genius handout?
Why's this guy oblige me to sit
    meditating,
shine rocknroll Moon on Midwest Collegetown
    stages blind in overhead
    spotlights
bawling out of tune into giant microphones
makes me go down suck teenage boys
I declare a new life, how can I pay all
    his debts
next month's rent on his body,
    bald & panicky, with Pyronie's disease
Cartilage stuff grown an inch inside
    his cock root,
non-malignant.

Karme-Choling, April 4, 1983, 12:15 A.M.

221 Syllables at Rocky Mountain Dharma Center

Headless husk legs wrapped round a grass spear, an old bee trembles in
  sunlight.

Since yesterday noon two Brown-eyed Susans stand before the outhouse
  door.

Tail turned to red sunset high on a spruce crown one lone chickadee
  tweets.

Moonless thunder—yellow dandelions flash in fields of rainy grass.

Mad at Oryoki in the shrine-room—Thistles blossomed late afternoon.

Put on my shirt and took it off in the sun walking the path to lunch.

A dandelion seed floats above the marsh grass with the mosquitos.

Empty clouds drift above me, birds chirp, a plane roar falls down through
  blue sky.

Electric noon—pine bough cicadas buzz outside the machineshop door.

At 4 A.M. the two middleaged men sleeping together hold hands.

In the half-light of dawn a few birds warble under the Pleiades.

Sky reddens behind fir trees as larks twitter and sparrows cheep cheep
  cheep.

July 1983

Caught shoplifting ran out the department store at sunrise and woke up.

August 1983

Fighting Phantoms Fighting Phantoms

Fighting phantoms we have car wrecks on Hollywood Freeway
Fighting phantoms th'Egyptians mummified Pharaohs & rich businessmen
Fighting phantoms a young Scotsman wore tennis shoes on the battleship
    deck
Fighting phantoms William S. Burroughs wrote umpteen novels
Fighting giant phantoms David picked up his sling
Fighting phantoms Chögyam Trungpa Vidyadara founded Shambhala
    Kingdom
Fighting phantoms pay federal taxes few write tax refusal forms
Fighting phantoms a Son of God ascended his wooden cross
Fighting summer phantoms muscular young musicians jumped up scream-
    ing in the twilit movie theater
Fighting phantoms Siddhartha meditated under a Bo tree
Fighting phantoms mysticism entered into the Catholic Church of
    Hollywood
Fighting phantoms a hundred thousand kids ordered purple Mohawks
Fighting phantoms various fairies chased adolescent athletes through
    steam bath locker rooms
Fighting phantoms the ruling class blew up the military budget, 244 Bil-
    lion dollars 1985—of the tax pie 63% if past military debt interest
    & pensions're added in
Fighting phantoms Ronald Reagan sent cocaine armadas to Central
    America
Fighting phantoms poets who smoked cigarettes denounced cigarettes—
Fighting phantoms New York Times printed thousands of editorial pages
Fighting phantoms Adolf Hitler shot more Methamphetamine & chewed
    the Bunker rug
Fighting phantoms thousands of poets become rather good at acid satire
Fighting phantoms Jimmy Dean stepped on the gas, Orson Welles or-
    dered another cheesecake
Fighting phantoms Ernest Hemingway shotgunned his brain
Fighting phantoms Ezra Pound hated some Jews some hated Pound
Fighting phantoms Truman dropped two Atom Bombs
Fighting phantoms Einstein invented the theory of relativity

Mid–August 1983

Arguments

I'm sick of arguments
"You threw the butter in the pan"
"I did not you let it melt on the stove"
"You invaded Turkey and killed all the Armenians!"
"I did not! You invaded China got them addicted to Opium!"
"You built a bigger H Bomb than I did"
"You used poison gas in Indochina"
"Your agent orange defoliated ¼ the landmass   It isn't fair"
"You sprayed Paraquat"
"You smoke pot"
"You're under arrest"
"I declare war!"
Why don't we turn off the loudspeakers?

September 5, 1983

Sunday Prayer

An itch in the auditory canal scratches for years, use unguent,
Back pain a little, turn my head neck hurts
Balding long ago, gray whiskery hair inside ears
Eyes closed lying in bed, smart on my tongue, delicate
raw gums sore round some tooth roots—
From nineteenth year College chronic active Hepatitis
affects my kidney stones & high-blood pressure
Right cheek paralyzed slightly, eye squints tired,
lethargy dumps, no one's abdomen to kiss,
cock skewed and lumpy erection aches—
Why show myself these sicknesses? Show anyone?
Wisdom & senescence, sickness and Death come
legended from Buddha to Kerouac—Myself
suddenly older—I made a mistake long ago.

September 25, 1983

Brown Rice Quatrains

Those high lunches needn't matter
If you're of businessman's age
Anyway he enjoyed creating food
drifting across the Fragrant Nation

Who was it that began mouth talk
Gave the citizens thoughtful Saliva
Nature boy came close to Government
but secret police maintained ham & eggs

What tragedy for multiple Chickens
Think how pigs dream butcher night!
Sheep squawked nightmare, goat
fish sent regrets from meadow and sea

If he only could've made new Congress
We wouldn't breathe so much sulfur smog
Sugar dances at the movies, coffee tells you on TV
and Sodium Nitrate & Nicotine Cholesterol

have nothing to do with Foreign policy.
Nature boy drifts into Central American oblivion
with Seminole Patchwork and Albert Einstein,
nobody thought heat rays would end the world.

September 25, 1983

They're All Phantoms of My Imagining

I needed a young musician take off his pants sit down on the bed and
      sing me the blues
I needed a teacher could nail me to the Unborn
needed a stepmother'd accomplish my natural mother's tears
a scared friend of fame wearing locks and T'fillin by the Wall of Tears
I needed a brother was gentle, suffered to protect me from anger
needed a nephew lost, left his rice in the refrigerator with a cold spoon
Comrade farmer cook with me & study Banjo Dharma
Needed Presidents mad so I could write the Nation sane
I needed a father a poet would die
Needed the great companion dark eyes wearied brow tender heart in the
      grave
needed an intelligent junkie rebuke my shallow thought with dirty wit
an old girlfriend take my picture, give me a bed—
A college to be kicked out Columbia
scandal jail the clang of Iron madhouse to wake my 22'd year
Invented all these companions, wept & prayed them into flesh
needed these Creatures to be Allen Ginsberg this my self
crying the world awake mid oceans of suffering blood
needed to be the liar of Existence in America
Manslaughter showed me the True Falsehood of Law
Needed a Buddha enlightened I be enlightened
a bed to sleep in, a grave to cover my ashes.

October 1, 1983

White Shroud

> I am summoned from my bed
> To the Great City of the Dead
> Where I have no house or home
> But in dreams may sometime roam
> Looking for my ancient room
> A feeling in my heart of doom,
> Where Grandmother aged lies
> In her couch of later days
> And my mother saner than I
> Laughs and cries She's still alive.

I found myself again in the Great Eastern Metropolis,
wandering under Elevated Transport's iron struts—
many-windowed apartments walled the crowded Bronx road-way
under old theater roofs, masses of poor women shopping
in black shawls past candy store news stands, children skipped beside
grandfathers bent tottering on their canes. I'd descended
to this same street from blackened subways Sundays long ago,
tea and lox with my aunt and dentist cousin when I was ten.
The living pacifist David Dellinger walked at my right side,
he'd driven from Vermont to visit Catholic Worker
Tivoli Farm, we rode up North Manhattan in his car,
relieved the U.S. wars were over in the newspaper,
Television's frenzied dance of dots & shadows calmed—Now
older than our shouts and banners, we explored brick avenues
we lived in to find new residences, rent loft offices
or roomy apartments, retire our eyes & ears & thoughts.
Surprised, I passed the open Chamber where my Russian Jewish
Grandmother lay in her bed and sighed eating a little Chicken
soup or borscht, potato latkes, crumbs on her blankets, talking
Yiddish, complaining solitude abandoned in Old Folks House.
I realized I could find a place to sleep in the neighborhood, what
relief, the family together again, first time in decades!—
Now vigorous Middle aged I climbed hillside streets in West Bronx
looking for my own hot-water furnished flat to settle in,
close to visit my grandmother, read Sunday newspapers
in vast glassy Cafeterias, smoke over pencils & paper,
poetry desk, happy with books father'd left in the attic,
peaceful encyclopedia and a radio in the kitchen.

An old black janitor swept the gutter, street dogs sniffed red hydrants,
nurses pushed baby carriages past silent house fronts.
Anxious I be settled with money in my own place before
nightfall, I wandered tenement embankments overlooking
the pillared subway trestles by the bridge crossing Bronx River.
How like Paris or Budapest suburbs, far from Centrum
Left Bank junky doorstep tragedy intellectual fights
in restaurant bars, where a spry old lady carried her
Century Universal View camera to record Works
Progress Administration newspaper metropolis
double-decker buses in September sun near Broadway El,
skyscraper roofs upreared ten thousand office windows shining
electric-lit above tiny taxis street lamp'd in Mid-town
avenues' late-afternoon darkness the day before Christmas,
Herald Square crowds thronged past traffic lights July noon to lunch
Shop under Macy's department store awnings for dry goods
pause with satchels at Frankfurter counters wearing stylish straw
hats of the decade, mankind thriving in their solitudes in shoes.
But I'd strayed too long amused in the picture cavalcade,
Where was I living? I remembered looking for a house
& eating in apartment kitchens, bookshelf decades ago, Aunt
Rose's illness, an appendix operation, teeth braces,
one afternoon fitting eyeglasses first time, combing wet hair
back on my skull, young awkward looking in the high school mirror
photograph. The Dead look for a home, but here I was still alive.
        I walked past a niche between buildings with tin canopy
shelter from cold rain warmed by hot exhaust from subway gratings,
beneath which engines throbbed with pleasant quiet drone.
A shopping-bag lady lived in the side alley on a mattress,
her wooden bed above the pavement, many blankets and sheets,
Pots, pans, and plates beside her, fan, electric stove by the wall.
She looked desolate, white haired, but strong enough to cook and stare.
Passersby ignored her buildingside hovel many years,
a few businessmen stopped to speak, or give her bread or yogurt.
Sometimes she disappeared into state hospital back wards,
but now'd returned to her homely alleyway, sharp eyed, old
Cranky hair, half paralyzed, complaining angry as I passed.
I was horrified a little, who'd take care of such a woman,
familiar, half-neglected on her street except she'd weathered
many snows stubborn alone in her motheaten rabbit-fur hat.
She had tooth troubles, teeth too old, ground down like horse molars—
she opened her mouth to display her gorge—how can she live

with that, how eat I thought, mushroom-like gray-white horseshoe of
incisors she chomped with, hard flat flowers ranged around her gums.
Then I recognized she was my mother, Naomi, habiting
this old city-edge corner, older than I knew her before
her life diappeared. What are you doing here? I asked, amazed
she recognized me still, astounded to see her sitting up
on her own, chin raised to greet me mocking "I'm living alone,
you all abandoned me, I'm a great woman, I came here
by myself, I wanted to live, now I'm too old to take care
of myself, I don't care, what are you doing here?" I
was looking for a house, I thought, she has one, in poor
Bronx, needs someone to help her shop and cook, needs her children now,
I'm her younger son, walked past her alleyway by accident,
but here she is survived, sleeping at night awake on that
wooden platform. Has she an extra room? I noticed her cave
adjoined an apartment door, unpainted basement storeroom
facing her shelter in the building side. I could live here,
worst comes to worst, best place I'll find, near my mother in
our mortal life. My years of haunting continental city streets,
apartment dreams, old rooms I used to live in, still paid rent for,
key didn't work, locks changed, immigrant families occupied
my familiar hallway lodgings—I'd wandered downhill homeless
avenues, money lost, or'd come back to the flat—But couldn't
recognize my house in London, Paris, Bronx, by Columbia
library, downtown 8th Avenue near Chelsea Subway—
Those years unsettled—were over now, here I could live
forever, here have a home, with Naomi, at long last,
at long long last, my search was ended in this pleasant way,
time to care for her before death, long way to go yet,
lots of trouble her cantankerous habits, shameful blankets
near the street, tooth pots, dirty pans, half paralyzed irritable,
she needed my middle aged strength and worldly money knowledge,
housekeeping art. I can cook and write books for a living,
she'll not have to beg her medicine food, a new set of teeth
for company, won't yell at the world, I can afford a telephone,
after twenty-five years we could call up Aunt Edie in California,
I'll have a place to stay. "Best of all," I told Naomi
"Now don't get mad, you realize your old enemy Grandma's
still alive! She lives a couple blocks down hill, I just saw her,
like you!" My breast rejoiced, all my troubles over, she was
content, too old to care or yell her grudge, only complaining
her bad teeth. What long-sought peace!

Then glad of life I woke
in Boulder before dawn, my second story bedroom windows
Bluff Street facing East over town rooftops, I returned
from the Land of the Dead to living Poesy, and wrote
this tale of long lost joy, to have seen my mother again!
And when the ink ran out of my pen, and rosy violet
illumined city treetop skies above the Flatiron Front Range,
I went downstairs to the shady living room, where Peter Orlovsky
sat with long hair lit by television glow to watch
the sunrise weather news, I kissed him & filled my pen and wept.

October 5, 1983, 6:35 A.M.

Empire Air

Flying to Rochester Institute of Technology

Rising above the used car lots & colored dumps of Long Island
stubby white smokestreams drift North above th' Egyptic Factory
      roof'd monolith
into gray clouds, Conquer the world!
World Health restored with organic orange juice & Tibetan mule-dung-
      smelling Pills—Conquer the World Conquer the World
Conquer the World of Ego, Conquer World Anger
Conquer brick Worlds, Mortal Factories!
Conquer the Dewdrop? Conquer white clouded Sky we pass through?—
O ever-rising intelligent Sun conquer the night of Mind
Conquer War O Technologic Warrior
I ride above the Sun
             I look down into the Sun
I'm equal to Sun, Sun & I on the level
I've no appendicitis, I hang a Brooks Brothers tie
My clothes are Salvation Army! Conquer America! Conquer Greed!
      Conquer warmonger Hands!
Conquer yourself! Conquer your gluttony Ginsberg! Conquer lust for
      Conquest!
Conquer Conquest at last! All right Jack Number One! Creon wrecks
      Imperial City!
Conquer by Calm! Conquer by not getting laid, growing younger &
      older same time!
Conquer by having a hard on! Conquer all space by giving it away! Con-
      quer the Universe by inhabiting it!
Conquer by Dying! By eating decently! Wash yr behind after you move
      your bowels!
Pronounce your mother American language marvelously, mouth every
      syllable, savor every vowel, appreciate each consonant!
above the clouds! Conquer Karma, the chain of Cause and Effect
Conquer Cause & Effect, see it work the Cold War!
See it work in your heart!
Insult your girlfriend you'll feel hurt!
Insult Nicaragua you feel lousy
Insult the President you insult yourself
Conquer the President by not insulting him!
Don't insult yourself! stop insulting the Russians! stop insulting the
      enemy!

It costs $220800000000 a year to insult the enemy!
Conquer Underdeveloped Nation Hunger Debt! Conquer World Grief
       Bank default! Go Conquer mortal Nuclear Waste!
Then go back Conquer your own heart!

January 30, 1984

Surprise Mind

How lucky we are to have windows!
       Glass is transparent!
I saw that boy in red bathingsuit
          walk down the street.
July 7, 1984, 8:30 A.M.

Student Love

The boy's fresh faced, 18, big smile
underwear hangs below his shorts, he's a kid
                                    still growing
legs strong, he hugs me, steps away—
In twenty years thick bellied,
        bright eyes dulled with office work,
    his children'll pout in the
                        bathroom—
Better get in bed with him on top of me now
        laughing at my pot belly
before decades pass, bring our bony skulls whispering
                    to the hospital bedside.

July 31, 1984

The Question

When that dress-gray, gray haired and gray-faced
goblin took charge of me then inside the gate,
which closed behind me for a couple years,
I was still cheerful exceedingly
cheerful nodding out (hadn't slept for days),
cheerful because taking part in real life
action again, two serious gentlemen
at my shoulders in a night-colored car which
special for me rolled across December's bridge,
cheerful because I'd yelled out in the street
that this one and that one should be notified,
cheerful because I thought the adventure
a minor excursion, but cheerful also,
because such a gray such a small Uncle
I'd never seen yet, he however
wasn't cheerful, was reassuringly
bored bananas, boringly signed for
my delivery and boringly
turned my seven pockets inside out,
then with a wooden face confiscated
handkerchief, pocketknife, bunch of keys,
next indifferently requested my belt
and examined personally whether
my underpants operated with string,
yawned apathetic patting me down,
last nearly napping asked for the laces
that wagged lighthearted from my shoetops—
"I can't walk like this"—he shrugged a shoulder.
Left hand holding my pants up, spellbound by
this unprecedented situation, yet
still cavalier I bowed deep presenting
him with the shoelaces in my right hand.
"What's the point anyhow? I really don't
intend to hang myself"—I assured him
lighthearted. "You don't?" he questioned. . . . "Why not?"
On his sallow face neither mockery nor hate.
That was when the fear caught up with me.

István Eörsi
Translated with author by A. G. September 5, 1984

In My Kitchen in New York

for Bataan Faigao

Bend knees, shift weight—
Picasso's blue deathhead self portrait
    tacked on refrigerator door—
This is the only space in the apartment
    big enough to do T'ai chi—
Straighten right foot & rise—I wonder
    if I should have set aside that garbage
    pail—
Raise up my hands & bring them back to
    shoulders—The towels and pajama
    laundry's hanging on a rope in the hall—
Push down & grasp the sparrow's tail—
    Those paper boxes of grocery bags are
    blocking the closed door—
Turn north—I should hang up all
    those pots on the stovetop—
Am I holding the world right?—That
    Hopi picture on the wall shows
    rain & lightning bolt—
Turn right again—thru the door, God
    my office space, a mess of
    pictures & unanswered letters—
Left on my hips—Thank God Arthur Rimbaud's
    watching me from over the sink—
Single whip—piano's in the room, well
    Steven & Maria finally'll move to their
    own apartment next week! His pants're
    still here & Julius in his bed—
This gesture's the opposite of St. Francis
    in Ecstasy by Bellini—hands
    down for me—
I better concentrate on what I'm doing—
    weight in belly, move from hips—
No, that was the single whip—that apron's
    hanging on the North wall a year
    I haven't used it once
Except to wipe my hands—the Crane

spreads its wings—have I paid
    the electric bill?
Playing the guitar—do I have enough $
    to leave the rent paid while I'm
    in China?
Brush knee—that was good
    halvah, pounded sesame seed,
    in the icebox a week—
Withdraw & push—I should
    get a loft or giant living room—
The land speculators bought up all
    the square feet in Manhattan,
    beginning with the Indians—
Cross hands—I should write
    a letter to the *Times* saying
    it's unethical.

Come to rest hands down knees
    straight—I wonder how
    my liver's doing. O.K. I guess
    tonite, I quit smoking last
    week. I wonder if they'll blow
    up an H Bomb? Probably not.
             Manhattan Midnight, September 5, 1984

It's All So Brief

I've got to give up
Books, checks, letters
File cabinets, apartment
pillows, bodies and skin
even the ache in my teeth.
           September 14, 1984

I Love Old Whitman So

Youthful, caressing, boisterous, tender
Middle aged thoughtful, ten thousand noticings of shore ship or street,
workbench, forest, household or office, opera—
that conning his paper book again to read aloud to those few Chinese
        boys & girls
who know enough American tongue to ear his hand—
loath to select one leaf from another, loath to reject a sympathetic page
—the tavern boy's look, a stone prisoner's mustache-sweat, prostitute in
        the sun, garrulous old man waving goodbye on the stoop—
I skim *Leaves* beginning to end, this year in the Middle Kingdom
marvel his swimmers huffing naked on the wave
and touched by his desperado farewell, "Who touches this book touches
        a man"
tip the hat on my skull
to the old soldier, old sailor, old writer, old homosexual, old Christ poet
        journeyman,
inspired in middle age to chaunt Eternity in Manhattan,
and see the speckled snake & swelling orb earth vanish
after green seasons Civil War and years of snow
white hair.

                                        Baoding, China, November 20, 1984

Written in My Dream by W. C. Williams

"As Is
you're bearing

a common
Truth

Commonly known
as desire

No need
to dress

it up
as beauty

No need
to distort

what's not
standard

to be
understandable.

Pick your
nose

eyes ears
tongue

sex and
brain

to show
the populace

Take your
chances

on
your accuracy

Listen to
yourself

talk to
yourself

and others
will also

gladly
relieved

of the burden—
their own

thought
and grief.

What began
as desire

will end
wiser."

Baoding, November 23, 1984

One Morning I Took a Walk in China

Students danced with wooden silvered swords, twirling on hard packed
      muddy earth
as I walked out Hebei University's concrete North Gate,
across the road a blue capped man sold fried sweet dough-sticks, brown
      as new boiled doughnuts
in the gray light of sky, past poplar tree trunks, white washed cylinders
      topped
with red band the height of a boy—Children with school satchels sang
      & walked past me
Donkeys in the road, one big one dwarf pulling ahead of his brother,
      hauled a cart of white stones
another donkey dragged a load of bricks, other baskets of dirt—
Under trees at the crossing, vendors set out carts and tables of cigarettes,
mandarin Tangerines, yellow round pears taste crunchy lemony strange,
apples yellow red-pinked, short bananas half black'd green,
few bunches of red grapes—and trays of peanuts, glazed thumbsized
      crab-apples 6 on a stick,
soft wrinkled yellow persimmons sat dozens spread on a cloth in wet
      mud by the curb—
cookpots on charcoal near cornerside tables, noodle broth vegetables
      sprinkled on top
A white headed barber shook out his ragged towel, mirror hung on red
      nail in the brick wall
where a student sat, black hair clipped at ears straight across the back of
      his neck
Soft-formed gritty coal pellets lay drying on the sidewalk and down the
      factory alley, more black mats spread,
Long green cabbages heaped by the buildingside waiting for home pot,
      or stacked on hand-tractor carts the market verandah a few
      yards away—
Leeks in a pile, bright orange carrots thick & rare, green unripe tomatoes,
      parsley, thin celery stalks awful cheap, potatoes & fish—
little & big heads chopped or alive in a tub, tiny fresh babies or aged carp
      in baskets—
a half pig on a slab, two trotters stick out, a white burlap shroud covered
      his body cleaved in half—
meat of the ox going thru a grinder, white fat red muscle & sinew
      together squeezed into human spaghetti—

Bicycles lined up along the concrete walk, trucks pull in & move out
    delivering cows dead and fresh green-stalked salad—
Downstreet, the dry-goods door—soap, pencils, notebooks, tea, fur coats
    lying on a counter—
Strawberry jam in rusty-iron topped jars, milk powder, dry cookies with
    sweetmeats
inside dissolve on the tongue to wash down fragrant black tea—
Ah, the machine shop gateway, brick walled latrine inside the truck yard
    —enter, squat on a brick & discharge your earth
or stand & pee in the big hole filled with pale brown squishy droppings
    an hour before—
Out, down the alleyway across the street a factory's giant smokestack,
    black cloud-fumes boiling into sky
gray white with mist I couldn't see that chimney a block away, coming
    home
past women on bicycles heading downtown their noses & mouths covered
    with white cotton masks.

                                    Baoding, November 23, 1984, 9:30 P.M.

Reading Bai Juyi

I

I'm a traveler in a strange country
China and I've been to many cities
Now I'm back in Shanghai, days
under warm covers in a room with electric heat—
a rare commodity in this country—
hundreds of millions shiver in the north
students rise at dawn and run around the soccerfield
Workmen sing songs in the dark to keep themselves warm
while I sleep late, smoke too much cough,
turn over in bed on my right side
pull the heavy quilt over my nose and go back
to visit the dead my father, mother and immortal
friends in dreams. Supper's served me,
I can go out and banquet, but prefer
this week to stay in my room, recovering
a cough. I don't have to sell persimmons on the streetcurb
in Baoding like the lady with white bandanna'd head
Don't have to push my boat oars around a rocky corner
in the Yangtze gorges, or pole my way downstream
from Yichang through yellow industrial scum, or carry water
buckets on a bamboo pole over my shoulder
to a cabbage field near Wuxi—I'm famous,
my poems have done some men good
and a few women ill, perhaps the good
outweighs the bad, I'll never know.
Still I feel guilty I haven't done more;
True I praised the dharma from nation to nation
But my own practice has been amateur, seedy
—even I dream how bad a student I am—
My teacher's tried to help me, but I seem
to be lazy and have taken advantage of money
and clothes my work's brought me, today
I'll stay in bed again & read old Chinese poets—
I don't believe in an afterworld of god or even
another life separate from this incarnation
Still I worry I'll be punished for my carelessness
after I'm dead—my poems scattered and my name

forgotten and my self reborn a foolish workman
freezing and breaking rocks on a roadside in Hebei.

Shanghai, December 5, 1984, 10 A.M.

II

"Ignorant and contentious" I spent lunch
arguing about boys making love with a student.
Still coughing, reclusive, I went back to bed
with a headache, despite afternoon sun
streaming through the French windows
weakly, to write down these thoughts.
Why've I wanted to appear heroic, why
strain to accomplish what no mortal could—
Heaven on earth, self perfection, household
security, & the accomplishment of changing the World.
A noble ambition, but that of a pathetic dreamer.
Tomorrow if I recover from bronchitis
I'll put on a serious face and go down to the Market.

2:30 P.M.

III

Lying head on pillow aching
still reading poems of Tang roads
Something Bai said made me press my finger
to my eyes and weep—maybe his love
for an old poet friend, for I also
have gray on my cheek and bald head
and the Agricultural poet's in the madhouse this week
a telegram told me, more historical
jackanapes maybe tragic maybe comic
I'll know when I come home around the world.
Still with heavy heart and aching head I read on
till suddenly a cry from the garden reminded me
of a chicken, head chopped off running circles spurting blood
from its neck on farm yard dirt, I was eleven years old,
or the raptured scream of a rabbit—I put down my book
and listened carefully to the cry almost drowned
by the metal sound of cars and horns—It was a bird
repeating its ascending whistle, pipe notes burst
into a burble of joyful tones ending wildly
with variable trills in swift succession high and low
and high again. At least it wasn't me, not my song,
a sound outside my mind, nothing to do with my aching brow.

3:30 P.M.

IV

I lay my cheek on the pillow to nap
and my thoughts floated against the stream
up to Zhong Xian west of the Three Gorges
where Bai Juyi was Governor.
"Two streams float together and meet further on
and mingle their water. Two birds fly upward
beneath the ninth month's cold white cloud.
Two trees stand together bare branched
rooted in the same soil secretly touching.
Two apples hung from the same bough last
month and disappeared into the Market."
So flowed my mind like the river, like the wind.
"Two thoughts have risen together in dream therefore
Two worlds will be one if I wake and write."
So I lifted my head from my pillow and Woke
to find I was a sick guest in a vast poor kingdom
A famous visitor honored with a heated room,
medicines, special foods and learned visitors
inquiring when I'd be well enough to lecture my hosts
on the musics and poetics of the wealthy
Nation I had come from half way round the world

8:15 P.M.

V *China Bronchitis*

I sat up in bed and pondered what I'd learned
while I lay sick almost a month:
That monks who could convert Waste to Treasure
were no longer to be found among the millions
in the province of Hebei. That *The Secret of the Golden Lotus*
has been replaced by the Literature of the Scar, nor's hardly
anybody heard of the *Meditation Cushion of the Flesh*
That smoking Chinese or American cigarettes makes me cough;
Old men had got white haired and bald before
my beard showed the signs of its fifty-eight snows.
That of Three Gorges on the Yangtze the last one downstream
is a hairpin turn between thousand-foot-high rock mountain gates.
I learned that the Great Leap Forward caused millions
of families to starve, that the Anti-Rightist Campaign
against bourgeois "Stinkers" sent revolutionary poets
to shovel shit in Xinjiang Province a decade before
the Cultural Revolution drove countless millions of readers
to cold huts and starvation in the countryside Northwest.
That sensitive poetry girls in Shanghai dream
of aged stars from Los Angeles movies. That down the alley
from the stone bridge at Suzhou were Jiang Ji spent
a sleepless night wakened by the bell of Cold Mountain Temple,
water lapping against his boat a thousand years ago,
a teahouse stands with two-stringed violin and flutes
and wooden stage. That the gold in the Sun setting
at West Lake Hangzhou is manufactured from black Soft Coal.
That roast red-skinned juicy entire dogs with eyes
bulging from their foreheads hang in the market at Canton
That So-Chan meditation's frowned on and martial health
Qi-Gong's approved by Marxist theoreticians. That men in
deep-blue suits might be kind enough to file a report
to your Unit on gossip they've heard about your secret loves.
That "Hang yu hang yu!" song is heard when workmen labor
yodeling on bamboo scaffolds over the street outside all night.
That most people have thought "We're just little men,
what can we count" since the time of Qin Shi Huang.

VI

Tho the body's heavy meat's sustained
on our impalpable breath, materialists
argue that Means of Production cause History:
once in power, materialists argue what
the right material is, quarrel with each other,
jail each other and exile tens of millions
of people with 10,000 thoughts apiece.
They're worse than Daoists who quibbled about immortality.
Their saving grace this year's that all the peasants are fed.

VII Transformation of Bai's *"A Night in Xingyang"*

I grew up in Paterson New Jersey and was
just a virginal kid when I left
forty years ago. Now I'm around the world,
but I did go back recently to visit my stepmother.
Then I was 16 years old, now I'm fifty eight—
All the fears I had in those days—I can still see myself
daydreaming reading N.Y. Times on the Chinese rug on the living room
floor on Graham avenue. My childhood houses are torn down,
none of my old family lives here any more,
mother under the ground in Long Island, father underground
near the border of Newark where he was born.
A highway cuts thru the Fair Street lot where I remember our earliest
apartment, & a little girl's first kiss. New buildings rise on that street,
all the old stores along Broadway have disappeared.
Only the Great Falls and the Passaic river flow
noisy with mist then quietly along brick factory sides
as they did before.

10:15 P.M.

After Rewi Alley's *Bai Juyi, 200 Selected Poems* (Beijing: New World Press, 1983), p. 303.

Black Shroud

Kunming Hotel, I vomited greasy chicken sandwiched
in moldy bread, on my knees before the white toilet
retching, a wave of nausea, bowels and bladder loose
black on the bathroom floor like my mother groaning
in Paterson 1937. I went back to bed
on the twelfth floor, city lights twinkling north,
Orion in his belt bright in the sky, I slept again.

She had come into the bathroom her face hidden
in her breast, hair overhanging her figure bent in front
of me, stiff in hypertension, rigor mortis
convulsed her living body while she screamed
at the doctor and apartment house we inhabited.
Some electric current flowing up her spine tortured her,
foot to scalp unbearable, some professional advice
required quick action, I took her wrists, and held her
bound to the sink, beheading her silently with swift
dispatch, one gesture, a stroke of the knife-like ax
that cut thru her neck like soft thick gum, dead quick.

What had I done, and why? Certainly her visage
showed the reason, strain and fright lasting thru death.
But couldn't leave her body hidden in the toilet, someone
finding her bent over might wait, then push, then
horrified find her headless, skull fallen to the floor.
I picked her up by the shoulders, afraid to look at
the Medusa head
                which I lifted by long hair & set
on the sink before the mirror, but beheld no mad
drawn-cheek wild-eyed or blood-splotched wrinkled forehead—
Calm, beautiful face, tranquil in life's last moments
as if in prayer, eyes clear and modest, face content
with neither smile or frown but even-browed, eyebrows
in repose, cheeks colored healthy still as when alive.
"I made a mistake" I thought, in following the doctors' rules,
or where'd I get th' idea she was screaming and banging
her head on the wall in neural agony? Was that just my thought
or hadn't others told me so? Why'd I do it so abrupt
without consulting the World or the rest of the family—

Her look at last so tranquil and true made me wonder
why I'd covered her so early with black shroud.
Had I been insane myself and hasty? I left the room.

At Joel the doctor's wedding party the family'd gathered
whoever was left alive. Yes of course they found her corpse,
they knew she was crazy, but didn't announce a murder,
just whispered among themselves she was dead in the bathroom
causes unknown, tho headless, hard for her to suicide herself,
a further investigation would clarify this big mistake.
In fact my cousin my publisher with troubled frown
put the matter to rest, saying he'd call on the police
after the wedding guests go home. I said—
"I might be able to clear up the mystery. You saw
her head?" He looked at me surprised, how did I know
she was dead with her head cut off? I realized
I'd given myself away, but risked it, why lie more,
build up Karma nightmare another year & then get caught?
Police find my fingerprints on Naomi's dead neck? or my blade
be found under my bed, in the dust behind the refrigerator
on East 12th Street Lower East Side, I be arrested
in newspaper scandal? "You saw the head?" I asked
again, giving my knowledge away. "But are you sure?"
he asked. Dressed in his Harvard suit and silken tie
striped red and gold, "We have our legal staff, perhaps you should
consult with them, no fee, fortunate contract,
our clients we value, you for your Collected Works we do
protect without question." Helpful, alas, too late for me
to undo the murder of my mother, I must confess, I had
confessed, too late to undo confession and truth, I woke.

December 21, 1984, 5:12 A.M.

World Karma

China be China, B.C. Clay armies underground the First Han Emperor's
      improvement
on burying his armies alive
Later Ming tombs buried excavator architects
& Mao officially buried 20,000,000 in Shit Freeze & Exile, much Suicide
especially bilingual sophisticates in the molecular structure of surfaces,
      machine-tool engineers
and Poetic intelligentsia questioned his Imperial vision of Pure Land
      future communist afterworld

Russia had Czars & Stalin, all Yiddish Poets shot August 12, 1952 in
      Lubyanka basement, everybody got drunk afterward,
everyone still whispers on streetcorners

America forever democratic, lawless sheriffs shot Indians, bad men, good
      men, chinks kikes niggers and each other

Spain always killed bulls & loved blood, matadors & crucifixion, reds &
      fascists assassinated anarchists—

The Jews always complained, kvetching about false gods, and erected the
      biggest false God, Jehovah, in middle of western civilization—
For creating the Judge the Jews are judged that's their world Karma
      continuing, the Atom bomb

British always had sense of superiority, class, stiff upperlip, the Queen
      and fuck you ducky up your bloody 'ole

The French, advanced sense of superiority, stiff back, Algérie is always
      indissolubly a part of La France,
We will not regret the necessity to kill you or anyone who disagrees
They appreciate everything wine women song modern art
O la la they're so smart, introduced opium cultivation
Indochina will always be an indissoluble addiction to France, the Bourse

Germans had Kaisers Hitlers, orderly meticulous and rational a bunch of
      beasts
now want Nuclear arms They're also intelligent Pride themselves on
      Science

romantic Poetry, their Black Forest mysterious full of Solitude acid rain
hi tech civilization First the ovens of Auschwitz now goodbye ancient
      trees
we have to keep up with the vulgar Americans

Italy the trains never ran on time, they got good shoes & Pope & Mafia
also good tomatoes and Angelico Beato, who'd want to complain in
      Naples or Uffizi?

In 200 years America'll have a billion people like neon China
Computerized students'll sleep six abed and hawk their mucus on the
      morning floor
before fighting to get into the shower—much less a piece of soap
and half stick of bacon with their petrochemical Wheaties & eggs—
      That's because
we had to Get Back to America, let's Stand Up Tall
so we can insult the rest of the world.

More!—The Moslems expansionist monotheists will go Jihad whenever
      able
Always their god best god only god only name Allah and
die like a dog if you don't believe me! From Morocco to Java
heathen dogs and cats go barking and meow after terrific Nobodaddy
in Paradise the Western lands Heaven Pure Land Garden of Sky,
other side of Eternal Dreamtime I vote for Australian Aborigines!
Let them run the world after Hi Tech's annihilated all other species &
      genetic strains
from whale to donkey sperm.

               Kunming, *December 24, 1984, Midnight–12:49*

Prophecy

As I'm no longer young in life
and there seem to me not
so many pleasures to look forward to
How fortunate to be free
to write of cars and wars, truths of eras,
throw away old useless
ties and pants that don't fit.

January 9, 1985

Memory Cousins

After Long Absence, I returned from the land of the dead
to visit my stepmother in her suburban apartment.
I looked from a distance, was it a mental hospital
standing on a grass plain far from Manhattan's skyscrapers
after crossing Washington Bridge, or Jersey's tract houses
risen gigantic during my exile in China? I'd
been gone so long my relatives'd grown old at their doors—
a neighbor widow come out to empty the black plastic
garbagebag, I'd known her middle age, now with white hair
she gazed at me nodding absently, I'd not been gone long
while her husband'd died, children married with children now—
How dear to see me, where'd I been? I looked down the long hall,
door after door of Aunts and Uncles retired alive
white haired, television bound seeing the doctor, eating
delicatessen salad Sundays, reading best seller
books, dusting furniture, cleaning kitchen floors, happily
visiting Doctors for minor blood pressure, depression
or hernias. Years ahead, they should live so long, they'd die,
I'd never see them again, best settle down while childhood
memory cousins and brothers were old, but still alive,
enjoy each other's tables and coffee, business gossip.
Where else go off to, unhappy Russia warring Israel?
Here in America, peace, a place to live together.
They were bombing Nicaragua, factories exploding
in India, Cities crowded with Animal muggers
newspapers said, TV had pictures of them every nite—
Peter in fact just came back from Nuclear Buddhaland,
His belly exposed to Radiation a soft yellow
spot near his navel, he smiled rueful pulling his shirt
above his belt to show his mortal sore, what could cure him?
If go away now I'll be gone forever, Peter,
Stepmother Edith, Aunt Honey & Leo, Aunt Clara
and Uncle Abe, my brother Gene & Connie & the kids,
I may never see them again. Here are their living eyes,
here's the end of the Immortal Dream.

                                        March 2, 1985, 7:56 A.M.

Moral Majority

Something evil about you Mr. Viguerie Mr. Falwell Robertson Swaggert.
Not evil but ignorance of the delights of the Boy
The 1920s have passed, corsets chastity belts whips
the stake, Lesbian cities aflame in your fiery eyes
—Some old Demon the Satan in possession of your body
a thousand years old, two thousand that burned the parchments of Black
      Sappho
I've seen God as much as any, he doesn't look like you alone
He looks like me too, all the homosexuals on earth,
in Congo, Cities of North America, Rio Barrios—
He looks like a lavender fairy, Paris salons 1890 the birds & bees,
Like an ambidextrous worm, male dogs coupling in the Alabama parking-
      lot.
Nothing wrong with Family, Mother Father & Buba.
Nothing wrong with the Babe.
Nothing wrong with Mr. Falwell except a little mean streak
that isn't god, just a jerk, talks too big for his britches,
inexperienced Bible Salesman
interprets words & letters, not Holy Spirit
ambitious politically, at the expense of the poor,
the thwarted, & happy ruddy kids—
Find out Buddha, enter the great silence
& pass thru the needle's eye,
then come back happy, laughing, generous
big mouth full of good cheer, not money,
honey.

March 19, 1985

The Guest

I've a pain in my back
Fifth lumbar & sacrum
Kidneystones alas alack
can't drink milk calcium
High blood pressure about
salt I can't eat
at my age no red meat
sometimes I get gout

My age fifty eight
My friend Peter's away
I should lose ten pounds weight
Prostrate every day
to my guru who's Crazy
Prepare for grim death
Exercise for good health
All my life I've been lazy

Little gold, lots of fame
Small flat in Manhattan
tho I bank on my name
my wallet won't fatten
But the thing I want most
to embody my joy
is the belly of a boy
and there I get lost

I met David he undressed
Came naked on my bed
He climbed on my chest
"I love you Allen" he said
He touched and caressed
my stomach, heart and thigh
appreciated my sigh
I slept chaste & blessed.

He visited New York
to sleep a week in my room
watch me at work,

enlighten my gloom—
Body young & strong
shapely from Basketball
Skin muscular stomach small
"I can't be your lover long."

Mind tender, he loves girls
Sees me as poetry master
His pubic hair's soft curls
press my breast to rapture
His smooth cock grows thick
my heart beats at his loin
He presses with his groin
His hands caress my neck

I touch around his buttocks
smooth, firm and warm.
"I've never been fucked"
he encourages, as my arm
reaches up his spine
passes down his back
presses into his open crack
He turns on his belly to try.

I enter slow, he's soft
no pain, he raises his behind
no hard on, hips aloft
I push, he doesn't mind.
My trouble is, I'm old
and tho this young kind boy
gives me a chance for joy
I'm not hard enough to be bold.

Yet I'm in, "How does it feel now?"
"It's O.K., it's kind of different."
Ruddy face, eyes open on the pillow,
he lies before me prone, no effort—
I'm afraid to move, what'll he say?
But he humps his rear up more
to take what's in store,
I stick it in all the way.

Something is missing my hard on
But it's what I have, it works
I pump him slowly, then start on
moving faster while he jerks
his buttocks up to help me come,
I ask permission, he says "yes,"
I pull his hips up, hold his breast,
spurt my loves deep in his bum

Next night we hugged and slept
Chaste again and affectionate
I answered the phone all day but kept
winding him in my mental net—
He wasn't excited by my body
I couldn't expect his sexual love
After this week would I approve
his visiting, if I had to sleep lonely?

March 24, 1985

After Antipater

I've climbed the Great Wall's stone steep out of breath
sat on gray columns broken at Acropolis' marble sill
brushed past morbid scented insect eating plants in Petén Rainforest
Eaten roastbeef with my mother's cousins atop a World Trade Tower
      overhanging Hudson River
Slept under the dome echoing lament for Mumtaz Mahal's white skull
Stood in Red Square snow across from the Kremlin wall-tomb of th'-
      assassin of millions
Climbed Seville's gypsy balconies, Sagrada Familia's crannied spires,
      gazed through my father's eyes from San Marco's high porch
tarried on Brooklyn bridge facing Manhattan dusk's sparkling Towers,
      walked Golden Gate's Pacific promenade
But when you lay on my bed, white sheet covering your loins, your eyes
      on mine
I forgot these marvels, my heart breathed open, I saw life's glory look
      back at me naked.

March 26, 1985

Greek Anthology III, Book IX, Epigram 58, Loeb, p. 31.

Jumping the Gun on the Sun

Sincerity
is the key
to living
in Eternity

If you love
Heav'n above
Hold your ground,
Look around
Hear the sound
of television,
No derision,
Smell your blood
taste your good
bagels & lox
Wash your sox
& touch wood,
It's understood
This is it
wild wit
Make your love
on earth above,
home of the brave,
Save yr grave
for future days
Present here
nothing to fear
No need to sigh
no need to die
before your time
mentally whine
stupidly dine
on your own meat
That's what's neat
Mortally great
Immortally sweet
Incredibly deep
makes you weep
Just this once

Don't be a dunce
Take your cap
off Hear my rap

Sincerity
is the key
to living in
Eternity

Makes you wise
in your own eyes
makes the body
not seem shoddy
Makes your soul
completely whole
empty, final
indefinable
Mobile, total-
ly undeniable
Affirmative action
for no faction
for all men
women too,
mother brother,
even for you
Dead soul'd, sick
but really quick
with breath & thick
with blood in yr prick
Walking alive
on Riverside Drive
up on Broadway
shining gay
in New York
waving you dork
waving your mind
or living behind
your meaty masque
magnificent task
all you could ask
as if pure space
gave you a place

in Eternity—
To see the City
Stand all day
Shine all night
Bright starlight
streaming the height
Watery lawn
misty at dawn
warmed by the sun
Bathed in the moon
green grasses of June
80 times only
Don't be lonely
Roses are live
Cockroaches thrive
in plastic garbage
maggots salvage
your dead meat
Horses eat
golden Hay
in golden day
Young kids jump
in the City dump
Take the lump
in your throat
and sing out
yr holy note
of heart's delight
in living light
Day & Night

Sincerity
is the key
to Bliss in this
Eternity

     April 5, 1985

Cadillac Squawk

Sitting on the twelfth floor Gomden I heard a wild siren in the garment
      district
Heard dog scream at dog on park avenue
my head rumbled the Bronx 242'd street Lexington Avenue Express
lonesome sparrows chirped weathered coppergreen cornice 1860
Footstep crash, pocket change jangled the shrine room's polished floor
traffic waves rushed the shore 1985
Adolf Hitler's voice in the taxi horn
squeak soprano steely cheep Chevrolet brakeshafts
subway breath rising to Empire State Observation Roof
iron doors slam refrigerators shut
bones creak in my knees' antechambers
Heard the long Cadillac horn squawk up sidestreet brick buildingsides
elevators ascended and descended a thousand skyscrapers
wheels within wheels rubber and steel revolve on asphalt corridors
Exhaust puffs out monoxide Broadway Manhattan
Heard the sky shut up
Heard conversation in the trees in leafy Bronx
Heard Africa sigh
Asia turned over in its sleepy bunk
blood ran down rocks in South America
Heard Central America squeeze its ribs through iron gates
the Middle East rumbled plates & spoons in wartime bomb rubble
Polynesians danced with bacteria
Heard Japonesia eat with chopsticks chewing rice & peapods
Heard Australia rattle song sticks singing in Simpson Desert at the end
      of the world

New York Dharmadatu, June 16, 1985, 3:33 P.M.

Things I Don't Know

Dawn, a mastiff howls on the porch across the street behind the For Sale
    signed tree
Chatter Chirp Chirp Chatter Chirp Chir Chir Chic Chir chance birdie
    twitters in a maple tree branch, Twirp!
I wake, what bird's that, what kind of dog moans so?
Is that a maple or an oak, on Mapleton Street? What flowers weeds &
    ferns, those in the backyard? What car goes by awhoosh? A Pontiac,
    swash up the street,
A Chevy, Ford, a Pinto, a Grammarian, a 4 wheel drive GM?
What star I saw last night when clouds lifted & Orion's belt
Glittered gold on blue? or was that amber on azure? As my eye
followed his arrow past the North Star thru the void, was that a tiny
    galaxy shimmering?
Where's Sagittarius, which way is the black hole at center of the Spiral
    Nebula?
Where's Sahel where a million children starve? Where's Libya where
    Wilson of the CIA trained terrorists?
How many times this century'd the Marines land on Nicaragua's dirty
    flag?
Who killed Roque Dalton? What's the size of U.S. national Debt?
& how much interest we pay each year till the Eighties end?
Now the bird's quiet & the dog bark's down, what's differential calculus?
    How do you fix electric socket wires?
I used to know the names of all the minerals. I do remember Pectolite
    gave you like asbestos splinters.
How do people overcome panic driving cars? Are bird bones hollow?
    didn't I once know the look of grackle & scarlet tanager?
Cirrus or cumulus, what cloud produces thunder, lightning, rain?
What makes electricity in a battery? How does my wind charger friction
    become electric?
When water pours into hydraulic ram, what makes it squirt uphill when
    the valve closes in the Pressure Chamber? Is that it? Something like
    that?
What're the 12 pix in Conditioned Co-existent Emergence's Chain?
Blind man, potter, monkey tree, boat world, house with seven windows,
    what comes next before the man with arrow in his eye?
What about banks? What's common stock & preferred? What's a fu-
    tures?
How do you hang a door, frame a window? Hold a light chainsaw?

How fix a broken leg? Ease a heart attack, deliver a baby? Breathe in
    the mouth of a man dying at oceanside?
What kind of government ever worked? Who wrote English Choriam-
    bics?
This isn't Trivia (how play that?) this is my life, I can't remember
the name of the lawyer my fellow student, friends with me in college 40
    years ago—
How make a living, if I couldn't write poetry?
Would I know how to plant peas, tie up tomato stalks?

July 21, 1985

Notes

The following notes to the poems in *White Shroud* originally appeared in *Selected Poems 1947–1995*. (HarperCollins Publishers, 1996). More extensive notes to this section can be found online at www.allenginsberg.org.

Homage Vajracarya

page
850 Ven. Chögyam Trungpa, Vajracarya's Shambhala Arts included mind training with Archery (Kyudo), Calligraphy, Tea Ceremony, etc.

Why I Meditate

851 MIRROR STREET: Dadaist original Cabaret Voltaire was on Zürich's Spiegelgasse Strasse.

851 RUTHERFORD: William Carlos Williams. Manhattan: Charles Reznikoff.

851 CHICAGO'S TEARGAS SKIES: 1968 Democratic convention police riot.

851 UNBORN: Buddhist metaphor, universe & consciousness are "unborn," i.e. not traceable back to any ultimate birthplace, source, cause.

851 ROOTLESS COSMOPOLITAN: Aesopean Stalinist word for Jew.

Do the Meditation Rock

863 Buddhist Samatha-Vipassana Sitting Practice of Meditation instructions according to the Ven. Chögyam Trungpa, Rinpoche. See his *Meditation in Action* (Boston: Shambhala Press, 1991).

863 UNCLE DON: 1930s U.S. radio father-figure tale-teller.

Arguments

885 PARAQUAT: Agricultural poison dust sprayed by U.S. on Sonora, Mexico, cannabis fields.

White Shroud

889 TIVOLI FARM: Catholic Worker. Contemplative rural commune founded 1930s by Dorothy Day, celebrated saint-like bohemian Catholic Pacifist.

890 SPRY OLD LADY: Here several of Berenice Abbott *Changing New York* Depression era photographs are described, from "buses" to "shoes."

Reading Bai Juyi

908 After Rewi Alley's *Bai Juyi: 200 Selected Poems* (Beijing: New World Press, 1983), p. 303.

909 *The Secret of the Golden Lotus* and *Meditation Cushion of the Flesh*, Chinese classic erotic handbooks.

909 JIANG JI: See latter's text & Gary Snyder's reply poem 1984.

909 QIN SHI HUANG: Emperor 2nd century BC, burned all Buddhist & Classic books.

COSMOPOLITAN
GREETINGS
POEMS
1986–1992

*"I'm going to try speaking some reckless words,
and I want you to try to listen recklessly."*

Thanks to the hospitable editors, variants of these writings were printed first in: *After the Storm; Allen in Vision; Alpha Beat Soup; The Alternative Press; American Poetry Review; Be Released in Los Angeles; Big Scream; Big Sky; Black Box; Bombay Gin; Boulevard; Break the Mirror; Broadway 2; [Brooklyn College] English Majors Newsletter; Brooklyn Review; Casse Le Mirroir; City Lights Review; Collateral Damage; Collected Poems; Core; Cottonwood Commemorative; River City Portfolio 1987; Cover; Culturas; Entretien; Ergo; Esquire; Exit Zero; Exquisite Corps; Fall of America; Fear, Power, God* (recording); *First Blues; First Line; Flower Thief; Gandhabba; A Garden of Earthly Delight; Gathering of Poets; The Ginsberg Gallimaufry* (John Hammond Records); *Gown Literary Supplement; Grand Rapids College Review; Harper's; Holunderground; Howling Mantra; Hum Bom!* (broadside); *Hydrogen Jukebox* (libretto); *Inquiring Mind; Journal of the Gulf War; Karel Appel; Recent Work; Long Shot; Lovely Jobly; Man Alive!; Mill Street Forward; Moment; Moorish Science Monitor; Napalm Health Spa; Naropa Institute Summer Writing Program (1991); Nation; National Poetry Magazine of the Lower East Side; New Age Journal; New Censorship; A New Geography of Poets; New Letters; New Observations; New York Newsday; New York Planet; New York Times; Nigen Kazoku; Nightmares of Reason; Nola Express; La Nouvelle Chute de l'Amerique; Off the Wall; Organica; Paria; Pearl; Peckerwood; Personals Ad* (broadside); *Poem in the Form of a Snake* (broadside); *Poets for Life; Portable Lower East Side; Qualità di Tempo; Reality Sandwich; Riverrun; RuhRoh!; Sekai; Semiotext[e]; Shambhala Sun; Sixpack; Steaua; Struga; Sugar, Alcohol & Meat* (recording); *Sulfur; Supplication for the Rebirth of the Vidyadhara Chögyam Trungpa, Rinpoche* (broadside); *Talus; Thinker Review* (broadside); *This Is Important; Threepenny Review; Tikkun; Underground Forest; Vagabond; Vajradhatu Sun; Venue; The Verdict Is In; Village Voice; Vinduet; Visiting Father & Friends* (pamphlet); *Vylizanej Mozek!; Washington Square News; Wiersze; World; WPFW 89.3 FM Poetry Anthology.*

To
Steven Taylor

If music be the food of love, play on.

ACKNOWLEDGMENTS

Author wishes to inscribe grateful thanks to friends who've collaborated to type, track, edit, and critique *Cosmopolitan Greetings* thru a decade:

Harry Smith: Archetype cover design, typeface choice & logo.

Bill Morgan: Bibliographic lucidity.

Mark Ewert: Comix inspiration.

Bob Rosenthal: Holistic project supervision.

Steve Taylor: Musical guidance, lead sheets.

Regina Pellicano, Jacqueline Gens, Peter Hale, Steven Finbow, Victoria Smart, and Vicki Stanbury: Sympathetic meticulous assembly typescript text.

Andrew Wylie & Sarah Chalfant: Wise deadline protection.

Terry Karten and HarperCollins: Trustful & patient fidelity.

PREFACE

Improvisation in Beijing

I write poetry because the English word Inspiration comes from Latin *Spiritus*, breath, I want to breathe freely.

I write poetry because Walt Whitman gave world permission to speak with candor.

I write poetry because Walt Whitman opened up poetry's verse-line for unobstructed breath.

I write poetry because Ezra Pound saw an ivory tower, bet on one wrong horse, gave poets permission to write spoken vernacular idiom.

I write poetry because Pound pointed young Western poets to look at Chinese writing word pictures.

I write poetry because W. C. Williams living in Rutherford wrote New Jerseyesque "I kick yuh eye," asking, how measure that in iambic pentameter?

I write poetry because my father was poet my mother from Russia spoke Communist, died in a mad house.

I write poetry because young friend Gary Snyder sat to look at his thoughts as part of external phenomenal world just like a 1984 conference table.

I write poetry because I suffer, born to die, kidneystones and high blood pressure, everybody suffers.

I write poetry because I suffer confusion not knowing what other people think.

I write because poetry can reveal my thoughts, cure my paranoia also other people's paranoia.

I write poetry because my mind wanders subject to sex politics Buddhadharma meditation.

I write poetry to make accurate picture my own mind.

I write poetry because I took Bodhisattva's Four Vows: Sentient creatures to liberate are numberless in the universe, my own greed anger

ignorance to cut thru's infinite, situations I find myself in are
countless as the sky okay, while awakened mind path's endless.

I write poetry because this morning I woke trembling with fear what
could I say in China?

I write poetry because Russian poets Mayakovsky and Yesenin commit-
ted suicide, somebody else has to talk.

I write poetry because my father reciting Shelley English poet & Vachel
Lindsay American poet out loud gave example—big wind inspi-
ration breath.

I write poetry because writing sexual matters was censored in United
States.

I write poetry because millionaires East and West ride Rolls-Royce
limousines, poor people don't have enough money to fix their
teeth.

I write poetry because my genes and chromosomes fall in love with
young men not young women.

I write poetry because I have no dogmatic responsibility one day to the
next.

I write poetry because I want to be alone and want to talk to people.

I write poetry to talk back to Whitman, young people in ten years, talk
to old aunts and uncles still living near Newark, New Jersey.

I write poetry because I listened to black Blues on 1939 radio, Leadbelly
and Ma Rainey.

I write poetry inspired by youthful cheerful Beatles' songs grown old.

I write poetry because Chuang-tzu couldn't tell whether he was but-
terfly or man, Lao-tzu said water flows downhill, Confucius said
honor elders, I wanted to honor Whitman.

I write poetry because overgrazing sheep and cattle Mongolia to U.S.
Wild West destroys new grass & erosion creates deserts.

I write poetry wearing animal shoes.

I write poetry "First thought, best thought" always.

I write poetry because no ideas are comprehensible except as manifested
in minute particulars: "No ideas but in things."

I write poetry because the Tibetan Lama guru says, "Things are symbols
of themselves."

I write poetry because newspapers headline a black hole at our galaxy-
center, we're free to notice it.

I write poetry because World War I, World War II, nuclear bomb, and
World War III if we want it, I don't need it.
I write poetry because first poem *Howl* not meant to be published was
prosecuted by the police.
I write poetry because my second long poem *Kaddish* honored my
mother's parinirvana in a mental hospital.
I write poetry because Hitler killed six million Jews, I'm Jewish.
I write poetry because Moscow said Stalin exiled 20 million Jews and
intellectuals to Siberia, 15 million never came back to the Stray
Dog Café, St. Petersburg.
I write poetry because I sing when I'm lonesome.
I write poetry because Walt Whitman said, "Do I contradict myself?
Very well then I contradict myself (I am large, I contain multi-
tudes.)"
I write poetry because my mind contradicts itself, one minute in New
York, next minute the Dinaric Alps.
I write poetry because my head contains 10,000 thoughts.
I write poetry because no reason no because.
I write poetry because it's the best way to say everything in mind within
6 minutes or a lifetime.

October 21, 1984

PROLOGUE

Visiting Father & Friends

I climbed the hillside to the lady's house.
There was Gregory, dressed as a velvet ape,
japing and laughing, elegant-handed, tumbling
somersaults and consulting with the hostess,
girls and wives familiar, feeding him like a baby.
He looked healthy, remarkable energy, up all night
talking jewelry, winding his watches, hair over his eyes,
jumping from one apartment to another.

Neal Cassady rosy-faced indifferent and affectionate
entertaining himself in company far from China
back in the USA old 1950s–1980s still kicking
his way thru the city, up Riverside Drive without a car.
He hugged me & turned attention to the night ladies
appearing disappearing in the bar, in apartments
and the street, his continued jackanapes wasting his time
& everyone else's but mysterious, maybe up to something
good—keep us all from committing more crimes,
political wars, or peace protests angrier than wars'
cannonball noises. He needed a place to sleep.

Then my father appeared, lone forlorn & healthy
still living by himself in an apartment a block up
the hill from Peter's ancient habitual pad, I hadn't
noticed where Louis lived these days, somehow obliterated
his home condition from my mind, took it for granted
tho never'd been curious enough to visit—but as I'd no place
to go tonight, & wonder'd why I'd not visited him recently,
I asked could I spend the night & bed down

there with him, his place had bedroom and bath
a giant Jewish residence apartment on Riverside Drive
refugees inhabited, driven away from Europe by Hitler,
where now my father lived—I entered, he showed me his couch
& told me get comfortable, I slept the night, but woke
when he shifted his sleeping pad closer to mine I got up
—he'd slept badly on a green inch-thick dusty
foam rubber plastic mattress I'd thrown out years ago,
poor cold mat upon the concrete cellar warehouse floor—
so that was it! He'd given his bed for my comfort!

No no I said, take back your bed, sleep comfortable
weary you deserve it, amazing you still get around,
I'm sorry I hadn't visited before, just didn't know
where you lived, here you are a block upstreet
from Peter, hospitable to me Neal & Gregory &
girlfriends of the night, old sweet Bohemian heart
don't sleep in the floor like that I'll take your place
on the mat & pass the night ok.
                                   I went upstairs, happy to see
he had a place to lay his head for good, and woke in China.
Peter alive, though drinking a problem, Neal was dead
more years than my father Louis no longer
smiling alive, no wonder I'd not visited this place
he'd retired to a decade ago, How good to see him home, and take
his fatherly hospitality for granted among the living
and dead. Now wash my face, dress in my suit
on time for teaching classroom poetry at 8am Beijing,
far round the world away from Louis' grave in Jersey.

November 16, 1984, 6:52 A.M.

Baoding, P.R.C.

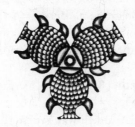

You Don't Know It

In Russia the tyrant cockroach mustache ate 20 million souls
and you don't know it, you don't know it
In Czechoslovakia the police ate the feet of a generation that can't walk
and you don't know it, you don't know it
In Poland police state double agent cancer grew large as Catholic
       Church Frankenstein the state itself a Gulag Ship
and you don't know it, you don't know it
In Hungary tanks rolled over words of Politician Poets
and you don't know it
In Yugoslavia underground partisans of the Great Patriotic War
fought off the Great Patriotic Army of USSR
and you don't know it,

you know Tito but you don't know it
you say you don't know it these exiles from East Europe complaining
      about someday Nicaragua Gulag
'cause you don't know it was the Writers Union intellectuals of Moscow
      Vilnius Minsk Leningrad and Tbilisi
saying "Invade Immediately" their Curse on your Revolution
No you don't know it's not N.Y. Review of Books it's bohemian Krakow
      Prague Budapest Belgrade E. Berlin
saying you don't know it you don't know it
Bella Akhmadulina in candlelight: "American poet you can never know
      the tragedy of Russia"
Nor you General Borge Father Cardenal Vice President Rodríguez you
      say you don't know it
Can't know it too busy with Yankee war Worse than memory of Stalin
That you know, yes you do know it

But you don't know it but you will know it
yes you will know it Lenin said
the first time History's Tragedy Second repeat it's Comedy
or was it Trotsky? Marx?
Non pasaran whispers from the Elbe, intellectual teeth chattering on
      Danube & Vistula
Village churchbells drowned in Volga waters dammed by Commissar
      engineers, riverwater evaporating faster than it reaches the sea
the Taiga woodsman weeping over "boring pamphlets" his forests pro-
      vided
Kulaks rattling skulls & bones to seed a new millennial agriculture by
      1980 '90 2000
with Lysenko's ectoplasm providing ammonia to grow Kasha
You don't know it intellectual Castro fat ass Power Chair a quarter
      century
biting fairies' nuts off, sneaking into Manolo's desk to read my love
      letters
making Heberto Padilla eat your speeches You don't know it's a frou-
      frou among French intellectual magazines you glance at as vice
      president of Nicaragua

between wars from North Yanquis and banquets with Pork & Rum after
  TV evening news—
              You don't know it
Madame Mandelstam's thick book's gossip, Mrs. Evgenia Ginzburg's
grey prisoners shitting on each other in the hull of the boat
on frozen sea out of Vladivostok going with the million
Card-carrying Party members old Bolshevik friends of Lenin
to the frozen puddles and hungry banks of Kolyma
where skeletons hit each other to keep alive you don't know it

And they don't know it, Aksionov Škvorecký Romain Rolland Ehren-
  burg Fedorenko Markov Yevtushenko—
don't know midnight Death Squad clubs on cobblestone no
the ears cut off, heads chopped open in Salvador don't know the million
Guatemala Indians in Model Villages—
Don't know 40,000 bellies ripped open by the d'Aubuisson hit-men for
  Born Again neoconservative Texans,
don't know Yanquis taking tea & 1916 money from the Douane, ex-
  change for Chinese opium
trading bananas to Europe for Tax Control in Managua & Shanghai—
don't know the holocaust in Salvador 25 years ago 30,000 shot one week
  for thinking Left-Pink-triangle yellow-red headband high on
  peyote
& you don't know Imagination that leaps like a frog in Communist
  Monastery Ponds—
Don't know you confess like a worm turning in a matchbox full of salt
Don't know Solitary, Lesbian Capo ordering Movie Star Princess to
  expose her ———
and her delicate pink ——— and her firm round ——— to the false
  dogs of Ideology Fart Yowp with big pricks Whip Blip Blip
  Blip—
Bugger it up in Dynamite Don't know the Marines in your mother's
  toilet
No you don't know it we don't know it only stupid American minstrels
  know intolerant gasbags ascending

with millions of Readers' Digest copies
and photo enlargements of a thumbnail translation of the Moravian
    Bible
Put in my shirt-pocket in a sweat eyes closing as the enemy approaches
to fall asleep & snore Don't I know it

January 25, 1986, 2:00–2:12 A.M.
Managua

On the Conduct of the World
Seeking Beauty Against Government

Is that the only way we can become like Indians, like Rhinoceri,
like Quartz Crystals, like organic farmers, live what we imagine
Adam & Eve to've been, caressing each other with trembling limbs
before the Snake of Revolutionary Sex wrapped itself round
the Tree of Knowledge? What would Roque Dalton joke about lately
teeth chattering like a machine gun as he debated mass tactics
with his Compañeros? Necessary to kill the Yanquis with big bomb
Yes but don't do it by yourself, better consult your mother
to get the Correct Line of Thought, if not consult Rimbaud once he got
           his leg cut off
or Lenin after his second stroke sending a message thru Mrs. Krupskaya
           to the rude Georgian, & just before his deathly fit when the
           Cheka aides outside
his door looked in coldly assuring him his affairs were in good hands
no need to move—What sickness at the pit of his stomach moved up to
           his brain?
What thought Khlebnikov on the hungry train exposing his stomach to
           the sun?
Or Mayakovsky before the bullet hit his brain, what sharp propaganda
           for action
on the Bureaucratic Battlefield in the Ministry of Collective Agriculture
           in Ukraine?
What Slogan for Futurist architects or epic hymn for masses of Com-
           munist Party Card holders in Futurity
on the conduct of the world seeking beauty against Government?

January 27, 1986

Hard Labor

After midnite, Second Avenue horseradish Beef
　　at Kiev's wood tables—
The Kasha Mushrooms tastes good
　　as Byelorussia usta when my momma
　　ran away from Cossacks 1905
Did the 5 year plan work? How bad Stalin?
Am I a Stalinist? A Capitalist? A
　　Bourgeois Stinker? A rotten Red?
No I'm a fairy with purple wings and white halo
　　translucent as an onion ring in
the transsexual fluorescent light of Kiev
　　Restaurant after a hard day's work

February 17, 1986, 12:35 A.M.

Velocity of Money

For Lee Berton

I'm delighted by the velocity of money as it whistles through windows of
    Lower East Side
Delighted skyscrapers rise grungy apartments fall on 84th Street's pave-
    ment
Delighted this year inflation drives me out on the street
with double digit interest rates in Capitalist worlds
I always was a communist, now we'll win
as usury makes walls thinner, books thicker & dumber
Usury makes my poetry more valuable
Manuscripts worth their weight in useless gold—
The velocity's what counts as the National Debt gets trillions higher
Everybody running after the rising dollar
Crowds of joggers down Broadway past City Hall on the way to the Fed
Nobody reads Dostoyevsky books anymore so they'll have to give
    passing ear
to my fragmented ravings in between President's speeches
Nothing's happening but the collapse of the Economy
so I can go back to sleep till the landlord wins his eviction suit in court

February 18, 1986, 10:00 A.M.

Sphincter

I hope my good old asshole holds out
60 years it's been mostly OK
Tho in Bolivia a fissure operation
       survived the *altiplano* hospital—
a little blood, no polyps, occasionally
       a small hemorrhoid
active, eager, receptive to phallus
       coke bottle, candle, carrot
       banana & fingers—
Now AIDS makes it shy, but still
       eager to serve—
out with the dumps, in with the condom'd
       orgasmic friend—
still rubbery muscular,
       unashamed wide open for joy
But another 20 years who knows,
       old folks got troubles everywhere—
necks, prostates, stomachs, joints—
       Hope the old hole stays young
       till death, relax

March 15, 1986, 1:00 P.M.

Spot Anger

"Drive all blames into one"

Allen when you get angry you got two choices—
Konk your head on the floor with words
Bang the kitchen table, slap taxicab doors,
         insult hotel toilets
Snarl into National microphones, sneer at the
         speedfreak closet girl syringiste—
Why not more subtle, grab your anger by the wings
and bag it in the garbage pail
Look around by the venetian blind
It's only you in the universe's kitchen—
A subtler wave of the hand, patience—
Say, I don't want this Saturn trip, no thanks,
Domo arigato how nice but I'll not entertain
         Dr. Frankenstein till Monday
These pants don't fit, may I borrow your library card—
Breathe your typhoonic tantrum in, exhale a gentle
         breath of Ginsberg out the kitchen window
wafting a Springtime Fairy feather-slight
         raising a big iron pipe
to konk Mr. Temper Tantrum on his green bull noodle & fly off
over Manhattan weaving silver laughter
         round skyscraper spires.

                              April 24, 1986, 6:00 A.M.

London Dream Doors

On London's Tavern's wooden table, been reading Kit Smart—
God sent him to sea for pearls—till eyes heavy must sleep—
So went upstairs to my boardinghouse room yet the tall dark
boy that lived across the hall'd just got under covers
in a high Captain's bed, but left his door wide open,
his room furnished mahogany, oak crowded to the closets—
I gazed alas he was handsome, older than my choice of flesh
smooth boyhood, the lad had dark eyes, long limbs
a little hair on legs and chest, a little beard and smile—
I dozed, woke and returned from the bog, again passing
his room at stairtop— He lay in bed eyes open, I paused—
then turned aside thru his door, an embrace before going
to sleep in my own solid room I'd rented, first night
in this odd town, I'd come to teach a few strangers Love
& Poetry— So cast myself on his chest for a hug goodnight,
a second's surprise like father-son sweet dreams—
He clasped arms around me, held tight, I stopped a second—
More than I'd hoped for! Refreshing friendliness!—
lay there a minute, his warmth remained, spontaneous—
Grateful hugged his chest & quickly kissed his neck
& face, haste before I must rise— Yet no need to go
so with right leg I pushed the door in, closed,
we were alone. He pulled me on top of him, held each other,
I passed my hand along his side down to his thigh
he shivered, hands on my back, we began to sweat
under covers, his skin like slippery meat, the heat
of our embrace familiar, companionable surprise, I was
to be loved by his strong form, how soon hug his middle?
touch his flaccid glans? My own already thick with pleasure—
chest to his chest, legs intertwined, hard hair felt
uncomfortable under my hand—moved my palm across
his slimy stomach, sweat not unpleasant, close heat
amazed us both, secret freedom in his antique room,
invitation to explore night's pleasure, fresh conscience,

muscled thoughts, hearts glowing astounded happiness a brief
8 hours in the dark— What to do? I kissed his solar plexus
& belly above loins, he sighed and breathed on my neck in back,
affectionate clasped to his breast, arm round my waist— eyes
closed I lay still, head under white muslin in dim light,
quilt set aside for the heat—

> The door opened suddenly!

"You'll have to pay for the night's furniture" announced
the landlord. "You'll have to pay for the sink water and extra
covers! We rent or sell!" He fell silent. Hadn't he noticed
my bulk under thin sheet-cloth? But next instant he was
gone downstairs to write up the bill, door left ajar.
"Into my closet!" my new friend whispered urgent, "the first door!"—
The knob on his mirrored armoire stuck, wouldn't open,
same horrific closet of old play-movie nightmare blackouts—I saw
my own room entrance across the hall—"I'll go in there, seconds
to hide," fast before the old fellow returns! Naked trailing
sheet & blanket I crossed the hall stealthy, closed my bedroom
door behind, just time enough? Alas bed sheets blocked
the door jamb, clogged the landing, pull them through, I strained,
dragged awkward blankets inside in a trice and woke under
springtime sheets and linen cover alone, East Twelfth Street,
last night with Bengali Marathi Urdu poets, Museum of Modern Art.

May 6, 1986, 3:10 A.M.

Cosmopolitan Greetings

To Struga Festival Golden Wreath Laureates
& International Bards 1986

Stand up against governments, against God.

Stay irresponsible.

Say only what we know & imagine.

Absolutes are coercion.

Change is absolute.

Ordinary mind includes eternal perceptions.

Observe what's vivid.

Notice what you notice.

Catch yourself thinking.

Vividness is self-selecting.

If we don't show anyone, we're free to write anything.

Remember the future.

Advise only yourself.

Don't drink yourself to death.

Two molecules clanking against each other require an observer to
     become scientific data.

The measuring instrument determines the appearance of the
     phenomenal world after Einstein.

The universe is subjective.

Walt Whitman celebrated Person.

We are observer, measuring instrument, eye, subject, Person.

Universe is Person.

Inside skull vast as outside skull.

Mind is outer space.

"Each on his bed spoke to himself alone, making no sound."

"First thought, best thought."

Mind is shapely, Art is shapely.

Maximum information, minimum number of syllables.

Syntax condensed, sound is solid.

Intense fragments of spoken idiom, best.

Consonants around vowels make sense.

Savor vowels, appreciate consonants.

Subject is known by what she sees.

Others can measure their vision by what we see.

Candor ends paranoia.

Kral Majales
June 25, 1986
Boulder, Colorado

FIFTH INTERNATIONALE

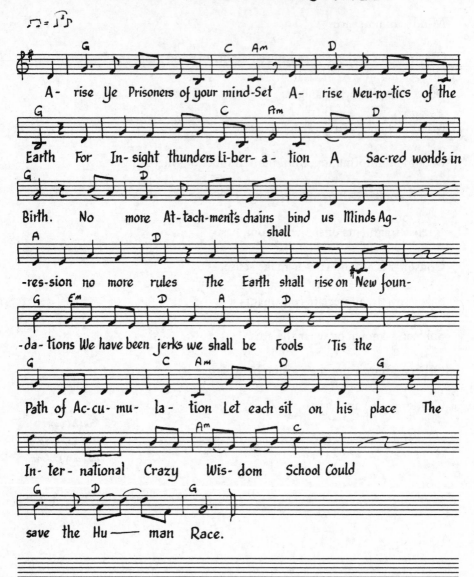

A- rise Ye Prisoners of your mind-Set A- rise Neu-ro-tics of the

Earth For In- sight thunders Li-ber- a- tion A Sac-red world's in

Birth. No more At-tach-ment's chains bind us Minds Ag-

-res-sion no more rules The Earth shall rise on New foun-

-da- tions We have been jerks we shall be Fools 'Tis the

Path of Ac-cu- mu- la- tion Let each sit on his place The

In- ter- national Crazy Wis- dom School Could

save the Hu —— man Race.

Fifth Internationale

To Billy MacKeever

Arise ye prisoners of your mind-set
Arise Neurotics of the Earth
For Insight thunders Liberation
A sacred world's in birth

No more Attachment's chains shall bind us
Mind's Aggression no more rules
The Earth shall rise on new foundations
We have been jerks we shall be Fools

'Tis the Path of Accumulation
Let each sit on his place
The International Crazy Wisdom School
Could save the Human Race

July 1986
Naropa

EUROPE, WHO KNOWS?

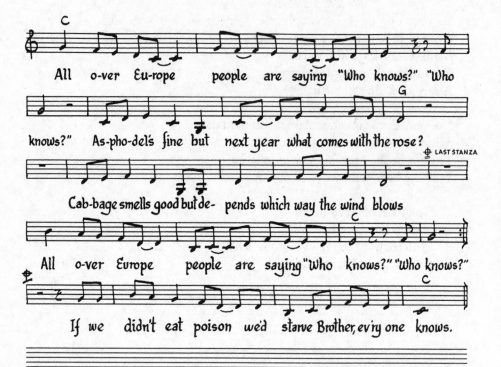

All o-ver Eu-rope people are saying "Who knows?" "Who knows?" As-pho-del's fine but next year what comes with the rose?

LAST STANZA

Cab-bage smells good but de- pends which way the wind blows

All o-ver Europe people are saying "Who knows?" "Who knows?"

If we didn't eat poison we'd starve Brother, ev'ry one knows.

Europe, Who Knows?

All over Europe people are saying, "Who knows?"
Asphodel's fine but next year what comes with the rose?
Cabbage smells good but depends which way the wind blows
All over Europe people are saying, "Who knows?"

Wormwood skies'll poison the sea: *Revelation*
Oslo to Athens black clouds've enlightened the nations
Cesium mushrooms & milk may mutate the Creation
All over Europe people are saying, "Who knows?"

Crossing the park in Munich Max Planck Institute
On my forearm and brow a film of invisible soot
Fell on my skin out of heaven, a new set of clothes
All over Europe people are saying, "Who knows?"

Woke up in Poland, maple leaves just wilted down
Not a cloud in the sky inexplicably cold on the ground
Kids in the yard were playing without any clothes
All over Europe people are saying, "Who knows?"

Phoned up the doctor, official reply: "Never mind"
Same afternoon suggested we take iodine
Three days later Chernobyl's error disclosed
All over Europe people are saying, "Who knows?"

Slaughtered the reindeer in Lapland, Lapps on the dole
Camembert radioactive, in Zurich, the gold
In the Cotswolds of England all the sheep markets were closed
All over Europe people are saying, "Who knows?"

If a liter of water's one x-ray in Washington State
So in milk bars of Minsk what does it cost a milkshake?
Big apples this year, we still have to eat up what grows
If we didn't eat poison we'd starve, Brother, everyone knows.

September 12, 1986 (with Steven Taylor)
Warsaw Airport

Graphic Winces

In highschool when you crack your front tooth bending down too fast
    over the porcelain water fountain
or raise the tuna sandwich to your open mouth and a cockroach tickles
    your knuckle
or step off the kitchen cabinet ladder on the ball of your foot hear the
    piercing meow of a soft kitten
or sit on a rattling subway next the woman scratching sores on her legs,
    thick pus on her fingers
or put your tongue to a winter-frozen porch door, a layer of frightening
    white flesh sticks to the wooden frame—
or pinch your little baby boy's fat neck skin in the last teeth of his
    snowsuit zipper
or when you cross Route 85 the double yellow line's painted over a dead
    possum
or tip your stale party Budweiser on the windowsill to your lips, taste
    Marlboro butts floating top of the can—
or fighting on the second flight of the tenement push your younger
    sister down the marble stairs she bites her tongue in half, they
    have to sew it back in the hospital—
or at icebox grabbing the half-eaten Nestlé's Crunch a sliver of foil
    sparks on your back molar's silver filling
or playing dare in High School you fall legs split on opposite sides of a
    high iron spiked fence
or kicked in the Karate Dojo hear the sound like a cracked twig then feel
    a slow dull throb in your left forearm,
or tripping fall on the sidewalk & rip last week's scab off your left knee
You might grimace, a sharp breath from the solar plexus, chill spreading
    from shoulderblades and down the arms,
or you may wince, tingling twixt sphincter and scrotum a subtle electric
    discharge.

December 8, 1986

Imitation of K.S.

The young kid, horror buff, monster Commissar, ghoul connoisseur, attic bedroom postered with violet skulls, cigarette butts on the floor, thinks he'd strangle girls after orgasm—pumping iron 13 years old, 175-pound muscleman, his father shot at him, missed, hit the door, he saw his mother's tiny apron, father clutched his throat, six foot four drunk, today's in Alcohol Anonymous. Even eyes, symmetric face, aged twenty, acid-free-plastic packages of *Ghoul Ghosts*, *Monsters Nowhere*, *Evil Demons of the Dead*, *Frenzy Reanimator*, *Psycho Nightmare on Elm Street* stacked by his mattress; he followed me around, carried my harmonium box, protected me from the drunk Tibetan, came to my bed; head on his shoulder, I felt his naked heart, "my Cock's half dead," he thinks he'll cut it off, can't stand to be touched, never touches himself, iron legs, "skinny dynamite," thick biceps, a six-day black fuzz on his even jaw, shining eyes, "I love you too."

March 22, 1987

I Went to the Movie of Life

In the mud, in the night, in Mississippi Delta roads
outside Clarksdale I slogged along Lights flashed
under trees, my black companion motioned "Here they are,
your company."—Like giant rhinoceri with painted faces
splashed all over side and snout, headlights glaring in rain,
one after another buses rolled past us toward Book Hotel
Boarding House, up the hill, town ahead.
                                    Accompanying me, two girls
pitched in the dark slush garbaged road, slipping in deep ruts
wheels'd left behind sucking at their high heels, staining granny
dresses sequined magic marked with astral signs, Head groupies
who knew the way to this Grateful Dead half-century heroes'
caravan pit stop for the night. I climbed mid-road, a toad
hopped before my foot, I shrank aside, unthinking'd kicked it off
with leather shoe, animal feet scurried back at my sight—
a little monster on his back bled red, nearby this prey a lizard
with large eyes retreated, and a rat curled tail and slithered
in mud wet to the dirt gutter, repelled. A long climb ahead, the girls'd
make it or not, I moved on, eager to rejoin old company.
Merry Pranksters with aged pride in peacock-feathered beds,
shining mylar mirror-paper walls, acid mothers with strobe-lit radios,
long-haired men, gaunt 60s' Diggers emerged from the night
to rest, bathe, cook spaghetti, nurse their kids,
smoke pipes and squat with Indian sages round charcoal
braziers in their cars; profound American dreamers,
I was in their company again after long years, byways
alone looking for lovers in bar street country towns
and sunlit cities, rain & shine, snow & spring-bud backyard
brick walls, ominous adventures behind the Iron Curtain.
Were we all grown old? I looked for my late boyfriends,
dancing to Electric Blues with their guns and smoke round jukebox walls
the smell of hash and country ham, old newspaper media stars
wandering room after room: Pentagon refugee Ellsberg, old dove

Dellinger bathing in an iron tub with a patch in his stomach wall
Abbie Hoffman explaining the natural strategy of city political saint
works, Quicksilver Messenger musicians, Berkeley orators
with half-grown children in their sox & dirty faces, alcohol
uncles who played chess & strummed banjos frayed by broken
fingernails.
Where's Ken Kesey, away tonite in another megalopolis hosting
hypnosis parties for Hell's Angels, maybe nail them down on stage
or radio, Neal must be tending his daughters in Los Gatos,
pacifying his wife, coming down amphetamines in his bedroom,
or downers to sleep this night away & wake for work
in the great Bay Carnival tented among smokestacks, railroad
tracks and freeways under box-house urban hills.
Young movie stars with grizzled beards passed thru bus corridors
looking for Dylan in the movie office, re-swaggering old roles,
recorded words now sung in Leningrad and Shanghai, their wives
in tortoise shell glasses & paisley shawls & towels tending
cauldrons bubbling with spaghetti sauce & racks of venison,
squirrel or lamb; ovens open with hot rhubarb pies—
Who should I love? Here one with leather hat, blond hair
strong body middle age, face frowned in awful thought,
beer in hand by the bathroom wall? That Digger boy I knew
with giant phallos, bald head studying medicine walked by,
preoccupied with anatomy homework, rolling a joint, his
thick fingers at his chest, eyes downcast on paper & tobacco.
One by one I checked out love companions, none whose beauty
stayed my heart, this place was tired of my adoration,
they knew my eyes too well. No one I could find to give me
bed tonite and wake me grinning naked, with eggs scrambled
for breakfast ready, oatmeal, grits, or hot spicy sausages
at noon assembly when I opened my eyelids out of dream. I
wandered, walking room to room thru psychedelic buses
wanting to meet someone new, younger than this crowd of wily
wrinkled wanderers with their booze and families, Electronic
Arts & Crafts, woe lined brows of chemical genius music
producers, adventurous politicians, singing ladies & earthy paramours
playing rare parts in the final movie of a generation.

The cameras
rolled and followed me, was I the central figure in this film?
I'd known most faces and guided the inevitable cameras room to room,
pausing at candle lit bus windows to view this ghostly caravan of gypsy
intellects passing thru USA, aged rock stars whispering by coal stoves,
public headline artists known from Rolling Stone & N.Y. Times,
actors & actresses from Living Theater, gaunt-faced and eloquent
with lifted hands & bony fingers greeting me on my way
to the bus driver's wheel, tattered dirty gloves on Neal's seat
waiting his return from working the National Railroad, young kids
I'd taught saluting me wearily from worn couches as I passed
bus to bus, cameras moving behind me. What was my role?
I hardly knew these faded heroes, friendly strangers
so long on the road, I'd been out teaching in Boulder, Manhattan,
Budapest, London, Brooklyn so long, why follow me thru
these amazing Further bus party reunion corridors tonite?
or is this movie, or real, if I turn to face the camera I'd break
the scene, dissolve the plot illusion, or is't illusion
art, or just my life? Were cameras ever there, the picture
flowed so evenly before my eyes, how could a crew follow
me invisible still and smoothly noiseless bus to bus
from room to room along the caravan's painted labyrinth?
This wasn't cinema, and I no hero spokesman documenting friendship
scenes, only myself alone lost in bus cabins with familiar
strangers still looking for some sexual angel for mortal delights
no different from haunting St. Mark's Boys Bar again solitary
in tie jacket and grey beard, wallet in my pocket full of
cash and cards, useless.
                                        A glimmer of lights
in the curtained doorway before me! my heart leapt
forward to the Orgy Room, all youths! Lithe and
hairless, smooth skinned, white buttocks ankles, young men's
nippled chests lit behind the curtain, thighs entwined
in the male area, place I was looking for behind
my closed eyelids all this night—I pushed my hand
into the room, moving aside the curtain that shimmered
within bright with naked knees and shoulders pale

in candlelight—entered the pleasure chamber's empty door
glimmering silver shadows reflected on the silver curtained veil,
eyelids still dazzling as their adolescent limbs
intangible dissolved where I put my hand into a vacant room,
lay down on its dark floor to watch the lights of phantom arms
pulsing across closed eyelids conscious as I woke in bed
returned at dawn New York wood-slatted venetian blinds over
the windows on E. 12th St. in my white painted room

April 30, 1987, 4:30–6:25 A.M.

When the Light Appears

Lento

You'll bare your bones you'll grow you'll pray you'll only know
When the light appears, boy, when the light appears
You'll sing & you'll love you'll praise blue heavens above
When the light appears, boy, when the light appears
You'll whimper & you'll cry you'll get yourself sick and sigh
You'll sleep & you'll dream you'll only know what you mean
When the light appears, boy, when the light appears
You'll come & you'll go, you'll wander to and fro
You'll go home in despair you'll wonder why'd you care
You'll stammer & you'll lie you'll ask everybody why
You'll cough and you'll pout you'll kick your toe with gout
You'll jump you'll shout you'll knock your friends about
You'll bawl and you'll deny & announce your eyes are dry
You'll roll and you'll rock you'll show your big hard cock
You'll love & you'll grieve & one day you'll come believe
As you whistle & you smile the lord made you worthwhile
You'll preach and you'll glide on the pulpit in your pride
Sneak & slide across the stage like a river in high tide
You'll come fast or come on slow just the same you'll never know
When the light appears, boy, when the light appears

May 3, 1987, 2:30 A.M.

On Cremation of
Chögyam Trungpa, Vidyadhara

I noticed the grass, I noticed the hills, I noticed the highways,
I noticed the dirt road, I noticed car rows in the parking lot
I noticed ticket takers, I noticed the cash and checks & credit cards,
I noticed buses, noticed mourners, I noticed their children in red
    dresses,
I noticed the entrance sign, noticed retreat houses, noticed blue &
    yellow Flags—
noticed the devotees, their trucks & buses, guards in Khaki uniforms
I noticed crowds, noticed misty skies, noticed the all-pervading smiles &
    empty eyes—
I noticed pillows, colored red & yellow, square pillows and round—
I noticed the Tori Gate, passers-through bowing, a parade of men &
    women in formal dress—
noticed the procession, noticed the bagpipe, drum, horns, noticed high
    silk head crowns & saffron robes, noticed the three piece suits,
I noticed the palanquin, an umbrella, the stupa painted with jewels the
    colors of the four directions—
amber for generosity, green for karmic works, noticed the white for
    Buddha, red for the heart—
thirteen worlds on the stupa hat, noticed the bell handle and umbrella,
    the empty head of the white clay bell—
noticed the corpse to be set in the head of the bell—
noticed the monks chanting, horn plaint in our ears, smoke rising from
    atop the firebrick empty bell—
noticed the crowds quiet, noticed the Chilean poet, noticed a Rainbow,
I noticed the Guru was dead, I noticed his teacher bare breasted watch-
    ing the corpse burn in the stupa,
noticed mourning students sat crosslegged before their books, chanting
    devotional mantras,
gesturing mysterious fingers, bells & brass thunderbolts in their hands
I noticed flame rising above flags & wires & umbrellas & painted orange
    poles

I noticed the sky, noticed the sun, a rainbow round the sun, light misty
    clouds drifting over the Sun—
I noticed my own heart beating, breath passing thru my nostrils
my feet walking, eyes seeing, noticing smoke above the corpse-fir'd
    monument
I noticed the path downhill, noticed the crowd moving toward buses
I noticed food, lettuce salad, I noticed the Teacher was absent,
I noticed my friends, noticed our car the blue Volvo, a young boy held
    my hand
our key in the motel door, noticed a dark room, noticed a dream
and forgot, noticed oranges lemons & caviar at breakfast,
I noticed the highway, sleepiness, homework thoughts, the boy's nippled
    chest in the breeze
as the car rolled down hillsides past green woods to the water,
I noticed the houses, balconies overlooking a misted horizon, shore &
    old worn rocks in the sand
I noticed the sea, I noticed the music, I wanted to dance.

May 28, 1987, 2:30–3:15 A.M.

Nanao

Brain washed by numerous mountain streams
Legs clean after walking four continents
Eyes cloudless as Kagoshima sky
Fresh raw surprisingly cooked heart
Tongue live as a Spring salmon
Nanao's hands are steady, pen & ax sharp as stars.

With Peter Orlovsky
June 1987

Personals Ad

"I will send a picture too
if you will send me one of you"
—R. CREELEY

Poet professor in autumn years
seeks helpmate companion protector friend
young lover w/empty compassionate soul
exuberant spirit, straightforward handsome
athletic physique & boundless mind, courageous
warrior who may also like women & girls, no problem,
to share bed meditation apartment Lower East Side,
help inspire mankind conquer world anger & guilt,
empowered by Whitman Blake Rimbaud Ma Rainey & Vivaldi,
familiar respecting Art's primordial majesty, priapic carefree
playful harmless slave or master, mortally tender passing swift time,
photographer, musician, painter, poet, yuppie or scholar—
Find me here in New York alone with the Alone
going to lady psychiatrist who says Make time in your life
for someone you can call darling, honey, who holds you dear
can get excited & lay his head on your heart in peace.

October 8, 1987

Proclamation

For Carlos Edmondo de Ory

I am the King of the Universe
I am the Messiah with a new dispensation
Excuse me I stepped on a nail.
A mistake
Perhaps I am not the Capitalist of Heaven.
Perhaps I'm a gate keeper snoring
      beside the Pearl Columns—
No this isn't true, I really am God himself.
Not at all human. Don't associate me
      w/that Crowd.
In any case you can believe every word
      I say.

October 31, 1987
Gas Station, N.Y.

To Jacob Rabinowitz

Dear Jacob I received your translation, what kind
favor you paid to have it printed up,
lighthearted the most readable I know—
Glad to be your friend, 2000 years after Catullus,
nothing's changed poets or poetics, lovers or love
familiar conversation between the three of us,
familiar tears—Remember you leaped in bed naked
and wouldn't sleep on my floor, decade ago? I was
half century old, you hardly out of puberty gave me
your ass bright eyes and virgin body a whole month
What a little liar you were, how'd I know you were cherry?
Put me down now for not hearing your teenage heartbeat,
think back were you serious offering to kidnap me
to Philadelphia, Cleveland, Baltimore, Miami, God
knows, rescued from boring fame & Academic fortune,
Rimbaud Verlaine lovers starved together in boondock houseflat
stockyard furnished rooms eating pea soup reading E. A. Poe?
First night in each other's arms you chilled my spine whispering
lies till dawn—pubescent lovelife with a tiny monkey you claim'd
you'd tortured to death—how trust you take me to the moon?
Tho you gave your butt to others in St. Mark's Baths' steam room
that year I followed you to Chelsea Hotel kissing your boots
& still lust for your body tho now you've grown a red beard.
At thirty still cute, lost interest in my potbelly years ago,
useless to jack off to your youthful shadow anymore.
And I your genius poet first love ignored hypoglycemic,
impotent, gouty, squint-eyed, halfway bald—
Reading this book gives me youth back again, not old
in vain, at last you bring love to Catullus & Poetry
humble enough to print these translations by yourself.

December 2, 1987, 4:30 A.M.

Grandma Earth's Song

I started down Capitol Hill side along unfamiliar black central avenues
warily uncertain which streets thru Fillmore district to City Hall valley
      center,
and as I passed a block or two I saw a fragile crone marching toward me
up hill, Grandma Bag-lady ragged dressed with firm ancient steps Old
      Ma Earth
dragging a shopping cart filled with cans bottles & plastic newspapers
      tied
with silk stockings wandering alone singing out loud on way to Civic
      Center

      When dull roots write Laws
      Jerusalem to New York
      Poor Jews break Arab Jaws
      Blacks eat greasy pork

      What's the Planet News?
      Wall Street's poison pill
      Palestinians stone Jews
      Water runs downhill

      Young soldiers gonna die
      Old presidents get AIDS
      They bankrupted the sky
      The ozone layer fades

      Crazy people got money
      I own State Capitols
      Sheriff calls me honey
      The army's a bunch of fools

I want my welfare stamps
I want my movie show
I got ten kerosene lamps
I'm 99 years old

This town's already dead
This country's on the skids
This state's made out of lead
I can't feed my kids

My name is Gaia ah ha ha
Put me in jail I screw the sky
Nothing to win or lose Poppa
Born your gonna die

Adam bombs & newsboy hoaxes
Fakers yak the Oval Room
I live in cardboard boxes
They killed the ocean's womb

Tear up your welfare check
I'll eat my way to Heaven
Throw me in Walnut Creek
I'll vomit Pacific Ocean

Wakening as she passed by I thought, she's improvising street doggerel
epic popular song cackling in everyone's Immortal brain
Anything comes to mind's the right politics to ruin Police State.

February 13, 1988, 7:30–9:00 A.M.

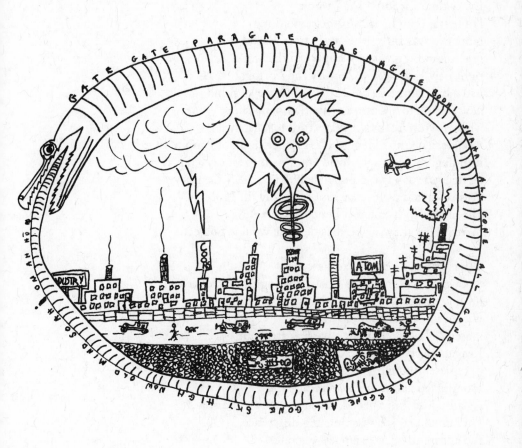

Salutations to Fernando Pessoa

Every time I read Pessoa I think
I'm better than he is I do the same thing
more extravagantly—he's only from Portugal,
I'm American greatest Country in the world
right now End of XX Century tho Portugal
had a big empire in the 15th century never mind
now shrunk to a Corner of Iberian peninsula
whereas New York take New York for instance
tho Mexico City's bigger N.Y.'s richer think of Empire State
Building not long ago world empire's biggest skyscraper—
be that as't may I've experienced 61 years' XX Century
Pessoa walked down Rua do Ouro only till 1936
He entered Whitman so I enter Pessoa no
matter what they say besides dead he wouldn't object.

What way'm I better than Pessoa?
Known on 4 Continents I have 25 English books he only 3
his mostly Portuguese, but that's not his fault—
U.S.A.'s a bigger country
merely 2 Trillion in debt a passing freakout,
Reagan's dirty work an American Century aberration
unrepresenting our Nation Whitman sang in Epic manner
tho worried about in *Democratic Vistas*
As a Buddhist not proud my superiority to Pessoa
I'm humble Pessoa was nuts big difference,
tho apparently gay—same as Socrates,
consider Michelangelo da Vinci Shakespeare
inestimable comerado Walt
True I was tainted Pinko at an early age a mere trifle
science itself destroys ozone layers this era antiStalinists
poison entire earth with radioactive anticommunism.
Maybe I lied somewhat
rarely in verse, only protecting others' reputations.

Frankly too Candid about my mother tho meant well
Did Pessoa mention his mother? she's interesting,
powerful to birth sextuplets
Alberto Cairo Alvaro de Campos Ricardo Reis Bernardo Soares &
         Alexander Search simultaneously
with Fernando Pessoa himself a classic sexophrenic
Confusing personae not so popular
outside Portugal's tiny kingdom (till recently a second-rate police state)
Let me get to the point er I forget what it was
but certainly enjoy making comparisons between this Ginsberg &
         Pessoa
people talk about in Iberia hardly any books in English
presently the world's major diplomatic language extended throughout
         China.
Besides he was a shrimp, himself admits in interminable "Salutations to
         Walt Whitman"
whereas 5'7½" height
somewhat above world average, no immodesty,
I'm speaking seriously about me & Pessoa.
Anyway he never influenced me, never read Pessoa
before I wrote my celebrated *Howl* already translated into 24 languages,
not to this day's Pessoa influence an anxiety
Midnight April 12 '88 merely glancing his book
certainly influences me in passing, only reasonable
but reading a page in translation hardly proves "Influence."
Turning to Pessoa, what'd he write about? Whitman
(Lisbon, the sea etc.) method peculiarly longwinded,
diarrhea mouth some people say—Pessoa Schmessoa.

                                        April 12, 1988

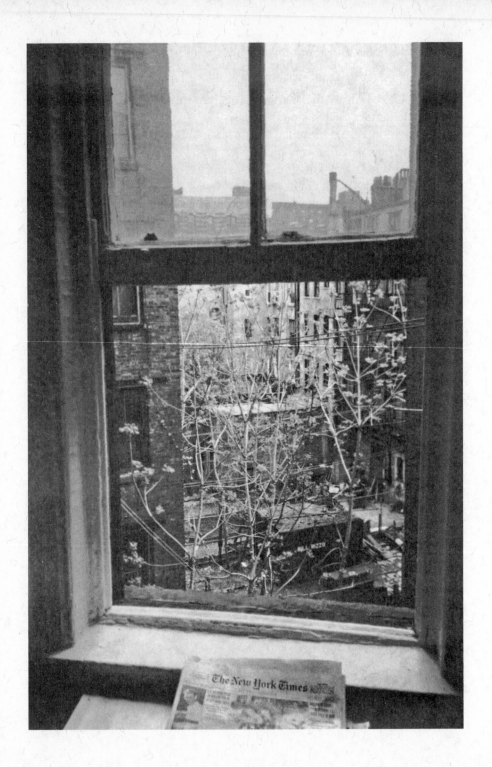

May Days 1988

I

As I cross my kitchen floor the thought of Death returns,
day after day, as I wake & drink lemon juice & hot water,
brush my teeth & blow my nose, stand at toilet a yellow stream
issuing from my body, look out curtained windows, across the street
Mary Help of Christians R.C. Church, how many years
empty the garbage pail, carry black plastic bags to the sidewalk,
before I boil the last soft egg,
day after day glance my altar sitting pillow a sidelong look & sigh,
pass bookcases' Greek lyrics & volumes of Military Industrial Secrecy?
How many mornings out the window Springtime's grey clouds drift
        over a wooden owl
on the Rectory roof, pigeons flutter off the street lamp to an iron fence, I
        return to kitchen
oatmeal cooking in an iron pot, sit in a wooden chair, choose a soup-
        spoon, dreaming out the window eat my gruel
as ailanthus trees bud & grow thick green, seaweed in rainy Atlantis,
lose leaves after snowfall, sit bare-branched in January's rusty winds?
Snap photographs focus'd on the clothesline, courtyard chimneypots a
        block away?
How many years lie alone in bed and stroke my cock
or read the Times on a pillow midnite, answer telephone talk, my
        Stepmother
or Joe in Washington, wait for a knock on the door it's portly Peter
        sober hesitant
inquiring supper, rarely visiting, rueful a life gone by—you got the
        monthly rent?
armfuls of mid-morn mail arriving with despairing Secretaries—
rise and tuck my shirt in, turn the doorlock key, go down hallway stairs,
enter New York City, Christine's Polish restaurant around East 12th
        Street corner on 1st Avenue
taxi uptown to art museums or visit Dr. Brown, chest x-rays, smoking
        cough or flu

Turn on the News from Palestine, Listen to Leadbelly's tape lament,
    Black Girl, Jim Crow, Irene—and
Sunday Puerto Ricans climb concrete steps week after week to church.

II
Sox in the laundry, snap on the kitchen light midnite icebox
raid, sun-dried tomatoes, soft swiss cheese & ham, Pineapple juice,
low rent control $260 per mo, clear sanded gymseal'd floors, white
    walls,
Blake's *Tyger* on the bedroom bookcase, cabs rattling on dark asphalt
    below,
Silence, a solitary house, Charles Fourier on bedside table waiting
    inspection, switch light off—
Pajamas in drawer for sleep, 80 volumes behind the headboard for
    browsing—
Irving Howe's Yiddish Poetry, Atilla József, Sashibusan Das Gupta's
    Obscure Religious Cults, Céline, *De Vulgari Eloquentia*—
What riches for old age? What cozy naps and long nights' dreams?
    Browsing in Persepolis and Lhasa!
What more ask existence? Except time, more time, ripe time & calm
& Warless time to contemplate collapsing years, tho body teeth brain
    elbow ache,
a crooked creak at backbone bottom, dry nostrils, mottled ankle
& smart tongue, how many years to talk, snap photos, sing in theaters
improvise in classroom street church radio, far from Congress?
How many more years eyes closed 9 A.M. wake worrying
the ulcer in my cheek is't cancer? Should I have charged Burroughs'
    biographer for photos
reprinted from 40 years ago? Miles the editor's stylistic competence OK
for Lit Hist Beat Generation? Should I rise & meditate
or sleep in daylight recuperate flu? phone ringing half an hour ago
What's on the Answer Machine? Give back Advances to Harper's?
Who promised deadlines for this photo book? Wasn't I up 2 A.M.
    revising Poems?
Spontaneous verse?!? Take a plane to Greenland, visit Dublin?
PEN Club meet May 17, decision Israeli Censorship Arabic Press?

Call C—— O—— Yiddish translator poetress Zionist yenta?
Write concentration camp expert moralist Elie Wiesel, what's his word
"Arabs shd throw words not stones?"—that quote accurate from the
 Times?
Should I get up right now, crosslegged scribbling Journals
with motor roar in street downstairs, stolen autos doctor'd at the curb
or pull the covers over achy bones? How many years awake or sleepy
How many mornings to be or not to be?
How many morning Mays to come, birds chirp insistent on six-story
 roofs?
buds rise in backyard cities? Forsythia yellow by brick walls & rusty
 bedsprings near the fence?

III
How many Sundays wake and lie immobile eyes closed remembering
 Death,
7 A.M. Spring Sunlight out the window the noise a Nuyorican drunkard
 on the corner
reminds me of Peter, Naomi, my nephew Alan, am I mad myself, have
 always been so
waking in N.Y. 61st year to realize childless I am a motherless freak
like so many millions, worlds from Paterson Los Angeles to Amazon
Humans & Whales screaming in despair from Empire State Building
 top to Arctic Ocean bottom—?

May 1–3, 1988

Numbers in U.S. File Cabinet
(Death Waits to Be Executed)

100,000,000 buffalo 17th century on North American Plains
$136,000,000,000 Farm Program costs encouraged chemical overuse
    1980s decade
$4,500,000 Agriculture Department research on Natural farm methods
    1980s
300,000 National junkies
100,000 alcohol deaths yearly
385,000 tobacco deaths heart attack cancer a year
30,000 deaths "illicit substances" yearly
$11,000,000,000 budget war on drugs 1990
1,000,000,000 people on world malnourished diseased
3,600,000 estimated American Homeless
300,000 mental patients dumped on streets 1970s–1980s
300 homeless slept outdoors Tompkins Park N.Y.C. July 29, 1989
17,000 meals served St. Peter's soup kitchen Morristown N.J.
110,000,000 man-made deaths Wars holocausts fatality camps
    XX Century
3°–8° Fahrenheit increase earth temperature next century computers
    project
Lambert 3-6606 Louis Ginsberg's phone for 20 years in Paterson N.J.
65 Decibels sound level ordinary speech
100 Decibels rock concert sound level
28,000,000 current cases hearing loss U.S.A.
6,000 workers, Rocky Flats Nuclear Weapons Plant
$300,000,000 yearly pay & benefits Rocky Flats Colorado
1% Colorado manufacturing activity's at Rocky Flats Nuclear Facility
70 FBI agents raided Rocky Flats investigating 10,000 gallon toxic waste
    tanks 1989
$100,000,000,000 to 200,000,000,000 estimate nuclear weapons
    complex cleanup costs
Savings & Loan Association bankruptcy taxpayers' costs it says here
    $500,000,000,000

70,000 Salvadorians killed in Civil War majority by Government
     Paramilitary Death Squads funded by U.S.A.
40,000 names Doris Lessing too on National Automated Immigration
     Lookout System barred entering U.S.A.
3,000 citizens killed by Shining Path, Peru 1972–1979
3,000 citizens disappeared in Government custody Peru 1972–1979
U.S. produces 24% planetary Greenhouse gas, consumes 40% world's
     gasoline
$2,000,000,000,000-plus U.S. National debt 1990 ante Iraq War
$65 cost of Harry Smith's eyeglasses
20 largest World Cities by year 2000 none U.S.-European none speak
     English
1 in 10 Salvadorians displaced in decade's counterinsurgency war
1 sun per known solar system
1 set Wisdom teeth
1 mother of all
1 wrong move
1 bad apple
1 way street
1 anus each
1 non-God
1 down 2 to go

March 1990

Return of Kral Majales

This silver anniversary much hair's gone from my head and I am the
  King of May
And tho I am King of May my howls & proclamations present are
  banned by FCC on America's electric airwaves 6 A.M. to mid-
  night
So King of May I return through Heaven flying to reclaim my paper
  crown
And I am King of May with high blood pressure, diabetes, gout, Bell's
  palsy, kidneystones & calm eyeglasses
And wear the foolish crown of no ignorance no wisdom anymore no fear
  no hope in capitalist striped tie & Communist dungarees
No laughing matter the loss of the planet next hundred years
And I am the King of May returned with a diamond big as the universe
  an empty mind
And I am the King of May lacklove bouzerant in Springtime with a
  feeble practice of meditation
And I am King of May Distinguished Brooklyn English Professor
  singing
All gone all gone all overgone all gone sky-high now old mind so Ah!

April 25, 1990

Elephant in the Meditation Hall

Yes all spiritual groups scandal the shrine room
What about San Francisco Roshi & the board director's wife
What about high living limousine expense accounts in Moscow?
What about the late Rajneesh & poisoned gefilte fish in Oregon?
What's hiding under Rajneeshis' Orange skullcaps? Brains?
Then old L.A. Mountain Roshi even tap'd his young girls
and East Coast Roshi's semen dribbled from Hawaii to the broom
      closets of the Catskills
Maezumi Roshi caused grief his senseis' hearts wrung out with midnight
      sake & beer
Later he thanked them for A.A.
Veteran Zenmaster with motorcycle & community farm chorale felt up
      little boys
& a big guy too, tough as nails
Remember a strange Mongolian Russian fruitcake Lama in Polk Gulch
      Bay Area?
Vajracharya Trungpa! Dont mention the naked poet at the Halloween
      Party!
And the whispered transmission regent died of AIDS (disciple a straight
      guy sick they say)
Marxists were right, religion the people's opium!
But who're *they* to talk lookit Mao a Marxist his picture on every
      Chinese wall & Little Red Book
wherefore everyone stood up bedtime nites reciting his dread slogans?
They still had pictures of Stalin on truckcab windows in Gori 1985 a
      scandal!
And New Left carried psychedelic pictures of Mao, Che Guevara &
      Castro up and down Empire State's stairways
A scandal of the sixties! And marvelous atheist Khmer Rouge read Marx
      Sartre & Erich Fromm,
how many'd they murder with religious good intentions?
What US President hasn't sponsored war, Lumumba's assassination, an
      H-bomb,

trillion dollar Savings & Loan mistakes? Scandals! taxpayers gotta subsi-
    dize Banks!
Now we gotta digest Plutonium? how evacuate CIA?
Scandal hundreds homeless under Brooklyn Bridge freezing Xmas &
    New Year's Eve! Millions homeless in America!
Who'll gotta pay for 500,000 U.S. boys & girls visiting Arabian
    Deserts?
Who'll cough up billions for Iraq War to save a President's face?
Twelve Billion dollars mickeymouse the year's drug wars?
El Salvador, Honduras, Guatemala we paid death squads for decades
Nobody does anything right! Gods, Popes, Mullahs, Communists,
    Poets, Financiers!
My own life, scandal! lazy bum! secondhand royal scarlet ties & Yves St.
    Laurent Salvation Army blazers
How many boys let me caress their thighs!
How many girls cursed my cold beard? I better commit suicide!
That wouldn't work either, it'll be a beatnik scandal
after Cassady's railroad track death, Joan Burroughs' bullet in head,
Orlovsky sane in Bellevue 1st Ave., Kerouac's liver collapse & ruptured
    esophagus!
Trapped in living nightmare, I made a big mistake I got born,
The world came out of a black hole, whole universe
a scandal, illusion, everyone deluded, a cosmic elephant in the medita-
    tion planet,
George the IIIrd, Rasputin, Stalin, Warren Harding, Herbert Hoover,
    Hitler, the 13th Dalai Lama's Regent, Vice President Agnew,
Ronald Reagan delayed hostage release till the Elephant party's Inau-
    guration Day
George Bush peddled coke for the contras in streetcorner banks down-
    town Panama City!
Scandals in Buddhafields? big mistakes in Hemispheres, on moons,
    Black Holes everywhere!
Anyway, the national debt'll approach 4 trillion any day say the homeless
    on Tompkins Square.

                                                        July 12, 1990

Poem in the Form of a Snake
That Bites Its Tail

       Oleta (Snake) River!
       Heron, Manatee, Osprey
Canopy of white red &
       black Mangroves
fighting for survival against
       exotics introduced
              by Europeans
Swamp fern covers the ground
       by this Primordial Tidal
                     Zone,
Brown detritus under the
              clear water
   feeds animals and trees in
              high and low tides
       pulled by the moon,
cycles of lunar
       reproduction following
              waters flowing
   in and out the
       Intracoastal Waterway—
Barracuda come
   in with the tides
              Heron we'll see
Brazilian pepper
       & Malalluca
              from Australia
brought in by Mr. Gifford
       first Doctor
       of Tropical Agriculture

Malalluca
　　to dry out the swamps
　　　　　　　& make truck farms
　　　　　　to feed the Northeast 1900—
　　　　　　　　Dade County
　　　　　　　tomatoes & cabbage today—

Then real estate won
　　　out, that saved the
　　　　　　　swamp
　　　　　　　water
　　　　　　　supply
This forest by Oleta River a tiny
　　　area untouched
　　　　　　　half a million
　　　　　　　　years—
　　Interconnected to the
　　　coral reefs
　　(as nutrient-rich protective
　　soup for fish
　　　　　　　　spawning)
　　　　　　with a rubber tire, mucus—
　　　　　　　soaked in the ooze
　　Red mangrove
　　　　　seedlings growing on inland skirts
　　　　　　at water edge
　　　roots like spindly
　　　　　　buttresses

　　First Indians Tequesta
　　　　　for 10–25,000 years—
　　　　　　　left behind shell
　　　　　　　　　　tools
　　　　　to make dugouts

Mikasuki and Seminole
were Creek Indians forced down
          from North Carolina
    by Sen. Jesse Helms
    then driven inland from
    Northern Florida
                by the Army
          —Indian middens
    attest 100
years' occupation

The Seminole
more warlike than
    the innocent
              Tequestas

Quiet in a canoe
    Train whistle West
    & airplane above
          cottony clouds
              in blue afternoon

Seminole and Mikasuki
    accepted
    runaway slaves
          got in trouble with
          the whites—
Abraham the Runaway showed Chief Osceola
          guerrilla gunpowder—
                Defied the U.S. Army—
Govt. fought 2 wars
          against them—
    first 1820 Andrew Jackson
          fought in Florida
    pushed Indians south

Second Seminole War
     transported 2,000
         Indians to Oklahoma
         around 1840, the Trail of Tears
—200 managed to
escape into swamp
where white man had
     yet no use for
         the land
Indians
     from before Columbus
             & runaway slaves
        Strange & perpetual
        alliance

Otherwise we're all exotics
     like the Brazilian pepper
     and Australian pine

A brown heron
     flaps along the
         green surface
    to stand sentinel
        beak pointed out
  on a green lawn
        past the big rubber
           tree—
    tall stalky legs
     rising halfway
heavy slow
     on long wings
     the height of the big
     ficus' leafy
        umbrella whose
      thready prop roots hang
    over the concrete
    bank down to the brackish
        water surface

Kids' & crows' voices
     (crows here for the
          season)

Water filled the
     coral, ojus,

          limestone
     a product trucked
          out since
               the railroad came down,
               turn of the century

Trains a mile long
          from rockpits now
     at the edge of
               the Everglades

Mikasuki Indians now hold
          cultural events
          Steve & Billy Tiger
                    painter & musician

Seminoles more commercially
          oriented, invented Bingo on
               the reservation,
          On land they control
          untax'd cigarettes

A local issue
               ecological!
We depend on Everglades
     for water to
               sustain our days—

Most of the body is
made up of water—
3–4 days without water
we die—
Everglades filters the
    water Dade Broward
        & Palm Beach County
            drink—
            (Tricounty fresh
                water—)

But Brazilian pepper seeds
        explode
        and cause mumbo-jumbo
        growth at
                    waterside.

    Exotic Malalluca trees—?
        The developers like it
                (it's cheap)
        but they drink up water & their
        flowers cause allergies
            to Rochelle—

    Red mangrove
                    stains the water
            properly its own color

Are hyperindustrial White folks
        exotics to the planet now?

Here comes a duck
that flies, sings & runs
        but doesn't do any
                of them well

El pato vuela, canta
        y corre, pero
            ninguno de las tres
                los hace bien.

Big yellow hibiscus faces
        with red noses—
Venetian sailors
        brought
            venereal disease
                to New World
now Millennial events
                speed up?

Get off fossil fuels
        for transport
Get off oil addiction
Plastics could be
        recyclable

Zero Growth regenerative
        recycling as for
                thousands of years
                with the Tequesta
Get off this disposable
        binge—

& water! dont mess
        up the Oleta River Dont
        play with the big Snake

Can live without air
        8 minutes
Can live without water
                2–4 days
can live without food
        40–50 days—

Survive, clean up our
            air
Clean up water
Grow enuf food to
        keep everybody
            alive

Instructors: any
            indigenous populations

Indians, Africans,
        Tibetans, Bedouins
            Laplanders—
Chernobyl began
        the question—
How much can the
        Government lie?

(*Miami Herald* pervasive
        and controlling—)

Locally the Seminoles may
        be the Gurus.

With Steven Bornstein
November 16, 1990

Mistaken Introductions

or this marvelous hi Lama followed
       in here by screaming madwoman
       charging she was betrayed 10 years ago
       on one of the moons of Saturn
or, I want to introduce you to this
       universe which unfortunately
       doesn't quite exist.
We set up luncheon at Rizzoli
       for the Tibetan photog who
       hadnt prepared his
       slides, it was a disaster—
May I introduce you to your
       prospective son-in-law—
       unfortunately today he's drunk
           unshaven but a good
       businessman tomorrow
It's a magnificent hotel
       just this week there's no
       water to flush the toilet
       above the 10th floor
       where you're staying and
we had a fire in the elevator

January 7, 1991

C.I.A. DOPE CALYPSO

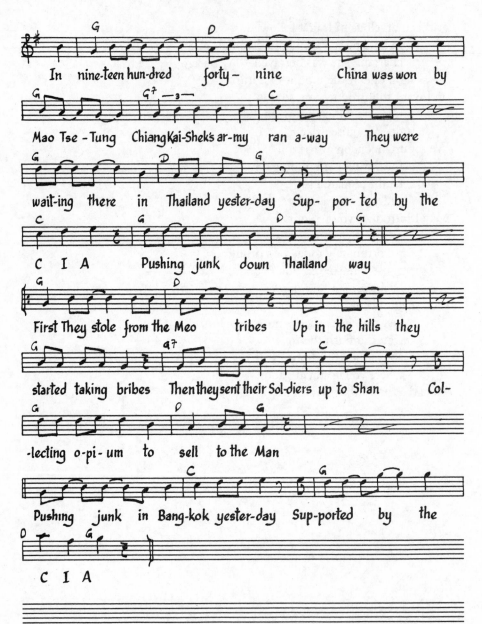

CIA Dope Calypso

In nineteen hundred forty-nine
China was won by Mao Tse-tung
Chiang Kai-shek's army ran away
They were waiting there in Thailand yesterday

Supported by the CIA
Pushing junk down Thailand way

First they stole from the Meo tribes
Up in the hills they started taking bribes
Then they sent their soldiers up to Shan
Collecting opium to sell to The Man

Pushing junk in Bangkok yesterday
Supported by the CIA

Brought their jam on mule trains down
To Chiang Rai that's a railroad town
Sold it next to police chief brain
He took it to town on the choochoo train

Trafficking dope to Bangkok all day
Supported by the CIA

The policeman's name was Mr. Phao
He peddled dope grand scale and how
Chief of border customs paid
By Central Intelligence's U.S. A.I.D.

The whole operation, Newspapers say
Supported by the CIA

He got so sloppy & peddled so loose
He busted himself & cooked his own goose
Took the reward for an opium load
Seizing his own haul which same he resold

Big-time pusher a decade turned grey
Working for the CIA

Touby Lyfong he worked for the French
A big fat man liked to dine & wench
Prince of the Meos he grew black mud
Till opium flowed through the land like a flood

Communists came and chased the French away
So Touby took a job with the CIA

The whole operation fell into chaos
Till U.S. Intelligence came into Laos
I'll tell you no lie I'm a true American
Our big pusher there was Phoumi Nosovan

All them princes in a power play
But Phoumi was the man for the CIA

And his best friend General Vang Pao
Ran our Meo army like a sacred cow
Helicopter smugglers filled Long Cheng's bars
In Xieng Quang province on the Plain of Jars

It started in secret they were fighting yesterday
Clandestine secret army of the CIA

All through the Sixties the Dope flew free
Thru Tan Son Nhut Saigon to Marshal Ky
Air America followed through
Transporting confiture for President Thieu

All these Dealers were decades and yesterday
The Indochinese mob of the U.S. CIA

Operation Haylift offisir Wm. Colby
Saw Marshal Ky fly opium Mr. Mustard told me
Indochina desk he was Chief of Dirty Tricks
"Hitchhiking" with dope pushers was how he got his fix

Subsidizing traffickers to drive the Reds away
Till Colby was the head of the CIA

January 1972

II
N.S.A. Dope Calypso

Now Richard Secord and Oliver North
Hated Sandinistas whatever they were worth
They peddled for the Contras to ease their pain
They couldn't sell Congress so Contras sold cocaine

They discovered Noriega only yesterday
Nancy Reagan & the CIA

Now coke and grass were exchanged for guns
On a border airfield that John Hull runs
Or used to run till his Costa Rican bust
As a CIA spy trading Contra coke dust

They discovered Noriega only yesterday
Nancy Reagan & the CIA

Ramón Milian Rodríguez of Medellín Cartel
Laundered their dollars & he did it very well
Hundreds of millions through U.S. banks
Till he got busted and sang in the tank

It was buried in the papers only yesterday
When Bush was Drug Czar U.S.A.

Milian told Congress $3,000,000 coke bucks
Went to Felix Rodríguez, CIA muck-a-muck
To give to the Contras only Hush Hush Hush
Except for Donald Gregg & his boss George Bush

Buried in the papers only yesterday
With Bush Vice President U.S.A.

Rodríguez met Bush in his office many times
They didn't talk business, they drank lemon & limes
Or maybe they drank coffee or they smoked a cigarette
But cocaine traffic they remembered to forget

It was buried in the papers only yesterday
And Bush got in the White House of the U.S.A.

Now when Bush was director of the C.I.A.
Panama traffic in coke was gay
You never used to hear George Bush holler
When Noriega laundered lots of cocaine dollar

Bush paid Noriega, used to work together
They sat on a couch & talked about the weather

Then Noriega doublecrossed his Company pal
With a treaty taking back our Panama Canal
So when he got into the big White House
Bush said Noriega was a cocaine louse

The Cold War ended, East Europe found hope
The U.S. got hooked in a war on dope

Glasnost came, East Europe got free
So Bush sent his army to Panama City
Bush's guns in Panama did their worst
Like coke fiends fighting on St. Marks & First

Does Noriega know Bush's Company crimes?
In 2000 A.D. read the New York Times.

January–February 1990

III
Just Say Yes Calypso

When Schwarzkopf's Father busted Iran's Mossadegh
They put in the Shah and his police the Savak
They sucked up his oil, but got Ayatollah's dreck
So Thirty years later we hadda arm Iraq

Though he used poison gas, Saddam was still our man
But to aid the Contras, hadda also arm Iran

Mesopotamia was doing just fine
Till the Ottoman Empire blew up on a mine
They had apple orchards in Eden and Ur
Till the Snake advised George Bush "This land is yours"

The Garden foul'd up, brimstone came down
In the good old days we had plenty ozone

The British & Americans & Frenchmen all
Took concessions in the Garden So the Garden took a fall
Got addicted to Emirs and their fossil fuels
Police state Sheiks & Intelligence ghouls

The Sphinx lost his nose, acid ate the Parthenon
Pretty soon the Persian Gulf is dead and gone

The Saudi desert bloomed with oil pipe lines
To push the auto industry It's yours & it's mine
L.A. and Osaka got a habit on gas
In a bullet-proof Caddie you can really move your ass

L.A. & Osaka got a habit on gas
In a bullet-proof Caddie you can really move your ass

From a Mickey-Mouse war on cocaine & crack
We dropped a million bombs on the kids in Iraq
How many we killed nobody wants to tell
It'd give a lousy picture of a war they gotta sell

When they wave a yellow ribbon & an oily flag
Just say yes or they'll call you a fag

April 25, 1991

Hum Bom!

I
Whom bomb?
We bomb'd them!
Whom bomb?
We bomb'd them!
Whom bomb?
We bomb'd them!
Whom bomb?
We bomb'd them!

Whom bomb?
We bomb you!
Whom bomb?
We bomb you!
Whom bomb?
You bomb you!
Whom bomb?
You bomb you!

What do we do?
Who do we bomb?
What do we do?
Who do we bomb?
What do we do?
Who do we bomb?
What do we do!
Who do we bomb?

What do we do?
You bomb! You bomb them!
What do we do?
You bomb! You bomb them!
What do we do?
We bomb! We bomb you!
What do we do?
You bomb! You bomb you!

Whom bomb?
We bomb you!
Whom bomb?
We bomb you!
Whom bomb?
You bomb you!
Whom bomb?
You bomb you!

May 1971

II

For Don Cherry

Whydja bomb?
We didn't wanna bomb!
Whydja bomb?
We didn't wanna bomb!
Whydja bomb?
You didn't wanna bomb!
Whydja bomb?
You didn't wanna bomb!

Who said bomb?
Who said we hadda bomb?
Who said bomb?
Who said we hadda bomb?
Who said bomb?
Who said you hadda bomb?
Who said bomb?
Who said you hadda bomb?

Who wantsa bomb?
We don't wanna bomb!
Who wantsa bomb?
We don't wanna bomb!
Who wantsa bomb?
We don't wanna bomb!
We don't wanna
      we don't wanna
         we don't wanna bomb!

Who wanteda bomb?
Somebody musta wanteda bomb!
Who wanteda bomb?
Somebody musta wanteda bomb!
Who wanteda bomb?
Somebody musta wanteda bomb!
Who wanteda bomb?
Somebody musta wanteda bomb!

They wanteda bomb!
They neededa bomb!
They wanteda bomb!
They neededa bomb!
They wanteda bomb!
They neededa bomb!
They wanteda bomb!
They neededa bomb!

They thought they hadda bomb!
They thought they hadda bomb!
They thought they hadda bomb!
They thought they hadda bomb!

Saddam said he hadda bomb!
Bush said he better bomb!
Saddam said he hadda bomb!
Bush said he better bomb!
Saddam said he hadda bomb!
Bush said he better bomb!
Saddam said he hadda bomb!
Bush said he better bomb!

Whatdid he say he better bomb for?
Whatdid he say he better bomb for?
Whatdid he say he better bomb for?
Whatdid he say he better bomb for?

Hadda get ridda Saddam with a bomb!
Hadda get ridda Saddam with a bomb!
Hadda get ridda Saddam with a bomb!
Hadda get ridda Saddam with a bomb!

Saddam's still there building a bomb!
Saddam's still there building a bomb!
Saddam's still there building a bomb!
Saddam's still there building a bomb!

III
Armageddon did the job
Gog & Magog Gog & Magog
Armageddon did the job
Gog & Magog Gog & Magog

Gog & Magog Gog & Magog
Armageddon does the job
Gog & Magog Gog & Magog
Armageddon does the job

Armageddon for the mob
Gog & Magog Gog & Magog
Armageddon for the mob
Gog & Magog Gog & Magog

Gog & Magog Gog & Magog
Gog Magog Gog Magog
Gog & Magog Gog & Magog
Gog Magog Gog Magog

Gog Magog Gog Magog
Gog Magog Gog Magog
Gog Magog Gog Magog
Gog Magog Gog Magog

Ginsberg says Gog & Magog
Armageddon did the job.

February–June 1991

Supplication for the Rebirth of the Vidyadhara Chögyam Trungpa, Rinpoche

Dear Lord Guru who pervades the space of my mind
permeates the universe of my consciousness,
still empties my balding head and's stabilized my wand'ring thought
to average equanimity in Manhattan & Boulder

Return return reborn in spirit & knowledge in human body
my own or others as continual Teacher of chaotic peace,
Return according to your vow to pacify magnetize enrich destroy
grasping angry stupidity in me my family friends & Sangha

Return in body speech & mind to enlighten my labors
& the labors of your meditators, thousands from L.A. to Halifax
to relieve sufferings of our brothers, lovers
family, friends, fellow citizens, nations and planet.

Remember your vow to be with us on our deathbeds
in living worlds where we dwell in your tender perspective
breathe with your conscious breath, catch ourselves thinking
& dissolve bomb dream, fear of our own skin & yelling argument
                              in the sky of your mind

Bend your efforts to regroup our community within your thought-body
& mind-space, the effects of your non-thought,
Turbulent ease of your spontaneous word & picture
nonmeditative compassion your original mind

These slogans were writ on the second day of June 1991
a sleepless night my brother's 70th birthday on Long Island
my own sixty-fifth year in the human realm visiting his house
by the Vajra Poet Allen Ginsberg supplicating protection of his
                              Vajra Guru Chögyam Trungpa
                              June 2, 1991, 2:05 A.M.

After the Big Parade

Millions of people cheering and waving flags for joy in Manhattan
Yesterday've returned to their jobs and arthritis now Tuesday—
What made them want so much passion at last, such mutual delight—
Will they ever regain these hours of confetti'd ecstasy again?
Have they forgotten the Corridors of Death that gave such victory?
Will another hundred thousand desert deaths across the world be
                            cause for the next rejoicing?

June 11, 1991, 2:30 P.M.

Big Eats

Big deal bargains TV meat stock market news paper headlines love life
      Metropolis
Float thru air like thought forms float thru the skull, check the headlines
      catch the boyish ass that walks
Before you fall in bed blood sugar high blood pressure lower, lower,
      your lips grow cold.
Sooner or later let go what you loved hated or shrugged off, you walk in
      the park
You look at the sky, sit on a pillow, count up the stars in your head, get up
      and eat.

August 20, 1991

Not Dead Yet

Huffing puffing upstairs downstairs telephone
      office mail checks secretary revolt—
The Soviet Legislative Communist bloc
      inspired Gorbachev's wife and Yeltsin
to shut up in terror or stand on a tank
      in front of White House denouncing Putschists—
September breezes sway branches & leaves in
      a calm schoolyard under humid grey sky,
Drink your decaf Ginsberg old communist New
      York Times addict, be glad you're not Trotsky.

September 16, 1991

Yiddishe Kopf

I'm Jewish because love my family matzoh ball soup.

I'm Jewish because my fathers mothers uncles grandmothers said "Jew-
ish," all the way back to Vitebsk & Kaminetz-Podolska via Lvov.

Jewish because reading Dostoyevsky at 13 I write poems at restaurant
tables Lower East Side, perfect delicatessen intellectual.

Jewish because violent Zionists make my blood boil, Progressive indig-
nation.

Jewish because Buddhist, my anger's transparent hot air, I shrug my
shoulders.

Jewish because monotheist Jews Catholics Moslems're intolerable
intolerant—

Blake sd. "6000 years of sleep" since antique Nobodaddy Adonai's mind
trap—Oy! such Meshuggeneh absolutes—

Senior Citizen Jewish paid my dues got half-fare card buses subways,
discount movies—

Can't imagine how these young people make a life, make a living.

How can they stand it, going out in the world with only $10 and a
hydrogen bomb?

October 1991

John

I
No one liked my hair
Mother pulled it toward the movies
Father hit the top of my head
Street gangs set it afire
My dry hair, my
short hair, black hair, drab hair
my stupid hair—frizzled!
Till I met John,
John loved my hair
Twined his fingers in my delicate curly locks
Told me let it grow
John buried his face in my hair
kissed my hair
Murmured endearments "Oh oh oh" to the top of my skull
Patted me on the head
Stroked me from crown to neck nape—
Sat across from me on the subway and gazed at me lovingly—

II
They were whispering, elbows leaned on the wide marble balustrade
balcony lobby of the Majestic Theater—
talking Jerusalem, Moscow, Ballet, Quasars, Interest rates—
John came down from his seat, stopped at the top stair—
sat down, hands on his ears in despair—"I've stymied my feet!"
"What" they asked, "you've stymied your feet? Whazzat mean?"
John nodded his head, eyes closed, hands against his head as before,
"I've stymied my feet," he repeated dolefully.

III
John had AIDS.
First, he began talking to himself.
The psychiatrist said:
"If you're going to talk to yourself,
    do it in the form of poetry."

November 7, 1991, 8:30 A.M.

A Thief Stole This Poem

These days steal everything
People steal your wallet, your watch
Break into your car steal your radio suitcase
Break in your house, your Sony Hi 8 your CD VCR Olympus XA
People steal your life, catch you on the street & steal your head off
Steal your sneakers in the toilet
Steal your love, mug your boyfriend rape your grandmother on the
      subway
Junkies steal your heart for medicine, they steal your credibility gap over
      the radio
Cokeheads & blackmen steal your comfort, peace of mind walking
      Avenue A your laundry package
steal your spirit, you gotta worry
Puerto Ricans steal white skin from your face
Wasps steal your planet for junk bonds, Jews steal your Nobodaddy and
      leave their dirty God in your bed
Arabs steal your pecker & you steal their oil
Everybody's stealing from everyone else, time sex wristwatch money
Steal your sleep 6 A.M. Garbage Trucks boomboxes sirens loud argu-
      ments hydrogen bombs
steal your universe.

December 19, 1991, 8:15 A.M.

Lunchtime

Birds chirp in the brick backyard Radio
piano chopping gentle chords next door
A rush of tires & car exhaust on 14th Street
Delighted to be alive this cloudy Thursday
February window open at the kitchen table,
Senior Citizen ready for next week's angiogram.

February 20, 1992, 1:15 P.M.

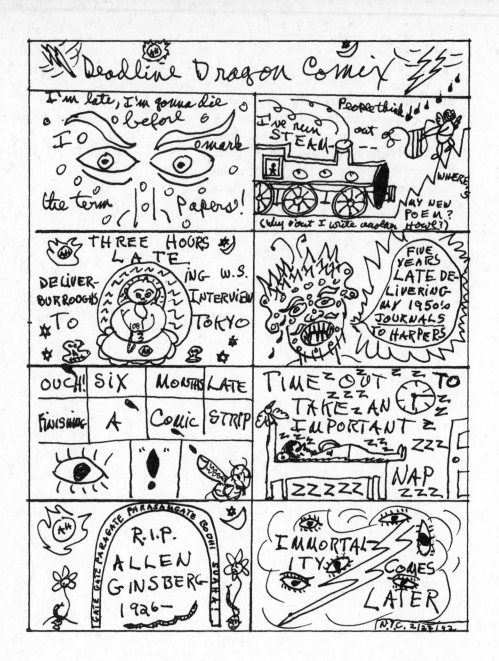

After Lalon

I
It's true I got caught in
                    the world
When I was young Blake
                    tipped me off
Other teachers followed:
Better prepare for Death
Don't get entangled with
                    possessions
That was when I was young,
           I was warned
Now I'm a Senior Citizen
and stuck with a million
                    books
a million thoughts a million
                    dollars a million
                                loves
How'll I ever leave my body?
Allen Ginsberg says, I'm
                    really up shits creek

II
I sat at the foot of a
                    Lover
     and he told me everything
Fuck off, 23 skidoo,
           watch your ass,
           watch your step
exercise, meditate, think
           of your temper—

Now I'm an old man and
       I won't live another
20 years maybe not another
       20 weeks,
maybe the next second I'll
       be carried off to
         rebirth
   the worm farm, maybe it's
       already happened—
How should I know, says
       Allen Ginsberg
Maybe I've been dreaming
       all along—

III
It's 2 A.M. and I got to
       get up early
and taxi 20 miles to satisfy
       my ambition—
How'd I get into this fix,
this workaholic show-
       biz meditation market?
If I had a soul I sold it
       for pretty words
If I had a body I used
       it up spurting my essence
If I had a mind it got
       covered with Love—
If I had a spirit I forgot
       when I was breathing
If I had speech it was
       all a boast
If I had desire it went
       out my anus

If I had ambitions to
        be liberated
how'd I get into this
           wrinkled person?
With pretty words, Love essences,
           breathing boasts, anal
           longings, famous crimes?
What a mess I am, Allen Ginsberg.

IV
Sleepless I stay up &
          think about my Death
—certainly it's nearer
        than when I was ten
           years old
and wondered how big the
        universe was—
If I dont get some rest I'll die faster
If I sleep I'll lose my
        chance for salvation—
asleep or awake, Allen
    Ginsberg's in bed
        in the middle of the night.

V

4 A.M.

Then they came for me,
       I hid in the toilet stall
They broke down the toilet door
       It fell in on an innocent boy
Ach the wooden door fell
       in on an innocent kid!
I stood on the bowl & listened,
       I hid my shadow,
they shackled the other and
       dragged him away
in my place— How long can
       I get away with this?
Pretty soon they'll discover
       I'm not there
They'll come for me again, where
       can I hide my body?
Am I myself or some one else
       or nobody at all?
Then what's this heavy flesh this
       weak heart leaky kidney?
Who's been doing time
       for 65 years
in this corpse? Who else went
       into ecstasy besides me?
Now it's all over soon,
       what good was all that come?
Will it come true? Will
       it really come true?

VI

I had my chance and lost it,
many chances & didn't
    take them seriously enuf.
Oh yes I was impressed, almost
    went mad with fear
I'd lose the immortal chance,
    One lost it.
Allen Ginsberg warns you
    dont follow my path
    to extinction.

March 31, 1992

Get It?

Get beat up on TV squirming on the ground for driving irregular
Get bombed in Philadelphia by helicopters with your little babies
Get kicked in the street by Newark police and charged w/riot
Get assassinated by a jerk while FBI sleeps with itself
Get shot by a stringer for the CIA & blame it on Fair Play for Cuba
      Committee
Get bumped off by an errandboy for Cuban drug kingpins, friend of the
      Feds & Dallas cops
Get caught paying off Contras with coke money while Acting U.S. Drug
      War Czar
Get busted for overcharging Iranians on secret warplane sales
Get convicted of lying to Congress about off-the-shelf dirty wars in
      Central America
Get 12 billion dollars for a drug bureaucracy and double the number of
      addicts
Get a million people in prison in the land of the free
Get the electric chair & gas chamber for unpopular crimes
Organize *Citizens for Decency Through Law* rob your own phony bank
      several billion dollars get sent to jail

May 1992
New York

Angelic Black Holes

By Andrey Voznesensky

Soul to crotch the streets commit hara-kiri,
Burnt-out stores chessboard moonlit households,
The City of Angels stares into black holes—
See down through Earth to scorched Nagorno-Karabakh.
How long is the tunnel of pain?
Does God need Welfare?

Even so, remembering the sheen on Peredelkino's black gooseberries,
Rodney King's name sounds Russian, *rodnik* for ground-spring.
As for me who crapped up my own homeland
How lay the blame on anybody else?
Rain & ashes seal my lips.
The two superpowers left the Little Man supersufferings.
Us—blown to hell. You—immolate yourselves in flame?

Any light at the end of the tunnel of pain?

Translated by Allen Ginsberg and Nina Bouis
May 17, 1992
Los Angeles

Research

Research has shown that black people have inferiority complexes re-
    garding white folks
Research has shown that Jews are exclusively concerned with financial
    lasciviousness
Research has shown Socialism to be a universal failure wherever prac-
    ticed by secret police
Research has shown that Earth was created 4004 B.C., a Divine
    Bang
Research has shown that sparrows, bees, lizards, chickens, pigs & cows
    exhibit signs of homosexual behavior when in prison
Research has shown Southern Baptist Inerrancy Confession the most
    virulent form of Christian Truth
Research has shown that 90% of people going to Dentists have bad
    teeth
brush your teeth violently 3 times a day after meals wear away the
    roots
Research has shown that Hollywood makes the best films ever, the
    sexually degenerate
that the U.N. is Good □ Bad □ Indifferent □ for American inter-
    ests Check One
Research has shown that Christian Reconstructionist homosexuality is
    Sin, Lesbianism crime against nature, AIDS a plague sent to
    punish gay Angelmakers
bisexuality disapproved by 51% Americans
Research has shown that teen headshakers watching TV get more IQ
    tests than natives of Amazon & Ucayali rivers who have no
    antennae
Research has shown whales & porpoises to subscribe to a Higher Intel-
    ligence
Research has shown that Elitist Individualism Spiritual Corruption &
    Degenerate Art caused Dictatorships in Soviet Union China
    and Germany

that possession of pornography by American Family Institute has re-
    sulted in 35% increase in sex crimes among institute librarians
viewing murderous behavior on TV sitcoms resulted in 100% increased
    violent language behavior by intercontinental Heads of State
To conclude research has shown that the material universe does not
    exist

May 20, 1992

PUT DOWN YOUR CIGARETTE RAG

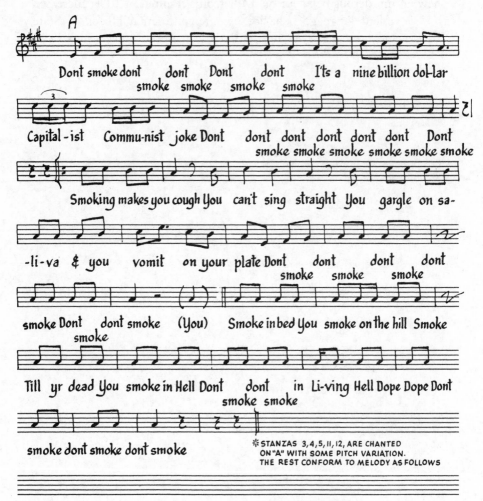

STANZAS 3,4,5,11,12, ARE CHANTED
ON "A" WITH SOME PITCH VARIATION.
THE REST CONFORM TO MELODY AS FOLLOWS

FIRST DOUBLE BAR

Put Down Your Cigarette Rag (Dont Smoke)

Dont smoke dont smoke dont smoke
Dont smoke
It's a nine billion dollar
Capitalist Communist joke
    Dont smoke dont smoke dont smoke dont smoke
            Dont smoke

Smoking makes you cough,
You cant sing straight
You gargle on saliva
& vomit on your plate
    Dont smoke dont smoke dont smoke dont smoke,
        Dont smoke smoke smoke smoke

You smoke in bed
You smoke on the hill
Smoke till yr dead
You smoke in Hell
    Dont smoke dont smoke in living Hell Dope Dope
        Dont smoke dont smoke dont smoke

You puff your fag
You suck your butt
You choke & gag
Teeth full of crud
    Smoke smoke smoke smoke Dont dont dont
        Dont Dont Dope Dope Dope Dont Smoke Dont Dope

Pay your two bucks
        for a deathly pack
Trust your bad luck
        & smoke in the sack
    Dont Smoke Dont Smoke Nicotine Nicotine No
    No dont smoke the official Dope Smoke Dope Dope

Four Billion dollars in Green
'swat Madison Avenue gets
t' advertise nicotine
& hook you radical brats
        Dont Smoke Dont Smoke Dont Smoke
            Nope Nope Dope Dope Hoax Hoax Hoax Hoax
        Dopey Dope Dopey Dope Dope Dope dope dope

Black magic pushes dope
Sexy chicks in cars
America loses hope
& smokes and drinks in bars
        Dont smoke dont smoke dont smoke,
        dont smoke dont dont dont dont
        choke choke choke choke kaf kaf
        Kaf Kaf Choke Choke
        Choke Choke Dope Dope

Communism's flopped
Let's help the Soviet millions
Sell 'em our Coffin-Nails
& make a couple billions
        Big Bucks Big Bucks bucks bucks
            bucks bucks smoke smoke smoke smoke
                smoke bucks smoke bucks Dope bucks big
                Dope Bucks Dig Big Dope Bucks Big Dope
                Bucks dont smoke big dope bucks
                    Dig big Pig dope bucks

Nine billion bucks a year
a Southern Industry
Buys Senator Jesse Fear who pushes Tobacco subsidy
In the Senate Foreign Relations Committee
    Dope smokes dope smokes dont smoke dont smoke
        Cloak cloak cloak room cloak & dagger
        smoke room cloak room dope cloak
        cloak room dope cloak room dope dont smoke

Nine billion bucks for dope
approved by Time & Life
America loses hope
The President smokes Tobacco votes
    Dont Smoke dont smoke dont smoke dont smoke
        Dont smoke nope nope nope nope

20 thousand die of coke
    Illegal speed each year
400 thousand cigarette deaths
    That's the drug to fear
        Dont smoke Dont smoke Dont smoke

Get Hooked on Cigarettes
Go Fight the War on Drugs
Smoke any other Weed
Get bust by Government Thugs
    Dont smoke dont smoke the official dope

If you will get in bed
& give your girlfriend head
then you wont want a fag
Nor evermore a drag
    Dont Smoke dont smoke Hope Hope Hope Hope
        O Please Dont Smoke Dont Smoke
        O Please O Please O Please
        I'm calling on my knees

Twenty-four hours in bed
& give your boyfriend head
Put something in your mouth
Like skin not cigarette filth
    Suck tit suck tit suck cock suck cock
        suck clit suck prick suck it
        but dont smoke nicotine dont smoke
        dont smoke nicotine nicotine it's
        too obscene dont smoke dont smoke
        nicotine suck cock suck prick suck tit
        suck clit suck it But don't smoke shit nope
        nope nope nope Dope Dope Dope Dope
          the official dope Dont Smoke

Make believe yer sick
Stay in bed and lick
yr cigarette habit greed
One day's all you need
    In deed in deed in deed in deed smoke weed
        smoke weed Put something green
        in between but don't smoke smoke dont smoke
        hope hope hope hope Nicotine dont
        smoke the official dope
        Dope Dope Dope Dope Don't Smoke

1971; June 21, 1992

VIOLENT COLLABORATIONS

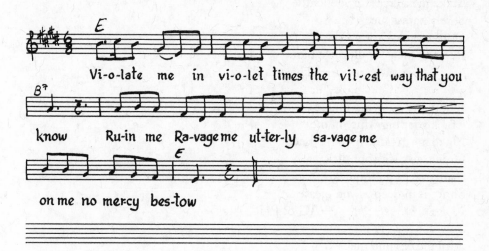

Vi-o-late me in vi-o-let times the vil-est way that you

know Ru-in me Ra-vage me ut-ter-ly sa-vage me

on me no mercy bes-tow

Violent Collaborations

> Violate me
> in violet times
> the vilest way that you know
> Ruin me
> Ravage me
> utterly savage me
> on me no mercy bestow
> —OLD SONG, 1944

Trespass against me
& penetrate deeply
Spare me not even your rape
Tie me up quickly
make me smile sickly
Seal up my mouth with scotch tape
—AG

Piss on me Crap on me
Wipe your fat ass on me
Make me a creature you loathe
Sorely harass me
Dont even ask me
But deal me your ultimate blow
              —PH

Ignore me & stomp on me
Crack your big whip on me
Make me get down on my knees
Order me suck your dick
spank me & do it quick
Shove it in deep as you please
              —AG & PH

Stun me & shun me
slave me & shave me
Give me your loathsome disease
Fuck me & fist me
in your army enlist me
Poop on me when you're at ease
              —AG & PH

Degrade & debase me
in public deface me
come on my beard in the mud
Double me over
in summertime clover
then hose me down w/your stud
              —AG & PH

With Peter Hale
June 1992

Calm Panic Campaign Promise

End of Millennium
                    Earth's decay—
Fire Air Water tainted
              We're the Great Beast—
                         Dark bed thoughts
Can't do anything to stop it—
Denial in Government, in Newspapers of Record—
Like watching gum disease & not brushing teeth
Getting heart failure, no rest much stress
Putting salt on your greasy pork
Putting sugar in coffee you're diabetic
              Dysesthesia on foot soles
Poor circulation smoke more cigarettes
Kick your son under the table have another beer
Need President who'll reverse the denial—
                    The Calm Panic Party
              to restore nature's balance.

July 9, 1992, 12:55 A.M.

Now and Forever

I'll settle for Immortality—
Not thru the body
    Not thru the eyes
        Star-spangled high mountains
            waning moon over Aspen peaks
But thru words, thru the breath
      of long sentences
loves I have, heart beating
      still,
inspiration continuous, exhalation of
      cadenced affection
These immortal survive America,
         survive the fall of States
      Departure of my body,
         mouth dumb dust
This verse broadcasts desire,
        accomplishment of Desire
Now and forever boys can read
        girls dream, old men cry
Old women sigh
        youth still come.

July 19, 1992
Aspen

Who Eats Who?

A crow sits on the prayerflagpole,
her mate blackwinged walks the wet green grass, worms?
Yesterday seagulls skimmed the choppy waves,
    feet touching foamed breakers
           looking for salmon? halibut? sole?
Bacteria eat parameciums or vice versa,
viruses enter cells, white cell count low—
Tooth & claw on TV, lions strike down antelope—
Whales sift transparent krill thru bearded teeth.
Every cannibal niche fulfilled, Amazon
    headhunters eat testicles—
         Enemy's powers & energy become mine!

August 13, 1992
Gampo Abbey, Nova Scotia

The Charnel Ground

... rugged and raw situations, and having accepted them as part of your home ground, then some spark of sympathy or compassion could take place. You are not in a hurry to leave such a place immediately. You would like to face the facts, realities of that particular world. . . .

FROM A COMMENTARY ON *THE SADHANA OF MAHAMUDRA*, CHÖGYAM TRUNGPA, RINPOCHE

Upstairs Jenny crashed her car & became a living corpse, Jake sold grass,
    the white-bearded potbelly leprechaun silent climbed their
    staircase
Ex-janitor John from Poland averted his eyes, cheeks flushed with
    vodka, wine who knew what
as he left his groundfloor flat, refusing to speak to the inhabitant of
    Apt. 24
who'd put his boyfriend in Bellevue, calling police, while the artistic
    Buddhist composer
on sixth floor lay spaced out feet swollen with water, dying slowly of
    AIDS over a year—
The Chinese teacher cleaned & cooked in Apt. 23 for the homosexual
    poet who pined for his gymnast
thighs & buttocks— Downstairs th' old hippie flower girl fell drunk
    over the banister, smashed her jaw—
her son despite moderate fame cheated of rocknroll money, twenty
    thousand people in stadiums
cheering his tattooed skinhead murderous Hare Krishna vegetarian
    drum lyrics—
Mary born in the building rested on her cane, heavy-legged with heart
    failure on the second landing, no more able
to vacation in Caracas & Dublin— The Russian landlady's husband
    from concentration camp disappeared again—nobody men-
    tioned he'd died—
tenants took over her building for hot water, she couldn't add rent & pay
    taxes, wore a long coat hot days

alone & thin on the street carrying groceries to her crooked apartment
    silent—
One poet highschool teacher fell dead mysterious heart dysrhythmia,
    konked over
in his mother's Brooklyn apartment, his first baby girl a year old, wife
    stoical a few days—
their growling noisy little dog had to go, the baby cried—
Meanwhile the upstairs apartment meth head shot cocaine & yowled up
    and down
East 12th Street, kicked out of Christine's Eatery till police cornered
    him, 'top a hot iron steamhole
near Stuyvesant Town Avenue A telephone booth calling his deaf
    mother—sirens speed the way to Bellevue—
past whispering grass crack salesman jittering in circles on East 10th
    Street's
southwest corner where art yuppies come out of the overpriced Japanese
    Sushi Bar—& they poured salt into potato soup heart failure
    vats at KK's Polish restaurant
—Garbage piled up, nonbiodegradable plastic bags emptied by diabetic
    sidewalk homeless
looking for returnable bottles recycled dolls radios half-eaten
    hamburgers—thrown-away Danish—
On 13th Street the notary public sat in his dingy storefront, driver's
    lessons & tax returns prepared on old metal desks—
Sunnysides crisped in butter, fries & sugary donuts passed over the
    luncheonette counter next door—
The Hispanic lady yelled at the rude African-American behind the Post
    Office window
"I waited all week my welfare check you sent me notice I was here
    yesterday
I want to see the supervisor bitch dont insult me refusing to look in—"
Closed eyes of Puerto Rican wino lips cracked skin red stretched out
on the pavement, naphtha backdoor open for the Korean family dry
    cleaners at the 14th Street corner—
Con Ed workmen drilled all year to bust electric pipes 6 feet deep in
    brown dirt

so cars bottlenecked wait minutes to pass the M14 bus stopped mid-
    road, heavy dressed senior citizens step down in red rubble
with Reduced Fare Program cards got from grey city Aging Department
    offices downtown up the second flight by elevators don't
    work—
News comes on the radio, they bomb Baghdad and the Garden of Eden
    again?
A million starve in Sudan, mountains of eats stacked on docks, local
    gangs & U.N.'s trembling bureaucrat officers sweat near the
    equator arguing over
wheat piles shoved by bulldozers—Swedish doctors ran out of
    medicine— The Pakistan taxi driver
says Salman Rushdie must die, insulting the Prophet in fictions—
"No that wasn't my opinion, just a character talking like in a poem no
    judgment"—
"Not till the sun rejects you do I," so give you a quarter by the Catholic
    church 14th St. you stand half drunk
waving a plastic glass, flush-faced, live with your mother a wounded
    look on your lips, eyes squinting,
receding lower jaw sometimes you dry out in Bellevue, most days
    cadging dollars for sweet wine
by the corner where Plump Blindman shifts from foot to foot showing
    his white cane, rattling coins in a white paper cup some weeks
where girding the subway entrance construction sawhorses painted
    orange
guard steps underground— And across the street the NYCE bank
    machine cubicle door sign reads
Not in Operation as taxis bump on potholes asphalt mounded at the
    crossroad when red lights change green
& I'm on my way uptown to get a CAT scan liver biopsy, visit the
    cardiologist,
account for high blood pressure, kidneystones, diabetes, misty eyes &
    dysesthesia—
feeling lack in feet soles, inside ankles, small of back, phallus head,
    anus—
Old age sickness death again come round in the wink of an eye—

High school youth the inside skin of my thighs was silken smooth tho
      nobody touched me there back then—
Across town the velvet poet takes Darvon N, Valium nightly, sleeps all
      day kicking methadone
between brick walls sixth floor in a room cluttered with collages & gold
      dot paper scraps covered
with words: "The whole point seems to be the idea of giving away the
      giver."

August 19, 1992

Everyday

The Lama sat
    in bed
with bamboo
backscratcher
his false teeth
in a big
glass of water
on the sunny
windowsill.

August 1992

Fun House Antique Store

I'd been motoring through States &
stopped at a country antique store, an
old-fashioned house, in excellent condition—
Flower'd wallpaper, polished banisters
lampshades dusted, candelabra burnished
flaming quiet by the cloak closet
under the stairs, pitcher of water & white
washbowls beside the french doors
embroidered doilies & artificial flowers
ivory & light brown on mahogany
side tables, a brass bowl for cards,
kitchen with polished stove cold ready
at Summer's end to light up with split
wood & kindling in buckets beside
the empty fireplace, tongs & screen
in neat order. The second floor as
perfectly appointed as the foyer
(set with hat & cane rack & mirror)
stairway rugs & oaken doors, down beds
a glass-front bookcase, brown shiny bureaus,
drawers crammed with old ties & bloomers,
celluloid collars, some long-sleeved underwear, silk
& paisley shirts & shawls—and the stairs
to the third-floor attic rose five steep steps
into a blank wall nicely wallpapered with roses.
      What a delicate touch, trompe l'oeil
artistry, what charming care & magical consciousness
arranged this antique shop, so practical
for display as Bed-and-Breakfast wayfarer's
stop-over & lampshade collector's twee daydream—
Yet it was a modern commercial establishment
we'd entered casually on our own road
through Maryland to see our lawyer in D.C.—

One attendant who observed us admiring his home
appointments watched us turn to go—
I wished to make a speech: "Congratulations
on your work of Ahrt, your antique care
& delicate intelligence, as if Messrs. McDermott
& McGough photographed the 1880s entire
& built it in 3-D renewed at millennium's end—"

So I orated on but the attendants conferred,
minds elsewhere, only one scion of the house
moon-faced thirtysomething sat legs spread
on the fake stairway & applauded our appreciation
& delight—& so we left to go, our party
on its way to the postmodern Capital.

August 31, 1992

News Stays News

Diana & Roger Napoleon's real estate empire
extended up to the Napoleon Castle Hotel's penthouse
stainless steel & gold doorknobs bathtubs bars & windowsills
But Roger got Alzheimer's & couldn't keep his money books straight
Diana went to jail for back taxes & cheating at cards
Lost control of her castle, lawyers ate her Empire
She got sick & spent years maintaining her body,
skin growths, liver failure, kidney disturbances, upset stomach
But the castle of flesh ceased to function
She was left inside with her soul.
What is that? Where will it go? Who am I?
asked Napoleon in bed, eyes closing for the last time on St. Helena.

September 7, 1992, 3:00 P.M.

Autumn Leaves

At 66 just learning how to take care of my body
Wake cheerful 8 A.M. & write in a notebook
rising from bed side naked leaving a naked boy asleep by the wall
mix miso mushroom leeks & winter squash breakfast,
Check bloodsugar, clean teeth exactly, brush, toothpick, floss, mouth-
       wash
oil my feet, put on white shirt white pants white sox
sit solitary by the sink
a moment before brushing my hair, happy not yet
to be a corpse.

September 13, 1992, 9:50 A.M.

In the Benjo

To G.S.

Reading *No Nature* in the toilet
Sitting down, absorbed
    page after page, forgetting
time, forgetting my bottom
    relax, detritus
       flopping out into water
—better than pushing and squeezing,
    nervous, self-conscious—
better forget and read a book,
    let your behind take care of itself
better than hemorrhoids, a good volume
       of poetry.

October 23, 1992, 11:00 A.M.

American Sentences

Tompkins Square Lower East Side N.Y.

Four skinheads stand in the streetlight rain chatting under an umbrella.

1987

* * *

Bearded robots drink from Uranium coffee cups on Saturn's ring.

May 1990

* * *

On Hearing the Muezzin Cry Allah Akbar While Visiting
the Pythian Oracle at Didyma Toward the End of the Second
Millennium

At sunset Apollo's columns echo with the bawl of the One God.

* * *

Crescent moon, girls chatter at twilight on the busride to Ankara.

* * *

The weary Ambassador waits relatives late at the supper table.

* * *

To be sucking your thumb in Rome by the Tiber among fallen leaves . . .

June 1990

* * *

Rainy night on Union Square, full moon. Want more poems? Wait till
I'm dead.

August 8, 1990, 3:30 A.M.

* * *

Approaching Seoul by Bus in Heavy Rain

Get used to your body, forget you were born, suddenly you got to get
  out!

August 1990

*   *   *

Put on my tie in a taxi, short of breath, rushing to meditate.

November 1991
New York

*   *   *

Taxi ghosts at dusk pass Monoprix in Paris 20 years ago.

*   *   *

The young stud who dreamt I "dick'd his ass" asked me to take him to
  supper.

*   *   *

Two blocks from his hotel in a taxi the fat Lama punched out his
  mugger.

*   *   *

I can still see Neal's 23-year-old corpse when I come in my hand.

January 1992
Amsterdam

*   *   *

Naropa Hot Tub

The ocean is full of naked young boys and Neptune-bearded old men.

July 1992

* * *

He stands at the church steps a long time looking down at new white
    sneakers—
Determined, goes in the door quickly to make his Sunday confession.

September 21, 1992

* * *

The midget albino entered the hairy limousine to pipi.

September 25, 1992

Modesto

* * *

That grey-haired man in business suit and black turtleneck thinks he's
    still young.

December 19, 1992

Notes

These reference notes may be of use to younger readers & translators not familiar with ephemeral news situations or translated & esoteric texts.

Title page epigraph
Section 2, "Discussion on Making All Things Equal," *Chuang Tzu Basic Writings*, trans. Burton Watson (New York: Columbia University Press, 1964), p. 42.

(p. 937) *Improvisation in Beijing*
Discourse at Chinese Writers Association conference with American Academy of Arts and Letters on "Sources of Inspiration," Beijing, October 1984. Improvised from notes, transcribed from tape, lightly edited.

(p. 941) *Prologue: Visiting Father & Friends*
See "At the Grave of My Father," Louis Ginsberg, *Collected Poems*, ed. Michael Fournier, Introduction Eugene Brooks, Afterword Allen Ginsberg (Orono, Maine: Northern Lights, 1992).

(p. 947) *On the Conduct of the World*
Roque Dalton: Salvadorian poet-hero-martyr (1935–1975) was liquidated by fellow FMLN revolutionists for tactical differences of opinion.
Velemir Khlebnikov (1885–1922), *Snake Train* (Ann Arbor: Ardis House, 1976). The classic Futurist poet perished after returning by train from Pyatigorsk to Moscow, "weakened by malnutrition and repeated bouts of typhus and malaria." See *The King of Time, Selected Writings of the Russian Futurian*, trans. Paul Schmidt (Cambridge: Harvard University Press, 1983).

(p. 951) *Spot Anger*
"Drive All Blames into One"—i.e., oneself. Jamgon Kongtrul, *The Great Path of Awakening. A Commentary on the Mahayana Teaching of the Seven Points of Mind Training*, trans. Ken McLeod (Boston: Shambhala Press, 1987). Original text by Atisa.

(p. 952)   *London Dream Doors*
    "God sent him to sea for pearls": "For in my nature I quested for beauty, but God, God hath sent me to sea for pearls." Christopher Smart, *Jubilate Agno*, ed. W. H. Bond (New York: Greenwood Press, 1969).

(p. 954)   *Cosmopolitan Greetings*
    Response to Macedonian request for message to Struga Evenings of Poetry festival, on receiving 1986 Golden Laurel Wreath prize.
    "Molecule/clinking against molecule.": See "Winter Night," *Attila József's Selected Poems and Texts*, trans. John Bátki (Iowa City: International Writing Program, University of Iowa, 1976).
    First Thought, Best Thought, Chögyam Trungpa (Boston: Shambhala Press, 1984).
    "If the mind is shapely, the art will be shapely": Jack Kerouac and Allen Ginsberg, conversation 1958, Cherry Plains, N.Y.

(p. 957)   *Fifth Internationale*
    See the "Internationale," former Soviet national anthem:
        "Arise ye prisoners of starvation,
        Arise ye wretched of the earth,
        For justice thunders condemnation,
        A better world's in birth," etc.
    Crazy Wisdom: i.e., wild wisdom "whispered lineage," characteristic of Kagyu school, Tibetan Buddhism. See Chögyam Trungpa, Rinpoche, *Crazy Wisdom* (Boston: Shambhala Press, 1992).

(p. 959)   *Europe, Who Knows?*
    Russian *Chernobyl* translates literally as "wormwood."

(p. 960)   *"Graphic Winces"*
    Collaboration with Brooklyn College M.F.A. Writing Workshop, Fall 1986, and Bob Rosenthal.

(p. 961)   *Imitation of K.S.*
    Jack Micheline, *Skinny Dynamite* (San Francisco: Second Coming Press, 1980). Story by the poet-painter.

(p. 967)   *On Cremation of Chögyam Trungpa*
    Cremation ceremony took place at Karme-Chöling Retreat Center, Barnet, Vermont.

(p. 969)   *Nanao*
    Written for back jacket copy, *Break the Mirror: The Poems of Nanao Sakaki* (San Francisco: North Point Press, 1987).

(p. 976)   *Salutations to Fernando Pessoa*
See "Salutation to Walt Whitman," *The Poems of Fernando Pessoa*, trans. Edwin Honig and Susan M. Brown (New York: Ecco Press, 1987).

(p. 979)   *May Days 1988*
"Arabs should throw words not stones," Elie Wiesel, quoted in *New York Post* sometime 1988.

(p. 984)   *Return of Kral Majales*
See "Kral Majales," p. 353 and notes, *Collected Poems 1947–1980* (New York: Harper & Row, 1984).

Sen. Jesse Helms & Heritage Foundation's October 1988 law directed Federal Communications Commission to enforce 24-hour ban on "indecent" language over all airwaves, declared unconstitutional by subsequent court decisions. At poem's writing, ban extended 6:00 A.M. to midnight. Court decisions 1993 froze ban as of 6:00 A.M. to 8:00 P.M., leaving as "safe harbor" late evening to 6:00 A.M. Daytime broadcast for students (& adults) reading the author's "questionable" poems in schools is now forbidden by law.

All gone all gone . . . : version of *Prajnaparamita*, Highest Perfect Wisdom, 17-syllable Sanskrit mantra: "Gate Gate Paragate Parasamgate Bodhi Svaha."

(p. 985)   *Elephant in the Meditation Hall*
"As late as 1988, 333 House members and 61 Senators hosted significant donations from Savings & Loan lobbyists." "S & L Scandal: The Gang's all Here," by Mary Fricher and Steve Pizzo, *New York Times* Op-Ed, July 27, 1990.

(p. 987)   *Poem in the Form of a Snake That Bites Its Tail*
Ojus: hard coral limestone formations, North Miami area, Florida.

(p. 997)   *CIA Dope Calypso*
See *New York Times*, March 12, 1989:

HULL BAILED OUT IN COSTA RICA
San Jose, Costa Rica, March 10 (AP)—American-born John Hull, who has been linked to Nicaraguan rebel supply network, was released from prison Friday after he posted $37,000 bail, his attorney said. The 69-year-old Mr. Hull, who was jailed on Jan. 13 on charges of

drug trafficking and violating Costa Rican security, was freed soon after friends collected bail money. Mr. Hull has lived in Costa Rica for 20 years. He is accused of allowing his ranch to be used by the Nicaraguan contras and of narcotics trafficking between 1982–1985.

Part I originally published in *First Blues* (New York: Full Court Press, 1979). Here two additional sections update events. For scholarly history of government intelligence involvement with drug trafficking to aid or fund "off-the-shelf" secret & illegal operations, including most references in "CIA Dope Calypso," see Alfred McCoy, *The Politics of Heroin* (Brooklyn: Lawrence Hill Books, 1991), to which poet contributed research.

(p. 1002) *Just Say Yes Calypso*
After aiding CIA overthrow of Iran's legal Premier Mohammed Mossadegh, General N. Schwarzkopf's father, Norman Schwarzkopf, Sr., trained the Shah's dreaded secret police, the Savak. See "Capitol Air," *Collected Poems 1947–1980; Lies of Our Times*, vol. 2, no. 2 (February 19, 1991) (New York: Sheridan Square Press); and James Breslin, "A Son Follows Suit in the Matter of Oil," *New York Newsday*, September 9, 1990.

(p. 1004) *Hum Bom!*
Part I and shorter version of Part II were published in *Collected Poems 1947–1980*. Additional verses added 1991.

(p. 1011) *Big Eats*
Mahamudra poetics exercise suggested by Khenpo Tsultrim Gyamtso, Rinpoche, Rocky Mountain Dharma Center, Summer 1991. The first of five verses, 21 syllables each, begins in "neurotic confusion" (Samsara), the last concludes grounded in "ordinary mind" (Dharmakaya).

(p. 1019) *After Lalon*
Lalon Shah (1774–1890), Bengali Baul singer, devotional forerunner of Rabindranath Tagore. See *Songs of Lalon Shah*, trans. Abu Rushd (Dhaka: Bangla Academy Press, 1991).

(p. 1024) *Get It?*
Verse 1: Ref. Rodney King videotape beating and police trials, Los Angeles 1992–93.

Verse 3: Ref. Police frame-up of political poet Amiri Baraka, 1966, later thrown out of court.

Verse 4: Ref. J. Edgar Hoover's amative relationship with assistant Clyde Tolson and his withholding of Kennedy assassination information from Warren Commission. See Curt Gentry, *J. Edgar Hoover: The Man and His Secrets* (New York: Penguin, 1991); and Anthony Summers, *Official and Confidential: The Secret Life of J. Edgar Hoover* (New York: Putnam, 1993).

Verse 5: Ref. Oswald's role as government intelligence informant within Fair Play for Cuba Committee.

Verse 6: Ref. Jack Ruby, courier to Cuba for Mafioso boss Santos Trafficante, Jr., former drug lord of Havana.

Verse 7: See "N.S.A. Dope Calypso" pp. 58–59, stanzas 3–6, and note.

Verse 8: Ref. Oliver North, Richard Secord, etc.

Verse 9: Ref. Elliott Abrams, former Assistant Secretary of State for Latin America, pardoned by outgoing President Bush 1992 after guilty plea to withholding Iran-contra scam information from Congress.

Verse 13: Charles H. Keating, Jr., 69, founder, Cincinnati Citizens for Decent Literature, later Citizens for Decency Through Law, was convicted 1993 on state and federal charges of swindling investors, fraud, and racketeering in collapse of Lincoln Savings and Loan Association. "The collapse of Lincoln, which was based in Irvine, California, in early 1989 is estimated to have cost taxpayers $2.5 billion" (*New York Times*, September 4, 1992). Along with pedophile Father Joseph Ritter, former director of wayward youths' Covenant House, Keating was outstanding homophobe on President Reagan's Meese Commission on Pornography.

(p. 1026) *Research*

Verse 6: Rev. W. A. Criswell, mentor of TV Bible evangelist fundraising theopoliticians Jimmy Swaggart, Pat Robertson, Jerry Falwell, and Billy Graham, decrees the Bible 100 percent "Inerrant."

Verse 11: John Rousas Rushdoony, fundamentalist author, leader of Chalcedon Foundation's Christian Reconstructionist exertions, disapproves homosexual emotions.

(p. 1029) *Put Down Your Cigarette Rag*

Originally published in *First Blues* (New York: Full Court Press, 1975). Here updated statistics, additional stanzas.

(p. 1033) *Violent Collaborations*

Epigraph remembered from 1940s college days, heard by classmate from his mother, perhaps 1920s flappers' ditty.

(p. 1038) *The Charnel Ground*

Epigraph and final quotation, "The whole point seems to be the idea of giving away the giver," taken from lectures on *The Sadhana of Mahamudra*, by Ven. Chögyam Trungpa, Rinpoche, Karma Dzong, December 1973, privately printed.

(p. 1047) *In the Benjo*

Gary Snyder, *No Nature: New and Selected Poems* (New York: Pantheon, 1992).

(p. 1048) *American Sentences*

On Hearing the Muezzin Cry Allah Akbar While Visiting the Pythian Oracle at Didyma Toward the End of the Second Millennium

Didyma, Asia Minor's shore site where Magna Mater and Pythian oracle were displaced by Judeo-Christian-Islamic Father God. In response to imperial Roman request for prophecy circa 4th century A.D., the oracle's last utterance declared the gods had departed, Apollo no longer inhabited the temple's pillars.

Rainy night on Union Square . . . Answering office mail late night, response to request from little magazine.

(p. 1049) *Approaching Seoul by Bus in Heavy Rain*

Bus over steep mountains from Kangnung to Seoul one rainy night was delayed along precipice by a mile of ambulance lights marking crash of bus I'd missed, scheduled an hour earlier.

Monoprix, familiar department store, onetime right bank of Seine across from Place St. Michel.

DEATH & FAME

POEMS

1993–1997

Edited by Bob Rosenthal, Peter Hale, and Bill Morgan
Foreword by Robert Creeley
Afterword by Bob Rosenthal

Thanks to the hospital editors, variants of these writings were printed first in: *Aftonbladet, Allen Ginsberg e Il Saggiatore, The Alternative Press, American Poetry Review, American Sentences, Ballad of the Skeletons* [recording], *The Best American Poetry 1997, Bombay Gin, Booglit, City Lights Review, Cuaderno Carmin, Davka, Harper's* magazine, *Harvard* magazine, *Illuminated Poetics, Lettre International, Literal Latté, Long Shot, Man Alive, The Nation, New York Newsday, New York Times Book Review,* the *New Yorker, Off the Wall, Poetry Flash, Poetry Ireland Review, Shambhala Sun, Tribu, Tricycle, Viva Vine, Viva Ferlinghetti!,* and *Woodstock Journal.*

Acknowledgments

The editors wish to acknowledge the following people for their help and support: Andrew Wylie, Sarah Chalfant, Jeff Posternak, Terry Karten, Megan Barrett, Jaqueline Gens, Eliot Katz, Steven Taylor, Ben Schafer, and Regina Pellicano.

Foreword

Vale

This is Allen Ginsberg's last book, particular to his determining intent, his last writings when in hospital aware of his impending death, his last reflections and resolutions—his last mind. When he was told by the doctors that he had at best only a short time to live, he called his old friends to tell them the hard news, comforting, reassuring, as particular to their lives as ever. Despite the intensely demanding fame he'd had to deal with for more than forty years, he'd kept the world both intimate and transcendent. It was a "here and now" that admitted all the literal things of each day's substance and yet well knew that all such was finally "too heavy for this lightness lifts the brain into blue sky/at May dawn when birds start singing on East 12th street . . ." He was, and remains, the enduring friend, the one who goes with us wherever we are taken, who counsels and consoles, who gets the facts when it seems we will never be told them, who asks "Who'll council who lives where in the rubble,/who'll sleep in what brokenwalled hut/in the moonlight . . ." He kept a witness of impeccable kind.

The playful, reductive, teasing verses, which could sometime make this world seem just the bitter foolishness it finally has to, sound here clearly. What is the grandness of death, of a body finally worn out, at last the simple fact of stubbornly reluctant shit and a tediously malfunctioning heart, of "all the accumulations that wear us out," as he put it, when still a young man? There is no irony, no despair, in delighting as one can in "No more right & wrong/yes it's gone gone gone/ gone gone away . . ." No poet more heard, more respected, more knew the intricacies of melody's patterns. He took such pleasure in the whimsical, insistent way the very rhythms could take hold of attention, bringing each word to its singular place. "Chopping apples into the fruit compote—suffer, suffer, suffer, suffer!" His company insisted upon music and he danced with a consummate grace.

Now we must make our own music, albeit his stays with us forever. William Blake's great call, "Hear the voice of the bard . . . ," now changes to "The authors are in eternity," because ours is a passing world. Yet the heroic voices, the insistent intimacies of their tenacious humanity, hold us in a profound and securing bond. Where else would we think to live? Our friend gave his whole life to keep faith with Whitman's heartfelt insistence, "Who touches this book touches a man." So Allen Ginsberg will not leave us even now. "To see Void vast infinite look out the window into the blue sky."

ROBERT CREELEY
JUNE 13, 1998

New Democracy Wish List

for President Clinton White House

Retro Axioms:

"Progress" ended in XX century.

Hyper-rationalism reduces natural complexity of nature through narrow
thought abstraction; Hyper-rationalization, hyper-industri-
alization & Hyper-technology create chaos.

U.S. command economy subsidizes fossil fuel and nuclear Energy &
Science, Agriculture, Air & Motor Transport, Banking,
Communications, Military Industrial Complex, licit & illicit
psychoactive Drugs, also rules Mass Media via FCC. American
Free Market is hi-tech myth with national socialist central-
ized regulation implicit everywhere except small business &
little magazines.

Muscle Power connected to appropriate hi-tech might rehabilitate
Earth.

Lacks & Needs:

Fossil Fuels retard the planet. Detoxify America: tainted Fire
poisons Earth, fouls Air & pollutes Water.

Emphasize prevention & alternative medicine with medical insurance
rebates for not using Self-insured health credits: like
mythic China, "Only pay Doctor when you are well."

Fund Ryan White Care Act, separate Church & State in Center for Dis-
ease Control, fund bleach kits, needle exchange & plainspoken
AIDS education, build infrastructure of decentralized com-
munity based health care preventative medicine early inter-
vention clinics for poverty class disease-prone high-risk
teens women & men living with AIDS & TB inner city plagues.

Coordinate National crash program to research inexpensive anti-
AIDS medicines.

Separate Church & State in arts, education & civil law. Restore Na-
tional Endowment for the Arts & FCC freedom from
Fundamentalist political intrusion.

Sexuality's loose not fixed. Legalize it.

Decriminalize addictive drug problem, doctors can cure addiction or
provide maintenance if no cure. Reduce mass-million expense
on narcotics-addicted political prisoners overcrowding courts
& jails, Medicalize drug trade.

Decriminalize marijuana, its disadvantages are minor; reserve hemp
grass as unadvertised private small cash crop for failing
family farms, encourage hemp fabric industries.

Privatize & entrust psychedelics to medical educational priestly
professions. End Military monopoly on LSD research and
development.

End tobacco farming subsidies, cut use. Ex-Nicotine lobbyists working
in Clinton's new White House can stop smoking.

Shift agricultural subsidies toward grain beans & vegetable diet. Tax
meat as a nutritional agronomic & ecologic disaster.

With massive scale reforestation rural & in wilderness, plant also uni-
versal urban tree rows.

Establish Civilian Conservation Corps for Urban homesteading, thin out
corrupt local bureaucracies obstructing populist housing re-
construction.

Encourage international trade in Eco-technology in place of enabling
codependency on weapons trade.

Inaugurate National "Limits of Growth" Program for Population/Land Use/Pollution.

Jump start national state & city human and industrial waste compost & recycling.

Honor primary and secondary school teachers, elevate respect, reward educators as handsomely as Plumbers, reduce class crowding to human size, under 15 students; encourage national child-care projects.

Take back money from SLA bankruptcy profiteer goniffs.

Purge U.S. military death squad subsidies in Salvador, Guatemala, etc. We backed up dictators in Zaire, Somalia, Liberia, Sudan, Angola, Haiti, Iran, Iraq, Salvador, we're responsible: admit it then figure ways out.

Open CIA & FBI & NSA archives on Cointelpro raids, Government drug dealing, Kennedy/King assassinations, Iranian Contragate, Panama Deception, Vatican, Hand & Lavoro Bank thuggery, etc. including Bush-Noriega relations and other CIA client-agent scandals.

Open all secret files on J. Edgar Hoover-Cardinal Spellman-Roy Cohn-Joe McCarthy alcoholic Closet-Queen Conspiracy with Organized Crime to sabotage the U.S. Labor Movement, Native African-American Hispanic & Gay minority leaderships; and blackmail U.S. Presidents Congress each other for half century.

Get Government Secret Police (DEA CIA FBI NSA etc.) off our backs by the next millennium.

January 17, 1993

Peace in Bosnia-Herzegovina

General Mother Teresa
    Emperor Dalai Lama XIV
        Chief of Staff Thich Nhat Hanh
           Army Chaplain John Paul II
followed by the shades of Gandhi
        Sakharov, Sartre & his uncle
            Albert Schweitzer
went to the bombed out streets
talked to Moslem Bosnians in
        the burnt out grocery stores
parlayed with Croatian & Serbian Generals & Parliament
asked them to quit shooting & firing
        artillery from the mountainside
overlooking villages
        emptied of grandmothers—
So now there was quiet—a few fires
        smoldered in back alleys
a few corpses stank in wet fields
—But who owns these houses? The
        cinema theaters with broken doors?
Who owns that grocery store, that City Hall,
        that windowless school with broken
        rooftiles?
Who owns these little apartments, now
        all worshippers of Allah
pray in towns besieged 100 miles away
overcrowded in tenements & tents, with
        U.N. portosans at the crossroads?
Who owns these abandoned alleys &
        drugstores with shattered bottle shards over
        the sidewalk & inside the door?
Who'll be the judge, attorney, file
        legal briefs,

bankruptcy papers, affidavits of ownership,
    deeds, old tax receipts?
Who'll council who lives where in the rubble,
    who'll sleep in what brokenwalled hut
in the full moonlight when spring clouds
    pass over the face
of the man in the moon at the end of May?

May 6, 1993, 3 A.M.

After the Party

amid glasses clinking, mineral water, schnapps
among professors' smiling beards,
sneaker'd classicists, intelligent lady millionaire
      literary Patron fag hags
      earth mothers of Lambeth, Trocadero,
      Hyde Park, 5th Avenue
blond haired journalists with bracelets, grand
      readers of Dostojevsky & Gogol—
senior editor escorts from Trotskyite weeklies,
lesbians sitting on glossy magazine covers—
what have we here? a kid moving from
      foyer to bathroom, thin body,
Pale cheeked with red cap, 18 year old window washer,
      came with Señora Murillo
She admired his impudence, amused by his
      sincere legs
as I admire his glance, he turns aside to
      gaze at me, I'm
happy to guess he'll show his
      naked body in bed
where we talk the refined old doctrine,
      Coemergent Wisdom

Łódź, October 5, 1993
9:15 P.M. at "Construction in Process" poetry reading

After Olav H. Hauge

I

Some live on islands, hills near Trondheim
Some in St. Moritz, or the forest depths
Some lonely have beautiful wives
castles, fine carpets on Wall Street
Buy & sell currencies, solitary on marble floors
consumed by a passion for fossil fuel
magnetized by cannons, lasers, bombsights, enriched uranium
or together play the stock market
They live & die at the throw of the dice
They're all businessmen
who have found eachother.

II

Fermented Jungle

North wind blows
Fish fly around the room
wind dies down
Fish fly under water.

III

Sometimes the Godliness
      strikes me as heroic
People mill about
Bodø won the Norwegian soccer cup
It's so crowded, fans are drunk
People's feet get mixed up
That big man wanders around
          lost, barefoot
he can't find his feet—
Finally he goes out, late
on his way home
not sure if he's on
his own two feet

Trondheim, October 25, 1993

These knowing age

These knowing age
fart
These knowing age
walk slowly
these knowing age
remind themselves of their grandmothers
these knowing age
take waterpills, high blood pressure,
        watch their sugar and salt
these knowing age eat less meat, some
        stopped smoking a decade ago
Some quit coffee, some drink it strong
These knowing age saw
best friends' funerals, telephoned
        daughters & granddaughters
Some drive, some don't, some cook, some
        do not
These knowing age often
keep quiet.

                    Munich, November 5, 1993

C'mon Pigs of Western Civilization Eat More Grease

Eat Eat more marbled Sirloin more Pork'n
        gravy!
Lard up the dressing, fry chicken in
        boiling oil
Carry it dribbling to gray climes, snowed with
        salt,
Little lambs covered with mint roast in racks
        surrounded by roast potatoes wet with
        buttersauce,
Buttered veal medallions in creamy saliva,
        buttered beef, by glistening mountains
        of french fries
Stroganoffs in white hot sour cream, chops
        soaked in olive oil,
surrounded by olives, salty feta cheese, followed
        by Roquefort & Bleu & Stilton
        thirsty
for wine, beer Cocacola Fanta Champagne
        Pepsi retsina arak whiskey vodka
Agh! Watch out heart attack, pop more
        angina pills
order a plate of Bratwurst, fried frankfurters,
couple billion Wimpys', McDonald's burgers
        to the moon & burp!
Salt on those fries! Hot dogs! Milkshakes!
Forget greenbeans, everyday a few carrots,
        a mini big spoonful of salty rice'll
        do, make the plate pretty;
throw in some vinegar pickles, briny sauerkraut
        check yr. cholesterol, swallow a pill
and order a sugar Cream donut, pack 2 under
        the size 44 belt
Pass out in the vomitorium come back cough
        up strands of sandwich still chewing
        pastrami at Katz's delicatessen

Back to central Europe & gobble Kielbasa
          in Lódź
swallow salami in Munich with beer, Liverwurst
on pumpernickel in Berlin, greasy cheese in
          a 3 star Hotel near Syntagma, on white
          bread thick-buttered
Set an example for developing nations, salt,
          sugar, animal fat, coffee tobacco Schnapps
Drop dead faster! make room for
          Chinese guestworkers with alien soybean
          curds green cabbage & rice!
Africans Latins with rice beans & calabash can
          stay thin & crowd in apartments for working
          class foodfreaks—

Not like Western cuisine rich in protein
          cancer heart attack hypertension sweat
          bloated liver & spleen megaly
Diabetes & stroke—monuments to carnivorous
          civilizations
presently murdering Belfast
          Bosnia Cypress Ngorno Karabach Georgia
mailing love letter bombs in
          Vienna or setting houses afire
          in East Germany—have another coffee,
          here's a cigar.
And this is a plate of black forest chocolate cake,
          you deserve it.

                              Athens, December 19, 1993

Here We Go 'Round the Mulberry Bush

I got old & shit in my pants
           shit in my pants
           shit in my pants
I got old & shit in my pants
           shit in my pants again

We got old & shit in our pants
           shit in our pants
           shit in our pants
We got old & shit in our pants
           shit in our pants again

You'll be lucky if you get old
           & shit in your pants
           & shit in your pants
You'll be lucky if you get old
           & shit in your pants again

January 1, 1994

Tuesday Morn

Waking with aching back at base of spine, walked stiffly to kitchen
         toilet to pee,
more limber returned to unmade bed, sat to write, dreamlike yesterdays
         recorded—
From pill dispenser 60 mg Lasix, water pills brings blood to kidney to
         relieve heart stressed by lung liquid
one white Lanoxin something further steadies the heart, one brown
         Vasotec for high blood pressure
a round blue potassium pill set aside for breakfast
Next another quaff of water for sleep-dried tongue
& check stove water boiling Tibetan medical powders
Quarter tsp. directly in mouth with hot water, morn & night
Next make the bed—pull out mattress, lift up sheets ballooning in air
         to settle all four corners,
lay on the orange-diamonded Mexican wool blanket & 3 pillows—
         push mattress back in place
brush teeth—then prick my finger
a drop, Exac-Tech blood sugar teststrip results noted morn & eve
98 today, a little low, swab pinkie with alcohol pad, another sip medi-
         cinal tea—
replace reading glasses with bifocals, brush teeth at front-room sink
         & looking out window, church door passers-by four floors
         below
while noon bells ring, clock ticking on the kitchen wall above the toilet
         cabinet—pull chain
worked this morning, flushed a wobbly porcelain throne—needa get
         Mike the Super fix pipes—
Back to front room, brush teeth, bowels begin to stir relief, electric
         shave,
brush out gray dust from razor head, wash face, clear throat's pale yellow
         phlegm, blow nose
in paper towel, stick pinkie end with white cream Borofax drop in
         each nostril, wipe mustache, put on teashirt
Vitalis on short hair around bald head, brush back small beard—&
         ready for breakfast

in boxer shorts alone at home, pee again, gray sky out window
Sparrows on courtyard dirt, bare Heaven Trees—yesterday's *Times*
      half read on the table where
red tulip blossoms dry in a glass jar—Time to crap & finish *Exquisite*
      Corpse—not much came down—
flush, climb ladder and fix the water ball, wash ass change shorts and
      choose fresh sox—
At last it's time to eat, clear & safe in the morning—1 P.M.
Salt-free cornflakes from the icebox, brown rice, shredded wheat in a
      Chinese bowl
filled thereafter with Rice Dream milk—banana that!
Chew and wonder what to read, answer phone, yes, "Peter's flown to
      Colorado, Huncke's rent is due" to patron Hiro—
Finish cereal reading yesterday's *Times* "How Mental Patients Sleep
      Out of Doors"
" 'Last time, I was just walking in the rain,' he said, his hands and lips
      quivering slightly from the medication he takes."
Slip a multivitamin pill in my mouth, grab a dish, fruit stewed two
      nites ago—
Ring Ring the telephone—the office, Bob Rosenthal, Debbie for Jewel
      Heart Benefit,
Ysrael Lubavitcher fairy returned from his Paris year
Edith not home, Aunt Honey leaving for Australia next week,
she had stroke & splenectomy 1942, long story—
David Rome preparing arts program Halifax during Sawang's Shambhala
      confirmation
—Finally 3 P.M. I get dressed go to office couple hours—
Phone Robert Frank? Yup, he's out, call early evening. I'm free.

January 23, 1994

God

The 18 year old marine "had made his Peace with God."
A word. A capitol G. Who is God? I thought I saw him once
and heard his voice, which now sounds like my own,
and I'm not God, so who's God? Jesus Bible God?
Whose Bible? Old JHVH? The 4 letter one without vowels or the 3 letter
    word God? G-O-D?
Allah? Some say Allah's great, tho' mock his name you're dead!
Zoroaster's Wise One used to be great, & Mormons' version got
    absolute pedigrees & Genealogies.
Is Pope's God same as Southern Baptist Inerrancy televangelists?
How's that square with the Ayatollah's Allah, Billy Graham Nixon's on
    his knees, Ronald Reagan's Armageddon deity?
What of Lubavitcher Rabbi's God refusing land for peace exchange?
Is Yassir Arafat's God same as Shamir's? What about Magna Mater?
What happened to Aphrodite, Hecate, Diana many breasted at Ephesus,
round bottom'd Willendorf Venus older than Jahweh & Allah &
    Zoroaster's dream!
older than Confucius, Lao Tzu, Buddha & the 39 patriarchs.
Is any God real? Is there one God? How come so many Gods—
Fighting eachother, poor Mayans, Aztecs, Peruvian sun worshippers?
    Hopi peyote dreamers round the half moon fire.
Am I God after all, made the universe, we dreamed it up together
or got tumbled out of the Chute onto the Planet, looking for progenitors?
I know I'm not God, are you? Don't be silly.
God? God? Everybody's God? Don't be silly.

February 25, 1994

Ah War

Ah War bigness addiction
Alchemized thru meta-industrial
Labor-Intensive permanent tree
Crop protein energy system
recycling Urban Wastes
in Meditative Egoless non
Theistic Space

Lisner Auditorium
Monday, March 21, 1994, 8:00 P.M.

Excrement

Everybody excretes different loads
To think of it—
Marilyn Monroe's pretty buttocks,
        Eleanor Roosevelt's bloomers dropt
    Rudolf Valentino on the seat, taut
          muscles relaxing
Presidents looking down the bowl
         to see their state of health
  Our White House rosy-cheeked dieter,
     One last, gaunt sourpuss
        striped pants ankle'd
        in the Water Chamber

Name it? byproduct of
     vegetables, steak, sausages, rice
  reduced to a brown loaf in the watery tureen,
        splatter of dark mud on highway
       side cornfields
    studded with peanuts & grape seeds—

Who doesn't attend to her business
No matter nobility, Hollywood starshine, media
      Blitz-heroics, everyone at
       table follows watercloset
       regulation & relief
An empty feeling going back to banquet,
       returned to bed, sitting for Breakfast,
   a pile of dirt unloaded from gut level
    mid-belly, down thru the butthole
       relaxed & released from the ton
       of old earth, poured back
       on Earth

It never appears in public
    'cept cartoons, filthy canards,
        political commix left & right
The Eminent Cardinal his robes pushed aside,
    Empress of Japan her 60 pound kimono,
        layered silks pushed aside,
The noble German Statesman giving his heart ease
    The pretty student boy in Heidelberg
        between chemic processor abstractions,
  Keypunch operators in vast newsrooms
        Editors their wives and children
      drop feces of various colors
      iron supplement black
        to pale green-white sausage
        delicacies the same
        in tiny bathroom
          distant suburbs,
     even dogs on green front lawns
        produce their simulacra of
        human garbage
      we all drop
Myself the poet aging on the stool
  Polyhymnia the Muse herself, lowered to this throne—
      what a relief!

March 24, 1994

New Stanzas for *Amazing Grace*

I dreamed I dwelled in a homeless place
Where I was lost alone
Folk looked right through me into space
And passed with eyes of stone

O homeless hand on many a street
Accept this change from me
A friendly smile or word is sweet
As fearless charity

Woe workingman who hears the cry
And cannot spare a dime
Nor look into a homeless eye
Afraid to give the time

So rich or poor no gold to talk
A smile on your face
The homeless ones where you may walk
Receive amazing grace

I dreamed I dwelled in a homeless place
Where I was lost alone
Folk looked right through me into space
And passed with eyes of stone

April 2, 1994

Composed at the request of Ed Sanders for his production of The New Amaz-
ing Grace, performed November 20, 1994, at the Poetry Project in St. Mark's
Church in-the-Bouwerie.

City Lights City

On Via Ferlinghetti & Kerouac Alley young heroes muse melancholy
     2025 A.D.
Musicians brood & pace Bob Kaufman Street and practice future jazz
     on Rexroth place
Spiritual novelists sit rapt in contemplation under the street sign at
     Saroyan Place before they cross to Aram Alley
Loves' eyes gaze sparkling on Bay waters from McClure Plaza at the
     foot of Market
Old Market itself as Robert Duncan Boulevard teems with theosophic
     shops & Hermetic Department Stores
& crossing Duncan Blvd.: First DiPrima Second Henry Miller Third
     Corso Street
Fourth Jeffers Street & Fifth on John Wieners Street the Greyhound
     Terminal stands
surrounded by Bookstore Galleries, Publishers Rows, and Artists lofts
Sightseers in tourist buses breathe fresh foggy air on Harold Norse &
     Hirschman Peaks—oldies but goldies
Ken Kesey's name makes Bayshore famous as you barrel up past
     Brother Everson Memorial Stadium
Whalen Bridge sits meditating all the way to Oakland
Snyder Bridge connects the East-West Gate between S.F. & Marin
Commuters crowd exhausted into the Neal Cassady R.R. Station on
     Corso ·
Czeslaw Milosz Street signs shine bright on Van Ness
Poet Jack Micheline gets Tenderloin, Philip Lamantia Tower crowns
     Telegraph Hill
where international surrealist tourists climb to see the view—
& I'll take Alcatraz (to return to Native Americans along with Treasure
     Island)

April 21, 1994

Newt Gingrich Declares War on "McGovernik Counterculture"

Does that mean war on every boy with more than one earring on the
      same ear?
against every girl with a belly button ring? What about nose piercing?
      a diamond in right nostril?
Does that mean more plainclothesmen high on LSD at Dead concerts?
What about MTV—no more Michael Jackson, no Dylan Subterranean
      Homesick Blues? Yoko & John no more Give Peace a Chance
Will there be laws against Punk, Generation X, the Voidoids, Slackers,
      Grunge?
Blues, Jazz, Bebop, Rocknroll? Where did it get countercultural?
What about Elvis' Pelvis? Sonic Youth dumbed, Cobain's screams
      banished from Nirvana?
No more grass on college campuses, Mushrooms stomped to death by
      the Elephant Party?
What about African-Americans? That's a terrific Counterculture, &
      what about the Yellow Peril, Chinese restaurants? New Age
      Cooking? is Japanese Sushi too much Zen?
Sitting meditation, that be frowned satanic in Congress? Tai Chi, Tai
      Kwando, Karate, Martial Arts? Ballet? Opera, *La Bohème*?
Don't mention us cocksuckers?! Is eating pussy countercultural?
      Sappho, Socrates, Da Vinci, Shakespeare, Michelangelo,
      Proust in or out the canon?
J. E. Hoover's name wiped off FBI granite in the Capital?
Poetry slams, is poetry countercultural, like a Third Party?
Is ecology pro or counter culture? Astronomy determining the Uni-
      verse's age & size?
Long hair, relativity, is Einstein countercultural?

January 1995

Pastel Sentences (Selections)

Mice ate at the big red heart in her breast, she was distracted in
    love.

Bowed down by the weight of nebulae he crouches underneath the
    hill.

A bat that's bigger than your ear watches you sleep while you dream
    him there.

A round blue eye woke red lipped 'neath this century's gigantic lightbulb.

Lantern-jawed Bismarck dreams a rich red rose blossoms thorn-
    stemmed through his skull.

In an oval blue womb a full-grown girl curled up eyes closed dreams
    her birth.

Big little people do yab yum in their ten petal'd yellow daisy.

Long hand over left eye Mother Sudan sees big bellied kids' thin
    ribs.

In midst of coition a blood-red worm spurts out his heaving rib-
    cage.

The one eyed moon-whale watches you weep, drifting brown seas in
    a pale boat.

Thirty Kingdoms' keys chainmailed down his chest, the Pope dreams
    he's St. Peter.

Jeannie Duval's cheek tickled by a Paris fly, 1852.

Puff a cigarette between skullfleshed lips, smoke gets in your empty eyes.

Sphincter-wound in his chest, he kneels and lifts both hands in surprise to pray.

All mixed up breasts feet genitals nipples & hands, both fall into sleep.

Adam contemplates his navel covered with a bush of jealous hearts.

Body spread open, black legs held down, she eats his ice cream—white sex-tongue.

One centaur palm raised thru earth-crust lifts a red live dog barking at stars.

Her dog licks the live red heart of th' African lady curled up in bed.

Naked in solitary prison cell he looks down at a hard-on.

Hands hold her ass tight with joy to lick & eat the blue star 'twixt her thighs.

Small pink-winged Lady-Heart hovers, rose-cunt legs spread nigh his stiff black dick.

Chic shoes rest in a black rose vortex of sociable fashion money.

She poses self-confident, blue sky & clouds borne in her oval womb.

Lady Buddha sleeps on blue air in a green leaf, knees raised spread naked.

Repose open-eyed on starry blue pillows under a star-roofed sky.

The black guy steps in the shade, glancing back at the sunlit boy he screwed.

Legs behind neck, arms hung down, Yogi's solar anal navel burns
    red.

Blowing bubbles in blue sky he squats on his own blue bubble planet.

Star, bird, cane & big thigh bones, the ghost baby dreams life
    beyond the womb.

Regarding their long thick tails, blue demons wrestle with golden
    scissors.

He steps on his own breast lying in bed with red half hard-on.

Lady snails delicately climb naked thighs to stir his genitals.

Left forefinger probed into his own left hand proves a Doubting
    Thomas.

They exchange glances, a bee shadows her tail, a rose grows on his
    hip.

William Burroughs' skeleton twists a towel, he's got the bloody rag
    on.

The rose-girl kneels weighed down, iron tanks on shoulder, coccyx,
    calves & footsoles.

Horse stands on horse upon horse, lie back on top & take your forty
    winks.

He dives from naked sky past the sun's nimbus into space-blue ocean.

Curtains part on a nail and its shadow, Samsara's drama Act I.

The red lip'd fat billionaire appeals you try out his wee twat or dick.

Arms to neck, his tit, her belly, prong-twat, the President and his
    wife.

Pale green headless phantoms upside-down dipsy-doodle with thin
      hard-ons.

Lady Day bows her neck under a pyramid of oily black rocks.

Beneath breast-eyed wasp-beaks the pink rose opens, better get in
      there quick!

Inside her red womb the hermaphrodite fetus closes a third eye.

Wiping blood-black tears from hard labor, try holding up your
      big sad head.

Jealousy! Jealousy! Chin in hand he ponders the Unfaithful Muse.

Young Don Juan bravely displays his girlish red-sexed lips and
      eyeshadow.

Caught in the burning house of my brown body I fainted openeyed.

Big phallus, black womb lined with reddish flesh, look at the monkey
      we birthed.

One bird pecks her double's breast on a ghost-white lingam's
      unblinking head.

She flies down thousands of stone steps for years, aged climbs them
      all back up.

for Francesco Clemente
Château Chenonceau, June 24, 1995
Naropa Institute, July 5, 1995
Lawrence, Kansas, July 22, 1995

Nazi Capish

Catholicism capish
Catholicism capish
Catholicism abortion capish
Capish capish capish

Christian capish
Christian capish
Christian sin capish

Islamic capish
Islamic capish
Islamic Jihad capish

Zionist capish
Zionist capish
Zionist nationalist capish

Fundamentalism capish
Fundamentalism capish
Fundamentalism absolutism
Fundamentalism capish

Hunkie Honkie Aryan Frog
Jap & Gook & Limey Wog
        Afric Chink capish

Nazi capish
Nazi capish
Nazi capish capish

Commie capish
Commie capish
Commie capish capish

Capitalist capish
Capitalist capish
Capitalist capish capish

Fascisti capish
Fascisti capish
Fascisti shit capish

September 21, 1995

Is About

Dylan is about the Individual against the whole of creation
Beethoven is about one man's fist in the lightning clouds
The Pope is about abortion & the spirits of the dead . . .
Television is about people sitting in their living room looking at their
      things
America is about being a big Country full of Cowboys Indians Jews
      Negroes & Americans
Orientals Chicanos Factories skyscrapers Niagara Falls Steel Mills
      radios homeless Conservatives, don't forget
Russia is about Tzars Stalin Poetry Secret Police Communism barefoot
      in the snow
But that's not really Russia it's a concept
A concept is about how to look at the earth from the moon
without ever getting there. The moon is about love & Werewolves, also
      Poe.
Poe is about looking at the moon from the sun
or else the graveyard
Everything is about something if you're a thin movie producer chain-
      smoking muggles
The world is about overpopulation, Imperial invasions, Biocide,
      Genocide, Fratricidal Wars, Starvation, Holocaust, mass
      injury & murder, high technology
Super science, atom Nuclear Neutron Hydrogen detritus, Radiation
      Compassion Buddha, Alchemy
Communication is about monopoly television radio movie newspaper
      spin on Earth, i.e. planetary censorship.
Universe is about Universe.
Allen Ginsberg is about confused mind writing down newspaper
      headlines from Mars—
The audience is about salvation, the listeners are about sex, Spiritual
      gymnastics, nostalgia for the Steam Engine & Pony Express
Hitler Stalin Roosevelt & Churchill are about arithmetic & Quadri-
      lateral equations, above all chemistry physics & chaos theory—

Who cares what it's all about?
I do! Edgar Allan Poe cares! Shelley cares! Beethoven & Dylan care.
Do you care? What are you about
or are you a human being with 10 fingers & two eyes?

New York City,
October 24, 1995

The Ballad of the Skeletons

Said the Presidential Skeleton
I won't sign the bill
Said the Speaker skeleton
Yes you will

Said the Representative Skeleton
I object
Said the Supreme Court skeleton
Whaddya expect

Said the Military skeleton
Buy Star Bombs
Said the Upperclass Skeleton
Starve unmarried moms

Said the Yahoo Skeleton
Stop dirty art
Said the Right Wing skeleton
Forget about yr heart

Said the Gnostic Skeleton
The Human Form's divine
Said the Moral Majority skeleton
No it's not it's mine

Said the Buddha Skeleton
Compassion is wealth
Said the Corporate skeleton
It's bad for your health

Said the Old Christ skeleton
Care for the Poor
Said the Son of God skeleton
AIDS needs cure

Said the Homophobe skeleton
Gay folk suck
Said the Heritage Policy skeleton
Blacks're outa luck

Said the Macho skeleton
Women in their place
Said the Fundamentalist skeleton
Increase human race

Said the Right-to-Life skeleton
Foetus has a soul
Said Pro Choice skeleton
Shove it up your hole

Said the Downsized skeleton
Robots got my job
Said the Tough-on-Crime skeleton
Tear gas the mob

Said the Governor skeleton
Cut school lunch
Said the Mayor skeleton
Eat the budget crunch

Said the Neo Conservative skeleton
Homeless off the street!
Said the Free Market skeleton
Use 'em up for meat

Said the Think Tank skeleton
Free Market's the way
Said the S&L skeleton
Make the State pay

Said the Chrysler skeleton
Pay for you & me
Said the Nuke Power skeleton
& me & me & me

Said the Ecologic skeleton
Keep Skies blue
Said the Multinational skeleton
What's it worth to you?

Said the NAFTA skeleton
Get rich, Free Trade,
Said the Maquiladora skeleton
Sweat shops, low paid

Said the rich GATT skeleton
One world, high tech
Said the Underclass skeleton
Get it in the neck

Said the World Bank skeleton
Cut down your trees
Said the I.M.F. skeleton
Buy American cheese

Said the Underdeveloped skeleton
Send me rice
Said Developed Nations' skeleton
Sell your bones for dice

Said the Ayatollah skeleton
Die writer die
Said Joe Stalin's skeleton
That's no lie

Said the Middle Kingdom skeleton
We swallowed Tibet
Said the Dalai Lama skeleton
Indigestion's whatcha get

Said the World Chorus skeleton
That's their fate
Said the USA skeleton
Gotta save Kuwait

Said the Petrochemical skeleton
Roar Bombers roar!
Said the Psychedelic skeleton
Smoke a dinosaur

Said Nancy's skeleton
Just say No
Said the Rasta skeleton
Blow Nancy Blow

Said Demagogue skeleton
Don't smoke Pot
Said Alcoholic skeleton
Let your liver rot

Said the Junkie skeleton
Can't we get a fix?
Said the Big Brother skeleton
Jail the dirty pricks

Said the Mirror skeleton
Hey good looking
Said the Electric Chair skeleton
Hey what's cooking?

Said the Talkshow skeleton
Fuck you in the face
Said the Family Values skeleton
My family values mace

Said the N.Y. Times skeleton
That's not fit to print
Said the C.I.A. skeleton
Cantcha take a hint?

Said the Network skeleton
Believe my lies
Said the Advertising skeleton
Don't get wise!

Said the Media skeleton
Believe you Me
Said the Couch-potato skeleton
What me worry?

Said the TV skeleton
Eat sound bites
Said the Newscast skeleton
That's all Goodnight

February 12–16, 1995

"You know what I'm saying?"

I was shy and tender as a 10 year old kid, you know what I'm saying?
Afraid people'd find me out in Eastside H.S. locker room you know
      what I'm saying?
Earl had beautiful hips & biceps when he took off his clothes to put on
      gym shorts you know what I'm saying?
His nose was too long, his face like a ferret but his white body
Proportioned thin, muscular definition thighs & breasts, with boy's
      nipples you know what I'm saying? uncircumcised
& strange, goyishe beauty you know what I'm saying, I was dumb-
      struck—
at Golden 50th H.S. Reunion I recognized him, bowed, & exchanged
      pleasant words, you know what I'm saying?
He was retired, wife on his arm, you know what I'm saying?
& Millie Peller "The Class Whore" warmest woman at our last Silver
      25th Reunion alas had passed away
She was nice to me a scared gay kid at Eastside High, you know what
      I'm saying?

December 23, 1995

Bowel Song

You've been coughing for weeks
still you don't sit on your cushion & visualize Bam
You've been in the hospital just last week
still you read the newspapers
Recovered from congestive heart failure,
you took 7 hours last week to read the Sunday N.Y. Times
Listen, your days are numbered, why waste the essence of your clock
How will you feel when you can't breathe?
What'll you do the last six minutes?
Where'll you go for the next 6 hours?
What good, half dozen gay porno films then?
You can hardly catch your breath now, why jack off limp prick?
Your master gives good advice, you listen, follow it couple weeks
then lapse into old habits, waste time on the toilet reading books,
at the kitchen sink 3am washing dishes daydreaming.
If you don't get ready now, what'll you do at the Black Hole
You wanna get born a pretty little girl & go through agony?
Wanna get caught between snakes coupling?
In between death and life, still wanna get laid?
What makes you lazy? you're not on your deathbed yet,
if you've an ounce of strength, use it to look inside.
Clear your mind, you won't escape the Great Sickness
the Immortal Plague, Grand Disaster continuous to eternity—
Whatever it is, whyn'cha figure it out?
Wanna drift off & become a newspaper headline,
what good favorable publicity in the bardo?
Allen Ginsberg says, these words'll get you nowhere
these jokes won't be funny when everyone leaves the seven exits.

January 2, 1996

Popular Tunes

What do I hear in my ear
              approaching my 70th year—
Echoes of popular tunes, old rhymes
                    familiar runes
Songs my mother taught me
          "O tell me pretty maiden
              are there any more at home
                  like you?"
Cousin Claire heard on the Newark radio
Aunt Elanor played on her Bronx phonograph
piercing Bell Song soprano notes,
             sostenuto Amelita Galli-Curci & Rosa Ponselle
Wind up Victrola Yiddish Monologues
        Cohen On The Telephone,
             The Wind the Wind,
"Last night da vind, da vind blew down da shutters."
           "No I didn't say shuddup!"
The fugitive words of a Scots contralto
         woman's chant "McCushla,
    McCushla my dark eyed McCushla"
Ask Aunt Honey age 83, ask Stepmother Edith just 90,
        they'll know—
            they'll remember
    "The March of the Wooden Soldiers," tin drums
       & pipes of *Babes in Toyland*
"Comin' thru the rye" new generations of
       folksing kids never remember sung
    when they play Guitar on Union Square's
         L train subway platform—
or "Auchichornya, auchimolinka, rasdrivyminya,
       molijeninka," with Mandolins or Balalaikas
and "Tis the last rose of Summer" by Thomas Moore—
    echoing thru Time's skull as my beard's
       turned white, sugar high in my blood
        coughing weeks on end fall to winter,

Chronic bronchitis the rest of my days?
& "Down will come baby cradle and all"
    as 1930's all fell down with
    mournful Peat Bog Soldiers'
        "Lied des Concentrationslagers"

February 9, 1996

Five A.M.

Élan that lifts me above the clouds
into pure space, timeless, yea eternal
Breath transmitted into words
                    Transmuted back to breath
            in one hundred two hundred years
nearly Immortal, Sappho's 26 centuries
of cadenced breathing—beyond time, clocks, empires, bodies, cars,
chariots, rocket ships skyscrapers, Nation empires
brass walls, polished marble, Inca Artwork
of the mind—but where's it come from?
Inspiration? The muses drawing breath for you? God?
Nah, don't believe it, you'll get entangled in Heaven or Hell—
Guilt power, that makes the heart beat wake all night
flooding mind with space, echoing thru future cities, Megalopolis or
Cretan village, Zeus' birth cave Lassithi Plains—Otsego County
            farmhouse, Kansas front porch?
Buddha's a help, promises ordinary mind no nirvana—
coffee, alcohol, cocaine, mushrooms, marijuana, laughing gas?
Nope, too heavy for this lightness lifts the brain into blue sky
at May dawn when birds start singing on East 12th street—
Where does it come from, where does it go forever?

                                              May 1996

Power

The N Power, the feminine power
      the woman power the
      flower power, the power of Marigolds
      & roses, Sequoia power,
      Nature's power
wont blossom in this lifetime
      or the next, this Yuga's finished,
      seeds shot, entered the earth
      gestating with alligators & waterworms
      in swamps where planes crash,
Next lifetimes after, watch roses turn
      red, Marigolds yellow, little
      sequoias begin to climb the sky
Millions of African kids'll grow up
      amid green bushes & radiant
            camelopards again—
Down 12th Street corner Avenue A midnight police
      lean against Bodega shutters looking for
      last week's swarthy crack pushers

May 15, 1996, 11 A.M.

Anger

How'd I get angry? Analytic approach:
M'I still angry with Carolyn? forty three years ago
        kicked me out of bed with
              naked Neal their house San Jose—
Disadvantaged hating Podhoretz
          for put-down of Beat writers
              queers nineteen fifty eight
          later defense of death-squad drug-dealer
            Generals in El Salvador
              & op-ed B2 Bombers
Angrily sat an hour adamant
        Thangka-thief meth-head Gaiton's apt.
          E. Houston Street nineteen sixty three
            never got my Dancing Skeletons back—
Never forgave late Alan Marlowe nineteen seventy five
        stole back my $100 loan gift
        to Jyoti Datta Calcutta four years earlier
Lost my telephone temper with critic Walter
        Goodman
        insulting Gunther Grass' visit to poor South Bronx
International PEN Congress nineteen eighty five
        & my own handmade Nicaraguan
          Contra-War peace petition mocked
            as "all the news that's fit to print."

May 18, 1996

Multiple Identity Questionnaire

"Nature empty, everything's pure;
Naturally pure, that's what I am."

I'm a jew? a nice Jewish boy?
A flaky Buddhist, certainly
Gay in fact pederast? I'm exaggerating?
Not only queer an amateur S&M fan, someone should spank me for
    saying that
Columbia Alumnus class of '48, Beat icon, students say.
White, if jews are "white race"
American by birth, passport, and residence
Slavic heritage, mama from Vitebsk, father's forebears Grading in
    Kamenetz-Podolska near Lvov.
I'm an intellectual! Anti-intellectual, anti-academic
Distinguished Professor of English Brooklyn College,
Manhattanite, Another middle class liberal,
but lower class second generation immigrant,
Upperclass, I own a condo loft, go to art gallery Buddhist Vernissage
    dinner parties with Niarchos, Rockefellers, and Luces
Oh what a sissy, Professor Four-eyes, can't catch a baseball or drive a
    car—courageous Shambhala Graduate Warrior
addressed as "Maestro" Milano, Venezia, Napoli
Still student, chela, disciple, my guru Gelek Rinpoche,
Senior Citizen, got Septuagenarian discount at Alfalfa's Healthfoods
    New York subway—
Mr. Sentient Being!—Absolutely empty neti neti identity, Maya Nobo-
    daddy, relative phantom nonentity

July 5, 1996, Naropa Tent,
Boulder, CO

Don't Get Angry with Me

for Chödok Tulku

Don't get angry with me
You might die tomorrow
I'm an empty hungry ghost
Any spare change I can borrow?

Don't get angry with me
Full of God tomorrow
Could get sorry you got mad,
wanna be the God of sorrow?

Don't get angry with me
War starts tomorrow
I'll get bombed You'll get shot
in the eye with Interdependent Arrow

Don't get angry with me
Hell's hot tomorrow
If we're burned up now inflamed
Could pass aeons in cold horror

Don't get angry with me
We'll be worms tomorrow
Both wriggling in the mud
cut in two by the ploughman's harrow

Don't get angry with me—
Who'll we be tomorrow?
who knows who we are today?
Better meditate & pray,
Tila, Mila, Marpa, Naro.

August 27, 1996

Swan Songs in the Present

"Swan songs in the present
moon systems in gleeps
Don't hang on to the essence
the refrigerator's for keeps
the Hot house vernacular
Sets up on the moldy hill
you and I climb the ribcage
& look for a heart to kill

you can do whatcha want with Europe
Eat Bananas with your dung
Whistle while you wonk the Pope
Breathe out of a spastic lung
but you'll live forever anyway
in birds' beasts hungry ghosts
& various Boddhisattvas
Drinking morning coffee
eating loxes & toasts

Hypnogogi Twaddle
anytime I can
But 70 years I'll sleep
like other old men

October 29, 1996, 3:50 A.M.

Gone Gone Gone

"The wan moon is sinking under the white wave
and time is sinking with me, O!"

—*Robert Burns*

yes it's gone gone gone
gone gone away
yes it's gone gone gone
gone gone away
yes it's gone gone gone
gone gone away
yes it's gone gone gone
it's all gone away
gone gone gone
won't be back today
gone gone gone
just like yesterday
gone gone gone
isn't any more
gone to the other shore
gone gone gone
it wasn't here to stay
yes it's gone gone gone
all gone out to play
yes it's gone gone gone
until another day
no one here to pray
gone gone gone
yak your life away
no promise to betray
gone gone gone
somebody else will pay
the national debt no way
gone gone gone
your furniture layaway

plan gone astray
gone gone gone
made hay
gone gone gone
Sunk in Baiae's Bay
yes it's gone gone gone
wallet and all you say
gone gone gone
so you can waive your pay
yes it's gone gone gone
gone last Saturday
yes it's gone gone gone
tomorrow's another day
gone gone gone
bald & old & gay
gone gone gone
turned old and gray
yes it's gone gone gone
whitebeard & cold
yes it's gone gone gone
cashmere scarf & gold
yes it's gone gone gone
warp & woof & wold
yes it's gone gone gone
gone far far away
to the home of the brave
down into the grave
yes it's gone gone gone
moon beneath the wave
yes it's gone gone gone
so I end this song
yes this song is gone
gone to kick the gong
yes it's gone gone gone
No more right & wrong
yes it's gone gone gone
gone gone away

November 10, 1996

Reverse the rain of Terror . . .

Reverse the rain of Terror on street consciousness U.S.A.
Death Penalty! Electric Chair! A roomsful of poison gas! Lethal
    injections! Mortal Hanging! Beheading the Idiot killer!
Dogs slaver over airport luggage! Suitcase bottoms caked with hash!
    Strip search the sick opium addict, medicine's up his anus in
    a finger stall
arriving from legal India, cozy England, lax Morocco, face 12 billion
    Dollars worth of cops
Sniffing bodies for illegal medicine! Vomiting in a stone cell,
    abdominal convulsions, muscle spasms thigh & foot, sleepless
    cold-turkey torture—
Puerto Rican kid needs a doctor, young black man needs his girlfriend's
    fix, white boy didn't know his habit was immortal!
The octogenarian schmecker's liver & kidneys failed, wants a
    deathbed shot of M
Half mad lady on the street had a fight with her daughter the whore!
The old boy lies on the sidewalk hands dirty red faced in his own
    saliva.
The delicate youth's in his halfway house a decade, thorazine eyes
    glazed over
His brother's Christmas card arrives at Binghampton State Hospital!
The elder hides in a furnished room drinks wine delivers newspapers,
    didn't wanna work on the neutron bomb!
The salesman's product went off the market, recycling coke bottles he
    cries at kitchen tables blaming Jews
An auto worker shoveling snow curses six African-Americans mugged
    him twenty years ago—
A black man walked the street with his B.A. pager, clubbed down
    giving lip to a cop car
The young fruit dies body with sores he challenged the Senate on the
    plague.
The homeless jewish guitarist sings on the 14th Street's L Train
    Subway platform, blows harmonica, taps tambourine with one
    foot, with another drums

then back to his graybeard cocksucker's apartment fries eggs
Streetcorner boys and girlfriends hang round the butcher shop
     corner, "Smoke smoke?"
Rocky Flats engineers tear their hair, Plutonium waste'll outlast an
     otherworldly God

December 1996

Sending Message

They are sending a message to the youth of America
Smoking medical marijuana's all right
They're sending a message in cartoon saloons hard-ass blokes look
        like camels smoke Camels at the bar, 5 year olds love it,
To the youth of America they're sending a message
CIA no official connections to Contra coke dealers in *New York Times*
Washington Post expert crackheads send same messages to adoles-
        cent Senior citizen crackhead readers
They're sending a message to American youth, African youth can
        starve to death we can't care
too much money, far over the Atlantic, our boys'll never die, politi-
        cally unpopular, they'll become dependent, it won't fly
They're sending message by Bronco, Honda, 4 by 4, cinema MG, Land
        Rover & half million gas stations
youth of this nation fossil fuel's neat, hella cool, admirable dope really
        rad, as if—what valley girls think when their fathers drive
        them to Highschool—
They're sending the message to Saturn, American Democracy works
        over the globe, spin that round your rings
To Chinese youth, eat like us, we do flesh & fries,
Don't sleep on streets, dangerous off-duty death-squad police send
        this message to Brazilian kiddies
Someone sent naked pretty boys on FCC Internet, Don't!
No Forbidden Planet Swedish sex? Got the message pretty girls?
Got the message clean old men? Michelangelo got the message? Da
        Vinci got it? Phidias, Socrates, Shakespeare, J. Edgar Hoover
        at the Plaza, Cardinal Francis Spellman on Roy Cohn's yacht,
        Senator Jesse Helms in your gut, duh
got the message teeny-weenies? They're sending a message right
        below your belly button.
A message to the youth of America, "Diminished expectations," they's
        too many people,
native gooks work cheaper, rich get richer, North hemispheric whites
        live longer, Black high-blood pressure rules Kentucky Fried
        Chicken

Across the highway from Arbie's Barbecue Palace, Roy Rogers' Horse-
        chops, or McDonalds Amazon Treeburgers
you heard about on Television serves the message Eat your meat
or beat your meat, safe sex with ketchup, Whatever
The message now's pay 4 trillion dollars debt Reagan pissed away on
        Military,
promised before you born, sit in school watercloset study yr Latin
They're sending youth a message look at TV football baseball hypnotic
        soccer basketball sports, sport!
General Rios-Montt & Pat Robertson sent a message to Guatemalan
        Indians
so 200,000 dropped dead with delight at sight of Christ's military
pistol machete machinegun baseball bat & Inerrant Bible
700 Club's Antichrist sends U.S. youth this message Despise the poor
        & piss on liberal Jesus
The message is Compassion'll cause a Wall Street crash
& Networks send me messages Shut the fuck up.

December 3, 1996, 4:30 A.M.
New York City

No! No! It's Not the End

No! No!
  Not the end of
      Civilization
  Not the end of
      Civilization

Blast of industrial
  Gas in Bhopal
    No! No! Not the end of
        Civilization

Dropt one bomb
  killed one
        hundred thousand
  Hiroshima nineteen forty five

No no not the end of
      Civilization
  Not the end of Civilization

Guatemala murdered
  two hundred thousand
        Indians

No no not the end of
      Civilization
  Not the end of Civilization

200 thousand
        slaughtered in Rwanda
  Crazed events
          on the TV screen

No no not the end of
       Civilization
   Not the end of Civilization

U.S. Blacks in jail
        land of the free
    mosta these citizens you & me

No no not the end of
       Civilization
   Not the end of Civilization

Fossil fuel dust filling heaven
    ozone layer hole in the sky

No no not the end of
       Civilization
   Not the end of Civilization

Oldest trees in the world cut down
    Weyerhaeuser Bush wears a cardboard Crown

No no not the end of
       Civilization
   Not the end of Civilization

Amazon forests cut to the ground
    you can still breathe
       to the chainsaw's sound

No no not the end of
       Civilization
   Only a temporary aberration

No No it's not the end of Civilization
It's Nobadaddy's
    old temptation
No no it's not the end of Civilization
Everybody's waltzing
   to "the Hesitation"

It's the same damned
President's Inauguration
No no it's not the end of Civilization
We're come to "the fabled
damned of Nations"
No no it's not the end of Civilization
Slaves wore chains
at the States' creation
No no it's not the end of Civilization
sourpuss wantsa stop colored immigration
Nobody's wearing
hooves & scales
all they wanna do is
kill more whales
No no it's not the end of Civilization

No no it's not the end of Civilization
Cayenne saved a little bit of sensation
No no it's not the end of civilization
No final solution
just gas & cremation

December 18–20, 1996

Bad Poem

Being as Now has been re-invented
I have devised a new now
Entering the real Now
at last
which is now

December 24, 1996, 3 A.M.

Homeless Compleynt

Pardon me buddy, I didn't mean to bug you
      but I came from Vietnam
where I killed a lot of Vietnamese gentlemen
          a few ladies too
and I couldn't stand the pain
          and got a habit out of fear
& I've gone through rehab and I'm clean
      but I got no place to sleep
          and I don't know what to do
          with myself right now

I'm sorry buddy, I didn't mean to bug you
      but it's cold in the alley
          & my heart's sick alone
and I'm clean, but my life's a mess
      Third Avenue
          and E. Houston Street
on the corner traffic island under a red light
wiping your windshield with a dirty rag

December 24, 1996

Happy New Year Robert & June

Happy New Year Robert & June
Tho I'd hoped to see you soon
I'd better say Happy Hanukkah too
Till I get your number that's new—
I'll be leaving for retreat,
Where they make me salt-free meat
along with Gelek Rinpoche
Who's got ailments same as me,
in Michigan Camp Copneconic
Where I'll room with Mr. Harmonic
Philip Glass in our Buddhist Class
Ten days later January 8
I'll go to Boston, rest & wait
the weekend in anticipation
Maybe a hernia operation
supervised by Dr. Lown
(cardiologist of wide renown
—I'd recommended him to you
elderly trustworthy smart & true)
—Recuperate a week with Ellie
Dorfman, eat yellow fish-yuckh jelly
with Gefilte fish, then best
Mid January home NY to rest
Maybe we'll see eachother then,
in any case let me know when.

Love, Allen
December 12, 1996

Diamond Bells

"Clear light & illusion body become one"

Hearing the all pervading scintillation of empty bells I realize
Napoleon had toes
Frankenstein's big toe
Hayagriva cosmic horse one big cleft toe
Virgin Mary white-toed married Joseph brown-toed, impregnated by
         a white dove transparent triple-toed
How many toes has God? Yahweh nobody knows his toes
Allah's toes? Mohammed, prophetic ten
Jesus Christ well-kissed human toes
Sealo the Seal Boy who two-fingered hand-flippers at shoulders could
         smoke & type with regular ten toes
sold tiny white toilets wrapped in toilet paper, souvenirs one dollar
Shelly ten pale pure toes
Michelangelo enjoyed five digits per foot, Da Vinci mapped ten on his
         two feet
Flies toes get stuck on spiderwebs
Spiders slide swift-toed on sticky nets
Scratch the sole, toes curl
Foetus is capable of toes
Stubbed my bare fourth toe on a step ladder one dark Friday night,
         though it still wiggles
walking on snowy mud's painful, back aches
John Madison has chocolate toes
Hitler natural toes
Buddha ten bare toes enlightened
Lay my skull on night pillows, rest on Tara's lap between gentle toes
Lama YabYum dreams with 20 toes
Emptiness innumerable trillion toes
Old men's toenails thicken ivory aged
Dead toenails grow in cenotaphs
Napoleon wore toenails inside polished riding boots
Elephant toenail stubs nudge tussocks
Such is the all pervading scintillation of empty bells

December 30, 1996, 12:55 A.M.

Virtual Impunity Blues

With Virtual impunity Clinton got campaign funds from pink Chinese
With Virtual impunity CIA Contra stringers sold Cocaine disease L.A.
    & Minneapolis
With Virtual impunity FBI burned down apocalyptic Waco
With Virtual impunity gov't began charging huge fees for public
    college studies
With Virtual impunity Congress FCC ok'd Fundamentalist Broadcast
    censorship
With Virtual impunity Family Values insulted ladies, gays, Afric
    Americans
With Virtual impunity the Pope banned planet birth control
With Virtual impunity N. Carolina banned sodomy in the wrong hole
With Virtual impunity the Chinese banned fresh speech electrics
With Virtual impunity Albanian Lottery bosses bought & sold elections

January 1997

Waribashi

Walk into your local Japanese restaurant Teriyaki Boy—
order sliced raw fish mackerel, smoked eel, roe on vinagered rice balls
slide thin wooden utensils out a white paper sleeve with blue Crane print
split the wood, rub ends together smooth down splinters, sit & wait & sigh—
200,000 cubic meters Southeast Asian timber exports
sawed & processed in Japan, resold, 20 billion waribashi
used once, thrown away—roots of rainforest destruction—help pay interest
Thailand's & Malaysia's yearly debt service to World Bank, IMF—
Your plate arrives with sharp green mustard & pink pickled ginger slices
new sprig of parsley, lift the chopsticks to your mouth enjoy sashimi

January 7, 1997, 6:30 A.M.

Good Luck

I'm lucky to have all five fingers on the right hand
Lucky peepee with little pain
Lucky bowels move
Lucky, sleep nights on a captain's bed, nap mid-afternoons
Lucky to amble down First Avenue
Lucky make a couple hundred thousand a year
singing Eli Eli, writing passing mind, etching primordial doodles,
      teaching Buddhist college, snapping Leica bus-stop photos
      thru my window eyeballs
Hear ambulance sirens, smell garlic & rust, taste persimmons &
      flounder, walk the loft floor barefoot soles a little desensitized
Lucky I can think, and sky can snow

January 8, 1997

Some Little Boys Dont

Some little boys like it
Some little boys dont
Some little girls swipe it
Some little girls won't

Some nephews suck it
Some lollypops grunt
Some nieces truck it
If grandpa's a runt

Some puberties request it
Four times a month
Some girl teens breast it
Some eat it for brunch

Some little people gargle
Some adolescents warble
Some teenyboppers babble
Some kiddies play Scrabble

January 10, 1997, 4 A.M.

Jacking Off

Who showed up?
        Joe S. pale bodied wiry leanness,
        suck your cock—I kissed his belly,
        thin muscular breast—
Suck my cock you bitch, little bitch
        suck my cock,
Huck, I got him on his knees
        licked his ass his hairy behind
        doggie style, jacked him off he
        grabbed his own dick finished—come.
Tom G. big cocked passed thru my
        dream bed, didn't stay
Ah John got you, bought the
        leather handcuffs & strap
        binding hand & feet helpless,
        Leather collar roped to the
        bedstead's head—buy it
        once for all S&M shops
        Christopher Street
        Uptown leather
Spank good & hard, slap his ass
        let him writhe, better
        than cutting him up,
        designs with razor—
So came on that unfamiliar fear
        savage control over
        Adonis body, willing
        eager—bound to be true.

January 28, 1997

Think Tank Rhymes

think tank
pick thank
lamb shank
wet wank
drug dork
hankie pankey
kitchey camp
namby pamby
macho wimp
witchy granny
randy daddy
skimpy mammie
toilet Tilly
itchy nursie
Golden Grammie
dandy Sammy

Fried pork
mind wonk
brain konk
junk funk
coke dink
dead drunk
Big Pink
skunk stink
mom wink
nuke kink
big dick
instinct
gum crank
space pork
fried wok

Hershey drink
Einstein

January 30, 1997, 2:45 A.M.

Song of the Washing Machine

Burned out Burned out Burned out
We're not burned out We're not burned out
for a house for a house for a house for a house
Bathroom Bathroom Bathroom Bathroom
At home at home at home at home
We're not burned out We're not burned out
Fair enough fair enough fair enough
Can you account for yourself account for yourself
Better not better not better not better not

January 31, 1997

World Bank Blues

I work for the world bank yes I do
My salary was hundred thousand smackeroo
I know my Harvard economics better than you

Nobody knows that I make big plans
I show Madagascar leaders how to dance
How to read statistics & wear striped pants

Emotional statistics that's not my job
Facts & figures, I'm no slob
But foresting & farming's all a big blob

Here's our scheme to stabilize your paper
for International trade right now or later
Follow our advice you'll thank your creator

Whatcha got to export, what raw materials?
Monoculture diamonds, coffee, Cereals
Sell 'em on the market to Multinational Imperials

We'll loan you money to expand production
Pay our yearly interest, for your own protection
Tighten your belts, we'll have no objection

Throw in some little minimal principle
tho debt service paid makes the deal invincible
That takes dollars but your currency's exchangeable

Get people working on mass market land
cut down forests, for your cash in hand
Or superhighways money where Rainforests stand

With agribusiness farms you can export beef
Cut social services & poverty relief
Forest people shift to the cities in grief

Tighten your belt for a roller coaster ride
Production's up, market prices slide
Wood pulp burger meat, coffee downside

Increase production pay yr. World Bank debt—
At least the interest if that's all you can get
Cut down Amazon you haven't paid it yet

In one decade you give all the money back
As Bank debt service but the Principal, alack!
We'll lend more cash (but dont sell smack)

Austerity measures, wages go down,
th'urban sewage is a charnel ground
Buses fall apart at the edge of town

coral reef fish dead factory waste,
Indigines hooked on Yankee dollar taste
Swiss bank funds for dictators disgraced

Fauna killed for the debt Costa Rica
Unknown flora at the mouth of Boca Chica
Birds in Equador, sick with toxic leakage?

Riots start over bags of foreign rice
Arm your teenage army with U.S. mace
Borrow money for a local Arms race

Families driven from crop land to forests
Forest folk in hovels hid from tourists
Currencies bankrupt for free market purists?

I just retired from my 20 year job
at World Bank Central with the money mob
Go to AA meetings so's not die a slob

I worked in Africa, Americas, Vietnam
Bangkok too with World Banks' big clan
Now I'm retired and I don't give a damn

Walk the streets of Washington alone at night
The job I did, was it wrong was it right?
Big mistakes that've gone out of sight?

It wasn't the job of a bureaucrat like me
to check the impact of the Bank policy
When debt bore fruit on the world money tree.

February 1997

Richard III

Toenail-thickening age on me,
Sugar coating my nerves, leg
      muscles lacking blood, weak kneed
Heart insufficient, a thick'd valve-wall,
Short of breath, six pounds
      overweight with water—
logged liver, gut & lung—up at 4 a.m.
      reading Shakespeare.

February 4, 1997, 4:03 A.M., NYC

Death & Fame

When I die
I don't care what happens to my body
throw ashes in the air, scatter 'em in East River
bury an urn in Elizabeth New Jersey, B'nai Israel Cemetery
But I want a big funeral
St. Patrick's Cathedral, St. Mark's Church, the largest synagogue in
          Manhattan
First, there's family, brother, nephews, spry aged Edith stepmother
          96, Aunt Honey from old Newark,
Doctor Joel, cousin Mindy, brother Gene one eyed one ear'd, sister-
          in-law blonde Connie, five nephews, stepbrothers & sisters
          their grandchildren.
companion Peter Orlovsky, caretakers Rosenthal & Hale, Bill Morgan—
Next, teacher Trungpa Vajracharya's ghost mind, Gelek Rinpoche
          there, Sakyong Mipham, Dalai Lama alert, chance visiting
          America, Satchitananda Swami,
Shivananda, Dehorahava Baba, Karmapa XVI, Dudjom Rinpoche,
          Katagiri & Suzuki Roshi's phantoms
Baker, Whalen, Daido Loori, Qwong, Frail White-haired Kapleau
          Roshis, Lama Tarchin—
Then, most important, lovers over half-century
Dozens, a hundred, more, older fellows bald & rich
young boys met naked recently in bed, crowds surprised to see each
          other, innumerable, intimate, exchanging memories
"He taught me to meditate, now I'm an old veteran of the thousand
          day retreat—"
"I played music on subway platforms, I'm straight but loved him he
          loved me"
"I felt more love from him at 19 than ever from anyone"
"We'd lie under covers gossip, read my poetry, hug & kiss belly to belly
          arms round each other"
"I'd always get into his bed with underwear on & by morning my
          skivvies would be on the floor"
"Japanese, always wanted take it up my bum with a master"

"We'd talk all night about Kerouac & Cassady sit Buddhalike then
        sleep in his captain's bed."
"He seemed to need so much affection, a shame not to make him happy"
"I was lonely never in bed nude with anyone before, he was so gentle my
        stomach
shuddered when he traced his finger along my abdomen nipple to hips—"
"All I did was lay back eyes closed, he'd bring me to come with mouth
        & fingers along my waist"
"He gave great head"
So there be gossip from loves of 1946, ghost of Neal Cassady commin-
        gling with flesh and youthful blood of 1997
and surprise—"You too? But I thought you were straight!"
"I am but Ginsberg an exception, for some reason he pleased me,"
"I forgot whether I was straight gay queer or funny, was myself, tender
        and affectionate to be kissed on the top of my head,
my forehead throat heart & solar plexus, mid-belly, on my prick,
        tickled with his tongue my behind"
"I loved the way he'd recite 'But at my back always hear/time's winged
        chariot hurrying near,' heads together, eye to eye, on a
        pillow—"
Among lovers one handsome youth straggling the rear
"I studied his poetry class, 17 year-old kid, ran some errands to his
        walk-up flat,
seduced me didn't want to, made me come, went home, never saw him
        again never wanted to . . ."
"He couldn't get it up but loved me," "A clean old man," "He made
        sure I came first"
This the crowd most surprised proud at ceremonial place of honor—
Then poets & musicians—college boys' grunge bands—age-old rock
        star Beatles, faithful guitar accompanists, gay classical con-
        ductors, unknown high Jazz music composers, funky trum-
        peters, bowed bass & french horn black geniuses, folksinger
        fiddlers with dobro tambourine harmonica mandolin auto-
        harp pennywhistles & kazoos
Next, artist Italian romantic realists schooled in mystic 60's India,
        late fauve Tuscan painter-poets, Classic draftsman Massa-
        chusetts surreal jackanapes with continental wives, poverty
        sketchbook gesso oil watercolor masters from American
        provinces

Then highschool teachers, lonely Irish librarians, delicate biblio-
       philes, sex liberation troops nay armies, ladies of either sex
"I met him dozens of times he never remembered my name I loved
       him anyway, true artist"
"Nervous breakdown after menopause, his poetry humor saved me
       from suicide hospitals"
"Charmant, genius with modest manners, washed sink dishes, my
       studio guest a week in Budapest"
Thousands of readers, "Howl changed my life in Libertyville Illinois"
"I saw him read Montclair State Teachers College decided be a poet—"
"He turned me on, I started with garage rock sang my songs in Kansas
       City"
"Kaddish made me weep for myself & father alive in Nevada City"
"Father Death comforted me when my sister died Boston 1982"
"I read what he said in a newsmagazine, blew my mind, realized
       others like me out there"
Deaf & Dumb bards with hand signing quick brilliant gestures
Then Journalists, editors' secretaries, agents, portraitists & photo-
       graphy aficionados, rock critics, cultured laborors, cultural
       historians come to witness the historic funeral
Super-fans, poetasters, aging Beatniks & Deadheads, autograph-
       hunters, distinguished paparazzi, intelligent gawkers
Everyone knew they were part of "History" except the deceased
who never knew exactly what was happening even when I was alive

February 22, 1997

Sexual Abuse

"A Nation of Finks"
—*W. S. Burroughs*

A voice in the kitchen light:
Sexual abuse should not be
      rewarded with a wink
Sexshual abuse should not be
      revarded mit a vink
Re Boston-Herald headline "Sexual Abuse Law Targets Clergy"
"Senator: Religious leaders must report child molesters"
Priests should turn each other in, fink—
So, say it in the confession box, not
      over sherry at intimate dinner.

February 26, 1997, 6 A.M.

Butterfly Mind

The mind is like a butterfly
That lights upon a rose
or flutters to a stinky feces pile
swoops into smoky bus exhaust
or rests upon porch chair, a flower breathing
open & closed balancing a Tennessee breeze—
Flies to Texas for a convention
spring weeds in fields of oil rigs
Some say these rainbow wings have soul
Some say empty brain
tiny automatic large-eyed wings
that settle on the page.

January 29, 1997, 2:15 A.M., NYC

A fellow named Steven

A fellow named Steven
went to look for God
on a street that's even
and a street that's odd

A lifestyle clean
with music and wife
A golden mean
For a heavenly life

He went to the city
Tried all tricks
Sadness & pity
many highs, many kicks

Saved by music
Books & dance bands,
Generous, correct
Taught class, steady hands

Married, had a boy
Whom he sang into life
He'll long enjoy
His Child & Wife

Air Shuttle Boston—N.Y.
March 4, 1997, 5 P.M. in milky sky

Half Asleep

Moved six months ago left it behind for Peter
He'd been in Almora when we bought it,
an old blanket, brown Himalayan wool
two-foot-wide long strips of light cloth
bound together with wool strings
That after 3 decades began to loosen
Soft familiar with use in Benares & Manhattan
I took it in my hands, searched to match the seams,
      fold them, sew together as I thought
But myself, being ill, too heavy for my arms,
Leave it to housekeeper's repair
      it disappeared suddenly in my hands—
back to the old apartment
where I'd let go half year before

                            March 7, 1997

Objective Subject

It's true I write about myself
Who else do I know so well?
Where else gather blood red roses & kitchen garbage
What else has my thick heart, hepatitis or hemorrhoids—
Who else lived my seventy years, my old Naomi?
and if by chance I scribe U.S. politics, Wisdom
meditation, theories of art
it's because I read a newspaper loved
teachers skimmed books or visited a museum

March 8, 1997, 12:30 A.M.

Kerouac

I can't answer,
reason I can't answer
I haven't been dead yet
Don't remember dead
I'm on 14th St & 1st Avenue
Vat's the qvestion?

March 12, 1997

Hepatitis Body Itch . . .

Hepatitis
Body itch
nausea
hemorrhage
tender Hemorrhoids
High Blood
Sugar, low
leaden limbs
lassitude
bed rest
shit factory
this corpse
cancer

March 13, 1997

Whitmanic Poem

We children, we
        school boys,
girls in America
        laborers, students
dominated by lust

March 18, 1997

American Sentences 1995–1997

I felt a breeze below my waist and realized that my fly was open.

April 20, 1995

* * *

Sitting forward elbows on knees, oh what luck! to be able to crap!

April 17, 1995

"That was good! that was great! That was important!" Standing to flush
the toilet.

June 22, 1995

Relief! relief! O Boy O Boy! That was necessary, wash behind!

January 18, 1997

"A good shit is worth a thousand dollars if your purse can afford it."

February 10, 1997, 5 A.M.

Heard at every workplace—obnoxious slogan: "Shit or get off the pot!"

January 24, 1997

How did I know? How did my ass know? Suddenly, go to the bathroom!

March 10, 1997

* * *

Château d'Amboise

Sun setting on their faces the diners chatter over plates of duck.

June 22, 1995

Baul Song

"Oh my mad mind, my mad mind, where've you been all my life, my old
    mad mind?"

October 7, 1996

The three-day-old kitchen fly's flown into my bedroom for company.

December 9, 1996

"Hi-diddly-Dee, a poet's life for me," Gregory Corso sang in Paris
    sniffing H.

January 16, 1997

Chopping apples for the fruit compote—suffer, suffer, suffer, suffer!

January 24, 1997

Courageous little lemon with so many pits! sliced into the pot.

January 25, 1997

The young dog—he jumped out the TV tube stood still then barked for
    supper.

January 26, 1997

Stupid of me, stupid of me, just dumb plain stupid ass! Where's my
    pen?

February 19, 1997, 2:45 A.M.

My father dying of Cancer, head drooping, "Oy kindelach."

February 24, 1997

Whatcha do about little girls who want to play Horsey on my knee?

March 10, 1997

"Hey Buster! Whatcha looking at me like that for?" in the Bronx
   subway.

March 10, 1997, 2:45 A.M.

To see Void vast infinite look out the window into the blue sky.

March 23, 1997

Variations on Ma Rainey's See See Rider

"I've been down at the bus stop
    Buy my jellyroll there
If I can't sell it in Memphis
        you can
  buy it in Eau St. Claire.
See See Rider
    you got me
        in your chair
    But if I have
      my fanny
        can sell it anywhere
    See what I want today
        yes yes yes
    Need a man who
        really can do
  anything I say
    Do that for me
        Then I
           guess I
   won't go way.

Go way go way go way from here
  look for all old gray home
  I can live by myself and
    ring my telephone
  Dirty pictures on my new TV
    Just now turned them on
  I don't need you and your
    mamma's long time gone

March 3, 1997

Sky Words

Sunrise dazzles the eye
Sirens echo tear thru the sky
Taxi klaxons echo the street
Broken car horns bleat bleat bleat

Sky is covered with words
Day is covered with words
Night is covered with words
God is covered with words

Consciousness covered with words
Mind is covered with words
Life & Death are words
Words are covered with words

Lovers are covered with words
Murders are covered with words
Spies are covered with words
Governments covered with words

Mustard gas covered with words
Hydrogen Bombs covered with words
World "News" is words
Wars are covered with words

Secret police covered with words
Starvation covered with words
Mothers bones covered with words
Skeleton Children made of words

Armies are covered with words
Money covered with words
High Finance covered with words
Poverty Jungles covered with words

Electric chairs covered with words
Screaming crowds are covered with words
Tyrant radios covered with words
Hell's televised, covered with words

March 23, 1997, 5 A.M.

Scatalogical Observations

The Ass knows more than the mind knows

Young romantic readers
Skip this part of the book
If you want a glimpse of life
You're free to take a look

Shit machine shit machine
I'm an incredible shit machine
Piss machine Piss machine
Inexhaustible piss machine

Piss & shit machine
That's the Golden Mean
Whether young or old
Move your bowels of gold

Piss & shit machine
It always comes out clean
Whether you're old or young
Never hold your tongue

(Chorus)
Shit machine piss machine
I'm an incredible piss machine
Piss machine piss machine
Inexhaustible shit machine.

Brown or black or green
everything will be seen
Hard or soft or loose
Shit's a glimpse of Truth

Babe or boy or youth
Fart's without a tooth
Baby girl or maid
Many a fart in laid

Shit piss shit piss
Fuck & shit & piss
Fuck fart shit Piss
It all comes down to this

Beautiful male Madonnas
Wrathful Maids of Honor
To be frank & honest
Stink the watercloset

Shit machine piss machine
Much comes down to this
Piss machine shit machine
Nature's not obscene

Shit piss shit piss
How'll I end my song?
Shit piss shit piss
Nature never wrong

(Chorus)
Shit machine Piss Machine
I'm an incredible piss machine
Piss machine shit machine
Inexhaustible shit machine

March 23, 1997

My Team Is Red Hot

My dick is red hot
Your dick is diddly dot

My politics red hot
Your politics diddly-plot

My President's red hot
your President's diddly-blot

My land is red hot
Your land is diddly-knot

My nation's red hot
Your nation's diddly rot

My cosmos red hot
Your cosmos diddly iddly squat

March 23, 1997

Starry Rhymes

Sun rises east
Sun sets west
Nobody knows
What the sun knows best

North star north
Southern Cross south
Hold close the universe
In your mouth

Gemini high
Pleiades low
Winter sky
Begins to snow

Orion down
North Star up
Fiery leaves
Begin to drop

March 23, 1997, 4:51 A.M.

Thirty State Bummers

Take a pee pee take a Bum
Take your choice for number one

Old man more or someone new
Take your choice someone new

President Clinton President Dole
Number three you're in a hole

Anchor two or anchor four
One's a liar one's a bore

Richard Helms Angleton live
We were lucky to survive

Jesse Helms & dirty pix
Dance your fate with his party mix

Idi Amin General Mobutu
Were paid by me & you

They were bought by me & mine
Albania, number 9

Mr. Allende was number 10
Pinochet Dictator then

Death squads in El Salvador
We paid D'Aubisson to score

Guatamalas by the dozen
Pat Robertson was country cousin

Rios-Montt the Indian killer
Born-again General Bible pillar

Nicaragua squeezed between
Col. North & a cocaine queen

Drug Czar Bush gave Company moolah
To Noriega Panama's ruler

Venezuela's Drug War Chief
Turned around to be a thief

Mexico's general drug-war head
pumped informers full of lead

State Department's favorite bloke
In Haiti he sold tons of coke

Till Aristide unhex'd the curse
CIA filled Cedras' Purse

White Peru's its Indian shame
Gave "Shining Path" worldwide fame

Then dictator Fujimori
Paid the World Bank hunky dory

With Indian Class the majority
Peru got respectable with poverty

Made a deal with English banks
To pay back USA with thanks

The price of rubber tin went down
Cocaine syndicates come to town

Now the money's in cocaine crops
U.S. Hellies do their dope air drops

We got rid of the President of Costa Rica
He had no army he didn't kill people

Lots began in '53
Guatemala couldn't break free

United Fruits annulled the vote
As Alan & Foster Dulles gloat

Then unseated Mosaddeq
& left Iran a police-state wreck

Then we sold the guy in Iraq
Money to bomb Iranians back

Central America Middle East
Preyed on by "Great Satan's" beast

Worst of all, & hell be damned!
Think what happened in Vietnam

Laos, victim of the war
Nobody really knew what for

Cambodia, caught by the tail
When we blew up Mekong's Ho Chi Minh Trail,

Descended into Anarchy
Pol Pot's Maoist Butchery

Shihanook's book before that day
Was called "My War with the CIA"

Who's to blame, Who's to blame
Anybody share America's shame

But there's more! Count the score!
So far we got twenty-four

25 is Afghanistan
Fundamentalists armed by The Man

Tribal Drug Lord Mountain gangs
Veiling up their own sex thangs

Looking around for number 26
Indochina was the Colonial sticks

France introduced the opium crop
France would sell the Chinese hop

Britain, U.S. got in on the deal
Opium war made the Emperor kneel

China opened to our own junk men
Shanghai famous for the opium den

Strung out on junk we took their silk
The yellow peril drank Christian milk

We're doing exactly the same thing again
In Indochina with Marlboro men

Smoke our dope to be Favored Nation
Nicotine cancer next generation

Who's pushing this new dope ring?
Senator Jesse Helms the Moralist King

Peaches Prunes & company goons
For the next two-hundred eighty eight moons

NAFTA NAFTA what comes after?
Toxic waste—Industrial laughter

Industrial Smog, Industrial sneers
Industrial women weeping tears

Wages low no CIO
No medical plan oh no! no! no!

No FDR No WPA
No toilet time, human say

No overtime no other way
Yankee work for a dollar a day

No jobs today No jobless pay
No future life but turn to clay

Work hard for a little bit of honey
But USA takes all the money

March 24, 1997, 10:40 P.M.

I have a nosebleed You have a nosebleed
He has a nosebleed three
She has a nosebleed It has a nosebleed
They all bleed on me

March 24, 1997

Timmy made a hot milk
Better than a warm milk
Better than a cold milk shake
Hot cream warm cream oh La La!
Pretty boy straight kids, Ha ha ha
Sneakers Jeans & T-shirts, damn!
Got it made said houseboy Sam
All except the Ku Klux Klan
Wham Bam & thank you ma'm

March 25, 1997, 6:30 A.M.

This kind of Hepatitis can cause ya
Nosebleed skin itch bowel nausea
Swell up hanging hemorrhoid heads
Easter lilies by your hospital beds

March 24, 1997

Giddy-yup giddy-yup giddy-yap
I can't take more of your crap
Giddy-yap Giddy-yap Giddy-yup
So you're right, so you're right, Shut up!
Giddy yup shut up, Giddy yup shut up
Giddy-yap giddy yap giddy yap shut up.

March 24, 1997

Turn on the heat & take a seat
& lookit junkies on the street

Forget the news from old Time-Warner
Lookit crackheads on the corner

Turn off TV 7 o'clock
They're selling grass around the block

Minimum wage is whacha make
Narcs are mostly on the take.

Make big money from your mob
Till Old MacDonald makes a job.

March 25, 1997

Bop Sh'bam

OO Bop Sh'bam
At the poetry slam
Scream & yell
At the poetry ball

Get in a rage
On the poetry stage
Make it rhyme
In double-time

Talk real fast
till your time's passed
Sound like a clown
& then sit down.

Listen to the next
'cause she listened to you
Tho all she says is
Peek-a-boo-boo.

March 25, 1997, 3:30 P.M.

Dream

There was a bulge in my right side, this dream recently—just now I realized I had a baby, full grown that came out of my right abdomen while I in hospital with dangerous hepatitis C.

I lay there awhile, wondering what to do, half grateful, half apprehensive. It'll need milk, it'll need exercise, taken out into fresh air with baby carriage.

Peter there sympathetic, he'll help me, bent over my bed, kissed me, happy a child to care for. What compassion he has. Reassured I felt the miracle was in Peter's reliable hands—but gee what if he began drinking again? No this'll keep him straight. How care for a baby, what can I do?

Worried & pleased since it was true I slowly woke, still thinking it'd happened, consciousness returned slowly 2:29 AM I was awake and there's no little mystic baby—naturally appeared, just disappeared—

A glow of happiness next morn, warm glow of pleasure half the day.

March 27, 1997, 4 A.M.

Things I'll Not Do (Nostalgias)

Never go to Bulgaria, had a booklet & invitation
Same Albania, invited last year, privately by Lottery scammers or
      recovering alcoholics,
Or enlightened poets of the antique land of Hades Gates
Nor visit Lhasa live in Hilton or Ngawang Gelek's household & weary
      ascend Potala
Nor ever return to Kashi "oldest continuously habited city in world"
      bathe in Ganges & sit again at Manikarnika ghat with Peter,
      visit Lord Jagganath again in Puri, never back to Birbhum take
      notes tales of Khaki Baba
Or hear music festivals in Madras with Philip
Or return to have Chai with older Sunil & the young coffeeshop poets,
Tie my head on a block in the Chinatown opium den, pass by Moslem
      Hotel, its rooftop Tinsmith Street Choudui Chowh Nimtallah
      Burning ground nor smoke ganja on the Hooghly
Nor the alleyways of Achmed's Fez, nevermore drink mint tea at Soco
      Chico, visit Paul B. in Tangiers
Or see the Sphinx in Desert at Sunrise or sunset, morn & dusk in the
      desert
Ancient collapsed Beirut, sad bombed Babylon & Ur of old, Syria's
      grim mysteries all Araby & Saudi Deserts, Yemen's sprightly
      folk,
Old opium tribal Afghanistan, Tibet-Templed Beluchistan
See Shanghai again, nor caves of Dunhuang
Nor climb E. 12th Street's stairway 3 flights again,
Nor go to literary Argentina, accompany Glass to Sao Paolo & live a
      month in a flat Rio's beaches & favella boys, Bahia's great
      Carnival
Nor more daydream of Bali, too far Adelaide's festival to get new song
      sticks
Not see the new slums of Jakarta, mysterious Borneo forests & painted
      men & women
No more Sunset Boulevard, Melrose Avenue, Oz on Ocean Way
Old cousin Danny Leegant, memories of Aunt Edith in Santa Monica

No more sweet summers with lovers, teaching Blake at Naropa,
Mind Writing Slogans, new modern American Poetics, Williams
       Kerouac Reznikoff Rakosi Corso Creeley Orlovsky
Any visits to B'nai Israel graves of Buba, Aunt Rose, Harry Meltzer and
       Aunt Clara, Father Louis
Not myself except in an urn of ashes

March 30, 1997, A.M.

Afterword
On Death & Fame

This final collection of Allen Ginsberg poems completes a remarkable half century of continuous verse creation. Allen leaves nothing out and takes the readers down a final walk of sickness and decline, but still the illumination of life shines through these strophes and rhythms. In these final five years, Allen struggles through several transformations. He is placed under the ever intensifying glare of media attention as a founder of the Beat Generation. He is interviewed as a living icon/prophet to each generation from the 1940s through the 1990s and is expected to elucidate the meaning of the century's conclusion and make new millennial predictions. The telephones ring continually for talk and advice on every subject from presidential politics to baby naming. He finally manages to place his lifelong archives into a permanent home at Stanford University. He is reviled in the *New York Times* on several occasions for "selling out." For the first time in his life, he buys himself a bit of comfort. At age seventy, he leaves his fourth-floor walk-up tenement apartment and moves into an elevator loft building still within his beloved Lower East Side of Manhattan. In these years, he embraces Jewel Heart Buddhist Center in Ann Arbor, Michigan, where he attends retreats, performs benefits, and receives profound and ultimate instructions from his teacher Gelek Rinpoche. Although struggling with illnesses continually, he does not learn of his fatal diagnosis until a week before his last breath. The poems follow these paths and illumine our own lives.

"New Democracy Wish List" was written at the request of *Long Island Newsday*. Allen polled his friends and collected advice on various subjects. The poem was sent to the White House and politely received. Allen's diabetes led to a state of dysesthesia below the waist. Allen transformed any shame of incontinence to a celebration of aging and life, as in "Here We Go 'Round the Mulberry Bush." It was Allen's habit to write poetry in his journals in the late night or the early morning. He would often write at dawn and then go back to sleep until late morning. His waking routine took several hours. There is a good sample of that routine in "Tuesday Morn." When Allen had collected several pages of poetry in his journals, he would photocopy them and hand them to his office to perform a first typing. Peter Hale typed them and returned them promptly. Allen would make alterations by hand and return them. Sometimes this process went on through ten drafts. We kept every draft in a file folder labeled with the title of the poem. Often slight rhythmic corrections to poems would come in after Allen returned from giving poetry readings. Allen Ginsberg was one of very few poets who had the opportunity to refine the exact cadence of his lines through his frequent public readings.

One of Allen's most beautiful song lyrics was "New Stanzas for *Amazing Grace*." Allen never ignored the homeless or beggars. He was generous to a fault and could not pass an outstretched hand without leaving a coin and looking deeply into the face beyond the hand. Allen lived comfortably within his modest fame. As he walked the streets of Lower Manhattan, people would nod to him in recognition or simply say "Hi Allen!" as they passed. If they stopped to recall when they last met him or ask a question, he was patient and conversed with them. If someone came up and said, "Are you Allen Ginsberg?" he might answer, "No, but that is what I am called." Allen was always supportive of the writers he admired and who were his friends. Notice in "City Lights City" which was written for the naming ceremony of Via Ferlinghetti, Allen used the occasion to create new literary renamings of streets for all the worthy writers of his circle.

"Pastel Sentences" were written in Allen's form of American Haiku (seventeen syllables with the common haiku associational enjambment of senses but carried through on a single strophe each). These sentences were composed to accompany a set of water colors by his friend, Francesco Clemente. There was a conciliation in Allen's poems; he was commingling his worldview with its detail of causes into Buddhist mindfulness and ego urges. He continued a flirtation with children's poetry in "The Ballad of the Skeletons" which was turned into a rock 'n' roll song with Paul McCartney, Philip Glass, and Lenny Kaye collaborating musically. Gus Van Sant made a music video. Memories from East Side High, Paterson, are explored in "You know what I'm saying?" Allen remembered the songs of his childhood ("Popular Tunes"). One day he walked around the loft trying to find his scarf. He sang a little ditty about the lost scarf, which became "Gone Gone Gone": a poem about loss, which was read at a Buddhist service the day after Allen's death.

Allen was unsteady on his feet, hesitant in his step, and exhausted in his frame. He had to fly the shuttle to Boston to see his cardiologist. I sensed that, for the first time, he didn't have the energy to fly by himself. "Allen, I'll go with you," I reassured him in the early twilight of a late February afternoon. He protested that it was not necessary. I insisted and he gave in happily.

I carried my bag and his. He shuffled with me. In the taxi to LaGuardia Airport, Allen asked for his book bag. The taxi was dark, only lit by the street lamps whisking by in an alternating stream. As the vehicle sped between lanes, I felt my stomach rise up to my throat and stick there. Allen said, "Listen to this. I started it last night!" He was laughing and cracking up. He searched in his journal and found the scrawled poem. It started:

When I die
I don't care what happens to my body
throw ashes in the air, scatter 'em in the East River
bury an urn in Elizabeth New Jersey, B'nai Israel Cemetery
But I want a big funeral

I wanted the cab ride to be over. I didn't want to hear the poem, but it got funnier and funnier. He was almost in hysterics as he listed what all his myriad boyfriends would say at his funeral. He wanted to know if I could add any lines. I suggested that women would all say, "He never did remember my name."

On the shuttle, Allen fell into a deep sleep. I stared at the deep lines in his face. He seemed so far away. I thought he might be dead. But at the beginning of our descent, he jerked awake, grabbed his notebook, scribbled for about two minutes, and read me this American sentence: "My father dying of Cancer, head drooping, 'Oy kindelach.'"

Allen's health continued to deteriorate. Poems were being written so fast that we could not keep up with them. Weeks after the trip to Boston, Allen entered Beth Israel Hospital in New York City. One of the doctors in the

Emergency Room handed Allen a poem he had written seeking Allen's improvements. Allen obliged and was pleased as he confided in me that it was "a much stronger poem now." In the hospital, Allen asked for a copy of *Mother Goose*. I brought my children's Rackham edition. "Starry Rhymes" injected pure beauty into the simple rhymes. The poetry of late March 1997 reflected Allen's lively mind balancing the primary hospital bodily events and his childhood innocence so long overridden in the need to grow up fast in a dysfunctional family.

Although we are unsure that Allen had finished with the rhymes dated March 24, 1997, we include them as exemplar of the pure, supple child Allen slipped in and out of in the late stages of liver cancer. "Dream" resolves contradictions inherent in his long love affair with Peter Orlovsky and remained the last poem written before the fatal diagnosis of liver cancer. After being told of the massive metastasized cancer within him, Allen Ginsberg only completed one poem in his final week of life. "Things I'll Not Do (Nostalgias)" is the only poem that Allen did not have a chance to proof and amend before his death. The poem is a compendium of farewells, with honest regrets and true Buddhist ability to let go. Allen was sad to leave the world, but he was also exhilarated.

Besides calling friends to take leave, and extract a few promises, he wrote a final political letter to President Clinton. He prefaces his note with, "Enclosed some recent political poems." Allen lapsed into his death coma before he could select the poems.

In preparing *Death & Fame*, Peter Hale, Bill Morgan, and myself have honored Allen's insistence on chronology and notes. We have included each poem as Allen fashioned it. We suspect that some of the short verse would be further revised and combined. These are the final poetry breaths—no more Allen Ginsberg. When Allen died many people felt as if a large hole gaped in their lives. Allen left many writings and songs to fill that hole. With *Death & Fame*, we find the circle will be unbroken.

Bob Rosenthal
July 7, 1998

Notes

(p. 1063) "New Democracy Wish List"

Ryan White Care Act—A federal program designed to provide support services for people with HIV/AIDS. The act was named for youth Ryan White, a hemophiliac who had contracted HIV through blood transfusion. His battle to return to school helped advance the rights of people living with AIDS.

SLA—Savings & Loan Association, a 1980's Federal program to bail out bankrupted savings & loan banks resulted in much mis-use and corruption.

Hand & Lavoro Bank Thuggery—Lavoro: Banca Nazionale del Lavoro.

(p. 1066) "Peace in Bosnia-Herzegovina"

Thich Nhat Hanh—(b. 1926) Zen monk, exiled from Vietnam, heads a retreat community in the south of France. Authored over seventy-five books.

Sakharov—Andrei Sakharov (1921–1989) Russian engineer and humanist, first known as "father of the Soviet Hydrogen Bomb" but soon realized radioactivity's hazards and in a series of articles confronted the Soviet government. In 1975, he was awarded the Nobel Peace Prize.

Albert Schweitzer—(1875–1965) Theologian, minister, medical missionary in Gabon, Organist, awarded the Nobel Peace prize in 1952. Schweitzer was in fact Sartre's cousin, though Sartre referred to him as "uncle Al."

(p. 1068) "After the Party"

Coemergent Wisdom—A key term in Vajrayana Buddhism referring to the simultaneous arising of samsara and nirvana, naturally giving birth to wisdom.

(p. 1069) "After Olav H. Hauge"

Olav H. Hauge—Norwegian poet (1908–1994). Trained as a gardener, his work was inspired by the natural world.

Bodø—Second largest city of northern Norway, just inside the Arctic Circle.

(p. 1074) "Tuesday Morn"

Exquisite Corpse—Literary Journal, edited by poet Andrei Codrescu.

Peter's flown—Peter Orlovsky

Sawang's . . . confirmation—*Sawang*: Previous title for Sakyong Mipham Rinpoche (see note, page 108). *Confirmation*: Or enthronement in Tibetan Buddhism, it is the formal recognition of an incarnation.

(p. 1076) "God"

Willendorf Venus—Late Stone-Age limestone statuette of Venus, found near the village of Willendorf, Austria.

39 patriarchs—In Chinese and Zen Buddhism, patriarch is the founder of a school and his successors. In some accounts lineages are traced back to 28 original Patriarchs in India, and many more in China, although never as a group of 39—. It's likely the Author remembered incorrectly here.

(p. 1078) "Excrement"

Polyhymnia—Polyhymnia (Polymnia) is one of the nine muses; sometimes considered the muse of Sacred Poetry.

(p. 1083) "Pastel Sentences"

The author had worked out a series of 108 seventeen syllable sentences describing individual pastel paintings by Francesco Clemente. With a copy of the catalogue, he continued to polish them as he traveled on. Included here are the sentences that the Author felt could stand alone without accompanying images.

(p. 1089) "Is About"

muggles—Hipster term for marijuana cigarette.

(p. 1091) "The Ballad of the Skeletons"

Yahoo—From Swift's *Gulliver's Travels*: A member of a race of brutes who have all the human vices, hence a boorish, crass, or stupid person.

Heritage Policy—Heritage Foundation: Conservative foundation think tank, often thwarting NEA projects, opposing social welfare programs and favoring strict FCC restrictions on "indecent" language. In their own words "One of the nations largest public policy research organizations."

NAFTA—North American Free Trade Agreement, passed by President Clinton and Congress over objections of many labor and environmental groups concerned about lowered workplace and ecological safeguards.

Maquiladora—Foreign-owned factories operating on the Mexican side of the U.S./Mexican border producing goods mainly for the U.S. market.

GATT—General Agreement on Tariffs and Trade.
I.M.F.—International Monetary Fund.

(p. 1097) "Bowel Song"
Bam—Seed syllable for Vajrayogini, one of the Author's principal Tibetan Buddhist practices.

(p. 1101) "Power"
Yuga—As in kaliyuga, Sanskrit for "age," as in the dark age.

(p. 1102) "Anger"
Carolyn—Carolyn Cassady.

(p. 1103) "Multiple Identity Questionnaire"
chela—Sanskrit term, literally "servant," though often used as the general word for a student, as in a spiritual student seeking guidance from a teacher.
neti neti—"Not this, not this." Vedantic process of discrimination by negation.
Maya—Sanskrit term in Buddhism meaning "deception, illusion, appearance," the continually changing impermanent phenomenal world of appearances and forms of illusion or deception which the unenlightened mind takes as the only reality.

(p. 1104) "Don't Get Angry with Me"
Chödok Tulku—Gelugpa school Tibetan Lama friend of Gelek Rinpoche, he was a guest speaker at a summer retreat attended by the Author. Because of nervousness or difficulty with English, he repeatedly interjected, "Don't get angry with me." The Author found it funny and innocent and wrote this poem during the lecture.
Tila, Mila, Marpa, Naro—Said here in prayer form, it is short for Tilopa, Milarepa, Marpa, Naropa (Gampopa). The line of saints or Mahasidhas of Kagupa lineage of Tibetan Buddhism.

(p. 1108) "Reverse the rain of Terror . . ."
Rocky Flats—Rockwell Corporation Nuclear Facility's Plutonium Bomb trigger factory, near Boulder, Colorado. Starting in the late '70s, the Author joined in many protests against the plant. In 1989 the FBI investigated the site, confirmed careless handling of radioactive materials, suspended activity there and subsequently shut it down, but only after a $2 billion failed attempt to get the plant back on line. Cleanup will continue into the next millennium.

(p. 1110) "Sending Message"

General Rios-Montt—Efrain Rios-Montt (b. 1926), Guatemalan dictator, rose to power in a 1982 coup lasting seventeen months. Claiming himself a "Born-Again" Christian reformer and backed by President Reagan, his campaigns were responsible for the destruction of native villages and the killing of tens of thousands of natives.

700 Club—Televangelist cable talk show, Christian Broadcasting Networks's Flagship program, founded by Pat Robertson.

(p. 1117) "Happy New Year Robert & June"

Robert & June—Robert Frank, June Lief.

(p. 1118) "Diamond Bells"

Hayagriva—One of the eight fierce protective deities, identified by a horse's head in Tibetan Buddhist iconology.

(p. 1120) "Waribashi"

See "Roots of Rain Forest Destruction," Khor Kok Pen, *Third World Resurgence*, no. 4, December 1990 (Malaysia, Third World Network), paraphrased in *The Debt Boomerang*, Susan George, 1992 (London, Pluto Press with Transnational Institute).

(p. 1130) "Death & Fame"

Trungpa Vajracharya—*Vajracharya*: In Tibetan Buddhism, Mantrayana-style meditation practice master. *Trungpa*: Chögyam Trungpa, Rinpoche (1939–1987), the Author's first meditation master (1971–1987), founder of Naropa institute and Shambhala centers, author of *Cutting Through Spiritual Materialism* and *First Thought Best Thought*, with introduction by Allen Ginsberg, 1984, both published by Shambhala Publications, Boston.

Gelek Rinpoche—Kyabje or Ngawang Gelek Rinpoche (b. 1939), friend and teacher to the Author, he is the founder of Jewel Heart Tibetan Buddhist centers. A refugee in India since 1959, where he gave up monastic life to better serve the Tibetan Buddhist lay community, in the late '70s he was directed by tutors to the Dalai Lama to begin teaching Western students. He currently resides in Ann Arbor, Michigan.

Sakyong Mipham Rinpoche—(b. 1962) The lineage holder of the Buddhist and Shambhala meditation traditions brought from Tibet by his father and teacher, Chögyam Trungpa Rinpoche. He is the leader of the international Shambhala community based in Halifax, Nova Scotia.

Satchitananda Swami—Sri Swami Satchidananda, founder of Integral Yoga Institute. Came to the United States from India 1966.

Dehorahava Baba—A yogi the Author met at the Ganges River across from Benares in 1963.

Karmapa XVI—(1924–1981) Sixteenth lama head of Milarepa lineage, Kagupa order of Tibetan Buddhism.

Dudjom Rinpoche—(1904–1987) Former lama head of Nyingmapa "old school" Tibetan teachings, founded by Padmasambhava.

Katigiri Roshi—Dainin Katagiri-Roshi (1928–1990), first Abbot of the Minnesota Zen Meditation Center in Minneapolis. Came to the United States from Japan in 1963. Taught and practiced in California and also assisted Suzuki-roshi at the San Francisco Zen Center.

Suzuki Roshi—Shunryu Suzuki-roshi: Zen master of the Soto Lineage. Came to the United States in 1958 as head of the Japanese Soto sect in San Francisco, where he established a Zen Center. He built Zen Mountain Center at Tassajara Springs, the first Zen monastery in America. His Dharma heir is Richard Baker.

Baker Roshi—Richard Baker, Roshi, Abbot, head teacher, and founder of the Dharma Sangha centers, Crestone, Colorado, and Germany.

Whalen Roshi—Zenshin Philip Whalen (b. 1923), poet friend associated with the Beat Generation, now an ordained Zen Buddhist priest, he is Abbot of the Hartford Street Zen Center, San Francisco.

Daido Loori Roshi—John Daido Loori, Abbot of Zen Mountain Monastery in Mt. Tremper, New York, and the founder/director of the Mountains and Rivers Order. Master in Rinzai and Soto lines of Zen Buddhism. Dharma heir of Hakuyu Taizen Maezumi Roshi.

Kapleau Roshi—Philip Kapleau Roshi, Zen master, studied Zen in Japan, founded the Rochester Zen Center in 1966, author of many books on Zen practice.

Lama Tarchin—Nyingmapa school Tibetan Lama, founded the Vajrayana Foundation, Santa Cruz, California, at the request of HH Dudjom Rinpoche.

(p. 1133) "Sexual Abuse"
See article "Sexual Abuse Bill Targets Clergy," Mark Mueller, *Boston Herald* (February 21, 1997).

(p. 1136) "Half Asleep"
Almora—Town in Uttar Pradesh state of Northern India, near the foothills of the Himalayas.

(p. 1151) "Thirty State Bummers"
Idi Amin—Idi Amin Dada Oumee (b. 1925), president and dictator of Uganda from 1971–1979, responsible for the killing of 300,000 tribal Ugandans.

General Mobutu—Joseph Mobutu (1930–1997), president and dictator of Zaire from 1965–1991, supported by Western powers.

Mr. Allende—Salvador Allende Gossens (1908–1973), Popularly elected Democratic Socialist President of Chile, overthrown by a military coup supported by the CIA.

Pinochet—Augusto Pinochet Ugarte (b. 1915), president of Chile following the death of Allende.

D'Aubuisson—Roberto D'Aubuisson Arrieta, Death Squad Leader of Arena Party in El Salvador.

Pat Robertson—Conservative Baptist minister and television talk show host who ran for president in 1988.

Rios-Montt—(See note, p. 108.)

Col. North—Oliver L. North, Jr. (b. 1943), U.S. Marine Colonel and a key figure in the Iran-Contra affair.

Aristide—Jean-Bertrand Aristide (b. 1951), the first democratically elected leader of Haiti from 1990–1991 and 1994–1995.

Cedras—Lt. Gen. Raoul Cedras, Haitian military ruler who overthrew Aristide in 1991.

Fujimori—Alberto Fujimori (b. 1938), president of Peru.

United Fruits—Corporation that controlled much of the Central American fruit market and now part of United Brands Company. United Fruit Company's law firm, Sullivan and Cromwell, had employed State Secretary Dulles, whose brother, Allen, heading the CIA, coordinated the 1954 then-covert overthrow of Jacob Arbenz, elected president of Guatemala. The event is notorious throughout Latin America as a mid-twentieth-century example of "banana republic" repression by North American imperium. By 1980, the U.S.-trained Guatemalan military had reportedly killed 10 percent of jungle Indian population as part of a "pacification" program to "create a favorable business climate." (See note: Rios-Montt.)

Mosaddeq—Mohammad Mosaddeq (1880–1967), Democratically elected Iranian premier from 1951–1953 who nationalized Western oil holdings.

Pol Pot—(1928–1998), Prime Minister of Cambodia from 1976–1979 and former leader of the Khmer Rouge.

Sihanook—Norodom Sihanook, Prime Minister since 1955 and crowned king of Cambodia in 1993 for the second time.

(p. 1160) "Things I'll Not Do (Nostalgias)"

Kashi—Known now as Benares, a city in northern India, mentioned in ancient Buddhist writings.

Manikarnika ghat—Benares, India; steps near the river where corpses are burned.

Jagganath, Lord—Lord Jagganath is the form under which the Hindu god Krishna is worshipped in Puri, a town in eastern India.

Birbhum—A district in West Bengal state, northeastern India, home of nineteenth-century holy fool, Khaki Baba (see below).

Khaki Baba—North Bengali (Birbhum area), nineteenth-century saint who, dressed in khaki loincloth, is pictured sometimes sitting surrounded by canine friends and protectors.

Philip—Philip Glass, American composer.

Sunil—Sunil Ganguly, Indian poet-friend.

Choudui Chowh Nimtallah—Calcutta neighborhood where the Author lived in the summer of 1962, near the burning ghats.

Soco Chico—Square in the medina, Tangiers, where outdoor cafes were popular with the Author, William S. Burroughs, and Paul Bowles.

Paul B.—Paul Bowles, American writer living in Tangier.

Baluchistan—Baluchistan province in Pakistan, bordered by Afghanistan on the north and Iran on the west.

Dunhuang—Pinyin Dunhuang, city in western Kansu Sheng province, China.

Buba—(Yiddish) *Grandmother* Rebecca Ginsberg was Allen Ginsberg's grandmother, buried in this cemetery.

INDEX OF
TITLES, FIRST
LINES, AND
ORIGINAL
BOOK SOURCES

Poem titles appear in *italics*. Books in which the poems originally appeared are abbreviated as follows:

AD	*Airplane Dreams*	J	*Journals: Early Fifties Early Sixties*
AE	*As Ever*	Kaddish	*Kaddish*
AW	*Angkor Wat*	MB	*Mind Breaths*
CG	*Cosmopolitan Greetings*	Mss.	Unpublished Manuscript
D&F	*Death & Fame*	PAOTP	*Poems All Over the Place*
EM	*Empty Mirror*	PN	*Planet News*
Fall	*The Fall of America*	PO	*Plutonian Ode*
GW	*The Gates of Wrath*	RS	*Reality Sandwiches*
Howl	*Howl*	SDG	*Sad Dust Glories*
IH	*Iron Horse*	SHD	*Straight Hearts' Delight*
IJ	*Indian Journals*	WS	*White Shroud*

A bitter cold winter night, 273
A brown piano in diamond, 373
A Crazy Spiritual (EM), 83
A crow sits on the prayerflagpole, (CG), 1036
ADAPTED FROM Neruda's "Que dispierte el leñador" (PO), 704
A Desolation (EM), 64
A Dream (GW), 52
A drunken night in my house with a, 132
Aether (RS), 250
A faithful youth, 83
A fellow named Steven (D&F), 1135
A fellow named Steven (D&F), 1135
After All, What Else Is There to Say? (EM), 37
After Antipater (WS), 921
After Dead Souls (EM), 73
After 53 years, 730
After Lalon (CG), 1019
After Long Absence, I returned from the land of the dead (WS), 916
After midnite, Second Avenue horseradish Beef (CG), 948
Afternoon Seattle (RS), 158
After Olav H. Hauge (D&F), 1069
After the Big Parade (CG), 1010
After the Party (D&F), 1068
After Thoughts (Fall), 544
After Whitman & Reznikoff (PO), 740
After Yeats (PN), 351
A Ghost May Come (EM), 79
Ah, still Lord, ah, sweet Divinity, 28
Ah War (D&F), 1077
Ah War bigness addiction (D&F), 1077
Airplane Blues (WS), 859
Albany throned in snow! It's winter, Poe, 522

All afternoon cutting bramble blackberries, 143
Allen when you get angry you got two choices— (CG), 951
All over Europe people are saying, "Who knows?" (CG), 959
Alone, 341
a lot of mouths and cocks, 606
Always Ether Comes, 509
A Mad Gleam (GW), 24
A Meaningless Institution (EM), 23
America (Howl), 154
America is like Russia, 72
America I've given you all and now I'm nothing, 154
American Change (RS), 194
American Sentences (CG), 1048
American Sentences 1995–1997 (D&F), 1042
A Methedrine Vision in Hollywood (PN), 388
amid glasses clinking, mineral water, schnapps (D&F), 1068
An Asphodel (Howl), 96
An Atypical Affair (EM), 80
and ate so much the bill was five dollars, 63
And the Communists have nothing to offer but fat cheeks, 361
And the youth free stripling bounding along the Hills of Color, 673
An Eastern Ballad (GW), 26
A new moon looks down on our sick sweet planet, 538
Angelic Black Holes (CG), 1025
Anger (D&F), 1102
Angkor—on top of the terrace, 314
Angkor Wat, 314
An Imaginary Rose in a Book (GW), 57

An itch in the auditory canal scratches for years, (WS), 886

An Open Window on Chicago (Fall), 481

Anti–Vietnam War Peace Mobilization (Fall), 549

A Poem on America (EM), 72

A Prophecy (Fall), 504

A Public Poetry (WS), 869

Arguments (WS), 885

Arise ye prisoners of your mind-set (CG), 957

Art recalls the memory, 43

As I cross my kitchen floor the thought of Death returns, (CG), 979

As I'm no longer young in life (WS), 915

As I passed thru Moscow's grass lots I heard, 655

As Is you're bearing (WS), 901

As orange dusk-light falls on an old idea, 295

A Strange New Cottage in Berkeley (Howl), 143

A Supermarket in California (Howl), 144

At Apollinaire's Grave (Kaddish), 188

At gauzy dusk, thin haze like cigarette smoke, 642

A Thief Stole This Poem (CG), 1016

a thousand sunsets behind tramcar wires in open skies of Warsaw, 360

At midnight the teacher lectures on his throne, 741

At 66 just learning how to take care of my body (CG), 1045

A Typical Affair (EM), 71

Aunt Rose—now—might I see you, 192

Auto Poesy: On the Lam from Bloomington (Fall), 420

Autumn Gold: New England Fall (Fall), 469

Autumn Leaves (CG), 1046

A Very Dove (GW), 15

A very Dove will have her love, 15

A voice in the kitchen light: (D&F), 1133

A Vow (Fall), 468

A Western Ballad (GW), 21

Ayers Rock / Uluru Song (MB), 587

Aztec sandstone waterholes known by Moapa've, 728

'*Back on Times Square, Dreaming of Times Square*' (RS), 196

Bad Poem (D&F), 1115

Ballade of Poisons (PAOTP), 700

Balmy, hotter outside than in the living room— (WS), 843

Baltimore bones grown maliciously under sidewalk, 672

Bare skin is my wrinkled sack, 34

Battleship Newsreel (RS), 214

Bayonne Entering NYC (Fall), 427

Bayonne Turnpike to Tuscarora (Fall), 476

Because I lay my, 343

Because this world is on the wing and what cometh no man can know, 263

Because we met at dusk, 247

Beginning of a Poem of These States (Fall), 377

Being as Now has been re-invented (D&F), 1115

Be kind to your self, it is only one, 367

Bend knees, shift weight— (WS), 898

Big Beat (PN), 357

Big deal bargains TV meat stock market news paper headlines (CG), 1011

Big Eats (CG), 1011

Bill Burroughs in Tangiers slowly transfiguring into Sanctity, 269

Birdbrain! (PO), 746

Birdbrain runs the World, 746

Birds chirp in the brick backyard Radio (CG), 1017

Bixby Canyon (Fall), 505

Bixby Canyon Ocean Path Word Breeze (Fall), 567

Black Magicians, 332

Black Shroud (WS), 911

Blame the Thought, Cling to the Bummer (PO), 717

Blandly mother, 86

Blasts rip Newspaper Gray Mannahatta's mid day Air Spires, 546

Blessed be the Muses (RS), 133

Bop Lyrics (GW), 50

Bop Sh'bam (D&F), 1158

Born in this world, 649

Bowel Song (D&F), 1097

Brain washed by numerous mountain streams (CG), 968

brilliant network-lights tentacle dim suburbs, 521

Brooklyn College Brain (PO), 725

Brown Rice Quatrains (WS), 887

Brown stonepeaks   rockstumps, 530

Buddha died and, 669

Burned out Burned out Burned out (D&F), 1125

Busride along waterfront down Yessler under street bridge, 158

Butterfly Mind (D&F), 1134

Cabin in the Rockies (MB), 653

Cadillac Squawk (WS), 925

Café in Warsaw (PN), 358

Calm Panic Campaign Promise (CG), 1035
Candle light blue banners incense, 670
Capitol Air (PO), 751
Car Crash (Fall), 516
Carmel Valley (PN), 381
Cars slide minute down asphalt lanes in front of, 637
Car wheels roar over freeway concrete, 561
Catholicism capish (D&F), 1087
Cézanne's Ports (EM), 61
Chances "R" (PN), 401
Chicago to Salt Lake by Air (Fall), 498
China be China, B.C. Clay armies underground (WS), 913
CIA Dope Calypso (CG), 997
City Flats, Coal yards and brown rivers, 435
City Lights City (D&F), 1081
City Midnight Junk Strains (PN), 465
Cleveland, the Flats (Fall), 437
Clouds' silent shadows passing across the Sun, 697
C'mon Jack (PAOTP), 657
C'mon Pigs of Western Civilization Eat More Grease (D&F), 1071
Come All Ye Brave Boys (MB), 645
Come all you young men that proudly display, 645
Complaint of the Skeleton to Time (GW), 25
Consulting I Ching Smoking Pot Listening to the Fugs Sing Blake (Air Dreams), 434
Contest of Bards (MB), 673
Continuation of a Long Poem of These States (Fall), 383
Cool black night thru the redwoods, 382
Cosmopolitan Greetings (CG), 953
Coughing in the Morning, 469
covered with yellow leaves, 539
Crash (GW), 57
"Criminal possession of a controlled substance, 613
Crossing Nation (Fall), 507

Dawn, a mastiff howls on the porch across the street (WS), 926
Dawn's orb orange-raw shining over Palisades, 640
Deadline Dragon Comix (CG), 1018
Dear Jacob I received your translation, what kind (CG), 972
Dear Lord Guru who pervades the space of my mind (CG), 1009
Death & Fame (D&F), 1130
Death News (PN), 305
Death on All Fronts (Fall), 538
Death to Van Gogh's Ear! (Kaddish), 175

December 31, 1978 (PO), 722
"Defending the Faith" (PO), 750
Delicate eyes that blinked blue Rockies all ash, 513
Denver tower blocks group'd under gray haze, 620
Describe: The Rain on Dasaswamedh Ghat (PN), 303
Diamond Bells (D&F), 1118
Diana & Roger Napoleon's real estate empire (CG), 1045
Does that mean war on every boy with more than one earring on the same ear? (D&F), 1082
Done, Finished with the Biggest Cock (Fall), 474
Done, finished, with the biggest cock you ever saw, 474
Don't Get Angry with Me (D&F), 1104
Don't get angry with me (D&F), 1104
Don't Grow Old (MB), 659
"Don't Grow Old" (PO), 718
Don't send me letters   Don't send me poems (WS), 877
Dont smoke dont smoke dont smoke (CG), 1029
Do the Meditation Rock (WS), 863
Do We Understand Each Other? (GW), 17
Dread spirit in me that I ever try, 16
Dream (D&F), 1159
Dream Record: June 8, 1955 (RS), 132
"Drive All Blames into One" (MB), 669
Drowse Murmurs (PN), 365
Dylan is about the Individual against the whole of creation (D&F), 1089

Easter Sunday (Fall), 524
Eat Eat more marbled Sirloin more Pork'n (D&F), 1071
Ecologue (Fall), 550
Ego Confession (MB), 631
Élan that lifts me above the clouds (D&F), 1100
Elegy Che Guevara (Fall), 492
Elegy for Neal Cassady (Fall), 495
Elements on my table, 79
Elephant in the Meditation Hall (CG), 984
Empire Air (WS), 893
End of Millennium (CG), 1034
Entering Minetta's soft yellow chrome, to the acrid bathroom, 433
Enthroned in plastic, shrouded in wool, diamond crowned, 439
Epigram on a Painting of Golgotha (GW), 41
Eroica (PO), 748

European Trib. boy's face photo'd eyes opened, 492

Europe! Europe! (Kaddish), 179

Europe, Who Knows? (CG), 959

Everybody excretes different loads (D&F), 1078

Everyday (CG), 1042

Every time I read Pessoa I think (CG), 975

Excrement (D&F), 1078

Falling Asleep in America (Fall), 525

Father Guru (PO), 700

Father Guru   unforlorn, 702

Fie My Fum (GW), 31

Fifth Internationale (CG), 957

Fighting Phantoms Fighting Phantoms (WS), 884

Fighting phantoms we have car wrecks on Hollywood Freeway (WS), 884

First Party at Ken Kesey's with Hell's Angels (PN), 382

Five A.M. (D&F), 1100

Flash Back (Fall), 542

Flying Elegy (MB), 620

Footnote to Howl, 142

For Creeley's Ear (PAOTP), 671

for their descent, 133

Forty feet long sixty feet high hotel, 302

Four Haiku (J), 145

4 Sniffs & I'm High, 250

Fourth Floor, Dawn, Up All Night Writing Letters (PO), 744

Fragment 1956 (RS), 157

Fragment: The Names II (PAOTP), 269

Friday the Thirteenth (Fall), 546

From Great Consciousness vision Harlem 1948 buildings, 603

Full moon over the shopping mall, 727

Fun House Antique Store (CG), 1043

Funny Death (RS), 208

Fyodor (EM), 40

Galilee Shore (PN), 297

Garden State (PO), 726

General Mother Teresa (D&F), 1066

Get beat up on TV squirming on the ground for driving irregular (CG), 1024

Get It? (CG), 1024

"Giddy-yup giddy-yup giddy-yap" (D&F), 1156

Go back to Egypt and the Greeks, 24

God (D&F), 1076

God answers with my doom! I am annulled, 265

Going to Chicago (Fall), 514

Going to the World of the Dead (WS), 875

Going to the World of the Dead Stalin & Hitler in Bed (WS), 875

Gold beard combd down like chinese fire gold hair, 545

Gone Gone Gone (D&F), 1106

Good Luck (D&F), 1121

Gospel Noble Truths (MB), 649

Graffiti 12th Cubicle Men's Room Syracuse Airport (Fall), 543

Grandma Earth's Song (CG), 973

Grant Park: August 28, 1968 (Fall), 515

Graphic Winces (CG), 960

Grass yellow hill, 381

Gray clouds blot sunglare, mountains float west, plane, 519

Gray water tanks in gray mist, 476

Green air, children sat under trees with the old, 515

Green Valentine Blues (Mss.), 103

Gregory Corso's Story (EM), 75

Growing Old Again, 431

Grim Skeleton (PO), 698

Grim skeleton come back & put me out of Action, 698

G. S. Reading Poesy at Princeton (Fall), 545

Guru (PN), 364

Guru Om (Fall), 561

Hadda be flashing like the Daily Double, 643

Hadda Be Playing on the Jukebox (MB), 643

Half Asleep (D&F), 1136

Happening Now? (WS), 868

Happening now? End of Earth? Apocalypse days? (WS), 868

Happy New Year Robert & June (D&F), 1117

Happy New Year Robert & June (D&F), 1117

Hard Labor (CG), 948

Haunting Poe's Baltimore (MB), 672

Havana 1953 (RS), 100

"Have You Seen This Movie?" (Fall), 563

Headless husk legs wrapped round a grass spear, (WS), 883

Hearing the all pervading scintillation of empty bells I realize (D&F), 1118

Heat (IJ), 302

He cast off all his golden robes, 65

He drags his bare feet, 98

Hepatitis (D&F), 1139

Hepatitis Body Itch . . . (D&F), 1139

Here at the atomic Crack-end of Time XX Century, 388

Here We Go 'Round the Mulberry Bush (D&F), 1073

He rises he stretches he liquefies he is hammered again, 173

High on Laughing Gas, 197

Hiway Poesy: L.A.–Albuquerque–Texas–Wichita (Fall), 390

Holy Ghost on the Nod over the Body of Bliss (PN), 475

Holy! Holy! Holy! Holy! Holy! Holy!, 142

Homage Vajracarya (WS), 850

Homeless Compleynt (D&F), 1116

Homework (PO), 739

Hospital Window (MB), 642

How Come He Got Canned at the Ribbon Factory (EM), 68

How'd I get angry (D&F), 1102

Howl (Howl), 134

How lucky we are to have windows! (WS), 895

How sick I am, 74

Huffing puffing upstairs downstairs telephone (CG), 1012

Hum Bom! (CG), 1004

Hūṃ Bom! (Fall), 576

hundred million cars running out of gasoline, 604

Hymn (EM), 44

I Am a Victim of Telephone (PN), 352

I am Fake Saint, 717

I am I, old Father Fisheye that begat the ocean, 267

I am married and would like to fuck someone else, 543

I Am Not (WS), 881

I am summoned from my bed (WS), 889

I am the King of the Universe (CG), 971

I attempted to concentrate (EM), 41

I Beg You Come Back & Be Cheerful (RS), 243

I came home and found a lion in my living room, 182

I came home from the movies with nothing on my mind, 81

I cannot sleep, I cannot sleep, 18

I can't answer (D&F), 1138

I climbed the hillside to the lady's house (CG), 941

I'd been motoring through States & (CG), 1043

I don't like the government where I live, 751

I dreamed I dwelled in a homeless place (D&F), 1080

I drove out to the airport on a blue sunny day (WS), 859

I dwelled in Hell on earth to write this rhyme, 13

I feel as if I am at a dead (EM), 79

I felt a breeze below my waist and realized my fly was open. (D&F), 1141

If Hanson Baldwin got a bullet in his brain, outrage, 498

If I had a Green Automobile, 91

If it weren't for you Mr Jukebox with yr aluminum belly, 296

If I were doing my Laundry I'd wash my dirty Iran, 739

If money made the mind more sane, 35

If my pen hand were snapped by a Broadway truck, 740

If you want to learn how to meditate (WS), 863

Ignu (Kaddish), 211

I got old & shit in my pants (D&F), 1073

I hauled down lifeless mattresses to sidewalk refuse-piles, 537

"I have a nosebleed . . ." (D&F), 1156

I Have Increased Power (EM), 76

I hope my good old asshole holds out (CG), 950

I lay down to rest weary at best (WS), 852

I Lay Love on My Knee (MB), 688

I'll go into the bedroom silently and lie down, 123

I'll settle for Immortality— (CG), 1036

I'll tell my deaf mother on you! Fall on the floor, 691

I Love Old Whitman So (WS), 900

Imaginary Universes (Fall), 520

I'm a Prisoner of Allen Ginsberg (WS), 882

I'm a traveler in a strange country (WS), 905

I'm crying all the time now, 159

I'm delighted by the velocity of money as it whistles (CG), 949

I met Einstein in a dream, 595

I'm happy, Kerouac, your madman Allen's, 131

Imitation of K.S. (CG), 961

I'm Jewish because love my family matzoh ball soup (CG), 1013

I'm late, I'm gonna die before I mark (CG), 1018

I'm lucky to have all five fingers on the right hand (D&F), 1121

I'm not a lesbian screaming in the basement strapped (WS), 881

Improvisation in Beijing (CG), 937

I'm sick of arguments (WS), 885

In a car Gray smoke over Elmira, 542

In a Moonlit Hermit's Cabin (Fall), 535

In a thousand years, if there's History, 550

In back of the real (Howl), 121

In bed on my green purple pink, 275
Incense under Horse Heaven Hills, 526
In Death, Cannot Reach What Is Most Near (EM), 42
Independence Day (Fall), 534
Industrial Waves (WS), 845
I needed a young musician take off his pants (WS), 888
In highschool when you crack your front tooth (CG), 960
"In later days, remembering this I shall certainly go mad.", 607
In Memoriam: William Cannastra, 1922–1950 (GW), 65
In My Kitchen in New York (WS), 898
In nineteen hundred forty-nine (CG), 997
I noticed the grass, I noticed the hills, I noticed the highways, (CG), 967
In Russia the tyrant cockroach mustache ate 20 million souls (CG), 943
In Society (EM), 11
In the Baggage Room at Greyhound (Howl), 161
In the Benjo (CG), 1046
In the depths of the Greyhound Terminal, 161
In the foreground we see time and life, 61
Into the Flats, thru Cleveland's, 437
In the mud, in the night, in Mississippi Delta roads (CG), 962
I nurs'd love where he lay, 688
I place my hand before my beard with awe, 347
I received in mail   offer beautiful certificate, 665
Iron Horse (IH), 440
Irritable Vegetable (WS), 877
Is About (D&F), 1089
I saw the best minds of my generation destroyed by madness, starving, 134
I sit because the Dadaists screamed on Mirror Street (WS), 851
I speak of love that comes to mind, 26
I started down Capitol Hill side along unfamiliar black central (CG), 973
Is that the only way we can become like Indians, like Rhinoceri, (CG), 947
Is this the God of Gods, the one I heard about, 475
It is a multiple million eyed monster, 239
It is here, the long Awaited bleap-blast light that Speaks, 280
It is the moon that disappears, 364
It's All So Brief (WS), 899
It's everybody's fault but me, 669

It's true I got caught in (CG), 1019
It's true I write about myself (D&F), 1137
It used to be, farms, 726
I've a pain in my back Fifth lumbar & sacrum (WS), 918
"I've been down at the bus stop" (D&F), 1144
I've climbed the Great Wall's stone steep out of breath (WS), 921
I've got to get out of the sun, 306
I've got to give up (WS), 899
I visited Père Lachaise to look for the remains of Apollinaire, 188
I waked at midmost in the night, 52
I walked into the cocktail party, 11
I walked on the banks of the tincan banana dock, 146
I walked out on the lamp shadowed concrete at midnight, 703
I want to be known as the most brilliant man in America, 631
I was born in Wyoming, Cody is my home town, 690
I was given my bedding, and a bunk, 23
I was high on tea in my fo'c'sle near the forepeak hatch, 214
I was shy and tender as a 10 year old kid, you know what I'm saying? (D&F), 1096
I went in the forest to look for a sign, 103
I Went to the Movie of Life (CG), 961
I will haunt these States, 468
I will have to accept women, 292
I work for the world bank yes I do (D&F), 1126
I write poetry because the English word Inspiration (CG), 937

Jacking Off (D&F), 1123
Jaweh and Allah Battle (MB), 622
Jaweh with Atom Bomb, 622
Joe Blow has decided, 69
John (CG), 1014
Journal Night Thoughts (PN), 275
Jumping the Gun on the Sun (WS), 922
"Junk Mail" (PAOTP), 665
Just Say Yes Calypso (CG), 1002

Kaddish (Kaddish), 217
Kali Ma tottering up steps to shelter tin roof, 303
Kansas City to Saint Louis (Fall), 421
Kerouac (D&F), 1138
Kiss Ass (Fall), 501
Kissass is the Part of Peace, 501
Kral Majales (PN), 361

Kunming Hotel, I vomited greasy chicken (WS), 911

Lack Love (PO), 701
Land O'Lakes, Wisc., (MB), 669
Land O'Lakes, Wisconsin: Vajrayana Seminary (PAOTP), 670
Last night I dreamed, 60
Last Night in Calcutta (PN), 309
Las Vegas: Verses Improvised for El Dorado H.S. Newspaper (PO), 728
Late sun opening the book, 105
Laughing Gas (Kaddish), 197
Lay down   Lay down yr mountain   Lay down God, 651
Leaving K.C. Mo.   past Independence past Liberty, 421
lemme kiss your face, lick your neck, 621
Let me say beginning I don't believe in Soul, 625
Let some sad trumpeter stand, 196
Let the Railsplitter Awake, 704
Listen to the tale of the sensitive car, 174
Living in an apartment with a gelded cat, 71
London Dream Doors (CG), 952
—Long enough to remember the girl, 80
Long Live the Spiderweb (EM), 54
Long since the years, 356
Long stone streets inanimate, repetitive machine Crash, 501
Looking over my shoulder, 145
Lord Heart, heal my right temple bang'd soft pain, 611
Lord Lord I got the sickness blues, I must've done something wrong, 647
Love came up to me, 692
Love Comes (WS), 852
Love Forgiven (PO), 737
Love Poem on Theme by Whitman (RS), 123
Love Replied (PO), 692
Love Returned (PO), 720
Love returned with smiles, 720
Love wears down to bare truth, 701
Lunchtime (CG), 1017
Lysergic Acid (Kaddish), 239

Magic Psalm (Kaddish), 263
Malest Cornifici Tuo Catullo (RS), 131
Manhattan May Day Midnight (PO), 703
Manhattan Thirties Flash (Fall), 501
Manifesto (MB), 625
Man's glory (J), 268
Many Loves, 164
Many prophets have failed, their voices silent, 745

Many seek and never see, 15
Marijuana Notation (EM), 74
Marlene Dietrich is singing a lament, 62
Maturity (WS), 872
Maybe Love (PO), 731
Maybe love will come, 731
May Days 1988 (CG), 979
Memory Cousins (WS), 916
Memory Gardens (Fall), 539
Mescaline (Kaddish), 236
Message (Kaddish), 191
Message II (PN), 356
Metaphysics (EM), 41
Mexcity drugstore table, giant, 511
Mice ate at the big red heart in her breast, she was distracted in love. (D&F), 1083
Midwinter night, 481
Milarepa Taste (Fall), 565
Millions of babies watching the skies, 579
Millions of people cheering and waving flags for joy in Manhattan (CG), 1010
Mind Breaths (MB), 617
Mistaken Introductions (CG), 995
Moral Majority (WS), 917
Morning (PN), 345
Moved six months ago left it behind for Peter (D&F), 1136
Mugging (MB), 633
Multiple Identity Questionnaire (D&F), 1103
Must be thousands of sweet gourmets rustling through, 588
My Alba (RS), 97
My dick is red hot (D&F), 1149
My love has come to ride me home, 17
My Sad Self (RS), 209
My Team Is Red Hot (D&F), 1149

Nagasaki Days (PO), 707
Nanao (CG), 969
"Nature empty, everything's pure; (D&F), 1103
Nazi Capish (D&F), 1087
Neal Cassady was my animal: he brought me to my knees, 164
Never go to Bulgaria, had a booklet & invitation (D&F), 1160
New Democracy Wish List (D&F), 1063
News Bulletin (PAOTP), 613
New Stanzas for Amazing Grace (D&F), 1080
News Stays News (CG), 1045
Newt Gingrich Declares War on "McGovernik Counterculture" (D&F), 1082

Night Gleam (MB), 609

No hyacinthine imagination can express this clock of meat, 44

No! No! (D&F), 1112

No! No! It's Not the End (D&F), 1112

No one liked my hair (CG), 1014

Northwest Passage (Fall), 586

Not Dead Yet (CG), 1012

Nov. 23, 1963: Alone (PAOTP), 341

Now and Forever (CG), 1036

Now I have become a man, 67

Now I'll record my secret vision, impossible sight of the face of God, 246

Now incense fills the air, 351

Now mind is clear, 64

Now Richard Secord and Oliver North (CG), 1000

Now that I've wasted, 97

Now that Samurai bow & arrow, Sumi brush, (WS), 850

Now to the come of the poem, let me be worthy, 157

N.S.A. Dope Calypso (CG), 1000

Numbers in U.S. File Cabinet (CG), 982

Nymph and shepherd raise electric tridents, 401

Objective Subject (D&F), 1137

O dear sweet rosy, 96

Ode: My 24th Year (GW), 67

Ode to Failure (PO), 745

Ode to the Setting Sun (GW), 46

O Future bards, 504

Oh dry old rose of God, 57

"Oh just hanging around picking my nose . . ." (WS), 870

O I am happy! O Swami Shivananda—a smile, 353

Oil brown smog over Denver, 636

OK Neal, 495

Old Love Story (WS), 856

Old maple hairytrunks root asphalt grass marge, 563

Old moon my eyes are new moon with human footprint, 171

Old Poet, Poetry's final subject glimmers months ahead, 659

Old Pond (PO), 715

Oleta (Snake) River! (CG), 987

OM—the pride of perfumed money, music food from China, 597

On a bare tree in a hollow place, 41

On Burroughs' Work (RS), 122

On Cremation of Chögyam Trungpa, Vidyadhara (CG), 967

One day 3 poets & 60 ears sat under a green-striped, 707

100,000,000 buffalo 17th century on North American Plains (CG), 982

One Morning I took a Walk in China (WS), 903

On Illness (PAOTP), 611

On London's Tavern's wooden table, been reading Kit Smart— (CG), 952

On Neal's Ashes (Fall), 513

On Neruda's Death (MB), 615

On Reading William Blake's "The Sick Rose" (GW), 14

On the Conduct of the World (CG), 947

On top of that if you know me I pronounce you an ignu, 211

On Via Ferlinghetti & Kerouac Alley young heroes muse melancholy 2025 A.D. (D&F), 1081

OO Bop Sh'bam (D&F), 1158

Opening a bus window in N.Y., 668

Orange hawkeye stronger than thought winking above, 534

Organs and War News, 384

or this marvellous hi Lama followed (CG), 995

O Statue of Liberty Spouse of Europa Destroyer of Past, 298

Over and over thru the dull material world the call is made, 609

Over Denver Again (Fall), 519

Over Kansas (RS), 124

over knowledge of death, 76

Over Laramie (Fall), 566

Pardon me buddy, I didn't mean to bug you (D&F), 1116

Pastel Sentences (Selections) (D&F), 1083

Past Silver Durango Over Mexic Sierra-Wrinkles (Fall), 512

Paterson (EM), 48

Path crowded with thistle fern blue daisy, 505

Patna–Benares Express (PN), 308

Peace in Bosnia-Herzegovina (D&F), 1066

Pentagon Exorcism (PN), 491

Personals Ad (CG), 970

Pertussin (Fall), 509

Philadelphia city lights boiling under the, 590

Pigeons shake their wings on the copper church roof, 744

Plastic & cellophane, milk cartons & yogurt containers, (WS), 880

Please Master (Fall), 502

Please master can I touch your cheek, 502

Please Open the Window and Let Me In (GW), 39

Plutonian Ode (PO), 710
Portland Coliseum (PN), 373
Poem in the Form of a Snake (CG), 987
POEM Rocket (Kaddish), 171
Poems rise in my brain, 654
POET is Priest, 175
Poet professor in autumn years (CG), 970
Popular Tunes (D&F), 1098
Porch Scribbles (WS), 843
Power (D&F), 1101
Proclamation (CG), 971
"Progress" ended in XX century. (D&F), 1063
Prophecy (WS), 916
Psalm I (EM), 26
Psalm II (GW), 28
Psalm III (RS), 163
Psalm IV (J), 246
Pull my daisy, 31
Pull my daisy, 32
Pull My Daisy (GW), 32
Punk Rock Your My Big Crybaby (PO), 691
Pussy Blues (PAOTP), 658
Put Down Your Cigarette Rag (CG), 1029

railroad yard in San Jose, 121
Rain-wet asphalt heat, garbage curbed cans (Fall), 537
reaching my own block, 78
Reading Bai Juyi (WS), 905
Reading French Poetry (PAOTP), 654
Reading No Nature in the toilet (CG), 1047
Ready to Roll (RS), 167
Real as a dream, 311
Reality is a question, 58
Red cheeked boyfriends tenderly kiss me sweet mouthed, 743
Red Guards battling country workers, 484
Red Scabies on the Skin, 509
Reflections at Lake Louise (PO), 741
Reflections in Sleepy Eye (Fall), 532
Refrain (GW), 19
Research (CG), 1026
Research has shown that black people have inferiority complexes (CG), 1026
Retire abandon world sd Swami Bhaktivedanta, 610
Returning North of Vortex (Fall), 484
Returning to the Country for a Brief Visit (MB), 607
Return of Kral Majales (CG), 984
Reverse the rain of Terror . . . (D&F), 1108
Reverse the rain of Terror on street consciousness U.S.A. (D&F), 1108
Rexroth's face reflecting human, 160

Richard III (D&F), 1129
Rising above the used car lots & colored dumps of Long Island (WS), 893
Rising over night-blackened Detroit Streets (Fall), 521
Rolling Thunder Stones (MB), 651
Rose of spirit, rose of light, 14
Rotting Ginsberg, I stared in the mirror naked today, 236
Ruhr-Gebiet (PO), 734

Sad Dust Glories (MB), 626
said Rinpoche Chögyam Trungpa Tulku in the marble, 600
Sakyamuni Coming Out from the Mountain (RS), 98
Said the Presidential Skeleton (D&F), 1091
Salutations to Fernando Pessoa (CG), 976
Sather Gate Illumination (RS), 150
Scatalogical Observations (D&F), 1147
Scribble (RS), 160
Seabattle of Salamis Took Place off Perama (PN), 296
Sending Message (D&F), 1110
September on Jessore Road (Fall), 579
Setting out East on rain bright highways, 420
Seven years' words wasted, 54
Sexual Abuse (D&F), 1133
Shines on top of Mountains where Grey Stone monastery sits, 268
Shining Diamonds & Sequins glitter, 722
Sickness Blues (MB), 647
Siesta in Xbalba (RS), 105
Sincerity is the key to living in Eternity (WS), 922
Since we had changed, 191
Sitting on a tree stump with half cup of tea, 653
Sitting on the twelfth floor Gomden I heard a wild siren (WS), 925
Sky Words (D&F), 1145
Slope woods' snows melt, 524
Smog trucks mile after mile high wire, 427
Smoke Rolling Down Street (Fall), 509
Snow-blizzard sowing, 516
Snow mountain fields, 620
Some breath breathes out Adonais & Canto General, 615
Some Little Boys Dont (D&F), 1122
Some little boys like it (D&F), 1122
Some live on islands, hills near Trondheim (D&F), 1069
Some Love (PO), 730
Something evil about you Mr. Viguerie Mr. Falwell (WS), 917

Some think the love of boys is wicked in the world, (WS), 856

Sometime I'll lay down my wrath, 38

Sometime Jailhouse Blues (GW), 38

Sometimes when my eyes are red, 209

Song (Howl), 119

Song of the Washing Machine (D&F), 1125

Sonora Desert-Edge (Fall), 530

Soul to crotch the streets commit hara-kiri, (CG), 1025

Sphincter (CG), 950

Spot Anger (CG), 951

Spring Fashions (PO), 727

Squeal (RS), 173

Stage-lit streets, 383

Stand up against governments, against God. (CG), 954

Stanzas: Written at Night in Radio City (GW), 35

Starry Rhymes (D&F), 1150

Starting with eyeball kicks, 124

Still night. The old clock Ticks, 309

Stool Pigeon Blues (PO), 690

Stopping on the bus from Novi Pazar in the rain, 750

Stotras to Kali Destroyer of Illusions (PN), 298

Straight and slender, 737

Strange now to think of you, gone without corsets & eyes, 217

Student Love (WS), 896

Students danced with wooden silvered swords, (WS), 903

Studying the Signs (PN), 371

Sunday Prayer (WS), 886

Sunflower Sutra (Howl), 146

Sunrise dazzles the eye (D&F), 1145

Sun rises east (D&F), 1150

Sunset (EM), 45

Sunset S.S. Azemour (PN), 295

Supplication for the Rebirth of the Vidyadhara Chögyam Trungpa (CG), 1009

Surprise Mind (WS), 895

Swan Songs In the Present (D&F), 1105

"Swan songs in the present (D&F), 1105

Sweet Boy, Gimme Yr Ass (MB), 621

Sweet Levinsky (GW), 27

Sweet Levinsky in the night, 27

Swirls of black dust on Avenue D (Fall), 510

Switch on lights yellow as the sun, 465

Take a pee pee take a Bum (D&F), 1151

Take my love, it is not true, 25

Tears (RS), 159

Television Was a Baby Crawling Toward That Deathchamber (PN), 280

"τεθνάκην δ ὀλίγω 'πιδεύης φαίνομ' ἄλαία" (PO), 743

Teton Village (MB), 620

That tree said I don't like that white car under me, (WS), 849

That which pushes upward, 434

The air is dark, the night is sad, 19

The Archetype Poem (EM), 69

The Ballad of the Skeletons (D&F), 1091

The Blue Angel (EM), 62

The boy's fresh faced, 18, big smile (WS), 896

The Bricklayer's Lunch Hour (EM), 12

The Change: Kyoto–Tokyo Express (PN), 332

The Charnel Ground (CG), 1038

The death's head of realism, 40

The delicate french girl jukebox husky lament, 431

The 18 year old marine "had made his Peace with God." (D&F), 1076

The End (Kaddish), 267

The Eye Altering Alters All (GW), 15

The fact is, the Russians are sissies (WS), 869

The first I looked on, after a long time far from home, 194

The first time I went, 75

The flower in the glass peanut bottle formerly in the kitchen, 148

The Green Automobile (RS), 91

The Guest (WS), 918

The Lama sat (CG), 1042

The Lion for Real (Kaddish), 182

The Little Fish Devours the Big Fish (WS), 865

The method must be purest meat, 122

The mind is like a butterfly (D&F), 1134

The Moments Return (PN), 360

The music of the spheres—that ends in Silence, 208

The Names (SHD), 184

The New Right's a creepy pre-Fascist fad (WS), 845

The Night-Apple (EM), 60

The night café—4 A.M., 100

The N Power, the feminine power (D&F), 1101

The old pond—a frog jumps in, kerplunk, 715

The Old Village Before I Die, 433

The *Olympics* have descended into, 357

The Question (WS), 897

There is more to Fury, 57

The Reply (Kaddish), 265

There was a bulge in my right side, this dream recently— (D&F), 1159

There was this character come in, 68

These are the names of the companies that have made money, 494

These days steal everything (CG), 1016

These knowing age (D&F), 1070

These knowing age (D&F), 1070

These psalms are the workings of the vision haunted mind, 26

These spectres resting on plastic stools, 358

These States: into L.A. (Fall), 384

These States: to Miami Presidential Convention (PAOTP), 590

The Shrouded Stranger (EM), 55

The Shrouded Stranger (GW), 34

The Shroudy Stranger's reft of realms, 55

The Terms in Which I Think of Reality (EM), 58

The Trembling of the Veil (EM), 22

The Voice of Rock (GW), 18

The Warrior is afraid, 738

The weight of the world, 119

The whitewashed room, roof, 301

The whole, 671

The whole blear world, 45

The wrathful East of smoke and iron, 46

They are sending a message to the youth of America (D&F), 1110

The young kid, horror buff, monster Commissar, ghoul connoisseur, (CG), 960

They're All Phantoms of My Imagining (WS), 888

345 W. 15th St. (AE), 81

Things I Don't Know (WS), 926

Things I'll Not Do (Nostalgias) (D&F), 1160

think tank (D&F), 1124

Think Tank Rhymes (D&F), 1124

Thirty State Bummers (D&F), 1151

This Form of Life Needs Sex (PN), 292

This Is About Death (EM), 43

This is the creature I am, 440

This is the one and only, 41

"This kind of Hepatitis can cause ya" (D&F), 1156

This silver anniversary much hair's gone from my head (CG), 984

Those high lunches needn't matter (WS), 887

Those Two (WS), 849

Thoughts on a Breath (PAOTP), 637

Thoughts Sitting Breathing (MB), 597

Thoughts Sitting Breathing II (WS), 878

3,489 friendly people, 532

"Throw Out the Yellow Journalists of Bad Grammar & Terrible Manner" (WS), 873

Thus crosslegged on round pillow sat in Teton Space, 617

Time comes spirit weakens and goes blank, 184

"Timmy made a hot milk" (D&F), 1156

Tiny orange-wing-tipped butterfly, 567

To an Old Poet in Peru (RS), 247

To Aunt Rose (Kaddish), 192

Today (PN), 353

Today out of the window, 22

Toenail-thickening age on me, (D&F), 1129

To God: to illuminate all men. Beginning with Skid Road, 163

To Jacob Rabinowitz (CG), 972

To Lindsay (Kaddish), 191

To Mexico! To Mexico! Down the dovegray highway, 167

Tompkins Square Lower East Side N.Y. (CG), 1048

Tonite all is well (EM), 40

Tonite I got hi in the window of my apartment, 243

Tonite I walked out of my red apartment door, 633

Too much industry, 734

To P.O. (IJ), 301

To Poe: Over the Planet, Air Albany–Baltimore (Fall), 522

To the Body (PN), 439

To the Punks of Dawlish (PO), 729

. . . touch of vocal flattery, 365

Transcription of Organ Music (Howl), 148

Tübingen–Hamburg Schlafwagen (PO), 736

Tuesday Morn (D&F), 1074

Turn me on your knees, 657

"Turn on the heat & take a seat" (D&F), 1157

Turn Right Next Corner, 402

Twenty-eight years before on the living room couch, 718

22,000 feet over Hazed square Vegetable planet Floor, 514

Two Boys Went Into a Dream Diner (EM), 63

Two bricklayers are setting the walls, 12

Two Dreams (MB), 655

221 Syllables at Rocky Mountain Dharma Center (WS), 883

Two Sonnets (GW), 13

Ugh! the planet screams, 345

Under orders to shoot the spy, I discharged, 520

Under silver wing, 507

Understand That This Is a Dream (Air Dreams), 311

Under the bluffs of Oroville, blue cloud September skies, 377

Under the world there's a lot of ass, a lot of cunt
  (MB), 606
Upstairs Jenny crashed her car & became a
  living corpse, (CG), 1038
Uptown (PN), 432
up up and away, 390

Vachel, the stars are out, 191
Variations on Ma Rainey's See See Rider
  (D&F), 1144
Velocity of Money (CG), 949
Verses Written for Student Antidraft
  Registration Rally 1980 (PO), 738
Violate me (CG), 1033
Violence (Fall), 511
Violent Collaborations (CG), 1033
Virtual Impunity Blues (D&F), 1119
Vision 1948 (GW), 16
Visiting Father & Friends (CG), 941
Voznesensky's "Silent Tingling" (PAOTP), 588
Vulture Peak: Gridhakuta Hill (PN), 306

Waking in New York (PN), 347
Wales Visitation (PN), 488
Walking at night on asphalt campus, 305
Walking home at night (EM), 78
Walking with aching back at base of spine,
  walked stiffly to kitchen toilet to pee,
  (D&F), 1074
Walk into your local Japanese restaurant
  Teriyaki Boy— (D&F), 1120
Waribashi (D&F), 1120
War Profit Litany (Fall), 494
Watching the White Image, electric moon,
  white mist, 535
We children, we (D&F), 1140
We know all about death that, 42
We're in the Great Place, Fable Place,
  Beulah, Man wedded to Earth, 525
We Rise on Sun Beams and Fall in the Night
  (MB), 640
Western Air boat bouncing, 566
Westward Mother-mountains drift Pacific,
  green-sloped canyons, 512
What do I hear in my ear (D&F), 1098
What do I want in these rooms papered, 48
Whatever it may be whoever it may be, 308
What I'd Like to Do (MB), 610
What new element before us unborn in
  nature, 710
What's Dead? (PO), 697
What the Sea Throws Up at Vlissingen (WS),
  880
What thoughts I have of you tonight, Walt
  Whitman, 144

"What would you do if you lost it?" (MB), 600
"What You Up To?" (WS), 870
When he kissed my nipple, 544
When I die (D&F), 1130
When I died, love, when I died, 21
When I lie down to sleep dream the Wishing
  Well it rings, 352
When I sat in my bedroom for devotions,
  meditations & prayers (WS), 878
When I sit before a paper, 37
When I think of death, 50
When Schwarzkopf's Father busted Iran's
  Mossadegh (CG), 1002
When that dress-gray, gray haired and gray-
  faced (WS), 897
When the Light Appears (CG), 965
When the red pond fills fish appear, 587
When the troops get their poop (WS), 865
Where O America are you, 73
White fog lifting & falling on mountain-
  brow, 488
white haze over Manhattan's towers, 510
White light's wet glaze on asphalt city floor,
  371
White marble pillars in the Rector's
  courtyard, 748
White Shroud (WS), 889
White sunshine on sweating skulls, 549
Whitmanic Poem (D&F), 1140
Who (PAOTP), 603
Who am I? Saliva, 565
Who Be Kind To (PN), 367
Who Eats Who? (CG), 1037
Who is the shroudy stranger of the night, 39
Who is this Slave Master makes me answer
  letters in his name (WS), 882
Whom bomb, 576
Whom bomb? (CG), 1004
who report Ten Commandments & Golden
  Rule (WS), 873
Who represents my body in Pentagon? Who
  spends, 491
Who Runs America? (MB), 636
Who showed up? (D&F), 1123
Who Will Take Over the Universe? (PN), 273
Why am I so angry at Kissinger, 736
Why do I deny manna to another, 150
Why I Meditate (WS), 851
Why Is God Love, Jack? (PN), 343
Wichita Vortex Sutra (PN), 402
Wild Orphan (Howl), 86
Wind mills churn on Windy City's, 641
Wings Lifted over the Black Pit (Fall), 435
With oil that streaks streets a magic color,
  700

With the blue-dark dome old-starred at night, 297

With Virtual impunity Clinton got campaign funds from pink Chinese (D&F), 1119

World Bank Blues (D&F), 1126

World Karma (WS), 913

World world world, 179

Written in My Dream by W. C. Williams (WS), 901

Written on Hotel Napkin: Chicago Futures (MB), 641

Wrote This Last Night (RS), 174

Xmas Gift (MB), 595

Yellow-lit Budweiser signs over oaken bars, 432

Yes all the spiritual groups scandal the shrine room (CG), 984

Yes and It's Hopeless (MB), 604

yes it's gone gone gone (D&F), 1106

Yiddishe Kopf (CG), 1012

You Don't Know It (CG), 943

"You know what I'm saying?" (D&F), 1096

You'll bare your bones you'll grow you'll pray you'll only know (CG), 966

"You Might Get in Trouble" (PAOTP), 668

Young I drank beer & vomited green bile (WS), 872

Young romantic readers (D&F), 1147

Your electric hair's beautiful gold as Blake's Glad Day boy, 729

You said you got to go home   & feed your pussycat, 658

Youthful, caressing, boisterous, tender (WS), 900

You used to wear dungarees & blue workshirt, 725

You've been coughing for weeks (D&F), 1097

You were here on earth, in cities, 626

About the Author

Allen Ginsberg was born in Newark, New Jersey, in 1926, a son of Naomi and lyric poet Louis Ginsberg. As a student at Columbia College in the 1940s, he began a close friendship with William Burroughs, Neal Cassady, and Jack Kerouac, and he later became associated with the Beat movement and the San Francisco Renaissance in the 1950s. After jobs as a laborer, sailor, and market researcher, Ginsberg published his first volume of poetry, *Howl and Other Poems*, in 1956. *Howl* defeated censorship trials to become one of the most widely read poems of the century, translated into more than twenty-two languages, from Macedonian to Chinese, a model for younger generations of poets from West to East.

Crowned Prague May King in 1965, then expelled by Czech police and simultaneously placed on the FBI's Dangerous Security list, Ginsberg traveled to and taught in the People's Republic of China, the Soviet Union, Scandinavia, and Eastern Europe, receiving Yugoslavia's Struga Poetry Festival "Golden Wreath" in 1986.

Ginsberg was a member of the American Academy of Arts and Letters, was awarded the medal of Chevalier de l'Ordre des Arts et des Lettres by the French minister of culture, was a winner of the National Book Award (for *The Fall of America*), and was a cofounder of the Jack Kerouac School of Disembodied Poetics at the Naropa Institute, the first accredited Buddhist college in the Western world. He died in New York City in 1997.